OUR NATIONAL INCOME ACCOUNTS AND <u>REAL GDP</u> SINCE 1929*

In this table, in which all amounts are in billions of dollars, we see historical data for the various components of nominal GDP. These are given in the first four columns. We then show the rest of the national income accounts going from GDP to NDP to NI to PI to DPI. The last column gives real GDP.

| | The Sum of Expenditures | | | | Equals | Less | Equals | Plus | Less | Equals | Less | | | Plus | Equals | Less | Equals | |
Year	Personal Consumption Expenditures	Gross Private Domestic Investment	Government Purchases of Goods and Services	Net Exports	Gross Domestic Product	Depreciation	Net Domestic Product	Net U.S. Income Earned Abroad	Statistical Discrepancy	National Income	Corporate Profits	Social Security Taxes	Taxes on Production and Imports Net of Subsidies	Net Transfers and Interest Earnings	Personal Income	Personal Income Taxes and Nontax Payment	Disposable Personal Income	Real GDP (2009 Dollars)
1989	3592.8	999.7	1151.9	−86.7	5657.7	836.1	4821.6	24.8	64.2	4782.2	414.2	385.2	371.4	1006.8	4618.2	566.1	4052.1	8777.0
1990	3825.6	993.5	1238.4	−77.9	5979.6	886.8	5092.8	34.6	91.3	5036.1	417.2	410.1	398.0	1093.7	4904.5	592.7	4311.8	8945.4
1991	3960.2	944.3	1298.2	−28.7	6174.0	931.1	5242.9	31.6	88.4	5186.1	451.3	430.2	429.6	1196.1	5071.1	586.6	4484.5	8938.9
1992	4215.7	1013.0	1345.4	−34.8	6539.3	959.7	5579.6	31.1	111.0	5499.7	475.3	455.0	453.3	1294.7	5410.8	610.5	4800.3	9256.7
1993	4471.0	1106.8	1366.1	−65.2	6878.7	1003.6	5875.1	32.0	152.3	5754.8	522.0	477.4	466.4	1357.8	5646.8	646.6	5000.2	9510.8
1994	4741.0	1256.5	1403.7	−92.5	7308.7	1055.6	6253.1	23.8	136.7	6140.2	621.9	508.2	512.7	1437.3	5934.7	690.5	5244.2	9894.7
1995	4984.2	1317.5	1452.2	−89.9	7664.0	1122.8	6541.2	28.7	90.4	6479.5	703.0	532.8	523.1	1555.9	6276.5	743.9	5532.6	10163.7
1996	5268.1	1432.1	1496.4	−96.4	8100.2	1176.0	6924.2	31.8	56.6	6899.4	786.1	555.1	545.5	1649.2	6661.9	832.0	5829.9	10549.5
1997	5560.7	1595.6	1554.2	−102.0	8608.5	1240.0	7368.5	24.1	12.2	7380.4	865.8	587.2	577.8	1725.4	7075.0	926.1	6148.9	11022.9
1998	5903.0	1735.3	1613.5	−162.7	9089.1	1310.3	7778.8	18.3	−60.2	7857.3	804.1	624.7	603.1	1762.3	7587.7	1026.4	6561.3	11513.4
1999	6316.9	1884.2	1726.0	−261.4	9665.7	1400.9	8264.8	27.1	−32.5	8324.4	830.2	661.3	628.4	1779.3	7983.8	1107.5	6876.3	12071.4
2000	6801.6	2033.8	1834.4	−380.1	10289.7	1514.2	8775.5	37.0	−94.5	8907.0	781.2	705.8	662.7	1875.5	8632.8	1232.3	7400.5	12565.2
2001	7106.9	1928.6	1958.8	−369.0	10625.3	1604.0	9021.3	51.8	−111.4	9184.5	754.0	733.2	669.0	1958.8	8987.1	1234.8	7752.3	12684.4
2002	7385.3	1925.0	2094.9	−425.0	10980.2	1662.1	9318.1	48.6	−70.1	9436.8	907.2	751.5	721.2	2092.6	9149.5	1050.3	8099.2	12909.7
2003	7764.6	2027.9	2220.8	−501.1	11512.2	1727.2	9785.0	68.0	−12.1	9865.1	1056.4	779.3	758.9	2217.1	9487.6	1000.9	8486.7	13270.0
2004	8257.8	2276.7	2357.4	−614.9	12277.0	1831.7	10445.3	90.0	−6.6	10541.9	1283.3	829.2	817.6	2437.4	10049.2	1046.0	9003.2	13774.0
2005	8790.3	2527.1	2493.7	−715.7	13095.4	1982.0	11113.4	93.5	−33.9	11240.8	1477.7	873.3	873.6	2594.1	10610.3	1208.5	9401.8	14235.6
2006	9297.5	2680.6	2642.2	−762.4	13857.9	2136.0	11721.9	68.5	−215.2	12005.6	1646.5	922.6	940.5	2893.8	11389.8	1352.1	10037.7	14615.2
2007	9744.4	2643.7	2801.9	−709.7	14480.3	2264.4	12215.9	126.4	20.0	12322.3	1529.0	961.4	980.0	3143.8	11995.7	1487.8	10507.9	14876.8
2008	10005.5	2424.8	3003.2	−713.2	14720.3	2363.4	12356.9	173.0	99.1	12430.8	1285.1	988.2	989.4	3262.5	12430.6	1107.6	10995.4	14833.6
2009	9842.9	1878.1	3089.1	−392.0	14417.9	2368.4	12049.5	147.2	72.2	12124.5	1392.6	964.4	967.8	3282.4	12082.1	1144.9	10937.2	14417.9
2010	10201.9	2100.8	3174.0	−518.4	14958.3	2381.6	12576.7	205.9	43.1	12739.5	1740.6	984.1	1001.2	3421.6	12435.2	1191.5	11243.7	14779.4
2011	10711.8	2232.1	3158.7	−568.8	15533.8	2452.6	13081.2	260.7	−53.8	13395.7	1877.7	918.2	1037.2	3628.7	13191.3	1403.9	11787.4	15052.4
2012	11149.6	2475.2	3167.0	−547.2	16244.6	2542.9	13701.7	252.9	−17.0	13971.6	2009.5	950.7	1065.6	3798.0	13743.8	1498.0	12245.8	15470.7
2013	11501.5	2670.0	3125.5	−497.3	16799.7	2646.6	14153.1	257.8	−122.2	14533.1	2102.1	1106.1	1088.0	3898.9	14135.8	1659.1	12476.7	15761.3
2014[a]	11973.1	2865.1	3232.4	−531.7	17538.9	2758.1	14780.8	258.4	47.3	14991.9	2227.3	1151.2	1103.4	4091.7	14601.7	1898.3	12703.4	16202.6
2015[a]	12389.4	3071.4	3289.4	−539.6	18210.6	2898.1	15312.5	259.3	69.6	15502.2	2351.2	1193.6	1151.3	4137.2	14943.3	1982.1	12961.2	16672.5

[a] Author's estimates.

*Note: Some rows may not add up due to rounding.

Commentary (by Joe Stenard)

Perspective on the Empire State Plaza, taken from 400 feet above, invites the student of economics to consider infrastructure, the crowding out effect, fiscal policy, trade-offs, and the interrelation of firms, households and government.

Conceived by Governor Nelson Rockefeller after being embarrassed when Princess Beatrix of the Netherlands visited Albany, the plaza's design was first doodled in pen on the back of a postcard and then revised in a European architectural style. The massive scale was designed to be appreciated from across the Hudson River.

As many as 9,500 citizens were uprooted when their homes and businesses were taken to build the mammoth government complex that defines Albany's skyline. Despite the displacement of thousands of loyal political voters, Albany Mayor Erastus Corning worked to engineer the "Pyramid to Pharaoh Rockefeller". After the 98.5-acre site was obtained using eminent domain, construction was begun in 1959 with an initial cost estimate of $250 million. Eventually, the total cost exceeded $2 Billion.

Paying for the construction of the plaza was done with borrowed funds and it was a major challenge to pass a state bond referendum for a city project. To this day, the construction of the Plaza — and the shocking speed with which an entire neighborhood was condemned through eminent domain — remains one of the most momentous and traumatic periods in the city's 400-year history.

DEFINITION of 'Crowding Out Effect' (taken from Investopedia.com)

An economic concept where increased public sector spending replaces, or drives down, private sector spending. Crowding out refers to when government must finance its spending with taxes and/or with deficit spending, leaving businesses with less money and effectively "crowding them out." One explanation of why crowding out occurs is government financing of projects with deficit spending through the use of borrowed money. Because the government borrows such large amounts of capital, its activities can increase interest rates. Higher interest rates discourage individuals and businesses from borrowing money, which reduces their spending and investment activities. (Citation: Investopedia.com)

Photo/John C. Glenn

Practice, Engage, and Assess

- **Enhanced eText**—Students actively read and learn, and with more engagement than ever before, through embedded and auto-graded practice, real-time data-graph updates, animations, author videos, and more.

- **Practice**—Algorithmically generated homework and study plan exercises with instant feedback ensure varied and productive practice, helping students improve their understanding and prepare for quizzes and tests. Draw-graph exercises encourage students to practice the language of economics.

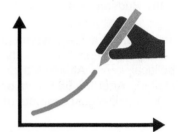

- **Learning Resources**—Personalized learning aids such as Help Me Solve This problem walkthroughs, Teach Me explanations of the underlying concept, and figure Animations provide on-demand help when students need it most.

- **Adaptive Study Plan**—Monitors each student's progress and offers a continuously personalized study plan based on his or her own homework, quiz, and test results. Includes unlimited practice exercises and the opportunity to prove mastery through quizzes based on recommended learning objectives.

- **Dynamic Study Modules**—With a focus on key topics, these modules work by continuously assessing student performance and activity in real time and, using data and analytics, provide personalized content to reinforce concepts that target each student's particular strengths and weaknesses.

- **Digital Interactives**—Focused on a single core topic and organized in progressive levels, each interactive immerses students in an assignable and auto-graded activity. Digital Interactives are also engaging lecture tools for traditional, online, and hybrid courses, many incorporating real-time data, data displays, and analysis tools for rich classroom discussions.

with MyEconLab ®

- **Learning Catalytics**—Generates classroom discussion, guides lectures, and promotes peer-to-peer learning with real-time analytics. Students can use any device to interact in the classroom, engage with content, and even draw and share graphs.

- **Real-Time Data Analysis Exercises**—Using current macro data to help students understand the impact of changes in economic variables, Real-Time Data Analysis Exercises communicate directly with the Federal Reserve Bank of St. Louis's FRED® site and update as new data are available.

- **Current News Exercises**—Every week, current microeconomic and macroeconomic news stories, with accompanying exercises, are posted to MyEconLab. Assignable and auto-graded, these multi-part exercises ask students to recognize and apply economic concepts to real-world events.

- **Experiments**—Flexible, easy-to-assign, auto-graded, and available in Single and Multiplayer versions, Experiments in MyEconLab make learning fun and engaging.

- **Reporting Dashboard**—View, analyze, and report learning outcomes clearly and easily. Available via the Gradebook and fully mobile-ready, the Reporting Dashboard presents student performance data at the class, section, and program levels in an accessible, visual manner.

- **LMS Integration**—Link from any LMS platform to access assignments, rosters, and resources, and synchronize MyLab grades with your LMS gradebook. For students, new direct, single sign-on provides access to all the personalized learning MyLab resources that make studying more efficient and effective.

- **Mobile Ready**—Students and instructors can access multimedia resources and complete assessments right at their fingertips, on any mobile device.

PEARSON

Roger LeRoy Miller

Economics Today
The Macro View

Custom Edition for Hudson Valley Community College

Taken from:
Economics Today: The Macro View, Eighteenth Edition
by Roger LeRoy Miller

Cover Art: Albany, photo courtesy of John C. Glenn.

Taken from:

Economics Today: The Macro View, Eighteenth Edition
by Roger LeRoy Miller
Copyright © 2016, 2014, 2012 by Pearson Education, Inc.
New York, NY 10013

This special edition published in cooperation with Pearson Learning Solutions.

Pearson Learning Solutions, 330 Hudson Street, New York, New York 10013
A Pearson Education Company
www.pearsoned.com

Printed in the United States of America

6 16

000200010271979822

RM

ISBN 10: 1-323-19276-X
ISBN 13: 978-1-323-19276-4

TKKNOK - An Allegory by Sam Stenard

Far across the blue ocean whose bottom is sand,
Where the sigglethrush hunt for fine places to land,
By the Mishler still fishing for figs in the deep,
And cacophonous caves where the Caterwall sleeps…

Far beyond all these places there exists a fine spot,
Where the sun's always shining quite bright and quite hot,
It's the land of the Neetches! The fine land of Knox!
All surrounded by mountains with glass on their tops.

Now these Knobbly-Kneed Neetches (as most know them best)
Are famous for the feathers on their wings and their breasts,
Very useful for catching a mid-morning breeze,
And the envy of those without knobs on their knees.

Also existing in this country of Knox,
Stands the Cliffs of Much Tallness, a pile of rocks
That reach their way upward, past the day's glow,
And casts a long shadow on things far below.

On the face of that cliff grows a plant that's quite rare:
The fresh Ju-Ju Fruit that is found only there.

The juice of this fruit turns Neetch feathers bright,
Makes them grow large and allows them their flight.
On these fine feathers they soar to great heights,
Eating the Ju-Jus with great beaky bites.

Searching the sky on one sunny day,
The Neetches in Charge were rather dismayed
To see their fellows in flight for so long;
They decided right there it mustn't go on.

So they came up with a plan,
A method, a way,
To keep Neetches on land
All through the day.

"We'll make a device, a great big machine!
That will fly up the rocks and pick the cliffs clean!"

"No need for Neetches flying about,
Exhausting themselves day in and day out;
All we need is a feather or two,
From each of the Neetches
To see our plan through."

The Neetches freely obeyed without fuss.
But faced a dilemma really quite rough:
That despite all their giving…
                              There wasn't enough!

When the Neetches in Charge again begged their fellows,
They found that their feathers had withered and yellowed.
For fewer feathers on the wings of the Neetches
Meant trouble ascending to the Cliff's highest reaches.

Yet it was here that the finest fruit could be found,
And without they must settle for the fruit on the ground.
But the juice of this fruit didn't make feathers so bright,
It actually did nothing but inhibit their flight.

So with feathers smaller than ever they'd seen,
It'd take two times the number to complete the machine!
Yet again they gave as the leaders implored,
Only to find that they still needed more.

But they had picked all the feathers, every last one.
And still the machine wasn't done.

Discussion questions written by Joe Stenard

Discuss:

1) What was the standard of living in Knox during the beginning of the poem?

2) Use the economic indicators of Unemployment, GDP and CPI to describe the conditions in Knox prior to the changes implemented by the Neeches in Charge.

3) What was the problem that dismayed the Neeches in Charge?

4) Describe the government program implemented in terms of Fiscal Policy.

5) Did taxes increase, decrease or stay the same?

6) Was the program a success? Explain.

7) Is it possible to support a spending program but oppose the tax policy that funds it? How about vice versa?

8) Compare this program to the Community Reinvestment Act (CRA) of 1995.

BRIEF CONTENTS

CONTENTS

PART 2 Introduction to Macroeconomics and Economic Growth

PART 4   Money, Stabilization, and Growth

PART 5 Global Economics

ONE-SEMESTER COURSE OUTLINE

Macroeconomic Emphasis
The Macro View

1. The Nature of Economics
2. Scarcity and the World of Trade-Offs
3. Demand and Supply
4. Extensions of Demand and Supply Analysis
5. Public Spending and Public Choice
6. Funding the Public Sector
7. The Macroeconomy: Unemployment, Inflation, and Deflation
8. Measuring the Economy's Performance
9. Global Economic Growth and Development
10. Real GDP and the Price Level in the Long Run
11. Classical and Keynesian Macro Analyses
12. Consumption, Real GDP, and the Multiplier
13. Fiscal Policy
14. Deficit Spending and the Public Debt
15. Money, Banking, and Central Banking
16. Domestic and International Dimensions of Monetary Policy
17. Stabilization in an Integrated World Economy
18. Policies and Prospects for Global Economic Growth
32. Comparative Advantage and the Open Economy
33. Exchange Rates and the Balance of Payments

Microeconomic Emphasis
The Micro View

1. The Nature of Economics
2. Scarcity and the World of Trade-Offs
3. Demand and Supply
4. Extensions of Demand and Supply Analysis
5. Public Spending and Public Choice
6. Funding the Public Sector
19. Demand and Supply Elasticity
20. Consumer Choice
21. Rents, Profits, and the Financial Environment of Business
22. The Firm: Cost and Output Determination
23. Perfect Competition
24. Monopoly
25. Monopolistic Competition
26. Oligopoly and Strategic Behavior
27. Regulation and Antitrust Policy in a Globalized Economy
28. The Labor Market: Demand, Supply, and Outsourcing
29. Unions and Labor Market Monopoly Power
30. Income, Poverty, and Health Care
31. Environmental Economics
32. Comparative Advantage and the Open Economy
33. Exchange Rates and the Balance of Payments

Balanced Micro-Macro

1. The Nature of Economics
2. Scarcity and the World of Trade-Offs
3. Demand and Supply
4. Extensions of Demand and Supply Analysis
5. Public Spending and Public Choice
6. Funding the Public Sector
20. Consumer Choice
21. Rents, Profits, and the Financial Environment of Business
22. The Firm: Cost and Output Determination
23. Perfect Competition
24. Monopoly
28. The Labor Market: Demand, Supply, and Outsourcing
29. Unions and Labor Market Monopoly Power
7. The Macroeconomy: Unemployment, Inflation, and Deflation
10. Real GDP and the Price Level in the Long Run
11. Classical and Keynesian Macro Analyses
12. Consumption, Real GDP, and the Multiplier
13. Fiscal Policy
14. Deficit Spending and the Public Debt
15. Money, Banking, and Central Banking
16. Domestic and International Dimensions of Monetary Policy
32. Comparative Advantage and the Open Economy
33. Exchange Rates and the Balance of Payments

PREFACE

This latest edition of *Economics Today—The Macro View* addresses cutting-edge issues while facilitating student learning. The text consistently focuses on demonstrating to students the relevance of economics to *their* own daily lives and on providing them with a variety of ways to evaluate their understanding of fundamental concepts covered in each chapter.

New to This Edition

- **Learning Objectives:** Learning Objectives have been further integrated into every chapter. Each major chapter section is accompanied with a learning objective, which helps to focus student reading comprehension and allows for self-assessment to ensure that students have grasped key concepts.

  All assessment in MyEconLab has also been aligned with Learning Objectives. This integration and alignment makes it simple to include or exclude portions of chapters in both the text and in MyEconLab.
- **Self Checks:** Self Checks appear at the end of every Learning Objective section. Self Checks consist of several fill-in-the-blank questions that allow students to check their understanding of the key concepts they just read before moving on. All answers are available in MyEconLab.
- **Fundamental Points**: At the end of every chapter, new numbered feature, *Fundamental Points*, provides students with a quick rundown of the most salient concepts they must understand for each chapter.
- **References:** Chapter endnotes now provide references and citations for all in-text examples for further exploration by instructors and students.

And New to MyEconLab

- **Videos:** Each chapter contains an Issues & Applications feature, which ties key chapter concepts to a real world example. Each Issues & Applications feature is now accompanied by a brief video that expands on the key point and real world applications of the feature. The videos contain visuals such as photos and graphs, which help to crystallize the key take-aways for the student.
- **Figure Animations:** Figure animations provide a step-by-step walk-through of select figures. Seventy percent of all figures are animated. Figure animations have been updated to reflect changes to the 18th edition.
- **Graphs Updated with Real-Time Data from FRED®:** Data graphs in the eText are continually updated with the latest data from FRED which is a comprehensive, up-to-date data set from the Federal Reserve Bank of St. Louis. Students can display a pop-up graph that shows new data plotted in the graph. The goal of this digital feature is to provide students with the most current macro data available so that they can observe the changing impacts of these important variables on the economy.

  Real-time data analysis exercises in MyEconLab also communicate directly with the Federal Reserve Bank of St. Louis's FRED® site and automatically update as new data are available. These exercises allow students to practice with data to better understand the current economic environment.

  Assessments using current macro data help students understand changes in economic variables and their impact on the economy. Real-Time Data Analysis exercises communicate directly with the Federal Reserve Bank of St. Louis's FRED® site and update as new data are available.
- **Dynamic Study Modules:** Dynamic Study Modules, available from within MyEconLab, continuously assess student performance on key topics in real time, and

provide additional and personalized practice content. Dynamic Study Modules exist for every chapter and are available on all mobile devices for on-the-go studying.

- **Digital Interactives:** *Digital Interactives* help to facilitate experiential learning through a set of interactives focused on core economic concepts. Fueled by data, decision-making, and personal relevance, each interactive progresses through a series of levels that build on foundational concepts, enabling a new immersive learning experience. The flexible and modular set-up of each interactive makes digital interactives suitable for classroom presentation, auto-graded homework, or both.
- **Learning Catalytics®:** Learning Catalytics® generate classroom discussion, guides lectures, and promotes peer-to-peer learning with real-time analytics. Now students can use any device to interact in the classroom, engage with content and even draw and share graphs.

Increased Emphasis on Public Policy

Many modern public policy issues in economics that are highlighted throughout the text are particularly relevant to today's students. These include:

- An evaluation of the **incentive effects** of student loans confronted by recent college graduates: Chapter 1 considers whether the substantial run-up of student loan debts has been rational for self-interested individuals who have pursued college and university degrees.
- An assessment of the soaring taxpayer cost of **Medicare subsidies**: Chapter 5 provides an analysis of likely expenses of the Medicare program to be faced by current students who will have to foot the bill as future taxpayers.
- A consideration of how a reduction in **consumption spending** of services has hampered the recovery from the 2007–2009 business contraction:

ISSUES & APPLICATIONS MyEconLab Video

Medicare's Soaring Bill for U.S. Taxpayers

CONCEPTS APPLIED
- Public Spending and Transfers
- Medicare
- Subsidies

One of the largest public spending and transfer programs in the United States is the Medicare program that provides government subsidies to elderly and other legally qualified recipients of assistance with health care expenses. Indeed, as the U.S. population continues to age and larger numbers of people qualify for subsidies, the amounts that current and future taxpayers can anticipate paying to fund the program continue to increase.

Chapter 12 documents how the slow growth of household expenditures on services has contributed to the weak economic growth confronted by recent degree earners.

What's New in *The Macro View*

In the macro portion of the text, coverage of the following has been included:

- Chapter 7 discusses the gradual decline in employment of males generated by a significant decline in male **labor force participation**.
- Chapter 8 explores important changes in the measurement of **investment** arising from the government's decision to include intangible investments, such as research and development expenditures and investments in intellectual property. This chapter also explains a **gross output** measure of domestic production of goods and services being tracked by the government.
- Chapter 9 evaluates the implications for U.S. **economic growth** of immigration policies that make it much easier for foreign sports stars to legally work in the United States than is the case for foreign scientists and engineers.
- Chapter 13 explains how differences in **impact fiscal multipliers versus cumulative fiscal multipliers** help to explain why substantial increases in discretionary government spending since 2008 have generated relatively small net increases in U.S. economic activity.

MAKING THE CONNECTION— FROM THE CLASSROOM TO THE REAL WORLD

Economics Today—The Macro View provides current examples with critical analysis questions that show students how economic theory applies to their diverse interests and lives. For the Eighteenth Edition, **more than 95 percent** of the examples are new.

DOMESTIC TOPICS AND EVENTS are presented through thought-provoking discussions, such as:

- Will Novel Materials Weave Innovative Clothing Fads?
- A Shift toward More Part-Time Employment
- A U.S. Comparative Advantage in Trash

EXAMPLE
Will Novel Materials Weave Innovative Clothing Fads?

The latest fads in clothing may be less related to their styling than to their content. Textile products now include antibacterial cotton, mosquito-repellent fibers, and fire-retardant acrylics. A number of firms already have thousands of patents for clothing containing these and other materials.

Perhaps the most innovative clothing items incorporate graphene, a material derived from graphite used in pencil leads. This material is very strong, light, and flexible and hence can be woven into clothing. Graphene also can be configured to absorb or emit light, thereby giving the wearer the capability either to blend in with surroundings or to glow like a firefly. In addition, graphene conducts heat and electricity, and this latter property may provide the basis for the most marketable clothing innovations.

Scientists already are testing articles of clothing that can allow the wearer to engage in phone conversations and connect to the Internet.

Thus, rethinking the composition of clothing offers the potential for an array of innovations. The main barrier that scientists must overcome is the high costs of the new textile materials. Graphene material currently costs about $60 per square inch—quite a bit more than a square inch of either cotton or polyester.

FOR CRITICAL THINKING
So far, does research in new textile materials appear to have yielded inventions or innovations? Explain.

Sources are listed at the end of this chapter.

IMPORTANT POLICY QUESTIONS help students understand public debates, such as:

- Why Online Sales Taxes Would Entail More Than Just Taxes
- Economic Policy Uncertainty as a Source of Shocks
- A Government Agency's Ideas for Reducing the Federal Deficit

POLICY EXAMPLE
Why Online Sales Taxes Would Entail More Than Just Taxes

Over the past few years, Congress has considered allowing the 45 states with sales taxes to require companies to collect such taxes when residents of those states purchase their products on the Internet. Proponents of the proposed legal change argue that it would establish a level playing field between sellers on the Web and sellers who predominantly utilize physical facilities.

A complication is that there would not really be "only" 45 different state sales tax rates to assess. Many states permit counties and cities to assess their own sales tax rates, too. Furthermore, each of these local jurisdictions within the 45 states has its own rules for defining how the rates apply to the values of purchases of many different goods and services. As a consequence, an online seller could confront different sales tax regulations for as many as 9,646 state, county, and city jurisdictions.

Current estimates indicate that for large online retailers, such as Amazon, the cost of complying with these many tax rules would amount to just over 2 percent of the dollar value of all sales. For small retailers, the compliance cost likely would exceed 13 percent of the total value of customers' purchases. Thus, compliance costs for small Web sellers could exceed the taxes they would transmit to the government.

FOR CRITICAL THINKING
Why might some small online retailers contemplate halting sales in some states, counties, and cities if required to collect sales taxes throughout the United States?

Sources are listed at the end of this chapter.

MyEconLab Concept Check

INTERNATIONAL EXAMPLE
The Global Black Market in Human Organs

Recent estimates indicate that at least 10,000 black market transactions in human organs occur around the world every year. Legal bans on the sale of organs effectively impose a ceiling price of $0 per unit. The consequences of these bans are global shortages of transplantable organs numbering in the hundreds of thousands. People in low-income nations in Eastern Europe and Asia often receive black market payments to donate "extra" kidneys. Some residents of China facing a waiting list of nearly 300,000 for organ transplants have resorted to buying organs of executed prisoners from their surviving

steal organs such as hearts or lungs intended for sale to people frantic enough to pay high prices to remain alive.

Black market prices of organs vary considerably. For kidneys, the prices range from $40,000 to $150,000, depending on the nation and location in which a black market kidney is purchased. The price of a heart in the global black market for human organs can reach nearly $1.5 million.

FOR CRITICAL THINKING
Why can prices in the black market for organs often vary within a wide range?

GLOBAL AND INTERNATIONAL POLICY EXAMPLES emphasize the continued importance of international perspectives and policy, such as:

- The Global Black Market in Human Organs
- Beijing Battles Pollution with a Car Congestion Fee
- French Soccer Teams Confront Dynamic Tax Analysis

INTERNATIONAL POLICY EXAMPLE
Beijing Battles Pollution with a Car Congestion Fee

In the city of Beijing, China, the concentration of dangerous airborne pollution particles has climbed as high as 900 micrograms per cubic meter of air, or 36 times greater than the World Health Organization's recommended maximum. Among the sources of particulate air pollution are emissions from a number of coal-fueled power plants and several oil refineries. Another key source is the exhaust pipes of more than 5.3 million gasoline-powered vehicles, which together account for about a third of the particulate pollutants in Beijing's atmosphere.

In an effort to reduce the vehicles' contribution to the city's pollution problem, the Beijing government is in the process of implementing a "car congestion fee." This fee effectively constitutes a charge that each vehicle

owner pays for the right to discharge particulates into the air—that is, an effluent fee. The intent of the fee is to raise the price of auto utilization for consumers and thereby push this price closer to the full cost—including the external cost added by air-pollution spillovers—to society.

FOR CRITICAL THINKING
Why do you suppose that Beijing's government also has banned private cars and trucks from the city's roadways one day each week based on the last digits on the vehicles' license plates?

Sources are listed at the end of this chapter.

HELPING STUDENTS FOCUS AND THINK CRITICALLY

New and revised pedagogical tools engage students and help them focus on the central ideas in economics today.

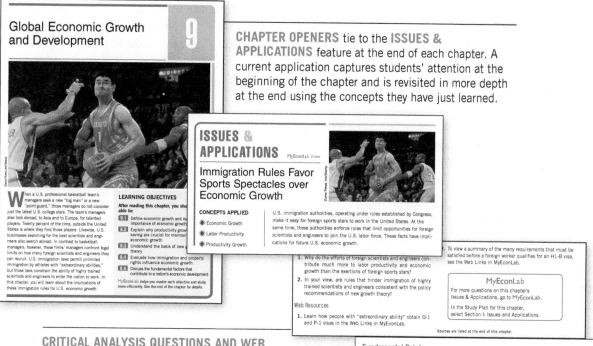

Global Economic Growth and Development | 9

CHAPTER OPENERS tie to the **ISSUES & APPLICATIONS** feature at the end of each chapter. A current application captures students' attention at the beginning of the chapter and is revisited in more depth at the end using the concepts they have just learned.

ISSUES & APPLICATIONS
MyEconLab Video

Immigration Rules Favor Sports Spectacles over Economic Growth

CONCEPTS APPLIED
- Economic Growth
- Labor Productivity
- Productivity Growth

U.S. immigration authorities, operating under rules established by Congress, make it easy for foreign sports stars to work in the United States. At the same time, these authorities enforce rules that limit opportunities for foreign scientists and engineers to join the U.S. labor force. These facts have implications for future U.S. economic growth.

1. Why do the efforts of foreign scientists and engineers contribute much more to labor productivity and economic growth than the exertions of foreign sports stars?

2. In your view, are rules that hinder immigration of highly trained scientists and engineers consistent with the policy recommendations of new growth theory?

Web Resources

1. Learn how people with "extraordinary ability" obtain O-1 and P-1 visas in the Web Links in MyEconLab.

2. To view a summary of the many requirements that must be satisfied before a foreign worker qualifies for an H1-B visa, see the Web Links in MyEconLab.

MyEconLab

For more questions on this chapter's Issues & Applications, go to MyEconLab.

In the Study Plan for this chapter, select Section I: Issues and Applications.

Sources are listed at the end of this chapter.

CRITICAL ANALYSIS QUESTIONS AND WEB RESOURCES provide further opportunities for discussion and exploration. Suggested answers for Critical Analysis questions are in the *INSTRUCTOR'S MANUAL*. Visit MyEconLab for additional practice and assignable questions for each chapter topic.
FUNDAMENTAL POINTS are placed at the beginning of chapter summaries to emphasize the key concepts within the chapter.

Fundamental Points

1. Economic growth is the annual rate of increase in per capita real GDP.
2. Improvements in labor productivity and a higher saving rate generate a higher rate of economic growth.
3. The key implication of new growth theory is that the greater the rewards from adoption of new technologies, the greater the pace of technological innovation.
4. Economists continue to disagree about the implications of immigration for economic growth, but one area of agreement is that failing to clearly define and protect property rights gives individuals less incentive to take risks, which reduces economic growth.
5. Historical evidence indicates nations typically pass through three stages of economic development: the agricultural stage, the manufacturing stage, and the service-sector stage, with rates of economic growth diminishing at each state.

The **END-OF-CHAPTER SUMMARY** shows students what they need to know and where to go in MyEconLab for more practice.
A VARIETY OF END-OF-CHAPTER PROBLEMS offer students opportunities to test their knowledge and review chapter concepts. Answers for odd-numbered questions are provided in MyEconLab, and **ALL QUESTIONS** are assignable in MyEconLab.

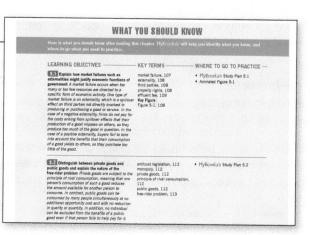

WHAT YOU SHOULD KNOW

Here is what you should know after reading this chapter. MyEconLab will help you identify what you know, and where to go when you need to practice.

LEARNING OBJECTIVES	KEY TERMS	WHERE TO GO TO PRACTICE
5.1 Explain how market failures such as externalities might justify economic functions of government A market failure occurs when too many or too few resources are directed to a specific form of economic activity. One type of market failure is an externality, which is a spillover effect on third parties not directly involved in producing or purchasing a good or service. In the case of a negative externality, firms do not pay for the costs arising from spillover effects that their production of a good imposes on others, so they produce too much of the good in question. In the case of a positive externality, buyers fail to take into account the benefits that their consumption of a good yields to others, so they purchase too little of the good.	market failure, 107 externality, 108 third parties, 108 property rights, 108 effluent fee, 109 Key Figure Figure 5-1, 108	• MyEconLab Study Plan 5.1 • Animated Figure 5-1
5.2 Distinguish between private goods and public goods and explain the nature of the free-rider problem Private goods are subject to the principle of rival consumption, meaning that one person's consumption of such a good reduces the amount available for another person to consume. In contrast, public goods can be consumed by many people simultaneously at no additional opportunity cost and with no reduction in quantity or quality. In addition, no individual can be excluded from the benefits of a public good even if that person fails to help pay for it.	antitrust legislation, 112 monopoly, 112 private goods, 112 principle of rival consumption, 112 public goods, 112 free-rider problem, 113	• MyEconLab Study Plan 5.2

SELF CHECKS encourage student interaction and provide an opportunity for them to check their understanding before moving on. Answers are in MyEconLab, and more practice questions can be found there as well.

YOU ARE THERE

In Finland, the Taxman Screams, "Less Ice Cream!"

Five-year-old Clara Hartikainen, of Espoo, Finland, is trying to be brave and hold back her tears as her mother tells her that the light blue truck that has always brought ice cream treats to her neighborhood is making its final stop. Her mother explains to Clara and her three-year-old brother that the company, which has long operated a fleet of dozens of ice cream trucks across the Scandinavian nation, has decided to park them, probably forever. Indeed, all ice cream producers throughout Finland have been reducing their production. Spaces in grocery freezers allocated to ice cream are shrinking across the land.

Finnish ice cream producers have been reducing the amount of ice cream supplied at all prevailing prices since the government began assessing special taxes on candies, ice cream, and soft drinks in 2010. Initially, the government had intended its tax on sugary delights to serve as a temporary fund-raising measure. Beginning in 2013, however, the government decided to make the tax permanent.

Clara's mother does not try to explain these details to her young children. All she can say is that perhaps every year for the rest of their lives, companies will be offering less ice cream—an estimated 20 percent less—for sale at any given price. The government's tax on sweets has reduced the supply of ice cream.

CRITICAL THINKING QUESTIONS

1. In which direction has Finland's market ice cream supply curve shifted?

2. The amount of the tax on ice cream is 0.75 euro per kilogram sold. What is the vertical amount of the shift in the market supply curve? Explain briefly.

Sources are listed at the end of this chapter.

YOU ARE THERE discusses real people making real personal and business decisions. Topics include:

- In Finland, the Taxman Screams, "Less Ice Cream!"
- In Kenya, Mobile-Phone Airtime Is Money
- Do Social Security Payments Boost Real GDP?

WHAT IF...? boxes can be found in every chapter. This feature aims to help students think critically about important real-world questions through the eyes of an economist.

- What If... the government "nudges" people to influence their decision making?
- What if... the federal government seeks to generate increases in aggregate demand and equilibrium levels of real GDP per year through public spending on all-electric and hybrid vehicles?
- What if... the Fed were to act as lender of *first* resort?

WHAT IF...

the government "nudges" people to influence their decision making?

Various economic studies have found evidence consistent with the idea that people sometimes put off making decisions that outside observers judge would make those individuals unambiguously better off. Researchers have found some evidence that people do not have unbounded willpower, meaning that their choices are not always consistent with their long-term goals. For instance, left to their own devices, some people never get around to contributing some of their earnings to a pension plan when

given the opportunity by their employers. In the United Kingdom, a law now requires people to contribute to an available pension plan unless they make a conscious decision not to do so. The British government thereby "nudges" people toward a choice that it perceives to be in their own best interest while giving them the ability to make a different decision if that is their preference. The result has been that more people have opted to contribute to pension plans than was true in previous years.

MYECONLAB: PRACTICE, ENGAGE, AND ASSESS

MyEconLab is a powerful assessment and tutorial system that works hand-in-hand with *Economics Today*. MyEconLab includes comprehensive homework, quiz, test, and tutorial options, allowing instructors to manage all assessment needs in one program.

For the Instructor

- Instructors can select a prebuilt course option, which creates a ready-to-go course with homework and quizzes already set up. Instructors can also choose to create their own assignments and add them to the preloaded course. Or, instructors can start from a blank course.
- All end-of-chapter problems are assignable and automatically graded in MyEconLab and, for most chapters, additional algorithmic, draw-graph, and numerical exercises are available to choose among.
- Instructors can also choose questions from the Test Bank and use the Custom Exercise Builder to create their own problems for assignment.
- The powerful Gradebook records each student's performance and time spent on the Tests and Study Plan, and generates reports by student or by chapter.

MyEconLab Real-Time Data Analysis
We offer real-time data exercises that students can complete in MyEconLab.

- **Real-Time Data Analysis Exercises** are marked with 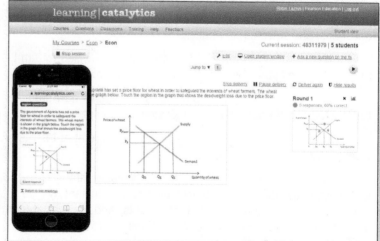 and allow instructors to assign problems that use up-to-the-minute data. Each RTDA exercise loads the appropriate and most currently available data from FRED, a comprehensive and up-to-date data set maintained by the Federal Reserve Bank of St. Louis. Exercises are graded based on that instance of data, and feedback is provided.

- In the eText available in MyEconLab, select figures labeled Real-Time Data now include a pop-up graph updated with real-time data from FRED.

- Current News Exercises provide a turn-key way to assign gradable news-based exercises in MyEconLab. Every week, Pearson scours the news and finds micro- and macroeconomic news stories (articles and videos), creates an accompanying exercise, and then posts it all to MyEconLab courses for possible assignment. Assigning and grading current news-based exercises that deal with the latest micro and macro events and policy issues has never been more convenient.

- Economics in the News is a turn-key solution to bringing current news into the classroom. Updated weekly during the academic year, this feature posts news articles with questions for further discussion.

- Experiments in MyEconLab are a fun and engaging way to promote active learning and mastery of important economic concepts. Pearson's experiments program is flexible and easy for instructors and students to use.
  - Single-player experiments allow your students to play an experiment against virtual players from anywhere at any time with an Internet connection.
  - Multiplayer experiments allow you to assign and manage a real-time experiment with your class.

  In both cases, pre- and post-questions for each experiment are available for assignment in MyEconLab.

Digital Interactives help to facilitate experiential learning through a set of interactives focused on core economic concepts. Fueled by data, decision-making, and personal relevance, each interactive progresses through a series of levels that build on foundational concepts, enabling a new immersive learning experience. The flexible and modular set-up of each interactive makes digital interactives suitable for classroom presentation, auto-graded homework, or both.

Learning Catalytics™ is a technology that has grown out of twenty years of cutting-edge research, innovation, and implementation of interactive teaching and peer instruction. Learning Catalytics is a "bring your own device" student engagement and classroom intelligence system. With Learning Catalytics you can:

- Engage students in real time, using open-ended tasks to probe student understanding.
  - Students use any modern web-enabled device they already have — laptop, smartphone, or tablet.
  - Eighteen different question types include: word clouds; graphing; short answer; matching; multiple choice; highlighting; and image upload.
  - Address misconceptions before students leave the classroom.
  - Understand immediately where students are and adjust your lecture accordingly.
- Improve your students' critical-thinking skills.
- Engage with and record the participation of every student in your classroom.
- Learning Catalytics gives you the flexibility to create your own questions to fit your course exactly or choose from a library of Pearson-created questions.

For more information, visit learningcatalytics.com.

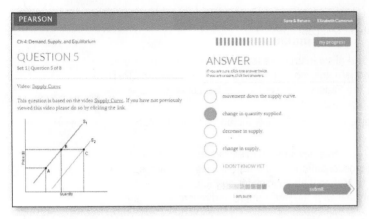

Dynamic Study Modules: Dynamic Study Modules continuously assess student performance on key topics in real time. Dynamic Study Modules exist for every chapter to provide additional practice for students around key concepts.

For the Student

Students are in control of their own learning through a collection of tests, practice, and study tools. Highlights include:

- Two Sample Tests per chapter are preloaded in MyEconLab, enabling students to practice what they have learned, to test their understanding, and to identify areas for further work.

- Based on each student's performance on homework, quizzes, and tests, MyEconLab generates a Study Plan that shows where the student needs further study.

- Learning Aids, such as step-by-step guided solutions, a graphing tool, content-specific links to the eText, animated graphs, and glossary flashcards, help students master the material.

To learn more, and for a complete list of digital interactives, visit www.myeconlab.com.

SUPPLEMENTAL RESOURCES

Student and instructor materials provide tools for success.

Test Bank (Parts 1, 2, and 3) offer more than 10,000 multiple-choice and short answer questions, all of which are available in computerized format in the TestGen software. The significant revision process by author Jim Lee of Texas A&M University–Corpus Christi and accuracy reviewer Conor Molloy of Suffolk County Community College ensure the accuracy of problems and solutions in these revised and updated Test Banks. The Test Bank author has connected the questions to the general knowledge and skill guidelines found in the Association to Advance Collegiate Schools of Business (AACSB) assurance of learning standards.

The Instructor's Manual, prepared by Jim Lee of Texas A&M University–Corpus Christi, includes lecture-ready examples; chapter overviews; objectives; outlines; points to emphasize; answers to all critical analysis questions; answers to all end-of-chapter problems; suggested answers to "You Are There" questions; and selected references.

PowerPoint lecture presentations for each chapter, revised by Jim Lee of Texas A&M University—Corpus Christi, include figures, key terms, and concepts from the text.

Clicker PowerPoint slides allow professors to instantly quiz students in class and receive immediate feedback through Clicker Response System technology.

The Instructor Resource Center puts supplements right at instructors' fingertips. Visit www.pearsonhighered.com/irc to register.

The CourseSmart eTextbook for the text is available through www.coursesmart.com. CourseSmart goes beyond traditional expectations by providing instant, online access to the textbooks and course materials you need at a lower cost to students. And, even as students save money, you can save time and hassle with a digital textbook that allows you to search the most relevant content at the very moment you need it. Whether you're evaluating textbooks or creating lecture notes to help students with difficult concepts, CourseSmart can make life a little easier. See how when you visit www.coursesmart.com/instructors.

ACKNOWLEDGMENTS

I am the most fortunate of economics textbook writers, for I receive the benefit of literally hundreds of suggestions from those of you who use *Economics Today*. Some professors have been asked by my publisher to participate in a more detailed reviewing process of this edition. I list them below. I hope that each one of you so listed accepts my sincere appreciation for the fine work that you have done.

Giuliana Andreopoulos Campanelli, *William Paterson University*
Kenneth Ardon, *Salem State University*
Kevin Beckwith, *Salem State University*
Barbara Blake Gonzalez, *Tidewater Community College*
Theologos Homer Bonitsis, *New Jersey Institute of Technology*
Walter Boyle Fayetteville, *Technical Community College*
James Buck, *East Carolina University*
Bill Burrows Lane, *Community College*
Joel Caron Salem, *State University*
Xudong Chen, *Baldwin Wallace University*
Joel Dalafave, *Bucks County Community College*
Tanya Downing, *Cuesta College*
Stephen Downing, *Danville Area Community College*
Brad Duerson, *DMACC*
Patricia Euzent, *University of Central Florida*
Jamie Falcon, *UMBC*
Elizabeth Faunce, *Immaculata University*
Maurita Fawls, *Portland Community College*
Julia Frankland, *Malone University*
Debora Frazier, *Walla Walla Community College*
George Goerner, *Mohawk Valley Community College*
Dennis Heiner, *College of Southern Idaho*
Stella Hofrenning, *Augsburg College*
Cedric Howie, *Schoolcraft College*
Peng Huang, *Ripon College*
Lillian Kamal, *University of Hartford*
Mohammad Kasraian, *Milwaukee Area Technical College*
Sukanya Kemp, *University of Akron*

James Leaman, *Eastern Mennonite University*
Bozena Leven, *TCNJ*
Jane Lopus, *Cal State University, East Bay*
Michael Machiorlatti, *Oklahoma City Community College*
John McArthur, *Wofford College*
Jeremy McCracken, *Tri County Technical College*
Charles Meyrick, *Housatonic Community College*
Ida Mirzaie, *Ohio State University*
Kevin Murphy, *Oakland University*
Tomi Ovaska, *Youngstown State University*
Lawrence Overlan, *Wentworth*
Joseph Patton, *Lynn University*
Teddi Paulson, *University of Jamestown*
Van Pham, *Salem State University*
Chris Phillips, *Somerset Community College*
Rod Raehsler, *Clarion University*
Paul Schoofs, *Ripon College*
Bill Schweizer, *University of Mount Union*
Jeff Shmidl, *Laramie County Community College*
Daniel Strang, *SUNY Geneseo*
Jialu Streeter, *Allegheny College*
Manjuri Talukdar, *Northern Illinois University*
Ian Taylor, *Tidewater Community College*
Ezgi Uzel, *SUNY Maritime College*
Reuben Veliz, *Marymount California University*
Don Weimer, *Milwaukee Area Technical College*
Oxana Wieland, *University of Minnesota Crookston*
Erik Zemljic, *Kent State University*

I also thank the reviewers of previous editions:

Rebecca Abraham, Cinda J. Adams, Esmond Adams, John Adams, Bill Adamson, Carlos Aguilar, John R. Aidem, Mohammed Akacem, Ercument Aksoy, M. C. Alderfer, John Allen, Ann Al-Yasiri, Charles Anderson, Leslie J. Anderson, Fatma W. Antar, Len Anyanwu, Rebecca Arnold, Mohammad Ashraf, Ali A. Ataiifar, Aliakbar Ataiifar, Leonard Atencio, John Atkins, Glen W. Atkinson, Thomas R. Atkinson, James Q. Aylesworth, John Baffoe-Bonnie, Kevin Baird, Maurice B. Ballabon, Charley Ballard, G. Jeffrey Barbour, Robin L. Barlett, Daniel Barszcz, Kari Battaglia, Robert Becker, Charles Beem, Glen Beeson, Bruce W. Bellner, Daniel K. Benjamin, Emil Berendt, Charles Berry, Abraham Bertisch, John Bethune, R. A. Blewett, Scott Bloom, John Bockino, M. L. Bodnar, Mary Bone, Karl Bonnhi, Thomas W. Bonsor, John M. Booth, Wesley F. Booth, Thomas Borcherding, Melvin Borland, Tom Boston, Barry Boyer, Maryanna Boynton, Ronald Brandolini, Fenton L. Broadhead, Elba Brown, William Brown, Michael Bull, Maureen Burton, Conrad P. Caligaris, Kevin Carey, James Carlson, Robert Carlsson, Dancy R. Carr, Scott Carson, Doris Cash, Thomas H. Cate, Richard J. Cebula, Catherine Chambers, K. Merry Chambers, Richard Chapman, Ronald Cherry, Young Back Choi, Marc Chopin, Carol Cies, Joy L. Clark, Curtis Clarke, Gary Clayton, Marsha Clayton, Dale O. Cloninger, Warren L. Coats, Ed Coen, Pat Conroy, James Cox, Stephen R. Cox, Eleanor D. Craig, Peggy Crane, Jerry Crawford, Patrick M. Crowley, Joanna Cruse, John P. Cullity, Will Cummings, Thomas Curtis, Margaret M. Dalton, Andrew J. Dane, Mahmoud Davoudi, Diana Denison, Edward Dennis, Julia G. Derrick, Sowjanya Dharmasankar, Carol Dimamro, William Dougherty, Barry Duman, Diane Dumont, Floyd Durham, G. B. Duwaji, James A. Dyal, Ishita Edwards, Robert P. Edwards, Alan E. Ellis, Miuke Ellis, Steffany Ellis, Frank Emerson, Carl Enomoto, Zaki Eusufzai, Sandy Evans, John L. Ewing-Smith, Frank Falero, Frank Fato, Abdollah Ferdowsi, Grant Ferguson, Victoria L. Figiel, Mitchell Fisher, David Fletcher, James Foley, John Foreman, Diana Fortier, Ralph G. Fowler, Arthur Friedberg, Peter Frost, Timothy S. Fuerst, Tom Fullerton, E. Gabriel, James Gale, Hamilton Galloway, Byron Gangnes, Frank Garland, Peter C. Garlick, Steve Garner, Neil Garston, Alexander Garvin, Joe Garwood, Doug Gehrke, Robert Gentenaar, J. P. Gilbert, Otis Gilley, Frank Glesber, Jack Goddard, Michael G. Goode, Allen C. Goodman, Richard J. Gosselin, Paul Graf, Anthony J. Greco, Edward Greenberg, Gary Greene, Peter A. Groothuis, Philip J. Grossman, Nicholas Grunt, William Gunther, Kwabena Gyimah-Brempong, Demos Hadjiyanis, Reza G. Hamzaee, Martin D. Haney, Mehdi Haririan, Ray Harvey,

Michael J. Haupert, E. L. Hazlett, Sanford B. Helman, William Henderson, Robert Herman, Gus W. Herring, Charles Hill, John M. Hill, Morton Hirsch, Benjamin Hitchner, Charles W. Hockert, R. Bradley Hoppes, James Horner, Grover Howard, Nancy Howe-Ford, Yu-Mong Hsiao, Yu Hsing, James Hubert, George Hughes, Joseph W. Hunt Jr., Scott Hunt, John Ifediora, R. Jack Inch, Christopher Inya, Tomotaka Ishimine, E. E. Jarvis, Ricot Jean, Parvis Jenab, Allan Jenkins, John Jensel, Mark Jensen, S. D. Jevremovic, J. Paul Jewell, Nancy Jianakoplos, Frederick Johnson, David Jones, Lamar B. Jones, Paul A. Joray, Daniel A. Joseph, Craig Justice, M. James Kahiga, Septimus Kai Kai, Devajyoti Kataky, Timothy R. Keely, Ziad Keilany, Norman F. Keiser, Brian Kench, Randall G. Kesselring, Alan Kessler, E. D. Key, Saleem Khan, M. Barbara Killen, Bruce Kimzey, Terrence Kinal, Philip G. King, E. R. Kittrell, David Klingman, Charles Knapp, Jerry Knarr, Tori Knight, Faik Koray, Janet Koscianski, Dennis Lee Kovach, Marie Kratochvil, Richard W. Kreissle, Peter Kressler, Paul J. Kubik, Michael Kupilik, Margaret Landman, Richard LaNear, Larry Landrum, Keith Langford, Theresa Laughlin, James M. Leaman, Anthony T. Lee, Jim Lee, Loren Lee, Bozena Leven, Donald Lien, George Lieu, Stephen E. Lile, Lawrence W. Lovick, Marty Ludlum, Laura Maghoney, G. Dirk Mateer, Robert McAuliffe, James C. McBrearty, Howard J. McBride, Bruce McClung, John McDowell, E. S. McKuskey, James J. McLain, Kevin McWoodson, John L. Madden, Mary Lou Madden, John Marangos, Dan Marburger, Glen Marston, John M. Martin, Paul J. Mascotti, James D. Mason, Paul M. Mason, Tom Mathew, Warren Matthews, Akbar Marvasti, Pete Mavrokordatos, Fred May, G. Hartley Mellish, Mike Melvin, Diego Mendez-Carbajo, Dan C. Messerschmidt, Michael Metzger, Herbert C. Milikien, Joel C. Millonzi, Glenn Milner, Daniel Mizak, Khan Mohabbat, Thomas Molloy, William H. Moon, Margaret D. Moore, William E. Morgan, Stephen Morrell, Irving Morrissett, James W. Moser, Thaddeaus Mounkurai, Martin F. Murray, Densel L. Myers, George L. Nagy, Solomon Namala, Ronald M. Nate, Jerome Neadly, James E. Needham, Claron Nelson, Douglas Nettleton, William Nook, Gerald T. O'Boyle, Greg Okoro, Dr. Larry Olanrewaju, Richard E. O'Neill, Lucian T. Orlowski, Diane S. Osborne, Joan Osborne, Melissa A Osborne, James O'Toole, Benny E. Overton, Jan Palmer, Zuohong Pan, Gerald Parker, Ginger Parker, Randall E. Parker, Mohammed Partapurwala, Kenneth Parzych, Elizabeth Patch, Norm Paul, Wesley Payne, Raymond A. Pepin, Martin M. Perline, Timothy Perri, Jerry Petr, Maurice Pfannesteil, Van Thi Hong Pham, James Phillips, Raymond J. Phillips, I. James Pickl, Bruce Pietrykowski, Dennis Placone, Mannie Poen, William L. Polvent, Robert Posatko, Greg Pratt, Leila J. Pratt, Steven Pressman, Rick Pretzsch, Reneé Prim, Robert E. Pulsinelli, Rod D. Raehsler, Kambriz Raffiee, Sandra Rahman, Jaishankar Raman, John Rapp, Richard Rawlins, Gautam Raychaudhuri, Ron Reddall, Mitchell Redlo, Charles Reichhelu, Robert S. Rippey, Charles Roberts, Ray C. Roberts, Leila Angelica Rodemann, Richard Romano, Judy Roobian-Mohr, Duane Rosa, Richard Rosenberg, Larry Ross, Barbara Ross-Pfeiffer, Marina Rosser, Philip Rothman, John Roufagalas, Stephen Rubb, Henry Ryder, Lewis Sage, Basel Saleh, Patricia Sanderson, Thomas N. Schaap, William A. Schaeffer, William Schamoe, David Schauer, A. C. Schlenker, David Schlow, Scott J. Schroeder, William Scott, Dan Segebarth, Paul Seidenstat, Swapan Sen, Augustus Shackelford, Richard Sherman Jr., Liang-rong Shiau, Gail Shields, David Shorow, Vishwa Shukla, R. J. Sidwell, Jonathan Silberman, David E. Sisk, Alden Smith, Garvin Smith, Howard F. Smith, Lynn A. Smith, Phil Smith, William Doyle Smith, Brian Sommer, Lee Spector, George Spiva, Richard L. Sprinkle, Alan Stafford, Amanda Stallings-Wood, Herbert F. Steeper, Diane L. Stehman, Columbus Stephens, William Stine, Allen D. Stone, Osman Suliman, J. M. Sullivan, Rebecca Summary, Terry Sutton, Joseph L. Swaffar, Thomas Swanke, Manjuri Talukdar, Frank D. Taylor, Daniel Teferra, Lea Templer, Gary Theige, Dave Thiessen, Robert P. Thomas, Deborah Thorsen, Richard Trieff, George Troxler, William T. Trulove, William N. Trumbull, Arianne K. Turner, Kay Unger, Anthony Uremovic, John Vahaly, Jim Van Beek, David Van Hoose, Lee J. Van Scyoc, Roy Van Til, Sharmila Vishwasrao, Craig Walker, Robert F. Wallace, Henry C. Wallich, Milledge Weathers, Ethel C. Weeks, Roger E. Wehr, Robert G. Welch, Terence West, James Wetzel, Wylie Whalthall, James H. Wheeler, Everett E. White, Michael D. White, Mark A. Wilkening, Raburn M. Williams, James Willis, George Wilson, Travis Wilson, Mark Wohar, Ken Woodward, Tim Wulf, Peter R. Wyman, Whitney Yamamura, Donald Yankovic, Alex Yguado, Paul Young, Shik Young, Mohammed Zaheer, Ed Zajicek, Charles Zalonka, Sourushe Zandvakili, Paul Zarembka, George K. Zestos, William J. Zimmer Jr.

As always, a revision of *Economics Today* requires me to put in the latest data at the last minute. If I did not have such an incredible editorial and production team, I wouldn't be able to do so. I do have a fantastic team both at the publisher—Pearson—and at our production house, Cenveo Publisher Services, working through them with my long-time Production Manager, John Orr of Orr Book Services. He again did a terrific job. I was fortunate to have Karen Carter, Project Manager at Pearson, lead the production team to as perfect a textbook as possible. To be sure, I was pushed hard by my Senior Acquisitions Editor, David Alexander, and I was helped greatly by Lindsey Sloan, the Program Manager on this project. The "pushing" all makes sense now.

I am greatly pleased with the design revision created by Cenveo Publisher Services. It is always a challenge to keep the traditional feel of this book, yet make it more exciting for today's students. I think that we succeeded. I appreciate the hard work of my copy editor, Joanne Boehme. And, of course, the proofreader *par excellence*, Robert Safranek, made sure that everything was perfect. As for the supplements for this edition, I wish to thank Andra Skaalrud for managing their production. On the marketing side, I appreciate the fine work performed by Alison Haskins and her team.

The online media materials, particularly great improvements in *MyEconLab*, were accomplished by Melissa Honig and Courtney Kamauf.

Jim Lee of Texas A&M University–Corpus Christi and Conor Molloy of Suffolk County Community College undertook the vast job of revising and improving the three test banks. The *Instructor's Manual* was masterfully revised by Jim Lee of Texas A&M University–Corpus Christi. Jim Lee also updated and improved PowerPoint presentations.

As always, my "super reviewer," Professor Dan Benjamin of Clemson University, really kept me honest, and my long-time assistant, Sue Jasin, did enough typing and retyping to fill a room with paper. I welcome comments and ideas from professors and students alike and hope that you enjoy this latest edition of *Economics Today*.

R. L. M.

The Nature of Economics

FINANCIAL AID OFFICE

Mark Humphrey/AP Images

Nearly 39 million U.S. residents are borrowers of student loans who still owe on these debts. The current aggregate volume of student loan debt is about $1.2 trillion. Thus, the average indebtedness of a college graduate or current enrollee with student loan debt exceeds $30,000. This is a substantial sum for a typical young person who is starting out in the world of work following graduation. In recent years, however, the wages of young people with student loans have stagnated even as average student loan debts have increased. In addition, an increasing number of borrowers who do graduate experience difficulties finding jobs that generate sufficient earnings to enable them to repay their debts. When people have borrowed to finance their college educations, have they failed to act in their own self-interest? In this chapter, you will contemplate the answer to this question.

LEARNING OBJECTIVES

After reading this chapter, you should be able to:

1.1 Define economics and discuss the difference between microeconomics and macroeconomics

1.2 Identify the three basic economic questions and the two opposing sets of answers

1.3 Evaluate the role that rational self-interest plays in economic analysis

1.4 Explain why economics is a science

1.5 Distinguish between positive and normative economics

MyEconLab helps you master each objective and study more efficiently. See the end of the chapter for details.

the number of college students majoring in economics rose by more than 50 percent during the past decade? One reason that students opt for extensive study of economics is that they find the subject fascinating. Another reason, however, is self-interest. On average, students who major in economics earn about 15 percent more than business management majors, 25 percent more than chemistry majors, and 50 percent more than psychology majors. Thus, students have a strong incentive to consider majoring in economics.

In this chapter, you will learn why contemplating the nature of self-interested responses to **incentives** is the starting point for analyzing choices people make in all walks of life. After all, how much time you devote to studying economics in this introductory course depends in part on the incentives established by your instructor's grading system. As you will see, self-interest and incentives are the underpinnings for all the decisions you and others around you make each day.

Incentives
Rewards or penalties for engaging in a particular activity.

1.1 Define economics and discuss the difference between microeconomics and macroeconomics

The Power of Economic Analysis

Simply knowing that self-interest and incentives are central to any decision-making process is not sufficient for predicting the choices that people will actually make. You also have to develop a framework that will allow you to analyze solutions to each economic problem—whether you are trying to decide how much to study, which courses to take, whether to finish school, or whether the U.S. government should provide more grants to universities or raise taxes. The framework that you will learn in this text is the *economic way of thinking*.

This framework gives you power—the power to reach informed judgments about what is happening in the world. You can, of course, live your life without the power of economic analysis as part of your analytical framework. Indeed, most people do. Economists believe, though, that economic analysis can help you make better decisions concerning your career, your education, financing your home, and other important matters.

In the business world, the power of economic analysis can help increase your competitive edge as an employee or as the owner of a business. As a voter, for the rest of your life you will be asked to make judgments about policies that are advocated by political parties. Many of these policies will deal with questions related to international economics, such as whether the U.S. government should encourage or discourage immigration or restrict other countries from selling their goods here.

Defining Economics

Economics is part of the social sciences and, as such, seeks explanations of real events. All social sciences analyze human behavior, as opposed to the physical sciences, which generally analyze the behavior of electrons, atoms, and other nonhuman phenomena.

Economics
The study of how people allocate their limited resources to satisfy their unlimited wants.

> *Economics is the study of how people allocate their limited resources in an attempt to satisfy their unlimited wants. As such, economics is the study of how people make choices.*

To understand this definition fully, two other words need explaining: *resources* and *wants*. **Resources** are things that have value and, more specifically, are used to produce goods and services that satisfy people's wants. **Wants** are all of the items that people would purchase if they had unlimited income.

Resources
Things used to produce goods and services to satisfy people's wants.

Wants
What people would buy if their incomes were unlimited.

Whenever an individual, a business, or a nation faces alternatives, a choice must be made, and economics helps us study how those choices are made. For example, you have to choose how to spend your limited income. You also have to choose how to spend your limited time. You may have to choose how many of your company's limited resources to allocate to advertising and how many to allocate to new-product research. In economics, we examine situations in which individuals choose how to do things, when to do things, and with whom to do them. Ultimately, the purpose of economics is to explain choices.

MyEconLab Concept Check

Microeconomics versus Macroeconomics

Economics is typically divided into two types of analysis: **microeconomics** and **macroeconomics.**

> **Microeconomics** *is the part of economic analysis that studies decision making undertaken by individuals (or households) and by firms. It is like looking through a microscope to focus on the small parts of our economy.*

> **Macroeconomics** *is the part of economic analysis that studies the behavior of the economy as a whole. It deals with economywide phenomena such as changes in unemployment, in the general price level, and in national income.*

Microeconomic analysis, for example, is concerned with the effects of changes in the price of gasoline relative to that of other energy sources. It examines the effects of new taxes on a specific product or industry. If the government establishes new health care regulations, how individual firms and consumers would react to those regulations would be in the realm of microeconomics. The effects of higher wages brought about by an effective union strike would also be analyzed using the tools of microeconomics.

In contrast, issues such as the rate of inflation, the amount of economywide unemployment, and the yearly growth in the output of goods and services in the nation all fall into the realm of macroeconomic analysis. In other words, macroeconomics deals with **aggregates,** or totals—such as total output in an economy.

Be aware, however, of the blending of microeconomics and macroeconomics in modern economic theory. Modern economists are increasingly using microeconomic analysis—the study of decision making by individuals and by firms—as the basis of macroeconomic analysis. They do this because even though macroeconomic analysis focuses on aggregates, those aggregates are the result of choices made by individuals and firms.

MyEconLab Concept Check
MyEconLab Study Plan

Microeconomics
The study of decision making undertaken by individuals (or households) and by firms.

Macroeconomics
The study of the behavior of the economy as a whole, including such economywide phenomena as changes in unemployment, the general price level, and national income.

Aggregates
Total amounts or quantities. Aggregate demand, for example, is total planned expenditures throughout a nation.

SELF CHECK — Visit MyEconLab to practice these and other problems and to get instant feedback in your Study Plan.

Economics is a social science that involves the study of how individuals choose among alternatives to satisfy their _____, which are what people would buy if their incomes were _____.

_____, the study of the decision-making processes of individuals (or households) and firms, and _____, the study of the performance of the economy as a whole, are the two main branches into which the study of economics is divided.

The Three Basic Economic Questions and Two Opposing Sets of Answers

1.2 Identify the three basic economic questions and the two opposing sets of answers

In every nation, three fundamental questions must be addressed irrespective of the form of its government or who heads that government, how rich or how poor the nation may be, or what type of **economic system**—the institutional mechanism through which resources are utilized to satisfy human wants—has been chosen.

Economic system
A society's institutional mechanism for determining the way in which scarce resources are used to satisfy human desires.

The Three Basic Questions

The three fundamental questions of economics concern the problem of how to allocate society's scarce resources:

1. *What and how much will be produced?* Some mechanism must exist for determining which items will be produced while others remain inventors' pipe dreams or individuals' unfulfilled desires.

2. *How will items be produced?* There are many ways to produce a desired item. It is possible to use more labor and fewer machines, or vice versa. It is possible, for instance, to produce an item with an aim to maximize the number of people employed. Alternatively, an item may be produced with an aim to minimize the total expenses that members of society incur. Somehow, a decision must be made about the mix of resources used in production, the way in which they are organized, and how they are brought together at a particular location.

3. *For whom will items be produced?* Once an item is produced, who should be able to obtain it? People use scarce resources to produce any item, so typically people value access to that item. Thus, determining a mechanism for distributing produced items is a crucial issue for any society.

Now that you know the questions an economic system must answer, how do current systems actually answer them? MyEconLab Concept Check

Two Opposing Sets of Answers

At any point in time, every nation has its own economic system. How a nation's residents go about answering the three basic economic questions depends on that nation's economic system.

CENTRALIZED COMMAND AND CONTROL Throughout history, one common type of economic system has been *command and control* (also called *central planning*) by a centralized authority, such as a king or queen, a dictator, a central government, or some other type of authority that assumes responsibility for addressing fundamental economic issues. Under command and control, this authority decides what items to produce and how many, determines how the scarce resources will be organized in the items' production, and identifies who will be able to obtain the items.

For instance, in a command-and-control economic system, a government might decide that particular types of automobiles ought to be produced in certain numbers. The government might issue specific rules for how to manage the production of these vehicles, or it might even establish ownership over those resources so that it can make all such resource allocation decisions directly. Finally, the government will then decide who will be authorized to purchase or otherwise utilize the vehicles.

Have the U.S. federal government's efforts to direct resources to specific green energy companies always fueled financial success for the recipient firms?

POLICY EXAMPLE
Government Green Energy Financing Flops

Since the end of the last decade, the federal government has considerably boosted its efforts to funnel resources toward so-called green energy technologies aimed at producing electrical power using nontraditional sources of energy. The U.S. Department of Energy typically commits itself to providing to specific green energy firms a certain amount of funds that the government has raised from federal taxes. Within certain prescribed limits, the green energy companies can then draw down these funds to help pay for their operations.

Within only a few years' time, a number of recipients of federal funding have already failed as on-going businesses. Table 1-1 at the top of the next page lists some of the companies to which the Department of Energy has offered funds and the amounts of dollar resources

that it initially committed to these companies. In addition to the six failed recipients listed in Table 1-1, more than two dozen other energy firms have recently been faltering and may have halted operations by the time you read these words. Thus, the government's command-and-control efforts to apply taxpayers' dollars to the harnessing of resources have failed to generate as much electricity production as anticipated.

FOR CRITICAL THINKING
Ultimately, who pays for such green energy projects that fail?

Sources are listed at the end of this chapter.

TABLE 1-1

Failed Green Energy Recipients of Federal Government Funding Offers

	Initial Federal Government Commitment ($ millions)
Solyndra	535.0
Abound Solar	400.0
A123 Systems	279.0
Ener1	118.5
ECOtality	115.0
Range Fuels	80.0

Source: U.S. Department of Energy.

THE PRICE SYSTEM The alternative to command and control is the *price system* (also called a *market system*), which is a shorthand term describing an economic system that answers the three basic economic questions via decentralized decision making. Under a pure price system, individuals and families own all of the scarce resources used in production. Consequently, choices about what and how many items to produce are left to private parties to determine on their own initiative, as are decisions about how to go about producing those items. Furthermore, individuals and families choose how to allocate their own incomes to obtain the produced items at prices established via privately organized mechanisms.

In the price system, which you will learn about in considerable detail in Chapters 3 and 4, prices define the terms under which people agree to make exchanges. Prices signal to everyone within a price system which resources are relatively scarce and which are relatively abundant. This *signaling* aspect of the price system provides information to individual buyers and sellers about what and how many items should be produced, how production of items should be organized, and who will choose to buy the produced items.

Thus, in a price system, individuals and families own the facilities used to produce automobiles. They decide which types of automobiles to produce, how many of them to produce, and how to bring labor and machines together within their facilities to generate the desired production. Other individuals and families decide how much of their earnings they wish to spend on automobiles.

MIXED ECONOMIC SYSTEMS By and large, the economic systems of the world's nations are mixed economic systems that incorporate aspects of both centralized command and control and a decentralized price system. At any given time, some nations lean toward centralized mechanisms of command and control and allow relatively little scope for decentralized decision making. At the same time, other nations limit the extent to which a central authority dictates answers to the three basic economic questions, leaving people mostly free to utilize a decentralized price system to generate their own answers.

A given country may reach different decisions at different times about how much to rely on command and control versus a price system to answer its three basic economic questions. Until 2008, for instance, the people of the United States preferred to rely mainly on a decentralized price system to decide which and how many automobiles to produce and how to produce them. Since then, the U.S. government has owned substantial fractions of auto companies and hence has exerted considerable command-and-control authority over U.S. vehicle production.

How is China confronting the issue of what economic system to adopt?

During the past decade, residents of China have debated the relative merits of two different economic systems. The first of these systems—the *Chongqing* system, named for a city in that nation's southwest—relies on government-owned enterprises to determine what, how, and for whom goods and services should be produced. Application of the Chongqing system to the steel industry has resulted in China's becoming the world's foremost steel producer. State-supported firms operate most of the nation's 2,700 steel mills, many of which produce more ribbed steel bars intended for reinforcing concrete than people desire to use.

The second system—the *Guangdon* system, named for a coastal province of China—places greater emphasis on allowing individuals who own and operate private businesses to decide what, how, and for whom production should take place. Under the Guangdon system,

instead of the government directing resources to produce more steel than people wish to consume, China's people would be free to shift scarce resources to production and distribution of a different item. For example, instead of making more underutilized steel, private firms could manufacture digital devices that many consumers would like to purchase.

FOR CRITICAL THINKING
Why might government-owned companies and private firms that produce steel respond differently if steel buyers purchase less?

Sources are listed at the end of this chapter.

MyEconLab Concept Check
MyEconLab Study Plan

SELF CHECK Visit MyEconLab to practice these and other problems and to get instant feedback in your Study Plan.

The three basic economic questions are _____ and how _____ will be produced, _____ will items be produced, and for _____ will items be produced?

The two opposing sets of answers are offered by alternative economy systems: (1) centralized _____ and (2) the _____ system.

1.3 Evaluate the role that rational self-interest plays in economic analysis

The Economic Approach: Systematic Decisions

Economists assume that individuals act *as if* they systematically pursue self-motivated interests and respond predictably to perceived opportunities to attain those interests. This central insight of economics was first clearly articulated by Adam Smith in 1776. Smith wrote in his most famous book, *An Inquiry into the Nature and Causes of the Wealth of Nations*, that "it is not from the benevolence [good will] of the butcher, the brewer, or the baker that we expect our dinner, but from their regard to their own interest." Thus, the typical person about whom economists make behavioral predictions is assumed to act *as though* he or she systematically pursues self-motivated interest.

The Rationality Assumption

Rationality assumption
The assumption that people do not intentionally make decisions that would leave them worse off.

The **rationality assumption** of economics, simply stated, is as follows:

> *We assume that individuals do not intentionally make decisions that would leave themselves worse off.*

The distinction here is between what people may think—the realm of psychology and psychiatry and perhaps sociology—and what they do. Economics does *not* involve itself in analyzing individual or group thought processes. Economics looks at what people actually do in life with their limited resources. It does little good to criticize the rationality assumption by stating, "Nobody thinks that way" or "I never think that way" or "How unrealistic! That's as irrational as anyone can get!" In a world in which people can be atypical in countless ways, economists find it useful to concentrate on discovering the baseline. Knowing what happens on average is a good place to start. In this way, we avoid building our thinking on exceptions rather than on reality.

Take the example of driving. When you consider passing another car on a two-lane highway with oncoming traffic, you have to make very quick decisions: You must estimate the speed of the car that you are going to pass, the speed of the oncoming cars, the distance between your car and the oncoming cars, and your car's potential rate of acceleration. If we were to apply a model to your behavior, we would use the rules of calculus. In actual fact, you and most other drivers in such a situation do not actually think of using the rules of calculus, but to predict your behavior, we could make the prediction *as if* you understood those rules.

How did a number of U.S. companies respond rationally to a significant increase in the federal tax rate on dividend payments to their shareholders?

EXAMPLE

Why Did Costco Borrow $3.5 Billion to Distribute to Its Shareholders?

In late 2012, owners of the wholesale-club operator Costco decided that the firm would borrow $3.5 billion, which the company then transmitted in the form of dividend payments to owners of the company's shares of stock. This dividend income received by Costco shareholders was subject to a federal tax rate of 15 percent that applied throughout 2012 instead of a 39.6 percent tax rate that went into effect at the beginning of 2013. After taking into account borrowing costs, this arrangement generated tens of millions of dollars of income tax savings for its shareholders.

More than 170 other U.S. companies seeking income tax savings for their shareholders also substantially boosted their dividends in 2012. In a response that many tax experts called "completely rational," these U.S. firms paid out about four times more dividends than they had in previous years. The companies sharply reduced dividend payments afterward. In effect, the companies shifted most of their dividend payments forward in time to reduce their owners' tax bills.

FOR CRITICAL THINKING
How do you think that individual taxpayers responded to the increase in dividend tax rates?

Sources are listed at the end of this chapter.

MyEconLab Concept Check

Responding to Incentives

If it can be assumed that individuals never intentionally make decisions that would leave them worse off, then almost by definition they will respond to changes in incentives. Indeed, much of human behavior can be explained in terms of how individuals respond to changing incentives over time.

Schoolchildren are motivated to do better by a variety of incentive systems, ranging from gold stars and certificates of achievement when they are young, to better grades with accompanying promises of a "better life" as they get older. Of course, negative incentives affect our behavior, too. Penalties, punishments, and other forms of negative incentives can raise the total cost of engaging in various activities.

MyEconLab Concept Check

Defining Self-Interest

Self-interest does not always mean increasing one's wealth measured in dollars and cents. We assume that individuals seek many goals, not just increased wealth measured in monetary terms. Thus, the self-interest part of our economic-person assumption includes goals relating to prestige, friendship, love, power, helping others, creating works of art, and many other matters. We can also think in terms of enlightened self-interest, whereby individuals, in the pursuit of what makes them better off, also achieve the betterment of others around them. In brief, individuals are assumed to want the ability to further their goals by making decisions about how items around them are used. The head of a charitable organization usually will not turn down an additional contribution, because accepting the funds yields control over how they are used, even though their use is for other people's benefit.

Thus, self-interest does not rule out doing charitable acts. Is it possible, nevertheless, that people are likely to be more charitable when their own self-interest clearly is involved?

EXAMPLE

Taking Care of Others—and Self

U.S. residents give more than $300 billion in annual charitable donations, or about 2 percent of the total income that their economic activities generate each year. Consequently, many people seem to incorporate into their self-interested motives some concerns for the well-being of other individuals. People tend to donate more to charity when their own personal interests also are involved. Charitable organizations have long recognized that people are likely to give more to charities that provide them with some form of entertainment in the process, perhaps by participating in raffles or auctions. Recently, these organizations have also begun operating charitable fund-raising programs through social networking sites that promote enjoyable interactions among participating donors.

In the United States, another self-interested incentive to donate to charities is that assessed dollar valuations of many charitable donations are tax deductible. Under this policy, people simultaneously can enjoy giving to others and reducing their own federal tax bills.

FOR CRITICAL THINKING

Why do you suppose economists have found evidence that people tend to give more to charities when they are currently in good health but reduce their giving when they anticipate they will shortly die?

Sources are listed at the end of this chapter.

MyEconLab Concept Check
MyEconLab Study Plan

SELF CHECK Visit MyEconLab to practice these and other problems and to get instant feedback in your Study Plan.

In economics, we assume that people do not _____ make decisions that will leave them _____ off.	The statement immediately preceding is known as the _____ assumption.

1.4 Explain why economics is a science·

Models, or theories
Simplified representations of the real world used as the basis for predictions or explanations.

Economics as a Science

Economics is a social science that employs the same kinds of methods used in other sciences, such as biology, physics, and chemistry. Like these other sciences, economics uses models, or theories. Economic **models**, or **theories**, are simplified representations of the real world that we use to help us understand, explain, and predict economic phenomena in the real world. There are, of course, differences between sciences. The social sciences—especially economics—make little use of laboratory experiments in which changes in variables are studied under controlled conditions. Rather, social scientists, and especially economists, usually have to test their models, or theories, by examining what has already happened in the real world.

Models and Realism

At the outset it must be emphasized that no model in *any* science, and therefore no economic model, is complete in the sense that it captures *every* detail or interrelationship that exists. Indeed, a model, by definition, is an abstraction from reality. It is conceptually impossible to construct a perfectly complete realistic model. For example, in physics we cannot account for every molecule and its position and certainly not for every atom and subatomic particle. Not only is such a model unreasonably expensive to build, but working with it would be impossibly complex.

The nature of scientific model building is that the model should capture only the *essential* relationships that are sufficient to analyze the particular problem or answer the particular question with which we are concerned. *An economic model cannot be faulted as unrealistic simply because it does not represent every detail of the real world.* A map of a city that shows only major streets is not faulty if, in fact, all you wish to know is how to pass through the city using major streets. As long as a model is able to shed light on the *central* issue at hand or forces at work, it may be useful.

A map is the quintessential model. It is *always* a simplified representation. It is *always* unrealistic. It is, however, also useful in making predictions about the world. If the model—the map—predicts that when you take Campus Avenue to the north, you always run into the campus, that is a prediction. If a simple model can explain observed behavior in repeated settings just as well as a complex model, the simple model has some value and is probably easier to use. MyEconLab Concept Check

Assumptions

Every model, or theory, must be based on a set of assumptions. Assumptions define the array of circumstances in which our model is most likely to be applicable. When some people predicted that sailing ships would fall off the edge of the earth, they used the *assumption* that the earth was flat. Columbus did not accept the implications of such a model because he did not accept its assumptions. He assumed that the world was round. The real-world test of his own model refuted the flat-earth model. Indirectly, then, it was a test of the assumption of the flat-earth model.

Is it possible to use our knowledge about assumptions to understand why driving directions sometimes contain very few details?

EXAMPLE

Getting Directions

Assumptions are a shorthand for reality. Imagine that you have decided to drive from your home in San Diego to downtown San Francisco. Because you have never driven this route, you decide to use a travel-planner device such as global-positioning-system equipment.

When you ask for directions, the electronic travel planner could give you a set of detailed maps that shows each city through which you will travel—Oceanside, San Clemente, Irvine, Anaheim, Los Angeles, Bakersfield, Modesto, and so on—with the individual maps showing you exactly how the freeway threads through each of these cities. You would get a nearly complete description of reality because the GPS travel planner will not have used many simplifying assumptions. It is more likely, however, that the travel planner will simply say, "Get on Interstate 5

going north. Stay on it for about 500 miles. Follow the signs for San Francisco. After crossing the toll bridge, take any exit marked 'Downtown.'" By omitting all of the trivial details, the travel planner has told you all that you really need and want to know. The models you will be using in this text are similar to the simplified directions on how to drive from San Diego to San Francisco—they focus on what is relevant to the problem at hand and omit what is not.

FOR CRITICAL THINKING
In what way do small talk and gossip represent the use of simplifying assumptions?

THE *CETERIS PARIBUS* ASSUMPTION: ALL OTHER THINGS BEING EQUAL Everything in the world seems to relate in some way to everything else in the world. It would be impossible to isolate the effects of changes in one variable on another variable if we always had to worry about the many other variables that might also enter the analysis. Similar to other sciences, economics uses the ***ceteris paribus* assumption.** *Ceteris paribus* means "other things constant" or "other things equal."

Consider an example taken from economics. One of the most important determinants of how much of a particular product a family buys is how expensive that product is relative to other products. We know that in addition to relative prices, other factors influence decisions about making purchases. Some of them have to do with income, others with tastes, and yet others with custom and religious beliefs. Whatever these other factors are, we hold them constant when we look at the relationship between changes in prices and changes in how much of a given product people will purchase.

MyEconLab Concept Check

Ceteris paribus [KAY-ter-us PEAR-uh-bus] assumption
The assumption that nothing changes except the factor or factors being studied.

Deciding on the Usefulness of a Model

We generally do not attempt to determine the usefulness, or "goodness," of a model merely by evaluating how realistic its assumptions are. Rather, we consider a model "good" if it yields usable predictions that are supported by real-world observations. In other words, can we use the model to predict what will happen in the world around us? Does the model provide useful implications about how things happen in our world?

Once we have determined that the model may be useful in predicting real-world phenomena, the scientific approach to the analysis of the world around us requires that

Empirical
Relying on real-world data in evaluating the usefulness of a model.

we consider evidence. Evidence is used to test the usefulness of a model. This is why we call economics an **empirical** science. *Empirical* means that evidence (data) is looked at to see whether we are right. Economists are often engaged in empirically testing their models.   MyEconLab Concept Check

Models of Behavior, *Not* Thought Processes

Take special note of the fact that economists' models do not relate to the way people *think*. Economic models relate to the way people *act*, to what they do in life with their limited resources. Normally, the economist does not attempt to predict how people will think about a particular topic, such as a higher price of oil products, accelerated inflation, or higher taxes. Rather, the task at hand is to predict how people will behave, which may be quite different from what they *say* they will do (much to the consternation of poll takers and market researchers). Thus, people's *declared* preferences are generally of little use in testing economic theories, which aim to explain and predict people's *revealed* preferences. The people involved in examining thought processes are psychologists and psychiatrists, not typically economists.   MyEconLab Concept Check

Behavioral Economics and Bounded Rationality

In recent years, some economists have proposed paying more attention to psychologists and psychiatrists. They have suggested an alternative approach to economic analysis. Their approach, known as **behavioral economics**, examines consumer behavior in the face of psychological limitations and complications that may interfere with rational decision making.

Behavioral economics
An approach to the study of consumer behavior that emphasizes psychological limitations and complications that potentially interfere with rational decision making.

BOUNDED RATIONALITY Proponents of behavioral economics suggest that traditional economic models assume that people exhibit three "unrealistic" characteristics:

1. *Unbounded selfishness.* People are interested only in their own satisfaction.

2. *Unbounded willpower.* Their choices are always consistent with their long-term goals.

3. *Unbounded rationality.* They are able to consider every relevant choice.

Bounded rationality
The hypothesis that people are *nearly*, but not fully, rational, so that they cannot examine every possible choice available to them but instead use simple rules of thumb to sort among the alternatives that happen to occur to them.

As an alternative, advocates of behavioral economics have proposed replacing the rationality assumption with the assumption of **bounded rationality**, which assumes that people cannot examine and think through every possible choice they confront. As a consequence, behavioral economists suggest, individuals cannot always pursue, on their own, their best long-term personal interests. They sometimes require help.

WHAT IF...

the government "nudges" people to influence their decision making?

Various economic studies have found evidence consistent with the idea that people sometimes put off making decisions that outside observers judge would make those individuals unambiguously better off. Researchers have found some evidence that people do not have unbounded willpower, meaning that their choices are not always consistent with their long-term goals. For instance, left to their own devices, some people never get around to contributing some of their earnings to a pension plan when

given the opportunity by their employers. In the United Kingdom, a law now requires people to contribute to an available pension plan unless they make a conscious decision not to do so. The British government thereby "nudges" people toward a choice that it perceives to be in their own best interest while giving them the ability to make a different decision if that is their preference. The result has been that more people have opted to contribute to pension plans than was true in previous years.

RULES OF THUMB A key behavioral implication of the bounded rationality assumption is that people should use so-called *rules of thumb:* Because every possible choice cannot be considered, an individual will tend to fall back on methods of making decisions that are simpler than trying to sort through every possibility.

A problem confronting advocates of behavioral economics is that people who *appear* to use rules of thumb may in fact behave *as if* they are fully rational. For instance, if a person faces persistently predictable ranges of choices for a while, the individual may rationally settle into repetitive behaviors that an outside observer might conclude to be consistent with a rule of thumb. According to the bounded rationality assumption, the person will continue to rely on a rule of thumb even if there is a major change in the environment that the individual faces. Time and time again, however, economists find that people respond to altered circumstances by fundamentally changing their behaviors. Economists also generally observe that people make decisions that are consistent with their own self-interest and long-term objectives.

BEHAVIORAL ECONOMICS: A WORK IN PROGRESS It remains to be seen whether the application of the assumption of bounded rationality proposed by behavioral economists will truly alter the manner in which economists construct models intended to better predict human decision making. So far, proponents of behavioral economics have not conclusively demonstrated that paying closer attention to psychological thought processes can improve economic predictions.

As a consequence, the bulk of economic analysis continues to rely on the rationality assumption as the basis for constructing economic models. Advocates of behavioral economics continue to explore ways in which psychological elements might improve analysis of decision making by individual consumers.

MyEconLab Concept Check
MyEconLab Study Plan

SELF CHECK   Visit MyEconLab to practice these and other problems and to get instant feedback in your Study Plan.

A _____, or _____, uses assumptions and is by nature a simplification of the real world. The usefulness of a _____ can be evaluated by bringing empirical evidence to bear on its predictions.

Most models use the _____ _____ assumption that all other things are held constant, or equal.

_____ economics emphasizes psychological constraints and complexities that potentially interfere with rational decision making. This approach utilizes the _____ _____ hypothesis that people are not quite rational, because they cannot study every possible alternative but instead use simple rules of thumb to decide among choices.

Positive versus Normative Economics

1.5 Distinguish between positive and normative economics

Economics uses *positive analysis*, a value-free approach to inquiry. No subjective or moral judgments enter into the analysis. Positive analysis relates to statements such as "If A, then B." For example, "If the price of gasoline goes up relative to all other prices, then the amount of it that people buy will fall." That is a positive economic statement. It is a statement of *what is*. It is not a statement of anyone's value judgment or subjective feelings.

Distinguishing between Positive and Normative Economics

For many problems analyzed in the "hard" sciences such as physics and chemistry, the analyses are considered to be virtually value-free. After all, how can someone's values enter into a theory of molecular behavior? Economists, however, face a different problem. They deal with the behavior of individuals, not molecules. That makes it more difficult to stick to what we consider to be value-free or **positive economics** without reference to our feelings.

When our values are interjected into the analysis, we enter the realm of **normative economics**, involving *normative analysis*. A positive economic statement is "If the price of gas rises, people will buy less." If we add to that analysis the statement "so we should not allow the price to go up," we have entered the realm of normative economics—we have expressed a value judgment. In fact, any time you see the word *should*, you will know that values are entering into the discussion. Just remember that positive

Positive economics
Analysis that is *strictly* limited to making either purely descriptive statements or scientific predictions; for example, "If A, then B." A statement of *what is*.

Normative economics
Analysis involving value judgments about economic policies; relates to whether outcomes are good or bad. A statement of *what ought to be*.

statements are concerned with *what is*, whereas normative statements are concerned with *what ought to be*.

Each of us has a desire for different things. That means we have different values. When we express a value judgment, we are simply saying what we prefer, like, or desire. Because individual values are diverse, we expect—and indeed observe—that people express widely varying value judgments about how the world ought to be.

MyEconLab Concept Check

A Warning: Recognize Normative Analysis

It is easy to define positive economics. It is quite another matter to catch all unlabeled normative statements in a textbook, even though an author goes over the manuscript many times before it is printed or electronically created. Therefore, do not get the impression that a textbook author will be able to keep all personal values out of the book. They will slip through. In fact, the very choice of which topics to include in an introductory textbook involves normative economics. There is no value-free way to decide which topics to use in her or his textbook. The author's values ultimately make a difference when choices have to be made. From your own standpoint, though, you might want to be able to recognize when you are engaging in normative as opposed to positive economic analysis. Reading this text will help equip you for that task.

MyEconLab Concept Check
MyEconLab Study Plan

SELF CHECK Visit MyEconLab to practice these and other problems and to get instant feedback in your Study Plan.

_____ economics is value-free and relates to statements that can be refuted, such as "If a, then b."	_____ economics involves people's values and typically uses the word *should*.

YOU ARE THERE

How a Tax Differential Aided a Texas Pro Basketball Team

Dwight Howard, a 26-year-old basketball center widely regarded as one of the five best professional players, has spent the past several years playing for National Basketball Association (NBA) teams in Orlando, Florida, and Los Angeles, California. Now he is trying to decide whether to stay in Los Angeles or move to Houston, Texas. The Los Angeles team has offered him a pre-tax salary of $23.6 million per year to continue with that team for the next several seasons. Houston's NBA team, in contrast, has offered a pre-tax salary of $22 million per year.

From the perspective of many sports enthusiasts, Howard has an easy choice to make. Most of them agree that the Los Angeles team is more likely than the one based in Houston to win NBA championships with Howard on their roster. Although Howard's presence on any team probably will generate greater fan interest, more fans likely will attend Los Angeles games to cheer for Howard than would attend Houston games. Fur-

thermore, Howard will be able to earn $1.6 million more per year before taxes if he stays in Los Angeles.

In the end, however, Howard's decision is to move to Houston. Texas has no state income tax, but California does. Thus, Howard's *after*-tax earnings will be more than $500,000 per year higher if he plays in Houston.

CRITICAL THINKING QUESTIONS

1. What is the nature of the incentive that appears to have predominated in influencing Howard's choice about where to play basketball?

2. Does Howard appear to have engaged in behavior consistent with the rationality assumption?

Sources are listed at the end of this chapter.

ISSUES & APPLICATIONS

MyEconLab Video

Incentive Effects of Student Loans for College Graduates

FINANCIAL AID OFFICE

Mark Humphrey/AP Images

CONCEPTS APPLIED

» Incentives

» Rationality Assumption

» Self-Interest

More than 70 percent of college graduates have at least some student loan debt. From today's perspective, the average inflation-adjusted debt of a typical graduate borrower has doubled since 1993, from $15,000 to more than $30,000. Such a substantial level of personal indebtedness has changed the incentives of indebted individuals with college degrees.

The Altered Incentives of Graduates with Student Loan Debts

The amount of $30,000 in debt is close to two-thirds of the annual income of a typical recent college graduate. It is also about the average price of a new automobile or, alternatively, the dollar amount of a 20 percent down payment on an average-priced house.

Not surprisingly, a number of young college graduates confronting student loan debts have viewed their substantial debts as disincentives to buying big-ticket items. Recent studies have shown that indebted graduates have been much less likely to purchase a house or a new car than debt-free graduates.

Has the Run-Up of Student Loan Debts Been Rational?

Even as the average level of indebtedness per student loan borrower has increased, so has the number of borrowers. Today more than twice as many college enrollees finance their educations using student loans than was the case a decade ago.

Some commentators have suggested that the observation of more people running up larger student loan debts is inconsistent with the rationality assumption employed by economists. Recall, however, that the rationality assumption requires only that people do not intentionally make decisions that cause them to be worse off. Most student borrowers have anticipated finding jobs that would enable them both to repay their student loans and to buy items such as houses and vehicles. Thus, they believed that borrowing to finance their education was in their own self-interest.

In recent years, nearly half of student loan borrowers have failed to complete their degrees and consequently

have not obtained jobs offering the anticipated higher incomes. A number of these individuals have not obtained any jobs. Their decisions to accumulate student loans did not involve any intent to make themselves worse off and hence were motivated by rational self-interest. Nevertheless, even though these decisions were rationally formulated at the time they were made, the outcome for many borrowers has, after the fact, been lower well-being.

For Critical Thinking

1. Why do you suppose that people with student loan debts wait longer to get married and to have children than people without debts?

2. Is regretting a previous decision inconsistent with the individual's self-interest at the time the decision was made?

Web Resources

1. To obtain information about default rates on student loans, see the Web Links in MyEconLab.

2. Read a discussion of how student loan debts compare with other forms of indebtedness in the Web Links in MyEconLab.

MyEconLab

For more questions on this chapter's Issues & Applications, go to MyEconLab.

In the Study Plan for this chapter, select Section I: Issues and Applications.

Sources are listed at the end of this chapter.

Fundamental Points

1. Economics is the study of how people allocate limited resources to satisfy unlimited wants.
2. The essential questions of economics are (a) What and how much will be produced? (b) How will items be produced? (c) For whom will items be produced? The opposing sets of answers are provided by a system of centralized command and control or the price system.
3. According to the rationality assumption utilized by economists, people do not intentionally make choices that cause them to be worse off.
4. Economists utilize models or theories, which are simplified representations of the real world, to formulate explanations or predictions.
5. Positive economics involves analysis that is strictly limited to making purely descriptive statements or scientific predictions, and normative economics involves analysis incorporating value judgments.

WHAT YOU SHOULD KNOW

Here is what you should know after reading this chapter. MyEconLab will help you identify what you know, and where to go when you need to practice.

LEARNING OBJECTIVES	KEY TERMS	WHERE TO GO TO PRACTICE
1.1 Define economics and discuss the difference between microeconomics and macroeconomics *Economics is the study of how individuals make choices to satisfy wants. Microeconomics is the study of decision making by individual households and firms, and macroeconomics is the study of nationwide phenomena such as inflation and unemployment.*	incentives, 2 economics, 2 resources, 2 wants, 2 microeconomics, 3 macroeconomics, 3 aggregates, 3	• MyEconLab Study Plan 1.1
1.2 Identify the three basic economic questions and the two opposing sets of answers *The three basic economic questions ask what and how much will be produced, how items will be produced, and for whom items will be produced. The two opposing answers to these questions are provided by the type of economic system: either centralized command and control or the price system.*	economic system, 3	• MyEconLab Study Plan 1.2
1.3 Evaluate the role that rational self-interest plays in economic analysis *Rational self-interest is the assumption that people never intentionally make decisions that would leave them worse off. Instead, they are motivated mainly by their self-interest, which can relate to monetary and nonmonetary goals, such as love, prestige, and helping others.*	rationality assumption, 6	• MyEconLab Study Plan 1.3

WHAT YOU SHOULD KNOW *continued*

LEARNING OBJECTIVES ───	KEY TERMS ───	WHERE TO GO TO PRACTICE ─
1.4 **Explain why economics is a science** *Economic models, or theories, are simplified representations of the real world. Economic models are never completely realistic because by definition they are simplifications using assumptions that are not directly testable. Nevertheless, economists can subject the predictions of economic theories to empirical tests in which real-world data are used to decide whether or not to reject the predictions.*	models, or theories, 8 *ceteris paribus* assumption, 9 empirical, 10 behavioral economics, 10 bounded rationality, 10	• MyEconLab Study Plan 1.4
1.5 **Distinguish between positive and normative economics** *Positive economics deals with what is, whereas normative economics deals with what ought to be. Positive economic statements are of the "if . . . then" variety. They are descriptive and predictive. In contrast, statements embodying values are within the realm of normative economics, or how people think things ought to be.*	positive economics, 11 normative economics, 11	• MyEconLab Study Plan 1.5

Log in to MyEconLab, take a chapter test, and get a personalized Study Plan that tells you which concepts you understand and which ones you need to review. From there, MyEconLab will give you further practice, tutorials, animations, videos, and guided solutions. For more information, visit http://www.myeconlab.com

PROBLEMS

All problems are assignable in MyEconLab. Answers to odd-numbered problems appear in MyEconLab.

1-1. Define economics. Explain briefly how the economic way of thinking—in terms of rational, self-interested people responding to incentives—relates to each of the following situations. (See pages 2, 6–7.)

   a. A student deciding whether to purchase a textbook for a particular class

   b. Government officials seeking more funding for mass transit through higher taxes

   c. A municipality taxing hotel guests to obtain funding for a new sports stadium

1-2. Some people claim that the "economic way of thinking" does not apply to issues such as health care. Explain how economics does apply to this issue by developing a "model" of an individual's choices. (See pages 8–9.)

1-3. Does the phrase "unlimited wants and limited resources" apply to both a low-income household and a middle-income household? Can the same phrase be applied to a very high-income household? (See page 2.)

1-4. In a single sentence, contrast microeconomics and macroeconomics. Next, categorize each of the following issues as a microeconomic issue, a macroeconomic issue, or not an economic issue. (See page 3.)

   a. The national unemployment rate

   b. The decision of a worker to work overtime or not

   c. A family's choice to have a baby

   d. The rate of growth of the money supply

   e. The national government's budget deficit

   f. A student's allocation of study time across two subjects

1-5. One of your classmates, Sally, is a hardworking student, serious about her classes, and conscientious about her grades. Sally is also involved, however, in volunteer activities and an extracurricular sport. Is Sally displaying rational behavior? Based on what you read in this chapter, construct an argument supporting the conclusion that she is. (See pages 6–8.)

1-6. Recently, a bank was trying to decide what fee to charge for "expedited payments"—payments the bank would transmit with extra speed so that customers could avoid late fees on cable TV bills, electric bills, and the like. To try to determine what fee customers were willing to pay for expedited payments, the bank conducted a survey. It was able to determine that many of the people surveyed already paid fees for expedited payment services that *exceeded* the maximum fees they said they were willing to pay. How does the bank's finding relate to economists' traditional focus on what people do, rather than what they *say* they will do? (See page 10.)

1-7. Explain, in your own words, the rationality assumption, and contrast it with the assumption of bounded rationality proposed by adherents of behavioral economics. (See pages 6–7, 10–11.)

1-8. Why does the assumption of bounded rationality suggest that people might use rules of thumb to guide their decision making instead of considering every possible choice available to them? (See page 10.)

1-9. Under what circumstances might people appear to use rules of thumb, as suggested by the assumption of bounded rationality, even though they really are behaving in a manner suggested by the rationality assumption? (See pages 10–11.)

1-10. For each of the following approaches that an economist might follow in examining a decision-making process, identify whether the approach relies on the rationality assumption or on the assumption of bounded rationality. (See page 10.)

   a. To make predictions about how many apps a person will download onto her tablet device, an economist presumes that the individual faces limitations that make it impossible for her to examine every possible choice among relevant apps.

   b. In evaluating the price that an individual will be willing to pay for a given quantity of a particular type of health-care service, a researcher assumes that the person considers all relevant health-care options in pursuit of his own long-term satisfaction with resulting health outcomes.

   c. To determine the amount of time that a person will decide to devote to watching online videos each week, an economist makes the assumption that the individual will feel overwhelmed by the sheer volume of videos available online and will respond by using a rule of thumb.

1-11. For each of the following approaches that an economist might follow in examining a decision-making process, identify whether the approach relies on the rationality assumption or on the assumption of bounded rationality. (See page 10.)

   a. An economic study of the number of online searches that individuals conduct before selecting a particular item to purchase online presumes that people are interested only in their own satisfaction, pursue their ultimate objectives, and consider every relevant option.

   b. An economist seeking to predict the effect that an increase in a state's sales tax rate will have on consumers' purchases of goods and services presumes that people are limited in their ability to process information about how the tax-rate increase will influence the after-tax prices those consumers will pay.

   c. To evaluate the impact of an increase in the range of choices that an individual confronts when deciding among devices for accessing the Internet, an economic researcher makes the assumption that the individual is unable to take into account every new Internet-access option available to her.

1-12. Which of the following predictions appear(s) to follow from a model based on the assumption that rational, self-interested individuals respond to incentives? (See pages 6–8.)

   a. For every ten exam points Myrna must earn in order to pass her economics course and meet her graduation requirements, she will study one additional hour for her economics test next week.

   b. A coin toss will best predict Leonardo's decision about whether to purchase an expensive business suit or an inexpensive casual outfit to wear next week when he interviews for a high-paying job he is seeking.

   c. Celeste, who uses earnings from her regularly scheduled hours of part-time work to pay for her room and board at college, will decide to purchase and download a newly released video this week only if she is able to work two additional hours.

1-13. Consider two models for estimating, in advance of an election, the shares of votes that will go to rival candidates. According to one model, pollsters' surveys of a randomly chosen set of registered voters before an election can be used to forecast the percentage of votes that each candidate will receive. The above model relies on the assumption that unpaid survey respondents will give truthful responses about how they will vote and that they will actually cast a ballot in the election. The other model uses prices of financial assets (legally binding IOUs) issued by the Iowa Electronic Markets, operated by the University of Iowa, to predict electoral outcomes. The final payments received by owners of these assets, which can be bought or sold during the weeks and days preceding an election, depend on the shares of votes the candidates actually end up receiving. This second model assumes that owners of these assets wish to earn the highest possible returns, and it predicts that the market prices of these assets provide an indication of the percentage of votes that each candidate will actually receive on the day of the election. (See pages 8–9.)

a. Which of these two models for forecasting electoral results is more firmly based on the rationality assumption of economics?

b. How would an economist evaluate which is the better model for forecasting electoral outcomes?

1-14. Write a sentence contrasting positive and normative economic analysis. (See pages 11–12.)

1-15. Based on your answer to Problem 1–14, categorize each of the following conclusions as resulting from positive analysis or normative analysis. (See pages 11–12.)

a. A higher minimum wage will reduce employment opportunities for minimum wage workers.

b. Increasing the earnings of minimum wage employees is desirable, and raising the minimum wage is the best way to accomplish this.

c. Everyone should enjoy open access to health care at no explicit charge.

d. Heath-care subsidies will increase the consumption of health care.

1-16. Consider the following statements, based on a positive economic analysis that assumes all other things remain constant. For each, list one other thing that might change and thus offset the outcome stated. (See pages 9, 11.)

a. Increased demand for laptop computers will drive up their price.

b. Falling gasoline prices will result in additional vacation travel.

c. A reduction of income tax rates will result in more people working.

REFERENCES

POLICY EXAMPLE: Government Green Energy Financing Flops

Chuck Jones, "Solar Companies Continue to Go Bankrupt," *Forbes*, April 9, 2013.

Lachian Markay, "ECOtality Fatality: Green Company Files for Bankruptcy after 115M Stimulus Funding Granted," *The Washington Times*, September 17, 2013.

Jeff St. John, "Xtreme Power, Grid-Scale Energy Storage Startup, Files for Bankruptcy," *Greentech Media*, January 23, 2014.

Eric Wesoff, "Rest in Peace: The List of Deceased Solar Companies," *Greentech Media*, April 6, 2013 (www.greentechmedia.com/articles/read/Rest-in-Peace-The-List-of-Deceased-Solar-Companies).

INTERNATIONAL POLICY EXAMPLE: In China, *Chongqing* Plus *Guangdon* Equals a Mixed Economy

David Mullings, "The Chongqing Model of Economic Development," *Jamaica Observer*, January 13, 2013.

Dan Steinbock, "One Growth Model, Many Chinas: Guangdong, Chongqing, and China's Regional Differences," *EconoMonitor*, Roubini Global Economics (www.economonitor.com/blog/2012/12/one-growth-model-many-chinas-guangdong-chongqing-and-chinas-regional-differences/).

Luo Wangshu and Ji Jin, "Foreign Investment Eyes Chongqing's Connections," *China Daily*, January 21, 2014.

EXAMPLE: Why Did Costco Borrow $3.5 Billion to Distribute to Its Shareholders?

"Costco Dividend Yield & Stock Price History," Dividend.com, February 10, 2014 (www.dividend.com/dividend_stocks/services/discount-variety-stores/cost-costco/)

Matt Krantz, "Investors Get a Tax Break with Early Dividends," *USA Today*, February 5, 2013.

Ian Salisbury, "Bigger Dividends in 2013? Experts Say the Tax Deal Isn't the Only Reason to Be Optimistic," *MarketWatch*, January 8, 2013 (www.marketwatch.com/story/bigger-dividends-in-2013-2013-01-08).

EXAMPLE: Taking Care of Others—and Self Entertainment Fundraising, "You Can Raise Money & Earn Huge Profits," Fall 2014 (www.entertainment.com/fundraising).

Michael Green, "Why Charities Need to Make Giving Fun," *The Guardian*, May 15, 2013.

Khadeeja Safdar, "The Specter of Death Makes People Less Charitable," *The Wall Street Journal*, July 3, 2013.

YOU ARE THERE: How a Tax Differential Aided a Texas Pro Basketball Team

Kay Bell, "Tax Lessons from Professional Athletes," DontMesswithTaxes.com, February 2, 2014 (http://dontmesswithtaxes.typepad.com/dont_mess_with_taxes/2014/02/tax-lessons-from-professional-athletes.html).

Ben Cohen, "Tax Break Could Give Texas Teams an Edge," *The Wall Street Journal*, July 2, 2013.

Tony Nitti, "Could State Taxes Cause Dwight Howard to Flee L.A. for Houston?" *Forbes*, May 23, 2013.

Staff Report, "Dwight Howard's Tax Savings," *The Washington Free Beacon*, July 10, 2013.

ISSUES & APPLICATIONS: Incentive Effects of Student Loans for College Graduates

Ben Casselman, "The Cost of Dropping Out," *The Wall Street Journal*, November 23, 2012.

Phil Izzo, "Number of the Week: Class of 2013, Most Indebted Ever," *The Wall Street Journal*, May 18, 2013.

Josh Mitchel and Ruth Simon, "Student Borrowers Retreat from Home Buying, Report Says," *The Wall Street Journal*, April 17, 2013.

Brett Nelson, "How to Deal with the $1 Trillion Student Loan Crisis," *Forbes*, January 20, 2014.

Reading and Working with Graphs

A graph is a visual representation of the relationship between variables. In this appendix, we'll deal with just two variables: an **independent variable**, which can change in value freely, and a **dependent variable**, which changes as a result of changes in the value of the independent variable. For example, even if nothing else is changing in your life, your weight depends on your intake of calories. The independent variable is caloric intake, and the dependent variable is weight.

A table is a list of numerical values showing the relationship between two (or more) variables. Any table can be converted into a graph, which is a visual representation of that list. Once you understand how a table can be converted to a graph, you will understand what graphs are and how to construct and use them.

Consider a practical example. A conservationist may try to convince you that driving at lower highway speeds will help you conserve gas. Table A-1 shows the relationship between speed—the independent variable—and the distance you can go on a gallon of gas at that speed—the dependent variable. This table does show a pattern. As the data in the first column get larger in value, the data in the second column get smaller.

Now let's take a look at the different ways in which variables can be related.

Direct and Inverse Relationships

Two variables can be related in different ways, some simple, others more complex. For example, a person's weight and height are often related. If we measured the height and weight of thousands of people, we would surely find that taller people tend to weigh more than shorter people. That is, we would discover there is a **direct relationship** between height and weight. By this we simply mean that an *increase* in one variable is usually associated with an *increase* in the related variable. This can easily be seen in panel (a) of Figure A-1 below.

Let's look at another simple way in which two variables can be related. Much evidence indicates that as the price of a specific commodity rises, the amount purchased decreases—there is an **inverse relationship** between the variable's price per unit and quantity

Independent variable
A variable whose value is determined independently of, or outside, the equation under study.

Dependent variable
A variable whose value changes according to changes in the value of one or more independent variables.

TABLE A-1

Gas Mileage as a Function of Driving Speed

Miles per Hour	Miles per Gallon
45	25
50	24
55	23
60	21
65	19
70	16
75	13

FIGURE A-1

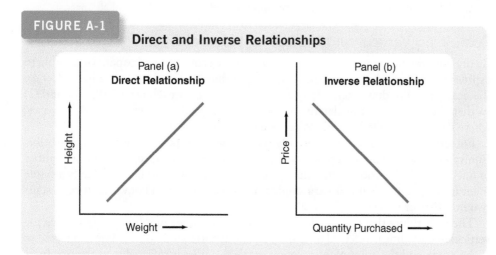

Direct and Inverse Relationships

Panel (a)
Direct Relationship

Height
Weight →

Panel (b)
Inverse Relationship

Price
Quantity Purchased →

Direct relationship
A relationship between two variables that is positive, meaning that an increase in one variable is associated with an increase in the other and a decrease in one variable is associated with a decrease in the other.

Inverse relationship
A relationship between two variables that is negative, meaning that an increase in one variable is associated with a decrease in the other and a decrease in one variable is associated with an increase in the other.

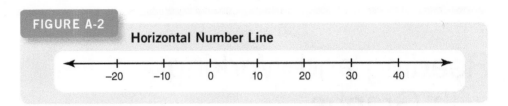

FIGURE A-2

Horizontal Number Line

Number line
A line that can be divided into segments of equal length, each associated with a number.

y axis
The vertical axis in a graph.

x axis
The horizontal axis in a graph.

Origin
The intersection of the *y* axis and the *x* axis in a graph.

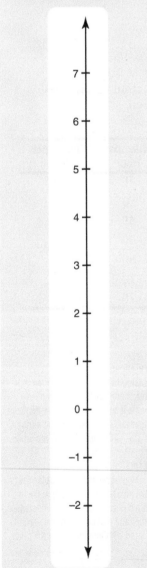

FIGURE A-3

Vertical Number Line

purchased. Such a relationship indicates that for higher and higher prices, smaller and smaller quantities will be purchased. We see this relationship in panel (b) of Figure A-1.

MyEconLab Concept Check
MyEconLab Study Plan

Constructing a Graph

Let us now examine how to construct a graph to illustrate a relationship between two variables.

A Number Line

The first step is to become familiar with what is called a **number line**. One is shown in Figure A-2 above. You should know two things about it:

1. The points on the line divide the line into equal segments.

2. The numbers associated with the points on the line increase in value from left to right. Saying it the other way around, the numbers decrease in value from right to left. However you say it, what you're describing is formally called an *ordered set of points*.

On the number line, we have shown the line segments—that is, the distance from 0 to 10 or the distance between 30 and 40. They all appear to be equal and, indeed, are each equal to $\frac{1}{2}$ inch. When we use a distance to represent a quantity, such as barrels of oil, graphically, we are *scaling* the number line. In the example shown, the distance between 0 and 10 might represent 10 barrels of oil, or the distance from 0 to 40 might represent 40 barrels. Of course, the scale may differ on different number lines. For example, a distance of 1 inch could represent 10 units on one number line but 5,000 units on another. Notice that on our number line, points to the left of 0 correspond to negative numbers and points to the right of 0 correspond to positive numbers.

Of course, we can also construct a vertical number line. Consider the one in Figure A-3 alongside. As we move up this vertical number line, the numbers increase in value; conversely, as we descend, they decrease in value. Below 0 the numbers are negative, and above 0 the numbers are positive. As on the horizontal number line, all the line segments are equal. This line is divided into segments such that the distance between –2 and –1 is the same as the distance between 0 and 1. MyEconLab Concept Check

Combining Vertical and Horizontal Number Lines

By drawing the horizontal and vertical lines on the same sheet of paper, we are able to express the relationships between variables graphically. We do this in Figure A-4 on the next page. We draw them (1) so that they intersect at each other's 0 point and (2) so that they are perpendicular to each other. The result is a set of coordinate axes, where each line is called an *axis*. When we have two axes, they span a *plane*.

For one number line, you need only one number to specify any point on the line. Equivalently, when you see a point on the line, you know that it represents one number or one value. With a coordinate value system, you need two numbers to specify a single point in the plane; when you see a single point on a graph, you know that it represents two numbers or two values.

The basic things that you should know about a coordinate number system are that the vertical number line is referred to as the **y axis**, the horizontal number line is referred to as the **x axis**, and the point of intersection of the two lines is referred to as the **origin**.

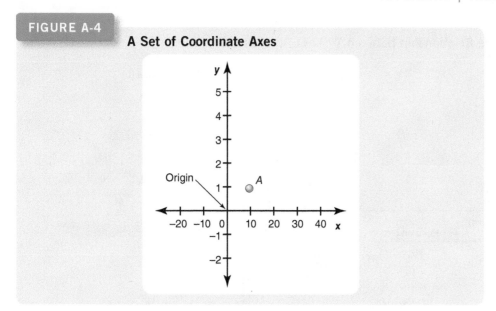

FIGURE A-4

A Set of Coordinate Axes

Any point such as A in Figure A-4 on the next page represents two numbers—a value of x and a value of y. We know more than that, though: We also know that point A represents a positive value of y because it is above the x axis, and we know that it represents a positive value of x because it is to the right of the y axis.

Point A represents a "paired observation" of the variables x and y; in particular, in Figure A-4, A represents an observation of the pair of values $x = 10$ and $y = 1$. Every point in the coordinate system corresponds to a paired observation of x and y, which can be simply written (x, y)—the x value is always specified first and then the y value. When we give the values associated with the position of point A in the coordinate number system, we are in effect giving the coordinates of that point. A's coordinates are $x = 10$, $y = 1$, or $(10, 1)$.

MyEconLab Concept Check
MyEconLab Study Plan

Graphing Numbers in a Table

Consider Table A-2 alongside. Column 1 shows different prices for T-shirts, and column 2 gives the number of T-shirts purchased per week at these prices. Notice the pattern of these numbers. As the price of T-shirts falls, the number of T-shirts purchased per week increases. Therefore, an inverse relationship exists between these two variables, and as soon as we represent it on a graph, you will be able to see the relationship. We can graph this relationship using a coordinate number system—a vertical and horizontal number line for each of these two variables. Such a graph is shown in panel (b) of Figure A-5 on the next page.

In economics, it is conventional to put dollar values on the y axis and quantities on the horizontal axis. We therefore construct a vertical number line for price and a horizontal number line, the x axis, for quantity of T-shirts purchased per week. The resulting coordinate system allows the plotting of each of the paired observation points. In panel (a), we repeat Table A-2, with a column added expressing these points in paired-data (x, y) form. For example, point J is the paired observation $(30, 9)$. It indicates that when the price of a T-shirt is \$9, 30 will be purchased per week.

If it were possible to sell parts of a T-shirt ($\frac{1}{2}$ or $\frac{1}{20}$ or of a shirt), we would have observations at every possible price. That is, we would be able to connect our paired observations, represented as lettered points. Let's assume that we can make T-shirts perfectly divisible so that the linear relationship shown in Figure A-5 also holds for fractions of dollars and T-shirts. We would then have a line that connects these points, as shown in the graph in Figure A-6 on the next page.

In short, we have now represented the data from the table in the form of a graph. Note that an inverse relationship between two variables shows up on a graph as a line or curve that slopes *downward* from left to right. (You might as well get used to the idea

TABLE A-2

T-Shirts Purchased

(1) Price of T-Shirts	(2) Number of T-Shirts Purchased per Week
\$10	20
9	30
8	40
7	50
6	60
5	70

FIGURE A-5

Graphing the Relationship between T-Shirts Purchased and Price

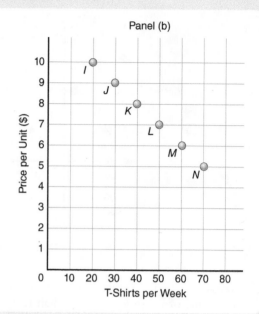

Panel (b)

Panel (a)

Price per T-Shirt	T-Shirts Purchased per Week	Point on Graph
$10	20	I (20, 10)
9	30	J (30, 9)
8	40	K (40, 8)
7	50	L (50, 7)
6	60	M (60, 6)
5	70	N (70, 5)

FIGURE A-6

Connecting the Observation Points

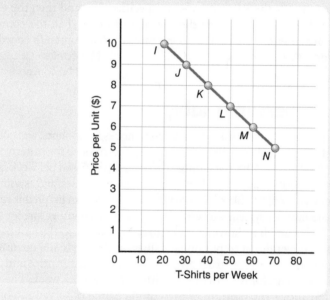

that economists call a straight line a "curve" even though it may not curve at all. Economists' data frequently turn out to be curves, so they refer to everything represented graphically, even straight lines, as curves.) MyEconLab Concept Check

MyEconLab Study Plan

The Slope of a Line (A Linear Curve)

An important property of a curve represented on a graph is its *slope*. Consider Figure A-7 on the next page, which represents the quantities of shoes per week that a seller is willing to offer at different prices. Note that in panel (a) of Figure A-7, as in Figure A-5 above,

FIGURE A-7

A Positively Sloped Curve

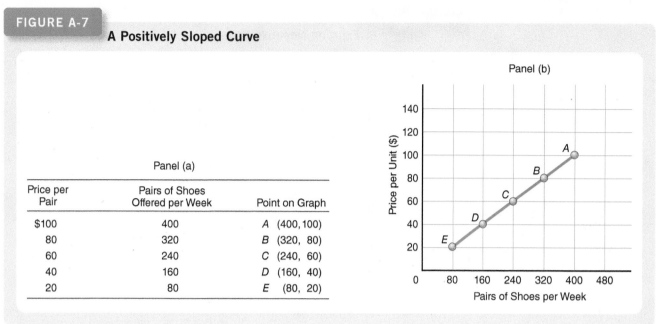

Panel (b)

Panel (a)

Price per Pair	Pairs of Shoes Offered per Week	Point on Graph
$100	400	A (400, 100)
80	320	B (320, 80)
60	240	C (240, 60)
40	160	D (160, 40)
20	80	E (80, 20)

we have expressed the coordinates of the points in parentheses in paired-data form. Let's consider how to measure slope between points along linear, or straight-line, curves.

Slopes of Linear (Straight-Line) Curves

The **slope** of a line is defined as the change in the y values divided by the corresponding change in the x values as we move along the line. Let's move from point E to point D in panel (b) of Figure A-7. As we move, we note that the change in the y values, which is the change in price, is $+20$, because we have moved from a price of $20 to a price of $40 per pair. As we move from E to D, the change in the x values is $+80$; the number of pairs of shoes willingly offered per week rises from 80 to 160 pairs. The slope, calculated as a change in the y values divided by the change in the x values, is therefore

$$\frac{20}{80} = \frac{1}{4}$$

It may be helpful for you to think of slope as a "rise" (movement in the vertical direction) over a "run" (movement in the horizontal direction). We show this abstractly in Figure A-8 below. The slope is the amount of rise divided by the amount of run. In

Slope
The change in the y value divided by the corresponding change in the x value of a curve; the "incline" of the curve.

MyEconLab Animation

FIGURE A-8

Figuring Positive Slope

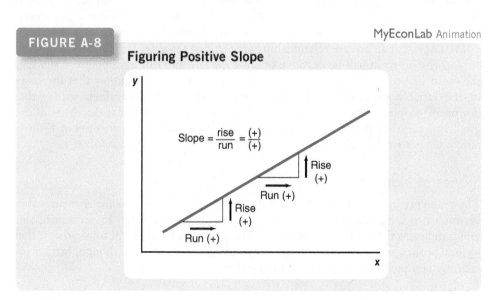

$$\text{Slope} = \frac{\text{rise}}{\text{run}} = \frac{(+)}{(+)}$$

Rise (+)

Run (+)

Rise (+)

Run (+)

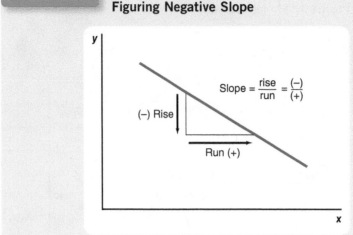

FIGURE A-9

Figuring Negative Slope

the example in Figure A-8, and of course in Figure A-7 on page 23, the amount of rise is positive and so is the amount of run. That's because it's a direct relationship. We show an inverse relationship in Figure A-9. The slope is still equal to the rise divided by the run, but in this case the rise and the run have opposite signs because the curve slopes downward. This fact means that the slope is negative and that we are dealing with an inverse relationship.

Now let's calculate the slope for a different part of the curve in panel (b) of Figure A-7. We will find the slope as we move from point B to point A. Again, we note that the slope, or rise over run, from B to A equals

$$\frac{20}{80} = \frac{1}{4}$$

A specific property of a straight line is that its slope is the same between any two points. In other words, the slope is constant at all points on a straight line in a graph.

We conclude that for our example in Figure A-7 on the previous page, the relationship between the price of a pair of shoes and the number of pairs of shoes willingly offered per week is *linear*, which simply means "in a straight line," and our calculations indicate a constant slope. Moreover, we calculate a direct relationship between these two variables, which turns out to be an upward-sloping (from left to right) curve. Upward-sloping curves have positive slopes—in this case, the slope is $+\frac{1}{4}$.

We know that an inverse relationship between two variables is a downward-sloping curve—rise over run will be negative because the rise and run have opposite signs, as shown in Figure A-9 above. When we see a negative slope, we know that increases in one variable are associated with decreases in the other. Therefore, we say that downward-sloping curves have negative slopes. Can you verify that the slope of the graph representing the relationship between T-shirt prices and the quantity of T-shirts purchased per week in Figure A-6 on page 22 is $-\frac{1}{10}$? **MyEconLab** Concept Check

Slopes of Nonlinear Curves

The graph presented in Figure A-10 on the next page indicates a *nonlinear* relationship between two variables, total profits and output per unit of time. Inspection of this graph indicates that, at first, increases in output lead to increases in total profits; that is, total profits rise as output increases. Beyond some output level, though, further increases in output cause decreases in total profits.

FIGURE A-10

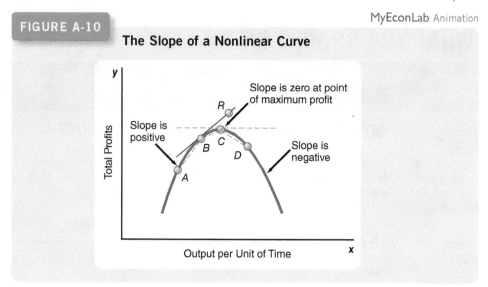

The Slope of a Nonlinear Curve

SLOPE VARIES ALONG A NONLINEAR CURVE Can you see how the curve in Figure A-10 rises at first, reaches a peak at point *C*, and then falls? This curve relating total profits to output levels appears mountain-shaped.

Considering that this curve is nonlinear (it is obviously not a straight line), should we expect a constant slope when we compute changes in *y* divided by corresponding changes in *x* in moving from one point to another? A quick inspection, even without specific numbers, should lead us to conclude that the slopes of lines joining different points in this curve, such as between *A* and *B*, *B* and *C*, or *C* and *D*, will *not* be the same. The curve slopes upward (in a positive direction) for some values and downward (in a negative direction) for other values. In fact, the slope of the line between any two points on this curve will be different from the slope of the line between any two other points. Each slope will be different as we move along the curve.

MEASURING SLOPE AT A POINT ALONG A NONLINEAR CURVE Instead of using a line between two points to discuss slope, mathematicians and economists prefer to discuss the slope *at a particular point*. The slope at a point on the curve, such as point *B* in the graph in Figure A-10 above, is the slope of a line tangent to that point. A tangent line is a straight line that touches a curve at only one point. For example, it might be helpful to think of the tangent at *B* as the straight line that just "kisses" the curve at point *B*.

To calculate the slope of a tangent line, you need to have some additional information besides the two values of the point of tangency. For example, in Figure A-10, if we knew that the point *R* also lay on the tangent line and we knew the two values of that point, we could calculate the slope of the tangent line. We could calculate rise over run between points *B* and *R*, and the result would be the slope of the line tangent to the one point *B* on the curve.

WHAT YOU SHOULD KNOW

Here is what you should know after reading this appendix. MyEconLab will help you identify what you know, and where to go when you need to practice.

LEARNING OBJECTIVES	KEY TERMS	WHERE TO GO TO PRACTICE
Direct and Inverse Relationships *In a direct relationship, a dependent variable changes in the same direction as the change in the independent variable. In an inverse relationship, the dependent variable changes in the opposite direction of the change in the independent variable.*	independent variable, 19 dependent variable, 19 direct relationship, 19 inverse relationship, 19	• MyEconLab Study Plan 1.6
Constructing a Graph *When we draw a graph showing the relationship between two economic variables, we are holding all other things constant (the Latin term for which is* ceteris paribus*).*	number line, 20 *y* axis, 20 *x* axis, 20 origin, 20	• MyEconLab Study Plan 1.7
Graphing Numbers *We obtain a set of coordinates by putting vertical and horizontal number lines together. The vertical line is called the* y *axis; the horizontal line, the* x *axis.*		• MyEconLab Study Plan 1.8
The Slopes of Linear and Nonlinear Curves *The slope of any linear (straight-line) curve is the change in the* y *values divided by the corresponding change in the* x *values as we move along the line. Otherwise stated, the slope is calculated as the amount of rise over the amount of run, where rise is movement in the vertical direction and run is movement in the horizontal direction. The slope of a nonlinear curve changes; it is positive when the curve is rising and negative when the curve is falling. At a maximum or minimum point, the slope of the nonlinear curve is zero.*	slope, 23 **Key Figures** Figure A-8, 23 Figure A-9, 24 Figure A-10, 25	• MyEconLab Study Plan 1.9 • Animated Figures A-8, A-9, A-10

Log in to MyEconLab, take an appendix test, and get a personalized Study Plan that tells you which concepts you understand and which ones you need to review. From there, MyEconLab will give you further practice, tutorials, animations, videos, and guided solutions. For more information, visit http://www.myeconlab.com

PROBLEMS

All problems are assignable in MyEconLab. Answers to odd-numbered problems appear in MyEconLab.

A-1. Explain which is the independent variable and which is the dependent variable for each of the following examples. (See page 19.)

    a. Once you determine the price of a flash drive at the college bookstore, you will decide how many flash drives to buy.

    b. You will decide how many credit hours to register for this semester once the university tells you how many work-study hours you will be assigned.

    c. You anticipate earning a higher grade on your next economics exam because you studied more hours in the weeks preceding the exam.

A-2. For each of the following items, state whether a direct or an inverse relationship is likely to exist. (See page 19.)

    a. The number of hours you study for an exam and your exam score

    b. The price of pizza and the quantity purchased

    c. The number of games the university basketball team won last year and the number of season tickets sold this year

A-3. Review Figure A-4 on page 21, and then state whether each of the following paired observations is on, above, or below the x axis and on, to the left of, or to the right of the y axis. (See page 21.)

    a. $(-10, 4)$

    b. $(20, -2)$

    c. $(10, 0)$

A-4. State whether each of the following functions specifies a direct or an inverse relationship. (See page 19.)

    a. $y = 5x$

    b. $y = 10 - 2x$

    c. $y = 3 + x$

    d. $y = -3x$

A-5. Given the function $y = 5x$, complete the following schedule and plot the curve. (See page 22.)

y	x
	−4
	−2
	0
	2
	4

A-6. Given the function $y = 8 - 2x$, complete the following schedule and plot the curve. (See page 23.)

y	x
	−4
	−2
	0
	2
	4

A-7. Calculate the slope of the function you graphed in Problem A-5. (See page 23.)

A-8. Calculate the slope of the function you graphed in Problem A-6. (See page 24.)

2

Scarcity and the World of Trade-Offs

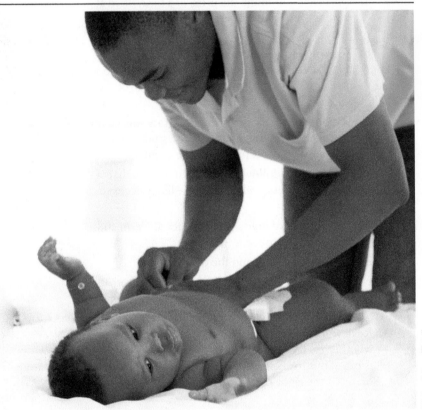

Michael Jung/Fotolia

LEARNING OBJECTIVES

After reading this chapter, you should be able to:

2.1 Evaluate why everyone, whether poor or affluent, faces the problem of scarcity

2.2 Explain why the scarcity problem causes people to consider opportunity costs and trade-offs among choices

2.3 Discuss why obtaining increasing increments of any particular good typically entails giving up more and more units of other goods

2.4 Explain why the economy faces a trade-off between consumption goods and capital goods

2.5 Distinguish between absolute and comparative advantage

MyEconLab helps you master each objective and study more efficiently. See the end of the chapter for details.

n years past, husbands normally were couples' main breadwinners. In more than 75 percent of marriages, husbands worked outside the home to earn most of couples' money income. Wives in these marriages tended to specialize in performing much of the unpaid work around the house. Today, in contrast, wives earn more money income outside the home than their husbands in close to 40 percent of marriages. The average wife is spending less time on unpaid housework, and the typical husband is allocating more of his time to such activities. In this chapter, you will contemplate the economic explanation for these shifting patterns in married couples' allocations of time to income-generating work outside their homes and to unpaid work within their homes.

DID YOU KNOW THAT... the U.S. Department of Agriculture estimates the overall cost of raising a child to the age of 18 averages about $300,000? Naturally, parental expenses on children tend to vary with family incomes. Lower-income families spend closer to $200,000 over the course of a child's first 17 years, while upper-income families spend nearly $500,000. Of course, these estimates do not include college expenses that parents also may incur beginning in the typical child's eighteenth year, which currently average about $39,000 per year for tuition, room and board, and other college costs.

Clearly, an individual who chooses to become a parent and incur these considerable expenses must sacrifice consuming items that the funds allocated to these child-related costs otherwise could have purchased. Specifically, the parent must give up spending all of these funds on the next-most-highly-valued purpose to which they otherwise could have been directed. As you will learn in this chapter, the next-most-highly-valued alternative to raising a child is the *opportunity cost* of parenting that child. Before you consider this idea, however, you must first learn about another important concept, known as *scarcity*.

Scarcity

Whenever individuals or communities cannot obtain everything they desire simultaneously, they must make choices. Choices occur because of *scarcity*. **Scarcity** is the most basic concept in all of economics. Scarcity means that we do not ever have enough of everything, including time, to satisfy our *every* desire. Scarcity exists because human wants always exceed what can be produced with the limited resources and time that nature makes available.

2.1 Evaluate why everyone, whether poor or affluent, faces the problem of scarcity

Scarcity
A situation in which the ingredients for producing the things that people desire are insufficient to satisfy all wants at a zero price.

What Scarcity Is Not

Scarcity is not a shortage. After a hurricane hits and cuts off supplies to a community, TV newscasts often show people standing in line to get minimum amounts of cooking fuel and food. A news commentator might say that the line is caused by the "scarcity" of these products. Cooking fuel and food, however, are always scarce—we cannot obtain all that we want at a zero price. Therefore, do not confuse the concept of scarcity, which is general and all-encompassing, with the concept of shortages, as evidenced by people waiting in line to obtain a particular product.

Scarcity is not the same thing as poverty. Scarcity occurs among the poor and among the rich. Even the richest person on earth faces scarcity. For instance, even the world's richest person has only limited time available. Low income levels do not create more scarcity. High income levels do not create less scarcity.

Scarcity is a fact of life, like gravity. And just as physicists did not invent gravity, economists did not invent scarcity—it existed well before the first economist ever lived. It has existed at all times in the past and will exist at all times in the future.

MyEconLab Concept Check

Scarcity and Resources

Scarcity exists because resources are insufficient to satisfy our every desire. Resources are the inputs used in the production of the things that we want. **Production** can be defined as virtually any activity that results in the conversion of resources into products that can be used in consumption. Production includes delivering items from one part of the country to another. It includes taking ice from an ice tray to put it in your soft-drink glass. The resources used in production are called *factors of production*, and some economists use the terms *resources* and *factors of production* interchangeably. The total quantity of all resources that an economy has at any one time determines what that economy can produce.

Production
Any activity that results in the conversion of resources into products that can be used in consumption.

Factors of production can be classified in many ways. Here is one such classification:

Land

The natural resources that are available from nature. Land as a resource includes location, original fertility and mineral deposits, topography, climate, water, and vegetation.

Labor

Productive contributions of humans who work.

Physical capital

All manufactured resources, including buildings, equipment, machines, and improvements to land that are used for production.

Human capital

The accumulated training and education of workers.

Entrepreneurship

The component of human resources that performs the functions of raising capital; organizing, managing, and assembling other factors of production; making basic business policy decisions; and taking risks.

1. *Land*. **Land** encompasses all the nonhuman gifts of nature, including timber, water, fish, minerals, and the original fertility of land. It is often called the *natural resource*.

2. *Labor*. **Labor** is the *human resource*, which includes productive contributions made by individuals who work, such as Web page designers, iPad applications creators, and professional football players.

3. *Physical capital*. **Physical capital** consists of the factories and equipment used in production. It also includes improvements to natural resources, such as irrigation ditches.

4. *Human capital*. **Human capital** is the economic characterization of the education and training of workers. How much the nation produces depends not only on how many hours people work but also on how productive they are, and that in turn depends in part on education and training. To become more educated, individuals have to devote time and resources, just as a business has to devote resources if it wants to increase its physical capital. Whenever a worker's skills increase, human capital has been improved.

5. *Entrepreneurship*. **Entrepreneurship** (actually a subdivision of labor) is the component of human resources that performs the functions of organizing, managing, and assembling the other factors of production to create and operate business ventures. Entrepreneurship also encompasses taking risks that involve the possibility of losing large sums of wealth. It includes new methods of engaging in common activities and generally experimenting with any type of new thinking that could lead to making more income. Without entrepreneurship, hardly any business organizations could continue to operate. MyEconLab Concept Check

Goods versus Economic Goods

Goods

All things from which individuals derive satisfaction or happiness.

Economic goods

Goods that are scarce, for which the quantity demanded exceeds the quantity supplied at a zero price.

Goods are defined as all things from which individuals derive satisfaction or happiness. Goods therefore include air to breathe and the beauty of a sunset as well as food, cars, and iPhones.

Economic goods are a subset of all goods—they are scarce goods, about which we must constantly make decisions regarding their best use. By definition, the desired quantity of an economic good exceeds the amount that is available at a zero price. Almost every example we use in economics concerns economic goods—cars, tablet devices, smartphones, socks, baseball bats, and corn. Weeds are a good example of *bads*—goods for which the desired quantity is much *less* than what nature provides at a zero price.

Services

Mental or physical labor or assistance purchased by consumers. Examples are the assistance of physicians, lawyers, dentists, repair personnel, housecleaners, educators, retailers, and wholesalers; items purchased or used by consumers that do not have physical characteristics.

Sometimes you will see references to "goods and services." **Services** are tasks that are performed by individuals, often for someone else, such as laundry, Internet access, hospital care, restaurant meal preparation, car polishing, psychological counseling, and teaching. One way of looking at services is to think of them as *intangible goods*.

MyEconLab Concept Check

Wants and Needs

Wants are not the same as needs. Indeed, from the economist's point of view, the term *needs* is objectively undefinable. When someone says, "I need some new clothes," there is no way to know whether that person is stating a vague wish, a want, or a life-saving requirement. If the individual making the statement were dying of exposure in a northern country during the winter, we might conclude that indeed the person does need clothes—perhaps not new ones, but at least some articles of warm clothing. Typically, however, the term *need* is used very casually in conversation. What people mean, usually, is that they desire something that they do not currently have.

Humans have unlimited wants. Just imagine that every single material want that you might have was satisfied. You could have all of the clothes, cars, houses, downloadable movies, yachts, and other items that you want. Does that mean that nothing else could add to your total level of happiness? Undoubtedly, you might continue to think of new goods and services that you could obtain, particularly as they came to market. You would also still be lacking in fulfilling all of your wants for compassion, friendship, love, affection, helping others, musical abilities, sports abilities, and the like.

In reality, every individual has competing wants but cannot satisfy all of them, given limited resources. This is the reality of scarcity. Each person must therefore make choices. Whenever a choice is made to produce or buy something, something else that is also desired is not produced or not purchased. In other words, in a world of scarcity, every want that ends up being satisfied causes one or more other wants to remain unsatisfied or to be forfeited.

MyEconLab Concept Check
MyEconLab Study Plan

SELF CHECK Visit MyEconLab to practice these and other problems and to get instant feedback in your Study Plan.

_____ is the situation in which human wants always exceed what can be produced with the limited resources and time that nature makes available.

We use scarce resources, such as _____, _____, _____, and _____ capital, and _____, to produce economic goods—goods that are desired but are not directly obtainable from nature to the extent demanded or desired at a zero price.

_____ are unlimited. They include all material desires and all nonmaterial desires, such as love, affection, power, and prestige.

The concept of _____ is difficult to define objectively for every person. Consequently, we simply consider every person's wants to be unlimited. In a world of **scarcity**, satisfaction of one want necessarily means nonsatisfaction of one or more other wants.

Opportunity Cost, Trade-Offs, and Choices

2.2 Explain why the scarcity problem causes people to consider opportunity costs and trade-offs among choices

The natural fact of scarcity implies that we must make choices. One of the most important results of this fact is that every choice made means that some opportunity must be sacrificed. Every choice involves giving up an opportunity to produce or consume something else.

Valuing Forgone Alternatives

Consider a practical example. Every choice you make to study economics for one more hour requires that you give up the opportunity to choose to engage in any one of the following activities: study more of another subject, listen to music, sleep, browse at a local store, read a novel, or work out at the gym. The most highly valued of these opportunities is forgone if you choose to study economics an additional hour.

Because there were so many alternatives from which to choose, how could you determine the value of what you gave up to engage in that extra hour of studying economics? First of all, no one else can tell you the answer because only *you* can put a value on the alternatives forgone. Only you know the value of another hour of sleep or of an hour looking for the latest digital music downloads—whatever one activity *you* would have chosen if you had not opted to study economics for that hour. That means that only you can determine the highest-valued, next-best alternative that you had to sacrifice in order to study economics one more hour. Only you can determine the value of the next-best alternative.

MyEconLab Concept Check

Opportunity Cost

The value of the next-best alternative is called **opportunity cost**. The opportunity cost of any action is the value of what is given up—the next-highest-ranked alternative—because a choice was made. What is important is the choice that you would have made if you

Opportunity cost
The highest-valued, next-best alternative that must be sacrificed to obtain something or to satisfy a want.

hadn't studied one more hour. Your opportunity cost is the *next-highest-ranked* alternative, not *all* alternatives.

> **In economics, cost is always a forgone opportunity.**

One way to think about opportunity cost is to understand that when you choose to do something, you lose something else. What you lose is being able to engage in your next-highest-valued alternative. The cost of your chosen alternative is what you lose, which is by definition your next-highest-valued alternative. This is your opportunity cost.

Why does ownership of scarce pieces of art pose a significant opportunity cost for the city of Detroit?

POLICY EXAMPLE

Bankrupt Detroit Confronts the Opportunity Cost of Art

Detroit is the largest city in U.S. history to enter into legal bankruptcy. In an effort to reduce expenses, the Detroit city government substantially reduced city services. As a consequence, the city's police department and ambulance services operate with skeleton staffs that often take an hour or longer to respond to emergency calls. Nevertheless, the city found itself with insufficient flows of on-going tax and fee revenues to cover its continuing flows of expenses, including payments on debts of about $18 billion owed to holders of bonds it had issued over the years.

The city's art museum, the Detroit Institute of Art, owns more than 60,000 pieces of art. Among these are 40 world-renowned pieces by artists such as Van Gogh, Rembrandt, and Matisse that experts have estimated could almost certainly be sold for about $2.5 billion. The market value of the Detroit Institute of Art's *entire* collection has

not been fully assessed, but there is general agreement that the value could exceed $20 billion. Thus, the opportunity cost of retaining the art collection held by the Detroit Institute of Art may be as high as the total amount required for the city to repay its outstanding debts and to increase the provision of police, ambulance and other city services.

FOR CRITICAL THINKING

Why do you suppose that the individual put in charge of discharging the city's bankruptcy has explored auctioning off pieces of art held by the Detroit Institute of Art?

Sources are listed at the end of this chapter.

MyEconLab Concept Check

The World of Trade-Offs

Whenever you engage in any activity using any resource, even time, you are *trading off* the use of that resource for one or more alternative uses. The extent of the trade-off is represented by the opportunity cost. The opportunity cost of studying economics has already been mentioned—it is the value of the next-best alternative. When you think of *any* alternative, you are thinking of trade-offs.

Let's consider a hypothetical example of a trade-off between the results of spending time studying economics and mathematics. For the sake of this argument, we will assume that additional time studying either economics or mathematics will lead to a higher grade in the subject to which additional study time is allocated. One of the best ways to examine this trade-off is with a graph. (If you would like a refresher on graphical techniques, study Appendix A at the end of Chapter 1 before going on.)

MyEconLab Concept Check

Graphical Analysis

In Figure 2-1 on the next page, the expected grade in mathematics is measured on the vertical axis of the graph, and the expected grade in economics is measured on the horizontal axis. We simplify the world and assume that you have a maximum of 12 hours per week to spend studying these two subjects and that if you spend all 12 hours on economics, you will get an A in the course. You will, however, fail mathematics. Conversely, if you spend all of your 12 hours studying mathematics, you will get an A in that subject, but you will flunk economics. Here the trade-off is a special case: one to one. A one-to-one trade-off means that the opportunity cost of receiving one grade higher in economics (for example, improving from a C to a B) is one grade lower in mathematics (falling from a C to a D).

FIGURE 2-1

Production Possibilities Curve for Grades in Mathematics and Economics (Trade-Offs)

We assume that only 12 hours can be spent per week on studying. If the student is at point *x*, equal time (6 hours a week) is spent on both courses, and equal grades of C will be received. If a higher grade in economics is desired, the student may go to point *y*, thereby receiving a B in economics but a D in mathematics. At point *y*, 3 hours are spent on mathematics and 9 hours on economics.

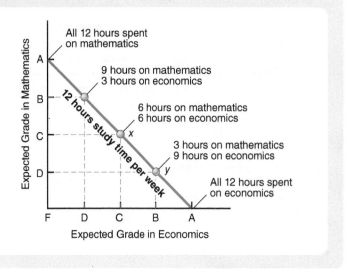

MyEconLab Concept Check

The Production Possibilities Curve (PPC)

The graph in Figure 2-1 above illustrates the relationship between the possible results that can be produced in each of two activities, depending on how much time you choose to devote to each activity. This graph shows a representation of a **production possibilities curve (PPC)**.

PRODUCTION POSSIBILITIES FOR COURSE GRADES Consider that you are producing a grade in economics when you study economics and a grade in mathematics when you study mathematics. Then the line that goes from A on one axis to A on the other axis therefore becomes a production possibilities curve. This line defines the maximum quantity of one good or service that can be produced, given that a specific quantity of another is produced. It is a curve that shows the possibilities available for increasing the output of one good or service by reducing the amount of another. In the example in Figure 2-1, your time for studying was limited to 12 hours per week. The two possible outputs were your grade in mathematics and your grade in economics.

The particular production possibilities curve presented in Figure 2-1 is a graphical representation of the opportunity cost of studying one more hour in one subject. It is a *straight-line production possibilities curve*, which is a special case. (The more general case will be discussed next.)

MEASURING TRADE-OFFS ALONG A PRODUCTION POSSIBILITIES CURVE If you decide to be at point *x* in Figure 2-1, you will devote 6 hours of study time to mathematics and 6 hours to economics. The expected grade in each course will be a C. If you are more interested in getting a B in economics, you will go to point *y* on the production possibilities curve, spending only 3 hours on mathematics but 9 hours on economics. Your expected grade in mathematics will then drop from a C to a D.

Note that these trade-offs between expected grades in mathematics and economics are the result of *holding constant* total study time as well as all other factors that might influence your ability to learn, such as computerized study aids. Quite clearly, if you were able to spend more total time studying, it would be possible to have higher grades in both economics and mathematics. In that case, however, we would no longer be on the specific production possibilities curve illustrated in Figure 2-1. We would have to draw a new curve, farther to the right, to show the greater total study time and a different set of possible trade-offs.

Why has the president of France proposed banning teachers from requiring homework?

Production possibilities curve (PPC)
A curve representing all possible combinations of maximum outputs that could be produced, assuming a fixed amount of productive resources of a given quality.

Recently, the president of France, François Hollande, proposed an increase in the amount of time that children spend in public schools—currently four days—by half of a day. An additional half-day at school, he argues, has a higher value to children in lower-income and single-parent families than do homework assignments. Hollande's rationale for this assessment is that the children in less advantaged homes with only one parent do not receive as much hands-on parental assistance with their homework. During an extra half-day spent in school, he reasons, all children will receive assistance from their teachers, thereby ensuring improved learning outcomes for disadvantaged students that they are not obtaining from homework.

Hollande argues that the value of time devoted to homework is actually the next-best alternative to the value of an extra day of school time.

He believes that the opportunity cost of homework, which is the value of an extra half of a school day, is too high to justify choosing homework over the additional time in school. Thus, Hollande concludes that homework should be eliminated and French schools should add an additional half-day of instructional time.

FOR CRITICAL THINKING

Is Hollande's argument strengthened or weakened by evidence that a majority of French lower-income and single parents view homework as a helpful mechanism for keeping some of their children's attention on learning during time outside school?

Sources are listed at the end of this chapter.

MyEconLab Concept Check
MyEconLab Study Plan

SELF CHECK   Visit MyEconLab to practice these and other problems and to get instant feedback in your Study Plan.

Scarcity requires us to choose. Whenever we choose, we lose the _____-_____-valued alternative.

Cost is always a forgone _____.

Another way to look at **opportunity cost** is the trade-off that occurs when one activity is undertaken rather than the _____-_____ alternative activity.

A _____ _____ curve graphically shows the trade-off that occurs when more of one output is obtained at the sacrifice of another. This curve is a graphical representation of, among other things, opportunity cost.

2.3 Discuss why obtaining increasing increments of any particular good typically entails giving up more and more units of other goods

The Economic Choices a Nation's People Face

The straight-line production possibilities curve presented in Figure 2-1 on the previous page can be generalized to demonstrate the related concepts of scarcity, choice, and trade-offs that our entire nation faces. As you will see, the production possibilities curve is a simple but powerful economic model because it can demonstrate these related concepts.

A Two-Good Example

The example we will use is the choice between the production of smartphones and tablet devices. We assume for the moment that these are the only two goods that can be produced in the nation.

Panel (a) of Figure 2-2 on the following page gives the various combinations of smartphones and tablet devices, or tablets, that are possible. If all resources are devoted to smartphone production, 50 million per year can be produced. If all resources are devoted to production of tablets, 60 million per year can be produced. In between are various possible combinations.   MyEconLab Concept Check

Production Trade-Offs

The nation's production combinations are plotted as points *A, B, C, D, E, F,* and *G* in panel (b) of Figure 2-2 on the following page. If these points are connected with a smooth curve, the nation's production possibilities curve (PPC) is shown, demonstrating the trade-off between the production of smartphones and tablets. These trade-offs occur *on* the PPC.

FIGURE 2-2

The Trade-Off between Smartphones and Tablet Devices

The production of smartphones and tablet devices is measured in millions of units per year. The various combinations are given in panel (a) and plotted in panel (b). Connecting the points *A–G* with a relatively smooth line gives society's production possibilities curve for smartphones and tablets. Point *R* lies outside the production possibilities curve and is therefore unattainable at the point in time for which the graph is drawn. Point *S* lies inside the production possibilities curve and therefore entails unemployed or underemployed resources.

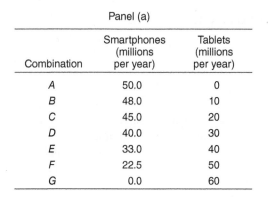

Panel (a)

Combination	Smartphones (millions per year)	Tablets (millions per year)
A	50.0	0
B	48.0	10
C	45.0	20
D	40.0	30
E	33.0	40
F	22.5	50
G	0.0	60

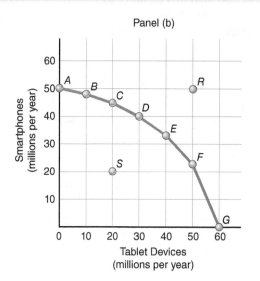

Panel (b)

Notice the major difference in the shape of the production possibilities curves in Figure 2-1 on page 33 and Figure 2-2. In Figure 2-1, there is a constant trade-off between grades in economics and in mathematics. In Figure 2-2, the trade-off between production of smartphones and tablet production is not constant, and therefore the PPC is a *bowed* curve. To understand why the production possibilities curve is typically bowed outward, you must understand the assumptions underlying the PPC.

MyEconLab Concept Check

Assumptions Underlying the Production Possibilities Curve

When we draw the curve that is shown in Figure 2-2, we make the following assumptions:

1. Resources are fully employed.

2. Production takes place over a specific time period—for example, one year.

3. The resource inputs, in both quantity and quality, used to produce smartphones or tablets are fixed over this time period.

4. Technology does not change over this time period.

Technology is defined as the total pool of applied knowledge concerning how goods and services can be produced by managers, workers, engineers, scientists, and artisans, using land, physical and human capital, and entrepreneurship. You can think of technology as the formula or recipe used to combine factors of production. (When better formulas are developed, more production can be obtained from the same amount of resources.) The level of technology sets the limit on the amount and types of goods and services that we can derive from any given amount of resources. The production possibilities curve is drawn under the assumptions that we use the best technology we currently have available and that this technology doesn't change over the time period under study.

Technology
The total pool of applied knowledge concerning how goods and services can be produced.

WHAT IF...

> **the government attempts to raise production of all goods by redirecting more available resources to the provision of health-care services?**

In recent years, a number of politicians and government officials have argued that providing more health-care services by diverting existing resources away from producing other goods and services will generate greater production of all items. In reality, with a given array of available resources and a fixed current technology, redirecting resources to the provision of more health-care services leaves *fewer* resources for producing other goods and services. Thus, the total volume of other goods and services produced must decrease when the government diverts resources to the provision of health-care services.

MyEconLab Concept Check

Being off the Production Possibilities Curve

Look again at panel (b) of Figure 2-2 on the previous page. Point *R* lies *outside* the production possibilities curve and is *impossible* to achieve during the time period assumed. By definition, the PPC indicates the *maximum* quantity of one good, given the quantity produced of the other good.

It is possible, however, to be at point *S* in Figure 2-2. That point lies beneath the PPC. If the nation is at point *S*, it means that its resources are not being fully utilized. This occurs, for example, during periods of relatively high unemployment. Point *S* and all such points inside the PPC are always attainable but imply unemployed or underemployed resources.

MyEconLab Concept Check

Efficiency

The production possibilities curve can be used to define the notion of efficiency. Whenever the economy is operating on the PPC, at points such as *A*, *B*, *C*, or *D*, we say that its production is efficient. Points such as *S* in Figure 2-2, which lie beneath the PPC, are said to represent production situations that are not efficient.

Efficiency can mean many things to many people. Even in economics, there are different types of efficiency. Here we are discussing *productive efficiency*. An economy is productively efficient whenever it is producing the maximum output with given technology and resources.

A simple commonsense definition of efficiency is getting the most out of what we have. Clearly, we are not getting the most out of what we have if we are at point *S* in panel (b) of Figure 2-2. We can move from point *S* to, say, point *C*, thereby increasing the total quantity of smartphones produced without any decrease in the total quantity of tablets produced. Alternatively, we can move from point *S* to point *E*, for example, and have both more smartphones and more tablets. Point *S* is called an **inefficient point,** which is defined as any point below the production possibilities curve.

MyEconLab Concept Check

Efficiency
The case in which a given level of inputs is used to produce the maximum output possible. Alternatively, the situation in which a given output is produced at minimum cost.

Inefficient point
Any point below the production possibilities curve, at which the use of resources is not generating the maximum possible output.

The Law of Increasing Additional Cost

In the example in Figure 2-1 on page 33, the trade-off between a grade in mathematics and a grade in economics was one to one. The trade-off ratio was constant. That is, the production possibilities curve was a straight line. The curve in Figure 2-2 is a more general case. We have re-created the curve in Figure 2-2 as Figure 2-3 on the next page. Each combination, *A* through *G*, of smartphones and tablets is represented on the PPC. Starting with the production of zero tablets, the nation can produce 50 million smartphones with its available resources and technology.

INCREASING ADDITIONAL COSTS When we increase production of tablet devices from zero to 10 million per year, the nation has to give up in smartphones an amount shown by

FIGURE 2-3

The Law of Increasing Additional Cost

Consider equal increments of production of tablets, as measured on the horizontal axis. All of the horizontal arrows—*aB*, *bC*, and so on—are of equal length (10 million). In contrast, the length of each vertical arrow—*Aa*, *Bb*, and so on—increases as we move down the production possibilities curve. Hence, the opportunity cost of going from 50 million tablets per year to 60 million (*Ff*) is much greater than going from zero units to 10 million (*Aa*). The opportunity cost of each additional equal increase in production of tablets rises.

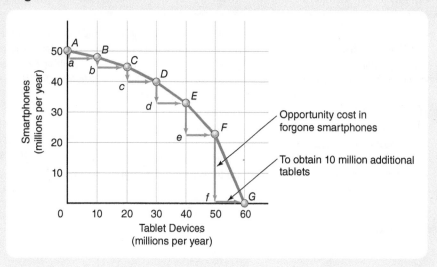

that first vertical arrow, *Aa*. In panel (a) of Figure 2-2, this distance is 2 million per year (50 million minus 48 million). Again, if we increase production of tablets by another 10 million units per year, we go from *B* to *C*. To do so, the nation has to give up the vertical distance *Bb*, or 3 million smartphones per year. By the time we go from 50 million to 60 million tablets, to obtain that 10 million increase, we have to forgo the vertical distance *Ff*, or 22.5 million smartphones. In other words, we see that the opportunity cost of the last 10 million tablets has increased to 22.5 million smartphones, compared to 2 million smartphones for the same increase in tablets when we started with none at all being produced.

What we are observing is called the **law of increasing additional cost**. When people take more resources and apply them to the production of any specific good, the opportunity cost increases for each additional unit produced.

Law of increasing additional cost
The fact that the opportunity cost of additional units of a good generally increases as people attempt to produce more of that good. This accounts for the bowed-out shape of the production possibilities curve.

EXPLAINING THE LAW OF INCREASING ADDITIONAL COST The reason that as a nation we face the law of increasing additional cost (shown as a production possibilities curve that is bowed outward) is that certain resources are better suited for producing some goods than other goods. Generally, resources are not *perfectly* adaptable for alternative uses. When increasing the output of a particular good, producers must use less suitable resources than those already used in order to produce the additional output. Hence, the cost of producing the additional units increases.

With respect to our hypothetical example here, at first the computing specialists at smartphone firms would shift over to producing tablet devices. After a while, though, the workers who normally design and produce smartphones would be asked to help design and manufacture tablet components. Typically, they would be less effective at making tablets than the people who previously specialized in this task.

In general, *the more specialized the resources, the more bowed the production possibilities curve*. At the other extreme, if all resources are equally suitable for smartphone production or production of tablets, the curves in Figures 2-2 (p. 35) and 2-3 above would approach the straight line shown in our first example in Figure 2-1 on page 33.

How has a U.S. government policy of requiring increased production of ethanol for use in vehicle fuels generated a production trade-off?

EXAMPLE

The Trade-Off from Redirecting Corn to Ethanol Production

Corn is a key resource used in producing both an array of food products and the ethanol that refiners blend into vehicle fuels. In recent years, the federal government has required the production of larger volumes of ethanol. The volume of corn resources available to manufacture both food products and ethanol has remained little changed during this period. The amount of corn required to produce ethanol, however, has risen from less than 20 percent of the nation's corn resources to about 40 percent of those resources within just a few years' time.

Because the nation's residents must produce more ethanol with nearly the same quantity of corn, they have had to reduce their output of food products. Hence, the government's ethanol-production requirement has generated a movement along the U.S. production possibilities curve. The result of the required increase in ethanol production has been a trade-off: a reduction in production of food items.

FOR CRITICAL THINKING

As the share of the nation's required ethanol production has increased each year, has the opportunity cost of ethanol in units of food products per unit of ethanol increased or decreased? Explain briefly.

Sources are listed at the end of this chapter.

MyEconLab Concept Check
MyEconLab Study Plan

SELF CHECK Visit MyEconLab to practice these and other problems and to get instant feedback in your Study Plan.

Trade-offs are represented graphically by a _____ _____ curve showing the maximum quantity of one good or service that can be produced, given a specific quantity of another, from a given set of resources over a specified period of time—for example, one year.

A **production possibilities curve** is drawn holding the quantity and quality of all resources _____ over the time period under study.

Points _____ the **production possibilities curve** are unattainable. Points _____ are attainable but represent an inefficient use or underuse of available resources.

Because many resources are better suited for certain productive tasks than for others, the production possibilities curve is bowed _____, reflecting the **law of increasing additional cost.**

2.4 Explain why the economy faces a trade-off between consumption goods and capital goods

Economic Growth, Production Possibilities, and the Trade-Off Between Present and Future

At any particular point in time, a society cannot be outside the production possibilities curve. *Over time*, however, it is possible to have more of everything. This occurs through economic growth. (An important reason for economic growth, capital accumulation, is discussed next. A more complete discussion of why economic growth occurs appears in Chapter 9.)

Economic Growth and the Production Possibilities Curve

Figure 2-4 on the next page shows the production possibilities curve for smartphones and tablet devices shifting outward. The two additional curves shown represent new choices open to an economy that has experienced economic growth. Such economic growth occurs for many reasons, including increases in the number of workers and productive investment in equipment.

Scarcity still exists, however, no matter how much economic growth takes place. At any point in time, we will always be on some production possibilities curve. Thus, we will always face trade-offs. The more we have of one thing, the less we can have of others.

If economic growth occurs in the nation, the production possibilities curve between smartphones and tablets moves outward, as shown in Figure 2-4. This takes time and does not occur automatically. One reason it will occur involves the choice about how much to consume today.

MyEconLab Concept Check

The Trade-Off between the Present and the Future

Consumption
The use of goods and services for personal satisfaction.

The production possibilities curve and economic growth can be combined to examine the trade-off between present **consumption** and future consumption. When we con-

FIGURE 2-4

Economic Growth Allows for More of Everything

If the nation experiences economic growth, the production possibilities curve between smartphones and tablets will move out as shown. This output increase takes time, however, and it does not occur automatically. This means, therefore, that we can have more of both smartphones and tablets only after a period of time during which we have experienced economic growth.

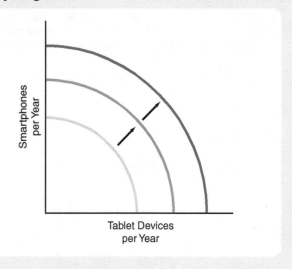

sume today, we are using up what we call consumption or consumer goods—food and clothes, for example.

WHY WE MAKE CAPITAL GOODS Why would we be willing to use productive resources to make things—capital goods—that we cannot consume directly? The reason is that capital goods enable us to produce larger quantities of consumer goods or to produce them less expensively than we otherwise could. Before fish are "produced" for the market, equipment such as fishing boats, nets, and poles is produced first. Imagine how expensive it would be to obtain fish for market without using these capital goods. Catching fish with one's hands is not an easy task. The cost per fish would be very high if capital goods weren't used.

FORGOING CURRENT CONSUMPTION Whenever we use productive resources to make capital goods, we are implicitly forgoing current consumption. We are waiting for some time in the future to consume the rewards that will be reaped from the use of capital goods. In effect, when we forgo current consumption to invest in capital goods, we are engaging in an economic activity that is forward-looking—we do not get instant utility or satisfaction from our activity.

THE TRADE-OFF BETWEEN CONSUMPTION GOODS AND CAPITAL GOODS To have more consumer goods in the future, we must accept fewer consumer goods today, because resources must be used in producing capital goods instead of consumer goods. In other words, an opportunity cost is involved. Every time we make a choice of more goods today, we incur an opportunity cost of fewer goods tomorrow, and every time we make a choice of more goods in the future, we incur an opportunity cost of fewer goods today. With the resources that we don't use to produce consumer goods for today, we invest in capital goods that will produce more consumer goods for us later. The trade-off is shown in Figure 2-5 on the next page. On the left in panel (a), you can see this trade-off depicted as a production possibilities curve between capital goods and consumption goods.

Assume that we are willing to give up $1 trillion worth of consumption today. We will be at point *A* in the left-hand diagram of panel (a). This will allow the economy to grow. We will have more future consumption because we invested in more capital goods today. In the right-hand diagram of panel (a), we see two consumer goods represented, food and entertainment. The production possibilities curve will move outward if individuals in the economy decide to restrict consumption now and invest in capital goods.

FIGURE 2-5

Capital Goods and Growth

In panel (a), people choose not to consume $1 trillion, so they invest that amount in capital goods. As a result, more of all goods may be produced in the future, as shown in the right-hand diagram in panel (a). In panel (b), people choose even more capital goods (point *C*). The result is that the production possibilities curve (PPC) moves even more to the right on the right-hand diagram in panel (b).

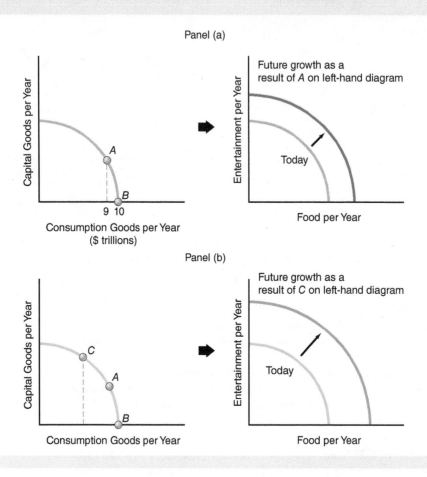

In panel (b) in Figure 2-5 above, we show the results of our willingness to forgo even more current consumption. We move from point *A* to point *C* in the left-hand side, where we have many fewer consumer goods today but produce many more capital goods. This leads to more future growth in this simplified model, and thus the production possibilities curve in the right-hand side of panel (b) shifts outward more than it did in the right-hand side of panel (a). In other words, the more we give up today, the more we can have tomorrow, provided, of course, that the capital goods are productive in future periods.

MyEconLab Concept Check
MyEconLab Study Plan

SELF CHECK Visit MyEconLab to practice these and other problems and to get instant feedback in your Study Plan.

_____ goods are goods that will later be used to produce consumer goods.

A trade-off is involved between current consumption and capital goods or, alternatively, between current consumption and future consumption. The _____ we invest in capital goods today, the greater the amount of consumer goods we can produce in the future and the _____ the amount of consumer goods we can produce today.

Specialization, Comparative Advantage, and Trade

2.5 Distinguish between absolute and comparative advantage

Specialization involves working at a relatively well-defined, limited endeavor, such as accounting or teaching. Most individuals do specialize. For example, you could change the oil in your car if you wanted to. Typically, though, you take your car to a garage and let the mechanic change the oil. You benefit by letting the garage mechanic specialize in changing the oil and in doing other repairs on your car.

The specialist normally will get the job finished sooner than you could and has the proper equipment to make the job go more smoothly. Specialization usually leads to greater productivity, not only for each individual but also for the nation.

Specialization
The organization of economic activity so that what each person (or region) consumes is not identical to what that person (or region) produces. An individual may specialize, for example, in law or medicine. A nation may specialize in the production of coffee, e-book readers, or digital cameras.

Comparative Advantage

Specialization occurs because different individuals experience different costs when they engage in the same activities. Some individuals can accurately solve mathematical problems at lower cost than others who might try to solve the same problems. Thus, those who solve math problems at lower cost sacrifice production of fewer alternative items. Some people can develop more high-quality iPad applications than others while giving up less production of other items, such as clean houses and neatly manicured yards.

Comparative advantage is the ability to perform an activity *at a lower opportunity cost*. You have a comparative advantage in one activity whenever you have a lower opportunity cost of performing that activity. Comparative advantage is always a *relative* concept. You may be able to change the oil in your car. You might even be able to change it faster than the local mechanic. But if the opportunity cost you face by changing the oil exceeds the mechanic's opportunity cost, the mechanic has a comparative advantage in changing the oil. The mechanic faces a lower opportunity cost for that activity.

You may be convinced that everybody can do more of everything than you can during the same period of time and using the same resources. In this extreme situation, do you still have a comparative advantage? The answer is yes. You do not have to be a mathematical genius to figure this out. The market tells you so very clearly by offering you the highest income for the job for which you have a comparative advantage. Stated differently, to find your comparative advantage, simply find the job that maximizes your income.

Often, those seeking appointments with physicians confront an opportunity cost. How has this opportunity cost provided entrepreneurs with potential profits to be earned from providing physician-appointment-scheduling services?

Comparative advantage
The ability to produce a good or service at a lower opportunity cost compared to other producers.

EXAMPLE

Too Sick to Call a Doc? ZocDoc and Practice Fusion Can Help

Scheduling an appointment with a physician requires incurring a substantial opportunity cost. Consequently, more people who are ill are using apps. These individuals sit quietly in bed and use digital devices to connect with the Web sites operated by companies such as ZocDoc and Practice Fusion. Once an ill person provides information about a preferred physician, these firms handle setting up an appointment. If the individual does not know which physician to contact, the companies utilize large physician databases to match the person's symptoms to an appropriate physician and book an appointment. While ZocDoc or

Practice Fusion utilizes its comparative advantage in handling these tasks, a person who feels ill can remain in bed, rest, and try to avoid feeling any worse than she already does.

FOR CRITICAL THINKING

What is the opportunity cost to people who spend time finding physicians and scheduling appointments when the next-best use of that time would have been earning income instead?

Sources are listed at the end of this chapter.

Absolute Advantage

Suppose you are the president of a firm and are convinced that you have the ability to do every job in that company faster than everyone else who works there. You might be able to enter data into a spreadsheet program faster than any of the other employees, file documents in order in a file cabinet faster than any of the file clerks, and wash windows faster than any of the window washers. Furthermore, you are able to manage the firm more effectively in less time than any other individual in the company.

Absolute advantage

The ability to produce more units of a good or service using a given quantity of labor or resource inputs. Equivalently, the ability to produce the same quantity of a good or service using fewer units of labor or resource inputs.

ABSOLUTE ADVANTAGE VERSUS COMPARATIVE ADVANTAGE If all of these self-perceptions were really true, then you would have an **absolute advantage** in all of these endeavors. In other words, if you were to spend a given amount of time in any one of them, you could produce more than anyone else in the company. Nonetheless, you would not spend your time doing these other activities. Why not? Because your time advantage in undertaking the president's managerial duties is even greater. Therefore, you would find yourself specializing in that particular task even though you have an *absolute* advantage in all these other tasks. Indeed, absolute advantage is irrelevant in predicting how you will allocate your time.

Only *comparative advantage*, not absolute advantage, matters in determining how you will allocate your time. Comparative advantage determines your choice because it involves the highest-valued alternative in a decision about time allocation.

COMPARATIVE ADVANTAGE IN SPORTS The coaches of sports teams often have to determine the comparative advantage of an individual player who has an absolute advantage in every aspect of the sport in question. Babe Ruth, who could hit more home runs and pitch more strikeouts per game than other players on the Boston Red Sox, was a pitcher on that professional baseball team.

After Ruth was traded to the New York Yankees, the owner and the manager decided to make him an outfielder, even though he could also pitch more strikeouts per game than other Yankees. They wanted "The Babe" to concentrate on his hitting because a home-run king would bring in more paying fans than a good pitcher would. Babe Ruth had an absolute advantage in both aspects of the game of baseball, but his comparative advantage was clearly in hitting homers rather than in practicing and developing his pitching game. MyEconLab Concept Check

Scarcity, Self-Interest, and Specialization

In Chapter 1, you learned about the assumption of rational self-interest. To repeat, for the purposes of our analyses we assume that individuals are rational in that they will do what is in their own self-interest. They will not consciously carry out actions that will make them worse off. In this chapter, you learned that scarcity requires people to make choices. We *assume* that they make choices based on their self-interest. When people make choices, they attempt to maximize benefits net of opportunity cost. In so doing, individuals choose their comparative advantage and end up specializing. MyEconLab Concept Check

The Division of Labor

Division of labor

The segregation of resources into different specific tasks. For instance, one automobile worker puts on bumpers, another doors, and so on.

In any firm that includes specialized human and nonhuman resources, there is a **division of labor** among those resources. The best-known example comes from Adam Smith (1723–1790), who in *The Wealth of Nations* illustrated the benefits of a division of labor in the making of pins, as depicted in the following example:

One man draws out the wire, another straightens it, a third cuts it, a fourth points it, a fifth grinds it at the top for receiving the head; to make the head requires two or three distinct operations; to put it on is a peculiar business, to whiten the pins is another; it is even a trade by itself to put them into the paper.

Making pins this way allowed 10 workers without very much skill to make almost 48,000 pins "of a middling size" in a day. One worker, toiling alone, could have made perhaps 20 pins a day. Therefore, 10 workers could have produced 200. Division of labor allowed for an increase in the daily output of the pin factory from 200 to 48,000! (Smith did not attribute all of the gain to the division of labor but credited also the use of machinery and the fact that less time was spent shifting from task to task.)

What we are discussing here involves a division of the resource called labor into different uses of labor. The different uses of labor are organized in such a way as to increase the amount of output possible from the fixed resources available. We can therefore talk about an organized division of labor within a firm leading to increased output. MyEconLab Concept Check

Comparative Advantage and Trade among Nations

Most of our analysis of absolute advantage, comparative advantage, and specialization has dealt with individuals. Nevertheless, it is equally applicable to groups of people.

TRADE AMONG REGIONS Consider the United States. The Plains states have a comparative advantage in the production of grains and other agricultural goods. Relative to the Plains states, the states to the east tend to specialize in industrialized production, such as automobiles. Not surprisingly, grains are shipped from the Plains states to the eastern states, and automobiles are shipped in the reverse direction. Such specialization and trade allow for higher incomes and standards of living.

If both the Plains states and the eastern states were separate nations, the same analysis would still hold, but we would call it international trade. Indeed, the European Union (EU) is comparable to the United States in area and population, but instead of one nation, the EU has 28. What U.S. residents call *interstate* trade, Europeans call *international* trade. There is no difference, however, in the economic results—both yield greater economic efficiency and higher average incomes.

INTERNATIONAL ASPECTS OF TRADE Political problems that normally do not occur within a particular nation often arise between nations. For example, if California avocado growers develop a cheaper method of producing avocados than growers in southern Florida use, the Florida growers will lose out. They cannot do much about the situation except try to lower their own costs of production or improve their product.

If avocado growers in Mexico, however, develop a cheaper method of producing avocados, both California and Florida growers can (and likely will) try to raise political barriers that will prevent Mexican avocado growers from freely selling their product in the United States. U.S. avocado growers will use such arguments as "unfair" competition and loss of U.S. jobs. Certainly, avocado-growing jobs may decline in the United States, but there is no reason to believe that U.S. jobs will decline overall. Instead, former U.S. avocado workers will move into alternative employment—something that 1 million people do every *week* in the United States. If the argument of U.S. avocado growers had any validity, every time a region in the United States developed a better way to produce a product manufactured somewhere else in the country, U.S. employment would decline. That has never happened and never will.

When nations specialize in an area of comparative advantage and then trade with the rest of the world, the average standard of living in the world rises. In effect, international trade allows the world to move from inside the global production possibilities curve toward the curve itself, thereby improving worldwide economic efficiency. Thus, all countries that engage in trade can benefit from comparative advantage, just as regions in the United States benefit from interregional trade. MyEconLab Concept Check

MyEconLab Study Plan

With a given set of resources, specialization results in _____ output. In other words, there are gains to specialization in terms of greater material well-being.

Individuals and nations specialize in their areas of _____ advantage in order to reap the gains of specialization.

Comparative advantages are found by determining which activities have the _____ opportunity costs—that is, which activities yield the highest return for the time and resources used.

A _____ of labor occurs when different workers are assigned different tasks. Together, the workers produce a desired product.

YOU ARE THERE

Frustrated by the Opportunity Cost of Time Spent in Meetings

Management studies have shown that the typical office worker spends just under eight hours per day at an employer's office but actually devotes less than half of that time to assigned work. Workers usually spend more than an hour each day reading and sending e-mails. The most significant allocations of their time, however, are face-to-face meetings with co-workers. The average office worker spends more than three hours per week in such meetings.

When Paul Betts was working as a software developer at Microsoft, he calculated that the typical meeting had an opportunity cost, measured in the wages that the company was paying employees to meet instead of work, of about $500. In frustration, he left that job to take a position at GitHub, which produces software apps that work teams can utilize to collaborate on projects remotely using digital devices. The apps produced by Betts and his colleagues also enable a company's employees to engage in discussions in online chat rooms as they work on their shared project, which largely eliminates e-mail communications as well.

Betts is happier at work, because he hardly e-mails or has any face-to-face meetings with co-workers during the working day. Furthermore, the products that he develops enable other companies to avoid incurring substantial opportunity costs associated with time that employees otherwise would devote to e-mailing or meeting.

CRITICAL THINKING QUESTIONS

1. Why do you think that some firms now require workers to stand during meetings?

2. How can companies readily assign a dollar value to the opportunity cost of time that employees spend e-mailing or meeting instead of getting work done?

Sources are listed at the end of this chapter.

ISSUES & APPLICATIONS

MyEconLab Video

Specialization Shifts within U.S. Marriages

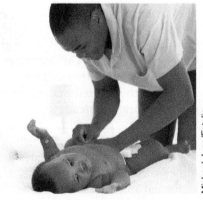

Michael Jung/Fotolia

CONCEPTS APPLIED

» Comparative Advantage

» Specialization

» Opportunity Cost

Over the past few decades, a larger share of married women have developed a comparative advantage over their husbands in the world of paid work. Accompanying this shift of earnings power in favor of wives in a larger percentage of marriages has been a reallocation of time devoted to unpaid housework by wives and their husbands.

FIGURE 2-6

The Share of Marriages in Which Wives Earn More Than Half of the Couple's Combined Income

The percentage of married couples for which wives contribute more than half of total earnings has increased during the past three decades.

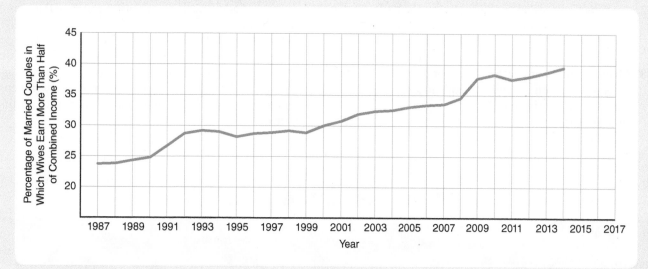

Source: Bureau of Labor Statistics; author's estimates.

An Earnings Shift from Husbands to Wives

As you learned in this chapter, people identify their comparative advantage for specialization by finding jobs that maximize their incomes. A comparative advantage for husbands over wives in the working world traditionally has been revealed by the fact that most husbands have earned more than half of couples' combined incomes.

Figure 2-6 above shows that this fact remains true for the majority of couples. Nevertheless, today wives earn more than half of the couples' combined incomes in nearly 40 percent of marriages, as compared with only about 24 percent in 1987. A relative shift of earnings power from husbands to wives has been taking place.

A Reallocation of Housework from Wives to Husbands

As more wives have developed a comparative advantage in performing tasks outside the home, the higher incomes that wives can earn from paid work have raised couples' opportunity costs of wives specializing in performing housework within the home. It is not surprising, therefore, that the amount of time that wives have devoted to housework has declined by 10 percent since 2003.

At the same time, as more husbands have lost their comparative advantage in the world of paid work, husbands' earnings power has declined relative to that of their wives. Thus, there has been a decrease in the opportunity cost of husbands engaging in unpaid housework instead of earning

income outside the home. This fact helps to explain why the amount of time that husbands spend performing unpaid housework has increased by 14 percent since 2003.

For Critical Thinking

1. How might the fact that more females than males now obtain college degrees contribute to the relative shift in earned incomes from husbands to wives?

2. Each day, the average wife spends about 35 minutes more on unpaid housework than her husband. If the percentage plotted in Figure 2-6 continues to increase over time, would you anticipate that this time differential would rise or fall?

Web Resources

1. Learn more about trends in earnings of women and wives in the Web Links in MyEconLab.

2. Read about developments in women's role in the world of paid work in the Web Links in MyEconLab.

> ## MyEconLab
>
> For more questions on this chapter's Issues & Applications, go to MyEconLab.
>
> In the Study Plan for this chapter, select Section I: Issues and Applications.

Sources are listed at the end of this chapter.

Fundamental Points

1. The wants of any individual, whether that person is affluent or poor, always exceed what can be produced with available limited resources and time, so all individuals regard resources as scarce.

2. A production possibilities curve depicts the trade-off that occurs when more of one item is obtained at the sacrifice of another item, which is a graphical representation of opportunity cost, or the cost of a forgone alternative.

3. Many resources are better suited for certain productive tasks than for others, and consequently, consistent with the law of increasing cost, an economy's production possibilities curve is bowed outward.

4. Choosing to produce more capital goods today requires giving up production of some consumption goods today but shifts the future production possibilities curve farther to the right and thereby enables production of additional consumption *and* capital goods in the future.

5. Whereas absolute advantage is the ability to produce more units of a good or service using a given quantity of labor or resource inputs, comparative advantage entails producing an item at a lower opportunity cost and thereby specializing in producing and trading that item.

WHAT YOU SHOULD KNOW

Here is what you should know after reading this chapter. MyEconLab will help you identify what you know, and where to go when you need to practice.

WHAT YOU SHOULD KNOW	KEY TERMS	WHERE TO GO TO PRACTICE
2.1 Evaluate why everyone, whether poor or affluent, faces the problem of scarcity *Even the richest people face scarcity because they have to make choices among alternatives. Despite their high levels of income or wealth, affluent people, like everyone else, want more than they can have (in terms of goods, power, prestige, and so on).*	Scarcity, 29 production, 29 land, 30 labor, 30 physical capital, 30 human capital, 30 entrepreneurship, 30 goods, 30 economic goods, 30 services, 30	• MyEconLab Study Plan 2.1
2.2 Explain why the scarcity problem causes people to consider opportunity costs and trade-offs among choices *Opportunity cost is the highest-valued alternative that one must give up to obtain an item. The trade-offs people face can be represented by a production possibilities curve (PPC). Moving along a PPC from one point to another entails incurring an opportunity cost of allocating scarce resources toward the production of one good instead of another good.*	opportunity cost, 31 production possibilities curve (PPC), 33 **Key Figure** Figure 2-1, 33	• MyEconLab Study Plan 2.2 • Animated Figure 2-1
2.3 Discuss why obtaining increasing increments of any particular good typically entails giving up more and more units of other goods *When people allocate additional resources to producing more units of a good, it must increasingly employ resources that would be better suited for producing other goods. As a result, the law of increasing additional cost holds. Each additional unit of a good can be obtained only by giving up more and more of other goods. Hence, the production possibilities curve is bowed outward.*	Technology, 35 efficiency, 36 inefficient point, 36 law of increasing additional cost, 37 **Key Figure** Figure 2-3, 37	• MyEconLab Study Plan 2.3 • Animated Figure 2-3

WHAT YOU SHOULD KNOW *continued*

LEARNING OBJECTIVES	KEY TERMS	WHERE TO GO TO PRACTICE
2.4 **Explain why the economy faces a trade-off between consumption goods and capital goods** *If we allocate more resources to producing capital goods today, then the production possibilities curve will shift outward by more in the future, which means that we can have additional future consumption goods. The trade-off is that producing more capital goods today entails giving up consumption goods today.*	consumption, 38 **Key Figure** Figure 2-4, 39	• MyEconLab Study Plan 2.4 • Animated Figure 2-4
2.5 **Distinguish between absolute and comparative advantage** *A person has an absolute advantage if she can produce more of a good than someone else who uses the same amount of resources. An individual can gain from specializing in producing a good if she has a comparative advantage in producing that good, meaning that she can produce the good at a lower opportunity cost than someone else.*	specialization, 41 comparative advantage, 41 absolute advantage, 42 division of labor, 42	• MyEconLab Study Plan 2.5

Log in to MyEconLab, take a chapter test, and get a personalized Study Plan that tells you which concepts you understand and which ones you need to review. From there, MyEconLab will give you further practice, tutorials, animations, videos, and guided solutions. For more information, visit http://www.myeconlab.com

PROBLEMS

All problems are assignable in MyEconLab. Answers to odd-numbered problems appear in MyEconLab.

2-1. Define opportunity cost. What is your opportunity cost of attending a class at 11:00 A.M.? How does it differ from your opportunity cost of attending a class at 8:00 A.M.? (See pages 31–32.)

2-2. If you receive a ticket to a concert at no charge, what, if anything, is your opportunity cost of attending the concert? How does your opportunity cost change if miserable weather on the night of the concert requires you to leave much earlier for the concert hall and greatly extends the time it takes to get home afterward? (See pages 31–32.)

2-3. You and a friend decide to spend $100 each on concert tickets. Each of you alternatively could have spent the $100 to purchase a textbook, a meal at a highly rated local restaurant, or several Internet movie downloads. As you are on the way

to the concert, your friend tells you that if she had not bought the concert ticket, she would have opted for a restaurant meal, and you reply that you otherwise would have downloaded several movies. Identify the relevant opportunity costs for you and your friend of the concert tickets that you purchased. Explain briefly. (See pages 31–32.)

2-4. After the concert discussed in Problem 2-3 is over and you and your friend are traveling home, you discuss how each of you might otherwise have used the four hours devoted to attending the concert. The four hours could have been used to study, to watch a sporting event on TV, or to get some extra sleep. Your friend decides that if she had not spent four hours attending the concert, she would have chosen to study, and you reply that you otherwise would have watched the televised sporting event. Identify the relevant opportunity costs for you and your friend for allocating your four hours to attending the concert. Explain briefly. (See pages 31–32.)

2-5. Recently, a woman named Mary Krawiec attended an auction in Troy, New York. At the auction, a bank was seeking to sell a foreclosed property: a large Victorian house suffering from years of neglect in a neighborhood in which many properties had been on the market for years yet remained unsold. Her $10 offer was the highest bid in the auction, and she handed over a $10 bill for a title to ownership. Once she acquired the house, however, she became responsible for all taxes on the property and for an overdue water bill of $2,000. In addition, to make the house habitable, she and her husband devoted months of time and unpaid labor to renovating the property. In the process, they incurred explicit expenses totaling $65,000. Why do you suppose that the bank was willing to sell the house to Ms. Krawiec for only $10? (*Hint:* Contemplate the bank's expected gain, net of all explicit and opportunity costs, if it had attempted to make the house habitable. (See pages 31–32.)

2-6. The following table illustrates the points a student can earn on examinations in economics and biology if the student uses all available hours for study. Plot this student's production possibilities curve. Does the PPC illustrate the law of increasing additional cost? (See page 33.)

Economics	Biology
100	40
90	60
80	75
70	85
60	93
50	98
40	100

2-7. Based on the information provided in Problem 2-6, what is the opportunity cost to this student of allocating enough additional study time on economics to move her grade up from a 90 to a 100? (See page 33.)

2-8. Consider a change in the table in Problem 2-6. The student's set of opportunities is now as follows: Does the PPC illustrate the law of increasing additional cost? What is the opportunity cost to this student for the additional amount of study time on economics required to move her grade from 60 to 70? From 90 to 100? (See page 33.)

Economics	Biology
100	40
90	50
80	60
70	70
60	80
50	90
40	100

2-9. Construct a production possibilities curve for a nation facing increasing opportunity costs for producing food and video games. Show how the PPC changes given the following events. (See page 35.)

a. A new and better fertilizer is invented.

b. Immigration occurs, and immigrants' labor can be employed in both the agricultural sector and the video game sector.

c. People invent a new programming language that is much less costly to code and is more memory-efficient.

d. A heat wave and drought result in a 10 percent decrease in usable farmland.

Consider the following diagram when answering Problems 2-10, 2-11, and 2-12.

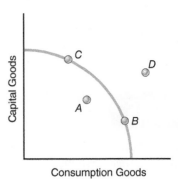

2-10. During a debate on the floor of the U.S. Senate, Senator Creighton states, "Our nation should not devote so many of its fully employed resources to producing capital goods because we already are not producing enough consumption goods for our citizens." Compared with the other labeled points on the diagram, which one could be consistent with the *current* production combination choice that Senator Creighton believes the nation has made? (See page 35.)

2-11. In response to Senator Creighton's statement reported in Problem 2-10, Senator Long replies, "We must remain at our current production combination if we want to be able to produce more consumption goods in the future." Of the labeled points on the diagram, which one could depict the *future* production combination Senator Long has in mind? (See page 35.)

2-12. Senator Borman interjects the following comment after the statements by Senators Creighton and Long reported in Problems 2-10 and 2-11: "In fact, both of my esteemed colleagues are wrong, because an unacceptably large portion of our nation's resources is currently unemployed." Of the labeled points on the diagram, which one is consistent with Senator Borman's position? (See page 35.)

2-13. A nation's residents can allocate their scarce resources either to producing consumption goods or to producing human capital—that is, providing themselves with training and education. (See pages 36–37.) The table at the top of next column displays the production possibilities for this nation:

Production Combination	Units of Consumption Goods	Units of Human Capital
A	0	100
B	10	97
C	20	90
D	30	75
E	40	55
F	50	30
G	60	0

a. Suppose that the nation's residents currently produce combination A. What is the opportunity cost of increasing production of consumption goods by 10 units? By 60 units?

b. Does the law of increasing additional cost hold true for this nation? Why or why not?

2-14. Like physical capital, human capital produced in the present can be applied to the production of future goods and services. Consider the table in Problem 2-13, and suppose that the nation's residents are trying to choose between combination C

and combination F. Other things being equal, will the future production possibilities curve for this nation be located farther outward if the nation chooses combination F instead of combination C? Explain. (See pages 38–40.)

2-15. You can wash, fold, and iron a basket of laundry in two hours and prepare a meal in one hour. Your roommate can wash, fold, and iron a basket of laundry in three hours and prepare a meal in one hour. Who has the absolute advantage in laundry, and who has an absolute advantage in meal preparation? Who has the comparative advantage in laundry, and who has a comparative advantage in meal preparation? (See page 41.)

2-16. Based on the information in Problem 2-15, should you and your roommate specialize in a particular task? Why? If so, who should specialize in which task? Show how much labor time you save if you choose to "trade" an appropriate task with your roommate as opposed to doing it yourself. (See page 41.)

2-17. Using only the concept of comparative advantage, evaluate this statement: "A professor with a Ph.D. in physics should never mow his or her own lawn, because this would fail to take into account the professor's comparative advantage." (See page 41.)

2-18. Country A and country B produce the same consumption goods and capital goods and currently have *identical* production possibilities curves. They also have the same resources at present, and they have access to the same technology. (See pages 38–41.)

a. At present, does either country have a comparative advantage in producing capital goods? Consumption goods?

b. Currently, country A has chosen to produce more consumption goods, compared with country B. Other things being equal, which country will experience the larger outward shift of its PPC during the next year?

REFERENCES

POLICY EXAMPLE: Bankrupt Detroit Confronts the Opportunity Cost of Art

Randy Kennedy, "Detroit Art Museum Offers Plan to Avoid Sale of Art," *The New York Times*, January 29, 2014.

Karen McVeigh, "Detroit Mired in Fresh Controversy Over Sale of 60,000-Piece Art Collection," *The Guardian*, August 14, 2013.

Abby Ohlheiser, "Detroit's Emergency Manager Could Sell the City's Art," *The Atlantic Wire*, August 5, 2013.

EXAMPLE: The Trade-Off from Redirecting Corn to Ethanol Production

James Conca, "It's Final—Corn Ethanol Is of No Use," *Forbes*, April 20, 2014.

Lisa Ingram, "Corn Ethanol Mandate Hurts Businesses, Consumers," *Louisville Courier-Journal*, March 23, 2014.

Charles Kenny, "Congress Wakes Up to the Bad News About Biofuels," *Bloomberg Businessweek*, January 6, 2014.

INTERNATIONAL POLICY EXAMPLE: Is the Opportunity Cost of Homework Too High in France?

"French President Wants to Ban Homework," *Circa*, November 21, 2013.

Irwin Stoomacher, "The French Plan to Eliminate Homework," *The Jersey Journal*, February 14, 2013.

Valerie Strauss, "The Trouble with Calls for Universal 'High-Quality' Pre-K," *The Washington Post*, February 1, 2014.

EXAMPLE: Too Sick to Call a Doc? ZocDoc and Practice Fusion Can Help

Jonah Comstock, "ZocDoc to Take Doctor Appointment Booking Nationwide by Yearend," *MobiHealthNews*, March 6, 2014.

Stephanie Baum, "Vitals CEO Flags Up to Five Consumer Health Care Trends That Could Impact Digital Health in 2014, *MedCityNews*, January 9, 2014.

Zina Moukheiber, "Practice Fusion Moves into ZocDoc Territory by Offering Appointment Bookings," *Forbes*, April 9, 2013.

YOU ARE THERE: Frustrated by the Opportunity Cost of Time Spent in Meetings

Francesca Donner, "Snapshot of the American Workday," *The Wall Street Journal*, June 21, 2013.

Rachel Feintzeig, "Before You Hit Send, Read This," *The Wall Street Journal*, August 9, 2013.

Mary Margaret Maule, "Wasting Time Means Wasting Money," *Northwest Herald*, April 29, 2014.

ISSUES & APPLICATIONS: Specialization Shifts within U.S. Marriages

Bryony Gordon, "Why Are Women Still Doing Most of the Housework," *The Telegraph*, February 9, 2014.

"More Married Women Make More Than Husbands," *Cleveland Plain Dealer*, May 29, 2013.

Richard Thalery, "Breadwinning Wives and Nervous Husbands," *The New York Times*, June 1, 2013.

Demand and Supply

3

Soleg/Fotolia

By developing novel techniques for extracting oil from beneath the earth's surface, U.S. firms have greatly expanded the volume of oil they produce. Several locations where oil is being extracted are far from ultimate consumers of the oil, so producers must arrange for the oil to be transported over hundreds of miles. The U.S. government held up plans to construct new pipelines to move all of this oil. In this chapter, you will learn why these events have led to higher prices for moving oil through existing pipelines and significant increases in oil shipments by barge, truck, and train.

LEARNING OBJECTIVES

After reading this chapter, you should be able to:

3.1 Explain the law of demand

3.2 Distinguish between changes in demand and changes in quantity demanded

3.3 Explain the law of supply

3.4 Distinguish between changes in supply and changes in quantity supplied

3.5 Understand how the interaction of the demand for and supply of a commodity determines the market price of the commodity and the equilibrium quantity of the commodity that is produced and consumed

MyEconLab helps you master each objective and study more efficiently. See end of chapter for details.

...as the inflation-adjusted prices of artificial Christmas trees have exhibited a net overall decrease since 1991, the annual number of real trees purchased has declined from 37 million in 1991 to fewer than 27 million? Lower prices of artificial Christmas trees induced many people who buy Christmas trees to substitute away from real Christmas trees to artificial ones.

If we use the economist's primary set of tools, *demand* and *supply*, we can develop a better understanding of why we sometimes observe relatively large decreases in the purchase, or consumption, of items such as real Christmas trees. We can also gain insight into why a persistent decrease in the price of items such as artificial Christmas trees ultimately induces a decrease in consumption of real Christmas trees. Demand and supply are two ways of categorizing the influences on the prices of goods that you buy and the quantities available. Indeed, demand and supply characterize much economic analysis of the world around us.

As you will see throughout this text, the operation of the forces of demand and supply takes place in *markets*. A **market** is an abstract concept summarizing all of the arrangements individuals have for exchanging with one another. Goods and services are sold in markets, such as the automobile market, the health care market, and the market for high-speed Internet access. Workers offer their services in the labor market. Companies, or firms, buy workers' labor services in the labor market. Firms also buy other inputs to produce the goods and services that you buy as a consumer. Firms purchase machines, buildings, and land. These markets are in operation at all times. One of the most important activities in these markets is the determination of the prices of all of the inputs and outputs that are bought and sold in our economy. To understand the determination of prices, you first need to look at the law of demand.

Market
All of the arrangements that individuals have for exchanging with one another. Thus, for example, we can speak of the labor market, the automobile market, and the credit market.

3.1 Explain the law of demand

Demand

Demand has a special meaning in economics. It refers to the quantities of specific goods or services that individuals, taken singly or as a group, will purchase at various possible prices, other things being constant. We can therefore talk about the demand for microprocessor chips, french fries, multifunction digital devices, children, and criminal activities.

The Law of Demand

Associated with the concept of demand is the **law of demand**, which can be stated as follows:

> *When the price of a good goes up, people buy less of it, other things being equal. When the price of a good goes down, people buy more of it, other things being equal.*

The law of demand tells us that the quantity demanded of any commodity is inversely related to its price, other things being equal. In an inverse relationship, one variable moves up in value when the other moves down. The law of demand states that a change in price causes a change in the quantity demanded in the *opposite* direction.

Notice that we tacked on to the end of the law of demand the statement "other things being equal." We referred to this in Chapter 1 as the *ceteris paribus* assumption. It means, for example, that when we predict that people will buy fewer digital devices if their price goes up, we are holding constant the price of all other goods in the economy as well as people's incomes. Implicitly, therefore, if we are assuming that no other prices change when we examine the price behavior of digital devices, we are looking at the *relative* price of digital devices.

The law of demand is supported by millions of observations of people's behavior in the marketplace. Theoretically, it can be derived from an economic model based on rational behavior, as was discussed in Chapter 1. Basically, if nothing else changes and the price of a good falls, the lower price induces us to buy more because we can enjoy additional net gains that were unavailable at the higher price. If you examine your own behavior, you will see that it generally follows the law of demand. MyEconLab Concept Check

Demand
A schedule showing how much of a good or service people will purchase at any price during a specified time period, other things being constant.

Law of demand
The observation that there is a negative, or inverse, relationship between the price of any good or service and the quantity demanded, holding other factors constant.

Relative Prices versus Money Prices

The **relative price** of any commodity is its price in terms of another commodity. The price that you pay in dollars and cents for any good or service at any point in time is called its **money price**.

THE RELATIVE PRICE OF A HOUSE You might hear from your grandparents, "My first new car cost only thirty-two hundred dollars." The implication, of course, is that the price of cars today is outrageously high because the average new car may cost $32,000. That, however, is not an accurate comparison.

What was the price of the average house during that same year? Perhaps it was only $18,000. By comparison, then, given that the average price of houses today is close to $180,000, the current price of a new car doesn't sound so far out of line, does it?

COMPARING RELATIVE PRICES OF DIGITAL STORAGE DRIVES The point is that money prices during different time periods don't tell you much. You have to calculate relative prices. Consider an example of the price of 500-gigabyte solid state drives versus the price of 500-gigabyte external hard drives from last year and this year. In Table 3-1 below, we show the money prices of solid state drives and external hard drives for two years during which they have both gone down.

This means that in today's dollars we have to pay out less for both solid state drives and external hard drives. If we look, though, at the relative prices of solid state drives and external hard drives, we find that last year, solid state drives were twice as expensive as external hard drives, whereas this year they are only one and a half times as expensive. Conversely, if we compare external hard drives to solid state drives, last year the price of external hard drives was 50 percent of the price of solid state drives, but today the price of external hard drives is about 67 percent of the price of solid state drives. In the one-year period, although both prices have declined in money terms, the relative price of external hard drives has risen in relation to that of solid state drives.

Sometimes relative price changes occur because the quality of a product improves, thereby bringing about a decrease in the item's effective *price per constant-quality unit*. The price of an item may also decrease simply because producers have reduced the item's quality. Thus, when evaluating the effects of price changes, we must always compare *price per constant-quality unit*.

How has the quantity of natural gas demanded responded to a significant reduction in the price of natural gas?

Relative price
The money price of one commodity divided by the money price of another commodity; the number of units of one commodity that must be sacrificed to purchase one unit of another commodity.

Money price
The price expressed in today's dollars; also called the *absolute* or *nominal price*.

EXAMPLE

The Law of Demand at Work in the Market for Natural Gas

Between 2008 and 2014, the price of natural gas declined from more than $8 per thousand cubic feet to about $4 per thousand cubic feet. In response to the price decline, more families and businesses switched to heating buildings with natural gas, and recently more trucking firms have been operating their vehicles with liquefied natural gas. As the price of natural gas has decreased, the

(continued)

TABLE 3-1

Money Price versus Relative Price

The money prices of both 500-gigabyte solid state drives and 500-gigabyte external hard drives have fallen. The relative price of external hard drives, however, has risen (or, conversely, the relative price of solid state drives has fallen).

	Money Price		Relative Price	
	Price Last Year	Price This Year	Price Last Year	Price This Year
Solid state drives	$300	$210	$\dfrac{\$300}{\$150} = 2.0$	$\dfrac{\$210}{\$140} = 1.50$
External hard drives	$150	$140	$\dfrac{\$150}{\$300} = 0.50$	$\dfrac{\$140}{\$210} = 0.67$

monthly quantity of natural gas consumed has correspondingly in-creased. The quantity of natural gas demanded each month throughout the United States is now more than 10 percent greater than in 2008.

FOR CRITICAL THINKING

Is there a direct or inverse relationship between the price of natural gas and the quantity of natural gas that people purchase? Explain.

Sources are listed at the end of this chapter.

MyEconLab Concept Check

The Demand Schedule

Let's take a hypothetical demand situation to see how the inverse relationship between the price and the quantity demanded looks (holding other things equal). We will con-sider the quantity of flash memory cards—utilized with various digital devices—demanded *per year*. Without stating the *time dimension*, we could not make sense out of this demand relationship because the numbers would be different if we were talking about the quantity demanded per month or the quantity demanded per decade.

In addition to implicitly or explicitly stating a time dimension for a demand rela-tionship, we are also implicitly referring to *constant-quality units* of the good or service in question. Prices are always expressed in constant-quality units in order to avoid the problem of comparing commodities that are in fact not truly comparable.

In panel (a) of Figure 3-1 below, we see that if the price is $1 apiece, 50 flash memory cards will be bought each year by our representative individual, but if the price is $5 apiece, only 10 flash memory cards will be bought each year. This reflects the law of demand. Panel (a) is also called simply demand, or a *demand schedule*, because it gives a schedule of alternative quantities demanded per year at different possible prices.

THE DEMAND CURVE Tables expressing relationships between two variables can be repre-sented in graphical terms. To do this, we need only construct a graph that has the price per constant-quality flash memory card on the vertical axis and the quantity measured in constant-quality flash memory cards per year on the horizontal axis. All we have to

---

FIGURE 3-1

The Individual Demand Schedule and the Individual Demand Curve

In panel (a), we show combinations *A* through *E* of the quantities of flash memory cards demanded, measured in constant-quality units at prices ranging from $5 down to $1 apiece. These combinations are points on the demand schedule. In panel (b), we plot combinations *A* through *E* on a grid. The result is the individual demand curve for flash memory cards.

Panel (a)

Combination	Price per Constant-Quality Flash Memory Card	Quantity of Constant-Quality Flash Memory Cards per Year
A	$5	10
B	4	20
C	3	30
D	2	40
E	1	50

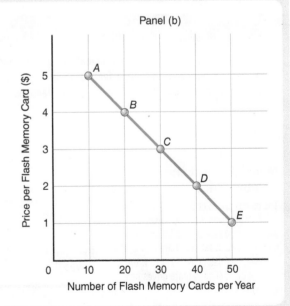

Panel (b)

do is take combinations *A* through *E* from panel (a) of Figure 3-1 on the previous page and plot those points in panel (b). Now we connect the points with a smooth line, and *voilà*, we have a **demand curve.** It is downward sloping (from left to right) to indicate the inverse relationship between the price of flash memory cards and the quantity demanded per year.

Our presentation of demand schedules and curves applies equally well to all commodities, including dental floss, bagels, textbooks, credit, and labor. Remember, the demand curve is simply a graphical representation of the law of demand.

INDIVIDUAL VERSUS MARKET DEMAND CURVES The demand schedule shown in panel (a) of Figure 3-1 and the resulting demand curve shown in panel (b) are both given for an individual. As we shall see, the determination of price in the marketplace depends on, among other things, the **market demand** for a particular commodity. The way in which we measure a market demand schedule and derive a market demand curve for flash memory cards or any other good or service is by summing (at each price) the individual quantities demanded by all buyers in the market. Suppose that the market demand for flash memory cards consists of only two buyers: buyer 1, for whom we've already shown the demand schedule, and buyer 2, whose demand schedule is displayed in column 3 of panel (a) of Figure 3-2 below. Column 1 shows the price, and

Demand curve
A graphical representation of the demand schedule. It is a negatively sloped line showing the inverse relationship between the price and the quantity demanded (other things being equal).

Market demand
The demand of all consumers in the marketplace for a particular good or service. The summation at each price of the quantity demanded by each individual.

FIGURE 3-2

MyEconLab Animation

The Horizontal Summation of Two Demand Curves

Panel (a) shows how to sum the demand schedule for one buyer with that of another buyer. In column 2 is the quantity demanded by buyer 1, taken from panel (a) of Figure 3-1 on page 54. Column 4 is the sum of columns 2 and 3.

We plot the demand curve for buyer 1 in panel (b) and the demand curve for buyer 2 in panel (c). When we add those two demand curves horizontally, we get the market demand curve for two buyers, shown in panel (d).

Panel (a)

(1) Price per Flash Memory Card	(2) Buyer 1's Quantity Demanded	(3) Buyer 2's Quantity Demanded	(4) = (2) + (3) Combined Quantity Demanded per Year
$5	10	10	20
4	20	20	40
3	30	40	70
2	40	50	90
1	50	60	110

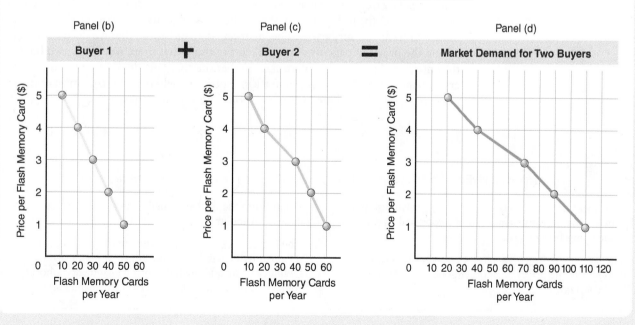

FIGURE 3-3

The Market Demand Schedule for Flash Memory Cards

In panel (a), we add up the existing demand schedules for flash memory cards. In panel (b), we plot the quantities from panel (a) on a grid.

Connecting them produces the market demand curve for flash memory cards.

Panel (a)

Price per Constant-Quality Flash Memory Card	Total Quantity Demanded of Constant-Quality Flash Memory Cards per Year (millions)
$5	2
4	4
3	6
2	8
1	10

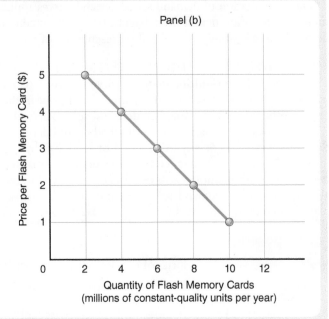

Panel (b)

column 2 shows the quantity demanded by buyer 1 at each price. These data are taken directly from Figure 3-1. In column 3, we show the quantity demanded by buyer 2. Column 4 shows the total quantity demanded at each price, which is obtained by simply adding columns 2 and 3. Graphically, in panel (d) of Figure 3-2, we add the demand curves of buyer 1 [panel (b)] and buyer 2 [panel (c)] to derive the market demand curve.

There are, of course, numerous potential consumers of flash memory cards. We'll simply assume that the summation of all of the consumers in the market results in a demand schedule, given in panel (a) of Figure 3-3 above, and a demand curve, given in panel (b). The quantity demanded is now measured in millions of units per year. Remember, panel (b) in Figure 3-3 shows the market demand curve for the millions of buyers of flash memory cards. The "market" demand curve that we derived in Figure 3-2 on the previous page was undertaken assuming that there were only two buyers in the entire market. That's why we assume that the "market" demand curve for two buyers in panel (d) of Figure 3-2 is not a smooth line, whereas the true market demand curve in panel (b) of Figure 3-3 is a smooth line with no kinks.

MyEconLab Concept Check
MyEconLab Study Plan

Visit MyEconLab to practice these and other problems and to get instant feedback in your Study Plan.

The law of demand posits an _____ relationship between the quantity demanded of a good and its price, other things being equal.

The law of _____ applies when other things, such as income and the prices of all other goods and services, are held constant.

We measure the demand schedule in terms of a time dimension and in _____-quality units.

The _____ _____ curve is derived by summing the quantity demanded by individuals at each price. Graphically, we add the individual demand curves horizontally to derive the total, or market, demand curve.

Shifts in Demand

Assume that the federal government gives every student registered in a college, university, or technical school in the United States a digital device that utilizes flash memory cards. The demand curve presented in panel (b) of Figure 3-3 on the previous page would no longer be an accurate representation of total market demand for flash memory cards. What we have to do is shift the curve outward, or to the right, to represent the rise in demand that would result from this program. There will now be an increase in the number of flash memory cards demanded at *each and every possible price*. The demand curve shown in Figure 3-4 below will shift from D_1 to D_2. Take any price, say, $3 per flash memory card. Originally, before the federal government giveaway of digital devices, the amount demanded at $3 was 6 million flash memory cards per year. After the government giveaway of digital devices, however, the new amount demanded at the $3 price is 10 million flash memory cards per year. What we have seen is a shift in the demand for flash memory cards.

Under different circumstances, the shift can also go in the opposite direction. What if colleges uniformly prohibited any of their students from using digital devices that utilize flash memory cards? Such a regulation would cause a shift inward—to the left—of the demand curve for flash memory cards. In Figure 3-4 below, the demand curve would shift to D_3. The quantity demanded would now be less at each and every possible price.

The Other Determinants of Demand

The demand curve in panel (b) of Figure 3-3 on the previous page is drawn with other things held constant, specifically all of the other factors that determine how many flash memory cards will be bought. There are many such determinants. We refer to these determinants as *ceteris paribus* **conditions,** and they include consumers' income; tastes and preferences; the prices of related goods; expectations regarding future prices and future incomes; and market size (number of potential buyers). Let's examine each of these determinants more closely.

Ceteris paribus **conditions**
Determinants of the relationship between price and quantity that are unchanged along a curve. Changes in these factors cause the curve to shift.

INCOME For most goods, an increase in income will lead to an increase in demand. That is, an increase in income will lead to a rightward shift in the position of the demand curve from, say, D_1 to D_2 in Figure 3-4. You can avoid confusion about shifts in curves by always relating a rise in demand to a rightward shift in the demand curve

MyEconLab Animation

FIGURE 3-4

Shifts in the Demand Curve

If some factor other than price changes, we can show its effect by moving the entire demand curve, say, from D_1 to D_2. We have assumed in our example that this move was precipitated by the government's giving digital devices that utilize flash memory cards to every registered college student in the United States. Thus, at *all* prices, a larger number of flash memory cards would be demanded than before. Curve D_3 represents reduced demand compared to curve D_1, caused by a prohibition of digital devices that utilize flash memory cards on campus.

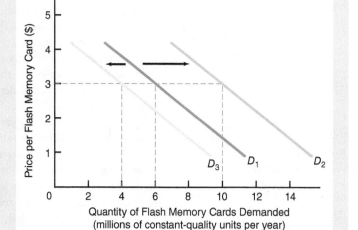

Normal goods
Goods for which demand rises as income rises. Most goods are normal goods.

Inferior goods
Goods for which demand falls as income rises.

and a fall in demand to a leftward shift in the demand curve. Goods for which the demand rises when consumer income rises are called **normal goods.** Most goods, such as shoes, smartphones, and flash memory drives, are "normal goods." For some goods, however, demand *falls* as income rises. These are called **inferior goods**. Beans might be an example. As households get richer, they tend to purchase fewer and fewer beans and purchase more and more fish. (The terms *normal* and *inferior* are merely part of the economist's lexicon. No value judgments are associated with them.)

Remember, a shift to the left in the demand curve represents a decrease in demand, and a shift to the right represents an increase in demand.

How have declines in incomes in European nations affected the demand for electricity in those countries?

INTERNATIONAL EXAMPLE

Lower European Incomes Reduce the Demand for Electricity

Recently, a number of European nations experienced decreases in their annual inflation-adjusted national income levels. Accompanying these income declines were reductions in these nations' purchases of electricity. For instance, in Spain, where total annual national income recently fell by 2.1 percent, electricity consumption decreased by 7.0 percent. In Italy, where national income decreased by 2.3 percent over the same year, purchases of electricity declined by 2.3 percent. Across all European nations that use the euro as their common currency, a 0.6 percent decline in these countries' aggregate income generated a reduction of more than 2 percent in electricity consumption. Thus, as incomes fell across Europe, the amount of electricity demanded showed a decrease, indicating that electricity is a normal good.

FOR CRITICAL THINKING
What do you suppose would happen to the demand for electricity if annual European income levels increased considerably?

Sources are listed at the end of this chapter.

TASTES AND PREFERENCES A change in consumer tastes in favor of a good can shift its demand curve outward to the right. When Pokémon trading cards became the rage, the demand curve for them shifted outward to the right. When the rage died out, the demand curve shifted inward to the left. Fashions depend to a large extent on people's tastes and preferences. Economists have little to say about the determination of tastes. That is, they don't have any "good" theories of taste determination or why people buy one brand of product rather than others. (Advertisers, however, have various theories they use to try to make consumers prefer their products over those of competitors.)

PRICES OF RELATED GOODS: SUBSTITUTES AND COMPLEMENTS Demand schedules are always drawn with the prices of all other commodities held constant. That is to say, when deriving a given demand curve, we assume that only the price of the good under study changes. For example, when we draw the demand curve for laptop computers, we assume that the price of tablet devices is held constant. When we draw the demand curve for home cinema speakers, we assume that the price of surround-sound amplifiers is held constant. When we refer to *related goods*, we are talking about goods for which demand is interdependent. If a change in the price of one good shifts the demand for another good, those two goods have interdependent demands.

There are two types of demand interdependencies: those in which goods are *substitutes* and those in which goods are *complements*. We can define and distinguish between substitutes and complements in terms of how the change in price of one commodity affects the demand for its related commodity.

Substitutes
Two goods are substitutes when a change in the price of one causes a shift in demand for the other in the same direction as the price change.

Butter and margarine are **substitutes.** Either can be consumed to satisfy the same basic want. Let's assume that both products originally cost $2 per pound. If the price of butter remains the same and the price of margarine falls from $2 per pound to $1 per pound, people will buy more margarine and less butter. The demand curve for butter shifts inward to the left. If, conversely, the price of margarine rises from $2 per pound to $3 per pound, people will buy more butter and less margarine. The demand curve for butter shifts outward to the right. In other words, an increase in the price of margarine will lead to an increase in the demand for butter, and an increase in the price of butter will lead to an increase in the demand for margarine. For substitutes, a change in the price of a substitute will cause a change in demand *in the same direction*.

How has the availability of lower-priced digital devices such as smartphones and tablet devices affected the demands for desktop computers and laptop computers?

EXAMPLE

The Great Substitution from Computers to Handheld Devices

Sales of smartphones began in 2007, and tablets were first offered for sale in 2008. Both of these digital devices have lower prices than desktop and laptop computers and can be utilized as substitutes. The consequences, as shown in Figure 3-5, have been a gradual decline in desktop computer sales since 2011 and a leveling off and recent decline in laptop computer sales since 2012. Sales of smartphones have eclipsed sales of desktop and of laptop computers since early 2011. Recently, sales of tablet devices also have outpaced sales of each type of computer.

FOR CRITICAL THINKING

Several new apps permit users of tablet devices to operate their tablets as if they were laptop computers. How is this development likely to affect the demand for laptops?

Sources are listed at the end of this chapter.

FIGURE 3-5

Purchases of Personal Computers versus Digital Devices since 2007

The number of smartphones purchased during each three-month interval has outpaced purchases of desktop computers since 2010 and laptop computers since 2011. Purchases of tablet devices rose above desktop-computer sales in 2012 and above laptop-computer purchases in 2013.

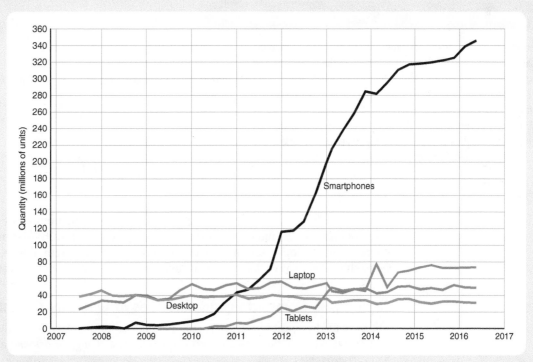

Source: Federal Communications Commission; author's estimates.

For **complements,** goods typically consumed together, the situation is reversed. Consider digital devices and online applications (apps). We draw the demand curve for apps with the price of digital devices held constant. If the price per constant-quality unit of digital devices decreases from, say, $500 to $300, that will encourage more people to purchase apps. They will now buy more apps, at any given app price, than before. The demand curve for apps will shift outward to the right. If, by contrast, the price of digital devices increases from $250 to $450, fewer people will purchase downloadable applications. The demand curve for apps will shift inward to the left.

Complements

Two goods are complements when a change in the price of one causes an opposite shift in the demand for the other.

To summarize, a decrease in the price of digital devices leads to an increase in the demand for apps. An increase in the price of digital devices leads to a decrease in the demand for apps. Thus, for complements, a change in the price of a product will cause a change in demand *in the opposite direction* for the other good.

EXPECTATIONS Consumers' expectations regarding future prices and future incomes will prompt them to buy more or less of a particular good without a change in its current money price. For example, consumers getting wind of a scheduled 100 percent increase in the price of flash memory cards next month will buy more of them today at today's prices. Today's demand curve for flash memory cards will shift from D_1 to D_2 in Figure 3-4 on page 57. The opposite would occur if a decrease in the price of flash memory cards was scheduled for next month (from D_1 to D_3).

Expectations of a rise in income may cause consumers to want to purchase more of everything today at today's prices. Again, such a change in expectations of higher future income will cause a shift in the demand curve from D_1 to D_2 in Figure 3-4.

Finally, expectations that goods will not be available at any price will induce consumers to stock up now, increasing current demand.

In what ways did recent actions by U.S. politicians and a federal agency affect expectations of the future prices of gun ammunition and, as a result, the current market demand for bullets?

POLICY EXAMPLE

An Expected Bullet Price Rise Boosts Current Ammo Demand

A number of U.S. politicians recently launched efforts to enact future tax increases on ammunition sold to private buyers. At the same time, the U.S. Department of Homeland Security announced plans to buy more than 1.6 billion rounds of gun ammunition over the next five years.

Both of these events caused private gun owners to anticipate a significant increase in future prices of bullets. A consequence of this expected rise in ammunition prices was a nearly 20 percent increase in the contemporaneous demand for bullets.

FOR CRITICAL THINKING
What would happen to the market demand for bullets if a different current event induced people to anticipate lower future ammunition prices?

Sources are listed at the end of this chapter.

MARKET SIZE (NUMBER OF POTENTIAL BUYERS) An increase in the number of potential buyers (holding buyers' incomes constant) at any given price shifts the market demand curve outward. Conversely, a reduction in the number of potential buyers at any given price shifts the market demand curve inward. MyEconLab Concept Check

Changes in Demand versus Changes in Quantity Demanded

We have made repeated references to demand and to quantity demanded. It is important to realize that there is a difference between a *change in demand* and a *change in quantity demanded*.

Demand refers to a schedule of planned rates of purchase and depends on a great many *ceteris paribus* conditions, such as incomes, expectations, and the prices of substitutes or complements. Whenever there is a change in a *ceteris paribus* condition, there will be a change in demand—a shift in the entire demand curve to the right or to the left.

A *quantity demanded* is a specific quantity at a specific price, represented by a single point on a demand curve. When price changes, quantity demanded changes according to the law of demand, and there will be a movement from one point to another along the same demand curve. Look at Figure 3-6 on the next page. At a price of $3 per flash memory card, 6 million flash memory cards per year are demanded. If the price falls to $1, quantity demanded increases to 10 million per year. This movement occurs

MyEconLab Animation

Movement along a Given Demand Curve

A change in price changes the quantity of a good demanded. This can
be represented as movement along a given demand schedule. If, in
our example, the price of flash memory cards falls from $3 to $1
apiece, the quantity demanded will increase from 6 million to
10 million flash memory cards per year.

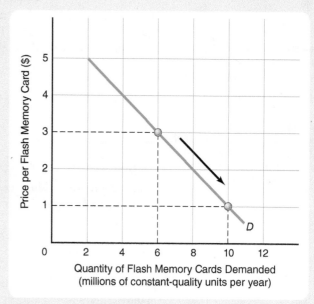

because the current market price for the product changes. In Figure 3-6, you can see
the arrow pointing down the given demand curve D.

When you think of demand, think of the entire curve. Quantity demanded, in contrast, is represented by a single point on the demand curve.

*A change or shift in demand is a movement of the entire curve. The **only** thing
that can cause the entire curve to move is a change in a determinant **other than**
the good's own price.*

In economic analysis, we cannot emphasize too much the following distinction that
must constantly be made:

*A change in a good's own price leads to a change in quantity demanded for any
given demand curve, other things held constant. This is a movement **along** the
curve.*

*A change in any of the **ceteris paribus** conditions for demand leads to a change
in demand. This causes a **shift of the curve.***

MyEconLab Concept Check
MyEconLab Study Plan

Visit MyEconLab to practice these and other problems and to get instant feedback in your Study Plan.

Demand curves are drawn with determinants other than
the price of the good held constant. These other determinants, called *ceteris paribus* conditions, are (1) _____,
(2) _____, (3) _____, (4) _____, and
(5) _____ at any given price. If any one of these
determinants changes, the demand curve will shift to
the right or to the left.

A change in demand comes about only because of a
change in the _____ _____ conditions of

demand. This change in demand is a shift in the demand
curve to the left or to the right.

A change in the quantity demanded comes about when
there is a change in the price of the good (other things
held constant). Such a change in quantity demanded
involves a _____ _____ a given demand
curve.

3.3 Explain the law of supply

Supply
A schedule showing the relationship between price and quantity supplied for a specified period of time, other things being equal.

Law of supply
The observation that the higher the price of a good, the more of that good sellers will make available over a specified time period, other things being equal.

Supply

The other side of the basic model in economics involves the quantities of goods and services that firms will offer for sale to the market. The **supply** of any good or service is the amount that firms will produce and offer for sale under certain conditions during a specified time period.

The Law of Supply

The relationship between price and quantity supplied, called the **law of supply**, can be summarized as follows:

> *At higher prices, a larger quantity will generally be supplied than at lower prices, all other things held constant. At lower prices, a smaller quantity will generally be supplied than at higher prices, all other things held constant.*

There is usually a direct relationship between price and quantity supplied. As the price rises, the quantity supplied rises. As the price falls, the quantity supplied also falls. Producers are normally willing to produce and sell more of their product at a higher price than at a lower price, other things being constant. At $5 per flash memory card, manufacturers would almost certainly be willing to supply a larger quantity than at $1 per flash memory card, assuming, of course, that no other prices in the economy had changed.

As with the law of demand, millions of instances in the real world have given us confidence in the law of supply. On a theoretical level, the law of supply is based on a model in which producers and sellers seek to make the most gain possible from their activities. For example, as a manufacturer attempts to produce more and more flash memory cards over the same time period, it will eventually have to hire more workers, pay overtime wages (which are higher), and heavily utilize its machines. Only if offered a higher price per flash memory card will the manufacturer be willing to incur these higher costs. That is why the law of supply implies a direct relationship between price and quantity supplied.

Why are many lobster boats in Maine tied up at dock even though there are more lobsters to catch than in prior years?

EXAMPLE

Why Many Lobster Boats Remain at Their Moorings

Since 2012, prices received by lobster fishermen have dropped by roughly 50 percent, to below $4 per pound. People who have made a living fishing for lobsters for their entire lives agree that there are more lobsters available to catch than they can remember. Nevertheless, the substantial price decline has significantly reduced their incentive to take out their boats and lower their nets. Indeed, another development that has become more commonplace than experienced fishermen can recall has been the decision by many of them to keep their boats at their moorings.

Naturally, as many fishermen have opted to keep their boats tied to docks, fewer lobsters have been caught. Thus, the quantity of lobsters supplied has declined in response to the decrease in the market price.

FOR CRITICAL THINKING
After the lobster prices declined, how did each lobster producer react?

Sources are listed at the end of this chapter.

MyEconLab Concept Check

The Supply Schedule

Just as we were able to construct a demand schedule, we can construct a *supply schedule*, which is a table relating prices to the quantity supplied at each price. A supply schedule can also be referred to simply as *supply*. It is a set of planned production rates that depends on the price of the product. We show the individual supply schedule for a

FIGURE 3-7

The Individual Producer's Supply Schedule and Supply Curve for Flash Memory Cards

Panel (a) shows that at higher prices, a hypothetical supplier will be willing to provide a greater quantity of flash memory cards. We plot the various price-quantity combinations in panel (a) on the grid in panel (b).

When we connect these points, we create the individual supply curve for flash memory cards. It is positively sloped.

Panel (a)

Combination	Price per Constant-Quality Flash Memory Card	Quantity of Flash Memory Cards Supplied (thousands of constant-quality units per year)
F	$5	55
G	4	40
H	3	35
I	2	25
J	1	20

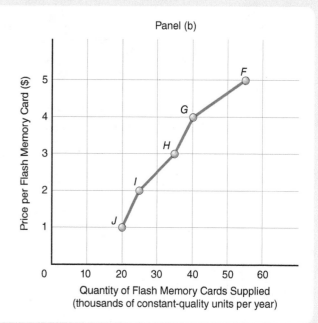

Panel (b)

hypothetical producer in panel (a) of Figure 3-7 above. At a price of $1 per flash memory card, for example, this producer will supply 20,000 flash memory cards per year. At a price of $5 per flash memory card, this producer will supply 55,000 flash memory cards per year.

THE SUPPLY CURVE We can convert the supply schedule from panel (a) of Figure 3-7 above into a **supply curve,** just as we earlier created a demand curve in Figure 3-1 on page 54. All we do is take the price-quantity combinations from panel (a) of Figure 3-7 and plot them in panel (b). We have labeled these combinations *F* through *J.* Connecting these points, we obtain an upward-sloping curve that shows the typically direct relationship between price and quantity supplied. Again, we have to remember that we are talking about quantity supplied *per year,* measured in constant-quality units.

Supply curve

The graphical representation of the supply schedule; a line (curve) showing the supply schedule, which generally slopes upward (has a positive slope), other things being equal.

THE MARKET SUPPLY CURVE Just as we summed the individual demand curves to obtain the market demand curve, we sum the individual producers' supply curves to obtain the market supply curve. Look at Figure 3-8 on next page, in which we horizontally sum two typical supply curves for manufacturers of flash memory cards. Supplier 1's data are taken from Figure 3-7 above. Supplier 2 is added. The numbers are presented in panel (a). The graphical representation of supplier 1 is in panel (b), of supplier 2 in panel (c), and of the summation in panel (d). The result, then, is the supply curve for flash memory cards for suppliers 1 and 2. We assume that there are more suppliers of flash memory cards, however. The total market supply schedule and total market supply curve for flash memory cards are represented in Figure 3-9 on page 65, with the curve in panel (b) obtained by adding all of the supply curves, such as those shown in panels (b) and (c) of Figure 3-8. Notice the difference between the

FIGURE 3-8

Horizontal Summation of Supply Curves

In panel (a), we show the data for two individual suppliers of flash memory cards. Adding how much each is willing to supply at different prices, we come up with the combined quantities supplied in column 4. When we plot the values in columns 2 and 3 on grids from panels (b) and (c) and add them horizontally, we obtain the combined supply curve for the two suppliers in question, shown in panel (d).

Panel (a)

(1) Price per Flash Memory Card	(2) Supplier 1's Quantity Supplied (thousands)	(3) Supplier 2's Quantity Supplied (thousands)	(4) = (2) + (3) Combined Quantity Supplied per Year (thousands)
$5	55	35	90
4	40	30	70
3	35	20	55
2	25	15	40
1	20	10	30

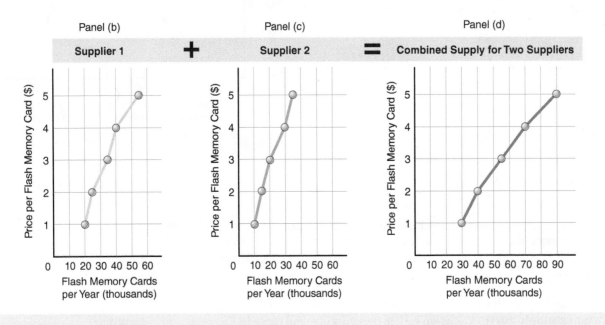

Panel (b)	Panel (c)	Panel (d)
Supplier 1 ＋	**Supplier 2** ＝	**Combined Supply for Two Suppliers**

market supply curve with only two suppliers in Figure 3-7 and the one with many suppliers—the entire true market—in panel (b) of Figure 3-9. (For simplicity, we assume that the true total market supply curve is a straight line.)

Note what happens at the market level when price changes. If the price is $3, the quantity supplied is 6 million. If the price goes up to $4, the quantity supplied increases to 8 million per year. If the price falls to $2, the quantity supplied decreases to 4 million per year. Changes in quantity supplied are represented by movements along the supply curve in panel (b) of Figure 3-9.

MyEconLab Concept Check
MyEconLab Study Plan

There is normally a _____ relationship between price and quantity of a good supplied, other things held constant.

The _____ curve normally shows a direct relationship between price and quantity supplied.

The _____ _____ curve is obtained by horizontally adding individual supply curves in the market.

FIGURE 3-9

The Market Supply Schedule and the Market Supply Curve for Flash Memory Cards

In panel (a), we show the summation of all the individual producers' supply schedules. In panel (b), we graph the resulting supply curve. It represents the market supply curve for flash memory cards and is upward sloping.

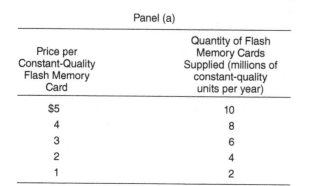

Panel (a)

Price per Constant-Quality Flash Memory Card	Quantity of Flash Memory Cards Supplied (millions of constant-quality units per year)
$5	10
4	8
3	6
2	4
1	2

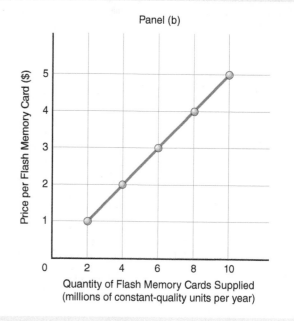

Panel (b)

Shifts in Supply

When we looked at demand, we found out that any change in anything relevant besides the price of the good or service caused the demand curve to shift inward or outward. The same is true for the supply curve. If something besides price changes and alters the willingness of suppliers to produce a good or service, we will see the entire supply curve shift.

Consider an example. There is a new method of manufacturing flash memory cards that significantly reduces the cost of production. In this situation, producers of flash memory cards will supply more product at *all* prices because their cost of so doing has fallen dramatically. Competition among manufacturers to produce more at each and every price will shift the supply curve outward to the right from S_1 to S_2 in Figure 3-10 on the next page. At a price of $3, the number supplied was originally 6 million per year, but now the amount supplied (after the reduction in the costs of production) at $3 per flash memory card will be 9 million a year. (This is similar to what has happened to the supply curve of digital devices in recent years as memory chip prices have fallen.)

Consider the opposite case. If the price of raw materials used in manufacturing flash memory cards increases, the supply curve in Figure 3-9 will shift from S_1 to S_3. At each and every price, the quantity of flash memory cards supplied will fall due to the increase in the price of raw materials.

The Other Determinants of Supply

When supply curves are drawn, only the price of the good in question changes, and it is assumed that other things remain constant. The other things assumed constant are the *ceteris paribus* conditions of supply. They include the prices of resources (inputs) used to produce the product, technology and productivity, taxes and subsidies,

3.4 Distinguish between changes in supply and changes in quantity supplied

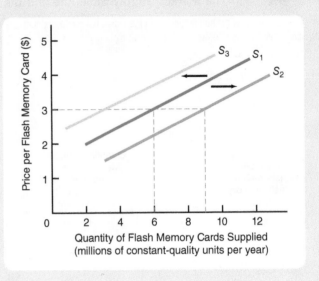

FIGURE 3-10

Shifts in the Supply Curve

If the cost of producing flash memory cards were to fall dramatically, the supply curve would shift rightward from S_1 to S_2 such that at all prices, a larger quantity would be forthcoming from suppliers. Conversely, if the cost of production rose, the supply curve would shift leftward to S_3.

producers' price expectations, and the number of firms in the industry. If *any* of these *ceteris paribus* conditions changes, there will be a shift in the supply curve.

TECHNOLOGY AND PRODUCTIVITY Supply curves are drawn by assuming a given technology, or "state of the art." When the available production techniques change, the supply curve will shift. For example, when a better production technique for flash memory cards becomes available, production costs will decrease, and the supply curve will shift to the right. A larger quantity will be forthcoming at each and every price because the cost of production is lower.

Why is the global supply of lithium anticipated to increase considerably by the end of the current decade?

EXAMPLE

How a New Production Technique Is Increasing Lithium Supply

Lithium is a key component of ion batteries that power mobile digital devices and electric vehicles. In years past, companies that produced lithium extracted the element from pegmatite, a coarse-grained rock formed from magma located below the earth's outer crust. Hence, firms that sold lithium operated mines in locations where deposits of pegmatite were concentrated. Mining the rocky pegmatite deposits and chemically separating the lithium were costly endeavors.

During the past two decades, lithium manufacturers have developed less expensive techniques for extracting lithium, using alternative inputs. Geologists have found that ancient lakebeds in South American nations, Tibet, and locales scattered across the western United States have brine deposits containing lithium. Special equipment pumps the brine into large evaporation ponds, and heat from the sun naturally extracts the lithium, which the companies collect with machines. Estimates indicate that, other things—including lithium prices—being equal, utilization of this new technology will permit lithium firms to expand annual production and sales of the element from 150,000 tons to 300,000 tons by 2020. Thus, the supply of lithium is likely to increase substantially within the next few years.

FOR CRITICAL THINKING

Other things being equal, what would happen to the supply of lithium if the prices of brine pumps were to increase significantly?

Sources are listed at the end of this chapter.

COST OF INPUTS USED TO PRODUCE THE PRODUCT If one or more input prices fall, production costs fall, and the supply curve will shift outward to the right. That is, more will be supplied at each and every price. The opposite will be true if one or more inputs become more expensive. For example, when we draw the supply curve of new tablet devices, we are holding the price of microprocessors (and other inputs) constant. When we draw the supply curve of blue jeans, we are holding the cost of cotton fabric fixed.

PRICE EXPECTATIONS A change in the expectation of a future relative price of a product can affect a producer's current willingness to supply, just as price expectations affect a consumer's current willingness to purchase. For example, suppliers of flash memory cards may withhold from the market part of their current supply if they anticipate higher prices in the future. The current amount supplied at each and every price will decrease.

TAXES AND SUBSIDIES Certain taxes, such as a per-unit tax, are effectively an addition to production costs and therefore reduce supply. If the supply curve is S_1 in Figure 3-9 on page 65, a per-unit tax increase would shift it to S_3. A per-unit **subsidy** would do the opposite. Every producer would get a "gift" from the government for each unit produced. This per-unit subsidy would shift the curve to S_2.

How has a tax on the sale of medical devices affected the market supply curve for these products?

Subsidy
A negative tax; a payment to a producer from the government, usually in the form of a cash grant per unit.

POLICY EXAMPLE

The Supply-Reducing Effect of Taxing Medical Devices

In January 2013, the U.S. government began assessing a special 2.3 percent tax rate on sales of medical devices, such as magnetic resonance imaging, or MRI, machines, sold to physicians, clinics, and hospitals. The official aim of the tax was to help raise funds to cover the costs of implementing the government's national health-care program. Another effect, however, is to reduce the supply of medical devices. Imposition of the tax causes producers of these devices to offer every device for sale at a price 2.3 percent higher than the pre-tax price. This fact implies that the market supply curve for medical devices has been shifted upward 2.3 percent at each quantity. Of course, an upward shift of the supply curve is the same as a leftward shift of the supply curve, or a decrease in the supply of medical devices.

How device manufacturers implement the reduction in supply varies from firm to firm. Some companies have canceled plans to build new production facilities. Others are closing some existing facilities. A few have cut back on the number of different types of devices they produce. All of these actions yield the same outcome: a decrease in the amount of devices supplied at each possible price.

FOR CRITICAL THINKING
How does the fact that fewer medical devices are offered for sale at each price following imposition of the tax affect the government's revenues from the tax?

Sources are listed at the end of this chapter.

NUMBER OF FIRMS IN THE INDUSTRY In the short run, when firms can change only the number of employees they use, we hold the number of firms in the industry constant. In the long run, the number of firms may change. If the number of firms increases, supply will increase, and the supply curve will shift outward to the right. If the number of firms decreases, supply will decrease, and the supply curve will shift inward to the left.

MyEconLab Concept Check

Changes in Supply versus Changes in Quantity Supplied

We cannot overstress the importance of distinguishing between a movement along the supply curve—which occurs only when the price changes for a given supply curve—and a shift in the supply curve—which occurs only with changes in *ceteris paribus* conditions. A change in the price of the good in question always (and only) brings about a change in the quantity supplied along a given supply curve. We move to a different point on the existing supply curve. This is specifically called a *change in quantity supplied*. When price changes, quantity supplied changes—there is a movement from one point to another along the same supply curve.

When you think of *supply*, think of the entire curve. Quantity supplied is represented by a single point on the supply curve.

*A change, or shift, in supply is a movement of the entire curve. The **only** thing that can cause the entire curve to move is a change in one of the **ceteris paribus** conditions.*

Consequently,

*A change in price leads to a change in the quantity supplied, other things being constant. This is a movement **along** the curve.*

*A change in any **ceteris paribus** condition for supply leads to a change in supply. This causes a **shift** of the curve.*

MyEconLab Concept Check
MyEconLab Study Plan

SELF CHECK Visit MyEconLab to practice these and other problems and to get instant feedback in your Study Plan.

If the price changes, we _____ _____ a curve—there is a change in quantity demanded or supplied. If some other determinant changes, we _____ a curve—there is a change in demand or supply.

The supply curve is drawn with other things held constant. If these *ceteris paribus* conditions of supply change, the supply curve will shift. The major *ceteris paribus* conditions are (1) _____, (2) _____, (3) _____, (4) _____, and (5) _____.

3.5 Understand how the interaction of the demand for and supply of a commodity determines the market price of the commodity and the equilibrium quantity of the commodity that is produced and consumed

Putting Demand and Supply Together

In the sections on demand and supply, we tried to confine each discussion to demand or supply only. You have probably already realized, however, that we can't view the world just from the demand side or just from the supply side. There is interaction between the two. In this section, we will discuss how they interact and how that interaction determines the prices that prevail in our economy and other economies in which the forces of demand and supply are allowed to work.

Let's first combine the demand and supply schedules and then combine the curves.

Demand and Supply Schedules Combined

Let's place panel (a) from Figure 3-3 (the market demand schedule) on page 56 and panel (a) from Figure 3-9 (the market supply schedule) on page 65 together in panel (a) of Figure 3-11 on the next page. Column 1 displays the price. Column 2 shows the quantity supplied per year at any given price. Column 3 displays the quantity demanded. Column 4 is the difference between columns 2 and 3, or the difference between the quantity supplied and the quantity demanded. In column 5, we label those differences as either excess quantity supplied (called a *surplus*, which we shall discuss shortly) or excess quantity demanded (commonly known as a *shortage*, also discussed shortly). For example, at a price of $1, only 2 million flash memory cards would be supplied, but the quantity demanded would be 10 million. The difference would be 8 million, which we label excess quantity demanded (a shortage). At the other end, a price of $5 would elicit 10 million in quantity supplied. Quantity demanded would drop to 2 million, leaving a difference of +8 million units, which we call excess quantity supplied (a surplus).

Now, do you notice something special about the price of $3? At that price, both the quantity supplied and the quantity demanded per year are 6 million. The difference, then, is zero. There is neither excess quantity demanded (shortage) nor excess quantity supplied (surplus). Hence the price of $3 is very special. It is called the **market clearing price**—it clears the market of all excess quantities demanded or supplied. There are no willing consumers who want to pay $3 per flash memory card but are

Market clearing, or equilibrium, price
The price that clears the market, at which quantity demanded equals quantity supplied; the price where the demand curve intersects the supply curve.

FIGURE 3-11

Putting Demand and Supply Together

In panel (a), we see that at the price of $3, the quantity supplied and the quantity demanded are equal, resulting in neither an excess quantity demanded nor an excess quantity supplied. We call this price the equilibrium, or market clearing, price. In panel (b), the intersection of the supply and demand curves is at *E*, at a price of $3 and a quantity of 6 million per year. At point *E*, there is neither an excess quantity demanded nor an excess quantity supplied. At a price of $1, the quantity supplied will be only 2 million per year, but the quantity demanded will be 10 million. The difference is excess quantity demanded at a price of $1. The price will rise, so we will move from point *A* up the supply curve and from point *B* up the demand curve to point *E*. At the other extreme, a price of $5 elicits a quantity supplied of 10 million but a quantity demanded of only 2 million. The difference is excess quantity supplied at a price of $5. The price will fall, so we will move down the demand curve and the supply curve to the equilibrium price, $3 per flash memory card.

Panel (a)

(1) Price per Constant-Quality Flash Memory Card	(2) Quantity Supplied (flash memory cards per year)	(3) Quantity Demanded (flash memory cards per year)	(4) Difference (2) – (3) (flash memory cards per year)	(5) Condition
$5	10 million	2 million	8 million	Excess quantity supplied (surplus)
4	8 million	4 million	4 million	Excess quantity supplied (surplus)
3	6 million	6 million	0	Market clearing price—equilibrium (no surplus, no shortage)
2	4 million	8 million	–4 million	Excess quantity demanded (shortage)
1	2 million	10 million	–8 million	Excess quantity demanded (shortage)

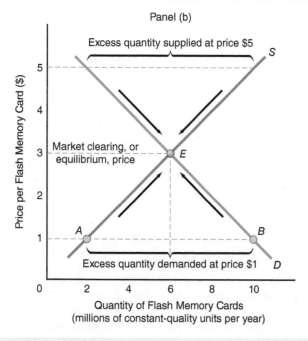

Panel (b)

turned away by sellers, and there are no willing suppliers who want to sell flash memory cards at $3 who cannot sell all they want at that price. Another term for the market clearing price is the *equilibrium price*, the price at which there is no tendency for change. Consumers are able to get all they want at that price, and suppliers are able to sell all they want at that price.

MyEconLab Concept Check

Equilibrium

Equilibrium
The situation when quantity supplied equals quantity demanded at a particular price.

We can define **equilibrium** in general as a point at which quantity demanded equals quantity supplied at a particular price. There tends to be no movement of the price or the quantity away from this point unless demand or supply changes. Any movement away from this point will set into motion forces that will cause movement back to it. Therefore, equilibrium is a stable point. Any point that is not an equilibrium is unstable and will not persist.

The equilibrium point occurs where the supply and demand curves intersect. The equilibrium price is given on the vertical axis directly to the left of where the supply and demand curves cross. The equilibrium quantity is given on the horizontal axis directly underneath the intersection of the demand and supply curves.

Panel (b) in Figure 3-3 (p. 56) and panel (b) in Figure 3-9 (p. 65) are combined as panel (b) in Figure 3-11 on the previous page. The demand curve is labeled *D*, the supply curve *S*. We have labeled the intersection of the supply curve with the demand curve as point *E*, for equilibrium. That corresponds to a market clearing price of $3, at which both the quantity supplied and the quantity demanded are 6 million units per year. There is neither excess quantity supplied nor excess quantity demanded. Point *E*, the equilibrium point, always occurs at the intersection of the supply and demand curves. This is the price *toward which* the market price will automatically tend to gravitate, because there is no outcome more advantageous than this price for both consumers and producers.

MyEconLab Concept Check

Shortages

The price of $3 depicted in Figure 3-11 on the previous page arises in a situation of equilibrium. If there were a non-market-clearing, or disequilibrium, price, this price would put into play forces that would cause the price to change toward the market clearing price, at which equilibrium would again be sustained. Look again at panel (b) in Figure 3-11. Suppose that instead of being at the equilibrium price of $3, for some reason the market price is $1. At this price, the quantity demanded of 10 million per year exceeds the quantity supplied of 2 million per year. We have an excess quantity demanded at the price of $1. This is usually called a **shortage.** Consumers of flash memory cards would find that they could not buy all they wished at $1 apiece. Forces, though, will cause the price to rise: Competing consumers will bid up the price, and suppliers will increase output in response. (Remember, some buyers would pay $5 or more rather than do without flash memory cards.) We would move from points *A* and *B* toward point *E*. The process would stop when the price again reached $3 per flash memory card.

Shortage
A situation in which quantity demanded is greater than quantity supplied at a price below the market clearing price.

Why is the market for nursing home workers likely to experience shortages?

EXAMPLE

America's Aging Contributes to a Nursing Home Labor Shortage

Today, one of every five workers is aged 55 or above. By 2020, one of every four workers will be in this age group as "baby boomers" choose to retire from work.

Economists anticipate that this trend in the age distribution of the U.S. population will fuel sporadic labor shortages for nursing homes. On one hand, as retired people age, more of them will move to nursing homes, which will seek to employ additional workers. Hence, the demand for nursing home workers will tend to rise over time. On the other hand, the supply of nursing home workers likely will tend to decrease. People who work in nursing homes often must perform physically draining tasks such as lifting elderly residents, and many older workers are unable to withstand such efforts on a continual basis. Hence, nursing homes often wish to employ younger workers, who in turn will make up a smaller share of the future U.S. workforce. As the demand for nursing home workers rises and the supply of young workers declines, short-term shortages are bound to occur from time to time.

Indeed, at the recently prevailing average wage rate of about $12 per hour, nursing homes have been seeking to hire more young people to staff their facilities. At this wage, they were unable to obtain the number of young workers they wish to hire. Thus, a temporary shortage of nursing home workers resulted.

FOR CRITICAL THINKING

Do you think that the average wage earned by nursing home workers eventually will fall below or rise above $12 per hour? Explain your reasoning.

Sources are listed at the end of this chapter.

At this point, it is important to recall a distinction made in Chapter 2:

Shortages and scarcity are not the same thing.

A shortage is a situation in which the quantity demanded exceeds the quantity supplied at a price that is somehow kept *below* the market clearing price. Our definition of scarcity was much more general and all-encompassing: a situation in which the resources available for producing output are insufficient to satisfy all wants. Any choice necessarily costs an opportunity, and the opportunity is lost. Hence, we will always live in a world of scarcity because we must constantly make choices, but we do not necessarily have to live in a world of shortages.

WHAT IF...

the government limits sellers to receiving a price that is below the equilibrium price?

In the absence of any government restrictions, when the quantity demanded of an item exceeds the quantity supplied at the currently prevailing price, consumers will bid up the price, and suppliers will respond by increasing their output of that item. If the government limits suppliers to receiving the currently prevailing price, then suppliers are prevented from responding in this way. Thus, the quantity supplied will remain below the quantity demanded. The shortage of the item will continue.

MyEconLab Concept Check

Surpluses

Now let's repeat the experiment with the market price at $5 rather than at the market clearing price of $3. Clearly, the quantity supplied will exceed the quantity demanded at that price. The result will be an excess quantity supplied at $5 per unit. This excess quantity supplied is often called a **surplus.** Given the curves in panel (b) in Figure 3-11, however, there will be forces pushing the price back down toward $3 per flash memory card. Competing suppliers will cut prices and reduce output, and consumers will purchase more at these new lower prices. If the two forces of supply and demand are unrestricted, they will bring the price back to $3 per flash memory card.

Surplus

A situation in which quantity supplied is greater than quantity demanded at a price above the market clearing price.

Shortages and surpluses are resolved in unfettered markets—markets in which price changes are free to occur. The forces that resolve them are those of competition: In the case of shortages, consumers competing for a limited quantity supplied drive up the price; in the case of surpluses, sellers compete for the limited quantity demanded, thus driving prices down to equilibrium. The equilibrium price is the only stable price, and the (unrestricted) market price tends to gravitate toward it.

What happens when the price is set below the equilibrium price? Here come the scalpers.

POLICY EXAMPLE

Should Shortages in the Ticket Market Be Solved by Scalpers?

If you have ever tried to get tickets to a playoff game in sports, a popular Broadway play, or a superstar's rap concert, you know about "shortages." The standard Super Bowl ticket situation is shown in Figure 3-12 on the next page. At the face-value price of Super Bowl tickets ($800), the quantity demanded (175,000) greatly exceeds the quantity supplied (80,000). Because shortages last only as long as prices and quantities do not change, markets tend to exhibit a movement out of this disequilibrium toward equilibrium. Obviously, the quantity of Super Bowl tickets cannot change, but the price can go as high as $6,000.

Enter the scalper. This colorful term is used because when you purchase a ticket that is being resold at a price higher than face value, the seller is skimming profit off the top ("taking your scalp"). If an event sells out and people who wished to purchase tickets at current prices were unable to do so, ticket prices by definition were lower than market clearing prices. Without scalpers, those individuals would not be able to attend the event. In the case of the Super Bowl, various forms of scalping occur nationwide. Tickets for a seat on the 50-yard line have been sold for as much as $6,000 apiece. In front of every Super Bowl arena, you can find ticket scalpers hawking their wares.

FOR CRITICAL ANALYSIS

What happens to ticket scalpers who are still holding tickets after an event has started?

Sources are listed at the end of this chapter.

(continued)

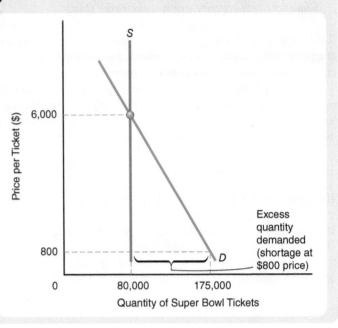

FIGURE 3-12

Shortages of Super Bowl Tickets

The quantity of tickets for a Super Bowl game is fixed at 80,000. At the price per ticket of $800, the quantity demanded is 175,000. Consequently, there is an excess quantity demanded at the below-market clearing price. In this example, prices can go as high as $6,000 in the scalpers' market.

SELF CHECK Visit MyEconLab to practice these and other problems and to get instant feedback in your Study Plan.

The market clearing price occurs at the _____ of the market demand curve and the market supply curve. It is also called the _____ price, the price from which there is no tendency to change unless there is a change in demand or supply.

Whenever the price is _____ than the equilibrium price, there is an excess quantity supplied (a surplus).

Whenever the price is _____ than the equilibrium price, there is an excess quantity demanded (a shortage).

YOU ARE THERE

In Finland, the Taxman Screams, "Less Ice Cream!"

Five-year-old Ciara Hartikainen, of Espoo, Finland, is trying to be brave and hold back her tears as her mother tells her that the light blue truck that has always brought ice cream treats to her neighborhood is making its final stop. Her mother explains to Ciara and her three-year-old brother that the company, which has long operated a fleet of dozens of ice cream trucks across the Scandinavian nation, has decided to park them, probably forever. Indeed, all ice cream producers throughout Finland have been reducing their production. Spaces in grocery freezers allocated to ice cream are shrinking across the land.

Finnish ice cream producers have been reducing the amount of ice cream supplied at all prevailing prices since the government began assessing special taxes on candies, ice cream, and soft drinks in 2010. Initially, the government had intended its tax on sugary delights to serve as a temporary fund-raising measure. Beginning in 2013, however, the government decided to make the tax permanent.

Ciara's mother does not try to explain these details to her young children. All she can say is that perhaps every year for the rest of their lives, companies will be offering less ice cream—an estimated 20 percent less—for sale at any given price. The government's tax on sweets has reduced the supply of ice cream.

CRITICAL THINKING QUESTIONS

1. In which direction has Finland's market ice cream supply curve shifted?

2. The amount of the tax on ice cream is 0.75 euro per kilogram sold. What is the vertical amount of the shift in the market supply curve? Explain briefly.

Sources are listed at the end of this chapter.

ISSUES & APPLICATIONS

MyEconLab Video

Higher Pipeline Prices Boost Demands for Substitute Oil Shipment Services

Soleg/Fotolia

CONCEPTS APPLIED

» Market Demand

» Market Clearing Price

» Substitutes

Since 2010, U.S. oil companies have dramatically increased production of oil. To sell the oil, the firms must arrange transportation to consumers located far from new oil fields in states such as North Dakota. Higher prices of pumping oil through pipelines have induced companies to increase their demands for substitute oil transport services.

Why Pipeline Prices Have Skyrocketed

Following discoveries of new U.S. oil fields and development of novel techniques of extracting oil from these and previously existing fields, U.S. oil production has soared. As a result, so has the market demand for oil shipment services.

A particularly speedy way to move oil over long distances is to pump it through pipelines. Federal regulators worried about potential environmental effects, however, have blocked construction of proposed new pipelines. As oil firms have bid against each other to move their oil through existing pipelines, the market prices of pipeline services have increased substantially.

Higher Demands for Substitute Oil Transport Services

The rise in pipeline prices has given oil firms incentives to utilize substitute services for moving oil around the nation. The three primary substitutes are conveyance via barges across waterways, shipment via trucks, and transportation via railroads.

Figure 3-13 on the next page displays the effects of higher pipeline prices on the amounts of oil shipments via these substitute transportation services. The figure shows that all three modes of transportation have experienced increased volumes of oil shipments. Although the barge and truck modes of transportation continue to account for the largest shares of substitute oil shipments, rail transport has exhibited the greatest proportional growth. Since 2009, the

number of rail carloads of oil shipped per year in the United States has risen from 2,700 to more than 600,000.

For Critical Thinking

1. What has happened to the market demand curves in the markets for barge, truck, and rail transportation services?

2. In the short run, have the markets for barge, truck, and rail transportation services experienced rightward shifts of their supply curves or movements along those supply curves?

Web Resources

1. Learn about adjustments to the higher demand for oil shipments in the market for barge transportation services in the Web Links in MyEconLab.

2. Contemplate how the increased demand for oil transportation has affected the markets for truck and rail transport in the Web Links in MyEconLab.

MyEconLab

For more questions on this chapter's Issues & Applications, go to MyEconLab.

In the Study Plan for this chapter, select Section I: Issues and Applications.

Sources are listed at the end of this chapter.

FIGURE 3-13

Shipments of Oil by Rail, Truck, and Barge since 2008

Since 2012, oil shipments utilizing mechanisms other than pipelines have increased dramatically.

Source: U.S. Energy Information Agency; author's estimates.

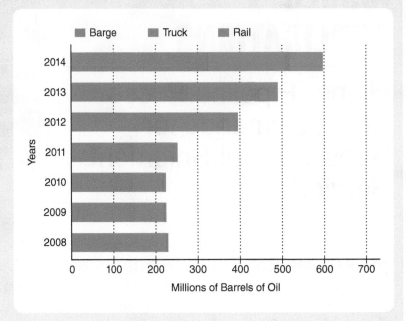

Fundamental Points

1. The law of demand is an inverse, or negative, relationship between the price of an item and the quantity of that item demanded, other things being equal.

2. A change in the quantity demanded, or movement along the demand curve for a good, comes about when there is a change in the good's own price. A change in a *ceteris paribus* condition other than the price of the good that affects demand shifts the demand curve.

3. The law of supply is a direct, or positive, relationship between the price of an item and the quantity of that item supplied, other things being equal.

4. A change in the quantity supplied, or movement along the demand curve for a good, comes about when there is a change in the good's own price. A change in a *ceteris paribus* condition other than the price of the good that affects supply shifts the supply curve.

5. The market clearing price of a good occurs at the crossing point of the market demand and supply curves, at which the quantity of the good demanded equals the quantity supplied. A surplus exists above that price, and a shortage exists below that price.

WHAT YOU SHOULD KNOW

Here is what you should know after reading this chapter. MyEconLab will help you identify what you know, and where to go when you need to practice.

LEARNING OBJECTIVES	KEY TERMS	WHERE TO GO TO PRACTICE
3.1 Explain the law of demand *Other things being equal, individuals will purchase fewer units of a good at a higher price and will purchase more units at a lower price.*	market, 52 demand, 52 law of demand, 52 relative price, 53 money price, 53 demand curve, 55 market demand, 55 **Key Figure** Figure 3-2, 55	• MyEconLab Study Plan 3.1 • Animated Figure 3-2

WHAT YOU SHOULD KNOW *continued*

LEARNING OBJECTIVES	KEY TERMS	WHERE TO GO TO PRACTICE

3.2 **Distinguish between changes in demand and changes in quantity demanded** *The demand schedule shows quantities purchased per unit of time at various possible prices. Graphically, the demand schedule is a downward-sloping demand curve. A change in the price of the good generates a change in the quantity demanded, which is a movement along the demand curve. Factors other than the price of the good that affect the amount demanded are (1) income, (2) tastes and preferences, (3) the prices of related goods, (4) expectations, and (5) market size (the number of potential buyers). If any of these ceteris paribus conditions of demand changes, there is a change in demand, and the demand curve shifts to a new position.*

ceteris paribus conditions, 57
normal goods, 58
inferior goods, 58
substitutes, 58
complements, 59
Key Figures
Figure 3-4, 57
Figure 3-6, 61

- MyEconLab Study Plan 3.2
- Animated Figures 3-4, 3-6

3.3 **Explain the law of supply** *According to the law of supply, sellers will produce and offer for sale more units of a good at a higher price, and they will produce and offer for sale fewer units of the good at a lower price.*

supply, 62
law of supply, 62
supply curve, 63
Key Figures
Figure 3-7, 63
Figure 3-8, 64

- MyEconLab Study Plan 3.3
- Animated Figures 3-7, 3-8

3.4 **Distinguish between changes in supply and changes in quantity supplied** *The supply schedule shows quantities produced and sold per unit of time at various possible prices. On a graph, the supply schedule is a supply curve that slopes upward. A change in the price of the good generates a change in the quantity supplied, which is a movement along the supply curve. Factors other than the price of the good that affect the amount supplied are (1) input prices, (2) technology and productivity, (3) taxes and subsidies, (4) price expectations, and (5) the number of sellers. If any of these ceteris paribus conditions changes, there is a change in supply, and the supply curve shifts to a new position.*

subsidy, 67
Key Figure
Figure 3-10, 66

- MyEconLab Study Plan 3.4
- Animated Figure 3-10

3.5 **Understand how the interaction of the demand for and supply of a commodity determines the market price of the commodity and the equilibrium quantity of the commodity that is produced and consumed** *The equilibrium price of a good and the equilibrium quantity of the good that are produced and sold are determined by the intersection of the demand and supply curves. At this intersection point, the quantity demanded by buyers of the good just equals the quantity supplied by sellers, so there is neither an excess quantity of the good supplied (surplus) nor an excess quantity of the good demanded (shortage).*

market clearing, or equilibrium, price, 68
equilibrium, 70
shortage, 70
surplus, 71
Key Figure
Figure 3-12, 72

- MyEconLab Study Plan 3.5
- Animated Figure 3-12

Log in to MyEconLab, take a chapter test, and get a personalized Study Plan that tells you which concepts you understand and which ones you need to review. From there, MyEconLab will give you further practice, tutorials, animations, videos, and guided solutions. For more information, visit http://www.myeconlab.com

PROBLEMS

All problems are assignable in MyEconLab. Answers to odd-numbered problems appear in MyEconLab.

3-1. Suppose that in a recent market period, the following relationship existed between the price of tablet devices and the quantity supplied and quantity demanded.

Price	Quantity Demanded	Quantity Supplied
$330	100 million	40 million
$340	90 million	60 million
$350	80 million	80 million
$360	70 million	100 million
$370	60 million	120 million

Graph the supply and demand curves for tablet devices using the information in the table. What are the equilibrium price and quantity? If the industry price is $340, is there a shortage or surplus of tablet devices? How much is the shortage or surplus? (See pages 68–70.)

3-2. Suppose that in a later market period, the quantities supplied in the table in Problem 3-1 are unchanged. The amount demanded, however, has increased by 30 million at each price. Construct the resulting demand curve in the illustration you made for Problem 3-1. Is this an increase or a decrease in demand? What are the new equilibrium quantity and the new market price? Give two examples of changes in *ceteris paribus* conditions that might cause such a change. (See page 57.)

3-3. Consider the market for cable-based Internet access service, which is a normal good. Explain whether the following events would cause an increase or a decrease in demand or an increase or a decrease in the quantity demanded. (See pages 57–61.)

  a. Firms providing wireless (an alternative to cable) Internet access services reduce their prices.

  b. Firms providing cable-based Internet access services reduce their prices.

  c. There is a decrease in the incomes earned by consumers of cable-based Internet access services.

  d. Consumers' tastes shift away from using wireless Internet access in favor of cable-based Internet access services.

3-4. In the market for flash memory drives (a normal good), explain whether the following events would cause an increase or a decrease in demand or an

increase or a decrease in the quantity demanded. Also explain what happens to the equilibrium quantity and the market clearing price. (See pages 57–61.)

  a. There are increases in the prices of storage racks for flash memory drives.

  b. There is a decrease in the price of computer drives that read the information contained on flash memory drives.

  c. There is a dramatic increase in the price of secure digital cards that, like flash memory drives, can be used to store digital data.

  d. A booming economy increases the income of the typical buyer of flash memory drives.

  e. Consumers of flash memory drives anticipate that the price of this good will decline in the future.

3-5. Give an example of a complement and a substitute in consumption for each of the following items. (See pages 59–60.)

  a. Bacon

  b. Tennis racquets

  c. Coffee

  d. Automobiles

3-6. For each of the following shifts in the demand curve and associated price change of a complement or substitute item, explain whether the price of the complement or substitute must have increased or a decreased. (See pages 59–60.)

  a. A rise in the demand for a dashboard global-positioning-system device follows a change in the price of automobiles, which are complements.

  b. A fall in the demand for e-book readers follows a change in the price of e-books, which are complements.

  c. A rise in the demand for tablet devices follows a change in the price of ultrathin laptop computers, which are substitutes.

  d. A fall in the demand for physical books follows a change in the price of e-books, which are substitutes.

3-7. Identify which of the following would generate an increase in the market demand for tablet devices, which are a normal good. (See pages 57–61.)

  a. A decrease in the incomes of consumers of tablet devices

b. An increase in the price of ultrathin computers, which are substitutes

c. An increase in the price of online apps, which are complements

d. An increase in the number of consumers in the market for tablet devices

3-8. Identify which of the following would generate a decrease in the market demand for e-book readers, which are a normal good. (See pages 57–60.)

a. An increase in the price of downloadable apps utilized to enhance the e-book reading experience, which are complements

b. An increase in the number of consumers in the market for e-book readers

c. A decrease in the price of tablet devices, which are substitutes

d. A reduction in the incomes of consumers of e-book readers

3-9. Consider the following diagram of a market for one-bedroom rental apartments in a college community. (See pages 68–70.)

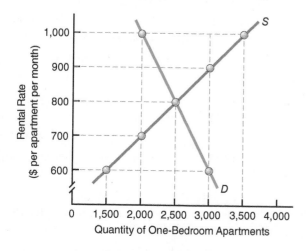

a. At a rental rate of $1,000 per month, is there an excess quantity supplied, or is there an excess quantity demanded? What is the amount of the excess quantity supplied or demanded?

b. If the present rental rate of one-bedroom apartments is $1,000 per month, through what mechanism will the rental rate adjust to the equilibrium rental rate of $800?

c. At a rental rate of $600 per month, is there an excess quantity supplied, or is there an excess

quantity demanded? What is the amount of the excess quantity supplied or demanded?

d. If the present rental rate of one-bedroom apartments is $600 per month, through what mechanism will the rental rate adjust to the equilibrium rental rate of $800?

3-10. Consider the market for paperbound economics textbooks. Explain whether the following events would cause an increase or a decrease in supply or an increase or a decrease in the quantity supplied. (See pages 65–68.)

a. The market price of paper increases.

b. The market price of economics textbooks increases.

c. The number of publishers of economics textbooks increases.

d. Publishers expect that the market price of economics textbooks will increase next month.

3-11. Consider the market for smartphones. Explain whether the following events would cause an increase or a decrease in supply or an increase or a decrease in the quantity supplied. Illustrate each, and show what would happen to the equilibrium quantity and the market price. (See pages 65–68.)

a. The price of touch screens used in smartphones declines.

b. The price of machinery used to produce smartphones increases.

c. The number of manufacturers of smartphones increases.

d. There is a decrease in the market demand for smartphones.

3-12. If the price of flash memory chips used in manufacturing smartphones decreases, what will happen in the market for smartphones? How will the equilibrium price and equilibrium quantity of smartphones change? (See pages 68–70.)

3-13. Assume that the cost of aluminum used by soft-drink companies increases. Which of the following correctly describes the resulting effects in the market for soft drinks distributed in aluminum cans? (More than one statement may be correct. See pages 65–68.)

a. The demand for soft drinks decreases.

b. The quantity of soft drinks demanded decreases.

c. The supply of soft drinks decreases.

d. The quantity of soft drinks supplied decreases.

REFERENCES

EXAMPLE: The Law of Demand at Work in the Market for Natural Gas

Larry Bell, "Natural Gas Could Fuel Our Future," *Newsmax*, February 10, 2014.

Diane Cardwell and Clifford Krauss, "Trucking Industry Is Set to Expand Its Use of Natural Gas," *The New York Times*, April 22, 2013.

"Difference Engine: Fuel for the Future?" *The Economist*, May 27, 2013.

INTERNATIONAL EXAMPLE: Lower European Incomes Reduce the Demand for Electricity

Jan Hromadko, "Power Firms Slowdown," *The Wall Street Journal*, May 14, 2012.

Rachel Morison and Julia Mengewein, "German Power Costs Seen Dropping for Fourth Year," Bloomberg, January 3, 2014.

"Taking Europe's Pulse," *The Economist*, July 18, 2013.

EXAMPLE: The Great Substitution from Computers to Handheld Devices

Enid Burns, "Tablets to Demote Laptops to Also-Ran Status This Year," E-Commerce Times, May 28, 2013.

Damon Poeter, "Grim News Again for PC Makers as Global Shipments Decline Again," PC Mag, July 10, 2013.

Aaron Ricadela, "PC Shipments Mark Steepest Decline with 10 Percent Drop," Bloomberg, January 10, 2014.

POLICY EXAMPLE: An Expected Bullet Price Rise Boosts Current Ammo Demand

Associated Press, "Ammunition Flies Off Store Shelves Amid New Restrictions, Fears," Foxnews.com, April 5, 2013.

Phil Bourjaily, "Rimfire Ammo Shortage Continues," *Field & Stream*, February 20, 2014.

Ashley Jones, "Bullet Run Leaves Many Low on Ammo," *The Wall Street Journal*, February 28, 2013.

EXAMPLE: Why Many Lobster Boats Remain at Their Moorings

"Debate Erupts Over How to Address Low Lobster Prices," Undercurrent News, March 3, 2014.

Taryn Luna, "With Warming Seas, Lobsters Become an Abundant Bargain," *The Boston Globe*, July 4, 2013.

James Surowiecki, "Clawback," *The New Yorker*, August 26, 2013.

EXAMPLE: How a New Production Technique Is Increasing Lithium Supply

John Daly, "America Finds Massive Source of Lithium in Wyoming," Mining.com, May 4, 2014. (www.mining.com/web/america-finds-massive-source-of-lithium-in-wyoming/)

Jason Hidalgo, "Recharging Nevada's Lithium Industry," *Reno Gazette-Journal*, April 7, 2014.

Melissa Pistilli, "Posco's Lithium Brine Processing Technology Could Be a Game Changer," Lithium Investing News, April 4, 2013.

POLICY EXAMPLE: The Supply-Reducing Effect of Taxing Medical Devices

Russ Britt, "Despite Bipartisan Howls, Medical-Device Tax Persists," MarketWatch, January 22, 2014.

John Graham, "Obamacare's Medical-Device Excise Tax: Early Evidence Suggests Significant Harm," *Forbes*, September 14, 2013.

J. K. Wall, "Indiana Device Makers Absorbing Obamacare Excise Tax," *Indianapolis Business Journal*, May 13, 2013.

EXAMPLE: America's Aging Contributes to a Nursing Home Labor Shortage

Judith Graham, "A Shortage of Caregivers," *The New York Times*, February 26, 2014.

James Hagerty, "As America Ages, Shortage of Help Hits Nursing Homes," *The Wall Street Journal*, April 14, 2013.

Jason Oliva, "Turnover Rates, Wages Worsen Labor Shortage for Nursing Aides," Home Health Care News, April 15, 2013.

POLICY EXAMPLE: Should Shortages in the Ticket Market Be Solved by Scalpers?

Ken Belson, "Super Bowl Tickets Are a Bargain at More Than $2,000," *The New York Times*, February 1, 2014.

Matt Fitzgerald, "Super Bowl 2014 Ticket Prices," Bleacher Report, January 28, 2014.

Jesse Lawrence, "24 Hours from Kick Off, Prices for Super Bowl Tickets Rising Rapidly, Quantity Shrinking," *Forbes*, February 1, 2014.

YOU ARE THERE: In Finland, the Taxman Screams, "Less Ice Cream!"

"Excise Duties on Sweets, Ice Cream, and Soft Drinks," Ministry of Finance, Finland, 2014. (http://www.vm.fi/vm/en/10_taxation/05_excise_duty/04_excise_duty_on_sweets_ice_cream_and_soft_drinks/index.jsp/)

"Government to Implement Planned Tax on Sweets, Ice Cream, and Soft Drinks," Helsingin Sanomat International Edition, February 9, 2013.

Juhana Rossi, "Finns Are in Bad Humor as Taxman Melts Ice Cream Man," *The Wall Street Journal*, August 28, 2013.

ISSUES & APPLICATIONS: Higher Pipeline Prices Boost Demands for Substitute Oil Shipment Services

James Conca, "Pick Your Poison for Crude—Pipeline, Rail, Truck, or Boat," *Forbes*, April 26, 2014.

Russell Gold, "Pipeline-Capacity Squeeze Reroutes Crude Oil," *The Wall Street Journal*, August 26, 2013.

Betsy Morris, "Boom Times on the Tracks: Rail Capacity, Spending Soar," *The Wall Street Journal*, March 26, 2013.

Micromonkey/Fotolia

4

Extensions of Demand and Supply Analysis

LEARNING OBJECTIVES

After reading this chapter, you should be able to:

4.1 Discuss the essential features of the price system

4.2 Evaluate the effects of changes in demand and supply on the market price and equilibrium quantity

4.3 Understand the rationing function of prices

4.4 Explain the effects of price ceilings

4.5 Explain the effects of price floors and government-imposed quantity restrictions

MyEconLab helps you master each objective and study more efficiently. See end of chapter for details.

During a period stretching across several months, a dangerous malady affected more than 700 recipients of therapeutic spinal injections of steroid drugs. Bacterial and fungal growths had contaminated the drug solutions. Once injected into nerve roots, these materials spread into defenseless spinal tissue. Many people experienced permanent nerve damage. Sixty-three people died. National media covered the story extensively for weeks, but only a handful of reports noted two key features: government controls over the prices of the spinal solutions and a shortage of drugs. When you have completed this chapter, you will understand how a form of price control called a *price ceiling* can create a shortage. You also will understand why shortages can induce some producers to sell lower-quality products, including tainted drugs that can harm people.

DID YOU KNOW THAT... more than 110,000 U.S. residents are on waiting lists for organ transplants? Many of these individuals must undergo physically and emotionally taxing treatments such as kidney dialysis because their organs are functioning poorly or not at all. These people are confronting *shortages* of transplantable organs. As you learned in Chapter 3, normally we would anticipate that in the face of a shortage in which the quantity supplied is less than the quantity demanded, the price of an item would increase. A rise in the price to its market clearing level, you learned, would bring quantities demanded and supplied back into equality. U.S. laws generally prevent people from selling organs for transplant into others' bodies, however. Consequently, the U.S. government effectively maintains *price ceilings* in the market for transplantable organs. Under the law, prices of kidneys and most other organs cannot rise above an explicit price of zero in order to eliminate a shortage.

What effects can a price ceiling have on the availability and consumption of a good or service? As you will learn in this chapter, we can use the supply and demand analysis developed in Chapter 3 to answer this question. You will find that when a government sets a ceiling below the equilibrium price, the result will be a shortage. Similarly, you will learn how we can use supply and demand analysis to examine the "surplus" of various agricultural products, the "shortage" of apartments in certain cities, and many other phenomena. All of these examples are part of our economy, which we characterize as a *price system*.

The Price System and Markets

4.1 Discuss the essential features of the price system

In a **price system**, otherwise known as a *market system*, relative prices are constantly changing to reflect changes in supply and demand for different commodities. The prices of those commodities are the signals to everyone within the price system as to what is relatively scarce and what is relatively abundant. In this sense, prices provide information.

Indeed, it is the *signaling* aspect of the price system that provides the information to buyers and sellers about what should be bought and what should be produced. In a price system, there is a clear-cut chain of events in which any changes in demand and supply cause changes in prices that in turn affect the opportunities that businesses and individuals have for profit and personal gain. Such changes influence our use of resources.

Price system
An economic system in which relative prices are constantly changing to reflect changes in supply and demand for different commodities. The prices of those commodities are signals to everyone within the system as to what is relatively scarce and what is relatively abundant.

Exchange and Markets

The price system features **voluntary exchange**, acts of trading between individuals that make both parties to the trade subjectively better off. The prices we pay for the desired items are determined by the interaction of the forces underlying supply and demand. In our economy, exchanges take place voluntarily in markets. A market encompasses the exchange arrangements of both buyers and sellers that underlie the forces of supply and demand. Indeed, one definition of a market is that it is a low-cost institution for facilitating exchange. A market increases incomes by helping resources move to their highest-valued uses. MyEconLab Concept Check

Voluntary exchange
An act of trading, done on a mutually agreed basis, in which both parties to the trade expect to be better off after the exchange.

Transaction Costs

Individuals turn to markets because markets reduce the cost of exchanges. These costs are sometimes referred to as **transaction costs**, which are broadly defined as the costs associated with finding out exactly what is being transacted as well as the cost of enforcing contracts. If you were Robinson Crusoe and lived alone on an island, you would never incur a transaction cost. For everyone else, transaction costs are just as real as the costs of production. Today, high-speed computers have allowed us to reduce transaction costs by increasing our ability to process information and keep records.

Consider some simple examples of transaction costs. A club warehouse such as Sam's Club or Costco reduces the transaction costs of having to go to numerous

Transaction costs
All of the costs associated with exchange, including the informational costs of finding out the price and quality, service record, and durability of a product, plus the cost of contracting and enforcing that contract.

specialty stores to obtain the items you desire. Financial institutions, such as commercial banks, have reduced the transaction costs of directing funds from savers to borrowers. In general, the more organized the market, the lower the transaction costs. Among those who constantly attempt to lower transaction costs are the much maligned middlemen.

MyEconLab Concept Check

The Role of Middlemen

As long as there are costs of bringing together buyers and sellers, there will be an incentive for intermediaries linking ultimate sellers and buyers, normally called middlemen, to lower those costs. This means that middlemen specialize in lowering transaction costs. Whenever producers do not sell their products directly to the final consumer, by definition, one or more middlemen are involved. Farmers typically sell their output to distributors, who are usually called wholesalers, who then sell those products to retailers such as supermarkets.

How is a Web-based company altering the transaction costs facing consumers of psychological therapy services?

EXAMPLE

Linking Patients to Therapists with Short Video Clips

Undergoing psychological treatment typically involves intensive one-on-one discussions with a therapist. Completing a regimen of psychological therapy entails hours of such discussions. Hence, new patients confront the difficult problem of finding a therapist with whom they likely will feel comfortable conversing about deeply personal issues. Many patients see at least three therapists before making a final choice, ruling out along the way therapists with treatment approaches or personal mannerisms not viewed as helpful by the patients. Conducting face-to-face therapist searches entails significant investments of time and out-of-pocket expenses on the part of patients.

A new middleman company, Therapick, helps consumers of psychological therapy services to identify and schedule appointments with new therapists. Therapick's Web site provides a directory of profile videos of therapists, which prospective patients can view to conduct initial assessments prior to scheduling initial appointments. In this way, Therapick provides a service that reduces the patients' transaction costs.

FOR CRITICAL THINKING

A number of therapists who provide videos to Therapick have perceived a more natural initial rapport with patients who have selected them using the Therapick site. How might Therapick's service also reduce therapists' transaction costs?

Sources are listed at the end of this chapter.

MyEconLab Concept Check
MyEconLab Study Plan

SELF CHECK   Visit MyEconLab to practice these and other problems and to get instant feedback in your Study Plan.

A key feature of the _____ system is _____ exchange, which involves trades between individuals that they both perceive to raise their well-being.	_____, also known as _____, specialize in linking ultimate sellers and buyers and lowering these parties' _____ costs.

4.2 Evaluate the effects of changes in demand and supply on the market price and equilibrium quantity

Changes in Demand and Supply

A key function of middlemen is to reduce transaction costs of buyers and sellers in markets for goods and services, and it is in markets that we see the results of changes in demand and supply. Market equilibrium can change whenever there is a *shock* caused by a change in a *ceteris paribus* condition for demand or supply. A shock to the supply and demand system can be represented by a shift in the supply curve, a shift in the demand curve, or a shift in both curves. Any shock to the system will result in a new set of supply and demand relationships and a new equilibrium. Forces will come into play to move the system from the old price-quantity equilibrium (now a disequilibrium situation) to the new equilibrium, where the new demand and supply curves intersect.

Effects of Changes in Either Demand or Supply

In many situations, it is possible to predict what will happen to both equilibrium price and equilibrium quantity when demand or supply changes. Specifically, whenever one curve is stable while the other curve shifts, we can tell what will happen to both price and quantity. Consider the possibilities in Figure 4-1 below. In panel (a), the supply curve remains unchanged, but demand increases from D_1 to D_2. Note that the results are an increase in the market clearing price from P_1 to P_2 and an increase in the equilibrium quantity from Q_1 to Q_2.

In panel (b) in Figure 4-1, there is a decrease in demand from D_1 to D_3. This results in a decrease in both the equilibrium price of the good and the equilibrium quantity. Panels (c) and (d) show the effects of a shift in the supply curve while the demand curve is unchanged. In panel (c), the supply curve has shifted rightward. The equilibrium price of the product falls, and the equilibrium quantity increases. In panel (d), supply has shifted leftward—there has been a supply decrease. The product's equilibrium price increases, and the equilibrium quantity decreases.

MyEconLab Animation

FIGURE 4-1

Shifts in Demand and in Supply: Determinate Results

In panel (a), the supply curve is unchanged at *S*. The demand curve shifts outward from to D_1 to D_2. The equilibrium price and quantity rise from P_1, Q_1 to P_2, Q_2, respectively. In panel (b), again the supply curve is unchanged at *S*. The demand curve shifts inward to the left, showing a decrease in demand from D_1 to D_3. Both equilibrium price and equilibrium quantity fall. In panel (c), the demand curve now remains unchanged at *D*.

The supply curve shifts from S_1 to S_2. The equilibrium price falls from P_1 to P_2. The equilibrium quantity increases, however, from Q_1 to Q_2. In panel (d), the demand curve is unchanged at *D*. Supply decreases as shown by a leftward shift of the supply curve from S_1 to S_3. The market clearing price increases from P_1 to P_3. The equilibrium quantity falls from Q_1 to Q_3.

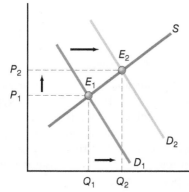

Panel (a) Increase in Demand

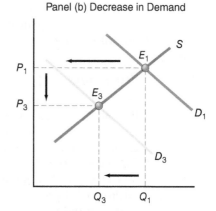

Panel (b) Decrease in Demand

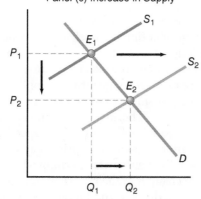

Panel (c) Increase in Supply

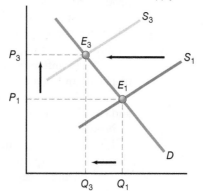

Panel (d) Decrease in Supply

MyEconLab Concept Check

Situations in Which Both Demand and Supply Shift

The examples in Figure 4-1 on the previous page show a theoretically determinate outcome of a shift either in the demand curve, holding the supply curve constant, or in the supply curve, holding the demand curve constant. When both the supply and demand curves change, the outcome is indeterminate for either equilibrium price or equilibrium quantity.

CHANGES OF DEMAND AND SUPPLY IN THE SAME DIRECTION When both demand and supply increase, the equilibrium quantity unambiguously rises, because the increase in demand and the increase in supply *both* tend to generate a rise in quantity. The change in the equilibrium price is uncertain without more information, because the increase in demand tends to increase the equilibrium price, whereas the increase in supply tends to decrease the equilibrium price.

Decreases in both demand and supply tend to generate a fall in quantity, so the equilibrium quantity falls. Again, the effect on the equilibrium price is uncertain without additional information, because a decrease in demand tends to reduce the equilibrium price, whereas a decrease in supply tends to increase the equilibrium price.

CHANGES OF DEMAND AND SUPPLY IN OPPOSITE DIRECTIONS We can be certain that when demand decreases and supply increases at the same time, the equilibrium price will fall, because *both* the decrease in demand and the increase in supply tend to push down the equilibrium price. The change in the equilibrium quantity is uncertain without more information, because the decrease in demand tends to reduce the equilibrium quantity, whereas the increase in supply tends to increase the equilibrium quantity. If demand increases and supply decreases at the same time, both occurrences tend to push up the equilibrium price, so the equilibrium price definitely rises. The change in the equilibrium quantity cannot be determined without more information, because the increase in demand tends to raise the equilibrium quantity, whereas the decrease in supply tends to reduce the equilibrium quantity. **MyEconLab** Concept Check

Price Flexibility and Adjustment Speed

We have used as an illustration for our analysis a market in which prices are quite flexible. Some markets are indeed like that. In others, however, price flexibility may take the form of subtle adjustments such as hidden payments or quality changes. For example, although the published price of floral bouquets may stay the same, the freshness of the flowers may change, meaning that the price per constant-quality unit changes. The published price of French bread might stay the same, but the quality could go up or down, perhaps through use of a different recipe, thereby changing the price per constant-quality unit. There are many ways to implicitly change prices without actually changing the published price for a *nominal* unit of a product or service.

We must also note that markets do not always return to equilibrium immediately. There may be a significant adjustment time. A shock to the economy in the form of an oil embargo, a drought, or a long strike will not be absorbed overnight. This means that even in unfettered market situations, in which there are no restrictions on changes in prices and quantities, temporary excess quantities supplied or excess quantities demanded may appear. Our analysis simply indicates what the market clearing price and equilibrium quantity ultimately will be, given a demand curve and a supply curve.

Nowhere in the analysis is there any indication of the speed with which a market will get to a new equilibrium after a shock. The price may even temporarily overshoot the new equilibrium level. Remember this warning when we examine changes in demand and in supply due to changes in their *ceteris paribus* conditions.

How have simultaneous shifts in demand and supply affected the equilibrium wage rate for airline pilots?

POLICY EXAMPLE

What Accounts for Upward Pressure on Wages of Airline Pilots?

The market clearing prices that airlines must pay for pilots—that is, the pilots' wage rates—have been surging upward. Several reasons account for the jump in equilibrium wage rate. One is that airline firms have been adding new routes to their national and global networks of regular flights among cities. In addition, airlines have been adding new flights to existing routes. To fly all of these additional flights of planes, the airlines require more pilots. Hence, as shown in Figure 4-2 below, the demand curve for airline pilots has shifted rightward.

At the same time, the U.S. government has mandated that all new pilots hired by airlines must have at least 1,500 hours of prior flight experience, which is nearly six times the amount of flight training previously required. The government also is requiring pilots to get more

daily rest time, thereby reducing the amount of time pilots can devote to flying planes. These government policy decisions have contributed to a reduction in the supply of airline pilots. On net, the equilibrium quantity of pilots employed by airlines has declined slightly, and the market clearing wage rate earned by pilots has increased.

FOR CRITICAL THINKING

During the coming decade, thousands of senior pilots will reach age 65, which is the federal government's mandatory pilot retirement age. How will this event likely affect the wages earned by airline pilots?

Sources are listed at the end of this chapter.

FIGURE 4-2

The Effects of a Simultaneous Decrease in the Supply of and Increase in the Demand for Airline Pilots

Airlines' addition of new routes to their national and global networks and of new flights to existing routes has boosted the demand for commercial airline pilots, as shown by the shift in the demand curve from D_1 to D_2. At the same time, U.S. government mandates requiring pilots to obtain more hours of flight experience and to get more daily rest time have generated reductions in the supply of airline pilots, depicted by the leftward shift in the supply curve from S_1 to S_2. On net, the equilibrium number of commercial airline pilots has decreased, from 140,000 to about 130,000. The average annual earnings of these pilots—that is, the price of the pilots to airlines—have risen from approximately $97,000 per year to $121,000 per year.

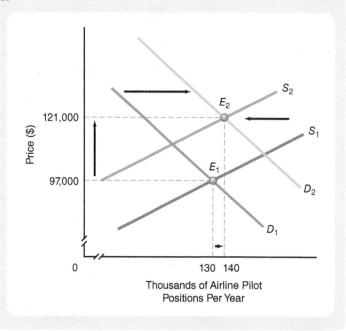

MyEconLab Concept Check
MyEconLab Study Plan

SELF CHECK   Visit MyEconLab to practice these and other problems and to get instant feedback in your Study Plan.

When the _____ curve shifts outward or inward with an unchanged _____ curve, equilibrium price and quantity increase or decrease, respectively. When the _____ curve shifts outward or inward given an unchanged _____ curve, equilibrium price moves in the direction opposite to equilibrium quantity.

When there is a shift in demand or supply, the new equilibrium price is not obtained _____. Adjustment takes _____.

The Rationing Function of Prices

The synchronization of decisions by buyers and sellers that leads to equilibrium is called the *rationing function of prices*. Prices are indicators of relative scarcity. An equilibrium price clears the market. The plans of buyers and sellers, given the price, are not frustrated. It is the free interaction of buyers and sellers that sets the price that eventually clears the market. Price, in effect, rations a good to demanders who are willing and able to pay the highest price. Whenever the rationing function of prices is frustrated by government-enforced price ceilings that set prices below the market clearing level, a prolonged shortage results.

There are ways other than price to ration goods. *First come, first served* is one method. *Political power* is another. *Physical force* is yet another. Cultural, religious, and physical differences have been and are used as rationing devices throughout the world.

RATIONING BY WAITING Consider first come, first served as a rationing device. We call this *rationing by queues*, where *queue* means "line." Whoever is willing to wait in line the longest obtains the good that is being sold at less than the market clearing price. All who wait in line are paying a higher *total outlay* than the money price paid for the good. Personal time has an opportunity cost. To calculate the total outlay expended on the good, we must add up the money price plus the opportunity cost of the time spent waiting.

Rationing by waiting may occur in situations in which entrepreneurs are free to change prices to equate quantity demanded with quantity supplied but choose not to do so. This results in queues of potential buyers. It may seem that the price in the market is being held below equilibrium by some noncompetitive force. That is not true, however. Such queuing may arise in a free market when the demand for a good is subject to large or unpredictable fluctuations, and the additional costs to firms (and ultimately to consumers) of constantly changing prices or of holding sufficient inventories or providing sufficient excess capacity to cover peak demands are greater than the costs to consumers of waiting for the good.

Common examples are waiting in line to purchase a fast-food lunch and queuing to purchase a movie ticket a few minutes before the next showing.

How long do Canadian health care consumers usually have to wait to obtain treatment from medical specialists?

INTERNATIONAL POLICY EXAMPLE

Want to See a Health Specialist in Canada? Hurry Up and Wait

In Canada, nonprice rationing is a key mechanism for rationing specialized health care. In contrast to the United States, where prices traditionally play a larger role in the rationing of medical services, the government-supervised Canadian health care system relies more on waiting lists. The average amount of time that a Canadian consumer must wait to see a health care specialist is about 18 weeks, which is nearly six times longer than the typical period that a U.S. consumer must wait.

FOR CRITICAL THINKING
Why do you think that wait times for specialized health care are shorter in the United States than in Canada?

Sources are listed at the end of this chapter.

RATIONING BY RANDOM ASSIGNMENT OR COUPONS *Random assignment* is another way to ration goods. You may have been involved in a rationing-by-random-assignment scheme in college if you were assigned a housing unit. Sometimes rationing by random assignment is used to fill slots in popular classes.

Rationing by *coupons* has also been used, particularly during wartime. In the United States during World War II, families were allotted coupons that allowed them to purchase specified quantities of rationed goods, such as meat and gasoline. To purchase such goods, they had to pay a specified price *and* give up a coupon.

The Essential Role of Rationing

In a world of scarcity, there is, by definition, competition for what is scarce. After all, any resources that are not scarce can be obtained by everyone at a zero price in as large a quantity as everyone wants, such as air to burn in internal combustion engines. Once scarcity arises, there has to be some method to ration the available resources, goods, and services. The price system is one form of rationing. The others we mentioned are alternatives. Economists cannot say which system of rationing is "best." They can, however, say that rationing via the price system leads to the most efficient use of available resources. As explained in Appendix B (which follows this chapter), this means that generally in a freely functioning price system, all of the gains from mutually beneficial trade will be captured.   MyEconLab Concept Check

MyEconLab Study Plan

SELF CHECK   Visit MyEconLab to practice these and other problems and to get instant feedback in your Study Plan.

Prices in a market economy perform a rationing function because they reflect relative scarcity, allowing the market to clear. Other ways to ration goods include _____ _____, _____ _____, _____ _____, _____ _____, and _____.

Even when businesspeople can change prices, some rationing by waiting may occur. Such _____ arises when there are large changes in demand coupled with high costs of satisfying those changes immediately.

Price Ceilings

4.4 Explain the effects of price ceilings

The rationing function of prices is prevented when governments impose price controls. **Price controls** often involve setting a **price ceiling**—the maximum price that may be allowed in an exchange. The world has had a long history of price ceilings applied to product prices, wages, rents, and interest rates. Occasionally, a government will set a **price floor**—a minimum price below which a good or service may not be sold. Price floors have most often been applied to wages and agricultural products. Let's first consider price ceilings.

Price controls
Government-mandated minimum or maximum prices that may be charged for goods and services.

Price ceiling
A legal maximum price that may be charged for a particular good or service.

Price floor
A legal minimum price below which a good or service may not be sold. Legal minimum wages are an example.

Price Ceilings and Black Markets

As long as a price ceiling is below the market clearing price, imposing a price ceiling creates a shortage, as can be seen in Figure 4-3 on the next page. At any price below the market clearing, or equilibrium, price of $1,000, there will always be a larger quantity demanded than quantity supplied—a shortage, as you will recall from Chapter 3. Normally, whenever quantity demanded exceeds quantity supplied—that is, when a shortage exists—there is a tendency for the price to rise to its equilibrium level. But with a price ceiling, this tendency cannot be fully realized because everyone is forbidden to trade at the equilibrium price.

NONPRICE RATIONING DEVICES The result is fewer exchanges and **nonprice rationing devices**. Figure 4-3 on the next page shows the situation for portable electric generators after a natural disaster: The equilibrium quantity of portable generators demanded and supplied (or traded) would be 10,000 units, and the market clearing price would be $1,000 per generator. If the government, though, essentially imposes a price ceiling by requiring the price of portable generators to remain at the predisaster level, which the government determines was a price of $600, the equilibrium quantity offered is only 5,000.

Nonprice rationing devices
All methods used to ration scarce goods that are price-controlled. Whenever the price system is not allowed to work, nonprice rationing devices will evolve to ration the affected goods and services.

FIGURE 4-3

Black Markets for Portable Electric Generators

The demand curve is *D*. The supply curve is *S*. The equilibrium price is $1,000. The government, however, steps in and imposes a maximum price of $600. At that lower price, the quantity demanded will be 15,000, but the quantity supplied will be only 5,000. There is a "shortage." The implicit price (including time costs) tends to increase to $1,400. If black markets arise, as they generally will, the equilibrium black market price will end up somewhere between $600 and $1,400. The actual quantity transacted will be between 5,000 and 10,000.

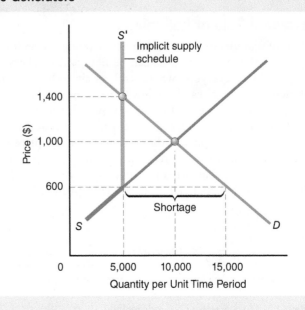

Because frustrated consumers will be able to purchase only 5,000 units, there is a shortage. The most obvious nonprice rationing device to help clear the market is queuing, or physical lines, which we have already discussed. To avoid physical lines, waiting lists may be established.

Black market

A market in which goods are traded at prices above their legal maximum prices or in which illegal goods are sold.

BLACK MARKETS Typically, an effective price ceiling leads to a **black market**. A black market is a market in which the price-controlled good is sold at an illegally high price through various methods. For example, if the price of gasoline is controlled at lower than the market clearing price, drivers who wish to fill up their cars may offer the gas station attendant a cash payment on the side (as happened in the United States in the 1970s and in China and India in the mid-2000s during price controls on gasoline).

If the price of beef is controlled at below its market clearing price, a customer who offers the butcher tickets for good seats to an upcoming football game may be allocated otherwise unavailable beef. Indeed, the true implicit price of a price-controlled good or service can be increased in an infinite number of ways, limited only by the imagination. (Black markets also occur when goods are made illegal.)

What accounts for a growing worldwide black market in human organs?

INTERNATIONAL EXAMPLE

The Global Black Market in Human Organs

Recent estimates indicate that at least 10,000 black market transactions in human organs occur around the world every year. Legal bans on the sale of organs effectively impose a ceiling price of $0 per unit. The consequences of these bans are global shortages of transplantable organs numbering in the hundreds of thousands. Many people have become desperate for replacement organs. People in low-income nations in Eastern Europe and Asia often receive black market payments to donate "extra" kidneys. Some residents of China facing a waiting list of nearly 300,000 for organ transplants have resorted to buying organs of executed prisoners from their surviving families. In some cases, criminal groups have even murdered people to

steal organs such as hearts or lungs intended for sale to people frantic enough to pay high prices to remain alive.

Black market prices of organs vary considerably. For kidneys, the prices range from $40,000 to $150,000, depending on the nation and location in which a black market kidney is purchased. The price of a heart in the global black market for human organs can reach nearly $1.5 million.

FOR CRITICAL THINKING

Why can prices in the black market for organs often vary within a wide range?

Sources are listed at the end of this chapter.

The Policy of Rent Ceilings

More than 200 U.S. cities and towns, including Berkeley, California, and New York City, operate under some kind of rent control. **Rent control** is a system under which the local government tells building owners how much they can charge their tenants for rent. In the United States, rent controls date back to at least World War II. The objective of rent control is to keep rents below levels that would be observed in a freely competitive market.

Rent control
Price ceilings on rents.

THE FUNCTIONS OF RENTAL PRICES In any housing market, rental prices serve three functions: (1) to promote the efficient maintenance of existing housing and to stimulate the construction of new housing, (2) to allocate existing scarce housing among competing claimants, and (3) to ration the use of existing housing by current demanders. Rent controls interfere with all of these functions.

Rent Controls and Construction Rent controls discourage the construction of new rental units. Rents are the most important long-term determinant of profitability, and rent controls artificially depress them. Consider some examples. In a recent year in Dallas, Texas, with a 16 percent rental vacancy rate but no rent control laws, 11,000 new rental housing units were built. In the same year in San Francisco, California, only 2,000 units were built, despite a mere 1.6 percent vacancy rate. The major difference? San Francisco has had stringent rent control laws. In New York City, most rental units being built are luxury units, which are exempt from controls.

Effects on the Existing Supply of Housing When rental rates are held below equilibrium levels, property owners cannot recover the cost of maintenance, repairs, and capital improvements through higher rents. Hence, they curtail these activities. In the extreme situation, taxes, utilities, and the expenses of basic repairs exceed rental receipts. The result has been abandoned buildings from Santa Monica, California, to New York City. Some owners have resorted to arson, hoping to collect the insurance on their empty buildings before the city claims them to pay back taxes.

Rationing the Current Use of Housing Rent controls also affect the current use of housing because they restrict tenant mobility. Consider a family whose children have gone off to college. That family might want to live in a smaller apartment. In a rent-controlled environment, however, giving up a rent-controlled unit can entail a substantial cost. In most rent-controlled cities, rents can be adjusted only when a tenant leaves. This means that a move from a long-occupied rent-controlled apartment to a smaller apartment can involve a hefty rent hike. In New York, this artificial preservation of the status quo came to be known as "housing gridlock."

ATTEMPTS TO EVADE RENT CEILINGS The distortions produced by rent ceilings lead to efforts by both property owners and tenants to evade the rules. These efforts lead to the growth of expensive government bureaucracies whose job it is to make sure that rent ceilings aren't evaded. In New York City, because rent on a rent-controlled apartment can be raised only if the tenant leaves, property owners have had an incentive to make life unpleasant for tenants in order to drive them out or to evict them on the slightest pretext. The city has responded by making evictions extremely costly for property owners. Eviction requires a tedious and expensive judicial proceeding.

Tenants, for their part, routinely try to sublet all or part of their rent-controlled apartments at fees substantially above the rent they pay to the owner. Both the city and the property owners try to prohibit subletting and often end up in the city's housing courts—an entire judicial system developed to deal with disputes involving rent-controlled apartments. The overflow and appeals from the city's housing courts sometimes clog the rest of New York's judicial system.

WHO LOSES AND WHO GAINS FROM RENT CEILINGS? The big losers from rent ceilings are clearly property owners. There is, however, another group of losers—low-income individuals, especially single mothers, trying to find apartments. Some observers now believe that rent ceilings have worsened the problem of homelessness in cities such as New York.

WHY BOTH LANDLORDS AND SOME TENANTS LOSE Often, owners of rent-controlled apartments charge "key money" before allowing a new tenant to move in. This is a large up-front cash payment, usually illegal but demanded nonetheless—just one aspect of the black market in rent-controlled apartments. Poor individuals have insufficient income to pay the hefty key money payment, nor can they assure the owner that their rent will be on time or even paid each month.

Because rent ceilings are usually below market clearing levels, apartment owners have little incentive to take any risk on low-income individuals as tenants. This is particularly true when a prospective tenant's chief source of income is a welfare check. Indeed, a large number of litigants in the New York housing courts are welfare mothers who have missed their rent payments due to emergency expenses or delayed welfare checks. Their appeals often end in evictions and a new home in a temporary public shelter—or on the streets.

BENEFICIARIES OF RENT CONTROLS Who benefits from rent ceilings? Ample evidence indicates that upper-income professionals benefit the most. These people can use their mastery of the bureaucracy and their large network of friends and connections to exploit the rent ceilings. Consider that in New York, actresses Mia Farrow and Cicely Tyson live in rent-controlled apartments, paying well below market rates. So do the former director of the Metropolitan Museum of Art and singer and children's book author Carly Simon.

Why did people with rent-controlled apartments in Mumbai, India, become millionaires overnight?

INTERNATIONAL EXAMPLE

Why Indian Landlords Are Paying Tenants Millions of Dollars to Break Leases

In 1947, government rent control rules in Mumbai, India, established maximum allowable rents in sections of the city based on 1940 market rent levels. Years later, the rules were altered to allow landlords the authority to raise rents above that level at a pace not to exceed 5 percent per year. For a number of residents, the consequence is rents at controlled levels less than $25 per month for 2,600 square feet in modern apartment buildings.

In recent years, some landlords have decided that the land occupied by rent-controlled apartment buildings has much greater value if the buildings are replaced with hotels or parking garages. Indeed, a number of landlords have determined that they can earn more from alternative structures than would have been possible by charging very high market rents. Consequently, the landlords are negotiating multimillion-dollar deals with people in rent-controlled apartments to break lease agreements. After buying back the rights to rent-controlled apartments for millions of dollars, the landlords can tear them down and replace them with hotels and parking decks—and still profit from the transactions.

FOR CRITICAL THINKING

Why do you think that since 1947 many more people have sought to rent apartments at $25 per month than landlords have been willing offer at that rate?

Sources are listed at the end of this chapter.

MyEconLab Concept Check
MyEconLab Study Plan

SELF CHECK Visit MyEconLab to practice these and other problems and to get instant feedback in your Study Plan.

Governments sometimes impose **price controls** in the form of price _____ and price _____.

An effective price _____ is an enforced regulation that sets the legal price below the market clearing price, which often leads to nonprice rationing devices and _____ markets.

_____ prices perform three functions: (1) allocating existing scarce housing among competing claimants, (2) promoting efficient maintenance of existing houses and stimulating new housing construction, and (3) rationing the use of existing houses by current demanders.

Effective rent _____ impede the functioning of rental prices. Construction of new rental units is discouraged.

Price Floors and Quantity Restrictions

4.5 Explain the effects of price floors and government-imposed quantity restrictions

Another way that government can seek to control markets is by imposing price floors or *quantity restrictions*. Let's begin by examining the effects of price floors, which governments most commonly impose in agricultural and labor markets.

Price Floors and Price Supports in Agriculture

During the Great Depression, the federal government swung into action to help farmers. In 1933, it established a system of price supports for many agricultural products. Since then, there have been price supports for wheat, feed grains, cotton, rice, soybeans, sorghum, and dairy products, among other foodstuffs.

IMPLEMENTING AGRICULTURAL PRICE SUPPORTS The nature of the supports is quite simple: The government simply chooses a *support price* for an agricultural product and then acts to ensure that the price of the product never falls below the support level.

Figure 4-4 below shows the market demand for and supply of milk. Without a price-support program, competitive forces would yield an equilibrium price of $0.08 per pound and an equilibrium quantity of 15.4 billion pounds per year. Clearly, if the government were to set the support price at or below $0.08 per pound, the quantity of milk demanded would equal the quantity of milk supplied at point *E*, because farmers could sell all they wanted at the market clearing price of $0.08 per pound.

AN EFFECTIVE AGRICULTURAL PRICE FLOOR What happens, though, when the government sets the support price *above* the market clearing price, at $0.10 per pound? At a support price of $0.10 per pound, the quantity demanded is only 15 billion pounds, but the quantity supplied is 16 billion pounds. The 1-billion-pound difference between them is called the *excess quantity supplied*, or *surplus*. As simple as this program seems, its existence creates a fundamental question: How can the government agency charged

---

MyEconLab Animation

FIGURE 4-4

Agricultural Price Supports

Free market equilibrium occurs at *E*, with an equilibrium price of $0.08 per pound and an equilibrium quantity of 15.4 billion pounds. When the government sets a support price at $0.10 per pound, the quantity demanded is 15 billion pounds and the quantity supplied is 16 billion pounds. The difference is the surplus, which the government buys.

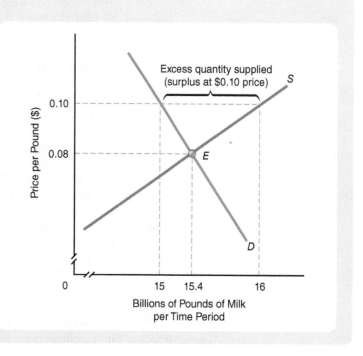

with administering the price-support program prevent market forces from pushing the actual price down to $0.08 per pound?

If production exceeds the amount that consumers want to buy at the support price, what happens to the surplus? Quite simply, if the price-support program is to work, the government has to buy the surplus—the 1-billion-pound difference. As a practical matter, the government acquires the 1-billion-pound surplus indirectly through a government agency. The government either stores the surplus or sells it to foreign countries at a greatly reduced price (or gives it away free of charge) under the Food for Peace program.

WHO BENEFITS FROM AGRICULTURAL PRICE SUPPORTS? Although agricultural price supports have traditionally been promoted as a way to guarantee "decent" earnings for low-income farmers, most of the benefits have in fact gone to the owners of very large farms. Price-support payments are made on a per-pound basis, not on a per-farm basis. Thus, traditionally, the larger the farm, the bigger the benefit from agricultural price supports. In addition, all of the benefits from price supports ultimately accrue to landowners on whose land price-supported crops grow.

Keeping Price Supports Alive under a New Name Back in the early 1990s, Congress indicated an intention to phase out most agricultural subsidies by the early 2000s. What Congress actually *did* throughout the 1990s, however, was to pass a series of "emergency laws" keeping farm subsidies alive. Some of these laws aimed to replace agricultural price supports with payments to many farmers for growing no crops at all, thereby boosting the market prices of crops by reducing supply. Nevertheless, the federal government and several state governments have continued to support prices of a number of agricultural products, such as peanuts, through "marketing loan" programs. These programs advance funds to farmers to help them finance the storage of some or all of their crops. The farmers can then use the stored produce as collateral for borrowing or sell it to the government and use the proceeds to repay debts.

Marketing loan programs raise the effective price that farmers receive for their crops and commit federal and state governments to purchasing surplus production. Consequently, they lead to outcomes similar to those of traditional price-support programs.

The Main Beneficiaries of Agricultural Subsidies In 2002, Congress enacted the Farm Security Act, which perpetuated marketing loan programs and other subsidy and price-support arrangements for such farm products as wheat, corn, rice, peanuts, and soybeans. All told, the more than $9 billion in U.S. government payments for these and other products amounts to about 25 percent of the annual market value of all U.S. farm production.

The government seeks to cap the annual subsidy payment that an individual farmer can receive at $360,000 per year, but some farmers are able to garner higher annual amounts by exploiting regulatory loopholes. The greatest share of total agricultural subsidies goes to the owners of the largest farming operations. At present, 10 percent of U.S. farmers receive more than 70 percent of agricultural subsidies.

The 2008 Food, Conservation, and Energy Act expanded on the 2002 legislation by giving farmers raising any of a number of crops a choice between subsidy programs. On the one hand, farmers could opt to participate in traditional programs involving a mix of direct payments and marketing loan programs. On the other hand, farmers could choose a program offering guaranteed revenues. If market clearing crop prices ended up higher than those associated with the government's revenue guarantee, farmers could sell their crops at the higher prices instead of collecting government subsidies. If equilibrium crop prices ended up below a level consistent with the government guarantee, however, farmers received direct subsidies to bring their total revenues up to the guaranteed level.

In 2014, Congress ended a number of direct subsidy payments to farmers. Under a new subsidy program, the government encourages farmers to purchase crop insurance policies. These policies provide farmers with extra payments if circumstances outside their control, such as too little or too much rain, harm their crops. Nevertheless, the government heavily subsidizes the farmers' insurance purchases.

How does the government administer a price floor in the market for raisins?

POLICY EXAMPLE

Regulating the Raisin Reserve

It is called the Farm Bill, and every time Congress votes to renew it as an update to the existing law governing agriculture subsidies, it lengthens. In 2015, it ran to over 1,000 pages. Buried within those pages is the "raisin reserve." Under 1937 rules renewed each time Congress authorizes passage of a new farm bill, the government establishes a fixed aggregate quantity of raisins that farmers can sell each year—namely, the raisin reserve.

Once the farmers have harvested and stored their raisins, the government ensures that they will receive a minimum price for them. Surplus raisins that farmers have on hand at the above-market-clearing price floor must be stored separately and can be sold only if the government

grants permission. In effect, the government expropriates the surplus raisins, which in recent years have amounted to between one-third and one-half of annual raisin crops. The government sells these surplus raisins in export markets and passes along all profits from these sales to the raisin farmers.

FOR CRITICAL THINKING

What determines the size of the government's raisin reserve? Explain briefly.

Sources are listed at the end of this chapter.

MyEconLab Concept Check

Price Floors in the Labor Market

The **minimum wage** is the lowest hourly wage rate that firms may legally pay their workers. Proponents favor higher minimum wages to ensure low-income workers a "decent" standard of living. Opponents counter that higher minimum wages cause increased unemployment, particularly among unskilled minority teenagers.

Minimum wage
A wage floor, legislated by government, setting the lowest hourly rate that firms may legally pay workers.

MINIMUM WAGES IN THE UNITED STATES The federal minimum wage started in 1938 at 25 cents an hour, about 40 percent of the average manufacturing wage at the time. Typically, its level has stayed at about 40 to 50 percent of average manufacturing wages. After holding the minimum wage at $5.15 per hour from 1997 to 2007, Congress enacted a series of phased increases in the hourly minimum wage, effective on July 24 of each year, to $5.85 in 2007, $6.55 in 2008, and $7.25 in 2009.

Many states and cities have their own minimum wage laws that exceed the federal minimum. A number of municipalities refer to their minimum wage rules as "living wage" laws. Governments of these municipalities seek to set minimum wages consistent with living standards they deem to be socially acceptable—that is, overall wage income judged to be sufficient to purchase basic items such as housing and food.

ECONOMIC EFFECTS OF A MINIMUM WAGE What happens when the government establishes a floor on wages? The effects can be seen in Figure 4-5 on the next page. We start off in equilibrium with the equilibrium wage rate of W_e and the equilibrium quantity of labor equal to Q_e. A minimum wage, W_m, higher than W_e, is imposed. At W_m, the quantity demanded for labor is reduced to Q_d, and some workers now become unemployed. Certain workers will become unemployed as a result of the minimum wage, but others will move to sectors where minimum wage laws do not apply. Wages will be pushed down in these uncovered sectors.

Explaining the Overall Decrease in Employment Note that the reduction in employment from Q_e to Q_d, or the distance from B to A, is less than the excess quantity of labor supplied at wage rate W_m. This excess quantity supplied is the distance between A and C, or the distance between Q_d and Q_s. The reason the reduction in employment is smaller than the excess quantity of labor supplied at the minimum wage is that the excess quantity of labor supplied also includes the *additional* workers who would like to work more hours at the new, higher minimum wage.

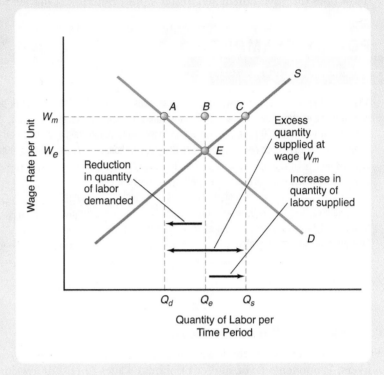

FIGURE 4-5

The Effect of Minimum Wages

The market clearing wage rate is W_e. The market clearing quantity of employment is Q_e, determined by the intersection of supply and demand at point E. A minimum wage equal to W_m is established. The quantity of labor demanded is reduced to Q_d. The reduction in employment from Q_e to Q_d is equal to the distance between B and A. That distance is smaller than the excess quantity of labor supplied at wage rate W_m. The distance between B and C is the increase in the quantity of labor supplied that results from the higher minimum wage rate.

In the long run (a time period that is long enough to allow for full adjustment by workers and firms), some of the reduction in the quantity of labor demanded will result from a reduction in the number of firms, and some will result from changes in the number of workers employed by each firm. Economists estimate that a 10 percent increase in the inflation-adjusted minimum wage decreases total employment of those affected by 1 to 2 percent.

Summing Up the Effects of an Above-Equilibrium Minimum Wage We can conclude from the application of demand and supply analysis that a minimum wage established above the equilibrium wage rate typically has two fundamental effects. On the one hand, it boosts the wage earnings of those people who obtain employment. On the other hand, the minimum wage results in unemployment for other individuals. Thus, demand and supply analysis implies that the minimum wage makes some people better off while making others worse off.

WHAT IF...

the government establishes both price floors and ceilings for different groups of employees at U.S. banks?

Bank employees whose market clearing wages otherwise would have been below the minimum wage must legally receive the legislated minimum wage instead, which generates surplus workers in bank labor markets as in other markets for labor. In recent years, however, bank regulators have used powers authorized by a new federal law to establish *maximum* permissible wages as well for bank employees. Those employees—

typically top managers—whose wages otherwise would be at market clearing levels exceeding the regulatory maximum must instead have their wages reset at the maximum legal level. Thus, in the market for the highest-ranking bank managers, the quantity of labor demanded by banks now exceeds the quantity of labor supplied. There is a shortage of labor in this market for managers.

Quantity Restrictions

Governments can impose quantity restrictions on a market. The most obvious restriction is an outright ban on the ownership or trading of a good. It is currently illegal to buy and sell human organs. It is also currently illegal to buy and sell certain psychoactive drugs such as cocaine, heroin, and methamphetamine. In some states, it is illegal to start a new hospital without obtaining a license for a particular number of beds to be offered to patients. This licensing requirement effectively limits the quantity of hospital beds in some states. From 1933 to 1973, it was illegal for U.S. citizens to own gold except for manufacturing, medicinal, or jewelry purposes.

Some of the most common quantity restrictions exist in the area of international trade. The U.S. government, as well as many foreign governments, imposes import quotas on a variety of goods. An **import quota** is a supply restriction that prohibits the importation of more than a specified quantity of a particular good in a one-year period. The United States has had import quotas on tobacco, sugar, and immigrant labor. For many years, there were import quotas on oil coming into the United States. There are also "voluntary" import quotas on certain goods. For instance, since the mid-2000s, the Chinese government has agreed to "voluntarily" restrict the amount of textile products China sends to the United States and the European Union.

Import quota
A physical supply restriction on imports of a particular good, such as sugar. Foreign exporters are unable to sell in the United States more than the quantity specified in the import quota.

MyEconLab Concept Check
MyEconLab Study Plan

SELF CHECK   Visit MyEconLab to practice these and other problems and to get instant feedback in your Study Plan.

With a price-_____ system, the government sets a minimum price at which, say, qualifying farm products can be sold. Any farmers who cannot sell at that price in the market can "sell" their surplus to the government. The only way a price-_____ system can survive is for the government or some other entity to buy up the excess quantity supplied at the support price.

When a _____ is placed on wages at a rate that is above market equilibrium, the result is an excess quantity of labor supplied at that minimum wage.

Quantity restrictions may take the form of _____ _____, which are limits on the quantity of specific foreign goods that can be brought into the United States for resale purposes.

YOU ARE THERE

A Zero-Price Price Ceiling Comes to an End in Los Angeles

John Anthony DiCiaccio, an engineer with Southwest Airlines, returns to the space in the Los Angeles LAX Airport parking lot where he had parked his all-electric Toyota Prius. DiCiaccio is dismayed to find on the windshield a sheet announcing an end to free parking for electric vehicles for up to 30 days in parking lots containing battery charging stations.

LAX Airport is ending the zero-price policy because it has created a major parking-space shortage. This shortage has arisen for three key reasons. First, some people really do park their cars for as long as 30 days in the designated spaces, which are among the most conveniently located parking spaces at the airport. Doing so enables them to avoid paying up to $30 per day to park their vehicles elsewhere. While those vehicles sit in spaces for a month at a time, the spaces are unavailable to other drivers. Second, many people driving hybrid vehicles that also run on gasoline have sought to avoid paid parking by interpreting the zero-price-for-

electric-cars policy as applying to hybrid cars as well. Third, more people actually have been buying electric vehicles.

Now so many people want to park their electric cars at a price of zero that traffic jams have developed in the zero-price lots as people driving electric and hybrid cars await open spaces. To bring an end to these mob scenes, the airport has decided to terminate this policy.

CRITICAL THINKING QUESTIONS

1. *Why does a zero-price restriction for a scarce good necessarily lead to a shortage?*

2. *Why do you suppose that some frequent LAX travelers bought electric cars?*

Sources are listed at the end of this chapter.

ISSUES & APPLICATIONS

MyEconLab Video

Micromonkey/Fotolia

Price Controls + Contaminated Drugs = Human Tragedy

CONCEPTS APPLIED

» Price Ceiling

» Shortage

» Price controls

National media outlets were all over the story. Hundreds of people had contracted a very rare spinal meningitis—an infection afflicting the tissue and nerves along their spinal cords. News reports quickly settled on a villain. A Massachusetts-based pharmacy had engaged in large-scale production of a steroid solution that had been sold to clinics and hospitals. Physicians who had injected doses of the solution into patients' nerve roots to relieve pain had unknowingly unleashed bacteria and fungal material into unprotected spinal tissue. Many who fell ill experienced permanent nerve damage, and dozens died.

An Economics Backstory: A Price Ceiling and a Shortage

Not widely reported was an economics backstory that preceded the Massachusetts pharmacy's sale of the contaminated drug. Months prior to the outbreak of spinal meningitis, a steady increase in demand for the drug had boosted the market clearing price of injectable steroid solution to and then above a ceiling price established by the U.S. federal government.

Of course, once the market price exceeded the government's ceiling price, the quantity of the drug demanded rose above the quantity of the steroid solution that pharmaceuticals companies normally manufacturing the product were willing to supply. A nationwide shortage of injectable steroid drugs developed. The magnitude of the shortage expanded as the demand for the steroid solution continued to increase.

Next: The Massachusetts Pharmacy and the Human Tragedy

At this point, the Massachusetts pharmacy entered the picture. Its owners offered to help fill the gap between the quantities demanded and supplied with its own version of the injectable steroid drug. The pharmacy could benefit from offering the steroid solution at the government's ceiling price, however, only by keeping its operating costs sufficiently low. Consequently, the pharmacy mixed the drug using substandard techniques and incompletely sterilized equipment. In so doing, the pharmacy engaged in a common response to a price ceiling by producing a lower-quality product as a substitute for a higher-quality product experiencing a shortage because of the price ceiling.

According to most of the national media, the involvement of the Massachusetts pharmacy—a readily identifiable villain—is the point at which the news story of a nationwide spinal meningitis outbreak "began." Nevertheless, there would have been no incentive for the "villain" to become involved in the spinal-steroid market in the absence of the government price ceiling and the resulting shortage. The ultimate root of this human tragedy is the steroid-solution price ceiling imposed by the federal government.

For Critical Thinking

1. Market prices of drugs periodically rise above ceilings that the federal government imposes on hundreds of pharmaceuticals, including a number of cancer drugs. Why do you think that about 300 drug shortages typically exist at any given time in the United States?

2. Why do you suppose that some economists argue that well-intentioned efforts by the government to hold down prices for sick patients can have the unintended effect of endangering many of those patients?

Web Resources

1. Take a look at the Food and Drug Administration's Web pages on drugs currently experiencing shortages in the Web Links in MyEconLab.

2. Learn about on-going shortages of medications used to combat tuberculosis in the Web Links in MyEconLab.

> ### MyEconLab
>
> For more questions on this chapter's Issues & Applications, go to MyEconLab.
>
> In the Study Plan for this chapter, select Section I: Issues and Applications.

Sources are listed at the end of this chapter.

Fundamental Points

1. The price system's key characteristic is voluntary exchange involving pairs of individuals, sometimes linked by intermediaries, or middlemen, that specialize in linking ultimate sellers and buyers and lowering their transaction costs.

2. The market clearing price ultimately adjusts to changes in the position of the demand curve or the supply curve.

3. In a market system, prices perform a rationing function because they reflect relative scarcity, which allows the market to clear with quantity demanded equal to quantity supplied.

4. Governments sometimes impose and enforce price controls such as effective price ceilings, in which the legal price is required to be below the market clearing price, with non-price rationing devices and black markets often resulting.

5. Governments commonly impose and enforce price floors that establish lower limits on legal prices above market clearing prices, which result in shortages, and quantity restrictions, such as import quotas that place limits on the amounts of sales of foreign goods.

WHAT YOU SHOULD KNOW

Here is what you should know after reading this chapter. MyEconLab will help you identify what you know, and where to go when you need to practice.

LEARNING OBJECTIVES	KEY TERMS	WHERE TO GO TO PRACTICE
4.1 Discuss the essential features of the price system *In the price system, prices respond to changes in supply and demand. Decisions on resource use depend on what happens to prices. Middlemen reduce transaction costs by bringing buyers and sellers together.*	price system, 81 voluntary exchange, 81 transaction costs, 81	• MyEconLab Study Plan 4.1
4.2 Evaluate the effects of changes in demand and supply on the market price and equilibrium quantity *With a given supply curve, an increase in demand causes increases in the market price and equilibrium quantity, and a decrease in demand induces decreases in the market price and equilibrium quantity. With a given demand curve, an increase in supply causes a fall in the market price and an increase in the equilibrium quantity, and a decrease in supply causes a rise in the market price and a decline in the equilibrium quantity. When both demand and supply shift at the same time, we must know the direction and amount of each shift in order to predict changes in the market price and the equilibrium quantity.*	**Key Figure** Figure 4-1, 83	• MyEconLab Study Plan 4.2 • Animated Figure 4-1
4.3 Understand the rationing function of prices *In the price system, prices ration scarce goods and services. Other ways of rationing include first come, first served; political power; physical force; random assignment; and coupons.*		• MyEconLab Study Plan 4.3

WHAT YOU SHOULD KNOW *continued*

LEARNING OBJECTIVES	KEY TERMS	WHERE TO GO TO PRACTICE
4.4 Explain the effects of price ceilings *Government-imposed price controls that require prices to be no higher than a certain level are price ceilings. If a government sets a price ceiling below the market price, then at the ceiling price the quantity of the good demanded will exceed the quantity supplied. There will be a shortage at the ceiling price. Price ceilings can lead to nonprice rationing devices and black markets.*	price controls, 87 price ceiling, 87 price floor, 87 nonprice rationing devices, 87 black market, 88 rent control, 89 **Key Figure** Figure 4-3, 88	• MyEconLab Study Plan 4.4 • Animated Figure 4-3
4.5 Explain the effects of price floors and government-imposed quantity restrictions *Government-mandated price controls that require prices to be no lower than a certain level are price floors. If a government sets a price floor above the market price, then at the floor price the quantity of the good supplied will exceed the quantity demanded. There will be a surplus at the floor price. Quantity restrictions can take the form of outright bans or licensing and import restrictions that restrict the amount supplied.*	minimum wage, 93 import quota, 95 **Key Figures** Figure 4-4, 91 Figure 4-5, 94	• MyEconLab Study Plan 4.5 • Animated Figures 4-4, 4-5

Log in to MyEconLab, take a chapter test, and get a personalized Study Plan that tells you which concepts you understand and which ones you need to review. From there, MyEconLab will give you further practice, tutorials, animations, videos, and guided solutions. For more information, visit www.myeconlab.com

PROBLEMS

All problems are assignable in MyEconLab. *Answers to odd-numbered problems appear in* MyEconLab.

4-1. In recent years, technological improvements have greatly reduced the costs of producing basic cell phones, and a number of new firms have entered the cell phone industry. At the same time, prices of substitutes for cell phones, such as smartphones and some tablet devices, have declined considerably. Construct a supply and demand diagram of the market for cell phones. Illustrate the impacts of these developments, and evaluate the effects on the market price and equilibrium quantity. (See pages 83–84.)

4-2. Advances in research and development in the pharmaceutical industry have enabled manufacturers to identify potential cures more quickly and therefore at lower cost. At the same time, the aging of our society has increased the demand for new drugs. Construct a supply and demand diagram of the market for pharmaceutical drugs. Illustrate the impacts of these developments, and evaluate the effects on the market price and the equilibrium quantity. (See pages 83–84.)

4-3. There are simultaneous changes in the demand for and supply of global-positioning-system (GPS) devices, with the consequences being an unambiguous increase in the market clearing price of these devices but no change in the equilibrium quantity. What changes in the demand for and supply of GPS devices could have generated these outcomes? Explain. (See pages 83–84.)

4-4. There are simultaneous changes in the demand for and supply of tablet devices, with the consequences being an unambiguous decrease in the equilibrium quantity of these devices but no change in the market clearing price. What changes in the demand for and supply of tablet devices could have generated these outcomes? Explain. (See pages 83–84.)

4-5. The following table depicts the quantity demanded and quantity supplied of studio apartments in a small college town.

Monthly Rent	Quantity Demanded	Quantity Supplied
$600	3,000	1,600
$650	2,500	1,800
$700	2,000	2,000
$750	1,500	2,200
$800	1,000	2,400

What are the market price and equilibrium quantity of apartments in this town? If this town imposes a rent control of $650 per month, how many studio apartments will be rented? (See pages 87–90.)

4-6. Suppose that the government places a ceiling on the price of a medical drug below the equilibrium price. (See pages 87–88.)

a. Show why there is a shortage of the medical drug at the new ceiling price.

b. Suppose that a black market for the medical drug arises, with pharmaceutical firms secretly selling the drug at higher prices. Illustrate the black market for this medical drug, including the implicit supply schedule, the ceiling price, the black market supply and demand, and the highest feasible black market price.

4-7. The table below illustrates the demand and supply schedules for seats on air flights between two cities:

Price	Quantity Demanded	Quantity Supplied
$200	2,000	1,200
$300	1,800	1,400
$400	1,600	1,600
$500	1,400	1,800
$600	1,200	2,000

What are the market price and equilibrium quantity in this market? Now suppose that federal authorities limit the number of flights between the two cities to ensure that no more than 1,200 passengers can be flown. Evaluate the effects of this quota if price adjusts. (Hint: What price per flight are the 1,200 passengers willing to pay? See page 95.)

4-8. The consequences of decriminalizing illegal drugs have long been debated. Some claim that legalization will lower the price of these drugs and reduce related crime and that more people will use these drugs. Suppose some of these drugs are legalized

so that anyone may sell them and use them. Now consider the two claims—that price will fall and quantity demanded will increase. Based on positive economic analysis, are these claims sound? (See page 95.)

4-9. In recent years, the government of Pakistan has established a support price for wheat of about $0.20 per kilogram of wheat. At this price, consumers are willing to purchase 10 billion kilograms of wheat per year, while Pakistani farmers are willing to grow and harvest 18 billion kilograms of wheat per year. The government purchases and stores all surplus wheat. (See pages 91–92.)

a. What are annual consumer expenditures on the Pakistani wheat crop?

b. What are annual government expenditures on the Pakistani wheat crop?

c. How much, in total, do Pakistani wheat farmers receive for the wheat they produce?

4-10. Consider the information in Problem 4-9 and your answers to that question. Suppose that the market clearing price of Pakistani wheat in the absence of price supports is equal to $0.10 per kilogram. At this price, the quantity of wheat demanded is 12 billion kilograms. Under the government wheat price-support program, how much more is spent each year on wheat harvested in Pakistan than otherwise would have been spent in an unregulated market for Pakistani wheat? (See pages 91–92.)

4-11. Consider the diagram below, which depicts the labor market in a city that has adopted a "living wage law" requiring employers to pay a minimum wage rate of $11 per hour. Answer the questions that follow. (See pages 93–94.)

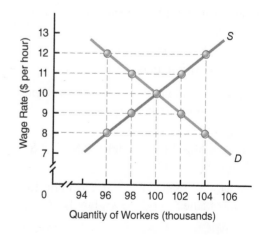

a. What condition exists in this city's labor market at the present minimum wage of $11 per hour? How many people are unemployed at this wage?

b. A city councilwoman has proposed amending the living wage law. She suggests reducing the minimum wage to $9 per hour. Assuming that the labor demand and supply curves were to remain in their present positions, how many people would be unemployed at a new $9 minimum wage?

c. A councilman has offered a counterproposal. In his view, the current minimum wage is too low and should be increased to $12 per hour. Assuming that the labor demand and supply curves remain in their present positions, how many people would be unemployed at a new $12 minimum wage?

4-12. A city has decided to impose rent controls, and it has established a rent ceiling below the previous equilibrium rental rate for offices throughout the city. How will the quantity of offices leased by building owners change? (See pages 89–90.)

4-13. In 2011, the government of a nation established a price support for wheat. The government's support price has been above the equilibrium price each year since, and the government has purchased all wheat over and above the amounts that consumers have bought at the support price. Every year since 2011, there has been an increase in the number of wheat producers in the market. No other factors affecting the market for wheat have changed. Predict what has happened every year since 2011, to each of the following (see page 91):

a. Amount of wheat supplied by wheat producers

b. Amount of wheat demanded by all wheat consumers

c. Amount of wheat purchased by the government

4-14. In advance of the recent increase in the U.S. minimum wage rate, the government of the state of Arizona decided to boost its own minimum wage by an additional $1.60 per hour. This pushed the wage rate earned by Arizona teenagers above the equilibrium wage rate in the teen labor market. What is the predicted effect of this action by Arizona's government on each of the following? (See pages 93–94.)

a. The quantity of labor supplied by Arizona teenagers

b. The quantity of labor demanded by employers of Arizona teenagers

c. The number of unemployed Arizona teenagers

REFERENCES

EXAMPLE: Linking Patients to Therapists with Short Video Clips

"The First Online Directory of Therapists," Therapick, 2014. (www.Therapick.com)

Pete Holley, "New Website Helps Patients Connect with Therapists," *Houston Chronicle*, July 19, 2013.

Caroline Winter, "Is Your Shrink on Vacation? Try Online Therapy" *Bloomberg Businessweek*, January 2, 2014.

POLICY EXAMPLE: What Accounts for Upward Pressure on Wages of Airline Pilots?

Justin Bachman, "Pilot Shortage Adds to Regional Airlines' Woes," *Bloomberg Businessweek*, March 7, 2014.

Susan Carey and Jack Nicas, "Airline-Pilot Shortage Arrives Ahead of Schedule," *The Wall Street Journal*, February 3, 2014.

Tanya Mohn, "New, Tougher Co-Pilot Rule Aims to Boost Plane Safety," *Forbes*, July 12, 2013.

INTERNATIONAL POLICY EXAMPLE: Want to See a Health Specialist in Canada? Hurry Up and Wait

"Canada Ranked Last among OECD Countries in Health Care Wait Times," CTV News, January 20, 2014.

Charlie Fidelman, "No Progress in Wait Times for Health Care in Canada," *Montreal Gazette*, June 11, 2013.

Sarah Hurtubise, "Canadians Wasted Over $1 Billion Just Waiting for Health Care," Daily Caller, March 24, 2014.

INTERNATIONAL EXAMPLE: The Global Black Market in Human Organs

Dan Bilefsky, "Black Market for Body Parts Spreads among Poor in Europe," *The New York Times*, June 28, 2013.

"Chopped Livers," *The Economist*, August 24, 2013.

Emily Thomas, "Black Market for Organs Reportedly Alive and Well on Facebook," Huffington Post, March 10, 2014.

INTERNATIONAL EXAMPLE: Why Indian Landlords are Paying Tenants Millions of Dollars to Break Leases

Rebecca Bundhun, "Mumbai's Bhendi Bazaar: A Slumdog Millionaire Overhaul," The National, September 8, 2013.

Pankaj Kapoor, "Is the Real Estate Bubble Big Enough to Naturally Burst in 2014?" *Forbes India*, January 2, 2014.

Pooja Thakur, "Mumbai's Boom Turns Renters into Millionaires," *Bloomberg Businessweek*, July 9–15, 2012.

POLICY EXAMPLE: Regulating the Raisin Reserve

"America's Raisin Regime: De miminus curat lex," *The Economist*, March 30, 2013.

"Raisin Growers File Lawsuit Against USDA, Inquisitr, January 22, 2014.

Claire Suddath, "The U.S. Government's Sweet Stash," *Bloomberg Businessweek*, July 9–15, 2013.

YOU ARE THERE: A Zero-Price Price Ceiling Comes to an End in Los Angeles

"Electric Vehicle Parking," Los Angeles World Airports, LAX, 2014. (www.lawa.org/welcome_lax.aspx?id=8705)

Antony Ingram, "LAX to Drop Free Parking for Electric Cars in March," Green Car Reports, January 7, 2013.

Hannah Karp, "It's Less Easy Being 'Green' as Los Angeles Yanks Plug on Free Parking for Electric Cars," *The Wall Street Journal*, January 4, 2013.

ISSUES & APPLICATIONS: Price Controls + Contaminated Drugs = Human Tragedy

"Current Drug Shortages Index," U.S. Food and Drug Administration, 2014. (www.fda.gov/drugs/drugsafety/drugshortages/ucm050792.htm)

Elizabeth Landau, "Fungal, Bacterial Growth Found in Steroid Injections," CNN Health, June 10, 2013.

Timothy Martin, "Dangers from Compounding Pharmacies Persist," *The Wall Street Journal*, September 9, 2013.

Consumer Surplus, Producer Surplus, and Gains from Trade within a Price System

A key principle of economics is that the price system enables people to benefit from the voluntary exchange of goods and services. Economists measure the benefits from trade by applying the concepts of *consumer surplus* and *producer surplus*, which are defined in the sections that follow.

Consumer Surplus

Let's first examine how economists measure the benefits that consumers gain from engaging in market transactions in the price system. Consider Figure B-1 below, which displays a market demand curve, D. We begin by assuming that consumers face a per-unit price of this item given by P_A. Thus, the quantity demanded of this particular product is equal to Q_A at point A on the demand curve.

Willingness to Pay

Typically, we visualize the market demand curve as indicating the quantities that all consumers are willing to purchase at each possible price. The demand curve also tells

---

FIGURE B-1

Consumer Surplus

If the per-unit price is P_A, then at point A on the demand curve D, consumers desire to purchase Q_A units. To purchase Q_1 units of this item, consumers would have been willing to pay the price P_1 for the last unit purchased, but they have to pay only the per-unit price P_A, so they gain a surplus equal to $P_1 - P_A$ for the last of the Q_1 units purchased. Likewise, to buy the last of the Q_2 units, consumers would have been willing to pay the price P_2, so they gain the surplus equal to $P_2 - P_A$ for the last of the Q_2 units purchased. Summing these and all other surpluses that consumers receive from purchasing each of the Q_A units at the price P_A yields the total consumer surplus at this price, shown by the blue-shaded area.

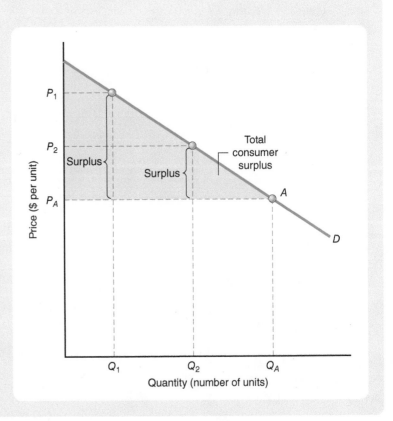

us the price that consumers are willing to pay for a unit of output at various possible quantities. For instance, if consumers buy Q_1 units of this good, they will be willing to pay a price equal to P_1 for the last unit purchased. If they have to pay only the price P_A for each unit they buy, however, consumers gain an amount equal to $P_1 - P_A$ for the last of the units Q_1 purchased. This benefit to consumers equals the vertical distance between the demand curve and the level of the market clearing price. Economists call this vertical distance a *surplus* value to consumers from being able to consume the last of the Q_1 units at the lower, market clearing price.

Likewise, if consumers purchase Q_2 units of this good, they will be willing to pay a price equal to P_2 for the last unit. Nevertheless, because they have to pay only the price P_A for each unit purchased, consumers gain an amount equal to $P_2 - P_A$. Hence, this is the surplus associated with the last of the Q_2 units that consumers buy.

MyEconLab Concept Check

Graphing Consumer Surplus

Of course, when consumers pay the same per-unit price P_A for every unit of this product that they purchase at point A, they obtain Q_A units. Thus, consumers gain surplus values—all of the vertical distances between the demand curve and the level of the market clearing price—for each unit consumed, up to the total of Q_A units. Graphically, this is equivalent to the blue-shaded *area under the demand curve but above the market clearing price* in Figure B-1 on the previous page. This entire area equals the total **consumer surplus,** which is the difference between the total amount that consumers *would have been willing to pay* for an item and the total amount that they actually pay.

MyEconLab Concept Check

Consumer surplus
The difference between the total amount that consumers would have been willing to pay for an item and the total amount that they actually pay.

Producer Surplus

Consumers are not the only ones who gain from exchange. Producers (suppliers) gain as well. To consider how economists measure the benefits to producers from supplying goods and services in exchange, look at Figure B-2 on the next page, which displays a market supply curve, S. Let's begin by assuming that suppliers face a per-unit price of this item given by P_B. Thus, the quantity supplied of this particular product is equal to Q_B at point B on the supply curve.

Willingness to Sell

The market supply curve tells us the quantities that all producers are willing to sell at each possible price. At the same time, the supply curve also indicates the price that producers are willing to accept to sell a unit of output at various possible quantities. For example, if producers sell Q_3 units of this good, they will be willing to accept a price equal to P_3 for the last unit sold. If they receive the price P_B for each unit they supply, however, producers gain an amount equal to $P_B - P_3$ for the last of the Q_3 units sold. This benefit to producers equals the vertical distance between the supply curve and the market clearing price, which is a *surplus* value from being able to provide the last of the Q_3 units at the higher, market clearing price.

Similarly, if producers supply Q_4 units of this good, they will be willing to accept a price equal to P_4 for the last unit. Producers actually receive the price P_B for each unit supplied, however, so they gain an amount equal to $P_B - P_4$. Hence, this is the surplus gained from supplying the last of the Q_4 units.

MyEconLab Concept Check

Graphing Producer Surplus

Naturally, when producers receive the same per-unit price P_B for each unit supplied at point B, producers sell Q_B units. Consequently, producers gain surplus values—all of the vertical distances between the level of the market clearing price and the supply

FIGURE B-2

Producer Surplus

If the per-unit price is P_B, then at point B on the supply curve S, producers are willing to supply Q_B units. To sell Q_3 units of this item, producers would have been willing to receive the price P_3 for the last unit sold, but instead they accept the higher per-unit price P_B, so they gain a surplus equal to $P_B - P_3$ for the last of the Q_3 units sold. Similarly, producers would have been willing to accept P_4 to provide Q_4 units, so they gain the surplus equal to $P_B - P_4$ for the last of the Q_4 units sold. Summing these and all other surpluses that producers receive from supplying each of the Q_B units at the price P_B yields the total producer surplus at this price, shown by the red-shaded area.

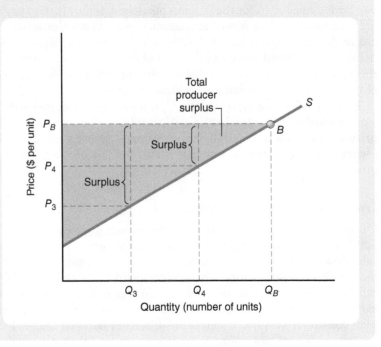

Producer surplus

The difference between the total amount that producers actually receive for an item and the total amount that they would have been willing to accept for supplying that item.

curve—for each unit supplied, up to the total of Q_B units. In Figure B-2 above, this is equivalent to the red-shaded *area above the supply curve but below the market clearing price*. This area is the total **producer surplus**, which is the difference between the total amount that producers actually receive for an item and the total amount that they *would have been willing to accept* for supplying that item. MyEconLab Concept Check

Gains from Trade within a Price System

The concepts of consumer surplus and producer surplus can be combined to measure the gains realized by consumers and producers from engaging in voluntary exchange. To see how, take a look at Figure B-3 on the next page. The market demand and supply curves intersect at point E, and as you have learned, at this point, the equilibrium quantity is Q_E. At the market clearing price P_E, this is both the quantity that consumers are willing to purchase and the quantity that producers are willing to supply.

In addition, at the market clearing price P_E and the equilibrium quantity Q_E the blue-shaded area under the demand curve but above the market clearing price is the amount of consumer surplus. Furthermore, the red-shaded area under the market clearing price but above the supply curve is the amount of producer surplus. The sum of *both* areas is the total value of the **gains from trade** —the sum of consumer surplus and producer surplus—generated by the mutually beneficial voluntary exchange of the equilibrium quantity Q_E at the market clearing price P_E.

Gains from trade

The sum of consumer surplus and producer surplus.

Consumer Surplus, Producer Surplus, and Gains from Trade

At point E, the demand and supply curves intersect at the equilibrium quantity Q_E and the market clearing price P_E. Total consumer surplus at the market clearing price is the blue-shaded area under the demand curve but above the market clearing price. Total producer surplus is the red-shaded area below the market clearing price but above the supply curve. The sum of consumer surplus and producer surplus at the market clearing price constitutes the total gain to society from voluntary exchange of the quantity Q_E at the market clearing price P_E.

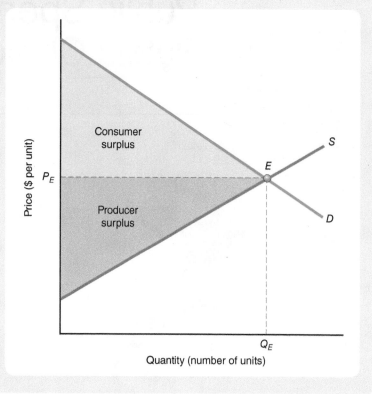

Price Controls and Gains from Trade

How do price controls affect gains from trade? Consider first the effects of imposing a ceiling price that is lower than the market clearing price. As you learned in Chapter 4, the results are an increase in quantity demanded and a decrease in quantity supplied, so a shortage occurs. The smaller quantity supplied by firms is the amount actually produced and available in the market for the item in question. Thus, consumers are able to purchase fewer units, and this means that consumer surplus may be lower than it would have been without the government's price ceiling. Furthermore, because firms sell fewer units at the lower ceiling price, producer surplus definitely decreases. Thus, the government's imposition of the price ceiling tends to reduce gains from trade.

Now consider the effects of the establishment of a price floor above the market clearing price of a good. As discussed in Chapter 4, the effects of imposing such a floor price are an increase in the quantity supplied and a decrease in the quantity demanded. The smaller quantity demanded by consumers is the amount actually traded in the market. Thus, consumers purchase fewer units of the good, resulting in a reduction in consumer surplus. In addition, firms sell fewer units, so producer surplus may decrease. Hence, the establishment of a price floor also tends to reduce gains from trade.

5

Public Spending and Public Choice

Wavebreak MediaMicro/Fotolia

LEARNING OBJECTIVES

After reading this chapter, you should be able to:

5.1 Explain how market failures such as externalities might justify economic functions of government

5.2 Distinguish between private goods and public goods and explain the nature of the free-rider problem

5.3 Describe political functions of government that entail its involvement in the economy

5.4 Analyze how public spending programs such as Medicare and spending on public education affect the consumption incentives

5.5 Discuss the central elements of the theory of public choice

MyEconLab helps you master each objective and study more efficiently. See end of chapter for details.

Each year, trustees of the Medicare program, which provides taxpayer-subsidized health care services to elderly patients and others who qualify, must issue projections about the program's financial future. These trustee projections have been released during most years since the program's 1965 date of establishment. The projections have almost always substantially underestimated Medicare's future expenses for federal taxpayers. Why are the trustees' projections of Medicare's costs consistently too low? After you have completed this chapter, you will possess sufficient understanding of the basic economics of Medicare to be able to answer this question.

the amount of time spent on the job each year by people employed by the federal government is the equivalent of about one fewer month than private employees work? Federal government employees work 4.7 fewer 40-hour workweeks than people who work for private employers. At the same time, the average federal employee earns an annual salary about 2 percent higher than a typical private worker's salary. Furthermore, the average federal employee's package of benefits—including health insurance, retirement contributions, and vacation pay—has a dollar value approximately 48 percent higher.

Many of us think of "government" as a monolithic institution. Nevertheless, governmental decision making involves choices made by people who occupy roles as politicians, appointed officials, and employees of government agencies. We can assume that these human beings are, like any others, motivated by self-interest. In this chapter, you will learn that a key requirement of any economic analysis of governmental behavior is to account for government's distinctive *incentive structure*—that is, its unique system of rewards and punishments. First, however, you must understand the rationales for agents of government to undertake actions that can influence others' choices.

Market Failures and Externalities

Throughout the book so far, we have alluded to the advantages of a price system. High on the list is economic efficiency.

> **5.1** Explain how market failures such as externalities might justify economic functions of government

Advantages of a Price System

In its ideal form, a price system allows all resources to move from lower-valued uses to higher-valued uses via voluntary exchange, by which mutually advantageous trades take place.

CONSUMER SOVEREIGNTY In a price system, consumers are sovereign. That is to say, they have the individual freedom to decide what they wish to purchase. Politicians and even business managers do not ultimately decide what is produced. Consumers decide. Some proponents of the price system argue that this is its most important characteristic.

BENEFITS OF COMPETITION AMONG SELLERS AND AMONG BUYERS Competition among sellers is beneficial to consumers because the availability of more than one seller protects consumers from coercion by a single seller. Likewise, competition among buyers benefits sellers because the availability of multiple potential buyers protects sellers from coercion by one consumer. MyEconLab Concept Check

Market Failures and Externalities

Sometimes the price system generates outcomes in which too few or too many resources go to specific economic activities. Such situations are **market failures**. Market failures prevent the price system from attaining economic efficiency and individual freedom. Market failures offer one of the strongest arguments in favor of certain economic functions of government, which we now examine.

In a pure market system, competition generates economic efficiency only when individuals know and must bear the true opportunity cost of their actions. In some circumstances, the price that someone actually pays for a resource, good, or service is higher or lower than the opportunity cost that all of society pays for that same resource, good, or service.

EXTERNALITIES Consider a hypothetical world in which there is no government regulation against pollution. You are living in a town that until now has had clean air. A steel mill moves into town. It produces steel and has paid for the inputs—land, labor, capital, and entrepreneurship. The price the mill charges for the steel reflects, in this example, only the costs that it incurs. In the course of production, however, the mill

Market failure
A situation in which the market economy leads to too few or too many resources going to a specific economic activity.

utilizes one input—clean air—by simply using it. This is indeed an input because in making steel, the furnaces emit smoke. The steel mill doesn't have to pay the cost of dirtying the air. Rather, the people in the community incur that cost in the form of dirtier clothes, dirtier cars and houses, and more respiratory illnesses.

The effect is similar to what would happen if the steel mill could take coal or oil or workers' services without paying for them. There is an **externality**, an external cost. Some of the costs associated with the production of the steel have "spilled over" to affect **third parties**, parties other than the buyer and the seller of the steel.

A fundamental reason that air pollution creates external costs is that the air belongs to everyone and hence to no one in particular. Lack of clearly assigned **property rights**, or the rights of an owner to use and exchange property, prevents market prices from reflecting all the costs created by activities that generate spillovers onto third parties.

EXTERNAL COSTS IN GRAPHICAL FORM To consider how market prices fail to take into account external costs in situations in which third-party spillovers exist without a clear assignment of property rights, look at panel (a) in Figure 5-1 below. Here we show the demand curve for steel as D. The supply curve is S_1. The supply curve includes only the costs that the firms in the market have to pay. Equilibrium occurs at point E, with a price of $800 per ton and a quantity equal to 110 million tons per year.

Producing steel, however, also involves externalities—the external costs that people who reside near steel mills pay in the form of dirtier clothes, cars, and houses and increased respiratory disease due to the air pollution emitted from the mills. In this case, the producers of steel use clean air without having to pay for it. Let's include these external costs in our graph to find out what the full cost of steel production would

Externality
A consequence of an economic activity that spills over to affect third parties. Pollution is an externality.

Third parties
Parties who are not directly involved in a given activity or transaction.

Property rights
The rights of an owner to use and to exchange property.

MyEconLab Animation

FIGURE 5-1

External Costs and Benefits

In panel (a) production of steel generates external costs. If steel producers ignore pollution, the equilibrium quantity of steel will be 110 million tons. If producers had to pay external costs, the supply curve would shift the vertical distance $A–E_1$, to S_2. If consumers of steel were forced to pay a price that reflected the spillover costs, the quantity demanded would fall to 100 million tons. In panel (b), inoculations against communicable diseases generate external benefits to those individuals who may not be inoculated but who will benefit because epidemics will not occur. If each individual ignores the external benefit of inoculations, the market clearing quantity will be 150 million. If buyers of inoculations took external benefits into account, however, the demand curve would shift to D_2, the new equilibrium quantity would be 200 million, and the equilibrium price of an inoculation would rise from $10 to $15.

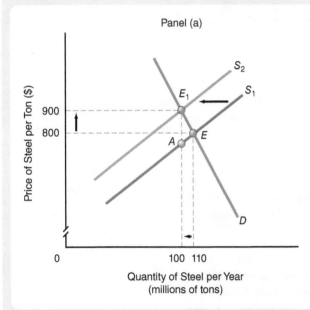

Panel (a)

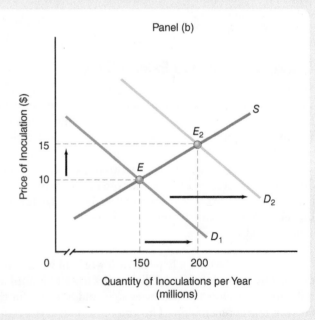

Panel (b)

really be if property rights to the air around the steel mill could generate payments for "owners" of that air. We do this by imagining that steel producers have to pay the "owners" of the air for the input—clean air—that the producers previously used at a zero price.

Recall from Chapter 3 that an increase in input prices shifts the supply curve upward and to the left. Thus, in panel (a) of the figure, the supply curve shifts from S_1 to S_2. External costs equal the vertical distance between A and E_1. In this example, if steel firms had to take into account these external costs, the equilibrium quantity would fall to 100 million tons per year, and the price would rise to $900 per ton. Equilibrium would shift from E to E_1. In contrast, if the price of steel does not account for external costs, third parties bear those costs—represented by the distance between A and E_1— in the form of dirtier clothes, houses, and cars and increased respiratory illnesses.

EXTERNAL BENEFITS IN GRAPHICAL FORM Externalities can also be positive. To demonstrate external benefits in graphical form, we will use the example of inoculations against communicable disease. In panel (b) of Figure 5-1 on the previous page, we show the demand curve as D_1 (without taking account of any external benefits) and the supply curve as S. The equilibrium price is $10 per inoculation, and the equilibrium quantity is 150 million inoculations.

We assume, however, that inoculations against communicable diseases generate external benefits to individuals who may not be inoculated but will benefit nevertheless because epidemics will not break out. If such external benefits were taken into account by those who purchase inoculations, the demand curve would shift from D_1 to D_2.

As a consequence of this shift in demand at point E_2, the new equilibrium quantity would be 200 million inoculations, and the new equilibrium price would be $15 per inoculation. If people who consider getting inoculations fail to take external benefits into account, individuals in society are not devoting enough resources to inoculations against communicable diseases.

RESOURCE MISALLOCATIONS OF EXTERNALITIES When there are external costs, the market will tend to *overallocate* resources to the production of the good or service in question, for those goods or services are implicitly priced deceptively low. In the steel example, too many resources will be allocated to steel production, because the steel mill owners and managers are not required to take account of the external cost that steel production is imposing on other individuals. In essence, the full cost of production is not borne by the owners and managers, so the price they charge the public for steel is lower than it would otherwise be. Of course, the lower price means that buyers are willing and able to buy more. More steel is produced and consumed than if the sellers and buyers were to bear external costs.

In contrast, when there are external benefits, the price is too low to induce suppliers to allocate resources to the production of that good or service (because the demand, which fails to reflect the external benefits, is relatively too low). Thus, the market *underallocates* resources to producing the good or service. Hence, in a market system, too many of the goods that generate external costs are produced, and too few of the goods that generate external benefits are produced.   MyEconLab Concept Check

How the Government Can Correct Negative Externalities

In theory, the government can take action to try to correct situations in which a lack of property rights allows third-party spillovers to create an externality. In the case of negative externalities, at least two avenues are open to the government: special taxes and legislative regulation or prohibition.

SPECIAL TAXES In our example of the steel mill, the externality problem arises because using the air for waste disposal is costless to the firm but not to society. The government could attempt to tax the steel mill commensurate with the cost to third parties from smoke in the air. This, in effect, would be a pollution tax or an **effluent fee**. The

Effluent fee
A charge to a polluter that gives the right to discharge into the air or water a certain amount of pollution; also called a *pollution tax*.

ultimate effect would be to reduce the supply of steel and raise the price to consumers, ideally making the price equal to the full cost of production to society.

Why is the government of China's capital city imposing a special fee on owners of cars and trucks?

INTERNATIONAL POLICY EXAMPLE

Beijing Battles Pollution with a Car Congestion Fee

In the city of Beijing, China, the concentration of dangerous airborne pollution particles has climbed as high as 900 micrograms per cubic meter of air, or 36 times greater than the World Health Organization's recommended maximum. Among the sources of particulate air pollution are emissions from a number of coal-fueled power plants and several oil refineries. Another key source is the exhaust pipes of more than 5.3 million gasoline-powered vehicles, which together account for about a third of the particulate pollutants in Beijing's atmosphere.

In an effort to reduce the vehicles' contribution to the city's pollution problem, the Beijing government is in the process of implementing a "car congestion fee." This fee effectively constitutes a charge that each vehicle owner pays for the right to discharge particulates into the air—that is, an effluent fee. The intent of the fee is to raise the price of auto utilization for consumers and thereby push this price closer to the full cost—including the external cost added by air-pollution spillovers—to society.

FOR CRITICAL THINKING

Why do you suppose that Beijing's government also has banned private cars and trucks from the city's roadways one day each week based on the last digits on the vehicles' license plates?

Sources are listed at the end of this chapter.

REGULATION Alternatively, to correct a negative externality arising from steel production, the government could specify a maximum allowable rate of pollution. This regulation would require that the steel mill install pollution abatement equipment at its facilities, reduce its rate of output, or some combination of the two. Note that the government's job would not be simple, for it would have to determine the appropriate level of pollution, which would require extensive knowledge of both the benefits and the cots of pollution control. MyEconLab Concept Check

How the Government Can Correct Positive Externalities

What can the government do when the production of one good spills *benefits* over to third parties? It has several policy options: financing the production of the good or producing the good itself, subsidies (negative taxes), and regulation.

GOVERNMENT FINANCING AND PRODUCTION If the positive externalities seem extremely large, the government has the option of financing the desired additional production facilities so that the "right" amount of the good will be produced. Again consider inoculations against communicable diseases. The government could—and often does—finance campaigns to inoculate the population. It could (and does) even produce and operate inoculation centers where inoculations are given at no charge.

REGULATION In some cases involving positive externalities, the government can require by law that individuals in the society undertake a certain action. For example, regulations require that all school-age children be inoculated before entering public and private schools. Some people believe that a basic school education itself generates positive externalities. Perhaps as a result of this belief, we have regulations—laws—that require all school-age children to be enrolled in a public or private school.

SUBSIDIES A subsidy is a negative tax. A subsidy is a per-unit payment made either to a business or to a consumer when the business produces or the consumer buys a good or a service. To generate more inoculations against communicable diseases, the government could subsidize everyone who obtains an inoculation by directly reimbursing those inoculated or by making per-unit payments to private firms that provide inoculations. Subsidies reduce the net price to consumers, thereby causing a larger quantity to be demanded.

Why might government subsidies fund construction of expensive bus shelters?

POLICY EXAMPLE

High Perceived Social Benefits Implied by Bus Shelter Subsidies

Grants Pass, Oregon, a town with just over 33,000 residents, has provided subsidies to finance construction of several new bus shelters. Each shelter has a single metal bench divided into three distinct seats by up-raised metal bars but no back support. In addition, each shelter has two posts supporting a roof to protect waiting bus passengers from rain. Otherwise, there are neither walls nor glass partitions to protect riders from wind. Each shelter is decorated with artwork intended to visually entice potential bus riders, however. The per-shelter subsidy amount is $65,000, or roughly the cost of building a small one- or two-bedroom house in Grants Pass.

The city government's aim in subsidizing these new shelters is to induce more people to ride buses around town. Getting numerous people into buses instead of individual vehicles, government officials have reasoned, will reduce traffic congestion. Reducing congestion on the roads, they believe, will yield a significant social benefit by enabling businesses to transport products more speedily—an external benefit that people adding to traffic with their private vehicles fail to take into account.

FOR CRITICAL THINKING

Why might it be that assigning a dollar value to the social benefits yielded by subsidies can sometimes be a difficult task?

Sources are listed at the end of this chapter.

MyEconLab Concept Check
MyEconLab Study Plan

SELF CHECK   Visit MyEconLab to practice these and other problems and to get instant feedback in your Study Plan.

External _____ lead to an overallocation of resources to the specific economic activity. Two possible ways of correcting these spillovers are _____ and _____.

External _____ result in an underallocation of resources to the specific activity. Three possible government corrections are _____ the production of the activity, _____ private firms or consumers to engage in the activity, and _____.

The Other Economic Functions of Government

5.2 Distinguish between private goods and public goods and explain the nature of the free-rider problem

Besides correcting for externalities, the government performs many other economic functions that affect the way exchange is carried out. In contrast, the political functions of government have to do with deciding how income should be redistributed among households and selecting which goods and services have special merits and should therefore be treated differently. The economic and political functions of government can and do overlap.

Let's look at four more economic functions of government.

Providing a Legal System

The courts and the police may not at first seem like economic functions of government. Their activities nonetheless have important consequences for economic activities in any country. You and I enter into contracts constantly, whether they be oral or written, expressed or implied. When we believe that we have been wronged, we seek redress of our grievances through our legal institutions. Moreover, consider the legal system that is necessary for the smooth functioning of our economic system. Our system has defined quite explicitly the legal status of businesses, the rights of private ownership, and a method of enforcing contracts. All relationships among consumers and businesses are governed by the legal rules of the game.

In its judicial function, then, the government serves as the referee for settling disputes in the economic arena. In this role, the government often imposes penalties for violations of legal rules.

Much of our legal system is involved with defining and protecting property rights. One might say that property rights are really the rules of our economic game. When property rights are well defined, meaning that the government enforces those rights and allows their transferral, the owners of property have an incentive to use that property efficiently. Any mistakes in their decisions about the use of property have negative consequences that the owners suffer. Furthermore, when property rights are well defined, owners of property have an incentive to maintain that property so that if they ever desire to sell it, it will fetch a better price.

What happens when the government fails to establish clear rights to private property and fails to enforce owners' rights fully? In such situations, at least some individuals and firms will create spillover effects for other individuals. Thus, externalities will result. In such cases, however, these externalities result from ambiguously assigned and weakly enforced property rights. The government, rather than the market, is at fault. MyEconLab Concept Check

Promoting Competition

Many economists argue that the only way to attain economic efficiency is through competition. One of the roles of government is to serve as the protector of a competitive economic system. Congress and the various state governments have passed **antitrust legislation**. Such legislation makes illegal certain (but not all) economic activities that might restrain trade—that is, that might prevent free competition among actual and potential rival firms in the marketplace. The avowed aim of antitrust legislation is to reduce the power of **monopolies**—firms that can determine the market price of the goods they sell. A large number of antitrust laws have been passed that prohibit specific anticompetitive actions. Both the Antitrust Division of the U.S. Department of Justice and the Federal Trade Commission attempt to enforce these antitrust laws. Various state judicial agencies also expend efforts at maintaining competition. MyEconLab Concept Check

Providing Public Goods

The goods used in our examples up to this point have been **private goods**. When I eat a cheeseburger, you cannot eat the same one. So you and I are rivals for that cheeseburger, just as much as contenders for the title of world champion are. When I use the services of an auto mechanic, that person cannot work at the same time for you. That is the distinguishing feature of private goods—their use is exclusive to the people who purchase them.

PRIVATE GOODS AND RIVAL CONSUMPTION The **principle of rival consumption** applies to most private goods. Rival consumption is easy to understand. Either you use such a private good or I use it.

Of course, private firms provide some goods and services that are not fully subject to the principle of rival consumption. For instance, you and a friend can both purchase tickets providing the two of you with the right to sit in a musical facility and listen to a concert during a specified period of time. Your friend's presence does not prohibit you from enjoying the music, nor does your presence prevent him from appreciating the concert. Nevertheless, the owner of the musical facility can prevent others who have not purchased tickets from entering the facility during the concert. Consequently, as long as nonpayers can be excluded from consuming an item, that item can also be produced and sold as a private good.

PUBLIC GOODS There is an entire class of goods that are not private goods. These are called **public goods**. Like musical concerts, public goods are items to which the principle of rival consumption does not apply. Hence, many individuals simultaneously can consume public goods *jointly*. What truly distinguishes public goods from all

Antitrust legislation
Laws that restrict the formation of monopolies and regulate certain anticompetitive business practices.

Monopoly
A firm that can determine the market price of a good. In the extreme case, a monopoly is the only seller of a good or service.

Private goods
Goods that can be consumed by only one individual at a time. Private goods are subject to the principle of rival consumption.

Principle of rival consumption
The recognition that individuals are rivals in consuming private goods because one person's consumption reduces the amount available for others to consume.

Public goods
Goods for which the principle of rival consumption does not apply and for which exclusion of nonpaying consumers is too costly to be feasible. They can be jointly consumed by many individuals simultaneously at no additional cost and with no reduction in quality or quantity. Furthermore, no one who fails to help pay for the good can be denied the benefit of the good.

private goods is that the costs required to exclude nonpayers from consuming public goods are so high that doing so is infeasible. National defense and police protection are examples. Suppose that your next-door neighbor were to pay for protection from a terrorist effort to explode a large bomb. If so, your neighbor's life and property could not be defended from such a threat without your life and property also receiving the same defense, even if you had failed to provide any payment for protection. Finding a way to avoid protecting you while still protecting your neighbor would be so expensive that such exclusion of defense for you and your property would be difficult.

CHARACTERISTICS OF PUBLIC GOODS The combination of two fundamental characteristics of public goods sets them apart from all other goods:

1. *Public goods can be used by more and more people at no additional opportunity cost and without depriving others of any of the services of the goods.* Once funds have been spent on national defense, the defense protection you receive does not reduce the amount of protection bestowed on anyone else. The opportunity cost of your receiving national defense once it is in place is zero because once national defense is in place to protect you, it also protects others.

2. *It is difficult to design a collection system for a public good on the basis of how much individuals use it.* Nonpayers can often utilize a public good without incurring any monetary cost, because the cost of excluding them from using the good is so high. Those who provide the public good find that it is not cost-effective to prevent nonpayers from utilizing it. For instance, taxpayers who pay to provide national defense typically do not incur the costs that would be entailed in excluding nonpayers from benefiting from national defense.

The fundamental problem of public goods is that the private sector has a difficult, if not impossible, time providing them. Individuals in the private sector have little or no incentive to offer public goods. It is difficult for them to make a profit doing so, because it is too costly and, hence, infeasible to exclude nonpayers. Consequently, true public goods must necessarily be provided by government. (Note, though, that economists do not categorize something as a public good simply because the government provides it.)

In the past, governments have purchased spacecraft and coordinated space flights, so why are private firms now planning to launch humans to locations far from the earth?

EXAMPLE

Will Private Rockets Blaze a Trail to an Asteroid Mining Rush?

On May 24, 2012, a company called Space Exploration Technologies made history by becoming the first private firm to dock a spacecraft with an orbital space station. In the process, it also contributed to growing interest in the idea of seeking out valuable minerals beyond the earth—in our solar system's asteroid belt.

Half a century ago, the science fiction author Robert Heinlein wrote novels portraying individuals and families flying spacecraft to asteroids in pursuit of profits from mining operations. Today, a company called Planetary Resources, Inc., is developing spacecraft-engineering plans for extracting nickel, iron, and other metal ores from asteroids. One possible approach would be to fly a spacecraft to a location in the asteroid belt populated with several asteroids containing both minerals to be mined and water for use by the firm's astronaut-miner employees. Another possibility would be for astronauts to utilize a spacecraft to nudge a large asteroid rich in minerals to a position closer to earth's orbit. This approach would enable miners to commute between the earth and the "parked" asteroid via shorter space-shuttle trips. Naturally, Planetary Resources intends to choose the approach that it determines is most likely to yield the largest stream of profits to the firm.

FOR CRITICAL THINKING
Do asteroid-mining activities possess the characteristics of public or private goods?

Sources are listed at the end of this chapter.

Free-rider problem
A problem that arises when individuals presume that others will pay for public goods so that, individually, they can escape paying for their portion without causing a reduction in production.

FREE RIDERS The nature of public goods leads to the **free-rider problem**, a situation in which some individuals take advantage of the fact that others will assume the burden of paying for public goods such as national defense. Suppose that citizens were taxed directly in proportion to how much they tell an interviewer that they value national defense. Some people who actually value national defense will probably tell interviewers that it has no value to them—they don't want any of it. Such people are trying to be free riders. We may all want to be free riders if we believe that someone else will provide the commodity in question that we actually value.

The free-rider problem often arises in connection with sharing the burden of international defense. A country may choose to belong to a multilateral defense organization, such as the North Atlantic Treaty Organization (NATO), but then consistently attempt to avoid contributing funds to the organization. The nation knows it would be defended by others in NATO if it were attacked but would rather not pay for such defense. In short, it seeks a free ride. MyEconLab Concept Check

Ensuring Economywide Stability

Our economy sometimes faces the problems of undesired unemployment and rising prices. The government, especially the federal government, has made an attempt to solve these problems by trying to stabilize the economy by smoothing out the ups and downs in overall business activity. The notion that the federal government should undertake actions to stabilize business activity is a relatively new idea in the United States, encouraged by high unemployment rates during the Great Depression of the 1930s and subsequent theories about possible ways that government could reduce unemployment. In 1946, Congress passed the Full-Employment Act, a landmark law concerning government responsibility for economic performance. It established three goals for government stabilization policy: full employment, price stability, and economic growth. These goals have provided the justification for many government economic programs during the post–World War II period. MyEconLab Concept Check
MyEconLab Study Plan

SELF CHECK Visit MyEconLab to practice these and other problems and to get instant feedback in your Study Plan.

The economic activities of government include (1) correcting for _____, (2) providing a _____ _____, (3) promoting _____, (4) producing _____ goods, and (5) ensuring _____ _____.

The principle of _____ _____ does not apply to public goods as it does to private goods.

Public goods have two characteristics: (1) Once they are produced, there is no additional _____ _____ when additional consumers use them, because your use of a public good does not deprive others of its simultaneous use; and (2) consumers cannot conveniently be _____ on the basis of use.

5.3 Describe political functions of government that entail its involvement in the economy

The Political Functions of Government

At least two functions of government are political or normative functions rather than economic ones like those discussed in the first part of this chapter. These two areas are (1) the provision and regulation of government-sponsored and government-inhibited goods and (2) income redistribution.

Government-Sponsored and Government-Inhibited Goods

Government-sponsored good
A good that has been deemed socially desirable through the political process. Museums are an example.

Through political processes, governments often determine that certain goods possess special merit and seek to promote their production and consumption. A **government-sponsored good** is defined as any good that the political process has deemed worthy of public support. Examples of government-sponsored goods in our society are sports stadiums, museums, ballets, plays, and concerts. In these areas, the government's role is the provision of these goods to the people in society who would not otherwise purchase them at market clearing prices or who would not purchase an amount of them judged to be sufficient. This provision may take the form of government production and distribution of the goods. It can also take the form of reimbursement for spending on government-sponsored goods or subsidies to producers or consumers for part of the goods' costs.

Governments do indeed subsidize such goods as professional sports, concerts, ballets, museums, and plays. In most cases, those goods would not be so numerous without subsidization.

WHAT IF...

the government provides subsidized student loans with repayments varying with recipients' wage rates?

Implementation of this idea, which some government officials recently have proposed for consideration, would alter the incentives of both prospective and actual borrowers of student loans. Students who enroll in programs providing degrees in fields that might help them land only the lowest-paying jobs would be more likely to take out student loans. They probably also would choose to borrow more, because they would not have to repay as much on their loans following gradua-

tion. Furthermore, even students who had borrowed to fund studies they hoped would lead to high-paying jobs would have an incentive to take lower-paying positions initially to reduce their required loan repayments. In the end, adoption of such a government student-loan policy could boost the number of borrowers and the amounts borrowed and almost certainly would lower the total volume of student loan repayments.

Government-inhibited goods are the opposite of government-sponsored goods. They are goods that, through the political process, have been deemed undesirable for human consumption. Heroin, cigarettes, gambling, and cocaine are examples. The government exercises its role with respect to these goods by taxing, regulating, or prohibiting their manufacture, sale, and use. Governments justify the relatively high taxes on alcohol and tobacco by declaring that they are socially undesirable. The best-known example of governmental exercise of power in this area is the stance against certain psychoactive drugs. Most psychoactives (except nicotine, caffeine, and alcohol) are either expressly prohibited, as is the case for heroin, cocaine, and opium, or heavily regulated, as in the case of prescription psychoactives. MyEconLab Concept Check

Government-inhibited good
A good that has been deemed socially undesirable through the political process. Heroin is an example.

Income Redistribution

Another relatively recent political function of government has been the explicit redistribution of income. This redistribution uses two systems: the progressive income tax (described in Chapter 6) and transfer payments. **Transfer payments** are payments made to individuals for which no services or goods are rendered in return. The two primary money transfer payments in our system are Social Security old-age and disability benefits and unemployment insurance benefits. Income redistribution also includes a large amount of income **transfers in kind**, rather than money transfers. Some income transfers in kind are food stamps, Medicare and Medicaid, government health care services, and subsidized public housing.

The government has also engaged in other activities as a form of redistribution of income. For example, the provision of public education is at least in part an attempt to redistribute income by making sure that the poor have access to education.

MyEconLab Concept Check
MyEconLab Study Plan

Transfer payments
Money payments made by governments to individuals for which no services or goods are rendered in return. Examples are Social Security old-age and disability benefits and unemployment insurance benefits.

Transfers in kind
Payments that are in the form of actual goods and services, such as food stamps, subsidized public housing, and medical care, and for which no goods or services are rendered in return.

SELF CHECK Visit MyEconLab to practice these and other problems and to get instant feedback in your Study Plan.

One set of political, or normative, activities of the government includes the provision and regulation of _____-_____ goods and _____-_____ goods.

Another key political function of government entails formulation of policies that bring about _____ redistribution.

5.4 Analyze how public spending programs such as Medicare and spending on public education affect the consumption incentives

Public Spending and Transfer Programs

The size of the public sector can be measured in many different ways. One way is to count the number of public employees. Another is to look at total government outlays. Government outlays include all government expenditures on employees, rent, electricity, and the like. In addition, total government outlays include transfer payments, such as welfare and Social Security.

What accounts for significant growth of the Social Security disability program?

POLICY EXAMPLE

Is the Social Security Disability Program Going Broke?

Since 1990, the number of people working has increased by just over 21 percent. During the same period, however, the number of people receiving Social Security disability payments who had previously been gainfully employed has risen by about 200 percent.

There is no evidence that proportionately more people are really experiencing long-term illnesses or injuries qualifying them for the Social Security disability program. Many low-income people who had qualified for other government transfer programs prior to the early 1990s gradually lost their eligibility for such assistance under tightened rules. During the years that followed, a nearly equivalent number of low-income people applied for and gained approval to receive Social Security disability payments. This shift of low-income people from other income-transfer programs to

the Social Security disability program accounted for more than half of the 200 percent growth of the disability rolls. Most studies indicate that the remainder of the program's growth not related to a higher population of workers has resulted from a tendency for officials to approve applications for assistance that would have been rejected in prior years.

FOR CRITICAL THINKING

Why do you suppose the government projects that employer and worker contributions will be insufficient to cover Social Security disability payments by no later than the beginning of 2017?

Sources are listed at the end of this chapter.

In Figure 5-2 below, you see that government outlays prior to World War I did not exceed 10 percent of annual national income. There was a spike during World War I, an increase during the Great Depression, and then a huge spike during World War II.

MyEconLab Animation

FIGURE 5-2

Total Government Outlays over Time

Total government outlays (federal, state, and local combined) remained small until the 1930s, except during World War I. After World War II, government outlays did not fall back to their historical average and quite recently have risen back close to their World War II levels.

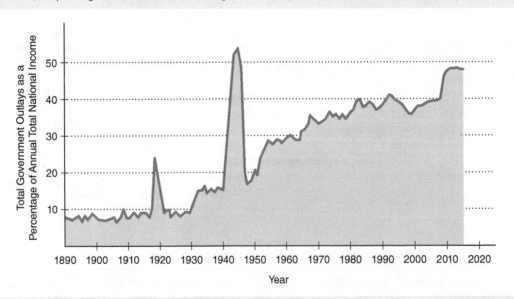

Sources: Facts and Figures on Government Finance, various issues; Economic Indicators, various issues.

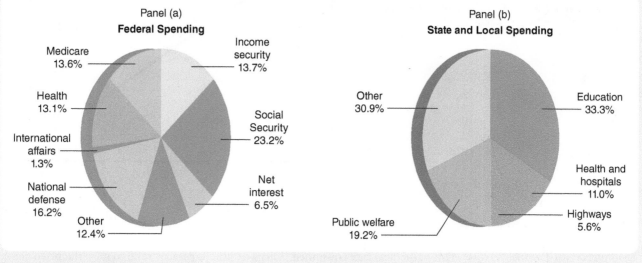

FIGURE 5-3

Federal Government Spending Compared to State and Local Spending

The federal government's spending habits are quite different from those of the states and cities. In panel (a), you can see that the most important categories in the federal budget are Medicare and other health-related spending, Social Security and other income-security programs, and national defense, which make up 79.7 percent. In panel (b), the most important category at the state and local level is education, which makes up 34.3 percent. "Other" includes expenditures in such areas as waste treatment, garbage collection, mosquito abatement, and the judicial system.

Panel (a)
Federal Spending

Medicare 13.6%
Income security 13.7%
Health 13.1%
Social Security 23.2%
International affairs 1.3%
Net interest 6.5%
National defense 16.2%
Other 12.4%

Panel (b)
State and Local Spending

Other 30.9%
Education 33.3%
Health and hospitals 11.0%
Highways 5.6%
Public welfare 19.2%

Sources: Economic Report of the President, Economic Indicators.

After World War II, government outlays as a percentage of total national income rose steadily before dropping in the 1990s, rising again in the early 2000s, and then jumping sharply beginning in 2008.

How do federal and state governments allocate their spending? A typical federal government budget is shown in panel (a) of Figure 5-3 above. The three largest categories are Medicare and other health-related spending, Social Security and other income-security programs, and national defense, which together constitute 79.8 percent of the total federal budget.

The makeup of state and local expenditures is quite different. As panel (b) shows, education is the biggest category, accounting for 33.3 percent of all expenditures.

Publicly Subsidized Health Care: Medicare

Figure 5-3 above shows that health-related spending is a significant portion of total government expenditures. Certainly, medical expenses are a major concern for many elderly people. Since 1965, that concern has been reflected in the existence of the Medicare program, which pays hospital and physicians' bills for U.S. residents over the age of 65 (and for those younger than 65 in some instances). In return for paying a tax on their earnings while in the workforce (2.9 percent of wages and salaries, plus 3.8 percent on certain income for high-income households), retirees are assured that the majority of their hospital and physicians' bills will be paid for with public monies.

THE SIMPLE ECONOMICS OF MEDICARE To understand how, in fewer than 50 years, Medicare became the second-biggest domestic government spending program in existence, a bit of economics is in order. Consider Figure 5-4 on the next page, which shows the demand for and supply of medical care.

The initial equilibrium price is P_0 and equilibrium quantity is Q_0. Perhaps because the government believes that Q_0 is not enough medical care for these consumers, suppose that the government begins paying a subsidy that eventually is set at M for each

FIGURE 5-4

The Economic Effects of Medicare Subsidies

When the government pays a per-unit subsidy M for medical care, consumers pay the price of services P_d for the quantity of services Q_m. Providers receive the price P_s for supplying this quantity. Originally, the federal government projected that its total spending on Medicare would equal an amount such as the area $Q_0 \times (P_0 - P_d)$. Because actual consumption equals Q_m, however, the government's total expenditures equal $Q_m \times M$.

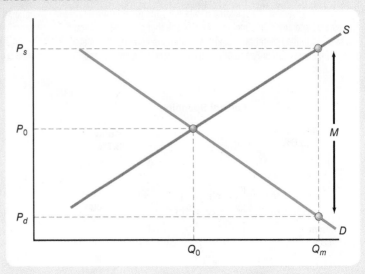

unit of medical care consumed. This will simultaneously tend to raise the price per unit of care received by providers (physicians, hospitals, and the like) and lower the perceived price per unit that consumers see when they make decisions about how much medical care to consume. As presented in the figure, the price received by providers rises to P_s, while the price paid by consumers falls to P_d. As a result, consumers of medical care want to purchase Q_m units, and suppliers are quite happy to provide it for them.

MEDICARE INCENTIVES AT WORK We can now understand the problems that plague the Medicare system today. First, one of the things that people observed during the 20 years after the founding of Medicare was a huge upsurge in physicians' incomes and medical school applications, the spread of private for-profit hospitals, and the rapid proliferation of new medical tests and procedures. All of this was being encouraged by the rise in the price of medical services from P_0 to P_s, as shown in Figure 5-4, which encouraged entry into this market.

Second, government expenditures on Medicare have routinely turned out to be far in excess of the expenditures forecast at the time the program was put in place or was expanded. The reasons for this are easy to see. Bureaucratic planners often fail to recognize the incentive effects of government programs. On the demand side, they fail to account for the huge increase in consumption (from Q_0 to Q_m) that will result from a subsidy like Medicare. On the supply side, they fail to recognize that the larger number of services can only be extracted from suppliers at a higher price, P_s. Consequently, original projected spending on Medicare was an area like $Q_0 \times (P_0 - P_d)$, because original plans for the program only contemplated consumption of Q_0 and assumed that the subsidy would have to be only $P_0 - P_d$ per unit. In fact, consumption rises to Q_m, and the additional cost per unit of service rises to P_s, implying an increase in the per-unit subsidy to M. Hence, actual expenditures turn out to be the far larger number $Q_m \times M$. Every expansion of the program, including the 2004 broadening of Medicare to cover obesity as a new illness eligible for coverage and the extension of Medicare to cover patients' prescription drug expenses beginning in 2006, has followed the same pattern.

Third, total spending on medical services has soared, consuming far more income than initially expected. Originally, total spending on medical services was $P_0 \times Q_0$. In the presence of Medicare, spending rises to $P_s \times Q_m$.

HEALTH CARE SUBSIDIES CONTINUE TO GROW Just how fast are Medicare subsidies growing? Medicare's cost has risen from 0.7 percent of U.S. national income in 1970 to more than 3.5 percent today, which amounts to nearly $550 billion per year. Because Medicare spending is growing much faster than total employer and employee contributions, future spending guarantees far outstrip the taxes to be collected in the future to pay for the system. (The current Medicare tax rate is 2.9 percent on all wages, with 1.45 percent paid by the employee and 1.45 percent paid by the employer. For certain income earned above $200,000 for individuals and $250,000 for married couples, a 3.8 percent Medicare tax rate applies.) Today, unfunded guarantees of Medicare spending in the future are estimated at more than $25 trillion (in today's dollars).

These amounts fail to reflect the costs of another federal health program called Medicaid. The Medicaid program is structured similarly to Medicare, in that the government also pays per-unit subsidies for health care to qualifying patients. Medicaid, however, provides subsidies only to people who qualify because they have lower incomes. At present, about 50 million people, or about one out of every six U.S. residents, qualify for Medicaid coverage. Medicaid is administered by state governments, but the federal government pays about 60 percent of the program's total cost from general tax revenues. The current cost of the program is more than $400 billion per year. In recent years, inflation-adjusted Medicaid spending has grown even faster than expenditures on Medicare, rising by more than 100 percent since 2000 alone.

In legislation enacted in 2010, the U.S. Congress further expanded by more than $100 billion per year the rate of growth of government health care spending, which already has been growing at an average pace of 8 percent per year.

MyEconLab Concept Check

Economic Issues of Public Education

In the United States, government involvement in health care is a relatively recent phenomenon. In contrast, state and local governments have assumed primary responsibility for public education for many years. Currently, these governments spend more than $900 billion on education—in excess of 6 percent of total U.S. national income. State and local sales, excise, property, and income taxes finance the bulk of these expenditures. In addition, each year the federal government provides tens of billions of dollars of support for public education through grants and other transfers to state and local governments.

THE NOW-FAMILIAR ECONOMICS OF PUBLIC EDUCATION State and local governments around the United States have developed a variety of complex mechanisms for funding public education. What all public education programs have in common, however, is the provision of educational services to primary, secondary, and college students at prices well below those that would otherwise prevail in the marketplace for these services.

So how do state and local governments accomplish this? The answer is that they operate public education programs that share some of the features of government-subsidized health care programs such as Medicare. Analogously to Figure 5-4 on the previous page, public schools provide educational services at a price below the market price. They are willing and able to produce the quantity of educational services demanded at this below-market price as long as they receive a sufficiently high per-unit subsidy provided by funds obtained from taxpayers.

THE INCENTIVE PROBLEMS OF PUBLIC EDUCATION Since the 1960s, various measures of the performance of U.S. primary and secondary students have failed to increase even as public spending on education has risen. Some measures of student performance have even declined.

Many economists argue that the incentive effects that have naturally arisen with higher government subsidies for public education help to explain this lack of improvement in student performance. A higher per-pupil subsidy creates a difference between the relatively high per-unit costs of providing the number of educational services that parents and students are willing to purchase and lower valuations of those services. As a consequence, some schools have provided services, such as after-school babysitting and various social services, that have contributed relatively little to student learning.

A factor that complicates efforts to assess the effects of education subsidies is that in most locales, parents who are unhappy with the quality of services provided at the subsidized price cannot transfer their child to a different public school. Thus, the individual public schools typically face little or no competition from unsubsidized providers of educational services.

How are federal college subsidies pushing up college tuition rates?

POLICY EXAMPLE

How College Aid Makes College More Expensive

During the past several years, the federal government has increased the amounts of grants and other subsidies that it provides to colleges and enrolled students. For instance, Pell Grants originally intended to help the poorest students when first issued in 1972, now go to nearly 50 percent of all college students. The average dollar amount of these grants has increased by more than 20 percent since 2008. Total federal aid to college students, including other grants and interest subsidies on student loans, has increased by more than 200 percent in the ten-year period ending in 2015.

The provision of these federal college subsidies reduces students' net out-of-pocket tuition prices, so more students enroll in colleges. The colleges, in turn, are willing to provide educational services for larger student bodies only if they receive tuition rates that exceed the students' out-of-pocket prices by the amount of each student's federal subsidy. In this way, tuition prices in the presence of federal subsidies are pushed above the tuition rates that would have prevailed in the absence of subsidies. In the case of Pell Grants, a recent study estimated that each $100 of subsidies boosts tuition prices by amounts that range from $17 to $66. Thus, consistent with the economic analysis of subsidies, providing federal college subsidies has pushed tuition prices above the level at which they would have been in the absence of subsidies.

FOR CRITICAL THINKING

Why do you suppose that some students perceive that the value of the educational services provided by colleges is less than the tuition price the colleges receive?

Sources are listed at the end of this chapter.

MyEconLab Concept Check
MyEconLab Study Plan

SELF CHECK Visit MyEconLab to practice these and other problems and to get instant feedback in your Study Plan.

Medicare subsidizes the consumption of medical care by the elderly, thus increasing the amount of such care consumed. People tend to purchase large amounts of _____-value, _____-cost services in publicly funded health care programs such as Medicare, because they do not directly bear the full cost of their decisions.

Basic economic analysis indicates that higher subsidies for public education have widened the differential between parents' and students' relatively _____ per-unit valuations of the educational services of public schools and the _____ costs that schools incur in providing those services.

5.5 Discuss the central elements of the theory of public choice

Collective Decision Making: The Theory of Public Choice

Governments consist of individuals. No government actually thinks and acts. Instead, government actions are the result of decision making by individuals in their roles as elected representatives, appointed officials, and salaried bureaucrats. Therefore, to understand how government works, we must examine the incentives of the people in government as well as those who would like to be in government—avowed or would-be candidates for elective or appointed positions—and special-interest lobbyists attempting to get government to do something. At issue is the analysis of **collective decision making**.

Collective decision making involves the actions of voters, politicians, political parties, interest groups, and many other groups and individuals. The analysis of collective decision making is usually called the **theory of public choice**. It has been given this name because it involves hypotheses about how choices are made in the public sector, as opposed to the private sector. The foundation of public-choice theory is the assumption that individuals will act within the political process to maximize their

Collective decision making
How voters, politicians, and other interested parties act and how these actions influence nonmarket decisions.

Theory of public choice
The study of collective decision making.

individual (not collective) well-being. In that sense, the theory is similar to our analysis of the market economy, in which we also assume that individuals act as though they are motivated by self-interest.

To understand public-choice theory, it is necessary to point out other similarities between the private market sector and the public, or government, sector. Then we will look at the differences.

Similarities in Market and Public-Sector Decision Making

In addition to the assumption of self-interest as the motivating force in both sectors, there are other similarities.

OPPORTUNITY COST Everything that is spent by all levels of government plus everything that is spent by the private sector must add up to the total income available at any point in time. Hence, every government action has an opportunity cost, just as in the market sector.

COMPETITION Although we typically think of competition as a private market phenomenon, it is also present in collective action. Given the scarcity constraint government faces, bureaucrats, appointed officials, and elected representatives will always be in competition for available government funds. Furthermore, the individuals within any government agency or institution will act as individuals do in the private sector: They will try to obtain higher wages, better working conditions, and higher job-level classifications. We assume that they will compete and act in their own interest, not society's.

SIMILARITY OF INDIVIDUALS Contrary to popular belief, the types of individuals working in the private sector and working in the public sector are not inherently different. The difference, as we shall see, is that the individuals in government face a different **incentive structure** than those in the private sector. For example, the costs and benefits of being efficient or inefficient differ in the private and public sectors.

Incentive structure
The system of rewards and punishments individuals face with respect to their own actions.

One approach to predicting government bureaucratic behavior is to ask what incentives bureaucrats face. Take the U.S. Postal Service (USPS) as an example. The bureaucrats running that government corporation are human beings with IQs not dissimilar to those possessed by workers in similar positions at Google or Apple. Yet the USPS does not function like either of these companies. The difference can be explained in terms of the incentives provided for managers in the two types of institutions. When the bureaucratic managers and workers at Google make incorrect decisions, work slowly, produce shoddy programs, and are generally "inefficient," the profitability of the company declines. The owners—millions of shareholders—express their displeasure by selling some of their shares of company stock. The market value, as tracked on the stock exchange, falls. This induces owners of shares of stock to pressure managers to pursue strategies more likely to boost revenues and reduce costs.

What about the USPS? If a manager, a worker, or a bureaucrat in the USPS gives shoddy service, the organization's owners—the taxpayers—have no straightforward mechanism for expressing their dissatisfaction. Despite the postal service's status as a "government corporation," taxpayers as shareholders do not really own shares of stock in the organization that they can sell.

Thus, to understand purported inefficiency in the government bureaucracy, we need to examine incentives and institutional arrangements—not people and personalities.

MyEconLab Concept Check

Differences between Market and Collective Decision Making

There are probably more dissimilarities between the market sector and the public sector than there are similarities.

GOVERNMENT GOODS AND SERVICES AT ZERO PRICE The majority of goods that governments produce are furnished to the ultimate consumers without payment required.

Government, or political, goods
Goods (and services) provided by the public sector; they can be either private or public goods.

Government, or political, goods can be either private or public goods. The fact that they are furnished to the ultimate consumer free of charge does *not* mean that the cost to society of those goods is zero, however. It only means that the price *charged* is zero. The full opportunity cost to society is the value of the resources used in the production of goods produced and provided by the government.

For example, none of us pays directly for each unit of consumption of defense or police protection. Rather, we pay for all these items indirectly through the taxes that support our governments—federal, state, and local. This special feature of government can be looked at in a different way. There is no longer a one-to-one relationship between consumption of government-provided goods and services and payment for these items. Indeed, most taxpayers will find that their tax bill is the same whether or not they consume government-provided goods.

USE OF FORCE All governments can resort to using force in their regulation of economic affairs. For example, governments can use *expropriation*, which means that if you refuse to pay your taxes, your bank account and other assets may be seized by the Internal Revenue Service. In fact, you have no choice in the matter of paying taxes to governments. Collectively, we decide the total size of government through the political process, but individually, we cannot determine how much service we pay for during any one year.

VOTING VERSUS SPENDING In the private market sector, a dollar voting system is in effect. This dollar voting system is not equivalent to the voting system in the public sector. There are at least three differences:

1. In a political system, one person gets one vote, whereas in the market system, each dollar a person spends counts separately.

Majority rule
A collective decision-making system in which group decisions are made on the basis of more than 50 percent of the vote. In other words, whatever more than half of the electorate votes for, the entire electorate has to accept.

2. The political system is run by **majority rule**, whereas the market system is run by **proportional rule**.

3. The spending of dollars can indicate intensity of want, whereas because of the all-or-nothing nature of political voting, a vote cannot.

Proportional rule
A decision-making system in which actions are based on the proportion of the "votes" cast and are in proportion to them. In a market system, if 10 percent of the "dollar votes" are cast for blue cars, 10 percent of automobile output will be blue cars.

Political outcomes often differ from economic outcomes. Remember that economic efficiency is a situation in which, given the prevailing distribution of income, consumers obtain the economic goods they want. There is no corresponding situation when political voting determines economic outcomes. Thus, a political voting process is unlikely to lead to the same decisions that a dollar voting process would yield in the marketplace.

Indeed, consider the dilemma every voter faces. Usually, a voter is not asked to decide on a single issue (although this happens). Rather, a voter is asked to choose among candidates who present a large number of issues and state a position on each of them. Just consider the average U.S. senator, who has to vote on several thousand different issues during a six-year term. When you vote for that senator, you are voting for a person who must make thousands of decisions during the next six years.

MyEconLab Concept Check
MyEconLab Study Plan

SELF CHECK Visit MyEconLab to practice these and other problems and to get instant feedback in your Study Plan.

The theory of _____ _____ examines how voters, politicians, and other parties collectively reach decisions in the public sector of the economy.

As in private markets, _____ _____ and _____ have incentive effects that influence public-

sector decision making. In contrast to private market situations, however, there is not a one-to-one relationship between consumption of a publicly provided good and the payment for that good.

YOU ARE THERE

China Confronts Contaminated Water

Guifan Sun, a dean at the China Medical University, is deeply concerned. A study he has conducted with several other researchers has concluded that almost 20 million people in China inhabit areas with arsenic water contamination that exceeds the World Health Organization's recommended limit. Of these people, as many as 6 million may be exposed to arsenic levels more than five times this limit. For these people, Sun argues, there is "urgency" for government action to address water-contamination problems—which extend beyond arsenic to ammonia, heavy metals, and other pollutants harmful to human beings. Water pollution also is damaging people's property, including farmlands and fisheries.

Sun and his colleagues have convinced the Chinese government's Ministry of Land and Resources to conduct follow-up studies. In the meantime the nation's State Council, or ruling cabinet, is considering implementing a tougher set of antipollution measures. The initially drafted rules include financial punishments for polluters and tighter regulatory limits on pollution to be imposed on companies that create water pollution as a by-product of their production processes.

CRITICAL THINKING QUESTIONS

1. What guidance does the economic theory of the correction of externalities offer regarding the amounts of financial penalties to be imposed on polluters?

2. Why might the Chinese government experience difficulties in determining exactly the "right" amount of water pollution to permit?

Sources are listed at the end of this chapter.

ISSUES & APPLICATIONS

MyEconLab Video

Medicare's Soaring Bill for U.S. Taxpayers

WavebreakMediaMicro/Fotolia

CONCEPTS APPLIED

» Public Spending and Transfers

» Medicare

» Subsidies

One of the largest public spending and transfer programs in the United States is the Medicare program that provides government subsidies to elderly and other legally qualified recipients of assistance with health care expenses. Indeed, as the U.S. population continues to age and larger numbers of people qualify for subsidies, the amounts that current and future taxpayers can anticipate paying to fund the program continue to increase.

Overly Rosy Medicare Assumptions

In the 1960s, projections of Medicare expenses to 1990 assumed no expansion in the eligible health care expenses covered by the program. The projections also assumed an unchanged quantity of health care demanded.

Nevertheless, during subsequent years, Congress enlarged the range of health care services for which Medicare subsidies are available. Furthermore, lower out-of-pocket prices to beneficiaries actually did generate substantial increases in the amounts of services demanded. Consequently, the actual annual taxpayer bills for Medicare in the early 1990s turned out to be almost ten times higher than projected.

More Realistic Estimates of Medicare's Overall Cost

Current projections are based on overly rosy assumptions. The government continues to presume that quantities of services demanded are unresponsive to artificially low out-of-pocket prices. Furthermore, the projections assume that, as required by the Balanced Budget Act of 1997, Medicare fees paid to physicians will not grow faster than the overall U.S. economic growth rate. Under these assumptions, the overall value of the expense to current and future U.S. taxpayers of funding Medicare into the indefinite future is about $21 trillion. In fact, however, Congress has voted fourteen times to postpone implementation of this provision of the 1997 law, actions that have allowed fee reimbursements for physicians to increase by more than 30 percent.

What if the too-rosy assumptions are eliminated? If so, the overall value of all Medicare expenses into the indefinite future is between $43 trillion and $100 trillion. Thus, a more realistic range of the total estimated bill facing U.S. taxpayers is two to five times greater than yielded by official government projections.

For Critical Thinking

1. Why is it unrealistic for government projections to assume that the quantity of health care services demanded will not increase when Medicare subsidies push down the out-of-pocket prices of people eligible for the program?

2. Why do you suppose that most observers anticipate that Medicare will be insolvent—meaning that current and future tax revenues will be insufficient to fund expenses—by no later than 2026?

Web Resources

1. For information about the numerous types of health care expenses subsidized by Medicare, see the Web Links in MyEconLab.

2. To contemplate one possible approach to preventing Medicare insolvency, see the Web Links in MyEconLab.

MyEconLab

For more questions on this chapter's Issues & Applications, go to MyEconLab.

In the Study Plan for this chapter, select Section I: Issues and Applications.

Sources are listed at the end of this chapter.

Fundamental Points

1. Externalities typically arise from failures to assign clearly and enforce fully private property rights. External costs lead to an overallocation of resources to the specific economic activity, whereas external benefits result in an underallocation of resources to the specific activity.

2. Public goods have two characteristics: (1) Once the items have been produced, additional use of the items by more consumers does not deprive other consumers of their benefits; and (2) no mechanism exists for charging consumers on the basis of their use of the items.

3. Political functions of government include providing government-sponsored goods, dissuading production and consumption of government-inhibited goods, and implementing policies that redistribute incomes.

4. Public subsidies for spending programs such as Medicare and public education boost the amounts of services consumed. Consumers do not bear the full cost of purchasing these higher quantities, and the result is larger amounts of lower-value, higher-cost services.

5. The theory of public choice considers the collective decisions of voters, politicians, and others in the public sector, in which, in contrast to private market situations, there is not a one-to-one relationship between consumption of publicly provided goods and the payment for the goods.

WHAT YOU SHOULD KNOW

Here is what you should know after reading this chapter. MyEconLab will help you identify what you know, and where to go when you need to practice.

LEARNING OBJECTIVES	KEY TERMS	WHERE TO GO TO PRACTICE
5.1 **Explain how market failures such as externalities might justify economic functions of government** *A market failure occurs when too many or too few resources are directed to a specific form of economic activity. One type of market failure is an externality, which is a spillover effect on third parties not directly involved in producing or purchasing a good or service. In the case of a negative externality, firms do not pay for the costs arising from spillover effects that their production of a good imposes on others, so they produce too much of the good in question. In the case of a positive externality, buyers fail to take into account the benefits that their consumption of a good yields to others, so they purchase too little of the good.*	market failure, 107 externality, 108 third parties, 108 property rights, 108 effluent fee, 109 **Key Figure** Figure 5-1, 108	• MyEconLab Study Plan 5.1 • Animated Figure 5-1
5.2 **Distinguish between private goods and public goods and explain the nature of the free-rider problem** *Private goods are subject to the principle of rival consumption, meaning that one person's consumption of such a good reduces the amount available for another person to consume. In contrast, public goods can be consumed by many people simultaneously at no additional opportunity cost and with no reduction in quality or quantity. In addition, no individual can be excluded from the benefits of a public good even if that person fails to help pay for it.*	antitrust legislation, 112 monopoly, 112 private goods, 112 principle of rival consumption, 112 public goods, 112 free-rider problem, 114	• MyEconLab Study Plan 5.2
5.3 **Describe political functions of government that entail its involvement in the economy** *As a result of the political process, government may seek to promote the production and consumption of government-sponsored goods. The government may also seek to restrict the production and sale of goods that have been deemed socially undesirable, called government-inhibited goods. In addition, the political process may determine that income redistribution is socially desirable.*	government-sponsored good, 114 government-inhibited good, 115 transfer payments, 115 transfers in kind, 115	• MyEconLab Study Plan 5.3
5.4 **Analyze how public spending programs such as Medicare and spending on public education affect the consumption incentives** *Medicare subsidizes the consumption of medical services. As a result, the quantity consumed is higher, as is the price sellers receive per unit of those services. Subsidies for programs such as Medicare and public education also encourages people to consume services that are very low in per-unit value relative to the cost of providing them.*	**Key Figures** Figure 5-2, 116 Figure 5-4, 118	• MyEconLab Study Plan 5.4 • Animated Figures 5-2, 5-4

WHAT YOU SHOULD KNOW *continued*

LEARNING OBJECTIVES	KEY TERMS	WHERE TO GO TO PRACTICE
5.5 Discuss the central elements of the theory of public choice *The theory of public choice applies to collective decision making, or the process through which voters and politicians interact to influence nonmarket choices. Certain aspects of public-sector decision making, such as scarcity and competition, are similar to those that affect private-sector choices. Others, however, such as legal coercion and majority-rule decision making, differ from those involved in the market system.*	collective decision making, 120 theory of public choice, 120 incentive structure, 121 government, or political, goods, 122 majority rule, 122 proportional rule, 122	• MyEconLab Study Plan 5.5

Log in to MyEconLab, take a chapter test, and get a personalized Study Plan that tells you which concepts you understand and which ones you need to review. From there, MyEconLab will give you further practice, tutorials, animations, videos, and guided solutions. For more information, visit http://www.myeconlab.com

PROBLEMS

All problems are assignable in MyEconLab. Answers to odd-numbered problems appear in MyEconLab.

5-1. Many people who do not smoke cigars are bothered by the odor of cigar smoke. If private contracting is impossible, will too many or too few cigars be produced and consumed? Taking *all* costs into account, is the market price of cigars too high or too low? (See pages 108–109.)

5-2. Suppose that repeated application of a pesticide used on orange trees causes harmful contamination of groundwater. The pesticide is applied annually in almost all of the orange groves throughout the world. Most orange growers regard the pesticide as a key input in their production of oranges. (See pages 108–109.)

    a. Use a diagram of the market for the pesticide to illustrate the implications of a failure of orange producers' costs to reflect the social costs of groundwater contamination.

    b. Use your diagram from part (a) to explain a government policy that might be effective in achieving the amount of orange production that fully reflects all social costs.

5-3. Now draw a diagram of the market for oranges. Explain how the government policy you discussed in part (b) of Problem 5-2 is likely to affect the market price and equilibrium quantity in the orange market. In what sense do consumers of oranges now "pay" for dealing with the spillover costs of pesticide production? (See pages 108–109.)

5-4. Suppose the U.S. government determines that cigarette smoking creates social costs not reflected in the current market price and equilibrium quantity of cigarettes. A study has recommended that the government can correct for the externality effect of cigarette consumption by paying farmers *not* to plant tobacco used to manufacture cigarettes. It also recommends raising the funds to make these payments by increasing taxes on cigarettes. Assuming that the government is correct that cigarette smoking creates external costs, evaluate whether the study's recommended policies might help correct this negative externality. (See page 110.)

5-5. A nation's government has determined that mass transit, such as bus lines, helps alleviate traffic congestion, thereby benefiting both individual auto commuters and companies that desire to move products and factors of production speedily along streets and highways. Nevertheless, even though several private bus lines are in service, the country's commuters are failing to take into account the social benefits of the use of mass transit. (See page 110.)

    a. Discuss, in the context of demand-supply analysis, the essential implications of commuters' failure to take into account the social benefits associated with bus ridership.

b. Explain a government policy that might be effective in achieving the socially efficient use of bus services.

5-6. Draw a diagram of this nation's market for automobiles, which are a substitute for buses. Explain how the government policy you discussed in part (b) of Problem 5-5 is likely to affect the market price and equilibrium quantity in the country's auto market. How are auto consumers affected by this policy to attain the spillover benefits of bus transit? (See page 110.)

5-7. Consider a nation with a government that does not provide people with property rights for a number of items and that fails to enforce the property rights it does assign for remaining items. Would externalities be more or less common in this nation than in a country such as the United States? Explain. (See pages 111–112.)

5-8. Many economists suggest that our nation's legal system is an example of a public good. Does the legal system satisfy the key properties of a public good? Explain your reasoning. (See page 113.)

5-9. Displayed in the diagram below are conditions in the market for residential Internet access in a U.S. state. The government of this state has determined that access to the Internet improves the learning skills of children, which it has concluded is an external benefit of Internet access. The government has also concluded that if these external benefits were to be taken into account, 3 million residences would have Internet access. Suppose that the state government's judgments about the benefits of Internet access are correct and that it wishes to offer a per-unit subsidy just sufficient to increase total Internet access to 3 million residences. What per-unit subsidy should it offer? Use the diagram to explain how providing this subsidy would affect conditions in the state's market for residential Internet access. (See page 110.)

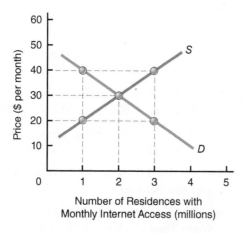

5-10. The French government recently allocated the equivalent of more than $120 million in public

funds to *Quaero* (Latin for "I search"), an Internet search engine analogous to Google or Yahoo. Does an Internet search engine satisfy the key characteristics of a public good? Why or why not? Based on your answer, is a publicly funded Internet search engine a public good or a government-sponsored good? (See pages 113–115.)

5-11. A government offers to let a number of students at public schools transfer to private schools under two conditions: It will transmit to private schools the same per-pupil subsidy it provides public schools, and the private schools will be required to admit the students at a below-market net tuition rate. Will the economic outcome be the same as the one that would have arisen if the government instead simply provided students with grants to cover the current market tuition rate at the private school? (Hint: Does it matter if schools receive payments directly from the government or from consumers? See pages 119–120.)

5-12. After a government implements a voucher program, granting funds that families can spend at schools of their choice, numerous students in public schools switch to private schools. The program's per-unit subsidy is exactly equal to the external benefit from private educational services. Is anyone likely to lose out nonetheless? If so, who? (See pages 119–120.)

5-13. Suppose that the current price of a tablet device is $300 and that people are buying 1 million drives per year. The government decides to begin subsidizing the purchase of new tablet devices. The government believes that the appropriate price is $260 per tablet, so the program offers to send people cash for the difference between $260 and whatever the people pay for each tablet they buy. (See page 117.)

a. If no consumers change their tablet-buying behavior, how much will this program cost the taxpayers?

b. Will the subsidy cause people to buy more, fewer, or the same number of tablets? Explain.

c. Suppose that people end up buying 1.5 million tablets once the program is in place. If the market price of tablets does not change, how much will this program cost the taxpayers?

d. Under the assumption that the program causes people to buy 1.5 million tablets and also causes the market price of tablets to rise to $320, how much will this program cost the taxpayers?

5-14. Scans of internal organs using magnetic resonance imaging (MRI) devices are often covered by subsidized health insurance programs such as Medicare. Consider the following table illustrating hypothetical quantities of individual MRI testing procedures demanded and supplied at various prices, and then answer the questions that follow. (See page 117.)

Price	Quantity Demanded	Quantity Supplied
$100	100,000	40,000
$300	90,000	60,000
$500	80,000	80,000
$700	70,000	100,000
$900	60,000	120,000

a. In the absence of a government-subsidized health plan, what is the equilibrium price of MRI tests? What is the amount of society's total spending on MRI tests?

b. Suppose that the government establishes a health plan guaranteeing that all qualified participants can purchase MRI tests at an effective price (that is, out-of-pocket cost) to the individual of $100 per test. How many MRI tests will people consume?

c. What is the per-unit price that induces producers to provide the number of MRI tests demanded at the government-guaranteed price of $100? What is society's total spending on MRI tests?

d. Under the government's coverage of MRI tests, what is the per-unit subsidy it provides? What is the total subsidy that the government pays to support MRI testing at its guaranteed price?

5-15. Suppose that, as part of an expansion of its State Care health system, a state government decides to offer a $50 subsidy to all people who, according to their physicians, should have their own blood pressure monitoring devices. Prior to this governmental decision, the market clearing price of blood pressure monitors in this state was $50, and the equilibrium quantity purchased was 20,000 per year. (See page 117.)

a. After the government expands its State Care plan, people in this state desire to purchase 40,000 devices each year. Manufacturers of blood pressure monitors are willing to provide 40,000 devices at a price of $60 per device. What out-of-pocket price does each consumer pay for a blood pressure monitor?

b. What is the dollar amount of the increase in total expenditures on blood pressure monitors in this state following the expansion in the State Care program?

c. Following the expansion of the State Care program, what *percentage* of total expenditures on blood pressure monitors is paid by the government? What percentage of total expenditures is paid by consumers of these devices?

5-16. A government agency is contemplating launching an effort to expand the scope of its activities. One rationale for doing so is that another government agency might make the same effort and, if successful, receive larger budget allocations in future years. Another rationale for expanding the agency's activities is that this will make the jobs of its workers more interesting, which may help the government agency attract better-qualified employees. Nevertheless, the agency will have to convince more than half of the House of Representatives and the Senate to approve a formal proposal to expand its activities. In addition, to expand its activities, the agency must have the authority to force private companies it does not currently regulate to be officially licensed by agency personnel. Identify which aspects of this problem are similar to those faced by firms that operate in private markets and which aspects are specific to the public sector. (See pages 120–122.)

REFERENCES

INTERNATIONAL POLICY EXAMPLE: Beijing Battles Pollution with a Car Congestion Fee

"Beijing Addresses Vehicle Emissions," United Press International, September 3, 2013.

"Beijing May Introduce Congestion Charge as Early as 2015," Bamboo Innovator, February 8, 2014.

Rose Yu, "Choking on Pollution, Beijing Eyes Car Congestion Fee," *The Wall Street Journal*, September 3, 2013.

POLICY EXAMPLE: High Perceived Social Benefits Implied by Bus Shelter Subsidies

John Darling, "$2 Bus Service Will Link Medford, Grants Pass," *Mail Tribune*, April 12, 2014.

"$1 Million Exposed Bus Stop Leaves Straphangers Out in the Rain," CBS News, March 28, 2013.

Joel Millman, "Six-Figure Bus Shelter Stirs Cries to Stop It," *The Wall Street Journal*, January 18, 2013.

EXAMPLE: Will Private Rockets Blaze a Trail to an Asteroid Mining Rush?

Tom McBrien, "Asteroid Mining Could Be Useful to Space Travel," *Michigan Daily*, February 11, 2014.

"Researchers Identify 12 'Easy' Candidates for Asteroid Mining," United Press International, August 13, 2013.

Mike Wall, "Private Asteroide-Mining Project Launching Tiny Satellites in 2014," Space.com, April 24, 2013. (www.space.com/20817-asteroid-mining-satellite-test-flight.html)

POLICY EXAMPLE: Is the Social Security Disability Program Going Broke?

Michael Boskin, "The 2016 Disability Insurance Time Bomb," *The Wall Street Journal*, July 13, 2013.

Chana Joffe-Walt, "Unfit for Work: The Startling Rise of Disability in America," National Public Radio, 2013. (http://apps.npr.org/unfit-for-work/)

Social Security and Medicare Boards of Trustees, "A Summary of the 2013 Annual Reports," 2014. (www.ssa.gov/oact/trsum/)

POLICY EXAMPLE: How College Aid Makes College More Expensive

Douglas Belkin, "More Students Subsidize Classmates' Tuition," *The Wall Street Journal*, January 13, 2014.

Veronique De Rugy, "Subsidized Loans Drive College Tuition, Student Debt to Record Levels," *Washington Examiner*, July 11, 2013.

Jon Marcus, "Federal Education Subsidies Benefit More Affluent Than Poor Americans," *Dallas News*, March 7, 2014.

YOU ARE THERE: China Confronts Contaminated Water

Josh Chin and Brian Speegle, "China's Bad Earth," *The Wall Street Journal*, July 27, 2013.

Josh Chin and Brian Speegle, "Nearly One-Fifth of China's Arable Land Is Contaminated," *The Wall Street Journal*, April 17, 2014.

Neil Gogh, "Pollutants from Plant Killed Fish in China," *The New York Times*, September 4, 2013.

Hamza Mohamed, "Millions Face Arsenic Contamination Risk in China, Study Finds," *The Guardian*, August 22, 2013.

ISSUES & APPLICATIONS: Medicare's Soaring Bill for U.S. Taxpayers

John Goodman and Laurence Kotlikoff, "Medicare by the Scary Numbers," *The Wall Street Journal*, June 24, 2013.

Mark Miller, "Medicare Cost Shifting: The Next Big Worry for Seniors," Reuters, February 25, 2014.

Jeanne Sahadi, "The Real Medicare Spending Problem," CNN Money, February 7, 2013.

Funding the Public Sector

Tyler Olson/Fotolia

LEARNING OBJECTIVES

After reading this chapter, you should be able to:

6.1 Distinguish between average tax rates and marginal tax rates

6.2 Explain the structure of the U.S. income tax system

6.3 Understand the key factors influencing the relationship between tax rates and the tax revenues governments collect

6.4 Explain how the taxes governments levy on purchases of goods and services affect market prices and equilibrium quantities

MyEconLab helps you master each objective and study more efficiently. See end of chapter for details.

Until recently, several dozens of people decided to renounce their U.S. citizenship each year. Some people did so for political reasons. Others did so simply because they preferred to be citizens of different countries. During the past few years, however, another reason has emerged: higher effective U.S. federal tax rates and increased costs of paying the associated taxes. A consequence of this new rationale for renouncing U.S. citizenship has been a rise in the number of people who decide not to remain citizens. The United States is now losing thousands of citizens each year—and taxes that would have been assessed on their incomes. In this chapter, you will learn why increases in effective income tax rates typically tend to depress to some extent the incomes to which those tax rates are applied.

the U.S. federal tax code—the set of rules governing all aspects of U.S. tax laws—is 3.8 million words long, or four times the length of Leo Tolstoy's epic novel *War and Peace*? The federal government collects income taxes, Social Security taxes, Medicare taxes, and so-called excise taxes. State and local governments assess sales taxes, property taxes, hotel occupancy taxes, and electricity, gasoline, water, and sewage taxes. When a person dies, the federal government and numerous state governments also collect estate taxes. Clearly, governments give considerable attention to their roles as tax collectors.

Paying for the Public Sector: Systems of Taxation

6.1 Distinguish between average tax rates and marginal tax rates

There are three sources of funding available to governments. One source is explicit fees, called *user charges*, for government services. The second and main source of government funding is taxes. Nevertheless, sometimes federal, state, and local governments spend more than they collect in taxes. To do this, they must rely on a third source of financing, which is borrowing. A government cannot borrow unlimited amounts, however. After all, a government, like an individual or a firm, can convince others to lend it funds only if it can provide evidence that it will repay its debts. A government must ultimately rely on taxation and user charges, the sources of its own current and future revenues, to repay its debts.

The Government Budget Constraint

Over the long run, therefore, taxes and user charges are any government's *fundamental* sources of revenues. The **government budget constraint** states that each dollar of public spending on goods, services, transfer payments, and repayments of borrowed funds during a given period must be provided by tax revenues and user charges collected by the government. This long-term constraint indicates that the total amount a government plans to spend and transfer today and into the future cannot exceed the total taxes and user charges that it currently earns and can reasonably anticipate collecting in future years. Taxation dwarfs user charges as a source of government resources, so let's begin by looking at taxation from a government's perspective.

How does Delaware depend on a specific type of user charge as a key source of revenues?

Government budget constraint
The limit on government spending and transfers imposed by the fact that every dollar the government spends, transfers, or uses to repay borrowed funds must ultimately be provided by the user charges and taxes it collects.

POLICY EXAMPLE

Be Sure to Claim Your Property from Delaware!

Businesses across the United States hold almost $42 billion in unclaimed properties—including empty houses with missing owners, dormant bank accounts whose owners cannot be located, uncashed checks, and unused gift-card balances. Most states have laws allowing their governments to take over such unclaimed properties after a legally specified number of years have passed and businesses have undertaken considerable efforts to locate rightful owners. Funds derived from taking control of such properties pass to the states as a type of user charge by which the states can supplement their primary revenue sources, such as taxes and other user charges.

Unlike most other states, Delaware views unclaimed property as a key source of funds, and it has acted on this perspective by seizing most unclaimed properties. During recent years, its finance department has seized more than $300 million of unclaimed properties annually and returned less than $20 million per year to rightful owners. Delaware has become so adept at locating and quickly seizing unclaimed properties that the share of its revenues derived from such seizures has risen from just over 2 percent in 1994 to about 15 percent today. Seizures of unclaimed properties now represent the state's third largest source of revenues, after individual and corporate income taxes.

FOR CRITICAL THINKING

Many states have slipped deeply into debt since 2008. How has this fact likely affected their incentives to seize unclaimed properties?

Sources are listed at the end of this chapter.

Implementing Taxation with Tax Rates

In light of the government budget constraint, a major concern of any government is how to collect taxes. Jean-Baptiste Colbert, the seventeenth-century French finance minister, said the art of taxation was in "plucking the goose so as to obtain the largest amount of feathers with the least possible amount of hissing." In the United States, governments have designed a variety of methods of plucking the private-sector goose.

THE TAX BASE AND THE TAX RATE To collect a tax, a government typically establishes a **tax base**, which is the value of goods, services, wealth, or incomes subject to taxation. Then it assesses a **tax rate**, which is the proportion of the tax base that must be paid to the government as taxes.

As we discuss shortly, for the federal government and many state governments, incomes are key tax bases. Therefore, to discuss tax rates and the structure of taxation systems in more detail, let's focus for now on income taxation.

MARGINAL AND AVERAGE TAX RATES If somebody says, "I pay 28 percent in taxes," you cannot really tell what that person means unless you know whether he or she is referring to average taxes paid or the tax rate on the last dollars earned. The latter concept refers to the **marginal tax rate**, with the word *marginal* meaning "incremental."

The marginal tax rate is expressed as follows:

$$\text{Marginal tax rate} = \frac{\text{change in taxes due}}{\text{change in taxable income}}$$

It is important to understand that the marginal tax rate applies only to the income in the highest **tax bracket** reached, with a tax bracket defined as a specified range of taxable income to which a specific and unique marginal tax rate is applied.

The marginal tax rate is not the same thing as the **average tax rate**, which is defined as follows:

$$\text{Average tax rate} = \frac{\text{total taxes due}}{\text{total taxable income}}$$

Why has the tax base of the federal government's Alternative Minimum Tax increased considerably since the late 1960s?

Tax base
The value of goods, services, wealth, or incomes subject to taxation.

Tax rate
The proportion of a tax base that must be paid to a government as taxes.

Marginal tax rate
The change in the tax payment divided by the change in income, or the percentage of *additional* dollars that must be paid in taxes. The marginal tax rate is applied to the highest tax bracket of taxable income reached.

Tax bracket
A specified interval of income to which a specific and unique marginal tax rate is applied.

Average tax rate
The total tax payment divided by total income. It is the proportion of total income paid in taxes.

EXAMPLE

The Expanding Tax Base for the Alternative Minimum Tax

In 1969, Congress established the Alternative Minimum Tax (AMT). Congress imposed the tax when U.S. Treasury officials discovered that 115 very-high-income households had invested in tax-free municipal bonds and thereby avoided paying any federal income taxes. The purpose of the AMT was to ensure that these few households did not utilize tax deductions to avoid paying at least some federal income taxes.

When Congress set up the AMT in 1969, it failed to ensure that the tax base—which it intended to be applied only to the highest incomes among U.S. households—was adjusted to take into account inflation. Since then, inflation alone has pushed up U.S. money incomes by more than 200 percent. Consequently, many households have become subject to the AMT. Today, more than 4 million households must pay the AMT.

The number of taxpayers affected by the AMT should not rise in future years, because in 2013, Congress finally adjusted the AMT tax base to inflation.

FOR CRITICAL THINKING

Currently, the federal government's AMT tax collections from the 4 million U.S. households whose incomes constitute its tax base amount to nearly $40 billion per year. Why do you suppose that Congress did not readjust the AMT tax base to encompass only 115 households, as was true in 1969?

Sources are listed at the end of this chapter.

Taxation Systems

No matter how governments raise revenues—from income taxes, sales taxes, or other taxes—all of those taxes fit into one of three types of taxation systems: proportional, progressive, or regressive, according to the relationship between the tax rate and income. To determine whether a tax system is proportional, progressive, or regressive, we simply ask, what is the relationship between the average tax rate and the marginal tax rate?

PROPORTIONAL TAXATION **Proportional taxation** means that regardless of an individual's income, taxes comprise exactly the same proportion. In a proportional taxation system, the marginal tax rate is always equal to the average tax rate. If every dollar is taxed at 20 percent, then the average tax rate is 20 percent, and so is the marginal tax rate.

Under a proportional system of taxation, taxpayers at all income levels end up paying the same *percentage* of their income in taxes. With a proportional tax rate of 20 percent, an individual with an income of $10,000 pays $2,000 in taxes, while an individual making $100,000 pays $20,000. Thus, the identical 20 percent rate is levied on both taxpayers.

Proportional taxation
A tax system in which, regardless of an individual's income, the tax bill comprises exactly the same proportion.

PROGRESSIVE TAXATION Under **progressive taxation**, as a person's taxable income increases, the percentage of income paid in taxes increases. In a progressive system, the marginal tax rate is above the average tax rate. If you are taxed 5 percent on the first $10,000 you earn, 10 percent on the next $10,000 you earn, and 30 percent on the last $10,000 you earn, you face a progressive income tax system. Your marginal tax rate is always above your average tax rate.

How much higher are average tax rates of the very-highest-income taxpayers than average tax rates of the 50 percent of taxpayers with the lowest incomes?

Progressive taxation
A tax system in which, as income increases, a higher percentage of the additional income is paid as taxes. The marginal tax rate exceeds the average tax rate as income rises.

POLICY EXAMPLE

Are U.S. Income Taxes Progressive? Ask the Top 400 Taxpayers

In recent years, the 50 percent of all U.S. taxpayers reporting the lowest annual incomes collectively earned about $1 trillion per year. This group normally pays a combined amount of individual income taxes equal to between $20 billion and $30 billion per year. Consequently, the average tax rate for these 70 million taxpayers ranges between 2 percent and 3 percent.

The 400 taxpayers who have received the highest annual taxable incomes in the United States, usually $80 billion to $85 billion as a group, have earned between 1 percent and 1.5 percent of the taxable income for U.S. individuals. The annual income tax payments of these 400 people—who together could occupy a single large apartment building—typically have been about $16 billion. Hence, the average tax rate for these 400

taxpayers ranges between 18 percent and 20 percent, which implies that their average tax rates are six to ten times higher than those of the 70 million people with lowest incomes. This fact implies that the 400 top taxpayers face marginal tax rates that considerably exceed their average tax rates. Thus, the U.S. income tax system is progressive.

FOR CRITICAL THINKING

Suppose the tax rates of the highest-income taxpayers and the 50 percent with lowest incomes were equalized. If so, would the U.S. income tax system become more or less progressive than it is today? Explain briefly.

Sources are listed at the end of this chapter.

REGRESSIVE TAXATION With **regressive taxation**, a smaller percentage of taxable income is taken in taxes as taxable income increases. The marginal rate is *below* the average rate. As income increases, the marginal tax rate falls, and so does the average tax rate. The U.S. Social Security tax is regressive. Once the legislative maximum taxable wage base is reached, no further Social Security taxes are paid. Consider a simplified hypothetical example: Suppose that every dollar up to $120,000 is taxed at 10 percent. After $120,000 there is no Social Security tax. Someone making $200,000 still pays only $12,000 in Social Security taxes. That person's average Social Security tax is 6 percent. The person making $120,000, by contrast, effectively pays 10 percent. The person making $1.2 million faces an average Social Security tax rate of only 1 percent in our simplified example.

Regressive taxation
A tax system in which as more dollars are earned, the percentage of tax paid on them falls. The marginal tax rate is less than the average tax rate as income rises.

MyEconLab Concept Check
MyEconLab Study Plan

Governments collect taxes by applying a tax _____ to a tax _____, which refers to the value of goods, services, wealth, or incomes. Income tax rates are applied to tax brackets, which are ranges of income over which the tax rate is constant.

The _____ tax rate is the total tax payment divided by total income, and the _____ tax rate is the change in the tax payment divided by the change in income.

Tax systems can be _____, _____, or _____, depending on whether the marginal tax rate is the same as, greater than, or less than the average tax rate as income rises.

6.2 Explain the structure of the U.S. income tax system

The Most Important Federal Taxes

What types of taxes do federal, state, and local governments collect? The two pie charts in Figure 6-1 below show the percentages of receipts from various taxes obtained by the federal government and by state and local governments. For the federal government, key taxes are individual income taxes, corporate income taxes, Social Security taxes, and excise taxes on items such as gasoline and alcoholic beverages. For state and local governments, sales taxes, property taxes, and personal and corporate income taxes are the main types of taxes.

The Federal Personal Income Tax

The most important tax in the U.S. economy is the federal personal income tax, which, as Figure 6-1 below indicates, accounts for 46 percent of all federal revenues. All U.S. citizens, resident aliens, and most others who earn income in the United States are required to pay federal income taxes on all taxable income, including income earned abroad.

The rates that are paid rise as income increases, as can be seen in Table 6-1 on the next page. Marginal income tax rates at the federal level have ranged from as low as

FIGURE 6-1

Sources of Government Tax Receipts

As panel (a) shows, about 92 percent of federal revenues comes from income and Social Security and other social insurance taxes. State government revenues, shown in panel (b), are spread more evenly across sources, with less emphasis on taxes based on individual income.

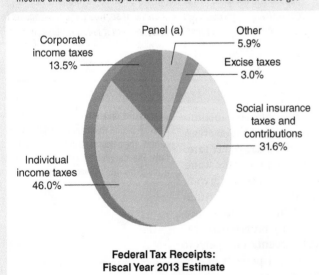

**Federal Tax Receipts:
Fiscal Year 2013 Estimate**

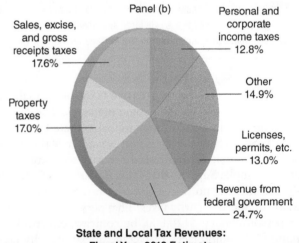

**State and Local Tax Revenues:
Fiscal Year 2013 Estimate**

Source: Economic Report of the President, Economic Indicators

TABLE 6-1	Single Persons		Married Couples	
Federal Marginal Income Tax Rates These rates applied in 2014.	Marginal Tax Bracket	Marginal Tax Rate	Marginal Tax Bracket	Marginal Tax Rate
	$0–$9,075	10%	$0–$18,150	10%
	$9,776–$36,900	15%	$18,151–$73,800	15%
	$36,901–$89,350	25%	$73,801–$148,850	25%
	$89,351–$186,350	28%	$148,851–$226,850	28%
	$186,351–$405,100	33%	$226,851–$405,600	33%
	$405,751 and up	35%	$357,601 and up	35%

Source: U.S. Department of the Treasury.

1 percent after the 1913 passage of the Sixteenth Amendment, which made the individual income tax constitutional, to as high as 94 percent (reached in 1944). There were 14 separate tax brackets prior to the Tax Reform Act of 1986, which reduced the number to three (now six, as shown in Table 6-1).

WHAT IF...

the federal government were to reduce the tax rates within the two lowest-income tax brackets in Table 6-1 while raising tax rates within the two highest-income tax brackets?

Altering tax rates in this way would cause marginal income tax rates to rise more sharply as an individual's income increased. Viewed across all taxpayers, the consequence would be that lower-income individuals would be required to pay a smaller percentage of their income as taxes than they do now. In contrast, higher-income individuals would owe larger percentages of their income as taxes than they currently do. Thus, the effect of simultaneously reducing tax rates within the lowest two income tax brackets and increasing tax rates within the highest two income tax brackets would be to make the federal income tax system more progressive.

MyEconLab Concept Check

The Treatment of Capital Gains

The difference between the purchase price and sale price of an asset, such as a share of stock or a plot of land, is called a **capital gain** if it is a profit and a **capital loss** if it is not. The federal government taxes capital gains, and as of 2015, there were several capital gains tax rates.

What appear to be capital gains are not always real gains. If you pay $100,000 for a financial asset in one year and sell it for 50 percent more 10 years later, your nominal capital gain is $50,000. But what if during those 10 years inflation has driven average asset prices up by 50 percent? Your *real* capital gain would be zero, but you would still have to pay taxes on that $50,000.

To counter this problem, many economists have argued that capital gains should be indexed to the rate of inflation. This is exactly what is done with the marginal tax brackets in the federal income tax code. Tax brackets for the purposes of calculating marginal tax rates each year are expanded at the rate of inflation, that is, the rate at which the average of all prices is rising. If the rate of inflation is 10 percent, therefore, each tax bracket is moved up by 10 percent. The same concept could be applied to capital gains and financial assets. So far, Congress has refused to enact such a measure.

MyEconLab Concept Check

Capital gain
A positive difference between the purchase price and the sale price of an asset. If a share of stock is bought for $5 and then sold for $15, the capital gain is $10.

Capital loss
A negative difference between the purchase price and the sale price of an asset.

The Corporate Income Tax

Figure 6-1 on the previous page shows that corporate income taxes account for 13.5 percent of all federal taxes collected. They also make up about 2 percent of all state and

TABLE 6-2

Federal Corporate Income Tax Schedule

These corporate tax rates were in effect through 2015.

Corporate Taxable Income	Corporate Tax Rate
$0–$50,000	15%
$50,001–$75,000	25%
$75,001–$100,000	34%
$100,001–$335,000	39%
$335,001–$10,000,000	34%
$10,000,001–$15,000,000	35%
$15,000,001–$18,333,333	38%
$18,333,334 and up	35%

Source: Internal Revenue Service.

local taxes collected. Corporations are generally taxed on the difference between their total revenues and their expenses. The federal corporate income tax structure is given in Table 6-2 above.

DOUBLE TAXATION Because individual stockholders must pay taxes on the dividends they receive, and those dividends are paid out of *after-tax* profits by the corporation, corporate profits are taxed twice. If you receive $1,000 in dividends, you have to declare them as income, and you must normally pay taxes on them. Before the corporation was able to pay you those dividends, it had to pay taxes on all its profits, including any that it put back into the company or did not distribute in the form of dividends.

Eventually, the new investment made possible by those **retained earnings**—profits not given out to stockholders—along with borrowed funds will be reflected in the value of the stock in that company. When you sell your stock in that company, you will have to pay taxes on the difference between what you paid for the stock and what you sold it for. In both cases, dividends and retained earnings (corporate profits) are taxed twice. In 2003, Congress reduced the double taxation effect somewhat by enacting legislation that allowed most dividends to be taxed at lower rates than are applied to regular income.

Retained earnings
Earnings that a corporation saves, or retains, for investment in other productive activities; earnings that are not distributed to stockholders.

WHO REALLY PAYS THE CORPORATE INCOME TAX? Corporations can function only as long as consumers buy their products, employees make their goods, stockholders (owners) buy their shares, and bondholders buy their bonds. Corporations per se do not do anything. We must ask, then, who really pays the tax on corporate income? This is a question of **tax incidence**. (The question of tax incidence applies to all taxes, including sales taxes and Social Security taxes.) The incidence of corporate taxation is the subject of considerable debate. Some economists suggest that corporations pass their tax burdens on to consumers by charging higher prices.

Tax incidence
The distribution of tax burdens among various groups in society.

Other economists argue that it is the stockholders who bear most of the tax. Still others contend that employees pay at least part of the tax by receiving lower wages than they would otherwise. Because the debate is not yet settled, we will not hazard a guess here as to what the correct conclusion may be. Suffice it to say that you should be cautious when you advocate increasing corporation income taxes. *People*, whether owners, consumers, or workers, end up paying all of the increase—just as they pay all of any tax. MyEconLab Concept Check

Social Security and Unemployment Taxes

Each year, taxes levied on payrolls account for an increasing percentage of federal tax receipts. These taxes, which are distinct from personal income taxes, are for Social

Security, retirement, survivors' disability, and old-age medical benefits (Medicare). The Social Security tax is imposed on earnings up to roughly $120,000 at a rate of 6.2 percent on employers and 6.2 percent on employees. That is, the employer matches your "contribution" to Social Security. (The employer's contribution is really paid by the employees, at least in part, in the form of a reduced wage rate.) As Chapter 5 explained, a Medicare tax is imposed on all wage earnings at a combined rate of 2.9 percent. The 2010 federal health care law also added a 3.8 percent Medicare tax on certain income above $200,000.

SOCIAL SECURITY TAXES Passage of the Federal Insurance Contributions Act (FICA) in 1935 brought Social Security taxes into existence. At that time, many more people paid into the Social Security program than the number who received benefits. Currently, however, older people drawing benefits make up a much larger share of the population. Consequently, in recent years, outflows of Social Security benefit payments have sometimes exceeded inflows of Social Security taxes. Various economists have advanced proposals to raise Social Security tax rates on younger workers or to reduce benefit payouts to older retirees and disabled individuals receiving Social Security payments. So far, however, the federal government has failed to address Social Security's deteriorating funding situation.

UNEMPLOYMENT INSURANCE TAXES There is also a federal unemployment insurance tax, which helps pay for unemployment insurance. This tax rate is 0.6 percent on the first $7,000 of annual wages of each employee who earns more than $1,500. Only the employer makes this tax payment. This tax covers the costs of the unemployment insurance system. In addition to this federal tax, some states with an unemployment system impose their own tax of up to about 3 percent, depending on the past record of the particular employer. An employer who frequently lays off workers typically will have a slightly higher state unemployment tax rate than an employer who never lays off workers.

MyEconLab Concept Check
MyEconLab Study Plan

SELF CHECK Visit MyEconLab to practice these and other problems and to get instant feedback in your Study Plan.

The federal government raises most of its revenues through _____ taxes and social insurance taxes and contributions. State and local governments raise most of their tax revenues from _____ taxes, _____ taxes, and income taxes.

Because corporations must first pay an income tax on most earnings, the personal income tax shareholders pay on dividends received (or realized capital gains) constitutes _____ taxation.

Both employers and employees must pay _____ _____ taxes and contributions at rates of 6.2 percent on roughly the first $120,000 in wage earnings, and a 2.9 percent _____ tax rate is applied to all wage earnings. The federal government and some state governments also assess taxes to pay for _____ insurance systems.

Tax Rates and Tax Revenues

6.3 Understand the key factors influencing the relationship between tax rates and the tax revenues governments collect

For most state and local governments, income taxes yield fewer revenues than taxes imposed on sales of goods and services. Figure 6-1 on page 134 shows that sales taxes, gross receipts taxes, and excise taxes generate almost one-fifth of the total funds available to state and local governments. Thus, from the perspective of many state and local governments, a fundamental issue is how to set tax rates on sales of goods and services to extract desired total tax payments.

Sales Taxes

Governments levy **sales taxes** on the prices that consumers pay to purchase each unit of a broad range of goods and services. Sellers collect sales taxes and transmit them to

Sales taxes

Taxes assessed on the prices paid on most goods and services.

Ad valorem taxation
Assessing taxes by charging a tax rate equal to a fraction of the market price of each unit purchased.

the government. Sales taxes are a form of **ad valorem taxation**, which means that the tax is applied "to the value" of the good. Thus, a government using a system of *ad valorem* taxation charges a tax rate equal to a fraction of the market price of each unit that a consumer buys. For instance, if the tax rate is 8 percent and the market price of an item is $100, then the amount of the tax on the item is $8.

A sales tax is therefore a proportional tax with respect to purchased items. The total amount of sales taxes a government collects equals the sales tax rate times the sales tax base, which is the market value of total purchases.

What complications would Internet sellers confront if states required them to collect sales taxes in every state in which they sell their products?

POLICY EXAMPLE

Why Online Sales Taxes Would Entail More Than Just Taxes

Over the past few years, Congress has considered allowing the 45 states with sales taxes to require companies to collect such taxes when residents of those states purchase their products on the Internet. Proponents of the proposed legal change argue that it would establish a level playing field between sellers on the Web and sellers who predominantly utilize physical facilities.

A complication is that there would not really be "only" 45 different state sales tax rates to assess. Many states permit counties and cities to assess their own sales tax rates, too. Furthermore, each of these local jurisdictions within the 45 states has its own rules for defining how the rates apply to the values of purchases of many different goods and services. As a consequence, an online seller could confront different sales tax regulations for as many as 9,646 state, county, and city jurisdictions.

Current estimates indicate that for large online retailers, such as Amazon, the cost of complying with these many tax rules would amount to just over 2 percent of the dollar value of all sales. For small retailers, the compliance cost likely would exceed 13 percent of the total value of customers' purchases. Thus, compliance costs for small Web sellers could exceed the taxes they would transmit to the government.

FOR CRITICAL THINKING
Why might some small online retailers contemplate halting sales in some states, counties, and cities if required to collect sales taxes throughout the United States?

Sources are listed at the end of this chapter.

MyEconLab Concept Check

Static Tax Analysis

Static tax analysis
Economic evaluation of the effects of tax rate changes under the assumption that there is no effect on the tax base, meaning that there is an unambiguous positive relationship between tax rates and tax revenues.

There are two approaches to evaluating how changes in tax rates affect government tax collections. **Static tax analysis** assumes that changes in the tax rate have no effect on the tax base. Thus, this approach implies that if a state government desires to increase its sales tax collections, it can simply raise the tax rate. Multiplying the higher tax rate by the tax base thereby produces higher tax revenues.

Governments often rely on static tax analysis. Sometimes this yields unpleasant surprises. For instance, in recent years states such as Delaware and Maryland have imposed special tax rates on so-called "millionaires"—usually defined as people earning hundreds of thousands of dollars per year. Agencies of state governments implementing these special taxes have applied the special tax rate to incomes subject to the tax and projected that additional tax revenues of tens of millions of dollars would be collected. In fact, however, many earners of income subjected to these special taxes responded by changing their state of residency. Consequently, the tax base of the high earners decreased, and the state governments imposing these taxes experienced much smaller increases in tax collections than they had projected. MyEconLab Concept Check

Dynamic Tax Analysis

Dynamic tax analysis
Economic evaluation of tax rate changes that recognizes that the tax base declines with ever-higher tax rates, so that tax revenues may eventually decline if the tax rate is raised sufficiently.

The problem with static tax analysis is that it ignores incentive effects created by new taxes or hikes in existing tax rates. According to **dynamic tax analysis**, a likely response to an increase in a tax rate is a *decrease* in the tax base. When a government pushes up its sales tax rate, for example, consumers have an incentive to cut back on their purchases of goods and services subjected to the higher rate, perhaps by buying them in a locale where there is a lower sales tax rate or perhaps no tax rate at all. As shown in Figure 6-2 on the next page, the maximum sales tax rate varies considerably from state to state.

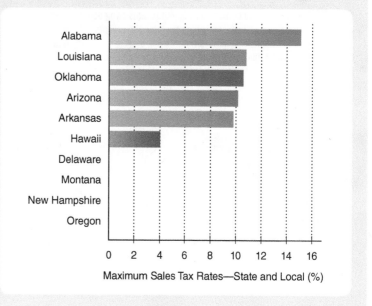

FIGURE 6-2

States with the Highest and Lowest Sales Tax Rates

A number of states allow counties and cities to collect their own sales taxes in addition to state sales taxes. This figure shows the maximum sales tax rates for selected states, including county and municipal taxes. Delaware, Montana, New Hampshire, and Oregon have no sales taxes.

Source: U.S. Department of Commerce.

Consider someone who lives in a state bordering Oregon. In such a border state, the sales tax rate can be as high as 8 percent, so a resident of that state has a strong incentive to buy higher-priced goods and services in Oregon, where there is no sales tax. Someone who lives in a high-tax county in Alabama has an incentive to buy an item online from an out-of-state firm to avoid paying sales taxes. Such shifts in expenditures in response to higher relative tax rates will reduce a state's sales tax base and thereby result in lower sales tax collections than the levels predicted by static tax analysis.

Dynamic tax analysis recognizes that increasing the tax rate could actually cause the government's total tax collections to *decline* if a sufficiently large number of consumers react to the higher sales tax rate by cutting back on purchases of goods and services included in the state's tax base. Some residents who live close to other states with lower sales tax rates might, for instance, drive across the state line to do more of their shopping. Other residents might place more orders with catalog companies or online firms located in other legal jurisdictions where their state's sales tax does not apply.

Why is dynamic tax analysis now important to French soccer players?

INTERNATIONAL POLICY EXAMPLE

French Soccer Teams Confront Dynamic Tax Analysis

In 2012, France announced a special top 75 percent tax rate for the "super rich"—people earning more than 1 million euros (about $1.3 million) per year. The government planned to impose this extra-high tax rate on this group only through 2014, albeit with the possibility of a further extension into future years.

One set of taxpayers affected by the 75 percent tax rate included super-rich players on French professional soccer teams. Soon, rumors began to swirl that many of the most highly paid French soccer players might contemplate departing their soccer clubs for teams based in other European nations with lower top tax rates. French soccer fans prevailed upon the government to exempt their favorite players and thereby remove their incentive

to flee the country. For a short while, the government wavered, but ultimately it declared that soccer players, like others among the country's super rich, would have to pay the special top rate. At that point, players on French teams openly began to search for positions with soccer clubs outside France—and the French income tax base gradually began to shrink.

FOR CRITICAL ANALYSIS

Why do you suppose that top-earning French film stars also have been moving to other countries?

Sources are listed at the end of this chapter.

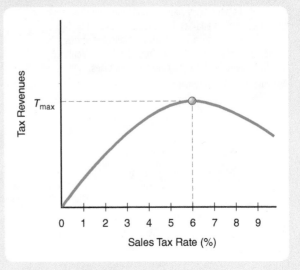

FIGURE 6-3

Maximizing the Government's Sales Tax Revenues

Dynamic tax analysis predicts that ever-higher tax rates bring about declines in the tax base, so that at sufficiently high tax rates the government's tax revenues begin to fall off. This implies that there is a tax rate, 6 percent in this example, at which the government can collect the maximum possible revenues, T_{max}.

Maximizing Tax Revenues

Dynamic tax analysis indicates that whether a government's tax revenues ultimately rise or fall in response to a tax rate increase depends on exactly how much the tax base declines in response to the higher tax rate. On the one hand, the tax base may decline by a relatively small amount following an increase in the tax rate, so that tax revenues rise. For instance, in the situation we imagine a government facing in Figure 6-3 above, a rise in the tax rate from 5 percent to 6 percent causes tax revenues to increase. On the other hand, the tax base may decline so much that total tax revenues decrease. In Figure 6-3, for example, increasing the tax rate from 6 percent to 7 percent causes tax revenues to *decline*.

What is most likely is that when the tax rate is already relatively low, increasing the tax rate causes relatively small declines in the tax base. Within a range of relatively low sales tax rates, therefore, increasing the tax rate generates higher sales tax revenues, as illustrated along the upward-sloping portion of the curve depicted in Figure 6-3. If the government continues to push up the tax rate, however, people increasingly have an incentive to find ways to avoid purchasing taxable goods and services. Eventually, the tax base decreases sufficiently that the government's tax collections decline with ever-higher tax rates.

Consequently, governments that wish to maximize their tax revenues should not necessarily assess a high tax rate. In the situation illustrated in Figure 6-3, above, the government maximizes its tax revenues at T_{max} by establishing a sales tax rate of 6 percent. If the government were to raise the rate above 6 percent, it would induce a sufficient decline in the tax base that its tax collections would decline. If the government wishes to collect more than T_{max} in revenues to fund various government programs, it must somehow either expand its sales tax base or develop another tax.

MyEconLab Concept Check
MyEconLab Study Plan

SELF CHECK   Visit MyEconLab to practice these and other problems and to get instant feedback in your Study Plan.

The _____ view of the relationship between tax rates and tax revenues implies that higher tax rates always generate increased government tax collections.

According to _____ tax analysis, higher tax rates cause the tax base to decrease. Tax collections will rise less than predicted by _____ tax analysis.

Dynamic tax analysis indicates that there is a tax rate that maximizes the government's tax collections. Setting the tax rate any higher would cause the tax base to _____ sufficiently that the government's tax revenues will _____.

Taxation from the Point of View of Producers and Consumers

6.4 Explain how the taxes governments levy on purchases of goods and services affect market prices and equilibrium quantities

Governments collect taxes on product sales at the source. They require producers to charge these taxes when they sell their output. This means that taxes on sales of goods and services affect market prices and quantities. Let's consider why this is so.

Taxes and the Market Supply Curve

Imposing taxes on final sales of a good or service affects the position of the market supply curve. To see why, consider panel (a) of Figure 6-4 below, which shows a gasoline market supply curve S_1 in the absence of taxation. At a price of $3.35 per gallon, gasoline producers are willing and able to supply 180,000 gallons of gasoline per week. If the price increases to $3.45 per gallon, firms increase production to 200,000 gallons of gasoline per week.

Both federal and state governments assess **excise taxes**—taxes on sales of particular commodities—on sales of gasoline. They levy gasoline excise taxes as a **unit tax**, or a constant tax per unit sold. On average, combined federal and state excise taxes on gasoline are about $0.40 per gallon.

Let's suppose, therefore, that a gasoline producer must transmit a total of $0.40 per gallon to federal and state governments for each gallon sold. Producers must continue to receive a net amount of $3.35 per gallon to induce them to supply 180,000 gallons each week, so they must now receive $3.75 per gallon to supply that weekly quantity. Likewise, gasoline producers now will be willing to supply 200,000 gallons each week only if they receive $0.40 more per gallon, or a total amount of $3.85 per gallon.

Excise tax
A tax levied on purchases of a particular good or service.

Unit tax
A constant tax assessed on each unit of a good that consumers purchase.

MyEconLab Animation

FIGURE 6-4

The Effects of Excise Taxes on the Market Supply and Equilibrium Price and Quantity of Gasoline

Panel (a) shows what happens if the government requires gasoline sellers to collect and transmit a $0.40 unit excise tax on gasoline. To be willing to continue supplying a given quantity, sellers must receive a price that is $0.40 higher for each gallon they sell, so the market supply curve shifts vertically by the amount of the tax. As illustrated in panel (b), this decrease in market supply causes a reduction in the equilibrium quantity of gasoline produced and purchased. It also causes a rise in the market clearing price, to $3.75, so that consumers pay part of the tax. Sellers pay the rest in lower profits.

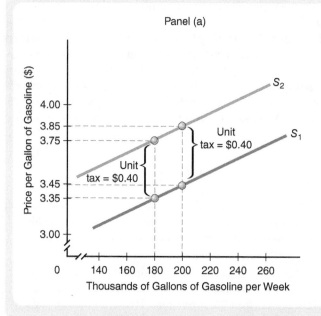

Panel (a)

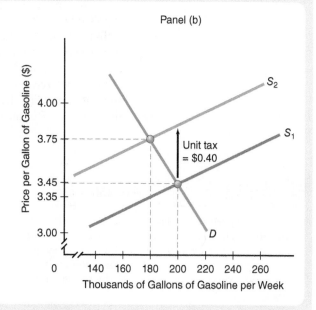

Panel (b)

As you can see, imposing the combined $0.40 per gallon excise taxes on gasoline shifts the supply curve vertically by exactly that amount to S_2 in panel (a). Thus, the effect of levying excise taxes on gasoline is to shift the supply curve vertically by the total per-unit taxes levied on gasoline sales. Hence, there is a decrease in supply. (In the case of an *ad valorem* sales tax, the supply curve would shift vertically by a proportionate amount equal to the tax rate.)   MyEconLab Concept Check

How Taxes Affect the Market Price and Equilibrium Quantity

Panel (b) of Figure 6-4 on the previous page shows how imposing $0.40 per gallon in excise taxes affects the market price of gasoline and the equilibrium quantity of gasoline produced and sold. In the absence of excise taxes, the market supply curve S_1 crosses the demand curve D at a market price of $3.45 per gallon. At this market price, the equilibrium quantity of gasoline is 200,000 gallons of gasoline per week.

The excise tax levy of $0.40 per gallon shifts the supply curve to S_2. At the original $3.45 per gallon price, there is now an excess quantity of gasoline demanded, so the market price of gasoline rises to $3.75 per gallon. At this market price, the equilibrium quantity of gasoline produced and consumed each week is 180,000 gallons.

What factors determine how much the equilibrium quantity of a good or service declines in response to taxation? The answer to this question depends on how responsive quantities demanded and supplied are to changes in price.

MyEconLab Concept Check

Who Pays the Tax?

In our example, imposing excise taxes of $0.40 per gallon of gasoline causes the market price to rise to $3.75 per gallon from $3.45 per gallon. Thus, the price that each consumer pays is $0.30 per gallon higher. Consumers pay three-fourths of the excise tax levied on each gallon of gasoline produced and sold in our example.

Gasoline producers must pay the rest of the tax. Their profits decline by $0.10 per gallon because costs have increased by $0.40 per gallon while consumers pay $0.30 more per gallon.

In the gasoline market, as in other markets for products subject to excise taxes and other taxes on sales, the shapes of the market demand and supply curves determine who pays most of a tax. The reason is that the shapes of these curves reflect the responsiveness to price changes of the quantity demanded by consumers and of the quantity supplied by producers.

In the example illustrated in Figure 6-4 on the previous page, the fact that consumers pay most of the excise taxes levied on gasoline reflects a relatively low responsiveness of quantity demanded by consumers to a change in the price of gasoline. Consumers pay most of the excise taxes on each gallon produced and sold because in this example the amount of gasoline they desire to purchase is relatively (but not completely) unresponsive to a change in the market price induced by excise taxes.   MyEconLab Concept Check
MyEconLab Study Plan

SELF CHECK   Visit MyEconLab to practice these and other problems and to get instant feedback in your Study Plan.

When the government levies a tax on sales of a particular product, firms must receive a higher price to continue supplying the same quantity as before, so the supply curve shifts _____. If the tax is a unit excise tax, the supply curve shifts _____ by the amount of the tax.

Imposing a tax on sales of an item _____ the equilibrium quantity produced and consumed and _____ the market price.

When a government assesses a unit excise tax, the market price of the good or service typically rises by an amount _____ than the per-unit tax. Hence, consumers pay a portion of the tax, and firms pay the remainder.

YOU ARE THERE

A Billboard Firm Grows by Helping Chicago Pay Its Bills

Jean-François Decaux's firm, JCDecaux, has become the world's top outdoor advertising company. The firm owns billboards and ad furnishings at bus shelters and other publicly visible locations in more than 1,800 cities around the globe, but the company has few operations in the United States. Decaux has determined that his firm must "create a new way in."

Decaux's approach is to take advantage of difficulties that the city of Chicago is experiencing in raising sufficient funds to cover government expenditures. Chicago's spending has been outpacing its revenues for a number of years. Today, one component of spending is rising rapidly: the city's payments to retired workers. Chicago's pension payments are now nearly $500 million per year, or about 14 percent of the city's expenditures. By 2016, these pension payments are likely to more than double. Hence, the city is searching for user charges to help provide a stable source of funding to supplement tax revenues. Decaux has offered the city

a deal. If Chicago allows his company to erect dozens of massive digital billboards on city-owned properties, his company will pay the city user charges amounting to 40 percent of JCDecaux's annual ad revenues. Decaux estimates that the company's payments to Chicago will add up to about $280 million per year—enough to cover roughly 25 percent of the city's required pension payments. Chicago agrees, and Decaux's company rushes to construct its bright digital billboards.

CRITICAL THINKING QUESTIONS

1. Why is Chicago borrowing hundreds of millions of dollars each year?
2. What steps must Chicago consider taking to satisfy its budget constraint?

Sources are listed at the end of this chapter.

ISSUES & APPLICATIONS

MyEconLab Video

An Effective Tax Hike Induces More People to Give Up U.S. Citizenship

Tyler Olson/Fotolia

CONCEPTS APPLIED

» Tax Rate

» Static Tax Analysis

» Dynamic Tax Analysis

Under current U.S. law, failure to report incomes earned abroad and to pay taxes on those incomes has exposed citizens to penalties that can be substantial—but that the government has not always fully enforced. Renewed enforcement of income tax requirements for U.S. citizens who earn incomes abroad has induced a growing number of people to give up their citizenship to avoid paying U.S. taxes and incurring related compliance costs.

The U.S. Government Renews Tax Enforcement Abroad

In March 2010, Congress passed the Foreign Account Tax Compliance Act. This law requires foreign financial institutions to identify customers who are U.S. citizens and to report them to the Internal Revenue Service (IRS). Failure to file such reports exposes the institutions to significant tax penalties on their own investments held within U.S. borders.

This U.S. government enforcement threat has induced many foreign financial institutions to report information about year-end account balances of U.S. citizens. The IRS uses this information to compile lists of citizens who likely

have earned incomes abroad and hence should file tax forms and payments. The IRS also uses the information to calculate estimates of their annual incomes from foreign sources.

A Jump in the Number of Ex-U.S. Citizens

The objective of the Foreign Account Tax Compliance Act was to ensure that U.S. citizens report all foreign incomes, apply applicable tax rates to those incomes, and transmit to the IRS all taxes they legally owe. Static tax analysis indicated to Congress that once all citizens were required to take into account all relevant income tax rates, the result would be a substantial increase in federal income tax collections.

FIGURE 6-5

Estimates of the Number of People Giving Up U.S. Citizenship

Both the U.S. State Department and the Federal Bureau of Investigation provide estimates of how many people renounce their U.S. citizenship each year. This figure displays the average of these agencies' estimates, which recently have increased considerably.

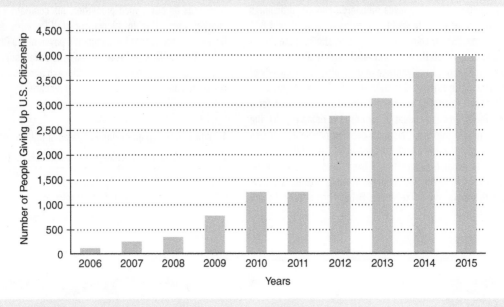

Sources: U.S. State Department; Federal Bureau of Investigation, author's estimates.

To be sure, the amount of federal income taxes collected from U.S. citizens who earn incomes abroad rose. The amount of the increase, however, was smaller than predicted. A key reason is that a surprisingly large number of U.S. citizens decided to give up their citizenship to avoid having to pay U.S. income taxes. As Figure 6-5 shows, after the new enforcement law was passed in 2010, the number of people choosing to renounce their U.S. citizenship more than doubled. Consequently, the U.S. government collected fewer taxes from citizens on their foreign incomes than had been estimated—because fewer people remained citizens.

For Critical Thinking

1. For some taxpayers, why might sudden enforcement of previously weakly enforced tax requirements be equivalent to an unexpected tax rate increase?

2. Why do you suppose that a growing number of foreign financial institutions are opting not to offer accounts to U.S. citizens?

Web Resources

1. Take a look at the foreign compliance requirements established by the Foreign Account Compliance Act in the Web Links in MyEconLab.

2. For a look at complications that the new U.S. law has created for individuals and businesses operating in the United Kingdom, see the Web Links in MyEconLab.

MyEconLab

For more questions on this chapter's Issues & Applications, go to MyEconLab.

In the Study Plan for this chapter, select Section I: Issues and Applications.

Sources are listed at the end of this chapter.

Fundamental Points

1. The average tax rate is the total tax payment divided by total income, and the marginal tax rate is the change in the tax payment divided by the change in income.

2. The federal government obtains most tax revenues from income taxes and social insurance taxes and contributions. State and local governments raise most of their tax revenues from sales taxes, property taxes, and income taxes.

3. The static view of the relationship between tax rates and tax revenues implies that higher tax rates always generate increased tax collections. The dynamic view indicates that higher tax rates cause the tax base to decrease, so that tax revenues will rise by a smaller amount.

4. A tax imposed on firms' sales shifts the supply curve upward, so the equilibrium quantity declines, and the market price rises. If demand and supply curves have typical shapes, consumers pay part of the tax through the increase in price, and firms pay the remainder.

WHAT YOU SHOULD KNOW

Here is what you should know after reading this chapter. MyEconLab will help you identify what you know, and where to go when you need to practice.

LEARNING OBJECTIVES	KEY TERMS	WHERE TO GO TO PRACTICE
6.1 **Distinguish between average tax rates and marginal tax rates** *The average tax rate is the ratio of total tax payments to total income. In contrast, the marginal tax rate is the change in tax payments induced by a change in total taxable income. Thus, the marginal tax rate applies to the last dollar that a person earns. In a progressive tax system, the marginal tax rate increases as income rises, so that the marginal tax rate exceeds the average tax rate. This contrasts with a regressive tax system, in which higher-income people pay lower marginal tax rates, resulting in a marginal tax rate that is less than the average tax rate. The marginal tax rate equals the average tax rate only under proportional taxation, in which the marginal tax rate does not vary with income.*	government budget constraint, 131 tax base, 132 tax rate, 132 marginal tax rate, 132 tax bracket, 132 average tax rate, 132 proportional taxation, 133 progressive taxation, 133 regressive taxation, 133	• MyEconLab Study Plan 6.1
6.2 **Explain the structure of the U.S. income tax system** *The U.S. federal government raises most of its annual tax revenues from individual and corporate income taxes and also collects Social Security and unemployment taxes. State governments raise revenues through a variety of different taxes, including personal and corporate income taxes, sales and excise taxes, and property taxes.*	capital gain, 135 capital loss, 135 retained earnings, 136 tax incidence, 136	• MyEconLab Study Plan 6.2
6.3 **Understand the key factors influencing the relationship between tax rates and the tax revenues governments collect** *Static tax analysis assumes that the tax base does not respond significantly to an increase in the tax rate, so it seems to imply that a tax rate hike must always boost a government's total tax collections. Dynamic tax analysis reveals, however, that increases in tax rates cause the tax base to decline. Thus, there is a tax rate that maximizes the government's tax revenues. If the government pushes the tax rate higher, tax collections decline.*	sales taxes, 137 *ad valorem* taxation, 138 static tax analysis, 138 dynamic tax analysis, 138 **Key Figure** Figure 6-3, 140	• MyEconLab Study Plan 6.3 • Animated Figure 6-3

WHAT YOU SHOULD KNOW *continued*

LEARNING OBJECTIVES ————————— KEY TERMS ————————— WHERE TO GO TO PRACTICE —

6.4 Explain how the taxes governments levy on purchases of goods and services affect market prices and equilibrium quantities *When a government imposes a per-unit tax on a good or service, a seller is willing to supply any given quantity only if the seller receives a price that is higher by exactly the amount of the tax. Hence, the supply curve shifts vertically by the amount of the tax per unit. In a market with typically shaped demand and supply curves, this results in a fall in the equilibrium quantity and an increase in the market price. To the extent that the market price rises, consumers pay a portion of the tax on each unit they buy. Sellers pay the remainder in lower profits.*

excise tax, 141
unit tax, 141
Key Figure
Figure 6-4, 141

• MyEconLab Study Plan 6.4
• Animated Figure 6-4

Log in to MyEconLab, take a chapter test, and get a personalized Study Plan that tells you which concepts you understand and which ones you need to review. From there, MyEconLab will give you further practice, tutorials, animations, videos, and guided solutions. For more information, visit http://www.myeconlab.com

PROBLEMS

All problems are assignable in MyEconLab. Answers to odd-numbered problems appear in MyEconLab.

6-1. A senior citizen gets a part-time job at a fast-food restaurant. She earns $8 per hour for each hour she works, and she works exactly 25 hours per week. Thus, her total pretax weekly income is $200. Her total income tax assessment each week is $40. She pays $3 in taxes for the final hour she works each week. (See page 132.)

  a. What is this person's average tax rate each week?

  b. What is the marginal tax rate for the last hour she works each week?

6-2. For purposes of assessing income taxes, there are three official income levels for workers in a small country: high, medium, and low. For the last hour on the job during a 40-hour workweek, a high-income worker pays a marginal income tax rate of 15 percent, a medium-income worker pays a marginal tax rate of 20 percent, and a low-income worker is assessed a 25 percent marginal income tax rate. Based only on this information, does this

nation's income tax system appear to be progressive, proportional, or regressive? (See page 133.)

6-3. Consider the table below when answering the questions that follow. Show your work, and explain briefly. (See page 132.)

Christino		Jarius		Meg	
Income	Taxes Paid	Income	Taxes Paid	Income	Taxes Paid
$1,000	$200	$1,000	$200	$1,000	$200
$2,000	$300	$2,000	$400	$2,000	$500
$3,000	$400	$3,000	$600	$3,000	$800

  a. What is Christino's marginal tax rate?

  b. What is Jarius's marginal tax rate?

  c. What is Meg's marginal tax rate?

6-4. Refer to the table in Problem 6-3 when answering the following questions. Show your work, and explain briefly. (See page 133.)

MyEconLab Visit http://www.myeconlab.com to complete these exercises online and get instant feedback.

a. Does Christino experience progressive, proportional, or regressive taxation?

b. Does Jarius experience progressive, proportional, or regressive taxation?

c. Does Meg experience progressive, proportional, or regressive taxation?

6-5. Suppose that a state has increased its sales tax rate every other year since 2005. Assume the state collected all sales taxes that residents legally owed. The table below summarizes its experience. What were total taxable sales in this state during each year displayed in the table? (See pages 137–138.)

Year	Sales Tax Rate	Sales Tax Collections
2005	0.03 (3 percent)	$9.0 million
2007	0.04 (4 percent)	$14.0 million
2009	0.05 (5 percent)	$20.0 million
2011	0.06 (6 percent)	$24.0 million
2013	0.07 (7 percent)	$29.4 million

6-6. The sales tax rate applied to all purchases within a state was 0.04 (4 percent) throughout 2012 but increased to 0.05 (5 percent) during all of 2013. The state government collected all taxes due, but its tax revenues were equal to $40 million each year. What happened to the sales tax base between 2012 and 2013? What could account for this result? (See pages 138–139.)

6-7. The British government recently imposed a unit excise tax of about $154 per ticket on airline tickets applying to flights to or from London airports. In answering the following questions, assume normally shaped demand and supply curves. (See pages 141–142.)

a. Use an appropriate diagram to predict effects of the ticket tax on the market clearing price of London airline tickets and on the equilibrium number of flights into and out of London.

b. What do you predict is likely to happen to the equilibrium price of tickets for air flights into and out of cities that are in close proximity to London but are not subject to the new ticket tax? Explain your reasoning.

6-8. To raise funds aimed at providing more support for public schools, a state government has just imposed a unit excise tax equal to $4 for each monthly unit of wireless phone services sold by each company operating in the state. The following diagram depicts the positions of the demand and supply curves for wireless phone services *before* the unit excise tax was imposed. Use this diagram

to determine the position of the new market supply curve now that the tax hike has gone into effect. (See pages 141–142.)

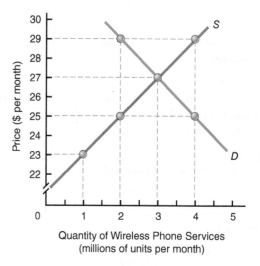

Quantity of Wireless Phone Services
(millions of units per month)

a. Does imposing the $4-per-month unit excise tax cause the market price of wireless phone services to rise by $4 per month? Why or why not?

b. What portion of the $4-per-month unit excise tax is paid by consumers? What portion is paid by providers of wireless phone services?

6-9. The following information applies to the market for a particular item in the *absence* of a unit excise tax (see pages 141–142):

Price ($ per unit)	Quantity Supplied	Quantity Demanded
4	50	200
5	75	175
6	100	150
7	125	125
8	150	100
9	175	75

a. According to the information in the table, in the *absence* of a unit excise tax, what is the market price? What is the equilibrium quantity?

b. Suppose that the government decides to subject producers of this item to a unit excise tax equal to $2 per unit sold. What is the new market price? What is the new equilibrium quantity?

c. What portion of the tax is paid by producers? What portion of the tax is paid by consumers?

REFERENCES

POLICY EXAMPLE: Be Sure to Claim Your Property from Delaware!

Nichole Dobo, "State Returns $83 Million in Unclaimed Property, Report Says," *The News Journal*, March 14, 2014.

Michael Kerman, "State Tax Snapshot: Unclaimed Property Lurks Beneath Delaware's Business Friendly Surface," Bloomberg, August 5, 2013.

Vipal Monga, "Tussle Imperils Delaware's Business-Friendly Image," *The Wall Street Journal*, June 19, 2013.

EXAMPLE: The Expanding Tax Base for the Alternative Minimum Tax

Jeff Brown, "Are You a Target for the Alternative Minimum Tax?" CNBC, January 27, 2014.

Mary Beth Franklin, "Permanent AMT Fix Protects Millions of Middle-Class Taxpayers," Investment News, January 6, 2013.

Dan Kadlec, "At Long Last, a Permanent Patch for a Dreaded Tax," *Time*, January 3, 2013.

POLICY EXAMPLE: Are U. S. Income Taxes Progressive? Ask the Top 400 Taxpayers

Internal Revenue Service "Top 400 Returns" list. (www.irs.gov/uac/SOI-Tax-Stats-Top-400-Individual-Income-Tax-Returns-with-the-Largest-Adjusted-Gross-Incomes)

POLICY EXAMPLE: Why Online Sales Taxes Would Entail More Than Just Taxes

Gordon Crovitz, "9,646 Tax Burdens on the Internet," *The Wall Street Journal*, April 28, 2013.

Howard Gleckman, "Retailers That Collect Online Sales Tax Lose Business," *Forbes*, April 29, 2014.

Robert Wood, "Online Sales Tax Inevitable, Senate Passes Marketplace Fairness Act," *Forbes*, March 23, 2013.

INTERNATIONAL POLICY EXAMPLE: French Soccer Teams Confront Dynamic Tax Analysis

Jonathan Howard, "Potential Impact of France's Super-Tax on Ligue 1," Business of Soccer, January 2, 2014.

Joseph Notte, "Some of France's Richest Taxed More Than 100 Percent," Microsoft Network Money, May 21, 2013.

Henry Samuel, "French Football Clubs 'Could Be Exempt from 75 Percent Supertax,' *The Telegraph*, September 11, 2013.

YOU ARE THERE: A Billboard Firm Grows by Helping Chicago Pay Its Bills

John Chase, "Details of Billboard Deal Raise Questions," *Chicago Tribune*, June 15, 2013.

Paul Merrion, "Digital Signs a Turn-On for Cash-Strapped City," Chicago Business, March 12, 2014.

Kristen Schweizer, "French Advertiser JCDecaux Begins U.S. Push with Chicago Billboards," *Bloomberg Businessweek*, May 30, 2013.

ISSUES & APPLICATIONS: An Effective Tax Hike Induces More People to Give Up U.S. Citizenship

Kelly Phillips Erb, "IRS Releases List of Americans Hoping to Expatriate, Number Tops 1,000," *Forbes*, August 11, 2013.

John McKinnon, "Top Earners Feel the Bite of Tax Increases," *The Wall Street Journal*, April 13, 2014.

Liam Pleven and Laura Saunders, "Number of Americans Renouncing Citizenship Surges," *The Wall Street Journal*, August 9, 2013.

The Macroeconomy: Unemployment, Inflation, and Deflation

7

CandyBox Images/Shutterstock

Prior to 2008, the likelihood of being gainfully employed in the United States appeared to be gender-neutral: The percentages of men and women who were employed in the United States typically were very nearly the same. Since then, however, the percentage of males employed often has been lower than the percentage of females employed. You will learn in this chapter why this fact helps to explain why men have experienced greater *unemployment*—the situation of seeking jobs but unable to find them—than women. You will also learn more about one reason why the entire U.S. male population more commonly has become less likely to be gainfully employed than the female population: Over time, fewer men have been trying to find jobs.

LEARNING OBJECTIVES

After reading this chapter, you should be able to:

7.1 Explain how the U.S. government calculates the official unemployment rate

7.2 Discuss the types of unemployment

7.3 Describe how price indexes are calculated and define the key types of price indexes

7.4 Evaluate who loses and who gains from inflation and distinguish between nominal and real interest rates

7.5 Understand key features of business fluctuations

MyEconLab helps you master each objective and study more efficiently. See the end of the chapter for details.

the number of people between the ages of 15 and 24 throughout the world who are *unemployed*—looking for positions, but so far unable to obtain jobs—amounts to nearly 300 million? Thus, the magnitude of global youth unemployment is close to the overall population of the United States.

Trying to understand determinants of unemployment and of the overall performance of either the national economy or the global economy is a central objective of macroeconomics. This branch of economics seeks to explain and predict movements in the average level of prices, unemployment, and total production of goods and services. This chapter introduces you to these key issues of macroeconomics.

7.1 Explain how the U.S. government calculates the official unemployment rate

Unemployment
The total number of adults (aged 16 years or older) who are willing and able to work and who are actively looking for work but have not found a job.

Unemployment

Unemployment is normally defined as the number of adults who are actively looking for work but do not have a job. Unemployment is costly in terms of lost output for the entire economy. At the end of the first decade of the twenty-first century, the unemployment rate rose by more than 4 percentage points and firms operated below 80 percent of their capacity. One estimate indicates that the amount of output that the economy lost due to idle resources was roughly 5 percent of the total production throughout the United States. (In other words, we were somewhere inside the production possibilities curve that we talked about in Chapter 2.)

That was the equivalent of more than an inflation-adjusted $700 billion of schools, houses, restaurant meals, cars, and movies that *could have been* produced. It is no wonder that policymakers closely watch the unemployment figures published by the Department of Labor's Bureau of Labor Statistics.

On a more personal level, the state of being unemployed often results in hardship and failed opportunities as well as a lack of self-respect. Psychological researchers believe that being fired creates at least as much stress as the death of a close friend. The numbers that we present about unemployment can never fully convey its true cost to the people of this or any other nation.

Historical Unemployment Rates

The unemployment rate, defined as the proportion of the measured **labor force** that is unemployed, hit a low of 1.2 percent of the labor force at the end of World War II, after having reached 25 percent during the Great Depression in the 1930s. You can see in Figure 7-1 on the next page what has happened to the unemployment rate in the United States since 1890. The highest level ever was reached in the Great Depression, but the unemployment rate was also high during the Panic of 1893.

MyEconLab Concept Check

Labor force
Individuals aged 16 years or older who either have jobs or are looking and available for jobs; the number of employed plus the number of unemployed.

Employment, Unemployment, and the Labor Force

Figure 7-2 on the next page presents the population of individuals 16 years of age or older broken into three segments: (1) employed, (2) unemployed, and (3) not in the civilian labor force (a category that includes homemakers, full-time students, military personnel, persons in institutions, and retired persons). The employed and the unemployed, added together, make up the labor force. In 2015, the labor force amounted to 146.6 million + 9.5 million = 156.1 million people. To calculate the

FIGURE 7-1

More Than a Century of Unemployment

The U.S. unemployment rate dropped below 2 percent during World Wars I and II but exceeded 25 percent during the Great Depression.

During the period following 2007, the unemployment rate rose to about 10 percent.

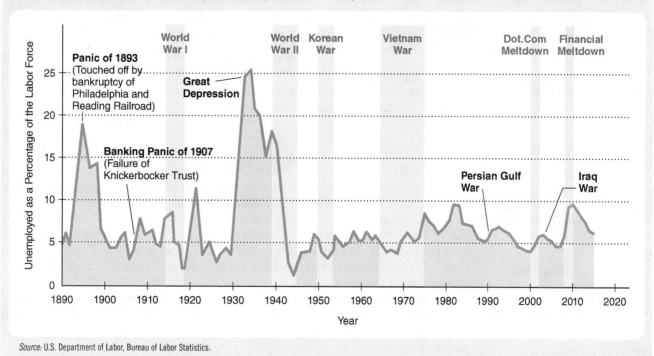

Source: U.S. Department of Labor, Bureau of Labor Statistics.

FIGURE 7-2

Adult Population

The population aged 16 and older can be broken down into three groups: people who are employed, those who are unemployed, and those not in the labor force.

Source: U.S. Department of Labor, Bureau of Labor Statistics.

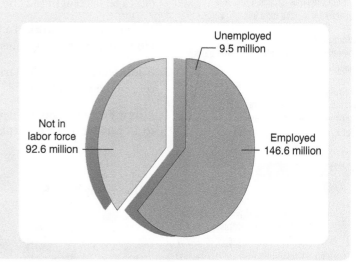

unemployment rate, we simply divide the number of unemployed by the number of people in the labor force and multiply by 100: 9.5 million/156.1 million × 100 = 6.1 percent.

Among people classified as employed, how have the shares of those classified as full-time workers versus part-time workers changed in recent years?

EXAMPLE

A Shift toward More Part-Time Employment

When the U.S. government reports on the number of people classified as *employed*, it adds together those working full-time—35 or more hours per week—and those working part-time—less than 35 hours per week. People who are classified as unemployed, therefore, are seeking work but find cannot find *either* full- or part-time jobs.

Since 2007, the share of employed people holding part-time jobs has increased from less than 17 percent to more than 19 percent today. If this shift in employment shares had not occurred, as many as 4 million more people otherwise would be working in full-time jobs.

FOR CRITICAL THINKING

Why do you suppose that the average weekly hours an average employed U.S. worker spends on the job have dropped slightly since 2007?

Sources are listed at the end of this chapter.

MyEconLab Concept Check

Stock
The quantity of something, measured at a given point in time—for example, an inventory of goods or a bank account. Stocks are defined independently of time, although they are assessed at a point in time.

Flow
A quantity measured per unit of time; something that occurs over time, such as the income you make per week or per year or the number of individuals who are fired every month.

Job loser
An individual in the labor force whose employment was involuntarily terminated.

Reentrant
An individual who used to work full-time but left the labor force and has now reentered it looking for a job.

Job leaver
An individual in the labor force who quits voluntarily.

New entrant
An individual who has never held a full-time job lasting two weeks or longer but is now seeking employment.

The Arithmetic Determination of Unemployment

Because there is a transition between employment and unemployment at any point in time—people are leaving jobs and others are finding jobs—there is a simple relationship between the employed and the unemployed, as can be seen in Figure 7-3 below. Job departures are shown at the top of the diagram, and job acquisitions are shown at the bottom. If the numbers of job departures and acquisitions are equal, the unemployment rate stays the same. If departures exceed acquisitions, the unemployment rate rises.

The number of unemployed is some number at any point in time. It is a **stock** of individuals who do not have a job but are actively looking for one. The same is true for the number of employed. The number of people departing jobs, whether voluntarily or involuntarily, is a **flow,** as is the number of people acquiring jobs.

CATEGORIES OF INDIVIDUALS WHO ARE WITHOUT WORK According to the Bureau of Labor Statistics, an unemployed individual will fall into any of four categories:

1. A **job loser**, whose employment was involuntarily terminated or who was laid off (40 to 60 percent of the unemployed)

2. A **reentrant**, who worked a full-time job before but has been out of the labor force (20 to 30 percent of the unemployed)

3. A **job leaver**, who voluntarily ended employment (less than 10 to around 15 percent of the unemployed)

4. A **new entrant**, who has never worked a full-time job for two weeks or longer (10 to 15 percent of the unemployed)

MyEconLab Animation

FIGURE 7-3

The Logic of the Unemployment Rate

Individuals who depart jobs but remain in the labor force are subtracted from the employed and added to the unemployed. When the unemployed acquire jobs, they are subtracted from the unemployed and added to the employed. In an unchanged labor force, if both flows are equal, the unemployment rate is stable. If more people depart jobs than acquire them, the unemployment rate increases, and vice versa.

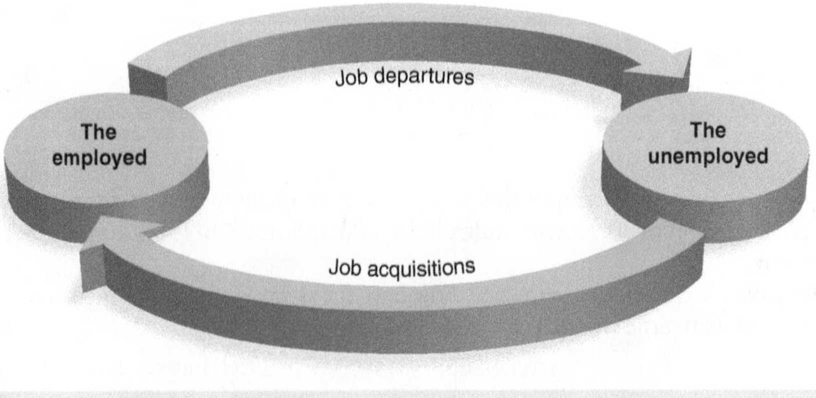

DURATION OF UNEMPLOYMENT If you are out of a job for a week, your situation is typically much less serious than if you are out of a job for, say, 14 weeks. An increase in the duration of unemployment can raise the unemployment rate because workers stay unemployed longer, thereby creating a greater number of them at any given time.

The most recent information on duration of unemployment paints the following picture: More than a third of those who become unemployed acquire a new job by the end of one month, approximately one-third more acquire a job by the end of two months, and only about a sixth are still unemployed after six months. Since the mid-1960s, the average annual duration of unemployment for all the unemployed has varied between 10 and 20 weeks. The overall average duration for the past 25 years has been 16 weeks.

When overall business activity goes into a downturn, the duration of unemployment tends to rise, thereby accounting for much of the increase in the estimated unemployment rate. In a sense, then, it is the increase in the *duration* of unemployment during a downturn in national economic activity that generates the bad news that concerns policymakers in Washington, D.C. Furthermore, the individuals who stay unemployed longer than six months are the ones who create pressure on Congress to "do something." What Congress does, typically, is extend and supplement unemployment benefits.

How has the duration of U.S. unemployment changed in recent years?

EXAMPLE

An Increase in the Duration of Unemployment

The average duration of unemployment has increased substantially during the past few years. In 2009, the average unemployment duration was approximately 17 weeks. Since then, the average duration has exceeded 30 weeks.

The main reason for this increase in average unemployment duration has been a sharp rise in the percentage of unemployed people who have been unable to find work for many weeks. The government classifies these people as *long-term unemployed*. In years past, the long-term unemployment rate—that is, the percentage of the labor force that has been unemployed for more than six months—averaged about 1 percent. Today, the long-term unemployment rate is close to 3 percent. This fact means that of the more than 9 million people who are unemployed, in excess of 3 million have been out of work for more than half of a year.

FOR CRITICAL THINKING

Why do you suppose that someone who has been counted among the long-term unemployed usually has a harder time finding a job than a person who otherwise has similar past work experience but who has been out of work only a few weeks? (Hint: Employers tend to be wary of hiring people whose work skills may have declined after lengthy intervals spent without jobs.)

Sources are listed at the end of this chapter.

THE DISCOURAGED WORKER PHENOMENON Critics of the published unemployment rate calculated by the federal government believe that it fails to reflect the true numbers of **discouraged workers** and "hidden unemployed." Though there is no agreed-on method to measure discouraged workers, the Department of Labor defines them as people who have dropped out of the labor force and are no longer looking for a job because they believe that the job market has little to offer them. To what extent do we want to include in the measured labor force those individuals who voluntarily choose not to look for work or those who take only a few minutes a day to scan the want ads and then decide there are no jobs?

Some economists argue that people who work part-time but are willing to work full-time should be classified as "semihidden" unemployed. Estimates range as high as 6 million workers at any one time. Offsetting this factor, though, is *overemployment*. An individual working 50 or 60 hours a week is still counted as only one full-time worker. Some people hold two or three jobs but still are counted as just one employed person.

Discouraged workers
Individuals who have stopped looking for a job because they are convinced that they will not find a suitable one.

LABOR FORCE PARTICIPATION The way in which we define unemployment and membership in the labor force will affect the **labor force participation rate**. It is defined as the proportion of noninstitutionalized (i.e., not in prisons, mental institutions, etc.) working-age individuals who are employed or seeking employment.

Labor force participation rate
The percentage of noninstitutionalized working-age individuals who are employed or seeking employment.

The U.S. labor force participation rate has risen somewhat over time, from 60 percent in 1950 to almost 64 percent today. The gender composition of the U.S. labor force has changed considerably during this time. In 1950, more than 83 percent of men and fewer than 35 percent of women participated in the U.S. labor force. Today, fewer than 70 percent of men and nearly 60 percent of women are U.S. labor force participants.

MyEconLab Concept Check

MyEconLab Study Plan

SELF CHECK Visit MyEconLab to practice these and other problems and to get instant feedback in your Study Plan.

_____ persons are adults who are willing and able to work and are actively looking for a job but have not found one. The unemployment rate is computed by dividing the number of unemployed by the total _____ _____, which is equal to those who are employed plus those who are unemployed.

The unemployed are classified as _____ _____, _____, _____ _____, and _____ _____ to the labor force. The flow of people departing

jobs and people acquiring jobs determines the stock of the unemployed as well as the stock of the employed.

The duration of unemployment affects the unemployment rate. If the duration of unemployment increases, the measured unemployment rate will _____, even though the number of unemployed workers may remain the same.

Whereas overall labor force participation on net has risen only modestly since World War II, there has been a major increase in _____ labor force participation.

7.2 Discuss the types of unemployment

The Major Types of Unemployment

After economists adjust unemployment to take into account seasonal variations—for instance, more construction industry unemployment during winter months—they classify unemployment into three basic types: frictional, structural, and cyclical. Economists also seek to measure full employment and a concept known as the natural rate of unemployment.

Frictional Unemployment

Of the more than 156 million people in the labor force, more than 50 million will either change jobs or take new jobs during the year. In the process, in excess of 22 million persons will report themselves unemployed at one time or another each year. This continuous flow of individuals from job to job and in and out of employment is called **frictional unemployment**. There will always be some frictional unemployment as resources are redirected in the economy, because job-hunting costs are never zero, and workers never have full information about available jobs. To eliminate frictional unemployment, we would have to prevent workers from leaving their present jobs until they had already lined up other jobs at which they would start working immediately. We also would have to guarantee first-time job seekers a job *before* they started looking.

MyEconLab Concept Check

Frictional unemployment
Unemployment due to the fact that workers must search for appropriate job offers. This activity takes time, and so they remain temporarily unemployed.

Structural Unemployment

Structural changes in our economy cause some workers to become unemployed for very long periods of time because they cannot find jobs that use their particular skills. This is called **structural unemployment**. Structural unemployment is not caused by general business fluctuations, although business fluctuations may affect it. Unlike frictional unemployment, structural unemployment is not related to the movement of workers from low-paying to high-paying jobs.

At one time, economists thought about structural unemployment only from the perspective of workers. The concept applied to workers who did not have the ability, training, and skills necessary to obtain available jobs. Today, it still encompasses these workers. In addition, however, economists increasingly look at structural unemployment from the viewpoint of employers, many of whom face government mandates requiring them to take such steps as providing funds for social insurance

Structural unemployment
Unemployment of workers over lengthy intervals resulting from skill mismatches with position requirements of employers and from fewer jobs being offered by employers constrained by governmental business regulations and labor market policies.

programs for their employees and announcing plant closings months or even years in advance.

There is now considerable evidence that government labor market policies influence how many job positions businesses wish to create, thereby affecting structural unemployment. In the United States, many businesses appear to have adjusted to these policies by hiring more "temporary workers" or establishing short-term contracts with "private consultants." Such measures may have increased the extent of U.S. structural unemployment in recent years.

How is the government of France trying to reduce structural unemployment?

INTERNATIONAL POLICY EXAMPLE

The French Government Buys Lower Structural Unemployment

Economists concur that structural unemployment is a significant contributor to the high French unemployment rate, which has recently exceeded 11 percent. Economists also are in general agreement that French government policies have helped to push up the structural unemployment rate. Chief among these policies is a requirement that employers offer their workers long-term contracts that come with strong protections against dismissal. In response to this requirement, French companies have been hesitant to hire as many workers as they otherwise might have employed. In particular, many firms have avoided hiring young people out of a fear of having to keep unproductive workers on their staffs for many years.

The French government wishes to reduce structural unemployment—but without reversing the policies that have contributed to its growth.

Thus, the government is using almost $1.5 billion in taxpayer funds to pay subsidies to companies that hire young people, thereby removing them from the ranks of the structurally unemployed. There is one important condition that firms have to satisfy: They must promise not to replace older workers on long-term contracts with younger workers whose wages are paid in part by the French government.

FOR CRITICAL THINKING

How might the French government's subsidy policy fail to reduce structural unemployment if funding subsidies for wages to young people requires raising taxes on employers? (Hint: Employers sometimes respond to tax increases by reducing the number of workers they hire.)

Sources are listed at the end of this chapter.

MyEconLab Concept Check

Cyclical Unemployment

Cyclical unemployment is related to business fluctuations. It is defined as unemployment associated with changes in business conditions—primarily recessions and depressions. The way to lessen cyclical unemployment would be to reduce the intensity, duration, and frequency of downturns in business activity. Economic policymakers attempt, through their policies, to reduce cyclical unemployment by keeping business activity on an even keel.

MyEconLab Concept Check

Cyclical unemployment
Unemployment resulting from business recessions that occur when aggregate (total) demand is insufficient to create full employment.

Full Employment and the Natural Rate of Unemployment

Does full employment mean that everybody has a job? Certainly not, for not everyone is looking for a job—full-time students and full-time homemakers, for example, are not. Is it always possible for everyone who is looking for a job to find one? No, because transaction costs (see Chapter 4) in the labor market are not zero. Transaction costs are those associated with any activity whose goal is to enter into, carry out, or terminate contracts. In the labor market, these costs involve time spent looking for a job, being interviewed, negotiating the terms of employment, and the like.

FULL EMPLOYMENT We will always have some frictional unemployment as individuals move in and out of the labor force, seek higher-paying jobs, and move to different parts of the country. **Full employment** is therefore a concept that implies some sort of balance or equilibrium in an ever-shifting labor market. Of course, this general notion of full employment must somehow be put into numbers so that economists and others can determine whether the economy has reached the full-employment point.

THE NATURAL RATE OF UNEMPLOYMENT In trying to assess when a situation of balance has been attained in the labor market, economists estimate the **natural rate of unemployment**, the rate that is expected to prevail in the long run once all workers and

Full employment
An arbitrary level of unemployment that corresponds to "normal" friction in the labor market.

Natural rate of unemployment
The rate of unemployment that is estimated to prevail in long-run macroeconomic equilibrium, when all workers and employers have fully adjusted to any changes in the economy.

employers have fully adjusted to any changes in the economy. If correctly estimated, the natural rate of unemployment should not include cyclical unemployment. Thus, the natural unemployment rate should include only frictional and structural unemployment.

A long-standing difficulty, however, has been a lack of agreement about how to estimate the natural unemployment rate. Until the late 2000s, most economists, including those with the president's Council of Economic Advisers and those at the Federal Reserve, had concluded that the natural unemployment rate was slightly above 5 percent.

Since the 2008–2009 recession, the actual unemployment rate has remained considerably above 5 percent. This fact suggests that perhaps the natural rate of unemployment has increased because of a rise in structural unemployment. Some economists propose that the collapse of the U.S. housing industry precipitated this rise. The housing meltdown, these economists suggest, left people possessing skills that were poorly matched to the requirements of jobs other than those in construction, housing finance, and real estate. In contrast, other economists contend that increases in the scope of government regulations and taxes have raised the costs confronted by firms when they contemplate hiring job applicants. Government policies, these economists argue, are to blame for a higher natural unemployment rate.

Of course, both explanations together could help to account for an upswing in structural unemployment. What has yet to be determined by economists is exactly how much higher than 5 percent the natural unemployment rate now may be. Some estimates indicate that it may be above 6 percent.

WHAT IF...

governments provide workers with payments no matter how long they stay unemployed?

Governments of many nations, including France, Italy, and the United States, operate taxpayer-funded programs that provide workers who face lengthy layoffs with part of their regular pay. The governments intend for these payments to replace a portion of lost wages so that workers can cover basic expenses until they find new positions. Such payments create an important disincentive effect, however. The payments discourage recipients from looking as hard for new jobs than they otherwise would have. After all, workers require wages from private employers to compensate them for the fact that they have to work instead of engaging in leisure activities. When laid-off workers receive payments from the government, they do not have to give up leisure pursuits, which leads many of the payment recipients to remain out of work. The result is increased structural unemployment and a higher natural rate of unemployment.

MyEconLab Concept Check
MyEconLab Study Plan

SELF CHECK Visit MyEconLab to practice these and other problems and to get instant feedback in your Study Plan.

_____ **unemployment** occurs because of transaction costs in the labor market. For example, workers do not have full information about vacancies and must search for jobs.

_____ **unemployment** occurs when there is a poor match of workers' skills and abilities with available jobs, perhaps because workers lack appropriate training or government labor rules reduce firms' willingness to hire.

The levels of frictional and structural unemployment are used in part to determine our (somewhat arbitrary) measurement of the _____ rate of unemployment.

7.3 Describe how price indexes are calculated and define the key types of price indexes

Inflation
A sustained increase in the average of all prices of goods and services in an economy.

Inflation and Deflation

During World War II, you could buy bread for 8 to 10 cents a loaf and have milk delivered fresh to your door for about 25 cents a half gallon. The average price of a new car was less than $700, and the average house cost less than $3,000. Today, bread, milk, cars, and houses all cost more—a lot more. Prices are about 17 times what they were in 1940. Clearly, this country has experienced quite a bit of *inflation* since then. We define **inflation** as an upward movement in the average level of prices. The opposite of inflation is **deflation**, defined as a downward movement in the average level of prices. Notice that these definitions depend on the *average* level of prices. This means that even during a period of inflation, some prices can be falling if other prices are rising at a faster rate. The prices of electronic equipment have dropped dramatically since the 1960s, even though there has been general inflation.

Deflation
A sustained decrease in the average of all prices of goods and services in an economy.

Inflation and the Purchasing Power of Money

By definition, the value of a dollar does not stay constant when there is inflation. The value of money is usually talked about in terms of **purchasing power**. A dollar's purchasing power is the real goods and services that it can buy. Consequently, another way of defining inflation is as a decline in the purchasing power of money. The faster the rate of inflation, the greater the rate of decline in the purchasing power of money.

One way to think about inflation and the purchasing power of money is to discuss dollar values in terms of *nominal* versus *real* values. The nominal value of anything is simply its price expressed in today's dollars. In contrast, the real value of anything is its value expressed in purchasing power, which varies with the overall price level. Let's say that you received a $100 bill from your grandparents this year. One year from now, the nominal value of that bill will still be $100. The real value will depend on what the purchasing power of money is after one year's worth of inflation. Obviously, if there is inflation during the year, the real value of that $100 bill will have diminished. For example, if you keep the $100 bill in your pocket for a year during which the rate of inflation is 3 percent, at the end of the year you will have to come up with $3 more to buy the same amount of goods and services that the $100 bill can purchase today.

To discuss what has happened to prices here and in other countries, we have to know how to measure inflation. MyEconLab Concept Check

Purchasing power
The value of money for buying goods and services. If your money income stays the same but the price of one good that you are buying goes up, your effective purchasing power falls.

Measuring the Rate of Inflation

How can we measure the rate of inflation? It is easy to determine how much the price of an individual commodity has risen: If last year a compact fluorescent light bulb cost $6.00, and this year it costs $9.00, there has been a 50 percent rise in the price of that light bulb over a one-year period. We can express the change in the individual light bulb price in one of several ways: The price has gone up $3.00. The price is one and a half (1.5) times as high. The price has risen by 50 percent. An *index number* of this price rise is simply the second way (1.5) multiplied by 100, meaning that the index today would stand at 150. We multiply by 100 to eliminate decimals because it is easier to think in terms of percentage changes using whole numbers. This is the standard convention adopted for convenience in dealing with index numbers or price levels.

MyEconLab Concept Check

Computing a Price Index

The measurement problem becomes more complicated when it involves a large number of goods, especially if some prices have risen faster than others and some have even fallen. What we have to do is pick a representative bundle, a so-called market basket, of goods and compare the cost of that market basket of goods over time. When we do this, we obtain a **price index**, which is defined as the cost of a market basket of goods today, expressed as a percentage of the cost of that identical market basket of goods in some starting year, known as the **base year**.

Price index
The cost of today's market basket of goods expressed as a percentage of the cost of the same market basket during a base year.

Base year
The year that is chosen as the point of reference for comparison of prices in other years.

$$\text{Price index} = \frac{\text{cost of market basket today}}{\text{cost of market basket in base year}} \times 100$$

In the base year, the price index will always be 100, because the year in the numerator and in the denominator of the fraction is the same. Therefore, the fraction equals 1, and when we multiply it by 100, we get 100. A simple numerical example is given in

TABLE 7-1

Calculating a Price Index for a Two-Good Market Basket

In this simplified example, there are only two goods—corn and digital devices. The quantities and base-year prices are given in columns 2 and 3. The 2007 cost of the market basket, calculated in column 4, comes to $1,300. The 2017 prices are given in column 5. The cost of the market basket in 2017, calculated in column 6, is $1,500. The price index for 2017 compared with 2007 is 115.38.

(1) Commodity	(2) Market Basket Quantity	(3) 2007 Price per Unit	(4) Cost of Market Basket in 2007	(5) 2017 Price per Unit	(6) Cost of Market Basket in 2017
Corn	100 bushels	$ 4	$ 400	$ 8	$ 800
Digital devices	2	450	900	350	700
		0			
Totals			**$1,300**		**$1,500**

$$\text{Price index} = \frac{\text{cost of market basket in 2017}}{\text{cost of market basket in base year 2007}} \times 100 = \frac{\$1,500}{\$1,300} \times 100 = 115.38$$

Table 7-1 above. In the table, there are only two goods in the market basket—corn and digital devices. The *quantities* in the basket are the same in the base year, 2007, and the current year, 2017. Only the *prices* change. Such a *fixed-quantity* price index is the easiest to compute because the statistician need only look at prices of goods and services sold every year rather than observing how much of these goods and services consumers actually purchase each year.

REAL-WORLD PRICE INDEXES Government statisticians calculate a number of price indexes. The most often quoted are the **Consumer Price Index (CPI)**, the **Producer Price Index (PPI)**, the **GDP deflator**, and the **Personal Consumption Expenditure (PCE) Index**. The CPI attempts to measure changes only in the level of prices of goods and services purchased by consumers. The PPI attempts to show what has happened to the average price of goods and services produced and sold by a typical firm. (There are also *wholesale price indexes* that track the price level for commodities that firms purchase from other firms.) The GDP deflator is the most general indicator of inflation because it measures changes in the level of prices of all new goods and services produced in the economy. The PCE Index measures average prices using weights from surveys of consumer spending.

THE CPI The Bureau of Labor Statistics (BLS) has the task of identifying a market basket of goods and services of the typical consumer. Today, the BLS uses the time period 1982–1984 as its base of market prices. The BLS has indicated an intention to change the base to 1993–1995 but has yet to do so. It has, though, updated the expenditure weights for its market basket of goods to reflect consumer spending patterns in 2001–2002. All CPI numbers since February 1998 reflect these expenditure weights.

Economists have known for years that there are possible problems in the CPI's market basket. Specifically, the BLS has been unable to account for the way consumers substitute less expensive items for higher-priced items. The reason is that the CPI is a fixed-quantity price index, meaning that the BLS implicitly ignores changes in consumption patterns that occur between years in which it revises the index. Until recently, the BLS has also been unable to take quality changes into account as they occur. Now, though, it is subtracting from certain list prices estimated effects of qualitative improvements and adding to other list prices to account for deteriorations in quality. An additional flaw is that the CPI usually ignores successful new products until long after they have been introduced. Despite these flaws, the CPI is widely followed because its level is calculated and published monthly.

How much do weights on food expenditures in CPI market baskets differ across countries, and why has this mattered during the past few years?

Consumer Price Index (CPI)
A statistical measure of a weighted average of prices of a specified set of goods and services purchased by typical consumers in urban areas.

Producer Price Index (PPI)
A statistical measure of a weighted average of prices of goods and services that firms produce and sell.

GDP deflator
A price index measuring the changes in prices of all new goods and services produced in the economy.

Personal Consumption Expenditure (PCE) Index
A statistical measure of average prices that uses annually updated weights based on surveys of consumer spending.

INTERNATIONAL EXAMPLE

Consuming More Food Boosts Some Nations' CPI Inflation Rates

The expenditure weight for home-consumed food—that is, food items purchased from grocery stores and taken home to prepare for meals—in the U.S. CPI's market basket is close to 8.5 percent. In contrast, the expenditure weights for food prepared at home are about 14.8 percent in the French CPI and 18.2 percent in the South African CPI. In India, the CPI weights for home-prepared food exceed 35 percent for urban residents and 55 percent for rural residents.

Since 2007, food prices have risen considerably faster than all other prices in about two-thirds of the world's nations. In many of these nations, which include South Africa and India, CPI weights for home-consumed food are higher than in advanced nations. As a consequence, measured rates of CPI inflation have been significantly higher in these countries.

FOR CRITICAL THINKING

Even if the base years for the CPIs were the same, why would it be a mistake to compare the value of the 2015 CPI for the United States with the 2015 CPI for India?

Sources are listed at the end of this chapter.

THE PPI There are a number of Producer Price Indexes, including one for foodstuffs, another for intermediate goods (goods used in the production of other goods), and one for finished goods. Most of the producer prices included are in mining, manufacturing, and agriculture. The PPIs can be considered general-purpose indexes for nonretail markets.

Although in the long run the various PPIs and the CPI generally show the same rate of inflation, that is not the case in the short run. Most often the PPIs increase before the CPI because it takes time for producer price increases to show up in the prices that consumers pay for final products. Changes in the PPIs are watched closely as a hint that CPI inflation is going to increase or decrease.

THE GDP DEFLATOR The broadest price index reported in the United States is the GDP deflator, where GDP stands for gross domestic product, or annual total national income. Unlike the CPI and the PPIs, the GDP deflator is *not* based on a fixed market basket of goods and services. The basket is allowed to change with people's consumption and investment patterns. In this sense, the changes in the GDP deflator reflect both price changes and the public's market responses to those price changes. Why? Because new expenditure patterns are allowed to show up in the GDP deflator as people respond to changing prices.

THE PCE INDEX Another price index that takes into account changing expenditure patterns is the Personal Consumption Expenditure (PCE) Index. The Bureau of Economic Analysis, an agency of the U.S. Department of Commerce, uses continuously updated annual surveys of consumer purchases to construct the weights for the PCE Index. Thus, an advantage of the PCE Index is that weights in the index are updated every year. The Federal Reserve has used the rate of change in the PCE Index as its primary inflation indicator because Fed officials believe that the updated weights in the PCE Index make it more accurate than the CPI as a measure of consumer price changes. Nevertheless, the CPI remains the most widely reported price index, and the U.S. government continues to use the CPI to adjust the value of Social Security benefits to account for inflation.

HISTORICAL CHANGES IN THE CPI Between World War II and the early 1980s, the Consumer Price Index showed a fairly dramatic trend upward. Figure 7-4 on the next page shows the annual rate of change in the CPI since 1860. Prior to World War II, there were numerous periods of deflation interspersed with periods of inflation. Persistent year-in and year-out inflation seems to be a post–World War II phenomenon, at least in this country. As far back as before the American Revolution, prices used to rise during war periods but then would fall back toward prewar levels afterward. This occurred after the Revolutionary War, the War of 1812, the Civil War, and to a lesser extent World War I. Consequently, the overall price level in 1940 wasn't much different from 150 years earlier.

FIGURE 7-4

Inflation and Deflation in U.S. History

For 80 years after the Civil War, the United States experienced alternating inflation and deflation. Here we show them as reflected by changes in the price level. Since World War II, the periods of inflation have not been followed by periods of deflation. Even during peacetime, the price index has continued to rise. The shaded areas represent wartime.

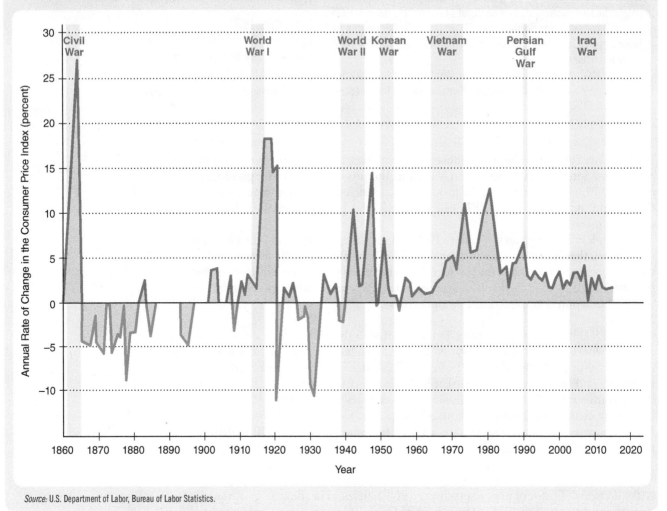

Source: U.S. Department of Labor, Bureau of Labor Statistics.

SELF CHECK Visit MyEconLab to practice these and other problems and to get instant feedback in your Study Plan.

Once we pick a market basket of goods, we can construct a **price index** that compares the cost of that market basket today with the cost of the same market basket in a _____ year.

The _____ _____ Index is the most often used price index in the United States. The **Producer Price Index (PPI)** is also widely mentioned.

The _____ _____ measures what is happening to the average price level of *all* new, domestically produced final goods and services in our economy.

The _____ _____ _____ Index uses annually updated weights from consumer spending surveys to measure average prices faced by consumers.

7.4 Evaluate who loses and who gains from inflation and distinguish between nominal and real interest rates

Anticipated Versus Unanticipated Inflation

To determine who is hurt by inflation and what the effects of inflation are in general, we have to distinguish between anticipated and unanticipated inflation. We will see that the effects on individuals and the economy are vastly different, depending on which type of inflation exists.

Anticipated inflation is the rate of inflation that most individuals believe will occur. If the rate of inflation this year turns out to be 5 percent, and that's about what most people thought it was going to be, we are in a situation of fully anticipated inflation.

Unanticipated inflation is inflation that comes as a surprise to individuals in the economy. For example, if the inflation rate in a particular year turns out to be 10 percent when, on average, people thought it was going to be 3 percent, there was unanticipated inflation—inflation greater than anticipated.

Some of the problems caused by inflation arise when it is unanticipated, because then many people are unable to protect themselves from its ravages. Keeping the distinction between anticipated and unanticipated inflation in mind, we can easily see the relationship between inflation and interest rates.

> **Anticipated inflation**
> The inflation rate that we believe will occur. When it does occur, we are in a situation of fully anticipated inflation.
>
> **Unanticipated inflation**
> Inflation at a rate that comes as a surprise, either higher or lower than the rate anticipated.

Inflation and Interest Rates

Let's start in a hypothetical world in which there is no inflation and anticipated inflation is zero. In that world, you may be able to borrow funds—to buy a house or a car, for example—at a **nominal rate of interest** of, say, 6 percent. If you borrow the funds to purchase a house or a car and your anticipation of inflation turns out to be accurate, neither you nor the lender will have been fooled. Each dollar you pay back in the years to come will be just as valuable in terms of purchasing power as the dollar you borrowed.

What you ordinarily want to know when you borrow is the *real* rate of interest that you will have to pay. The **real rate of interest** is defined as the nominal rate of interest minus the anticipated rate of inflation. In effect, we can say that the nominal rate of interest is equal to the real rate of interest plus an *inflationary premium* to take account of anticipated inflation. That inflationary premium covers depreciation in the purchasing power of the dollars repaid by borrowers. (Whenever there are relatively high rates of anticipated inflation, we must add an additional factor to the inflationary premium—the product of the real rate of interest times the anticipated rate of inflation. Usually, this last term is omitted because the anticipated rate of inflation is not high enough to make much of a difference.) MyEconLab Concept Check

> **Nominal rate of interest**
> The market rate of interest observed in contracts expressed in today's dollars.
>
> **Real rate of interest**
> The nominal rate of interest minus the anticipated rate of inflation.

Does Inflation Necessarily Hurt Everyone?

Most people think that inflation is bad. After all, inflation means higher prices, and when we have to pay higher prices, are we not necessarily worse off? The truth is that inflation affects different people differently. Its effects also depend on whether it is anticipated or unanticipated.

UNANTICIPATED INFLATION: CREDITORS LOSE AND DEBTORS GAIN In most situations, unanticipated inflation benefits borrowers because the nominal interest rate they are being charged does not fully compensate creditors for the inflation that actually occurred. In other words, the lender did not anticipate inflation correctly. Whenever inflation rates are underestimated for the life of a loan, creditors lose and debtors gain. Periods of considerable unanticipated (higher than anticipated) inflation occurred in the late 1960s and all of the 1970s. During those years, creditors lost and debtors gained.

PROTECTING AGAINST INFLATION Lenders attempt to protect themselves against inflation by raising nominal interest rates to reflect anticipated inflation. Adjustable-rate mortgages in fact do just that: The interest rate varies according to what happens to interest rates in the economy. Workers can protect themselves from inflation by obtaining **cost-of-living adjustments (COLAs)**, which are automatic increases in wage rates to take account of increases in the price level.

To the extent that you hold non-interest-bearing cash, you will lose because of inflation. If you have put $100 in a mattress and the inflation rate is 5 percent for the year, you will have lost 5 percent of the purchasing power of that $100. If you have your funds in a non-interest-bearing checking account, you will suffer the same fate. Individuals attempt to reduce the cost of holding cash by putting it into interest-bearing accounts, some of which pay nominal rates of interest that reflect anticipated inflation.

> **Cost-of-living adjustments (COLAs)**
> Clauses in contracts that allow for increases in specified nominal values to take account of changes in the cost of living.

THE RESOURCE COST OF INFLATION Some economists believe that the main cost of inflation is the opportunity cost of resources used to protect against distortions that inflation introduces as firms attempt to plan for the long run. Individuals have to spend time and resources to figure out ways to adjust their behavior in case inflation is different from what it has been in the past. That may mean spending a longer time working out more complicated contracts for employment, for purchases of goods in the future, and for purchases of raw materials to be delivered later.

Repricing, or menu, cost of inflation
The cost associated with recalculating prices and printing new price lists when there is inflation.

Inflation requires that price lists be changed. This is called the **repricing, or menu, cost of inflation**. The higher the rate of inflation, the higher the repricing cost of inflation, because prices must be changed more often within a given period of time.

MyEconLab Concept Check
MyEconLab Study Plan

SELF CHECK Visit MyEconLab to practice these and other problems and to get instant feedback in your Study Plan.

Whenever inflation is _____ than anticipated, creditors lose and debtors gain. Whenever the rate of inflation is _____ than anticipated, creditors gain and debtors lose.

Holders of cash lose during periods of inflation because the _____ _____ of their cash depreciates at the rate of inflation.

The _____ interest rate is the market rate of interest observed in contracts expressed in today's dollars, whereas the _____ interest rate equals the _____ interest rate minus the _____ rate of inflation.

7.5 Understand key features of business fluctuations

Changing Inflation and Unemployment: Business Fluctuations

Some years unemployment goes up, and some years it goes down. Some years there is a lot of inflation, and other years there isn't. We have fluctuations in all aspects of our macroeconomy. The ups and downs in economywide economic activity are sometimes called **business fluctuations**. When business fluctuations are positive, they are called **expansions**—speedups in the pace of national economic activity. The opposite of an expansion is a **contraction**, which is a slowdown in the pace of national economic activity. The top of an expansion is usually called its *peak*, and the bottom of a contraction is usually called its *trough*. Business fluctuations used to be called *business cycles*, but that term no longer seems appropriate because *cycle* implies regular or automatic recurrence, and we have never had automatic recurrent fluctuations in general business and economic activity. What we have had are contractions and expansions that vary greatly in length. For example, the 10 post–World War II expansions have averaged 57 months, but three of those exceeded 90 months, and two lasted less than 25 months.

Business fluctuations
The ups and downs in business activity throughout the economy.

Expansion
A business fluctuation in which the pace of national economic activity is speeding up.

Contraction
A business fluctuation during which the pace of national economic activity is slowing down.

Recession
A period of time during which the rate of growth of business activity is consistently less than its long-term trend or is negative.

Depression
An extremely severe recession.

If the contractionary phase of business fluctuations becomes severe enough, we call it a **recession**. An extremely severe recession is called a **depression**. Typically, at the beginning of a recession, there is a marked increase in the rate of unemployment, and the duration of unemployment increases. In addition, people's incomes start to decline. In times of expansion, the opposite occurs.

In Figure 7-5 on the next page, you see that typical business fluctuations occur around a growth trend in overall national business activity shown as a straight upward-sloping line. Starting out at a peak, the economy goes into a contraction (recession). Then an expansion starts that moves up to its peak, higher than the last one, and the sequence starts over again.

A Historical Picture of Business Activity in the United States

Figure 7-6 on the next page traces changes in U.S. business activity from 1880 to the present. Note that the long-term trend line is shown as horizontal, so all changes in business activity focus around that trend line. Major changes in business activity in the

FIGURE 7-5

The Idealized Course of Business Fluctuations

A hypothetical business cycle would go from peak to trough and back again in a regular cycle. Real-world business cycles are not as regular as this hypothetical cycle.

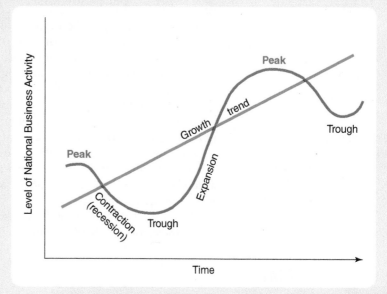

FIGURE 7-6

National Business Activity, 1880 to the Present

Variations around the trend of U.S. business activity have been frequent since 1880.

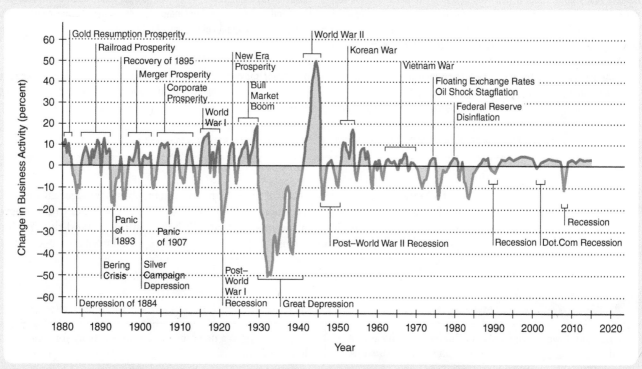

Sources: American Business Activity from 1790 to Today, 67th ed., AmeriTrust Co., January 1996, plus author's estimates.

United States occurred during the Great Depression, World War II, and, most recently, the sharp 2008-2009 recession. Note that none of the actual business fluctuations in Figure 7-6 exactly mirror the idealized course of a business fluctuation shown in Figure 7-5 above.

Explaining Business Fluctuations: External Shocks

As you might imagine, because changes in national business activity affect everyone, economists for decades have attempted to understand and explain business fluctuations. For years, one of the most obvious explanations has been external events that tend to disrupt the economy. In many of the graphs in this chapter, you have seen that World War II was a critical point in this nation's economic history. A war is certainly an external shock—something that originates outside our economy.

In trying to help account for shocks to economic activity that may induce business fluctuations and thereby make fluctuations easier to predict, the U.S. Department of Commerce and private firms and organizations tabulate indexes (weighted averages) of **leading indicators**. These are events that economists have noticed typically occur *before* changes in business activity. For example, economic downturns often follow such events as a reduction in the average workweek, an increase in unemployment insurance claims, a decrease in the prices of raw materials, or a drop in the quantity of money in circulation.

How is the U.S. Bureau of the Census striving to provide people with leading economic indicators—only to be outdone by private firms?

Leading indicators
Events that have been found to occur before changes in business activity.

POLICY EXAMPLE

Want to Be Led by an Indicator? There Are Apps for That!

Since 2012, people have been able to visit digital app stores to obtain the U.S. Census Bureau's "America's Economy" app. This app provides data on 19 key leading indicators of economic activity, including retail sales, durable goods sales, construction spending, and international trade volumes. U.S. taxpayer funding supports the Census Bureau's development of the app and its staff's real-time updating of the data that it provides users, so the Census Bureau makes the app available at no explicit charge.

Those searching for the best free leading-indicator apps, however, can quickly find privately produced apps that provide many more economic indicators. For instance, A2ZEconomy's Indicators Online© app, which can be downloaded at no explicit charge, provides data on dozens of indicators of economic activity. For people who are not satisfied following only a few dozen leading indicators, Cascade Software's "Economy for iPad" app, which provides information on about 45,000 economic indicators, is available at a one-time charge of $3.99. Alternatively, A2ZEconomy's "premium" version of its app, which additionally provides thousands of novel leading indicators developed by the company, is available at an annual charge of $99.99.

FOR CRITICAL THINKING
Why might someone be willing to pay for access to leading indicators offered by private firms instead of downloading a free Census Bureau app?

Sources are listed at the end of this chapter.

To better understand the role of shocks in influencing business fluctuations, we need a theory of why national economic activity changes. The remainder of the macro chapters in this book develop the models that will help you understand the ups and downs of our business fluctuations.

MyEconLab Concept Check
MyEconLab Study Plan

SELF CHECK Visit MyEconLab to practice these and other problems and to get instant feedback in your Study Plan.

The ups and downs in economywide business activity are called _____ _____, which consist of **expansions** and **contractions** in overall business activity.

The lowest point of a contraction is called the _____. The highest point of an expansion is called the _____.

A _____ is a downturn in business activity for some length of time.

One possible explanation for business fluctuations relates to _____ _____, such as wars, dramatic increases in the prices of raw materials, and earthquakes, floods, and droughts.

A Small-Business Skills Mismatch and Structural Unemployment

More than 99 percent of U.S. companies are small businesses. A typical small business employs fewer than 20 workers. These facts taken together suggest why small businesses account for only one-fifth of all U.S. jobs. At any given time, though, in past years small businesses typically have accounted for more than six of every ten new positions that U.S. employers fill each year.

Paul McDonald, a senior executive director with the professional staffing firm Robert Half International, Inc., has just overseen a study of the biggest management challenges facing small businesses. He has discovered that for 60 percent of small businesses, the main challenge is finding skilled workers. Many small businesses have adopted the latest technologies for producing goods or delivering services. Consequently, they require workers who are able to perform skilled tasks, such as using digital technologies to adapt designs to customer orders or to develop logistical plans for providing services to clients. Most small firms do not have significant budgets for training people to

perform these tasks and must search for workers who already possess required skills. McDonald's survey indicates a mismatch of the skills of workers looking for jobs and the skills that the majority of small businesses wish their workers to have. This skills mismatch may help to account for the fact today that small businesses are providing only just over four of every ten new jobs and leaving positions unfilled—resulting in higher structural unemployment.

CRITICAL THINKING QUESTIONS

1. Why might small businesses reduce hiring if wages for scarce skilled workers rise? (Hint: What does the demand curve for skilled workers look like?)

2. How might federal small-business regulations affect structural unemployment?

Sources are listed at the end of this chapter.

ISSUES & APPLICATIONS

MyEconLab Video

The U.S. Male Work Withdrawal

CandyBox Images/Shutterstock

CONCEPTS APPLIED

» Employment

» Unemployment

» Labor Force Participation

The share of the U.S. male population that is gainfully employed has been shrinking. Events since 2008 help to explain a sharp drop in the male employment percentage. The significant recession that occurred that year generated substantial employment reductions in the construction and manufacturing industries, in which men hold most of the jobs. Nevertheless, a general reduction in male employment as a share of the male population has been under way for some time. It is not isolated to recent years but instead has been occurring over several decades.

The Gradual Decline of Male Employment

Figure 7-7 on the next page documents the substantial decline in U.S. male employment in relation to the population of men. It shows that during the past 60 years, the percentage of the U.S. male population that is employed has fallen by about 20 percentage points.

If 20 percent more U.S. male residents were working today, in excess of 20 million additional men would be

employed. Instead of about 75 million employed males, at least 95 million would hold jobs.

A Persistent Drop in Male Labor Force Participation

Why are so many men no longer gainfully employed? Is there a vast conspiracy among employers not to hire men?

FIGURE 7-7

The U.S. Male Employment-Population Ratio

Since reaching a peak just above 85 percent in the early 1950s, male employment as a percentage of the male population has dropped by about 20 percentage points.

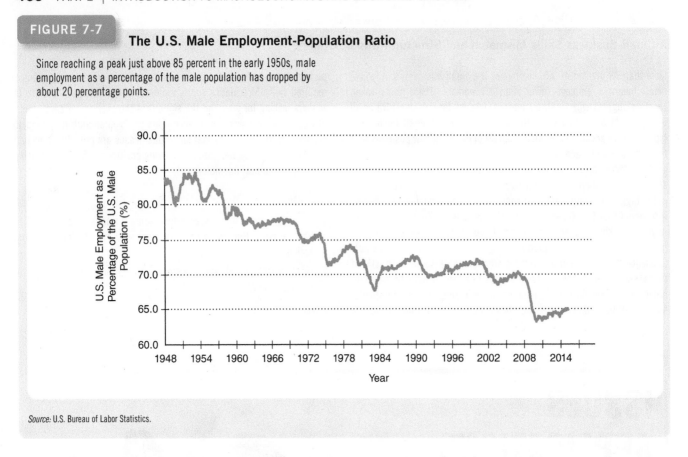

Source: U.S. Bureau of Labor Statistics.

In fact, the primary reason is that a smaller percentage of men are entering the *labor force* and even attempting to find jobs. Sixty years ago, more than 86 percent of adult men participated in the labor force. Today, this figure has dropped to about 70 percent. Thus, the fundamental reason we now observe so many fewer men employed relative to the population is that a significantly smaller percentage of men are choosing to seek jobs.

For Critical Thinking

1. Why does the overall level of employment often tend to increase as overall labor force participation rises?

2. If male unemployment were to decrease at the same time that male labor force participation declines, does the male unemployment rate necessarily drop? Explain briefly. (Hint: The male unemployment rate equals the number of unemployed males divided by the number of males in the labor force.)

Web Resources

1. Take a look at the U.S. male labor force participation rate in the Web Links in MyEconLab.

2. Consider ratios of female to male labor force participation rates in most of the world's nations in the Web Links in MyEconLab.

> ### MyEconLab
>
> For more questions on this chapter's Issues & Applications, go to MyEconLab.
>
> In the Study Plan for this chapter, select Section I: Issues and Applications

Sources are listed at the end of this chapter.

Fundamental Points

1. Unemployment is the number of adults who are part of the labor force and actively looking for a job but have not found one. The unemployment rate is equal to the number of unemployed divided by the sum of the number of employed and the number unemployed.

2. Unemployment can be classified into three types: frictional, structural, and cyclical.

3. An annual inflation rate is the percentage change in a measure of the overall price level during a year. Examples of key price indexes are the Consumer Price Index (CPI), the Producer Price Index (PPI), and the Personal Consumption Expenditure (PCE) Index.

4. The nominal interest rate is the market rate of interest observed in contracts expressed in today's dollars,

whereas the real interest rate is equal to nominal interest rate minus the anticipated rate of inflation.

5. Business fluctuations, or the expansions and contractions in overall business activity in the economy, reach a peak at the highest point of an expansion and drop to a trough at the lowest point of a contraction.

WHAT YOU SHOULD KNOW

Here is what you should know after reading this chapter. MyEconLab will help you identify what you know, and where to go when you need to practice.

LEARNING OBJECTIVES	KEY TERMS	WHERE TO GO TO PRACTICE
7.1 **Explain how the U.S. government calculates the official unemployment rate** *The total number of workers who are officially unemployed consists of noninstitutionalized people aged 16 or older who are willing and able to work and who are actively looking for work but have not found a job. To calculate the unemployment rate, the government determines what percentage this quantity is of the labor force, which consists of all noninstitutionalized people aged 16 years or older who either have jobs or are available for and actively seeking employment.*	unemployment, 150 labor force, 150 stock, 152 flow, 152 job loser, 152 reentrant, 152 job leaver, 152 new entrant, 152 discouraged workers, 153 labor force participation rate, 153 **Key Figure** Figure 7-3, 152	• MyEconLab Study Plan 7.1 • Animated Figure 7-3
7.2 **Discuss the types of unemployment** *Temporarily unemployed workers who are searching for appropriate job offers are frictionally unemployed. The structurally unemployed lack the skills currently required by prospective employers. People unemployed due to business contractions are cyclically unemployed.*	frictional unemployment, 154 structural unemployment, 154 cyclical unemployment, 155 full employment, 155 natural rate of unemployment, 155	• MyEconLab Study Plan 7.2
7.3 **Describe how price indexes are calculated and define the key types of price indexes** *To calculate any price index, economists multiply 100 times the ratio of the cost of a market basket of goods and services in the current year to the cost of the same market basket in a base year. The Consumer Price Index (CPI) is a weighted average of prices of items purchased by a typical urban consumer. The Producer Price Index (PPI) is a weighted average of prices of goods sold by a typical firm. The GDP deflator measures changes in the overall level of prices of all goods produced during a given interval. The Personal Consumption Expenditure (PCE) Index is a measure of average prices using weights from surveys of consumer spending.*	inflation, 156 deflation, 157 purchasing power, 157 price index, 157 base year, 157 Consumer Price Index (CPI), 158 Producer Price Index (PPI), 158 GDP deflator, 158 Personal Consumption Expenditure (PCE) Index, 158 **Key Figure** Figure 7-4, 160	• MyEconLab Study Plan 7.3 • Animated Figure 7-4

WHAT YOU SHOULD KNOW *continued*

LEARNING OBJECTIVES	KEY TERMS	WHERE TO GO TO PRACTICE
7.4 Evaluate who loses and who gains from inflation and distinguish between nominal and real interest rates *The nominal interest rate applies to contracts expressed in current dollars. The real interest rate is net of inflation anticipated to erode the value of nominal interest payments during the period that a loan is repaid. Hence, the real interest rate equals the nominal interest rate minus the expected inflation rate.* *Creditors lose as a result of unanticipated inflation, because the real value of the interest payments they receive will turn out to be lower than they had expected. Borrowers gain when unanticipated inflation occurs, because the real value of their interest and principal payments declines. Key costs of inflation include expenses of protecting against inflation, costs of altering business plans because of unexpected changes in prices, and menu costs of repricing goods and services.*	anticipated inflation, 161 unanticipated inflation, 161 nominal rate of interest, 161 real rate of interest, 161 cost-of-living adjustments (COLAs), 161 repricing, or menu, cost of inflation, 162	• MyEconLab Study Plan 7.4
7.5 Understand key features of business fluctuations *Business fluctuations are increases and decreases in business activity. A positive fluctuation is an expansion, which is an upward movement in business activity from a trough, or low point, to a peak, or high point. A negative fluctuation is a contraction, which is a drop in the pace of business activity from a previous peak to a new trough.*	business fluctuations, 162 expansion, 162 contraction, 162 recession, 162 depression, 162 leading indicators, 164 **Key Figure** Figure 7-6, 163	• MyEconLab Study Plan 7.5 • Animated Figures 7-5, 7-6

PROBLEMS

All problems are assignable in MyEconLab; exercises that update with real-time data are marked with 🌐 . Answers to odd-numbered problems appear in MyEconLab.

7-1. Suppose that you are given the following information (see page 151.):

Total population	300.0 million
Adult, noninstitutionalized, nonmilitary population	200.0 million
Unemployment	7.5 million

  a. If the labor force participation rate is 70 percent, what is the labor force?

b. How many workers are employed?

c. What is the unemployment rate?

7-2. Suppose that you are given the following information (see page 151):

Labor force	206.2 million
Adults in the military	1.5 million
Nonadult population	48.0 million
Employed adults	196.2 million
Institutionalized adults	3.5 million
Nonmilitary, noninstitutionalized adults not in labor force	40.8 million

a. What is the total population?

b. How many people are unemployed, and what is the unemployment rate?

c. What is the labor force participation rate?

7-3. Suppose that the U.S. nonmilitary, noninstitutionalized adult population is 224 million, the number employed is 156 million, and the number unemployed is 8 million. (See page 151.)

a. What is the unemployment rate?

b. Suppose there is a difference of 60 million between the adult population and the combined total of people who are employed and unemployed. How do we classify these 60 million people? Based on these figures, what is the U.S. labor force participation rate?

7-4. During the course of a year, the labor force consists of the same 1,000 people. Employers have chosen not to hire 20 of these people in the face of government regulations making it too costly to employ them. Hence, they remain unemployed throughout the year. At the same time, every month during the year, 30 different people become unemployed, and 30 other different people who were unemployed find jobs. (See pages 150–155.)

a. What is the frictional unemployment rate?

b. What is the unemployment rate?

c. Suppose that a system of unemployment compensation is established. Each month, 30 new people (not including the 20 that employers have chosen not to employ) continue to become unemployed, but each monthly group of newly unemployed now takes two months to find a job. After this change, what is the frictional unemployment rate?

d. After the change discussed in part (c), what is the unemployment rate?

7-5. Suppose that a nation has a labor force of 100 people. In January, Amy, Barbara, Carine, and Denise are unemployed. In February, those four find jobs, but Evan, Francesco, George, and Horatio become unemployed. Suppose further that every month, the previous four who were unemployed find jobs and four different people become unemployed. Throughout the year, however, three people—Ito, Jack, and Kelley—continually remain unemployed because firms facing government regulations view them as too costly to employ. (See page 154.)

a. What is this nation's frictional unemployment rate?

b. What is its structural unemployment rate?

c. What is its unemployment rate?

7-6. In a country with a labor force of 200, a different group of 10 people becomes unemployed each month, but becomes employed once again a month later. No others outside these groups are unemployed. (See pages 150–155.)

a. What is this country's unemployment rate?

b. What is the average duration of unemployment?

c. Suppose that establishment of a system of unemployment compensation increases to two months the interval that it takes each group of job losers to become employed each month. Nevertheless, a different group of 10 people still becomes unemployed each month. Now what is the average duration of unemployment?

d. Following the change discussed in part (c), what is the country's unemployment rate?

7-7. A nation's frictional unemployment rate is 1 percent. Its cyclical rate of unemployment is 3 percent, and its structural unemployment rate is 4 percent. What is this nation's overall rate of unemployment? (See pages 150–155.)

7-8. In 2014, the cost of a market basket of goods was $2,000. In 2016, the cost of the same market basket of goods was $2,100. Use the price index formula to calculate the price index for 2016 if 2014 is the base year. (See pages 157–158.)

7-9. Suppose that in 2015, a typical U.S. student attending a state-supported college bought 10 textbooks at a price of $100 per book and enrolled in 25 credit hours of coursework at a price of $360 per credit hour. In 2016, the typical student continued to purchase 10 textbooks and enroll in 25 credit hours, but the price of a textbook rose to $110 per book, and the tuition price increased to $400 per credit hour. The base year for computing a "student price index" using this information is 2015. What is the value of the student price index in 2015? In 2016? Show your work. (See pages 157–158.)

7-10. Between 2015 and 2016 in a particular nation, the value of the consumer price index—for which the base year is 2012—rose by 9.091 percent, to a value of 120 in 2016. What was the value of the price index in 2015? (See pages 157–158.)

7-11. Consider the following price indexes: 90 in 2015, 100 in 2016, 110 in 2017, 121 in 2018, and 150 in 2019. Answer the following questions. (See pages 157–158.)

a. Which year is likely the base year?

b. What is the inflation rate from 2016 to 2017?

c. What is the inflation rate from 2017 to 2018?

d. If the cost of a market basket in 2016 is $2,000, what is the cost of the same basket of goods and services in 2015? In 2019?

7-12. The real interest rate is 4 percent, and the nominal interest rate is 6 percent. What is the anticipated rate of inflation? (See page 161.)

7-13. Currently, the price index used to calculate the inflation rate is equal to 90. The general expectation throughout the economy is that next year its value will be 99. The current nominal interest rate is 12 percent. What is the real interest rate? (See page 161.)

7-14. At present, the nominal interest rate is 7 percent, and the expected inflation rate is 5 percent. The current year is the base year for the price index used to calculate inflation. (See page 161.)

    a. What is the real interest rate?

    b. What is the anticipated value of the price index next year?

7-15. Suppose that in 2019 there is a sudden, unanticipated burst of inflation. Consider the situations faced by the following individuals. Who gains and who loses? (See pages 161–162.)

    a. A homeowner whose wages will keep pace with inflation in 2019 but whose monthly mortgage payments to a savings bank will remain fixed

    b. An apartment landlord who has guaranteed to his tenants that their monthly rent payments during 2019 will be the same as they were during 2018

    c. A banker who made an auto loan that the auto buyer will repay at a fixed rate of interest during 2019

    d. A retired individual who earns a pension with fixed monthly payments from her past employer during 2019

7-16. Consider the diagram below. The line represents the economy's growth trend, and the curve represents the economy's actual course of business fluctuations. For each part below, provide the letter label from the portion of the curve that corresponds to the associated term. (See page 162.)

    a. Contraction

    b. Peak

    c. Trough

    d. Expansion

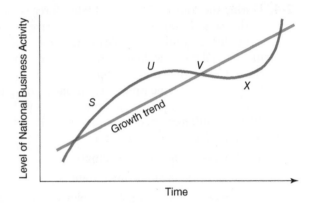

REFERENCES

EXAMPLE: A Shift toward More Part-Time Employment

Tomaz Cajner, Dennis Mawhirter, Christopher Nekarda, and David Ratner, "Why Is Involuntary Part-Time Work Elevated?" FEDS Notes, Board of Governors of the Federal Reserve System, April 14, 2014.

Peter Morici, "Part-Time Jobs Dominate Jobs Picture," CNBC, September 4, 2013.

Aimee Picchi, "Job Growth Is Coming from Low-Paying Industries," MSN Money, August 5, 2013.

EXAMPLE: An Increase in the Duration of Unemployment

Ben Casselman, "Long-Term Jobless Left Out of the Recovery," *The Wall Street Journal*, September 2, 2013.

Diane Stafford, "Long-Term Unemployment Plagues Many Job Hunters," *Kansas City Star*, April 7, 2014.

Rob Valletta, "Long-Term Unemployment: What Do We Know?" Federal Reserve Bank of San Francisco *Economic Letter*, February 4, 2013.

INTERNATIONAL POLICY EXAMPLE: The French Government Buys Lower Structural Unemployment

Liz Alderman, "Hollande Vows to Tackle Rising Unemployment, but the French Are Skeptical," *The New York Times*, August 7, 2013.

Clea Caulcutt, "Discord in France," Inside Higher Ed, January 24, 2014.

William Horobin, "France to Push State-Backed Jobs to Meet Unemployment Goal," *The Wall Street Journal*, August 1, 2013.

INTERNATIONAL EXAMPLE: Consuming More Food Boosts Some Nations' CPI Inflation Rates

"America's Shrinking Grocery Bill," *Bloomberg Businessweek*, March 4–10, 2013.

Brendan Greeley and Kartik Goyal, "For India's Inflation Crisis, See Onion Prices," *Bloomberg Businessweek*, July 25, 2013.

Josh Kerr, "Food Prices Far Outpace Consumer Price Index," June 27, 2013.

OECD Stat Abstracts, 2014. (http://stats.oecd.org/Index .aspx?QueryId=22377)

POLICY EXAMPLE: Want to Be Led by an Indicator? There Are Apps for That! https://itunes.apple.com/us/ app/americas-economy-for-iphone/id551790789?mt=8 https://itunes.apple.com/us/app/economy-for-ipad/ id396544244?mt=8 www.a2zeconomy.com/www/index .html

YOU ARE THERE: A Small-Business Skills Mismatch and Structural Unemployment

Elizabeth Laderman, "Small Businesses Hit Hard by Weak Job Gains," Federal Reserve Bank of San Francisco *Economic Letter*, September 9, 2013.

Robert Half International, Inc., "Small Businesses, Big Recruiting Challenges," Press Release, August 6, 2013.

Steve Matthews and Jason Philyaw, "Fed's Fischer Says Job Growth Has Been Hurt by Skills Mismatch," *Bloomberg Businessweek*, April 16, 2014.

ISSUES & APPLICATIONS: The U.S. Male Work Withdrawal

Tami Luhby, "Men Are Disappearing from the Workforce," CNN Money, June 19, 2013.

Rich Morin, "The Disappearing Male Worker," Pew Research Center, September 3, 2013.

Mark Peters and David Wessell, "More Men in Prime Working Years Don't Have Jobs," *The Wall Street Journal*, February 5, 2014.

Measuring the Economy's Performance

George Taylor/Everett Collection Inc/Alamy

LEARNING OBJECTIVES

After reading this chapter, you should be able to:

8.1 Describe the circular flow of income and output

8.2 Define gross domestic product (GDP) and explain its limitations

8.3 Explain the expenditure and income approaches to tabulating GDP

8.4 Discuss the key components of national income

8.5 Distinguish between nominal GDP and real GDP

MyEconLab helps you master each objective and study more efficiently. See the end of the chapter for details.

Recently, the Bureau of Economic Analysis (BEA), the government agency that measures annual U.S. economic activity, decided that previous years' levels had been about 3 percent too small. Previously overlooked, the BEA decided, was *intangible* investment—capital expenditures on nonphysical goods, such as research and development spending and investments in intellectual property products, such as software. Inclusion of these forms of investment has been a complicated undertaking, however. Before you can understand why this has been so, you must first learn about the overall approach to measuring aggregate economic activity, which is a key topic of this chapter.

recent research studies by economists have concluded that for high- and low-income individuals alike, people's sense of well-being increases as their incomes rise? This finding contradicts claims dating from the 1970s that once a person's "basic needs" are met, higher average income does not translate into increased feelings of satisfaction. Undoubtedly, economists will continue to argue about whether higher incomes yield happier people. Most economists do agree about the importance of utilizing objective measures of a nation's economic performance. The government utilizes what has become known as **national income accounting**. How this measurement is done is the main focus of this chapter. First, though, we need to look at the flow of income within an economy, for it is the flow of goods and services from businesses to consumers and of payments from consumers to businesses that constitutes economic activity.

National income accounting
A measurement system used to estimate national income and its components. One approach to measuring an economy's aggregate performance.

The Simple Circular Flow

8.1 Describe the circular flow of income and output

The concept of a circular flow of income (ignoring taxes) involves two principles:

1. In every economic exchange, the seller receives exactly the same amount that the buyer spends.

2. Goods and services flow in one direction and money payments flow in the other.

In the simple economy shown in Figure 8-1 below, there are only businesses and households. It is assumed that businesses sell their *entire* output in the current period to households and that households spend their *entire* income in the current period on consumer products. Households receive their income by selling the use of whatever factors of production they own, such as labor services.

FIGURE 8-1

MyEconLab Animation

The Circular Flow of Income and Product

Businesses provide final goods and services to households (upper clockwise loop), who in turn pay for them (upper counterclockwise loop). Payments flow in a counterclockwise direction and can be thought of as a circular flow. The dollar value of output is identical to total income because profits are defined as being equal to total business receipts minus business outlays for wages, rents, and interest. Households provide factor services to businesses and receive income (lower loops).

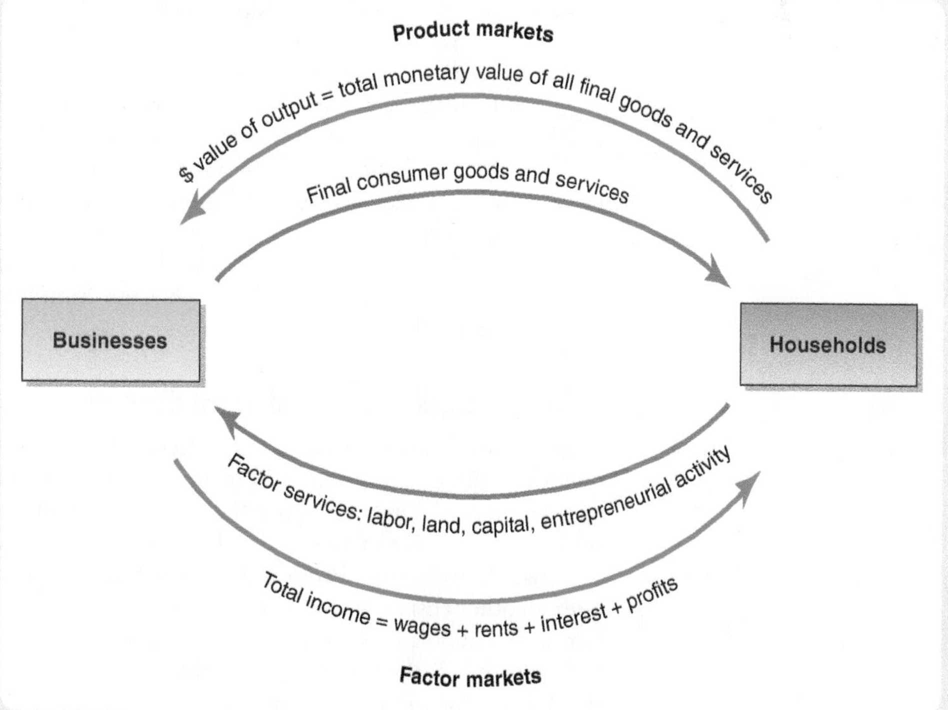

Product markets

$ value of output = total monetary value of all final goods and services

Final consumer goods and services

Businesses

Households

Factor services: labor, land, capital, entrepreneurial activity

Total income = wages + rents + interest + profits

Factor markets

Profits Explained

We have indicated in Figure 8-1 on the previous page that profit is a cost of production. You might be under the impression that profits are not part of the cost of producing goods and services, but profits are indeed a part of this cost because entrepreneurs must be rewarded for providing their services or they won't provide them. Their reward, if any, is profit. The reward—the profit—is included in the cost of the factors of production. If there were no expectations of profit, entrepreneurs would not incur the risk associated with the organization of productive activities. That is why we consider profits a cost of doing business. Just as workers expect wages, entrepreneurs expect profits.   MyEconLab Concept Check

Total Income or Total Output

Total income
The yearly amount earned by the nation's resources (factors of production). Total income therefore includes wages, rent, interest payments, and profits that are received by workers, landowners, capital owners, and entrepreneurs, respectively.

Final goods and services
Goods and services that are at their final stage of production and will not be transformed into yet other goods or services. For example, wheat ordinarily is not considered a final good because it is usually used to make a final good, bread.

The arrow that goes from businesses to households at the bottom of Figure 8-1 is labeled "Total income." What would be a good definition of **total income**? If you answered "the total of all individuals' income," you would be right. All income, however, is actually a payment for something, whether it be wages paid for labor services, rent paid for the use of land, interest paid for the use of capital, or profits paid to entrepreneurs. It is the amount paid to the resource suppliers. Therefore, total income is also defined as the annual *cost* of producing the entire output of **final goods and services**.

The arrow going from households to businesses at the top of Figure 8-1 represents the dollar value of output in the economy. This is equal to the total monetary value of all final goods and services for this simple economy. In essence, it represents the total business receipts from the sale of all final goods and services produced by businesses and consumed by households. Business receipts are the opposite side of household expenditures. When households purchase goods and services, those payments become a *business receipt*. Every transaction, therefore, simultaneously involves an expenditure and a receipt.

PRODUCT MARKETS Transactions in which households buy goods take place in the product markets—that's where households are the buyers and businesses are the sellers of consumer goods. *Product market* transactions are represented in the upper loops in Figure 8-1. Note that consumer goods and services flow to household demanders, while money flows in the opposite direction to business suppliers.

FACTOR MARKETS *Factor market* transactions are represented by the lower loops in Figure 8-1. In the factor market, households are the sellers. They sell resources such as labor, land, capital, and entrepreneurial ability. Businesses are the buyers in factor markets. Business expenditures represent receipts or, more simply, income for households. Also, in the lower loops of Figure 8-1, factor services flow from households to businesses, while the payments for these services flow in the opposite direction from businesses to households. Observe also the flow of money income (counterclockwise) from households to businesses and back again from businesses to households: It is an endless circular flow.   MyEconLab Concept Check

Why the Dollar Value of Total Output Must Equal Total Income

Total income represents the income received by households in payment for the production of goods and services. Why must total income be identical to the dollar value of total output? First, as Figure 8-1 shows, spending by one group is income to another. Second, it is a matter of simple accounting and the economic definition of profit as a cost of production. Profit is defined as what is *left over* from total business receipts after all other costs—wages, rents, interest—have been paid. If the dollar value of total output is $1,000 and the total of wages, rent, and interest for producing that output is $900, profit is $100. Profit is always the *residual* item that makes total income equal to the dollar value of total output.   MyEconLab Concept Check

MyEconLab Study Plan

In the circular flow model of income and output, households sell _____ services to businesses that pay for those services. The receipt of payments is total _____. Businesses sell goods and services to households that pay for them.

The dollar value of total output is equal to the total monetary value of all _____ goods and services produced.

The dollar value of final output must always equal total income. The variable that adjusts to make this so is known as _____.

National Income Accounting

8.2 Define gross domestic product (GDP) and explain its limitations

We have already mentioned that policymakers require information about the state of the national economy. Economists use historical statistical records on the performance of the national economy for testing their theories about how the economy really works. Thus, national income accounting is important. Let's start with the most commonly presented statistic on the national economy.

Gross Domestic Product (GDP)

Gross domestic product (GDP) represents the total market value of the nation's annual final product, or output, produced by factors of production located within national borders. We therefore formally define GDP as the total market value of all final goods and services produced in an economy during a year. We are referring here to the value of a *flow of production*. A nation produces at a certain rate, just as you receive income at a certain rate. Your income flow might be at a rate of $20,000 per year or $100,000 per year. Suppose you are told that someone earns $5,000. Would you consider this a good salary? There is no way to answer that question unless you know whether the person is earning $5,000 per month or per week or per day. Thus, you have to specify a time period for all flows. Income received is a flow. You must contrast this with, for example, your total accumulated savings, which are a stock measured at a point in time, not over time. Implicit in just about everything we deal with in this chapter is a time period—usually one year. All the measures of domestic product and income are specified as *rates* measured in dollars per year.

Gross domestic product (GDP)
The total market value of all final goods and services produced during a year by factors of production located within a nation's borders.

MyEconLab Concept Check

Stress on Final Output

GDP does not count **intermediate goods** (goods used up entirely in the production of final goods) because to do so would be to count them twice. For example, even though grain that a farmer produces may be that farmer's final product, it is not the final product for the nation. It is sold to make bread. Bread is the final product.

Intermediate goods
Goods used up entirely in the production of final goods.

We can use a numerical example to clarify this point further. Our example will involve determining the value added at each stage of production. **Value added** is the dollar value contributed to a product at each stage of its production. In Table 8-1 on the following page, we see the difference between total value of all sales and value added in the production of a donut. We also see that the sum of the values added is equal to the sale price to the final consumer. It is the 45 cents that is used to measure GDP, not the 97 cents. If we used the 97 cents, we would be double counting from stages 2 through 5, for each intermediate good would be counted at least twice—once when it was produced and again when the good it was used in making was sold. Such double counting would greatly exaggerate GDP.

Value added
The dollar value of an industry's sales minus the value of intermediate goods (for example, raw materials and parts) used in production.

What determines the value added of a Starbucks grande latte in China?

INTERNATIONAL EXAMPLE

The Total Value Added for a Starbucks Grande Latte in China

Even though the typical resident of China earns less than 20 percent as much income as the average U.S. resident, the price of a Starbucks coffee drink is usually at least 25 percent higher in China than in the United States. Hence, sale of a Starbucks coffee drink contributes a greater value added in China.

Consider a Starbucks "grande latte" drink sold in China. As is normally the case for most drinks offered for sale, the $0.64 value added from raw materials for the Chinese version of the grande latte is only a small part of the total value added. This component of value added is higher than in the United States, however, because expenses incurred in transporting raw materials are higher in China. An additional $0.40 value added is contributed through utilization of coffee-making equipment and associated operating expenses. Labor employed in producing a grande latte yields another $0.41 value added.

A significant portion of the value added comes from the ability to obtain the drink from a Starbucks outlet in a convenient location in a city such as Beijing. This portion of the total value added to a grande latte drink, which includes overall store operating and managerial expenses, rents, taxes, and sufficient profits to compensate the outlet owner for time devoted to the business, totals $3.35. Summing all of these values added yields $4.80 for a Chinese Starbucks grande latte.

FOR CRITICAL THINKING

What portion of the total value added of a Chinese Starbucks grande latte arises from the resources devoted to physically making the drink? Explain.

Sources are listed at the end of this chapter.

TABLE 8-1

Sales Value and Value Added at Each Stage of Donut Production

(1) Stage of Production	(2) Dollar Value of Sales	(3) Value Added
Stage 1: Fertilizer and seed	$.03]————————	$.03
Stage 2: Growing	.07]————————	.04
Stage 3: Milling	.12]————————	.05
Stage 4: Baking	.30]————————	.18
Stage 5: Retailing	.45]————————	.15

Total dollar value of all sales $.97   Total value added $.45

Stage 1: A farmer purchases 3 cents' worth of fertilizer and seed, which are used as factors of production in growing wheat.

Stage 2: The farmer grows the wheat, harvests it, and sells it to a miller for 7 cents. Thus, we see that the farmer has added 4 cents' worth of value. Those 4 cents represent income over and above expenses incurred by the farmer.

Stage 3: The miller purchases the wheat for 7 cents and adds 5 cents as the value added. That is, there is 5 cents for the miller as income. The miller sells the ground wheat flour to a donut-baking company.

Stage 4: The donut-baking company buys the flour for 12 cents and adds 18 cents as the value added. It then sells the donut to the final retailer.

Stage 5: The donut retailer sells donuts at 45 cents apiece, thus creating an additional value of 15 cents.

We see that the total value of the transactions involved in the production of one donut is 97 cents, but the total value added is 45 cents, which is exactly equal to the retail price. The total value added is equal to the sum of all income payments.

Exclusion of Financial Transactions, Transfer Payments, and Secondhand Goods

Remember that GDP is the measure of the dollar value of all final goods and services produced in one year. Many more transactions occur that have nothing to do with final goods and services produced. There are financial transactions, transfers of the ownership of preexisting goods, and other transactions that should not (and do not) get included in our measure of GDP.

FINANCIAL TRANSACTIONS There are three general categories of purely financial transactions: (1) the buying and selling of securities, (2) government transfer payments, and (3) private transfer payments.

Securities When you purchase shares of existing stock in Apple, Inc., someone else has sold it to you. In essence, there was merely a *transfer* of ownership rights. You paid $100 to obtain the stock. Someone else received the $100 and gave up the stock. No producing activity was consummated at that time, unless a broker received a fee for performing the transaction, in which case only the fee is part of GDP. The $100 transaction is not included when we measure GDP.

Government Transfer Payments Transfer payments are payments for which no productive services are concurrently provided in exchange. The most obvious government transfer payments are Social Security benefits and unemployment compensation. The recipients add nothing to current production in return for such transfer payments (although they may have contributed in the past to be eligible to receive them). Government transfer payments are not included in GDP.

Private Transfer Payments Are you receiving funds from your parents in order to attend school? Has a wealthy relative ever given you a gift of cash? If so, you have been the recipient of a private transfer payment. This payment is merely a transfer of funds from one individual to another. As such, it does not constitute productive activity and is not included in GDP.

TRANSFER OF SECONDHAND GOODS If I sell you my two-year-old laptop computer, no current production is involved. I transfer to you the ownership of a computer that was produced years ago. In exchange, you transfer to me $350. The original purchase price of the computer was included in GDP in the year I purchased it. To include the price again when I sell it to you would be counting the value of the computer a second time.

OTHER EXCLUDED TRANSACTIONS Many other transactions are not included in GDP for practical reasons:

- Household production—housecleaning, child care, and other tasks performed by people in their *own* households and for which they receive no payments through the marketplace

- Otherwise legal underground transactions—those that are legal but not reported and hence not taxed, such as paying housekeepers in cash that is not declared as income to the Internal Revenue Service

- Illegal underground activities—these include prostitution, illegal gambling, and the sale of illicit drugs

Why have underground economic activities increased in recent years (see the Policy Example at the top of the next page)?   MyEconLab Concept Check

Recognizing the Limitations of GDP

Like any statistical measure, gross domestic product is a concept that can be both well used and misused. Economists find it especially valuable as an overall indicator of a

Why Might 10 Percent of the U.S. Economy Be "Underground"?

Recent estimates indicate that between 10 percent and 13 percent of all U.S. economic activity is not included in official gross domestic product figures. These new estimates are higher than those for the previous decade of this century, during which economists estimated that between 7 percent and 10 percent of final transactions in newly produced items went unrecorded.

There is general agreement that government programs and policies explain much of the shift from recorded to unrecorded activity. The slow recovery from the recent recession has induced some people to remain officially unemployed to be able to collect government benefits but to unofficially perform income-earning services. In addition, since 2000 the number of U.S. residents who must meet federal and state licensing requirements has increased from less than 20 percent to more than 30 percent. Many people do not wish to go incur expenses required to obtain licenses and hence may opt to perform income-generating services illegally. In addition, recent increases in a variety of tax rates assessed by the federal government and by many state governments may have induced more individuals to opt for cash payments "off the books." Numerous employers also may prefer such arrangements to avoid higher tax payments associated with incomes paid to workers.

FOR CRITICAL THINKING

Why do you suppose that economists estimate that underground activities reduce federal tax payments by as much as $500 billion per year? (Hint: The federal government finances most of its spending by taxing reported incomes.)

Sources are listed at the end of this chapter.

---

nation's economic performance. It is important, however, to realize that GDP has significant weaknesses.

GDP EXCLUDES NONMARKET PRODUCTION Because it includes only the value of goods and services traded in markets, GDP excludes *nonmarket* production, such as the household services of homemakers discussed earlier. This can cause some problems in comparing the GDP of an industrialized country with the GDP of a highly agrarian nation in which nonmarket production is relatively more important.

It also causes problems if nations have different definitions of legal versus illegal activities. For instance, a nation with legalized gambling will count the value of gambling services, which has a reported market value as a legal activity. In a country where gambling is illegal, though, individuals who provide such services will not report the market value of gambling activities, and so they will not be counted in that country's GDP. This can complicate comparing GDP in the nation where gambling is legal with GDP in the country that prohibits gambling.

GDP IS NOT A DIRECT MEASURE OF HUMAN WELL-BEING Furthermore, although GDP is often used as a benchmark measure for standard-of-living calculations, it is not necessarily a good measure of the well-being of a nation. No measured figure of total national annual income can take account of changes in the degree of labor market discrimination, declines or improvements in personal safety, or the quantity or quality of leisure time. Measured GDP also says little about our environmental quality of life.

The now-defunct Soviet Union showed that large-scale production of such items as minerals, electricity, and irrigation for farming can have negative effects on the environment. Examples were: deforestation from strip mining, air and soil pollution from particulate emissions or nuclear accidents, and erosion of the natural balance between water and salt in bodies of water such as the Aral Sea. Other nations, such as China and India, have also experienced greater pollution problems as their levels of GDP have increased. Hence, it is important to recognize the following point:

GDP is a measure of the value of production in terms of market prices and an indicator of economic activity. It is not a measure of a nation's overall welfare.

Nonetheless, GDP is a relatively accurate and useful measure of the economy's domestic economic activity, measured in current dollars. Understanding GDP is thus an important first step for analyzing changes in economic activity over time.

WHAT IF...

governments were to de-emphasize GDP in favor of more subjective measures of a nation's economic performance?

If governments were to utilize subjective measures such as survey data on average self-reported levels of economic welfare, many more normative, value-laden judgments would be involved. For instance, proposed welfare-based measures employ subjective quality scores for nations' residents in categories such as people's satisfaction with their life status, the state of the natural environment, and their balance of labor versus leisure. The range of possibilities of quantitative measures for scoring a nation's aggregate economic welfare is so wide that it would be very difficult to interpret what particular magnitudes of such measures would mean. GDP has its limitations, but it has an important advantage: Although choices must be made about how to measure GDP and which types of transactions to include or exclude, GDP is a relatively objective measure of aggregate economic activity.

MyEconLab Concept Check
MyEconLab Study Plan

SELF CHECK   Visit MyEconLab to practice these and other problems and to get instant feedback in your Study Plan.

_____ _____ _____ is the total market value of final goods and services produced in an economy during a one-year period by factors of production within the nation's borders. It represents the dollar value of the flow of final production over a one-year period.

To avoid double counting, we look only at final goods and services produced or, equivalently, at _____ _____.

In measuring GDP, we must _____ (1) purely financial transactions, such as the buying and selling of securities; (2) government transfer payments and private transfer payments; and (3) the transfer of secondhand goods.

Many other transactions are excluded from measured _____, among them household services rendered by homemakers, underground economy transactions, and illegal economic activities, even though many of these result in the production of final goods and services.

GDP is a useful measure for tracking changes in the _____ _____ of overall economic activity over time, but it is not a measure of the well-being of a nation's residents because it fails to account for nonmarket transactions, the amount and quality of leisure time, environmental or safety issues, labor market discrimination, and other factors that influence general welfare.

Two Main Methods of Measuring GDP

The definition of GDP is the total dollar value of all final goods and services produced during a year. How, exactly, do we go about actually computing this number?

The circular flow diagram presented in Figure 8-1 on page 173 gave us a shortcut method for calculating GDP. We can look at the *flow of expenditures*, which consists of consumption, investment, government purchases of goods and services, and net expenditures in the foreign sector (net exports). In this **expenditure approach** to measuring GDP, we add the dollar value of all final goods and services. We could also use the *flow of income*, looking at the income received by everybody producing goods and services. In this **income approach**, we add the income received by all factors of production.

Deriving GDP by the Expenditure Approach

To derive GDP using the expenditure approach, we must look at each of the separate components of expenditures and then add them together. These components are consumption expenditures, investment, government expenditures, and net exports.

CONSUMPTION EXPENDITURES How do we spend our income? As households or as individuals, we spend our income through consumption expenditure (C), which falls into three categories: **durable consumer goods**, **nondurable consumer goods**, and **services**. Durable goods are *arbitrarily* defined as items that last more than three years. They include automobiles, furniture, and household appliances. Nondurable goods are all the rest, such as food and gasoline. Services are intangible commodities: medical care, education, and the like.

8.3 Explain the expenditure and income approaches to tabulating GDP

Expenditure approach
Computing GDP by adding up the dollar value at current market prices of all final goods and services.

Income approach
Measuring GDP by adding up all components of national income, including wages, interest, rent, and profits.

Durable consumer goods
Consumer goods that have a life span of more than three years.

Nondurable consumer goods
Consumer goods that are used up within three years.

Services
Mental or physical labor or assistance purchased by consumers. Examples are the assistance of physicians, lawyers, dentists, repair personnel, housecleaners, educators, retailers, and wholesalers; items purchased or used by consumers that do not have physical characteristics.

Housing expenditures constitute a major proportion of anybody's annual expenditures. Rental payments on apartments are automatically included in consumption expenditure estimates. People who own their homes, however, do not make rental payments. Consequently, government statisticians estimate what is called the *implicit rental value* of existing owner-occupied homes. It is roughly equal to the amount of rent you would have to pay if you did not own the home but were renting it from someone else.

Gross private domestic investment

The creation of capital goods, such as factories and machines, that can yield production and hence consumption in the future. Also included in this definition are changes in business inventories and repairs made to machines or buildings.

Investment

Any use of today's resources to expand tomorrow's production or consumption.

GROSS PRIVATE DOMESTIC INVESTMENT We now turn our attention to **gross private domestic investment** (I) undertaken by businesses. When economists refer to investment, they are referring to additions to productive capacity. **Investment** may be thought of as an activity that uses resources today in such a way that they allow for greater production in the future and hence greater consumption in the future. When a business buys new equipment or puts up a new factory, it is investing. It is increasing its capacity to produce in the future.

In estimating gross private domestic investment, government statisticians also add consumer expenditures on *new* residential structures because new housing represents an addition to our future productive capacity in the sense that a new house can generate housing services in the future.

The layperson's notion of investment often relates to the purchase of stocks and bonds. For our purposes, such transactions simply represent the *transfer of ownership* of assets called stocks and bonds. Thus, you must keep in mind the fact that in economics, investment refers *only* to *additions* to productive capacity, not to transfers of assets.

Producer durables, or capital goods

Durable goods having an expected service life of more than three years that are used by businesses to produce other goods and services.

Fixed investment

Purchases by businesses of newly produced producer durables, or capital goods, such as production machinery and office equipment.

Inventory investment

Changes in the stocks of finished goods and goods in process, as well as changes in the raw materials that businesses keep on hand. Whenever inventories are decreasing, inventory investment is negative. Whenever they are increasing, inventory investment is positive.

FIXED VERSUS INVENTORY INVESTMENT In our analysis, we will consider the basic components of investment. We have already mentioned the first one, which involves a firm's purchase of equipment or construction of a new factory. These are called **producer durables,** or **capital goods**. A producer durable, or a capital good, is simply a good that is purchased not to be consumed in its current form but to be used to make other goods and services. The purchase of equipment and factories—capital goods—is called **fixed investment**.

The other type of investment has to do with the change in inventories of raw materials and finished goods. Firms do not immediately sell off all their products to consumers. Some of this final product is usually held in inventory waiting to be sold. Firms hold inventories to meet future expected orders for their products. Inventories consist of all finished goods on hand, goods in process, and raw materials. When a firm increases its inventories, it is engaging in **inventory investment**.

The reason we can think of a change in inventories as being a type of investment is that an increase in such inventories provides for future increased consumption possibilities. When inventory investment is zero, the firm is neither adding to nor subtracting from the total stock of goods or raw materials on hand. Thus, if the firm keeps the same amount of inventories throughout the year, inventory *investment* has been zero.

Why are some economists promoting a new measure of the economy's total production that assigns a greater role to business expenditures?

POLICY EXAMPLE

A New Output Measure Intentionally Double Counts Business Spending

Recall that gross domestic product counts only spending on goods and services in those items' final forms. Thus, GDP represents the overall value added in production. This approach avoids double counting business spending on intermediate steps of producing those final products. Some economists argue that this avoidance of double counting is misguided. In their view, *all* aggregate business investment expenditures on intermediate inputs—supplies, raw materials, tools and equipment, and the like—should be included in any meaningful measure of the economy's

total productive activity. The entirety of such purchases by firms from other firms, these economists contend, is required to transform resources across production stages. In their view, such business spending consequently should be summed in obtaining an overall U.S. output measure.

Toward this end, the U.S. Bureau of Economic Analysis now tracks an alternative to GDP called *Gross Output*, which includes all forms of business-to-business expenditures. Not surprisingly, double counting business spending across all stages of production boosts the relative importance of such expenditures. Gross private domestic investment accounts for only about 25 percent of GDP, but aggregate business expenditures make up more than 50 percent of Gross Output.

less efficiently, what happens to the GDP and Gross Output measures of total production? Explain.

·Sources are listed at the end of this chapter.

FOR CRITICAL THINKING
If firms' spending on intermediate inputs used to produce an unchanged market value of final output increases because the firms now use inputs

---

GOVERNMENT EXPENDITURES In addition to personal consumption expenditures, there are government purchases of goods and services (*G*). The government buys goods and services from private firms and pays wages and salaries to government employees. Generally, we value goods and services at the prices at which they are sold. Many government goods and services, however, are not sold in the market. Therefore, we cannot use their market value when computing GDP.

Until recently, the values of all government-produced goods were considered equal to their *costs*. For example, the value of a newly built road was considered equal to its construction cost for inclusion in GDP for the year it was built. In recent years, in contrast, national income accountants have "imputed" the values of many government-produced items. For instance, the accountants value public education, fire protection, and police services in terms of prices observed in markets for privately produced education, fire protection, and security services. Three decades ago, imputed values of such government-provided activities made up a negligible portion of GDP. Today, imputed values constitute about 15 percent of GDP.

NET EXPORTS (FOREIGN EXPENDITURES) To obtain an accurate representation of GDP, we must include the foreign sector. As U.S. residents, we purchase foreign goods called *imports*. The goods that foreign residents purchase from us are our *exports*. To determine the *net* expenditures from the foreign sector, we subtract the value of imports from the value of exports to get net exports (*X*) for a year:

$$\text{Net exports } (X) = \text{total exports} - \text{total imports}$$

To understand why we subtract imports rather than ignoring them altogether, recall that we want to estimate *domestic* output, so we have to subtract U.S. expenditures on the goods produced in other nations.   MyEconLab Concept Check

Presenting the Expenditure Approach
We have just defined the components of GDP using the expenditure approach. When we add them all together, we get a definition for GDP, which is as follows:

$$\text{GDP} = C + I + G + X$$

where C = consumption expenditures

I = investment expenditures

G = government expenditures

X = net exports

THE HISTORICAL PICTURE To get an idea of the relationship among *C, I, G,* and *X*, look at Figure 8-2 on the next page, which shows GDP, personal consumption expenditures, government purchases, and gross private domestic investment plus net exports since 1929. When we add up the expenditures of the household, business, government, and foreign sectors, we get GDP.

DEPRECIATION AND NET DOMESTIC PRODUCT We have used the terms *gross domestic product* and *gross private domestic investment* without really indicating what *gross* means. The

MyEconLab Real-time data
MyEconLab Animation

FIGURE 8-2

GDP and Its Components

Here we see a display of gross domestic product, personal consumption expenditures, government purchases, and gross private domestic investment plus net exports for the years since 1929. (Note that the scale of the vertical axis changes as we move up the axis.) During the Great Depression of the 1930s, gross private domestic investment *plus* net exports was negative because we were investing very little at that time. Since the late 1990s, the sum of gross private domestic investment and net exports has been highly variable.

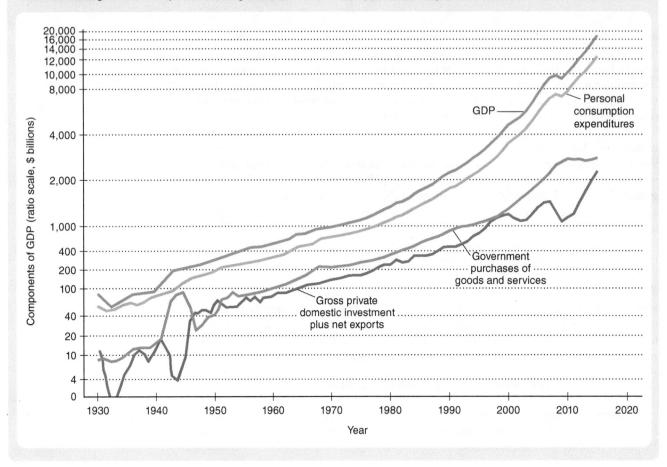

dictionary defines it as "without deductions," the opposite of *net*. You might ask, deductions for what? The deductions are for something we call **depreciation**. In the course of a year, machines and structures wear out or are used up in the production of domestic product. For example, houses deteriorate as they are occupied, and machines need repairs or they will fall apart and stop working. Most capital, or durable, goods depreciate.

An estimate of the amount that capital goods have depreciated during the year is subtracted from gross domestic product to arrive at a figure called **net domestic product (NDP)**, which we define as follows:

$$NDP = GDP - \text{depreciation}$$

Depreciation is also called **capital consumption allowance** because it is the amount of capital stock that has been consumed over a one-year period. In essence, it equals the amount a business would have to put aside to repair and replace deteriorating machines. Because we know that

$$GDP = C + I + G + X$$

Depreciation
Reduction in the value of capital goods over a one-year period due to physical wear and tear and also to obsolescence; also called *capital consumption allowance*.

Net domestic product (NDP)
GDP minus depreciation.

Capital consumption allowance
Another name for depreciation, the amount that businesses would have to put aside in order to take care of deteriorating machines and other equipment.

we know that the formula for NDP is

$$NDP = C + I + G + X - \text{depreciation}$$

Alternatively, because net $I = I - $ depreciation,

$$NDP = C + \text{net } I + G + X$$

Net investment measures *changes* in our capital stock over time and is positive nearly every year. Because depreciation does not vary greatly from year to year as a percentage of GDP, we get a similar picture of what is happening to our national economy by looking at either NDP or GDP data.

Net investment is an important variable to observe over time nonetheless. If everything else remains the same in an economy, changes in net investment can have dramatic consequences for future economic growth (a topic we cover in more detail in Chapter 9). Positive net investment by definition expands the productive capacity of our economy.

This capacity expansion means that there is increased capital, which will generate even more income in the future. When net investment is zero, we are investing just enough to offset depreciation. Our economy's productive capacity remains unchanged. Finally, when net investment is negative, we can expect negative economic growth prospects in the future. Negative net investment means that our productive capacity is actually declining—we are disinvesting. This actually occurred during the Great Depression.

Can we measure levels of economic activity for groupings of people within geographic areas smaller than nations?

Net investment
Gross private domestic investment minus an estimate of the wear and tear on the existing capital stock. Net investment therefore measures the change in the capital stock over a one-year period.

EXAMPLE

Using GDP to Assess the Size and Growth of Cities' Economies

GDP accounting can be used to measure economic activity within any desired region, including states and cities. Indeed, each year the Bureau of Economic Analysis releases GDP data for U.S. metropolitan areas. Table 8-2 lists the ten U.S. metropolitan areas with the largest annual GDP levels, which exceed the levels of GDP per year in many of the world's nations.

FOR CRITICAL THINKING
Why do you suppose that the annual GDP levels displayed in Table 8-2 exceed the levels of GDP for several individual U.S. states?

Sources are listed at the end of this chapter.

TABLE 8-2

Top Ten U.S. Metropolitan Areas Ranked by GDP per Year	Metropolitan Area	GDP ($ billions)
	New York City	1,358.4
	Los Angeles	765.8
	Chicago	571.0
	Houston	449.4
	Washington, D.C.	448.7
	Dallas	420.3
	Philadelphia	364.0
	San Francisco	360.4
	Boston	336.2
	Atlanta	294.6

Source: Bureau of Economic Analysis.

Deriving GDP by the Income Approach

If you go back to the circular flow diagram in Figure 8-1 on page 173, you see that product markets are at the top of the diagram and factor markets are at the bottom. We can calculate the value of the circular flow of income and product by looking at expenditures—which we just did—or by looking at total factor payments. Factor payments are called income. We calculate **gross domestic income (GDI)**, which we will see is identical to gross domestic product (GDP). Using the income approach, we have four categories of payments to individuals: wages, interest, rent, and profits.

Gross domestic income (GDI)
The sum of all income—wages, interest, rent, and profits—paid to the four factors of production.

1. *Wages.* The most important category is, of course, wages, including salaries and other forms of labor income, such as income in kind and incentive payments. Because GDI measures all income, there is no deduction from wages for Social Security taxes (whether paid by employees or employers).

2. *Interest.* Here interest payments do not equal the sum of all payments for the use of funds in a year. Instead, interest is expressed in *net* rather than in gross terms. The interest component of total income is only net interest received by households plus net interest paid to us by foreign residents. Net interest received by households is the difference between the interest they receive (from savings accounts, certificates of deposit, and the like) and the interest they pay (to banks for home mortgages, credit cards, and other loans).

3. *Rent.* Rent is all income earned by individuals for the use of their real (nonmonetary) assets, such as farms, houses, and stores. As stated previously, we have to include here the implicit rental value of owner-occupied houses. Also included in this category are royalties received from copyrights, patents, and assets such as oil wells.

4. *Profits.* Our last category includes total gross corporate profits plus *proprietors' income.* Proprietors' income is income earned from the operation of unincorporated businesses, which include sole proprietorships, partnerships, and producers' cooperatives. It is unincorporated business profit.

All of the payments listed are *actual* factor payments made to owners of the factors of production. When we add them together, though, we do not yet have gross domestic income. We have to take account of two other components: **indirect business taxes**, such as sales and business property taxes, and depreciation, which we have already discussed.

Indirect business taxes
All business taxes except the tax on corporate profits. Indirect business taxes include sales and business property taxes.

INDIRECT BUSINESS TAXES Indirect taxes are the (nonincome) taxes paid by consumers when they buy goods and services. When you buy a book, you pay the price of the book plus any state and local sales tax. The business is actually acting as the government's agent in collecting the sales tax, which it in turn passes on to the government. Such taxes therefore represent a business expense and are included in gross domestic income.

DEPRECIATION Just as we had to deduct depreciation to get from GDP to NDP, so we must *add* depreciation to go from net domestic income to gross domestic income. Depreciation can be thought of as the portion of the current year's GDP that is used to replace physical capital consumed in the process of production. Because somebody has paid for the replacement, depreciation must be added as a component of gross domestic income.

Nonincome expense items
The total of indirect business taxes and depreciation.

The last two components of GDP—indirect business taxes and depreciation—are called **nonincome expense items**.

FIGURE 8-3

Gross Domestic Product and Gross Domestic Income, 2015

By using the two different methods of computing the output of the economy, we come up with gross domestic product and gross domestic income, which are by definition equal. One approach focuses on expenditures, or the flow of product. The other approach concentrates on income, or the flow of costs.

Sources: U.S. Department of Commerce and author's estimates.

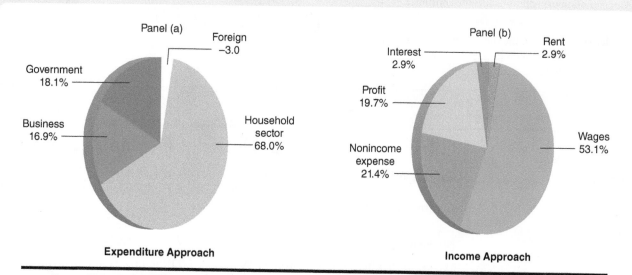

Panel (a)

Government 18.1%
Foreign −3.0
Household sector 68.0%
Business 16.9%

Expenditure Approach

Panel (b)

Interest 2.9%
Rent 2.9%
Profit 19.7%
Wages 53.1%
Nonincome expense 21.4%

Income Approach

Expenditure Point of View—Product Flow / Income Point of View—Cost Flow		Expenditure by Different Sectors: / Domestic Income (at Factor Cost):	
Household sector		*Wages*	
Personal consumption expenses	$12,389.4	All wages, salaries, and supplemental employee compensation	$9,678.2
Government sector		*Rent*	
Estimated value of goods and services	3,289.4	All rental income of individuals plus implicit rent on owner-occupied dwellings	527.3
Business sector		*Interest*	
Gross private domestic investment (including depreciation)	3,071.4	Net interest received by households	845.9
Foreign sector		*Profit*	
Net exports of goods and services	−539.6	Proprietorial income	1,028.3
		Corporate profits before taxes deducted	2,351.2
		Nonincome expense items	
		Indirect business taxes	918.0
		Depreciation	2,898.1
		Statistical discrepancy	−36.4
Gross domestic income	$18,210.6	Gross domestic product	$18,210.6

Figure 8-3 above shows a comparison between estimated gross domestic product and gross domestic income for 2015. Whether you decide to use the expenditure approach or the income approach, you will come out with the same number. There are sometimes statistical discrepancies, but they are usually relatively small.

MyEconLab Concept Check
MyEconLab Study Plan

The _____ approach to measuring GDP requires that we add up consumption expenditures, gross private investment, government purchases, and net exports. Consumption expenditures include consumer _____, consumer _____, and _____.

To derive GDP using the income approach, we add up all factor payments, including _____, _____, _____, and _____.

To get an accurate measure of GDP using the income approach, we must also add _____ _____ _____ and _____ to those total factor payments.

8.4 Discuss the key components of national income

Other Components of National Income Accounting

Gross domestic income or product does not really tell us how much income people have access to for spending purposes. To get to those kinds of data, we must make some adjustments, which we now do.

National Income (NI)

We know that net domestic product (NDP), or GDP minus depreciation, is the total market value of goods and services available to consume and to add to the capital stock. NDP, however, includes indirect business taxes and transfers, which should not count as part of income earned by U.S. factors of production, but does not include various business incomes that should. We therefore subtract from NDP indirect taxes and transfers and add other business income adjustments. Because U.S. residents earn income abroad and foreign residents earn income in the United States, we also add *net* U.S. income earned abroad. The result is what we define as **national income (NI)**—income earned by all U.S. factors of production.   MyEconLab Concept Check

National income (NI)
The total of all factor payments to resource owners. It can be obtained from net domestic product (NDP) by subtracting indirect business taxes and transfers and adding net U.S. income earned abroad and other business income adjustments.

Personal Income (PI)

National income does not actually represent what is available to individuals to spend because some people obtain income for which they have provided no concurrent good or service and others earn income but do not receive it. In the former category are mainly recipients of transfer payments from the government, such as Social Security, welfare, and food stamps. These payments represent shifts of funds within the economy by way of the government, with no goods or services concurrently rendered in exchange. For the other category, income earned but not received, the most obvious examples are corporate retained earnings that are plowed back into the business, contributions to social insurance, and corporate income taxes.

When transfer payments are added and when income earned but not received is subtracted, we end up with **personal income (PI)**—income *received* by the factors of production prior to the payment of personal income taxes.   MyEconLab Concept Check

Personal income (PI)
The amount of income that households actually receive before they pay personal income taxes.

Disposable Personal Income (DPI)

Everybody knows that you do not get to take home all your salary. To obtain **disposable personal income (DPI)**, we subtract all personal income taxes from personal income. This is the income that individuals have left for consumption and saving.

MyEconLab Concept Check

Disposable personal income (DPI)
Personal income after personal income taxes have been paid.

Deriving the Components of GDP

Table 8-3 on the next page shows how to derive the various components of GDP. It explains how to go from gross domestic product to net domestic product to national

TABLE 8-3		Billions of Dollars
Going from GDP to Disposable Income, 2015	Gross domestic product (GDP)	18,210.6
	Minus depreciation	−2,898.1
	Net domestic product (NDP)	15,312.5
	Plus net U.S. income earned abroad	+259.3
	Less statistical discrepancy	−69.6
	National income (NI)	115,502.2
	Minus corporate taxes, Social Security contributions, taxes on production and imports net of subsidies	−4,696.1
	Plus net transfers and interest earnings	4,137.2
	Personal income (PI)	14,943.3
	Minus personal income taxes	−1,982.1
	Disposable personal income (DPI)	12,961.2

Sources: U.S. Department of Commerce and author's estimates.

income to personal income and then to disposable personal income. On the frontpapers of your book, you can see the historical record for GDP, NDP, NI, PI, and DPI for selected years since 1929.

We have completed our rundown of the different ways that GDP can be computed and of the different variants of the nation's income and product. What we have not yet touched on is the difference between the nation's income measured in this year's dollars and its income representing real goods and services.   MyEconLab Concept Check

MyEconLab Study Plan

SELF CHECK   Visit MyEconLab to practice these and other problems and to get instant feedback in your Study Plan.

To obtain _____ _____, we subtract indirect business taxes and transfers from net domestic product and add other business income adjustments and net U.S. income earned abroad.

To obtain _____ _____, we must add government transfer payments, such as Social Security benefits and food stamps. We must subtract income earned but not

received by factor owners, such as corporate retained earnings, Social Security contributions, and corporate income taxes.

To obtain disposable personal income, we subtract all personal _____ _____ from personal income. Disposable personal income is income that individuals actually have for consumption or saving.

Distinguishing Between Nominal and Real Values

8.5 Distinguish between nominal GDP and real GDP

So far, we have shown how to measure *nominal* income and product. When we say "nominal," we are referring to income and product expressed in the current "face value" of today's dollar. Given the existence of inflation or deflation in the economy, we must also be able to distinguish between the **nominal values** that we will be looking at and the **real values** underlying them. Nominal values are expressed in current dollars. Real income involves our command over goods and services—purchasing power—and therefore depends on money income and a set of prices. Thus, real income refers to nominal income corrected for changes in the weighted average of all prices. In other words, we must make an adjustment for changes in the price level.

Consider an example. Nominal income *per person* in 1960 was only about $2,800 per year. In 2015, nominal income per person was about $57,000. Were people really that badly off in 1960? No, for nominal income in 1960 is expressed in 1960 prices, not in

Nominal values

The values of variables such as GDP and investment expressed in current dollars, also called *money values;* measurement in terms of the actual market prices at which goods and services are sold.

Real values

Measurement of economic values after adjustments have been made for changes in the average of prices between years.

the prices of today. In today's dollars, the per-person income of 1960 would be closer to $15,000, or about 26 percent of today's income per person. This is a meaningful comparison between income in 1960 and income today. Next we will show how we can translate nominal measures of income into real measures by using an appropriate price index, such as the Consumer Price Index or the GDP deflator discussed in Chapter 7.

Correcting GDP for Price Changes

If a tablet device costs $200 this year, 10 tablet devices will have a market value of $2,000. If next year they cost $250 each, the same 10 tablet devices will have a market value of $2,500. In this case, there is no increase in the total quantity of tablet devices, but the market value will have increased by one-fourth. Apply this to every single good and service produced and sold in the United States, and you realize that changes in GDP, measured in *current* dollars, may not be a very useful indication of economic activity.

If we are really interested in variations in the *real* output of the economy, we must correct GDP (and just about everything else we look at) for changes in the average of overall prices from year to year. Basically, we need to generate an index that approximates the average prices and then divide that estimate into the value of output in current dollars to adjust the value of output to what is called **constant dollars**, or dollars corrected for general price level changes. This price-corrected GDP is called *real GDP*.

How much has correcting for price changes caused real GDP to differ from nominal GDP during the past few years?

Constant dollars
Dollars expressed in terms of real purchasing power, using a particular year as the base or standard of comparison, in contrast to current dollars.

EXAMPLE

Correcting GDP for Price Index Changes, 2005–2015

Let's take a numerical example to see how we can adjust GDP for changes in the price index. We must pick an appropriate price index in order to adjust for these price level changes. We mentioned the Consumer Price Index, the Producer Price Index, and the GDP deflator in Chapter 7. Let's use the GDP deflator to adjust our figures. Table 8-4 on the next page gives 11 years of GDP figures. Nominal GDP figures are shown in column 2. The price index (GDP deflator) is in column 3, with base year of 2009, when the GDP deflator equals 100. Column 4 shows real (inflation-adjusted) GDP in 2009 dollars.

The formula for real GDP is

$$Real\ GDP = \frac{nominal\ GDP}{price\ index} \times 100$$

The step-by-step derivation of real (constant-dollar) GDP is as follows: The base year is 2009, so the price index for that year must equal 100. In 2009, nominal GDP was $14,417.9 billion, and so was real GDP expressed in 2009 dollars. In 2010, the price index increased to 101.21047.

Thus, to correct 2010's nominal GDP for inflation, we divide the price index, 101.21047, into the nominal GDP figure of $14,958.3 billion and then multiply it by 100. The rounded result is $14,779.4 billion, which is 2010 GDP expressed in terms of the purchasing power of dollars in 2009. What about a situation when the price index is lower than in 2009? Look at 2005. Here the price index shown in column 3 is only 91.99050. That means that in 2005, the average of all prices was almost 92 percent of prices in 2009. To obtain 2005 GDP expressed in terms of 2009 purchasing power, we divide nominal GDP, $13,095.4 billion, by 91.99050 and then multiply by 100. The rounded result is a larger number—$14,235.6 billion. Column 4 in Table 8-3 is a better measure of how the economy has performed than column 2, which shows nominal GDP changes.

FOR CRITICAL THINKING

Based on the information in Table 8-4, in what years was the economy in a recession? Explain briefly.

Sources are listed at the end of this chapter.

MyEconLab Concept Check

Plotting Nominal and Real GDP

Nominal GDP and real GDP since 1970 are plotted in Figure 8-4 on the following page. There is quite a big gap between the two GDP figures, reflecting the amount of inflation that has occurred. Note that the choice of a base year is arbitrary. We have chosen 2009 as the base year in our example. This happens to be the base year currently used by the government for the GDP deflator. MyEconLab Concept Check

Correcting GDP for Price Index Changes

To correct GDP for price index changes, we first have to pick a price index (the GDP deflator) with a specific year as its base. In our example, the base year is 2009. The price index for that year is 100. To obtain 2009 constant-dollar GDP, we divide the price index into nominal GDP and multiply by 100. In other words, we divide column 3 into column 2 and multiply by 100. This gives us column 4, which (taking into account rounding of the deflator) is a measure of real GDP expressed in 2009 purchasing power.

(1) Year	(2) Nominal GDP (billions of dollars per year)	(3) Price Index (base year 2009 = 100)	(4) = [(2) ÷ (3)] × 100 Real GDP (billions of dollars per year, in constant 2009 dollars)
2005	13,095.4	91.99050	14,235.6
2006	13,857.9	94.81841	14,615.2
2007	14,480.3	97.33478	14,876.8
2008	14,720.3	99.23619	14,833.6
2009	14,417.9	100.00000	14,417.9
2010	14,958.3	101.21047	14,779.4
2011	15,533.8	103.19816	15,052.4
2012	16,244.6	105.00236	15,470.7
2013	16,799.7	106.58829	15,761.3
2014	17,538.9	108.24744	16,202.6
2015	18,210.6	109.22537	16,672.5

Sources: U.S. Department of Commerce, Bureau of Economic Analysis, and author's estimates.

MyEconLab Real-time data
MyEconLab Animation

Nominal and Real GDP

Here we plot both nominal and real GDP. Real GDP is expressed in the purchasing power of 2009 dollars. The gap between the two represents price level changes.

Source: U.S. Department of Commerce.

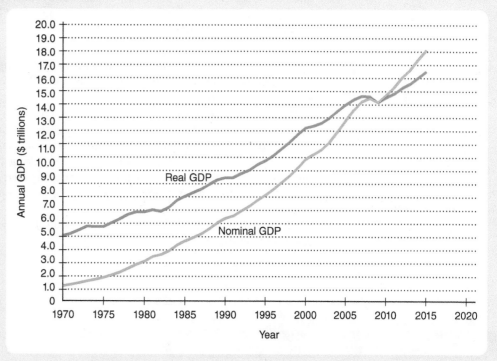

Per Capita Real GDP

Looking at changes in real GDP as a measure of economic growth may be deceiving, particularly if the population size has changed significantly. If real GDP over a 10-year period went up 100 percent, you might jump to the conclusion that the real income of a typical person in the economy had increased by that amount. But what if during the same period the population increased by 200 percent? Then what would you say? Certainly, the amount of real GDP per person, or *per capita real GDP*, would have fallen, even though *total* real GDP had risen. To account not only for price changes but also for population changes, we must first deflate GDP and then divide by the total population, doing this for each year. If we were to look at certain less developed countries, we would find that in many cases, even though real GDP has risen over the past several decades, per capita real GDP has remained constant or fallen because the population has grown just as rapidly or even more rapidly. MyEconLab Concept Check

Comparing GDP throughout the World

It is relatively easy to compare the standard of living of a family in Los Angeles with that of one living in Boston. Both families get paid in dollars and can buy the same goods and services at Wal-Mart, McDonald's, and Costco. It is not so easy, however, to make a similar comparison between a family living in the United States and one in, say, Indonesia. The first problem concerns currency comparisons. Indonesian residents get paid in rupiah, their national currency, and buy goods and services with those rupiah. How do we compare the average standard of living measured in rupiah with that measured in dollars?

Foreign exchange rate
The price of one currency in terms of another.

FOREIGN EXCHANGE RATES In earlier chapters, you have encountered international examples that involved local currencies, but the dollar equivalent has always been given. The dollar equivalent is calculated by looking up the **foreign exchange rate** that is published daily in major newspapers throughout the world. If you know that you can exchange $1.33 per euro, the exchange rate is 1.33 to 1 (or otherwise stated, a dollar is worth 0.75 euros). So, if French incomes per capita are, say, 34,500 euros, that translates, at an exchange rate of $1.33 per euro, to $45,885. For years, statisticians calculated relative GDPs by simply adding up each country's GDP in its local currency and dividing by the respective dollar exchange rate.

Purchasing power parity
Adjustment in exchange rate conversions that takes into account differences in the true cost of living across countries.

TRUE PURCHASING POWER The problem with simply using foreign exchange rates to convert other countries' GDPs and per capita GDPs into dollars is that not all goods and services are bought and sold in a world market. Restaurant food, housecleaning services, and home repairs do not get exchanged across countries. In countries that have very low wages, those kinds of services are much cheaper than foreign exchange rate computations would imply. Government statistics claiming that per capita income in some poor country is only $300 a year seem shocking. Such a statistic, though, does not tell you the true standard of living of people in that country. Only by looking at what is called **purchasing power parity** can you hope to estimate other countries' true standards of living compared to ours.

Given that nations use different currencies, how can we compare nations' levels of real GDP per capita?

INTERNATIONAL EXAMPLE

Purchasing Power Parity Comparisons of World Incomes

A few years ago, the International Monetary Fund accepted the purchasing power parity approach as the correct one. It started presenting international statistics on each country's GDP relative to every other's based on purchasing power parity relative to the U.S. dollar. The results were surprising. As you can see from Table 8-5 on the top of next page, China's per capita GDP is higher based on purchasing power parity than when measured at market foreign exchange rates.

FOR CRITICAL THINKING
What is the percentage increase in China's per capita GDP when one switches from foreign exchange rates to purchasing power parity?

Sources are listed at the end of this chapter.

TABLE 8-5

Comparing GDP Internationally

Country	Annual GDP Based on Purchasing Power Parity (billions of U.S. dollars)	Per Capita GDP Based on Purchasing Power Parity (U.S. dollars)	Per Capita GDP Based on Foreign Exchange Rates (U.S. dollars)
United States	17,058	54,000	54,000
Germany	3,019	44,540	46,100
France	2,239	37,580	42,250
Japan	4,194	37,630	46,140
United Kingdom	2,196	35,760	39,110
Italy	1,948	34,100	34,400
Russia	2,676	23,200	13,860
Brazil	2,421	14,750	11,690
China	10,815	11,850	6,560
Indonesia	1,701	9,260	3,580

Source: World Bank.

MyEconLab Concept Check
MyEconLab Study Plan

SELF CHECK Visit MyEconLab to practice these and other problems and to get instant feedback in your Study Plan.

To correct **nominal GDP** for price changes, we first select a base year for our price index and assign it the number _____. Then we construct an index based on how a weighted average of prices has changed relative to that base year. For example, if in the next year a weighted average of the prices indicates that prices have increased by 10 percent, we would assign it the number _____. We then divide each year's price index, so constructed, into its respective nominal GDP figure (and multiply by 100).

We can divide the _____ into real GDP to obtain per capita real GDP.

Statisticians often calculate relative GDP by adding up each country's GDP in its local currency and dividing by the dollar _____ _____. Because not all goods and services are bought and sold in the world market, however, we must correct exchange rate conversions of other countries' GDP figures to take into account differences in the true _____ of _____ across countries.

YOU ARE THERE

Purchasing Power Parity in Bus Tickets Eludes Brazilians

Samy Dana, a professor at a business school in São Paulo, Brazil, has been evaluating whether concerns about city bus prices expressed by protestors have justification. After examining data provided by the United Bank of Switzerland (UBS), Professor Dana has found evidence of a sharp difference in the purchasing power required for fares to ride Brazilian city buses.

UBS has performed purchasing-power-parity conversions of prices of various goods and services, including city bus rides. To measure the purchasing power requirements for different items, UBS has converted prices paid in national currencies to numbers of minutes required to earn equivalent amounts of incomes denominated in those currencies. In Mumbai, India, for instance, an average resident must work 3 minutes to earn sufficient wages to pay for a city bus ticket. The purchasing-power-parity prices are 3 minutes of work in Los Angeles and in Beijing, China, and 5 minutes of work in New York City and Paris. In Brazil's two largest

cities, São Paulo and Rio de Janeiro, the purchasing-power-parity price is at least twice as high as in these and most other cities around the world, at 10 minutes of work required to generate sufficient income to pay bus fares. Thus, when measured in terms of purchasing power income parities, Brazilian bus rides between two points rank among the most expensive on the planet.

CRITICAL THINKING QUESTIONS

1. *How do purchasing power parities enable global price comparisons?*
2. *Could the purchasing power parities for per capita real GDP levels in Table 8-5 above be expressed in terms of work time instead of U.S. dollars? Explain.*

Sources are listed at the end of this chapter.

ISSUES & APPLICATIONS

MyEconLab Video

Beyonce Boosts Real GDP Growth!

George Taylor/Everett Collection Inc/Alamy

CONCEPTS APPLIED

» Business Fixed Investment

» Real GDP

» Real GDP Growth

For purposes of national income accounting, business fixed investment has traditionally included primarily purchases of newly produced producer durables, or capital goods. These are material, or *tangible*, items such as manufacturing equipment and digital devices. Nevertheless, over the years, a growing chorus of economists argued that because investment is broadly defined as the use of current resources to expand future productive capabilities, business fixed investment should include *intangible* investment. Intangible investment includes firms' spending on items as improvements in their organizational structure, such as giving managers more power to make decisions. Furthermore, intangible investment encompasses research expenditures for development of new processes or products, such as spending on preliminary models of new products that firms later discard. In addition, it includes firms' spending on employee education.

The Effects of Intangible Investment on Real GDP Growth Rates

In 2013, the Bureau of Economic Analysis (BEA) decided to include various forms of intangible investment in its computations of business fixed investment. Because this decision added to investment expenditures, a consequence was that measured real GDP suddenly increased. To prevent the increase from showing up all at once in the year that the BEA made this computational change, the BEA revised prior years to reflect the addition of intangible investment.

Following its revisions, the BEA evaluated the effects of the intangibles-investment inclusion on measured average real GDP growth rates between 2007 and 2009 and between 2009 and 2012. The alteration in the BEA's GDP computation reduced the measured severity of the recession between 2007 and 2009. Instead of falling an average of 3.2 percent per year during this interval, as originally measured, real GDP declined by 2.9 percent annually. The revisions also increased the magnitude of the postrecession recovery between 2009 and 2012, with the new measure of real GDP rising at an average annual rate of 2.3 percent instead of the previously measured average rate of 2.1 percent per year.

A Complication: More Subjective Real GDP Computations

Many business expenses on intangible investment, such as companies' research and development spending, are readily measurable. The inflation-adjusted dollar values of other intangible investments are much harder to gauge, however. For instance, the BEA has included a category of intangible investment that it calls "intellectual property products." These products include items such as artwork, copyrighted recorded musical performances, and copyrighted recorded video presentations that will yield streams of royalty returns to firms over a number of years.

The difficulty for the BEA is that there is no way to know during the year in which firms produce artwork, musical tracks, or videos what today's value of the future streams of returns on those investments will actually turn out to be. Consequently, the BEA must estimate the values of those streams of returns. For instance, when a recording studio produces and releases new songs by Beyonce, the BEA must project the likely future returns that the recording studio will receive on this investment. Likewise, when a TV production company releases a new comedy series, the BEA effectively must guess whether the show will last several years and generate returns in reruns for many years.

That is, the BEA must project whether that show will be the next Andy Griffith Show or Seinfeld or instead be canceled the following year. Clearly, the BEA's projections of the values that such forms of intangible investment contribute to current real GDP are subject to judgmental errors. Hence, the intangible-investment component of real GDP has added uncertainty to real GDP computations that previously did not exist.

For Critical Thinking

1. Why do you think that the BEA decided to count as intangible investment only the estimated values of copyrighted artwork, musical performances, and videos while excluding estimated values of similar items posted on the Web for free download?

2. Why do you suppose that some economists have expressed concerns about the possibility that GDP may become a more subjective measure of economic activity as intangible investment becomes a larger fraction of GDP in the future?

Web Resources

1. For a discussion of the changes that the BEA made to its GDP computations, see the Web Links in MyEconLab.

2. To learn about the BEA's treatment of intellectual property products as a component of intangible investment, see the Web Links in MyEconLab.

MyEconLab

For more questions on this chapter's Issues & Applications, go to MyEconLab.

In the Study Plan for this chapter, select Section I: Issues and Applications.

Sources are listed at the end of this chapter.

Fundamental Points

1. In the circular flow model of income and output, households sell factor services to businesses that pay for those services and provide households with income payments, and the businesses produce and sell goods and services in exchange for payments from households.

2. Gross domestic product is the aggregate value of final goods and services produced by factors of production within the nation's borders during a one-year period and measured using market prices.

3. The expenditure approach to GDP sums consumption, gross private investment, government purchases, and net exports. The income approach adds incomes derived from wages, rents, interest, profits, and nonincome expenses, including indirect business taxes and depreciation.

4. National income equals net domestic product less indirect business taxes and transfers plus other business income adjustments and net U.S. income abroad. Adding transfer payments and subtracting income earned but not received by factor owners yields personal income.

5. A given year's figure for U.S. real GDP is obtained by dividing that year's price index into that year's nominal GDP figure and multiplying by 100. GDP comparisons across countries can be done by (1) adding up each country's GDP in its local currency and dividing by the dollar exchange rate or (2) accounting for differences in the true cost of living.

WHAT YOU SHOULD KNOW

Here is what you should know after reading this chapter. MyEconLab will help you identify what you know, and where to go when you need to practice.

LEARNING OBJECTIVES	KEY TERMS	WHERE TO GO TO PRACTICE—
8.1 **Describe the circular flow of income and output** *The circular flow of income and output captures two principles: (1) In every transaction, the seller receives the same amount that the buyer spends; and (2) goods and services flow in one direction, and money payments flow in the other direction. Households ultimately purchase the nation's total output of final goods and services. They make these purchases using income—wages, rents, interest, and profits—earned from selling labor, land, capital, and entrepreneurial services, respectively. Hence, income equals the value of output.*	national income accounting, 173 total income, 174 final goods and services, 174 **Key Figure** Figure 8-1, 173	• MyEconLab Study Plan 8.1 • Animated Figure 8-1

WHAT YOU SHOULD KNOW *continued*

LEARNING OBJECTIVES	KEY TERMS	WHERE TO GO TO PRACTICE
8.2 **Define gross domestic product (GDP) and explain its limitations** *A nation's gross domestic product is the total market value of its final output of goods and services produced within a given year using factors of production located within the nation's borders. Because GDP measures the value of a flow of production during a year in terms of market prices, it is not a measure of a nation's wealth.*	gross domestic product (GDP), 175 intermediate goods, 175 value added, 175	• MyEconLab Study Plan 8.2
8.3 **Explain the expenditure and income approaches to tabulating GDP** *To calculate GDP using the expenditure approach, we sum consumption spending, investment expenditures, government spending, and net export expenditures. Thus, we add up the total amount spent on newly produced goods and services to obtain the dollar value of the output produced and purchased during the year.*	expenditure approach, 179 income approach, 179 durable consumer goods, 179 nondurable consumer goods, 179 services, 179 gross private domestic investment, 180 investment, 180 producer durables, or capital goods, 180 fixed investment, 180 inventory investment, 180 depreciation, 182 net domestic product (NDP), 182 capital consumption allowance, 182 net investment, 183 gross domestic income (GDI), 184 indirect business taxes, 184 nonincome expense items, 184 **Key Figure** Figure 8-2, 182	• MyEconLab Study Plan 8.3 • Animated Figure 8-2
8.4 **Discuss the key components of national income** *To tabulate GDP using the income approach, we add total wages and salaries, rental income, interest income, profits, and nonincome expense items—indirect business taxes and depreciation—to obtain gross domestic income, which is equivalent to gross domestic product. Thus, the total value of all income earnings (equivalent to total factor costs) equals GDP.*	national income (NI), 186 personal income (PI), 186 disposable personal income (DPI), 186	• MyEconLab Study Plan 8.4
8.5 **Distinguish between nominal GDP and real GDP** *Nominal GDP is the value of newly produced output during the current year measured at current market prices. Real GDP adjusts the value of current output into constant dollars by correcting for changes in the overall level of prices from year to year. To calculate real GDP, we divide nominal GDP by the price index (the GDP deflator) and multiply by 100.*	nominal values, 187 real values, 187 constant dollars, 188 foreign exchange rate, 190 purchasing power parity, 190 **Key Figure** Figure 8-4, 189	• MyEconLab Study Plan 8.5 • Animated Figure 8-4

Log in to MyEconLab, take a chapter test, and get a personalized Study Plan that tells you which concepts you understand and which ones you need to review. From there, MyEconLab will give you further practice, tutorials, animations, videos, and guided solutions. For more information, visit http://www.myeconlab.com

PROBLEMS

All problems are assignable in MyEconLab; exercises that update with real-time data are marked with ⊕. Answers to odd-numbered problems appear in MyEconLab.

8-1. Explain in your own words why the flow of gross domestic product during a given interval must always be equivalent to the flow of gross domestic income within that same period. (See page 174.)

8-2. In the first stage of manufacturing each final unit of a product, a firm purchases a key input at a price of $4 per unit. The firm then pays a wage rate of $3 for the time that labor is exerted, combining an additional $2 of inputs for each final unit of output produced. The firm sells every unit of the product for $10. What is the contribution of each unit of output to GDP in the current year? (See page 175.)

8-3. Each year after a regular spring cleaning, Maria spruces up her home a little by retexturing and repainting the walls of one room in her house. In a given year, she spends $25 on magazines to get ideas about wall textures and paint shades, $45 on newly produced texturing materials and tools, $35 on new paintbrushes and other painting equipment, and $175 on newly produced paint. Normally, she preps the walls, a service that a professional wall-texturing specialist would charge $200 to do, and applies two coats of paint, a service that a painter would charge $350 to do, on her own. (See pages 175–177.)

a. When she purchases her usual set of materials and does all the work on her home by herself in a given spring, how much does Maria's annual spring texturing and painting activity contribute to GDP?

b. Suppose that Maria hurt her back this year and is recovering from surgery. Her surgeon has instructed her not to do any texturing work, but he has given her the go-ahead to paint a room as long as she is cautious. Thus, she buys all the equipment required to both texture and paint a room. She hires someone else to do the texturing work but does the painting herself. How much would her spring painting activity add to GDP?

c. As a follow-up to part (b), suppose that as soon as Maria bends down to dip her brush into the paint, she realizes that painting will be too hard on her back after all. She decides to hire someone else to do all the work using the materials she has already purchased. In this case, how much will her spring painting activity contribute to GDP?

8-4. Each year, Johan typically does all his own landscaping and yard work. He spends $200 per year on mulch for his flower beds, $225 per year on flowers and plants, $50 on fertilizer for his lawn, and $245 on gasoline and lawn mower maintenance. The lawn and garden store where he obtains his mulch and fertilizer charges other customers $500 for the service of spreading that much mulch in flower beds and $50 for the service of distributing fertilizer over a yard the size of Johan's. Paying a professional yard care service to mow his lawn would require an expenditure of $1,200 per year, but in that case Johan would not have to buy gasoline or maintain his own lawn mower. (See pages 175–177.)

a. In a normal year, how much does Johan's landscaping and yard work contribute to GDP?

b. Suppose that Johan has developed allergy problems this year and will have to reduce the amount of his yard work. He can wear a mask while running his lawn mower, so he will keep mowing his yard, but he will pay the lawn and garden center to spread mulch and distribute fertilizer. How much will all the work on Johan's yard contribute to GDP this year?

c. As a follow-up to part (b), at the end of the year, Johan realizes that his allergies are growing worse and that he will have to arrange for all his landscaping and yard work to be done by someone else next year. How much will he contribute to GDP next year?

8-5. Consider the following hypothetical data for the U.S. economy in 2018 (all amounts are in trillions of dollars; see pages 179–182).

Consumption	11.0
Indirect business taxes	.8
Depreciation	1.3
Government spending	3.8
Imports	2.7
Gross private domestic investment	4.0
Exports	2.5

a. Based on the data, what is GDP? NDP? NI?

b. Suppose that in 2019, exports fall to $2.3 trillion, imports rise to $2.85 trillion, and gross private domestic investment falls to $3.25 trillion. What will GDP be in 2019, assuming that other values do not change between 2018 and 2019?

8-6. Look back at Table 8-4 on page 189, which explains how to calculate real GDP in terms of 2009 constant dollars. Change the base year to 2005. Recalculate the price index, and then recalculate real GDP—that is, express column 4 of Table 8-4 in terms of 2005 dollars instead of 2009 dollars. (See pages 188–189.)

8-7. Consider the following hypothetical data for the U.S. economy in 2018 (in trillions of dollars), and assume that there are no statistical discrepancies or other adjustments. (See pages 184–187.)

Profit	2.8
Indirect business taxes and transfers	.8
Rent	.7
Interest	.8
Wages	8.2
Depreciation	1.3
Consumption	12.0
Exports	1.5
Government transfer payments	2.0
Personal income taxes and nontax payments	1.7
Imports	1.7
Corporate taxes and retained earnings	.5
Social Security contributions	2.0
Government spending	3.8

a. What is gross domestic income? GDP?

b. What is gross private domestic investment?

c. What is personal income? Personal disposable income?

8-8. Which of the following are production activities that are included in GDP? Which are not? (See pages 175–178.)

a. Mr. King performs the service of painting his own house instead of paying someone else to do it.

b. Mr. King paints houses for a living.

c. Mrs. King earns income from parents by taking baby photos in her digital photography studio.

d. Mrs. King takes photos of planets and stars as part of her astronomy hobby.

e. E*Trade charges fees to process Internet orders for stock trades.

f. Mr. Ho spends $10,000 on shares of stock via an Internet trade order and pays a $10 brokerage fee.

g. Mrs. Ho receives a Social Security payment.

h. Ms. Hernandez makes a $300 payment for an Internet-based course on stock trading.

i. Mr. Langham sells a used laptop computer to his neighbor.

8-9. Explain what happens to contributions to GDP in each of the following situations. (See page 177.)

a. A woman who makes a living charging for investment advice on her Internet Web site marries one of her clients, to whom she now provides advice at no charge.

b. A man who had washed the windows of his own house every year decides to pay a private company to wash those windows this year.

c. A company that had been selling used firearms illegally finally gets around to obtaining an operating license and performing background checks as specified by law prior to each gun sale.

8-10. Explain what happens to the official measure of GDP in each of the following situations. (See page 177.)

a. Air quality improves significantly throughout the United States, but there are no effects on aggregate production or on market prices of final goods and services.

b. The U.S. government spends considerably less on antipollution efforts this year than it did in recent years.

c. The quality of cancer treatments increases, so patients undergo fewer treatments, which hospitals continue to provide at the same price per treatment as before.

8-11. Which of the following activities of a computer manufacturer during the current year are included in this year's measure of GDP? (See page 177.)

a. The manufacturer produces a chip in June, uses it as a component in a computer in August, and sells the computer to a customer in November.

b. A retail outlet of the firm sells a computer completely built during the current year.

c. A marketing arm of the company receives fee income during the current year when a buyer of one of its computers elects to use the computer manufacturer as her Internet service provider.

8-12. A number of economists contend that official measures of U.S. gross private investment expenditures are understated. For instance, household spending on education, such as college tuition expenditures, is counted as consumption. Some economists suggest that these expenditures, which amount to 6 percent of GDP, should be counted as investment instead. Based on this 6 percent estimate and the GDP computations detailed in Figure 8-3 on page 185, how many billions of dollars would shift from consumption to investment if this suggestion was adopted? (See page 185.)

8-13. Consider the table below for the economy of a nation whose residents produce five final goods. (See pages 187–188.)

Good	2015		2019	
	Price	Quantity	Price	Quantity
Shampoo	$ 2	15	$ 4	20
External hard drives	200	10	250	10
Books	40	5	50	4
Milk	3	10	4	3
Candy	1	40	2	20

Assuming a 2015 base year:

a. What is nominal GDP for 2015 and 2019?

b. What is real GDP for 2014 and 2019?

8-14. Consider the following table for the economy of a nation whose residents produce four final goods. (See pages 187–188.)

Good	2017		2018	
	Price	Quantity	Price	Quantity
Computers	$1,000	10	$800	15
Bananas	6	3,000	11	1,000
Televisions	100	500	150	300
Cookies	1	10,000	2	10,000

Assuming a 2018 base year:

a. What is nominal GDP for 2017 and 2018?

b. What is real GDP for 2017 and 2018?

8-15. In the table for Problem 8-14, if 2018 is the base year, what is the price index for 2017? (Round decimal fractions to the nearest tenth; see pages 187–188.)

8-16. Suppose that early in a year, a hurricane hits a town in Florida and destroys a substantial number of homes. A portion of this stock of housing, which had a market value of $100 million (not including the market value of the land), was uninsured. The owners of the residences spent a total of $5 million during the rest of the year to pay salvage companies to help them save remaining belongings. A small percentage of uninsured owners had sufficient resources to spend a total of $15 million during the year to pay construction companies to rebuild their homes. Some were able to devote their own time, the opportunity cost of which was valued at $3 million, to work on rebuilding their homes. The remaining people, however, chose to sell their land at its market value and abandon the remains of their houses. What was the combined effect of these transactions on GDP for this year? (Hint: Which transactions took place in the markets for *final* goods and services?) In what ways, if any, does the effect on GDP reflect a loss in welfare for these individuals? (See page 177.)

8-17. Suppose that in 2017, geologists discover large reserves of oil under the tundra in Alaska. These new reserves have a market value estimated at $50 billion at current oil prices. Oil companies spend $1 billion to hire workers and move and position equipment to begin exploratory pumping during that same year. In the process of loading some of the oil onto tankers at a port, one company accidentally spills some of the oil into a bay and by the end of the year pays $1 billion to other companies to clean it up. The oil spill kills thousands of birds, seals, and other wildlife. What was the combined effect of these events on GDP for this year? (Hint: Which transactions took place in the markets for *final* goods and services?) In what ways, if any, does the effect on GDP reflect a loss in national welfare? (See page 177.)

8-18. Consider the diagram below, and answer the following questions. (See pages 188–189.)

a. What is the base year? Explain.

b. Has this country experienced inflation or deflation since the base year? How can you tell?

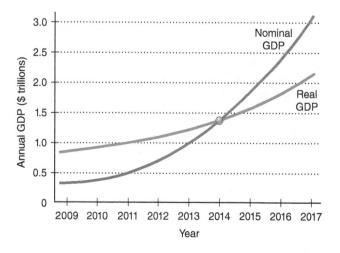

REFERENCES

INTERNATIONAL EXAMPLE: The Total Value Added for a Starbucks Grande Latte in China

Laurie Burkitt, "The Extra-Caffeinated Cost of a Starbucks Latte in China," *The Wall Street Journal*, September 4, 2013.

Lindsey Goodwin, "How Much Is Starbucks Coffee?" About.com Coffee/Tea (http://coffeetea.about.com/od/orderingcoffee/a/How-Much-Is-Starbucks-Coffee.htm/), 2014, updated periodically.

"Starbucks Latte (Grande) Prices," Humuch? (http://www.humuch.com/prices/Starbucks-Latte-grande-size/_____/818), 2014, Updated Periodically.

Matt Schiavenza, "Why Is Starbucks So Expensive in China?" *The Atlantic*, September 6, 2013.

POLICY EXAMPLE: Why Might 10 Percent of the U.S. Economy Be "Underground"?

Patrice Lewis, "The Burgeoning Underground Economy," World Net Daily, January 31, 2014.

James Surowiecki, "The Underground Economy," *The New Yorker*, April 29, 2013.

Joshua Zumbrun, "More Americans Work in the Underground Economy," *Bloomberg Businessweek*, March 28, 2013.

POLICY EXAMPLE: A New Output Measure Intentionally Double Counts Business Spending

John Aziz, "Is the Economy Really Twice As Large As We Thought," *The Week*, April 25, 2014.

Danielle Kurtzleben, "The U.S. Government Could Soon Reshape How We Measure the Economy," Vox, April 24, 2014. (http://www.vox.com/2014/4/24/5646978/how-the-us-government-might-be-reshaping-how-we-measure-the-economy)

Mark Skousen, "At Last, a Better Economic Measure," *The Wall Street Journal*, April 22, 2014.

EXAMPLE: Using GDP to Assess the Size and Growth of Cities' Economies

Bureau of Economic Analysis, "GDP by Metropolitan Area," 2014. (http://www.bea.gov/newsreleases/regional/gdp_metro/gdp_metro_newsrelease.htm)

William Mauldin, "Washington Drops below Houston in Top 10 U.S. Cities," *The Wall Street Journal*, September 17, 2013.

Matthew O'Brien, "Here Are the 10 Biggest U.S. Cities by GDP—and How They've Grown Since 2009," *The Atlantic*, September 19, 2013.

YOU ARE THERE: Purchasing Power Parity in Bus Tickets Eludes Brazilians

Joshua Goodman, "Brazilians Foil a Bus Fare Hike, But Commuting's Still Costly," *Bloomberg Businessweek*, July 3, 2013.

Simon Romero, "Bus-Fare Protests Hit Brazil's Two Biggest Cities," *The New York Times*, June 13, 2013.

Jonathan Watts, "Fury and Frustration in Brazil as Fares Rise and Transport Projects Flounder," *The Guardian*, February 6, 2014.

ISSUES & APPLICATIONS: Beyonce Boosts Real GDP Growth!

Peter Coy, "The Rise of the Intangible Economy: U.S. GDP Counts R&D, Artistic Creation," *Bloomberg Businessweek*, July 18, 2013.

Arnold Kling, "GDP and Measuring the Intangible," The American, February 26, 2014.

Sarah Portlock and Eric Morath, "GDP Revisions Aim to Account for Value of Art," *The Wall Street Journal*, April 26, 2013.

Global Economic Growth and Development

Zuma Press, Inc/Alamy

When a U.S. professional basketball team's managers seek a new "big man" or a new "point guard," those managers do not consider just the latest U.S. college stars. The team's managers also look abroad, to Asia and to Europe, for talented players. Twenty percent of the time, outside the United States is where they find those players. Likewise, U.S. businesses searching for the best scientists and engineers also search abroad. In contrast to basketball managers, however, these firms' managers confront legal limits on how many foreign scientists and engineers they can recruit. U.S. immigration laws permit unlimited immigration by athletes with "extraordinary abilities," but those laws constrain the ability of highly trained scientists and engineers to enter the nation to work. In this chapter, you will learn about the implications of these immigration rules for U.S. *economic growth*.

LEARNING OBJECTIVES

After reading this chapter, you should be able to:

9.1 Define economic growth and recognize the importance of economic growth rates

9.2 Explain why productivity growth and saving are crucial for maintaining economic growth

9.3 Understand the basis of new growth theory

9.4 Evaluate how immigration and property rights influence economic growth

9.5 Discuss the fundamental factors that contribute to a nation's economic development

MyEconLab helps you master each objective and study more efficiently. See the end of the chapter for details.

DID YOU KNOW THAT... between 2008 and 2010, U.S. per capita real GDP, measured in 2009 base-year dollars, *fell* by nearly $3,000? Prior to the 2008 financial meltdown and recession, per capita real GDP had very nearly reached $50,000. It proceeded to drop to $47,000 by 2010 before increasing once more in subsequent years. Not until 2014 had per capita real GDP finally grown sufficiently to pass the $50,000 threshold. In this chapter, you will learn that the rate of growth of per capita real GDP is economists' primary measure of *economic growth.*

9.1 Define economic growth and recognize the importance of economic growth rates

How Do We Define Economic Growth?

Recall from Chapter 2 that we can show economic growth graphically as an outward shift of a production possibilities curve, as is seen in Figure 9-1 below. If there is economic growth between 2017 and 2037, the production possibilities curve will shift outward toward the red curve. The distance that it shifts represents the amount of economic growth, defined as the increase in the productive capacity of a nation. Although it is possible to come up with a measure of a nation's increased productive capacity, it would not be easy. Therefore, we turn to a more readily obtainable definition of economic growth.

Most people have a general idea of what economic growth means. When a nation grows economically, its citizens must be better off in at least some ways, usually in terms of their material well-being. Typically, though, we do not measure the well-being of any nation solely in terms of its total output of real goods and services or in terms of real GDP without making some adjustments. After all, Indonesia has a real GDP more than 10 times as large as that of the small European nation of Luxembourg. The population in Indonesia, though, is more than 470 times greater than that of Luxembourg. Consequently, we view Indonesia as a poorer country and Luxembourg as a richer country. Thus, when we measure economic growth, we must adjust for population growth. Our formal definition becomes this:

Economic growth
Increases in per capita real GDP measured by its rate of change per year.

Economic growth *occurs when there are increases in* **per capita** *real GDP, measured by the rate of change in per capita real GDP per year.*

Figure 9-2 on the next page presents the historical record of real GDP per person in the United States.

MyEconLab Animation

FIGURE 9-1

Economic Growth

If there is growth between 2017 and 2037, the production possibilities curve for the entire economy will shift outward from the blue line labeled 2015 to the red line labeled 2037. The distance that it shifts represents an increase in the productive capacity of the nation.

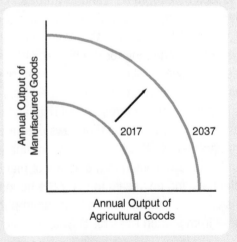

FIGURE 9-2

The Historical Record of U.S. Economic Growth

The graph traces per capita real GDP in the United States since 1900. Data are given in 2009 dollars.

Source: U.S. Department of Commerce.

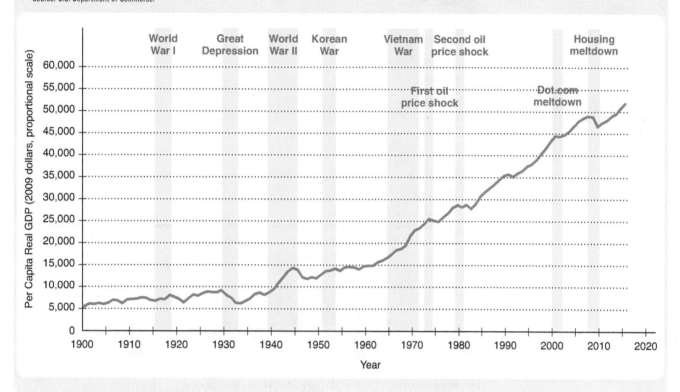

Problems in Definition

Our definition of economic growth says nothing about the *distribution* of output and income. A nation might grow very rapidly in terms of increases in per capita real GDP, while its poor people remain poor or become even poorer. Therefore, in assessing the economic growth record of any nation, we must be careful to pinpoint which income groups have benefited the most from such growth. Another important consideration is how much economic growth differs across countries.

Real standards of living can go up without any positive economic growth. This can occur if individuals are, on average, enjoying more leisure by working fewer hours but producing as much as they did before. For example, if per capita real GDP in the United States remained at $55,000 a year for a decade, we still could not conclude that U.S. residents were no better off at the end of the decade. What if, during that same 10-year period, average hours worked fell from 37 per week to 33 per week? That would mean that during the 10 years under study, individuals in the labor force were "earning" 4 more hours of leisure a week.

How much does economic growth differ across countries?

INTERNATIONAL EXAMPLE

Growth Rates around the World

Table 9-1 on the next page shows the average annual rate of growth of real GDP per person in selected countries since 1970. During this time period, the United States has been positioned in the lower range of the pack. Thus, even though we are one of the world's richest countries, in recent years our rate of economic growth has been in the lower range.

FOR CRITICAL THINKING

"The largest change is from zero to one." Does this statement have anything to do with relative growth rates in poorer versus richer countries?

Sources are listed at the end of this chapter.

TABLE 9-1

Per Capita Real GDP Growth Rates in Various Countries

Country	Average Annual Rate of Growth of Real GDP Per Capita, 1970–2015 (%)
Sweden	1.5
France	1.6
Germany	1.6
United States	1.7
Canada	1.9
Turkey	1.9
Japan	2.0
Brazil	2.2
India	3.3
Indonesia	4.4
Malaysia	4.9
China	7.2

Sources: World Bank, International Monetary Fund, and author's estimates.

Nothing so extreme as this example has occurred in this country, but something similar has. Average hours worked per week fell steadily until the 1960s, when they leveled off. That means that during much of the history of this country, the increase in per capita real GDP *understated* the growth in living standards that we were experiencing because we were enjoying more and more leisure as time passed.   MyEconLab Concept Check

Is Economic Growth Bad?

Some commentators on our current economic situation believe that the definition of economic growth ignores its negative effects. Some psychologists even contend that economic growth makes us worse off. They say that the more the economy grows, the more "needs" are created so that we feel worse off as we become richer. Our expectations are rising faster than reality, so we presumably always suffer from a sense of disappointment. Also, economists' measurement of economic growth does not take into account the spiritual and cultural aspects of the good life. As with all activities, both costs and benefits are associated with growth. You can see some of those listed in Table 9-2 below.

Any measure of economic growth that we use will be imperfect. Nonetheless, the measures that we do have allow us to make comparisons across countries and over

TABLE 9-2

Costs and Benefits of Economic Growth

Benefits	Costs
Reduction in illiteracy	Environmental pollution
Reduction in poverty	Breakdown of the family
Improved health	Isolation and alienation
Longer lives	Urban congestion
Political stability	

time and, if used judiciously, can enable us to gain important insights. Per capita real GDP, used so often, is not always an accurate measure of economic well-being, but it is a serviceable measure of productive activity.   MyEconLab Concept Check

The Importance of Growth Rates

Notice in Table 9-1 on the previous page that the growth rates in real per capita income for most countries differ very little—generally by only a few percentage points. You might want to know why such small differences in growth rates are important. What does it matter if we grow at 3 percent rather than at 4 percent per year? The answer is that in the long run, it matters a lot.

A small difference in the rate of economic growth does not matter very much for next year or the year after. For the more distant future, however, it makes considerable difference. The power of *compounding* is impressive. Let's see what happens with three different annual rates of growth: 3 percent, 4 percent, and 5 percent. We start with $1 trillion per year of U.S. GDP at some time in the past. We then compound this $1 trillion, or allow it to grow at these three different growth rates. The difference is huge. In 50 years, $1 trillion per year becomes $4.38 trillion per year if compounded at 3 percent per year. Just one percentage point more in the growth rate, 4 percent, results in a real GDP of $7.11 trillion per year in 50 years, almost double the previous amount. Two percentage points' difference in the growth rate—5 percent per year—results in a real GDP of $11.5 trillion per year in 50 years, or nearly three times as much. Obviously, very small differences in annual growth rates result in great differences in cumulative economic growth. That is why nations are concerned if the growth rate falls even a little in absolute percentage terms.

Thus, when we talk about growth rates, we are talking about compounding. In Table 9-3 below, we show how $1 compounded annually grows at different interest rates. We see in the 3 percent column that $1 in 50 years grows to $4.38. We merely multiplied $1 trillion times 4.38 to get the growth figure in our earlier example. In the 5 percent column, $1 grows to $11.50 after 50 years. Again, we multiplied $1 trillion times 11.50 to get the growth figure for 5 percent in the preceding example.

TABLE 9-3

One Dollar Compounded Annually at Different Interest Rates

Here we show the value of a dollar at the end of a specified period during which it has been compounded annually at a specified interest rate. For example, if you took $1 today and invested it at 5 percent per year, it would yield $1.05 at the end of one year. At the end of 10 years, it would equal $1.63, and at the end of 50 years, it would equal $11.50.

Number of Years	3%	4%	5%	6%	8%	10%	20%
1	1.03	1.04	1.05	1.06	1.08	1.10	1.20
2	1.06	1.08	1.10	1.12	1.17	1.21	1.44
3	1.09	1.12	1.16	1.19	1.26	1.33	1.73
4	1.13	1.17	1.22	1.26	1.36	1.46	2.07
5	1.16	1.22	1.28	1.34	1.47	1.61	2.49
6	1.19	1.27	1.34	1.41	1.59	1.77	2.99
7	1.23	1.32	1.41	1.50	1.71	1.94	3.58
8	1.27	1.37	1.48	1.59	1.85	2.14	4.30
9	1.30	1.42	1.55	1.68	2.00	2.35	5.16
10	1.34	1.48	1.63	1.79	2.16	2.59	6.19
20	1.81	2.19	2.65	3.20	4.66	6.72	38.30
30	2.43	3.24	4.32	5.74	10.00	17.40	237.00
40	3.26	4.80	7.04	10.30	21.70	45.30	1,470.00
50	4.38	7.11	11.50	18.40	46.90	117.00	9,100.00

Interest Rate (column group header spanning 3% through 20%)

Rule of 70
A rule stating that the approximate number of years required for per capita real GDP to double is equal to 70 divided by the average rate of economic growth.

THE RULE OF 70 Table 9-3 on the previous page indicates that how quickly the level of a nation's per capita real GDP increases depends on the rate of economic growth. A formula called the **rule of 70** provides a shorthand way to calculate approximately how long it will take a country to experience a significant increase in per capita real GDP. According to the rule of 70, the approximate number of years necessary for a nation's per capita real GDP to increase by 100 percent—that is, to *double*—is equal to 70 divided by the average rate of economic growth. Thus, at an annual growth rate of 10 percent, per capita real GDP should double in about 7 years.

As you can see in Table 9-3, at a 10 percent growth rate, in 7 years per capita real GDP would rise by a factor of 1.94, which is very close to 2, or very nearly the doubling predicted by the rule of 70. At an annual growth rate of 8 percent, the rule of 70 predicts that nearly 9 years will be required for a nation's per capita real GDP to double. Table 9-3 verifies that this prediction is correct. Indeed, the table shows that after 9 years an exact doubling will occur at a growth rate of 8 percent.

The rule of 70 implies that at lower rates of economic growth, much more time must pass before per capita real GDP will double. At a 3 percent growth rate, just over 23 (70 ÷ 3) years must pass before per capita real income doubles. At a rate of growth of only 1 percent per year, 70 (70 ÷ 1) years must pass. This means that if a nation's average rate of economic growth is 1 percent instead of 3 percent, 47 more years—about two generations—must pass for per capita real GDP to double. Clearly, the rule of 70 verifies that even very slight differences in economic growth rates are important.

WHAT IF...

the U.S. rate of economic growth remains stalled at about 1 percent per year instead of the previous average annual rate of 1.7 percent?

Between 1970 and 2015, the average annual rate of growth of per capita real GDP was 1.7 percent. At that rate of growth, the rule of 70 indicates that per capita real GDP will double just about every 40 years. Hence, at that annual growth rate, U.S. per capita real GDP next would be doubled around the year 2056. In contrast, at a rate of economic growth of 1 percent, which is about the growth rate experienced in recent years, the rule of 70 indicates that about 70 years would be required for the next doubling of per capita real GDP to occur—that is, shortly after the year 2085.

MyEconLab Concept Check
MyEconLab Study Plan

SELF CHECK Visit MyEconLab to practice these and other problems and to get instant feedback in your Study Plan.

Economic growth can be defined as the increase in _____ _____ real GDP, measured by its rate of change per year.

The _____ of economic growth are reductions in illiteracy, poverty, and illness and increases in life spans and political stability. The _____ of economic growth may include environmental pollution, alienation, and urban congestion.

Small percentage-point differences in growth rates lead to _____ differences in per capita real GDP over time. These differences can be seen by examining a compound interest table such as the one in Table 9-3 on page 203.

9.2 Explain why productivity growth and saving are crucial for maintaining economic growth

Productivity Growth and Saving: Fundamental Determinants of Economic Growth

Both productivity growth and the national saving rate influence the rate of economic growth. Let's consider each of these elements individually.

Productivity Increases: The Heart of Economic Growth

Let's say that you are required to type 10 term papers and homework assignments a year. You have a digital device, but you do not know how to touch-type. You end up spending an average of two hours per typing job. The next summer, you buy a touch-typing tutorial to use on your digital device and spend a few minutes a day improving your speed. The following term, you spend only 1 hour per typing assignment, thereby saving 10 hours a semester. You have become more productive. This concept of productivity summarizes your ability (and everyone else's) to produce the same output with fewer inputs. Thus, **labor productivity** is normally measured by dividing total real domestic output (real GDP) by the number of workers or the number of labor hours. By definition, labor productivity increases whenever average output produced per worker (or per hour worked) during a specified time period increases.

Labor productivity
Total real domestic output (real GDP) divided by the number of workers (output per worker).

Clearly, there is a relationship between economic growth and increases in labor productivity. If you divide all resources into just capital and labor, economic growth can be defined simply as the cumulative contribution to per capita GDP growth of three components: the rate of growth of capital, the rate of growth of labor, and the rate of growth of capital and labor productivity. If everything else remains constant, improvements in labor productivity ultimately lead to economic growth and higher living standards.

Figure 9-3 below displays estimates of the relative contributions of the growth of labor and capital and the growth of labor and capital productivity to economic growth in the United States, nations in South Asia, and Latin American countries. The growth of labor resources, through associated increases in labor force participation, has contributed to the expansion of output that has accounted for at least half of economic growth in all three regions. Total capital is the sum of physical capital, such as tools and machines, and human capital, which is the amount of knowledge acquired from research and education.

Figure 9-3 shows the separate contributions of the growth of these forms of capital, which together have accounted for more than a third of the growth rate of per capita incomes in the United States, South Asia, and Latin America. In these three parts of the world, growth in overall capital and labor productivity has contributed the remaining 7 to 18 percent.

How might a nation's growth prospects be affected by population aging? See the next page.

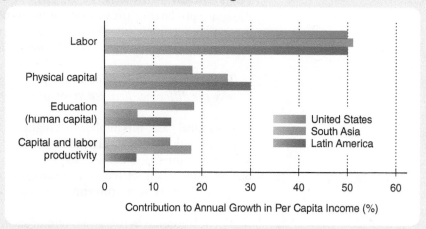

FIGURE 9-3

Factors Accounting for Economic Growth in Selected Regions

In the United States, South Asia, and Latin America, growth in labor resources is the main contributor to economic growth.

Source: International Monetary Fund.

INTERNATIONAL EXAMPLE

Figure 9-4 below displays for selected nations the percentages of populations that are aged 65 and older. Many observers have suggested that the increasing percentage of elderly in the populations of Japan, the United States, and nations in Western Europe necessarily will translate into declining rates of economic growth in these countries. At the same time, these commentators argue, economic growth prospects will improve in nations with smaller elderly population percentages, such as Colombia, Egypt, and India. The observers' reasoning is that older workers are constrained in their physical capabilities, which reduces their labor productivity in relation to that of younger workers. The observers conclude, therefore, that labor productivity and economic growth will tend to be lower in the nations with larger percentages of elderly populations.

FOR CRITICAL THINKING

How could changes in immigration affect the percentage of elderly in the population? (Hint: Are most new immigrants old?)

Sources are listed at the end of this chapter.

FIGURE 9-4

Percentage of the Population Aged 65 and Above in Selected Nations

In developed nations, such as Japan, Western European countries, and the United States, the percentage of the population that is elderly is much higher than in emerging nations such as Colombia, Egypt, and India.

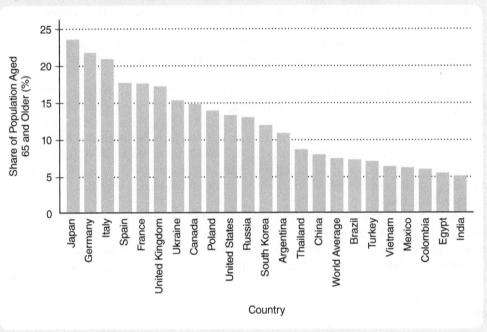

MyEconLab Concept Check

The Fundamental Role of Saving for Economic Growth

Alongside productivity growth, one of the most important factors that affect the rate of economic growth and hence long-term living standards is the rate of saving. A basic proposition in economics is that if you want more tomorrow, you have to consume less today.

> *To have more consumption in the future, you have to consume less today and save the difference between your income and your consumption.*

On a national basis, this implies that higher saving rates eventually mean higher living standards in the long run, all other things held constant. Although the U.S. saving rate has recently increased, concern has been growing that we still are not saving enough. Saving is important for economic growth because without saving, we cannot have investment. If there is no investment in our capital stock, there would be much less economic growth.

The relationship between the rate of saving and per capita real GDP is shown in Figure 9-5 on the next page. Among the nations with the highest rates of saving are China, Germany, Japan, and South Korea.

FIGURE 9-5

Relationship between Rate of Saving and Per Capita Real GDP

This diagram shows the relationship between per capita real GDP and the rate of saving expressed as the average share of annual real GDP saved.

Source: World Bank.

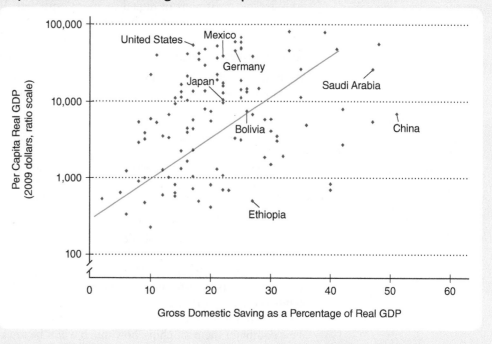

MyEconLab Concept Check
MyEconLab Study Plan

SELF CHECK Visit MyEconLab to practice these and other problems and to get instant feedback in your Study Plan.

Improvements in _____ productivity, all other things being equal, lead to _____ economic growth and higher living standards.

One fundamental determinant of the rate of growth is the rate of _____. To have more consumption in the future, we have to _____ rather than consume. In general, countries that have had higher rates of _____ have had higher rates of growth in per capita real GDP.

New Growth Theory and The Determinants of Growth

9.3 Understand the basis of new growth theory

A simple arithmetic definition of economic growth has already been given. The per capita growth rates of capital and labor plus the per capita growth rate of their productivity constitute the rate of economic growth. Economists have had good data on the growth of the physical capital stock in the United States as well as on the labor force. When you add those two growth rates together, however, you still do not get the total economic growth rate in the United States. The difference has to be due to improvements in productivity. Economists typically labeled this "improvements in technology," and that was that. More recently, proponents of what is now called **new growth theory** argue that technology cannot simply be viewed as an outside factor without explanation. Technology must be understood in terms of what drives it. What are the forces that make productivity grow in the United States and elsewhere?

New growth theory
A theory of economic growth that examines the factors that determine why technology, research, innovation, and the like are undertaken and how they interact.

Growth in Technology

Consider some startling statistics about the growth in technology. Microprocessor speeds may increase from 4,000 megahertz to 10,000 megahertz by the year 2025. By that same year, the size of the thinnest circuit line within a transistor may decrease by 90 percent. The typical memory capacity (RAM) of digital devices will jump from 8 gigabytes, or more than 100 times the equivalent text in the Internal Revenue Code, to more than 400 gigabytes. Recent developments in phase-change memory technologies and in new techniques for storing bits of data on molecules and even individual atoms promise even greater expansions of digital memory capacities. Predictions are that computers may become as powerful as the human brain by 2030.   MyEconLab Concept Check

Technology: A Separate Factor of Production

We now recognize that technology must be viewed as a separate factor of production that is sensitive to rewards. Indeed, one of the major foundations of new growth theory is this:

> ***When the rewards are greater, more technological advances will occur.***

Let's consider several aspects of technology here, the first one being research and development.   MyEconLab Concept Check

Research and Development

A certain amount of technological advance results from research and development (R&D) activities that have as their goal the development of specific new materials, new products, and new machines. How much spending a nation devotes to R&D can have an impact on its long-term economic growth. Part of how much a nation spends depends on what businesses decide is worth spending. That in turn depends on their expected rewards from successful R&D. If your company develops a new way to produce computer memory chips, how much will it be rewarded? The answer depends on what you can charge others to use the new technique.

Patent

A government protection that gives an inventor the exclusive right to make, use, or sell an invention for a limited period of time (currently, 20 years).

PATENTS To protect new techniques developed through R&D, we have a system of **patents**, in which the federal government gives the patent holder the exclusive right to make, use, and sell an invention for a period of 20 years. One can argue that this special protection given to owners of patents increases expenditures on R&D and therefore adds to long-term economic growth. Figure 9-6 below shows that U.S. patent grants fell during the 1970s, increased steadily after 1982, surged following 1995, dropped in 2004 and 2005, and increased again starting in 2010.

How has a change in U.S. patent law affected the incentives that inventors confront regarding when to file a patent application with the U.S. Patent and Trademark Office?

MyEconLab Animation

U.S. Patent Grants

The U.S. Patent and Trademark Office gradually began awarding more patent grants between the early 1980s and the mid-1990s. Since 1995, the number of patents granted each year has risen in most years, except the mid and late 2000s.

Source: U.S. Patent and Trademark Office.

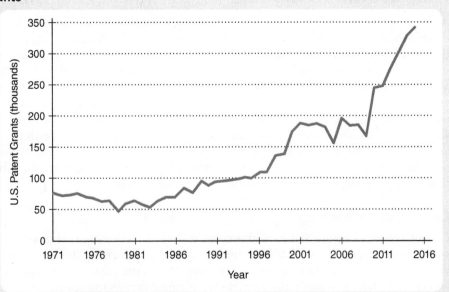

POLICY EXAMPLE

Have an Invention in Mind? First, Think about Patent Timing!

Recently, Congress decided to align U.S. patent rules more closely with those in much of the rest of the world. Previously, the government's U.S. Patent and Trademark Office (USPTO) awarded a patent to an individual or a company that could offer proof of being the first to invent a new product. Now the USPTO awards patents to the individual or company that is the first to file an application providing acceptable evidence of a novel invention.

This rule change has considerably altered inventors' incentives. In years past, an individual or firm sought to publish articles about a new product early in the process of developing it, because the act of publishing such information helped to establish the claim to the invention. Now, however, inventors have an incentive to be more secretive. In addition,

inventors approach lawyers to discuss when to file for a patent as soon as the inventors have begun developing a product. In such cases, patent attorneys typically counsel clients to file "provisional" patents. Obtaining a provisional patent ensures that the inventor is the first to file the application, rather than someone else who might learn of the product and beat the true inventor to a patent.

FOR CRITICAL THINKING

Why might the new law reduce costly court battles over who first invented a product?

Sources are listed at the end of this chapter.

POSITIVE EXTERNALITIES AND R&D As we discussed in Chapter 5, positive externalities are benefits from an activity that are enjoyed by someone besides the instigator of the activity. In the case of R&D spending, a certain amount of the benefits go to other companies that do not have to pay for them. In particular, according to economists David Coe of the International Monetary Fund and Elhanan Helpman of Harvard University, about a quarter of the global productivity gains of R&D investment in the top seven industrialized countries goes to other nations. For every 1 percent rise in the stock of R&D in the United States alone, for example, productivity in the rest of the world increases by about 0.25 percent.

One country's R&D expenditures benefit other countries because they are able to import capital goods—say, digital devices and telecommunications networks—from technologically advanced countries and then use them as inputs in making their own industries more efficient. In addition, countries that import high-tech goods are able to imitate the technology. MyEconLab Concept Check

The Open Economy and Economic Growth

People who study economic growth today emphasize the importance of the openness of the economy. Free trade encourages a more rapid spread of technology and industrial ideas. Moreover, open economies may experience higher rates of economic growth because their own industries have access to a bigger market. When trade barriers are erected in the form of quotas and the like, domestic industries become isolated from global technological progress. This occurred for many years in Communist countries and in most developing countries in Africa, Latin America, and elsewhere. Figure 9-7 on the next page shows the relationship between economic growth and openness as measured by the level of tariff barriers. MyEconLab Concept Check

Innovation and Knowledge

We tend to think of technological progress as, say, the invention of the transistor. But invention means little by itself. **Innovation** is required. Innovation involves the transformation of something new, such as an invention, into something that benefits the economy either by lowering production costs or by providing new goods and services. Indeed, the new growth theorists believe that real wealth creation comes from innovation and that invention is but a facet of innovation.

Historically, technologies have moved relatively slowly from invention to innovation to widespread use. The dispersion of new technology remains for the most part slow and uncertain. The inventor of the transistor thought it might be used to make better hearing aids. At the time it was invented, the *New York Times*'s sole reference to it was in a small weekly column called "News of Radio." When the laser was invented,

Innovation
Transforming an invention into something that is useful to humans.

FIGURE 9-7

The Relationship between Economic Growth and Tariff Barriers to International Trade

Nations with low tariff barriers are relatively open to international trade and have tended to have higher average annual rates of real GDP per capita growth since 1965.

Source: World Bank.

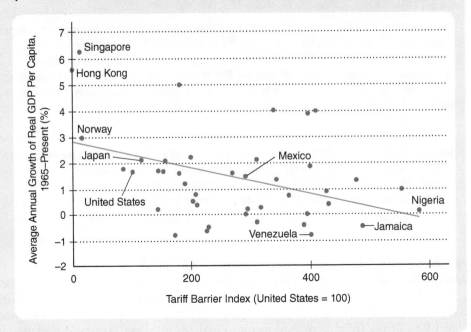

no one really knew what it could be used for. It was initially used to help in navigation, measurement, and chemical research. Today, it is used in the reproduction of music, printing, surgery, telecommunications, and optical data transmittal and storage. Tomorrow, who knows?

Typically, thousands of raw ideas emerge each year at a large firm's R&D laboratories. Only a few hundred of these ideas develop into formal proposals for new processes or products. Of these proposals, the business selects perhaps a few dozen that it deems suitable for further study to explore their feasibility. After careful scrutiny, the firm concludes that only a handful of these ideas are inventions worthy of being integrated into actual production processes or launched as novel products. The firm is fortunate if one or two ultimately become successful marketplace innovations.　　　MyEconLab Concept Check

The Importance of Ideas and Knowledge

Economist Paul Romer has added at least one other important factor that determines the rate of economic growth. He contends that production and manufacturing knowledge is just as important as the other determinants and perhaps even more so. He considers knowledge a factor of production that, like capital, has to be paid for by forgoing current consumption. Economies must therefore invest in knowledge just as they invest in machines. Because past investment in capital may make it more profitable to acquire more knowledge, there may be an investment-knowledge cycle in which investment spurs knowledge and knowledge spurs investment.

A once-and-for-all increase in a country's rate of investment may permanently raise that country's growth rate. (According to traditional theory, a once-and-for-all increase in the rate of saving and therefore in the rate of investment simply leads to a new steady-state standard of living, not one that continues to increase.)

Another way of looking at knowledge is that it is a store of ideas. According to Romer, ideas are what drive economic growth. In fact, we have become an idea economy. Consider Apple, Inc. A relatively small percentage of that company's labor force is involved in actually building products. Rather, a majority of Apple's employees are attempting to discover new ideas that can be translated into computer code that can then be turned into products. The major conclusion that Romer and other new growth theorists draw is this:

Economic growth can continue as long as we keep coming up with new ideas.

How do new textile materials promise a wave of clothing innovations?

EXAMPLE

Will Novel Materials Weave Innovative Clothing Fads?

The latest fads in clothing may be less related to their styling than to their content. Textile products now include antibacterial cotton, mosquito-repellent fibers, and fire-retardant acrylics. A number of firms already have thousands of patents for clothing containing these and other materials.

Perhaps the most innovative clothing items incorporate graphene, a material derived from graphite used in pencil leads. This material is very strong, light, and flexible and hence can be woven into clothing. Graphene also can be configured to absorb or emit light, thereby giving the wearer the capability either to blend in with surroundings or to glow like a firefly. In addition, graphene conducts heat and electricity, and this latter property may provide the basis for the most marketable clothing innovations.

Scientists already are testing articles of clothing that can allow the wearer to engage in phone conversations and connect to the Internet.

Thus, rethinking the composition of clothing offers the potential for an array of innovations. The main barrier that scientists must overcome is the high costs of the new textile materials. Graphene material currently costs about $60 per square inch—quite a bit more than a square inch of either cotton or polyester.

FOR CRITICAL THINKING
So far, does research in new textile materials appear to have yielded inventions or innovations? Explain.

Sources are listed at the end of this chapter.

MyEconLab Concept Check

The Importance of Human Capital

Knowledge, ideas, and productivity are all tied together. One of the threads is the quality of the labor force. Increases in the productivity of the labor force are a function of increases in human capital, the fourth factor of production discussed in Chapter 2. Recall that human capital consists of the knowledge and skills that people in the workforce acquire through education, on-the-job training, and self-teaching. To increase your own human capital, you have to invest by forgoing income-earning activities while you attend school. Society also has to invest in the form of teachers and education.

According to the new growth theorists, human capital is becoming nearly as important as physical capital, particularly when trying to explain international differences in living standards. It is therefore not surprising that one of the most effective ways that developing countries can become developed is by investing in secondary schooling.

One can argue that policy changes that increase human capital will lead to more technological improvements. One of the reasons that concerned citizens, policymakers, and politicians are looking for a change in the U.S. schooling system is that our educational system seems to be falling behind those of other countries. This lag is greatest in science and mathematics—precisely the areas required for developing better technology.

MyEconLab Concept Check
MyEconLab Study Plan

SELF CHECK Visit MyEconLab to practice these and other problems and to get instant feedback in your Study Plan.

_____ _____ theory argues that the greater the rewards, the more rapid the pace of technology. And greater rewards spur research and development.

The openness of a nation's economy to international _____ seems to correlate with its rate of economic growth.

Invention and innovation are not the same thing. _____ are useless until _____ transforms them into goods and services that people find valuable.

According to _____ _____ theory, economic growth can continue as long as we keep coming up with new ideas.

Increases in _____ capital can lead to greater rates of economic growth. These come about by increased education, on-the-job training, and self-teaching.

9.4 Evaluate how immigration and property rights influence economic growth

Immigration, Property Rights, and Growth

New theories of economic growth have also shed light on two additional factors that play important roles in influencing a nation's rate of growth of per capita real GDP: immigration and property rights.

Population and Immigration as They Affect Economic Growth

There are several ways to view population growth as it affects economic growth. On the one hand, population growth can result in a larger labor force and increases in human capital, which contribute to economic growth. On the other hand, population growth can be seen as a drain on the economy because for any given amount of GDP, more population means lower per capita GDP. According to Harvard economist Michael Kremer, the first of these effects is historically more important. His conclusion is that population growth drives technological progress, which then increases economic growth. The theory is simple: If there are 50 percent more people in the United States, there will be 50 percent more geniuses. And with 50 percent more people, the rewards for creativity are commensurately greater. Otherwise stated, the larger the potential market, the greater the incentive to develop human capital.

A larger market also provides an incentive for well-trained people to immigrate, which undoubtedly helps explain why the United States attracts a disproportionate number of top scientists from around the globe.

Does immigration help spur economic growth? Yes, according to the late economist Julian Simon, who pointed out that "every time our system allows in one more immigrant, on average, the economic welfare of American citizens goes up. . . . Additional immigrants, both the legal and the illegal, raise the standard of living of U.S. natives and have little or no negative impact on any occupational or income class." He further argued that immigrants do not displace natives from jobs but rather create jobs through their purchases and by starting new businesses. Immigrants' earning and spending simply expand the economy.

Not all researchers agree with Simon, and few studies have tested the theories he and Kremer have advanced. This area is currently the focus of much research.

MyEconLab Concept Check

Property Rights and Entrepreneurship

If you were in a country where bank accounts and businesses were periodically expropriated by the government, how willing would you be to leave your financial assets in a savings account or to invest in a business? Certainly, you would be less willing than if such actions never occurred.

In general, the more securely private property rights (see page 108) are assigned, the more capital accumulation there will be. People will be willing to invest their savings in endeavors that will increase their wealth in future years. Attaining this outcome requires that property rights in their wealth be sanctioned and enforced by the government. In fact, some economic historians have provided evidence that it was the development of well-defined private property rights and legal structures that allowed Western Europe to increase its growth rate after many centuries of stagnation. The ability and certainty with which they can reap the gains from investing also determine the extent to which business owners in other countries will invest capital in developing countries. The threat of loss of property rights that hangs over some developing nations undoubtedly stands in the way of foreign investments that would allow these nations to develop more rapidly.

The legal structure of a nation is closely tied to the degree with which its citizens use their own entrepreneurial skills. In Chapter 2, we identified entrepreneurship as the fifth factor of production. Entrepreneurs are the risk takers who seek out new ways to do things and create new products. To the extent that entrepreneurs are allowed to capture the rewards from their entrepreneurial activities, they will seek to engage in those activities. In countries where such rewards cannot be captured because of a lack of property rights, there will be less entrepreneurship. Typically, this results in fewer investments and a lower rate of growth. We shall examine the implications this has for policymakers in Chapter 18.

MyEconLab Concept Check
MyEconLab Study Plan

SELF CHECK Visit MyEconLab to practice these and other problems and to get instant feedback in your Study Plan.

While some economists argue that population growth reduces _____ growth, others contend that the opposite is true. The latter economists consequently believe that immigration should be encouraged rather than discouraged.

Well-defined and protected _____ rights are important for fostering entrepreneurship. In the absence of well-defined _____ rights, individuals have less incentive to take risks, and economic growth rates suffer.

Economic Development

How did developed countries travel paths of growth from extreme poverty to relative riches? That is the essential issue of **development economics**, which is the study of why some countries grow and develop and others do not and of policies that might help developing economies get richer. It is not enough simply to say that people in different countries are different and that is why some countries are rich and some countries are poor. Economists do not deny that different cultures have different work ethics, but they are unwilling to accept such a pat and fatalistic answer.

Look at any world map. About four-fifths of the countries you will see on the map are considered relatively poor. The goal of economists who study development is to help the more than 4.5 billion people today with low living standards join the more than 2.5 billion people who have at least moderately high living standards.

9.5 Discuss the fundamental factors that contribute to a nation's economic development

Development economics
The study of factors that contribute to the economic growth of a country.

Putting World Poverty into Perspective

Most U.S. residents cannot even begin to understand the reality of poverty in the world today. At least one-half, if not two-thirds, of the world's population lives at subsistence level, with just enough to eat for survival. Indeed, the World Bank estimates that nearly 20 percent of the world's people live on less than $1.50 per day. The official poverty line in the United States is above the annual income of at least half the human beings on the planet. This is not to say that we should ignore domestic problems with the poor and homeless simply because they are living better than many people elsewhere in the world. Rather, it is necessary for us to maintain an appropriate perspective on what are considered problems for this country relative to what are considered problems elsewhere.

MyEconLab Concept Check

The Relationship between Population Growth and Economic Development

The world's population is growing at the rate of about 2 people a second. That amounts to 172,800 a day or 63.1 million a year. Today, there are more than 7 billion people on earth. By 2050, according to the United Nations, the world's population will be close to leveling off at around 9 billion. Panel (a) of Figure 9-8 on the next page shows population growth. Panel (b) emphasizes an implication of panel (a), which is that almost all the growth in population is occurring in developing nations. Many developed countries are expected to lose population over the next several decades.

Ever since the Reverend Thomas Robert Malthus wrote *An Essay on the Principle of Population* in 1798, excessive population growth has been a concern. Modern-day Malthusians are able to generate great enthusiasm for the concept that population growth is bad. Over and over, media commentators and a number of scientists tell us that rapid population growth threatens economic development and the quality of life.

MyEconLab Animation

FIGURE 9-8

Expected Growth in World Population by 2050

Panel (a) displays the percentages of the world's population residing in the various continents by 2050 and shows projected population growth for these continents and for selected nations. It indicates that Asia and Africa are expected to gain the most in population by the year 2050.

Panel (b) indicates that population will increase in developing countries before beginning to level off around 2050, whereas industrially advanced nations will grow very little in population in the first half of this century.

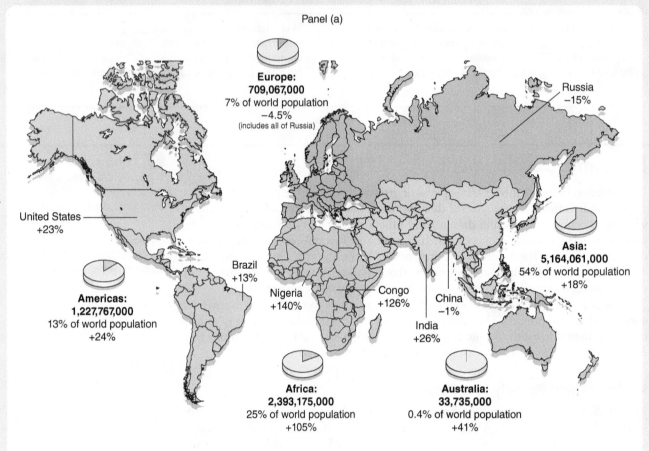

Panel (a)

Europe:
709,067,000
7% of world population
−4.5%
(includes all of Russia)

Russia
−15%

United States
+23%

Brazil
+13%

Nigeria
+140%

Congo
+126%

China
−1%

India
+26%

Asia:
5,164,061,000
54% of world population
+18%

Americas:
1,227,767,000
13% of world population
+24%

Africa:
2,393,175,000
25% of world population
+105%

Australia:
33,735,000
0.4% of world population
+41%

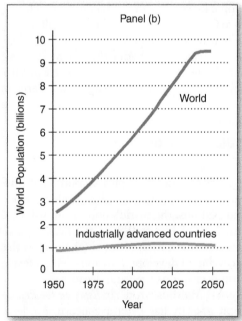

Panel (b)

World

Industrially advanced countries

Source: United Nations.

MALTHUS WAS PROVED WRONG Malthus predicted that population would outstrip food supplies. This prediction has never been supported by the facts, according to economist Nicholas Eberstadt of the American Enterprise Institute for Public Policy Research. As the world's population has grown, so has the world's food stock, measured by calories per person. In addition, the price of food, corrected for inflation, has generally been falling for more than a century. The production of food has been expanding faster than the increase in demand caused by increased population.

GROWTH LEADS TO SMALLER FAMILIES Furthermore, economists have found that as nations become richer, average family size declines. Otherwise stated, the more economic development occurs, the slower the population growth rate becomes. Population growth certainly has dropped in Western Europe and in the former Soviet Union, where populations in some countries are actually declining. Predictions of birthrates in developing countries have often turned out to be overstated if those countries experience rapid economic growth. Past birthrate overpredictions have occurred for this reason in nations such as Chile, Hong Kong, Mexico, and Taiwan.

Recent research on population and economic development has revealed that social and economic modernization has been accompanied by a decline in childbearing significant enough to be called a demographic transition. Modernization reduces infant mortality, which in turn reduces the incentive for couples to have many children to make sure that a certain number survive to adulthood. Modernization also lowers the demand for children for a variety of reasons, not the least being that couples in more developed countries do not need to rely on their children to take care of them in old age.   MyEconLab Concept Check

The Stages of Development: Agriculture to Industry to Services

If we analyze the development of modern rich nations, we find that they went through three stages. First is the agricultural stage, when most of the population is involved in agriculture. Then comes the manufacturing stage, when much of the population becomes involved in the industrialized sector of the economy. Finally, there is a shift toward services. That is exactly what happened in the United States: The so-called tertiary, or service, sector of the economy continues to grow, whereas the manufacturing sector (and its share of employment) is declining in relative importance.

Of particular significance, however, is the requirement for specialization in a nation's comparative advantage (see Chapter 2). The doctrine of comparative advantage is particularly appropriate for the developing countries of the world. If trading is allowed among nations, a country is best off if it produces what it has a comparative advantage in producing and imports the rest (for more details, see Chapter 19). This means that many developing countries should continue to specialize in agricultural production or in labor-intensive manufactured goods.   MyEconLab Concept Check

Keys to Economic Development

According to one theory of development, a country must have a large natural resource base in order to develop. This theory goes on to assert that much of the world is running out of natural resources, thereby limiting economic growth and development. Only the narrowest definition of a natural resource, however, could lead to such an opinion. In broader terms, a natural resource is something occurring in nature that we can use for our own purposes. As emphasized by new growth theory, natural resources therefore include human capital—education and experience. Also, natural resources change over time. Several hundred years ago, for example, they did not include hydroelectric power—no one knew that such a natural resource existed or how to bring it into existence.

Natural resources by themselves are not a prerequisite for or a guarantee of economic development, as demonstrated by Japan's extensive development despite a lack of domestic oil resources and by Brazil's slow pace of development in spite of a vast array of natural resources. Resources must be transformed into something usable for either investment or consumption.

Economists have found that four factors seem to be highly related to the pace of economic development:

1. *Establishing a system of property rights.* As noted earlier, if you were in a country where bank accounts and businesses were periodically confiscated by the government, you would be reluctant to leave some of your wealth in a savings account or to invest in a business. Confiscation of private property rarely takes place in developed countries. It has occurred in numerous developing countries, however. For example, private property has been nationalized in Venezuela and in Cuba. Economists have found that other things being equal, the more secure private property rights are, the more private capital accumulation and economic growth there will be.

2. *Developing an educated population.* Both theoretically and empirically, we know that a more educated workforce aids economic development because it allows individuals to build on the ideas of others. Thus, developing countries can advance more rapidly if they increase investments in education. Or, stated in the negative, economic development is difficult to sustain if a nation allows a sizable portion of its population to remain uneducated. Education allows impoverished young people to acquire skills that enable them to avoid poverty as adults.

3. *Letting "creative destruction" run its course.* The twentieth-century Harvard economist Joseph Schumpeter championed the concept of "creative destruction," through which new businesses ultimately create new jobs and economic growth after first destroying old jobs, old companies, and old industries. Such change is painful and costly, but it is necessary for economic advancement. Many governments in developing nations have had a history of supporting current companies and industries by discouraging new technologies and new companies from entering the marketplace. The process of creative destruction has not been allowed to work its magic in these countries.

Limiting protectionism. Open economies experience faster economic development than economies closed to international trade. Trade encourages people and businesses to discover ways to specialize so that they can become more productive and earn higher incomes. Increased productivity and subsequent increases in economic growth are the results. Thus, having fewer trade barriers promotes faster economic development.

MyEconLab Concept Check

MyEconLab Study Plan

SELF CHECK Visit MyEconLab to practice these and other problems and to get instant feedback in your Study Plan.

Although many people believe that population growth hinders economic development, there is little evidence to support that notion. What is clear is that economic development tends to lead to a reduction in the rate of _____ growth.

Historically, there are three stages of economic development: the _____ stage, the _____ stage, and the _____-_____ stage, when a large part of the workforce is employed in providing services.

Although one theory of economic development holds that a sizable natural resource base is the key to a nation's development, this fails to account for the importance of the human element: The _____ _____ must be capable of using a country's natural resources.

Fundamental factors contributing to the pace of economic development are a well-defined system of _____ _____, training, and _____, allowing new generations of companies and industries to _____ older generations, and promoting an open economy by allowing _____ _____.

YOU ARE THERE

Is U.S. Immigration Policy Creating a "Skills Gap"?

The family of Rosario Marin, who served as the forty-first treasurer of the United States, emigrated from Mexico when she was 14. Marin recognizes the important contributions that immigrants have made to U.S. economic growth. For instance, immigrants or their children founded more than 25 percent of high-tech firms and about 40 percent of Fortune 500 companies.

Marin is concerned about what she perceives to be a growing immigrant "skills gap." The source of the problem, she argues, is an immigration policy that discourages U.S. companies from hiring immigrants who could make economic contributions. Marin points out that many firms are unable to hire any well-qualified foreign workers because of legislated caps on the total number of available work permits. Even companies that are able apply for a permit to hire qualified foreign workers must pay application fees exceeding $1,000 per worker.

Limiting immigration of foreign residents with skills while allowing many who lack skills could help explain the deteriorating earnings performances of immigrants. Those immigrants who arrived between 1960 and 1969 and initially earned 20 percent less than the average U.S. resident now earn about 20 percent more. Since the mid-1980s, however, the average U.S. immigrant's earnings have remained at least 20 percent below those of the typical U.S. resident.

1. How could higher barriers to immigration of highly skilled immigrants tend to reduce overall U.S. labor productivity and, consequently, economic growth?

2. What relationship might exist between the entry of highly skilled immigrants and the production of new ideas and knowledge that promote economic growth?

Sources are listed at the end of this chapter.

ISSUES & APPLICATIONS

MyEconLab Video

Zuma Press, Inc/Alamy

Immigration Rules Favor Sports Spectacles over Economic Growth

CONCEPTS APPLIED

» Economic Growth

» Labor Productivity

» Productivity Growth

U.S. immigration authorities, operating under rules established by Congress, make it easy for foreign sports stars to work in the United States. At the same time, these authorities enforce rules that limit opportunities for foreign scientists and engineers to join the U.S. labor force. These facts have implications for future U.S. economic growth.

Immigration Rules for Sports Stars versus Scientists and Engineers

Nearly one of every five players participating in the National Basketball Association's professional teams is a foreign resident granted a special work permit called an O-1 or P-1 visa. U.S. immigration law classifies these men as athletes of "extraordinary ability." The rules do not require professional sports teams to try first to hire U.S. residents as players. The rules also set no upper limit on the numbers of O-1 or P1 visas that may be granted to foreign athletes who play professional basketball or other sports such as baseball or hockey.

Foreign scientists and engineers must obtain a different type of work permit—an H1-B visa. A company can obtain this permit to hire a foreign scientist or engineer only after it has proved that no similarly qualified U.S. citizens could fill the firm's position. In addition, there is an overall cap on the number of these work permits that can be issued nationwide during a given year. Each year, this cap prevents firms from hiring as many foreign scientists and engineers as they desire to employ.

Economic Growth Implications of U.S. Immigration Rules

Professional sports stars provide entertainment services that are consumption goods used up immediately. Thus, granting professional sports teams the right to obtain O-1 and P-1 visas to hire foreign players possessing "extraordinary ability" to produce these entertainment services offers a negligible contribution to future U.S. economic growth.

In contrast, many U.S. companies utilize the services of foreign scientists and engineers to produce capital goods, which in turn can be utilized to produce more consumption *and* capital goods in the future. Services provided by foreign scientists and engineers also contribute to technological improvements that boost labor productivity. This productivity growth fuels additional economic growth. Consequently, promoting the immigration of foreign sports stars while hindering immigration of foreign scientists and engineers tends to reduce prospects for future U.S. economic growth.

For Critical Thinking

1. Why do the efforts of foreign scientists and engineers contribute much more to labor productivity and economic growth than the exertions of foreign sports stars?

2. In your view, are rules that hinder immigration of highly trained scientists and engineers consistent with the policy recommendations of new growth theory?

Web Resources

1. Learn how people with "extraordinary ability" obtain O-1 and P-1 visas in the Web Links in MyEconLab.

2. To view a summary of the many requirements that must be satisfied before a foreign worker qualifies for an H1-B visa, see the Web Links in MyEconLab.

MyEconLab

For more questions on this chapter's Issues & Applications, go to MyEconLab.

In the Study Plan for this chapter, select Section I: Issues and Applications.

Sources are listed at the end of this chapter.

Fundamental Points

1. Economic growth is the annual rate of increase in per capita real GDP.
2. Improvements in labor productivity and a higher saving rate generate a higher rate of economic growth.
3. The key implication of new growth theory is that the greater the rewards from adoption of new technologies, the greater the pace of technological innovation.
4. Economists continue to disagree about the implications of immigration for economic growth, but one area of agreement is that failing to clearly define and protect property rights gives individuals less incentive to take risks, which reduces economic growth.
5. Historical evidence indicates nations typically pass through three stages of economic development: the agricultural stage, the manufacturing stage, and the service-sector stage, with rates of economic growth diminishing at each state.

WHAT YOU SHOULD KNOW

Here is what you should know after reading this chapter. MyEconLab will help you identify what you know, and where to go when you need to practice.

LEARNING OBJECTIVES	KEY TERMS	WHERE TO GO TO PRACTICE
9.1 Define economic growth and recognize the importance of economic growth rates *The rate of economic growth is the annual rate of change in per capita real GDP. This measure reflects growth in overall production of goods and services and population growth. It is an average measure that does not account for possible changes in the distribution of income or welfare costs or benefits. Economic growth compounds over time. Thus, over long intervals, small differences in growth can accumulate to produce large disparities in per capita incomes.*	economic growth, 200 rule of 70, 204 **Key Figures** Figure 9-1, 200 Figure 9-2, 201	• MyEconLab Study Plan 9.1 • Animated Figures 9-1, 9-2
9.2 Explain why productivity growth and saving are crucial for maintaining economic growth *The fundamental factors contributing to economic growth are growth in a nation's pool of labor, growth of its capital stock, and growth in the productivity of its capital and labor. Higher productivity growth influences near-term changes in economic growth by unambiguously contributing to greater annual increases in a nation's per capita real GDP. Higher saving rates contribute to greater investment and hence increased capital accumulation and economic growth.*	Labor productivity, 205 **Key Figure** Figure 9-5, 207	• MyEconLab Study Plan 9.2

WHAT YOU SHOULD KNOW *continued*

LEARNING OBJECTIVES ————	KEY TERMS ————	WHERE TO GO TO PRACTICE ———
9.3 **Understand the basis of new growth theory** *This theory examines why individuals and businesses conduct research into inventing and developing new technologies and how this innovation process affects economic growth. A key implication of the theory is that ideas and knowledge are crucial elements of the growth process.*	new growth theory, 207 patent, 208 innovation, 209 **Key Figures** Figure 9-6, 208 Figure 9-7, 210	• MyEconLab Study Plan 9.3 • Animated Figures 9-6, 9-7
9.4 **Evaluate how immigration and property rights influence economic growth** *Immigration increases a nation's population, which can have the effect of pushing down per capita GDP. Nevertheless, the resulting increase in labor resources and their employment in production contribute to economic growth. More secure property rights provide a foundation for capital accumulation and increased economic growth.*		• MyEconLab Study Plan 9.4
9.5 **Discuss the fundamental factors that contribute to a nation's economic development** *Key features shared by nations that attain higher levels of economic development are protection of property rights, significant opportunities for their residents to obtain training and education, policies that permit new companies and industries to replace older ones, and the avoidance of protectionist barriers that hinder international trade.*	development economics, 213	• MyEconLab Study Plan 9.5 • Animated Figure 9-8

Log in to MyEconLab, take a chapter test, and get a personalized Study Plan that tells you which concepts you understand and which ones you need to review. From there, MyEconLab will give you further practice, tutorials, animations, videos, and guided solutions. For more information, visit http://www.myeconlab.com

PROBLEMS

All problems are assignable in MyEconLab; exercises that update with real-time data are marked with . *Answers to odd-numbered problems appear in* MyEconLab.

9-1. The graph to the right shows a production possibilities curve for 2018 and two potential production possibilities curves for 2019, denoted 2019_A and 2019_B. (See page 200.)

  a. Which of the labeled points corresponds to maximum feasible 2018 production that is more likely to be associated with the curve denoted 2019_A?

  b. Which of the labeled points corresponds to maximum feasible 2018 production that is more likely to be associated with the curve denoted 2019_B?

MyEconLab Visit **www.myeconlab.com** to complete these exercises online and get instant feedback. Exercises that update with real-time data are marked with .

9-2. A nation's capital goods wear out over time, so a portion of its capital goods become unusable every year. Last year, its residents decided to produce no capital goods. It has experienced no growth in its population or in the amounts of other productive resources during the past year. In addition, the nation's technology and resource productivity have remained unchanged during the past year. Will the nation's economic growth rate for the current year be negative, zero, or positive? (See page 205.)

9-3. In the situation described in Problem 9-2, suppose that vocational training during the past year enables the people of this nation to repair all capital goods so that they continue to function as well as new. All other factors are unchanged, however. In light of this single change to the conditions faced in this nation, will the nation's economic growth rate for the current year be negative, zero, or positive? (See page 205.)

9-4. Consider the following data. What is the per capita real GDP in each of these countries? (See pages 201–203.)

Country	Population (millions)	Real GDP ($ billions)
A	10	55
B	20	60
C	5	70

9-5. Suppose that during the next 10 years, real GDP triples and population doubles in each of the nations in Problem 9-4. What will per capita real GDP be in each country after 10 years have passed? (See page 202.)

9-6. Consider the following table displaying annual growth rates for nations X, Y, and Z, each of which entered 2015 with real per capita GDP equal to $20,000. (See pages 201–203.)

	Annual Growth Rate (%)			
Country	2015	2016	2017	2018
X	7	1	3	4
Y	4	5	7	9
Z	5	5	3	2

a. Which nation most likely experienced a sizable earthquake in late 2015 that destroyed a significant portion of its stock of capital goods, but was followed by speedy investments in rebuilding the nation's capital stock? What is this nation's per capita real GDP at the end of 2018, rounded to the nearest dollar?

b. Which nation most likely adopted policies in 2015 that encouraged a gradual shift in production from capital goods to consumption goods? What is this nation's per capita real GDP at the end of 2018, rounded to the nearest dollar?

c. Which nation most likely adopted policies in 2015 that encouraged a quick shift in production from consumption goods to capital goods? What is this nation's per capita real GDP at the end of 2018, rounded to the nearest dollar?

9-7. Per capita real GDP grows at a rate of 3 percent in country F and at a rate of 6 percent in country G. Both begin with equal levels of per capita real GDP. Use Table 9-3 on page 203 to determine how much higher per capita real GDP will be in country G after 20 years. How much higher will real GDP be in country G after 40 years? (See page 203.)

9-8. Since the early 1990s, the average rate of growth of per capita real GDP in Mozambique has been 3 percent per year, as compared with a growth rate of 8 percent in China. Refer to Table 9-3 on page 203. If a typical resident of each of these nations begins this year with a per capita real GDP of $3,000 per year, about how many more dollars' worth of real GDP per capita would the person in China be earning 10 years from now than the individual in Mozambique? (See page 203.)

9-9. On the basis of the information in Problem 9-10 and reference to Table 9-3 on page 203, about how many more dollars' worth of real GDP per capita would the person in China be earning 50 years from now than the individual in Mozambique? (See page 203.)

9-10. In 2016, a nation's population was 10 million. Its nominal GDP was $40 billion, and its price index was 100. In 2017, its population had increased to 12 million, its nominal GDP had risen to $57.6 billion, and its price index had increased to 120. What was this nation's economic growth rate during the year? (See page 203.)

9-11. Between the start of 2016 and the start of 2017, a country's economic growth rate was 4 percent. Its population did not change during the year, nor did its price level. What was the rate of increase of the country's nominal GDP during this one-year interval? (See page 203.)

9-12. In 2016, a nation's population was 10 million, its real GDP was $1.21 billion, and its GDP deflator had a value of 121. By 2017, its population had increased to 12 million, its real GDP had risen to $1.5 billion, and its GDP deflator had a value of 125. What was the percentage change in per capita real GDP between 2016 and 2017? (See page 203.)

9-13. A nation's per capita real GDP was $2,000 in 2015, and the nation's population was 5 million in that year. Between 2015 and 2016, the inflation rate in this country was 5 percent, and the nation's annual rate of economic growth was 10 percent. Its population remained unchanged. What was per capita real GDP in 2016? What was the *level* of real GDP in 2016? (See page 203.)

9-14. Brazil has a population of about 200 million, with about 145 million over the age of 15. Of these, an estimated 25 percent, or 35 million people, are functionally illiterate. The typical literate individual reads only about two nonacademic books per year, which is less than half the number read by the typical literate U.S. or European resident. Answer the following questions solely from the perspective of new growth theory (see page 205):

a. Discuss the implications of Brazil's literacy and reading rates for its growth prospects in light of the key tenets of new growth theory.

b. What types of policies might Brazil implement to improve its growth prospects? Explain.

REFERENCES

INTERNATIONAL EXAMPLE: Aging Nations and Labor Productivity

Robert Ayres, "The Economic Conundrum of an Aging Population," Worldwatch Institute, October 2, 2013.

Michael Heath, "Lowe Says Aging Workers, Slow Productivity Risks Economic Growth," Bloomberg, March 12, 2014.

Neil Shah, "Will Baby Boomers Drag Down Growth?" *The Wall Street Journal*, April 11, 2013.

POLICY EXAMPLE: Have an Invention in Mind? First, Think about Patent Timing!

Laura Baverman, "Patent Law Changes Alter Entrepreneurs' Planning," *USA Today*, September 19, 2013.

"IP Alert: U.S. Patent Law Changes Taking Effect as of December 18, 2013," Fitch Even News, January 2, 2014.

Raymond Van Dyke, "Caveat Inventor: The New Patent Paradigm," E-Commerce Times, March 15, 2013.

EXAMPLE: Will Novel Materials Weave Innovative Clothing Fads?

Olivia Fleming, "Never Catch a Cold on the Subway Again! New Antibacterial Clothing Line Protects Wearers from Germs on Their Daily Commute," *Daily Mail*, February 19, 2014.

"Material Benefits," The Economist, September 7, 2013.

Gautam Naik, "Wonder Material Ignites Scientific Gold Rush," *The Wall Street Journal*, August 23, 2013.

YOU ARE THERE: Is U.S. Immigration Policy Creating a "Skills Gap"?

Emily Badger, "Why More Skilled Immigration Would Be Good for American Workers, Too," *The Washington Post*, March 19, 2014.

"Correlations: Immigrants Fall Behind," *Bloomberg Businessweek*, June 23, 2013.

Rosario Marin, "Immigration Reform and the Skills Gap," *The Wall Street Journal*, June 6, 2013.

ISSUES & APPLICATIONS: Immigration Rules Favor Sports Spectacles over Economic Growth

Stuart Anderson, "H-1B Visas Essential to Attracting and Retaining Talent in America," National Foundation for American Policy, May 2013. (www.nfap.com/pdf/NFAP%20Policy%20Brief%20H-1B%20Visas%20May%202013.pdf)

Fergus Cullen, "Those 'Guest Workers' of the NBA and NHL," *The Wall Street Journal*, June 18, 2013.

U.S. National Science Foundation, Science and Engineering Indicators 2014, Chapter 3: "Science and Engineering Labor Force." (http://www.nsf.gov/statistics/seind14/content/chapter-3/chapter-3.pdf)

10

Real GDP and the Price Level in the Long Run

Joy Durham/Danita Delimont/Alamy

LEARNING OBJECTIVES

After reading this chapter, you should be able to:

10.1 Discuss the concept of long-run aggregate supply and describe the effect of economic growth on the long-run aggregate supply curve

10.2 Explain why the aggregate demand curve slopes downward and list key factors that cause this curve to shift

10.3 Evaluate the meaning of long-run equilibrium for the economy as a whole and explain why economic growth can cause deflation

10.4 Evaluate likely reasons for persistent inflation in recent decades

MyEconLab helps you master each objective and study more efficiently. See the end of the chapter for details.

The island nation of Greenland encompasses a large, icy surface area but possesses the smallest human population of any country on earth. Until recently, the country also had a small set of available productive resources. Only in recent years have Greenland's residents been farming potatoes, let alone mining uranium. Today, the melting of glacial ice and the introduction of new technologies for growing foods and extracting minerals such as uranium have expanded considerably the range of resources available for people to apply to productive endeavors. In this chapter, you will learn how such an expansion of productive resources over a long-run time horizon can influence a nation's capability to produce final goods and services and, hence, its real GDP. You will also learn about the effects of a resource expansion on a nation's overall price level.

since 2007, U.S. real GDP has grown an average of less than $190 billion per year, or only about 1.2 percent per year? As a consequence, during this period, the United States has experienced the slowest overall growth in inflation-adjusted economic activity since the Great Depression of the 1930s. In this chapter, you will learn about how to analyze the essential implications of subdued real GDP growth using the tools of *aggregate supply* and *aggregate demand*.

Output Growth and the Long-Run Aggregate Supply Curve

In Chapter 2, we showed the derivation of the production possibilities curve (PPC). At any point in time, the economy can be inside or on the PPC but never outside it. Along the PPC, a country's resources are fully employed in the production of goods and services, and the sum total of the inflation-adjusted value of all final goods and services produced is the nation's real GDP. Economists refer to the total of all planned production for the entire economy as the **aggregate supply** of real output.

The Long-Run Aggregate Supply Curve

Put yourself in a world in which nothing has been changing, year in and year out. The price level has not changed. Technology has not changed. The prices of inputs that firms must purchase have not changed. Labor productivity has not changed. All resources are fully employed, so the economy operates on its production possibilities curve, such as the one depicted in panel (a) of Figure 10-1 below. This is a world that is fully adjusted and in which people have all the information they are ever going to have about that world. The **long-run aggregate supply curve** (*LRAS*) in this world is some amount of real GDP—say, $18 trillion of real GDP—which is the value of the flow of production of final goods and services measured in **base-year dollars**.

We can represent long-run aggregate supply by a vertical line at $18 trillion of real GDP. This is what you see in panel (b) of the figure below. That curve, labeled *LRAS*, is a vertical line determined by technology and **endowments**, or resources that exist in our economy. It is the full-information and full-adjustment level of real output of

10.1 Discuss the concept of long-run aggregate supply and describe the effect of economic growth on the long-run aggregate supply curve

Aggregate supply
The total of all planned production for the economy.

Long-run aggregate supply curve
A vertical line representing the real output of goods and services after full adjustment has occurred. It can also be viewed as representing the real GDP of the economy under conditions of full employment—the full-employment level of real GDP.

Base-year dollars
The value of a current sum expressed in terms of prices in a base year.

Endowments
The various resources in an economy, including both physical resources and such human resources as ingenuity and management skills.

MyEconLab Animation

FIGURE 10-1

The Production Possibilities Curve and the Economy's Long-Run Aggregate Supply Curve

At a point in time, a nation's base of resources and its technological capabilities define the position of its production possibilities curve (PPC), as shown in panel (a). This defines the real GDP that the nation can produce when resources are fully employed, which determines the position of the long-run aggregate supply curve (*LRAS*) displayed in panel (b). Because people have complete information and input prices adjust fully in the long run, the *LRAS* is vertical.

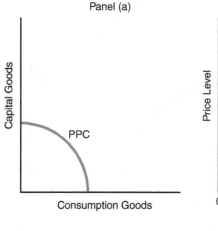

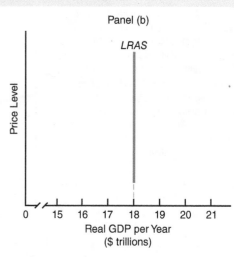

goods and services. It is the level of real GDP that will continue being produced year after year, forever, if nothing changes.

THE *LRAS* CURVE AND FULL-EMPLOYMENT REAL GDP Another way of viewing the *LRAS* is to think of it as the full-employment level of real GDP. When the economy reaches full employment along its production possibilities curve, no further adjustments will occur unless a change occurs in the other variables that we are assuming to be stable.

Some economists suggest that the *LRAS* occurs at the level of real GDP consistent with the natural rate of unemployment, the unemployment rate that occurs in an economy with full adjustment in the long run. As we discussed in Chapter 7, many economists like to think of the natural rate of unemployment as consisting of frictional and structural unemployment.

WHY THE *LRAS* CURVE IS VERTICAL To understand why the *LRAS* is vertical, think about the long run. To an economist examining the economy as a whole, the long run is a sufficiently long period that all factors of production and prices, including wages and other input prices, can change.

A change in the level of prices of goods and services has no effect on real GDP per year in the long run, because higher prices will be accompanied by comparable changes in input prices. Suppliers will therefore have no incentive to increase or decrease their production of goods and services. Remember that in the long run, everybody has full information, and there is full adjustment to price level changes. (Of course, this is not necessarily true in the short run, as we shall discuss in Chapter 11.) MyEconLab Concept Check

Economic Growth and Long-Run Aggregate Supply

In Chapter 9, you learned about the determinants of growth in per capita real GDP: the annual growth rate of labor, the rate of year-to-year capital accumulation, and the rate of growth of the productivity of labor and capital. As time goes by, population gradually increases, and labor force participation rates may even rise. The capital stock typically grows as businesses add such capital equipment as new information-technology hardware. Furthermore, technology improves. Thus, the economy's production possibilities increase, and as a consequence, the production possibilities curve shifts outward, as shown in panel (a) of Figure 10-2 below.

The result is economic growth: Aggregate real GDP and per capita real GDP increase. This means that in a growing economy such as ours, the *LRAS* will shift outward to the right, as in panel (b) below. We have drawn the *LRAS* for the year 2017 to

MyEconLab Animation

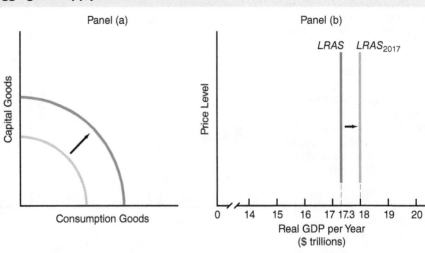

FIGURE 10-2

The Long-Run Aggregate Supply Curve and Shifts in It

In panel (a), we repeat a diagram that we used in Chapter 2, on page 39, to show the meaning of economic growth. Over time, the production possibilities curve shifts outward. In panel (b), we demonstrate the same principle by showing the long-run aggregate supply curve initially as a vertical line at $17.3 trillion of real GDP per year. As our productive abilities increase, the *LRAS* moves outward to *LRAS*$_{2017}$ at $18 trillion.

FIGURE 10-3

A Sample Long-Run Growth Path for Real GDP

Year-to-year shifts in the long-run aggregate supply curve yield a long-run trend path for real GDP growth. In this example, from 2017 onward, real GDP grows by a steady 3 percent per year.

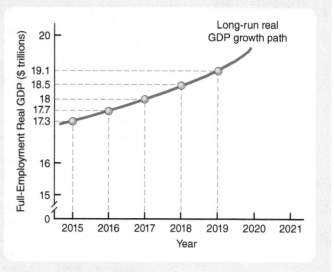

the right of our original *LRAS* of $17.3 trillion of real GDP. We assume that between now and 2017, real GDP increases to $18 trillion, to give us the position of the $LRAS_{2017}$ curve. Thus, it is to the right of today's *LRAS* curve.

We may conclude that in a growing economy, the *LRAS* shifts ever farther to the right over time. If the *LRAS* happened to shift rightward at a constant pace, real GDP would increase at a steady annual rate. As shown in Figure 10-3 above, this means that real GDP would increase along a long-run, or *trend*, path that is an upward-sloping line. Thus, if the *LRAS* shifts rightward from $17.3 trillion to $18 trillion between now and 2017 and then increases at a steady 3 percent annual rate every year thereafter, in 2018 long-run real GDP will equal $18.5 trillion, in 2019 it will equal $19.1 trillion, and so on.

Why has the *LRAS* curve for Greece been shifting to the left during the past few years?

INTERNATIONAL EXAMPLE

Greece Experiences a Series of Leftward Shifts in Its LRAS Curve

Greek real GDP per year, which is slightly less than 1 percent of the U.S. real GDP level, has *decreased* in every year since an economic crisis that began in 2008. The average annual rate of reduction in real GDP in Greece has been about 4.6 percent. Consequently, since 2008 the Greek *LRAS* curve has been shifting *leftward* at an average pace of approximately 4.6 percent per year.

FOR CRITICAL THINKING
Has the Greek production possibilities curve been shifting outward or inward in recent years? Explain your answer.

Sources are listed at the end of this chapter.

SELF CHECK

The **long-run aggregate supply curve**, *LRAS*, is a _____ line determined by amounts of available resources such as labor and capital and by technology and resource productivity. The position of the *LRAS* gives the full-information and full-adjustment level of real GDP per year.

The _____ rate of unemployment occurs at the long-run level of real GDP per year given by the position of the *LRAS*.

If labor or capital increases from year to year or if the productivity of either of these resources rises from one year to the next, the *LRAS* shifts _____. In a growing economy, therefore, real GDP per year gradually _____ over time.

10.2 Explain why the aggregate demand curve slopes downward and list key factors that cause this curve to shift

Total Expenditures and Aggregate Demand

In equilibrium, individuals, businesses, and governments purchase all the goods and services produced, valued in trillions of real dollars. As explained in Chapters 7 and 8, GDP is the dollar value of total expenditures on domestically produced final goods and services. Because all expenditures are made by individuals, firms, or governments, the total value of these expenditures must be what these market participants decide it shall be.

The Importance of Spending Decisions for the Level of Real GDP

The decisions of individuals, managers of firms, and government officials determine the annual dollar value of total expenditures. You can certainly see this in your role as an individual. You decide what the total dollar amount of your expenditures will be in a year. You decide how much you want to spend and how much you want to save. Thus, if we want to know what determines the total value of GDP, the answer is clear: the spending decisions of individuals like you, firms, and local, state, and national governments. In an open economy, we must also include foreign individuals, firms, and governments (foreign residents, for short) that decide to spend their money income in the United States.

Simply stating that the dollar value of total expenditures in this country depends on what individuals, firms, governments, and foreign residents decide to do really doesn't tell us much, though. Two important issues remain:

1. What determines the total amount that individuals, firms, governments, and foreign residents want to spend?

2. What determines the equilibrium price level and the rate of inflation (or deflation)?

Aggregate demand
The total of all planned expenditures in the entire economy.

The *LRAS* tells us only about the economy's long-run real GDP. To answer these additional questions, we must consider another important concept. This is **aggregate demand**, which is the total of all *planned* real expenditures in the economy.

MyEconLab Concept Check

The Aggregate Demand Curve

Aggregate demand curve
A curve showing planned purchase rates for all final goods and services in the economy at various price levels, all other things held constant.

The **aggregate demand curve**, *AD*, gives the various quantities of all final commodities demanded at various price levels, all other things held constant. Recall the components of GDP that you studied in Chapter 8: consumption spending, investment expenditures, government purchases, and net foreign demand for domestic production. They are all components of aggregate demand. Throughout this chapter and the next, whenever you see the aggregate demand curve, realize that it is a shorthand way of talking about the components of GDP that are measured by government statisticians when they calculate total economic activity each year. In Chapter 12, you will look more closely at the relationship between these components and, in particular, at how consumption spending depends on income.

The aggregate demand curve gives the total amount, measured in base-year dollars, of *real* domestic final goods and services that will be purchased at each price level—everything produced for final use by households, businesses, the government, and foreign (non-U.S.) residents. It includes iPads, socks, shoes, medical and legal services, digital devices, and millions of other goods and services that people buy each year.

DEPICTING THE AGGREGATE DEMAND CURVE A graphical representation of the aggregate demand curve is seen in Figure 10-4 on the next page. On the horizontal axis, real GDP is measured. For our measure of the price level, we use the GDP price deflator on the vertical axis.

MyEconLab Animation

The Aggregate Demand Curve

The aggregate demand curve, *AD*, slopes downward. If the price level is 110, we will be at point *A* with $18 trillion of real GDP demanded per year. As the price level increases to 115 and to 120, we move up the aggregate demand curve to points *B* and *C*.

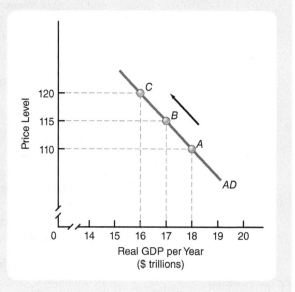

The aggregate demand curve is labeled *AD*. If the GDP deflator is 110, aggregate quantity demanded is $18 trillion per year (point *A*). At the price level 115, it is $17 trillion per year (point *B*). At the price level 120, it is $16 trillion per year (point *C*). The higher the price level, the lower the total real amount of final goods and services demanded in the economy, everything else remaining constant, as shown by the arrow along *AD* in Figure 10-4. Conversely, the lower the price level, the higher the total real GDP demanded by the economy, everything else staying constant.

PLANNED SPENDING IN THE U.S. ECONOMY Let's take the year 2015. Estimates based on U.S. Department of Commerce preliminary statistics reveal the following information:

- Nominal GDP was estimated to be $18,210.6 billion.

- The price level as measured by the GDP deflator was about 109.2 (base year is 2009, for which the index equals 100).

- Real GDP was approximately $16,672.5 billion in 2009 dollars.

What can we say about 2015? Given the dollar cost of buying goods and services and all of the other factors that go into spending decisions by individuals, firms, governments, and foreign residents, the total amount of planned spending on final goods and services by firms, individuals, governments, and foreign residents was $16,672.5 billion in 2015 (in terms of 2009 dollars).   MyEconLab Concept Check

What Happens When the Price Level Rises?

What if the price level in the economy rose to 160 tomorrow? What would happen to the amount of real goods and services that individuals, firms, governments, and foreigners wish to purchase in the United States? We know from Chapter 3 that when the price of one good or service rises, the quantity of it demanded will fall. But here we are talking about the *price level*—the average price of *all* goods and services in the economy.

The answer is still that the total quantities of real goods and services demanded would fall, but the reasons are different. When the price of one good or service goes up, the consumer substitutes other goods and services. For the entire economy, when the price level goes up, the consumer doesn't simply substitute one good for another, for now we are dealing with the demand for *all* goods and services in the nation. There are *economywide* reasons that cause the aggregate demand curve to slope downward. They involve at least three distinct forces: the *real-balance effect*, the *interest rate effect*, and the *open economy effect*.

THE REAL-BALANCE EFFECT A rise in the price level will have an effect on spending. Individuals, firms, governments, and foreign residents carry out transactions using money, a portion of which consists of currency and coins that you have in your pocket (or stashed away) right now. Because people use money to purchase goods and services, the amount of money that people have influences the amount of goods and services they want to buy.

An Example If you find a $100 bill on the sidewalk, the amount of money you have increases. Given your now greater level of money, or cash, balances—currency in this case—you will almost surely increase your spending on goods and services.

Similarly, if your pocket is picked while you are at the mall, your desired spending would be affected. For instance, if your wallet had $150 in it when it was stolen, the reduction in your cash balances—in this case, currency—would no doubt cause you to reduce your planned expenditures. You would ultimately buy fewer goods and services.

Contemplating the Real-Balance Effect This response is sometimes called the **real-balance effect** (or *wealth effect*) because it relates to the real value of your cash balances. While your *nominal* cash balances may remain the same, any change in the price level will cause a change in the *real* value of those cash balances—hence the real-balance effect on total planned expenditures.

When you think of the real-balance effect, just think of what happens to your real wealth if you have, say, a $100 bill hidden under your mattress. If the price level increases by 5 percent, the purchasing power of that $100 bill drops by 5 percent, so you have become less wealthy. You will reduce your purchases of all goods and services by some small amount.

THE INTEREST RATE EFFECT There is a more subtle but equally important effect on your desire to spend. A higher price level leaves people with too few money balances. Hence, they try to borrow more (or lend less) to replenish their real money holdings. This drives up interest rates. Higher interest rates raise borrowing costs for consumers and businesses. They will borrow less and consequently spend less. The fact that a higher price level pushes up interest rates and thereby reduces borrowing and spending is known as the **interest rate effect**.

Higher interest rates make it more costly for people to finance purchases of houses and cars. Higher interest rates also make it less profitable for firms to install new equipment and to erect new office buildings. Whether we are talking about individuals or firms, a rise in the price level will cause higher interest rates, which in turn reduce the amount of goods and services that people are willing to purchase. Therefore, an increase in the price level will tend to reduce total planned expenditures. (The opposite occurs if the price level declines.)

THE OPEN ECONOMY EFFECT: THE SUBSTITUTION OF FOREIGN GOODS Recall from Chapter 8 that GDP includes net exports—the difference between exports and imports. In an open economy, we buy imports from other countries and ultimately pay for them through the foreign exchange market. The same is true for foreign residents who purchase our goods (exports).

Given any set of exchange rates between the U.S. dollar and other currencies, an increase in the price level in the United States makes U.S. goods more expensive relative to foreign goods. Foreign residents have downward-sloping demand curves for U.S. goods. When the relative price of U.S. goods goes up, foreign residents buy fewer U.S. goods and more of their own. At home, relatively cheaper prices for foreign goods cause U.S. residents to want to buy more foreign goods instead of domestically produced goods. Thus, when the domestic price level rises, the result is a fall in exports and a rise in imports. That means that a price level increase tends to reduce net exports, thereby reducing the amount of real goods and services purchased in the United States. This is known as the **open economy effect**. MyEconLab Concept Check

Real-balance effect
The change in expenditures resulting from a change in the real value of money balances when the price level changes, all other things held constant; also called the *wealth effect*.

Interest rate effect
One of the reasons that the aggregate demand curve slopes downward: Higher price levels increase the interest rate, which in turn causes businesses and consumers to reduce desired spending due to the higher cost of borrowing.

Open economy effect
One of the reasons that the aggregate demand curve slopes downward: Higher price levels result in foreign residents desiring to buy fewer U.S.-made goods, while U.S. residents now desire more foreign-made goods, thereby reducing net exports. This is equivalent to a reduction in the amount of real goods and services purchased in the United States.

What Happens When the Price Level Falls?

What about the reverse? Suppose now that the GDP deflator falls to 100 from an initial level of 120. You should be able to trace the three effects on desired purchases of goods and services. Specifically, how do the real-balance, interest rate, and open economy effects cause people to want to buy more? You should come to the conclusion that the lower the price level, the greater the total planned spending on goods and services.

The aggregate demand curve, *AD*, shows the quantity of aggregate output that will be demanded at alternative price levels. It is downward sloping, just like the demand curve for individual goods. The higher the price level, the lower the real amount of total planned expenditures, and vice versa. MyEconLab Concept Check

Demand for All Goods and Services versus Demand for a Single Good or Service

Even though the aggregate demand curve, *AD*, in Figure 10-4 on page 227 looks similar to the one for individual demand, *D*, for a single good or service that you encountered in Chapters 3 and 4, the two are not the same. When we derive the aggregate demand curve, we are looking at the entire economic system. The aggregate demand curve, *AD*, differs from an individual demand curve, *D*, because we are looking at total planned expenditures on *all* goods and services when we construct *AD*. MyEconLab Concept Check

Shifts in the Aggregate Demand Curve

In Chapter 3, you learned that any time a nonprice determinant of demand changes, the demand curve will shift inward to the left or outward to the right. The same analysis holds for the aggregate demand curve, except we are now talking about the non-price-level determinants of aggregate demand. So, when we ask the question, "What determines the position of the aggregate demand curve?" the fundamental proposition is as follows:

Any non-price-level change that increases aggregate spending (on domestic goods) shifts AD to the right. Any non-price-level change that decreases aggregate spending (on domestic goods) shifts AD to the left.

The list of potential determinants of the position of the aggregate demand curve is long. Some of the most important "curve shifters" for aggregate demand are presented in Table 10-1 below.

TABLE 10-1

Determinants of Aggregate Demand

Aggregate demand consists of the demand for domestically produced consumption goods, investment goods, government purchases, and net exports. Consequently, any change in total planned spending on any one of these components of real GDP will cause a change in aggregate demand. Some possibilities are listed here.

Changes That Cause an Increase in Aggregate Demand	Changes That Cause a Decrease in Aggregate Demand
An increase in the amount of money in circulation	A decrease in the amount of money in circulation
Increased security about jobs and future income	Decreased security about jobs and future income
Improvements in economic conditions in other countries	Declines in economic conditions in other countries
A reduction in real interest rates (nominal interest rates corrected for inflation) not due to price level changes	A rise in real interest rates (nominal interest rates corrected for inflation) not due to price level changes
Tax decreases	Tax increases
A drop in the foreign exchange value of the dollar	A rise in the foreign exchange value of the dollar

How has a varying amount of circulating money affected aggregate demand?

POLICY EXAMPLE

Oscillating Amounts of Money in Circulation Cause Aggregate Demand to Gyrate

The quantity of money in circulation in the United States has increased every year since 2000. The rate of growth in the amount of circulating money increased sharply between 2000 and 2001, however, from about 6 percent per year to more than 10 percent per year, which generated a significant increase in aggregate demand. The annual rate of growth in the quantity of money in circulation gradually tapered off, until by 2004 it had dropped to as low as 3 percent, which contributed to slower growth in aggregate demand.

From 2005 to 2008, the rate of growth in the amount of circulating money gradually increased once more, from close to 3 percent per year to almost 10 percent per year. This increase in money growth considerably hastened the speed at which the U.S. aggregate demand curve shifted rightward. Then in 2008, the growth rate of the quantity of money in circulation plummeted to about 2 percent, which contributed to a sudden

near halt in the rightward movement of the aggregate demand curve. A rapid repeat run-up in the money growth rate then took place beginning late 2009. The rate of growth of the quantity of money in circulation gradually increased until it peaked at 10 percent per year by early 2012, which contributed once more to higher aggregate demand. Since 2012, the money growth rate has been closer to its long-term average of about 6 percent per year, and the growth of aggregate demand in the United States has been much more stable.

FOR CRITICAL THINKING

How did decreased job security on the part of many U.S. households through-out most of 2009 likely affect U.S. aggregate demand during that year?

Sources are listed at the end of this chapter.

MyEconLab Concept Check
MyEconLab Study Plan

SELF CHECK Visit MyEconLab to practice these and other problems and to get instant feedback in your Study Plan.

Aggregate demand is the total of all planned _____ in the economy, and **aggregate supply** is the total of all planned _____ in the economy. The aggregate demand curve shows the various quantities of total planned _____ on final goods and services at various price levels; it is downward sloping.

There are three reasons why the aggregate demand curve is downward sloping. They are the _____-_____ effect, the _____ _____ effect, and the _____ _____ effect.

The _____-_____ effect occurs because price level changes alter the real value of cash balances, thereby

causing people to desire to spend more or less, depending on whether the price level decreases or increases.

The _____ _____ effect is caused by interest rate changes that mimic price level changes. At higher interest rates, people seek to buy _____ houses and cars, and at lower interest rates, they seek to buy _____.

The **open economy effect** occurs because of a shift away from expenditures on _____ goods and a shift toward expenditures on _____ goods when the domestic price level increases.

10.3 Evaluate the meaning of long-run equilibrium for the economy as a whole and explain why economic growth can cause deflation

Long-Run Equilibrium and the Price Level

As noted in Chapter 3, equilibrium occurs where the demand and supply curves intersect. The same is true for the economy as a whole, as shown in Figure 10-5 on the next page: The equilibrium price level occurs at the point where the aggregate demand curve *(AD)* crosses the long-run aggregate supply curve *(LRAS)*. At this equilibrium price level of 120, the total of all planned real expenditures for the entire economy is equal to actual real GDP produced by firms after all adjustments have taken place. Thus, the equilibrium depicted in Figure 10-5 is the economy's *long-run equilibrium.*

The Long-Run Equilibrium Price Level

Note in Figure 10-5 that if the price level were to increase to 140, actual real GDP of $18 trillion would exceed total planned real expenditures real GDP of $17 trillion. Inventories of unsold goods would begin to accumulate, and firms would stand ready to offer more services than people wish to purchase. As a result, the price level would tend to fall.

FIGURE 10-5

Long-Run Economywide Equilibrium

For the economy as a whole, long-run equilibrium occurs at the price level where the aggregate demand curve crosses the long-run aggregate supply curve. At this long-run equilibrium price level, which is 120 in the diagram, total planned real expenditures equal real GDP at full employment, which in our example is a real GDP of $18 trillion.

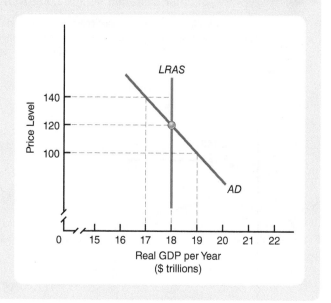

In contrast, if the price level were 100, then $19 trillion of total planned real expenditures by individuals, businesses, and the government would exceed actual real GDP of $18 trillion. Inventories of unsold goods would begin to be depleted. The price level would rise toward 120, and higher prices would encourage firms to expand production and replenish inventories of goods available for sale. MyEconLab Concept Check

The Effects of Economic Growth on the Price Level

We now have a basic theory of how real GDP and the price level are determined in the long run when all of a nation's resources can change over time and all input prices can adjust fully to changes in the overall level of prices of goods and services that firms produce. Let's begin by evaluating the effects of economic growth on the nation's price level.

ECONOMIC GROWTH AND SECULAR DEFLATION Take a look at panel (a) of Figure 10-6 on the next page, which shows what happens, other things being equal, when the *LRAS* shifts rightward over time. If the economy were to grow steadily during, say, a 10-year interval, the long-run aggregate supply schedule would shift to the right, from $LRAS_1$ to $LRAS_2$. In panel (a), this results in a downward movement along the aggregate demand schedule. The equilibrium price level falls, from 120 to 80.

Thus, if all factors that affect total planned real expenditures are unchanged, so that the aggregate demand curve does not noticeably move during the 10-year period of real GDP growth, the growing economy in the example would experience deflation. This is known as **secular deflation**, or a persistently declining price level resulting from economic growth in the presence of relatively unchanged aggregate demand.

SECULAR DEFLATION IN THE UNITED STATES In the United States, between 1872 and 1894, the price of bricks fell by 50 percent, the price of sugar by 67 percent, the price of wheat by 69 percent, the price of nails by 70 percent, and the price of copper by nearly 75 percent. Founders of a late-nineteenth-century political movement called *populism* offered a proposal for ending deflation: They wanted the government to issue new money backed by silver. As noted in Table 10-1 on page 229, an increase in the quantity of money in circulation causes the aggregate demand curve to shift to the right. It is clear from panel (b) of Figure 10-6 on the next page that the increase in the quantity of money would indeed have pushed the price level back upward, because the *AD* curve would shift from AD_1 to AD_2.

Secular deflation

A persistent decline in prices resulting from economic growth in the presence of stable aggregate demand.

FIGURE 10-6

Secular Deflation versus Long-Run Price Stability in a Growing Economy

Panel (a) illustrates what happens when economic growth occurs without a corresponding increase in aggregate demand. The result is a decline in the price level over time, known as *secular deflation*. Panel (b) shows that, in principle, secular deflation can be eliminated if the aggregate demand curve shifts rightward at the same pace that the long-run aggregate supply curve shifts to the right.

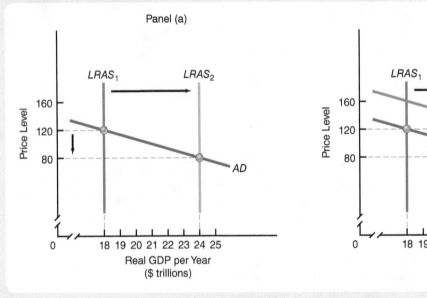

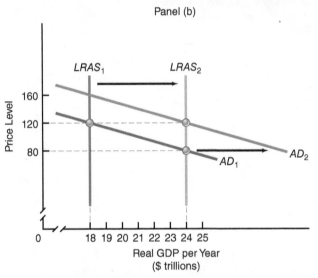

Nevertheless, money growth remained low for several more years. Not until the early twentieth century would the United States put an end to secular deflation, namely, by creating a new monetary system.

WHAT IF...

a nation's real GDP were to decrease over a prolonged period while its aggregate demand curve shifted rightward?

If a country's real GDP growth rate were negative—implying a reduction in real GDP each year—then its long-run aggregate supply curve would shift leftward. If the nation's aggregate demand curve shifted rightward during the same interval, the combination of both occurrences would place continual upward pressure on the equilibrium price level. In effect, the opposite of secular deflation would take place. The country would experience persistent inflation even as its real GDP continued to shrink.

MyEconLab Concept Check
MyEconLab Study Plan

SELF CHECK   Visit MyEconLab to practice these and other problems and to get instant feedback in your Study Plan.

When the economy is in long-run equilibrium, the price level adjusts to equate total planned real _____ by individuals, businesses, the government, and foreign (non-U.S.) residents with total planned _____ by firms.

Economic growth causes the long-run aggregate supply schedule to shift _____ over time. If the position of the aggregate demand curve does not change, the long-run equilibrium price level tends to _____, and there is **secular deflation.**

10.4 Evaluate likely reasons for persistent inflation in recent decades

Causes of Inflation

Of course, so far during your lifetime, deflation has not been a problem in the United States. Instead, what you have experienced is inflation. Figure 10-7 on the next page shows annual U.S. inflation rates for the past few decades. Clearly, inflation rates have been variable. The other obvious fact, however, is that inflation rates

FIGURE 10-7

Inflation Rates in the United States

Annual U.S. inflation rates rose considerably during the 1970s but declined to lower levels after the 1980s. The inflation rate has declined significantly in recent years after creeping upward during the early and middle 2000s.

Sources: Economic Report of the President; Economic Indicators, various issues.

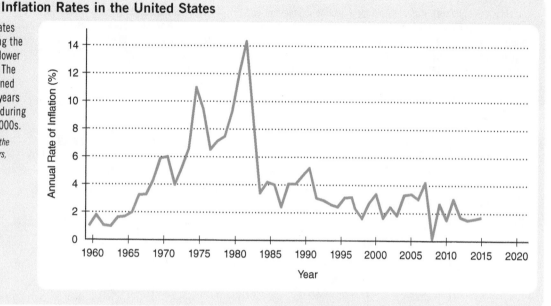

have been consistently *positive*. The price level in the United States has *risen* almost every year. For today's United States, secular deflation has not been a big political issue. If anything, it is secular *inflation* that has plagued the nation.

Supply-Side Inflation?

What causes such persistent inflation? The model of aggregate demand and long-run aggregate supply provides two possible explanations for inflation. One potential rationale is depicted in panel (a) of Figure 10-8 on the next page. This panel shows a rise in the price level caused by a *decline in long-run aggregate supply*. Hence, one possible reason for persistent inflation would be continual reductions in economywide production.

A leftward shift in the aggregate supply schedule could be caused by several factors, such as reductions in labor force participation, higher marginal tax rates on wages, or the provision of government benefits that give households incentives *not* to supply labor services to firms. Tax rates and government benefits have increased during recent decades, but so has the U.S. population. The significant overall rise in real GDP that has taken place during the past few decades tells us that population growth and productivity gains undoubtedly have dominated other factors. In fact, the aggregate supply schedule has actually shifted *rightward*, not leftward, over time. Consequently, this supply-side explanation for persistent inflation *cannot* be the correct explanation.

Demand-Side Inflation

This leaves only one other explanation for the persistent inflation that the United States has experienced in recent decades. This explanation is depicted in panel (b) of Figure 10-8 on the next page. If aggregate demand increases for a given level of long-run aggregate supply, the price level must increase. The reason is that at an initial price level such as 120, people desire to purchase more goods and services than firms are willing and able to produce, given currently available resources and technology. As a result, the rise in aggregate demand leads only to a general rise in the price level, such as the increase to a value of 140, depicted in the figure.

From a long-run perspective, we are left with only one possibility: Persistent inflation in a growing economy is possible only if the aggregate demand curve shifts rightward over time at a faster pace than the rightward progression of the long-run

FIGURE 10-8

Explaining Persistent Inflation

As shown in panel (a), it is possible for a decline in long-run aggregate supply to cause a rise in the price level. Long-run aggregate supply *increases* in a growing economy, however, so this cannot explain the observation of persistent U.S. inflation. Panel (b) provides the actual explanation of persistent inflation in the United

States and most other nations today, which is that increases in aggregate demand push up the long-run equilibrium price level. Thus, it is possible to explain persistent inflation if the aggregate demand curve shifts rightward at a faster pace than the long-run aggregate supply curve.

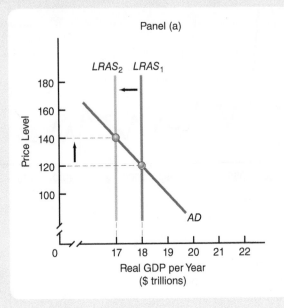

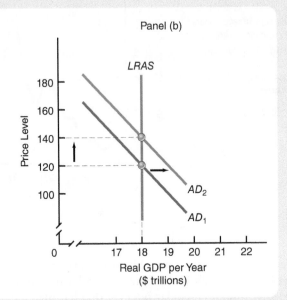

aggregate supply curve. Thus, in contrast to the experience of people who lived in the latter portion of the nineteenth century, when aggregate demand grew too slowly relative to aggregate supply to maintain price stability, your grandparents, parents, and you have lived in times when aggregate demand has grown too *speedily*. The result has been a continual upward drift in the price level, or long-term inflation.

Figure 10-9 on the next page shows that U.S. real GDP has grown in most years since 1970. Nevertheless, this growth has been accompanied by a higher price level every single year.

How do the relatively different speeds at which Brazil's long-run aggregate supply and aggregate demand curves have shifted rightward account for diverging movements in the nation's rate of real GDP growth and its inflation rate?

INTERNATIONAL EXAMPLE

Why Brazil's Inflation Rate Exceeds Its Real GDP Growth Rate

During the past few years, annual real GDP growth in Brazil has declined each year, from more than 7 percent per year in 2010 to less than 1 percent most recently. Over the same period, Brazil's inflation rate has increased from about 4 percent per year to more than 6 percent per year.

The considerably slowed growth of real GDP indicates that Brazil's long-run aggregate supply curve has been shifting rightward by a much smaller amount each year. The fact that the price level has been rising even as the *LRAS* curve has shifted slightly rightward indicates that the aggregate demand curve has been shifting rightward at a faster pace than the *LRAS*

curve. Indeed, the increased rate of growth of the price level indicates that the *AD* curve has been shifting rightward at a considerably faster pace.

FOR CRITICAL THINKING
What would happen to the Brazilian inflation rate in future years if the LRAS curve were to begin shifting rightward at a more rapid pace than the AD curve?

Sources are listed at the end of this chapter.

FIGURE 10-9

This figure shows the points where aggregate demand and aggregate supply have intersected each year from 1970 to the present. The United States has experienced economic growth over this period, but not without inflation.

Sources: Economic Report of the President; Economic Indicators, various issues; author's estimates.

Real GDP and the Price Level in the United States, 1970 to the Present

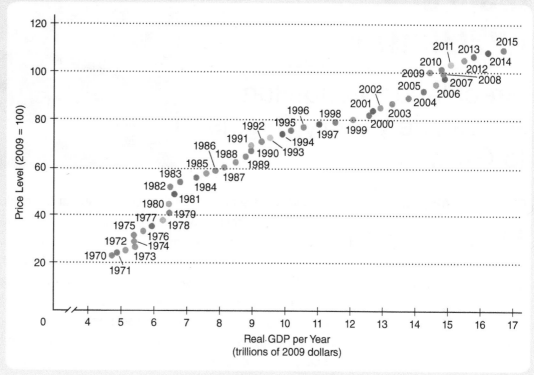

MyEconLab Concept Check
MyEconLab Study Plan

SELF CHECK Visit MyEconLab to practice these and other problems and to get instant feedback in your Study Plan.

Inflation can be caused by an increase in aggregate _____ or by a decrease in aggregate _____.

_____-side inflation cannot account for persistent inflation in a growing economy, but _____-side inflation can occur even as real GDP increases.

Because the U.S. economy has grown in recent decades, the persistent inflation during those years has been caused by the aggregate demand curve shifting _____ at a faster pace than the long-run aggregate supply curve.

YOU ARE THERE

Do Businesses Want to Transport Products? Sorry, the Bridge Is Out

Bob Wilson, owner of a fleet of 20 trucks based in Pennsylvania, plans to reroute several of his company's trucks. These trucks carry metal ingots along separate highway routes from a Reading plant to Boston, Massachusetts, and from a Latrobe factory to Birmingham, Alabama. The Pennsylvania state government has declared bridges along both routes to be impassable by the firm's heavy trucks and loads of freight, however. Wilson calculates that the longer detours required to cross rivers at different bridges will delay ingot deliveries and boost the per-truckload transportation expense by more than $1,000. Wilson confronts additional rerouting costs across Pennsylvania, in which one of every four bridges requires major repair work or replacement.

Across all 50 states, more than 11 percent of highway or railroad bridges, which have an average age of 42 years, are unsuitable for trucks or trains to carry heavy loads. Rerouting the transport of physical items is slowing the transport of products to customers. With fewer functioning bridges

available, companies that sell physical goods cannot complete delivery of as many units of these items per unit of time as was feasible in previous years, other things being equal. As more bridges are added to the deficiency lists around the country, the nation's economic growth prospects diminish.

CRITICAL THINKING QUESTIONS

1. As more highway and rail bridges become deficient, what is happening to the pace at which the U.S. production possibilities curve shifts outward over time?

2. How are bridge deficiencies affecting the extent to which the U.S. long-run aggregate supply curve shifts rightward each year?

Sources are listed at the end of this chapter.

ISSUES & APPLICATIONS

MyEconLab Video

Greenland's Long-Run Aggregate Supply Begins to Grow

Joy Durham/Danita Delimont/Alamy

CONCEPTS APPLIED

» Endowments

» Aggregate Supply

» Long-Run Aggregate Supply Curve

Greenland—a semi-independent protectorate of Denmark—has a physical surface mostly colored by various shades of white and gray tinged with some hues of green. The island nation is covered with glacial ice and a few fringes of forested and agricultural lands. Because the ice, which is hundreds of feet deep, has long blocked access to any resources lying within the island's interior, many inhabitants have specialized in fishing the waters surrounding the country. Thus, the nation's meager agricultural production and the annual catches by its fishing industry have accounted for the bulk of its output of final goods and services. Recently, however, the nation's production possibilities have begun to expand, which is generating an increase in the nation's aggregate supply.

Melting and Technologies Uncover Newly Available Resources

Two developments have contributed to an outward shift of Greenland's production possibilities curve. First, some of the island's glacial ice, which in many locations is hundreds of feet deep, has melted in recent years. Second, new technologies have been developed for penetrating the ice and the frozen ground beneath it.

The result has been access to many resources long suspected but previously unavailable for productive use. Iron ores, rubies, oil and gas, and various rare minerals such as uranium have been found buried beneath the island's somewhat lessened glacial covering. As these resources have been extracted at a growing pace, the nation's production possibilities and long-run aggregate supply have expanded at an increasing rate.

An Influx of People Enlarges Greenland's Most Scarce Resource

One of the scarcest resources in Greenland since the island's initial settlement in the year 982 has been human beings. The nation's Arctic waters are so cold that few people riding in boats bother with life jackets, because if they fell into the water they could not survive for long even if the jackets kept them afloat. Water routes into the island's interior freeze over during much of each year and open up only during seasonal thaws. Gales can sweep across portions of the island for weeks at a time. Until now, a population of only about 57,000 people—the smallest population of any nation on the planet—has sought to live and work under these harsh conditions.

Today, many new workers from countries across the globe—including Australia, Canada, China, the United Kingdom, and the United States—are moving to Greenland to extract its newly available mineral endowments. This enlargement of the island's human resources is further expanding its production possibilities and generating increases in long-run aggregate supply.

For Critical Thinking

1. In what direction is Greenland's LRAS curve currently shifting? Explain.

2. If aggregate demand were to remain unchanged, what likely would happen to Greenland's inflation rate during the coming years? Why?

Web Resources

1. For a summary of developments in Greenland's minerals industry, see the Web Links in MyEconLab.

2. To learn about the economy of Greenland, see the Web Links in MyEconLab.

MyEconLab

For more questions on this chapter's Issues & Applications, go to MyEconLab.

In the Study Plan for this chapter, select Section I: Issues and Applications.

Sources are listed at the end of this chapter.

Fundamental Points

1. The long-run aggregate supply curve, *LRAS*, is a vertical line positioned at the level of real GDP per year at which the economy operates given available resources such as labor and capital and given current technology and resource productivity.

2. The aggregate demand curve depicts quantities of total planned expenditures on final goods and services at various price levels. The aggregate demand curve slopes downward because of the real-balance effect, the interest rate effect, and the open economy effect.

3. In a long-run equilibrium for the economy as a whole, the price level adjusts to equate total planned real expenditures by individuals, businesses, the government, and foreign (non-U.S.) residents with total planned production by firms.

4. Inflation can be caused either by an increase in aggregate demand or by a decrease in aggregate supply. Persistent inflation in a growing economy cannot occur with steady leftward shifts of aggregate supply but can occur with steady rightward shifts of aggregate demand.

WHAT YOU SHOULD KNOW

Here is what you should know after reading this chapter. MyEconLab will help you identify what you know, and where to go when you need to practice.

LEARNING OBJECTIVES	KEY TERMS	WHERE TO GO TO PRACTICE
10.1 Discuss the concept of long-run aggregate supply and describe the effect of economic growth on the long-run aggregate supply curve *The long-run aggregate supply curve is vertical at the amount of real GDP that firms plan to produce when they have full information and when complete adjustment of input prices to any changes in output prices has taken place. The production possibilities curve shifts rightward when the economy grows, and so does the nation's long-run aggregate supply curve. In a growing economy, the changes in full-employment real GDP defined by the shifting long-run aggregate supply curve define the nation's long-run, or trend, growth path.*	aggregate supply, 223 long-run aggregate supply curve, 223 base-year dollars, 223 endowments, 223 **Key Figures** Figure 10-1, 223 Figure 10-2, 224 Figure 10-3, 225	• MyEconLab Study Plan 10.1 • Animated Figures 10-1, 10-2, 10-3
10.2 Explain why the aggregate demand curve slopes downward and list key factors that cause this curve to shift *The real-balance effect occurs when a rise in the price level reduces the real value of cash balances, which induces people to cut back on planned spending. The interest rate effect caused by a higher price level induces people to cut back on borrowing and spending. Finally, a rise in the price level at home causes domestic goods to be more expensive relative to foreign goods, so there is a fall in exports and a rise in imports, both of which cause domestic planned expenditures to fall. These three factors together account for the downward slope of the aggregate demand curve, which shifts if there is any other change in total planned real expenditures at any given price level.*	aggregate demand, 226 aggregate demand curve, 226 real-balance effect, 228 interest rate effect, 228 open economy effect, 228 **Key Figure** Figure 10-4, 227	• MyEconLab Study Plan 10.2 • Animated Figure 10-4

WHAT YOU SHOULD KNOW *continued*

LEARNING OBJECTIVES	KEY TERMS	WHERE TO GO TO PRACTICE
10.3 Evaluate the meaning of long-run equilibrium for the economy as a whole and explain why economic growth can cause deflation *In a long-run economywide equilibrium, the price level adjusts until total planned real expenditures equal actual real GDP. Thus, the long-run equilibrium price level is determined at the point where the aggregate demand curve intersects the long-run aggregate supply curve. If the aggregate demand curve is stationary during a period of economic growth, the long-run aggregate supply curve shifts rightward along the aggregate demand curve. The long-run equilibrium price level falls, so there is secular deflation.*	secular deflation, 231 **Key Figures** Figure 10-5, 231 Figure 10-6, 232	• MyEconLab Study Plan 10.3 • Animated Figures 10-5, 10-6
10.4 Evaluate likely reasons for persistent inflation in recent decades *Inflation can result from a fall in long-run aggregate supply, but in a growing economy, long-run aggregate supply generally rises. Thus, a much more likely cause of persistent inflation is a pace of aggregate demand growth that exceeds the pace at which long-run aggregate supply increases.*	**Key Figures** Figure 10-7, 233 Figure 10-8, 234	• MyEconLab Study Plan 10.4 • Animated Figures 10-7, 10-8

Log in to MyEconLab, take a chapter test, and get a personalized Study Plan that tells you which concepts you understand and which ones you need to review. From there, MyEconLab will give you further practice, tutorials, animations, videos, and guided solutions. For more information, visit http://www.myeconlab.com

PROBLEMS

All problems are assignable in MyEconLab. Answers to odd-numbered problems appear in MyEconLab.

10-1. Many economists view the natural rate of unemployment as the level observed when real GDP is given by the position of the long-run aggregate supply curve. How can there be positive unemployment in this situation? (See page 223.)

10-2. Suppose that the long-run aggregate supply curve is positioned at a real GDP level of $18 trillion in base-year dollars, and the long-run equilibrium price level (in index number form) is 115. What is the full-employment level of *nominal* GDP? (See page 231.)

10-3. Continuing from Problem 10-2, suppose that the full-employment level of *nominal* GDP in the following year rises to $21.85 trillion. The long-run equilibrium price level, however, remains unchanged. By how much (in real dollars) has the long-run aggregate supply curve shifted to the right in the following year? By how much, if any, has the aggregate demand curve shifted to the right? (Hint: The equilibrium price level can stay the same only if *LRAS* and *AD* shift rightward by the same amount.) (See page 232.)

10-4. Suppose that the position of a nation's long-run aggregate supply curve has not changed, but its long-run equilibrium price level has increased. Which of the following factors might account for this event? (See page 232.)

   a. A rise in the value of the domestic currency relative to other world currencies

   b. An increase in the quantity of money in circulation

   c. An increase in the labor force participation rate

   d. A decrease in taxes

   e. A rise in real incomes of countries that are key trading partners of this nation

   f. Increased long-run economic growth

10-5. Identify the combined shifts in long-run aggregate supply and aggregate demand that could explain the following simultaneous occurrences. (See page 232.)

   a. An increase in equilibrium real GDP and an increase in the equilibrium price level

   b. A decrease in equilibrium real GDP with no change in the equilibrium price level

   c. An increase in equilibrium real GDP with no change in the equilibrium price level

   d. A decrease in equilibrium real GDP and a decrease in the equilibrium price level

10-6. Suppose that during the past 3 years, equilibrium real GDP in a country rose steadily, from $450 billion to $500 billion, but even though the position of its aggregate demand curve remained unchanged, its equilibrium price level steadily declined, from 110 to 103. What could have accounted for these outcomes, and what is the term for the change in the price level experienced by this country? (See page 232.)

10-7. Suppose that during a given year, the quantity of U.S. real GDP that can be produced in the long run rises from $17.9 trillion to $18.0 trillion, measured in base-year dollars. During the year, no change occurs in the various factors that influence aggregate demand. What will happen to the U.S. long-run equilibrium price level during this particular year? (See page 232.)

10-8. Assume that the position of a nation's aggregate demand curve has not changed, but the long-run equilibrium price level has declined. Other things being equal, which of the following factors might account for this event? (See page 232.)

   a. An increase in labor productivity

   b. A decrease in the capital stock

   c. A decrease in the quantity of money in circulation

   d. The discovery of new mineral resources used to produce various goods

   e. A technological improvement

10-9. Suppose that there is a sudden rise in the price level. What will happen to economywide planned spending on purchases of goods and services? Why? (See pages 227–228.)

10-10. Assume that the economy is in long-run equilibrium with complete information and that input prices adjust rapidly to changes in the prices of goods and services. If there is a rise in the price level induced by an increase in aggregate demand, what happens to real GDP? (See page 232.)

10-11. Consider the diagram below when answering the questions that follow. (See page 231.)

   a. Suppose that the current price level is P_2. Explain why the price level will decline toward P_1.

   b. Suppose that the current price level is P_3. Explain why the price level will rise toward P_1.

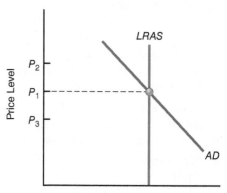

Real GDP per Year (base-year dollars)

10-12. Explain whether each of the following events would cause a movement along or a shift in the position of the *LRAS* curve, other things being equal. In each case, explain the direction of the movement along the curve or shift in its position. (See page 224.)

   a. Last year, businesses invested in new capital equipment, so this year the nation's capital stock is higher than it was last year.

   b. There has been an 8 percent increase in the quantity of money in circulation that has shifted the *AD* curve.

   c. A hurricane of unprecedented strength has damaged oil rigs, factories, and ports all along the nation's coast.

   d. Inflation has occurred during the past year as a result of rightward shifts of the *AD* curve.

10-13. Explain whether each of the following events would cause a movement along or a shift in the *AD* curve, other things being equal. In each case, explain the direction of the movement along the curve or shift in its position. (See pages 227–229.)

   a. Deflation has occurred during the past year.

   b. Real GDP levels of all the nation's major trading partners have declined.

   c. There has been a decline in the foreign exchange value of the nation's currency.

   d. The price level has increased this year.

10-14. This year, a nation's long-run equilibrium real GDP and price level both increased. Which of the following combinations of factors might simultaneously account for *both* occurrences? (See page 232.)

   a. An isolated earthquake at the beginning of the year destroyed part of the nation's capital stock, and the nation's government significantly reduced its purchases of goods and services.

   b. There was a technological improvement at the end of the previous year, and the quantity of money in circulation rose significantly during the year.

   c. Labor productivity increased throughout the year, and consumers significantly increased their total planned purchases of goods and services.

   d. The capital stock increased somewhat during the year, and the quantity of money in circulation declined considerably.

10-15. Explain how, if at all, each of the following events would affect equilibrium real GDP and the long-run equilibrium price level. (See page 232.)

   a. A reduction in the quantity of money in circulation

   b. An income tax rebate (the return of previously paid taxes) from the government to households, which they can apply only to purchases of goods and services

   c. A technological improvement

   d. A decrease in the value of the home currency in terms of the currencies of other nations

10-16. For each question, suppose that the economy *begins* at the long-run equilibrium point *A* in the diagram below. Identify which of the other points on the diagram—points *B*, *C*, *D*, or *E*—could represent a *new* long-run equilibrium after the described events take place and move the economy away from point *A*. (See page 232.)

   a. Significant productivity improvements occur, and the quantity of money in circulation increases.

   b. No new capital investment takes place, and a fraction of the existing capital stock depreciates and becomes unusable. At the same time, the government imposes a large tax increase on the nation's households.

   c. More efficient techniques for producing goods and services are adopted throughout the economy at the same time that the government reduces its spending on goods and services.

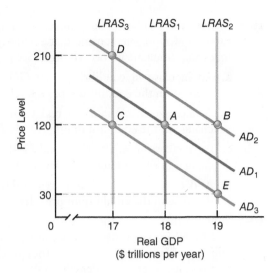

10-17. In Ciudad Barrios, El Salvador, the latest payments from relatives working in the United States have finally arrived. When the credit unions open for business, up to 150 people are already waiting in line. After receiving the funds their relatives have transmitted to these institutions, customers go off to outdoor markets to stock up on food or clothing or to appliance stores to purchase new stereos or televisions. Similar scenes occur throughout the developing world, as each year migrants working in higher-income, developed nations send around $200 billion of their earnings back to their relatives in less developed nations. Evidence indicates that the relatives, such as those in Ciudad Barrios, typically spend nearly all of the funds on current consumption. (See page 232.)

   a. Based on the information supplied, are developing countries' income inflows transmitted by migrant workers primarily affecting their economies' long-run aggregate supply curves or aggregate demand curves?

   b. How are equilibrium price levels in nations that are recipients of large inflows of funds from migrants likely to be affected? Explain your reasoning.

REFERENCES

INTERNATIONAL EXAMPLE: Greece Experiences a Series of Leftward Shifts in Its LRAS Curve

"Greek GDP Shrinks More Than Expected in the First Quarter," FocusEconomics, June 12, 2013. (www .focus-economics.com/en/economy/news/Greece-GDP-GDP_shrinks_more_than_expected_in_the_ first_quarter-2013-06-12)

Phillip Inman and Helena Smith, "Greek Economy to Shrink 25 Percent by 2014," *The Guardian*, September 18, 2013.

Cyrus Sanati, "Greece's Economy Is Still a Huge Mess," CNN Money, April 11, 2014.

POLICY EXAMPLE: Oscillating Amounts of Money in Circulation Cause Aggregate Demand to Gyrate

Federal Reserve Bank of St. Louis, *Monetary Trends*, various issues.

INTERNATIONAL EXAMPLE: Why Brazil's Inflation Rate Exceeds Its Real GDP Growth Rate

"Brazil's Economy's Wrong Numbers: More Inflation, Less Growth," The Economist, January 19, 2013.

Joe Leahy, "Brazil's Inflation Pace Hits 8-Year High," *Financial Times*, February 7, 2013.

Matthew Malinowski, "Brazil Economists Cut 2014 Growth Forecast for Third Week," Bloomberg, February 24, 2014.

YOU ARE THERE: Want to Transport Products? Sorry, the Bridge Is Out

Marisol Bello, "Bridge Collapse Shines Light on Aging Infrastructure," *USA Today*, May 24, 2013.

Rob Garver, "America's Ten Most Dangerous Infrastructure Problems," MSN Money, January 23, 2014.

Bob Tita, "A Slowdown on the Road to Recovery," *The Wall Street Journal*, October 13, 2013.

ISSUES & APPLICATIONS: Greenland's Long-Run Aggregate Supply Begins to Grow

James Areddy, "Race for Resources: Warm to Investors, Greenland Opens Up," *The Wall Street Journal*, August 22, 2013.

Peter Levring, "Greenland Bets on Mining as Global Warming Hits Fishing Industry," *Bloomberg Businessweek*, April 17, 2013.

Andrew Mason, "Mining in Greenland: The Long Road to Economic Independence," Global Business Reports, March 25, 2014.

11

Classical and Keynesian Macro Analyses

Cliff Hide News/Alamy

LEARNING OBJECTIVES

After reading this chapter, you should be able to:

11.1 Describe the short-run determination of equilibrium real GDP and the price level in the classical model

11.2 Discuss the essential features of Keynesian economics and explain the short-run aggregate supply curve

11.3 Explain what factors cause shifts in the short-run and long-run aggregate supply curves

11.4 Evaluate the effects of aggregate demand and supply shocks on equilibrium real GDP in the short run

11.5 Determine the causes of short-run variations in the inflation rate

MyEconLab helps you master each objective and study more efficiently. See the end of the chapter for details.

round the world, the sales revenues of nations' largest companies are accounting for increasing shares of the countries' levels of real GDP. An extreme example is Finland, in which one firm— Nokia—has contributed more than 20 percent to the country's real GDP growth since the late 1990s. Of course, no single firm's sales revenues make up anything close to such a substantial share of U.S. real GDP. Nevertheless, even in the United States the sales share of real GDP contributed by the largest firms has grown considerably during the past few decades. Does this fact mean that sales fluctuations at a set of very large firms can generate noticeable movements in U.S. real GDP? To contemplate the answer to this question, you first must learn about different theories of short-term variations in real GDP, which are key topics of this chapter.

the price of a bottle containing 6.5 ounces of Coca-Cola remained unchanged at 5 cents from 1886 to 1959? The prices of many other goods and services changed at least slightly during that 73-year period, and since then the prices of most items, including Coca-Cola, have generally moved in an upward direction. Nevertheless, prices of final goods and services have not always adjusted immediately in response to changes in aggregate demand. Consequently, one approach to understanding the determination of real GDP and the price level emphasizes *incomplete* adjustment in the prices of many goods and services. The simplest version of this approach was first developed by a twentieth-century economist named John Maynard Keynes (pronounced like *canes*). It assumes that in the short run, prices of most goods and services are nearly as rigid as the price of Coca-Cola from 1886 to 1959. Although the modern version of the Keynesian approach allows for greater flexibility of prices in the short run, incomplete price adjustment still remains a key feature of the modern Keynesian approach.

The Keynesian approach does not retain the long-run assumption, which you encountered in Chapter 10, of fully adjusting prices. Economists who preceded Keynes employed this assumption in creating an approach to understanding variations in real GDP and the price level that Keynes called the *classical model.* Like Keynes, we shall begin our study of variations in real GDP and the price level by considering the earlier, classical approach.

The Classical Model

The classical model, which traces its origins to the 1770s, was the first systematic attempt to explain the determinants of the price level and the national levels of real GDP, employment, consumption, saving, and investment. Classical economists—Adam Smith, J. B. Say, David Ricardo, John Stuart Mill, Thomas Malthus, A. C. Pigou, and others—wrote from the 1770s to the 1930s. They assumed, among other things, that all wages and prices were flexible and that competitive markets existed throughout the economy.

11.1 Describe the short-run determination of equilibrium real GDP and the price level in the classical model

Say's Law

Every time you produce something for which you receive income, you generate the income necessary to make expenditures on other goods and services. That means that an economy producing $18 trillion of real GDP, measured in base-year dollars (the value of current goods and services expressed in terms of prices in a base year), simultaneously produces the income with which these goods and services can be purchased. As an accounting identity, *actual* aggregate output always equals *actual* aggregate income. Classical economists took this accounting identity one step further by arguing that total national supply creates its own national demand. They asserted what has become known as **Say's law**:

> *Supply creates its own demand. Hence, it follows that* desired *expenditures will equal* actual *expenditures.*

Say's law
A dictum of economist J. B. Say that supply creates its own demand. Producing goods and services generates the means and the willingness to purchase other goods and services.

THE IMPLICATION OF SAY'S LAW What does Say's law really mean? It states that the very process of producing specific goods (supply) is proof that other goods are desired (demand). People produce more goods than they want for their own use only if they seek to trade them for other goods. Someone offers to supply something only because he or she has a demand for something else.

The implication of this, according to Say, is that no general glut, or overproduction, is possible in a market economy. From this reasoning, it seems to follow that full employment of labor and other resources would be the normal state of affairs in such an economy.

Say acknowledged that an oversupply of some goods might occur in particular markets. He argued that such surpluses would simply cause prices to fall, thereby decreasing production as the economy adjusted. The opposite would occur in markets in which shortages temporarily appeared.

SAY'S LAW IN A MODERN ECONOMY All this seems reasonable enough in a simple barter economy in which households produce most of the goods they want and trade for the rest. This is shown in Figure 11-1 below, in which there is a simple circular flow. What about a more sophisticated economy, however, in which people work for others and money is used instead of barter? Can these complications create the possibility of unemployment? Does the fact that laborers receive money income, some of which can be saved, lead to unemployment? No, said the classical economists to these last two questions. They based their reasoning on a number of key assumptions.   MyEconLab Concept Check

Assumptions of the Classical Model

The classical model makes four major assumptions:

1. *Pure competition exists.* No single buyer or seller of a commodity or an input can affect its price.

2. *Wages and prices are flexible.* The assumption of pure competition leads to the notion that prices, wages, and interest rates are free to move to whatever level supply and demand dictate (as the economy adjusts). Although no *individual* buyer can set a price, the community of buyers or sellers can cause prices to rise or to fall to an equilibrium level.

3. *People are motivated by self-interest.* Businesses want to maximize their profits, and households want to maximize their economic well-being.

4. *People cannot be fooled by money illusion.* Buyers and sellers react to changes in relative prices. That is to say, they do not suffer from **money illusion**. For example, workers will not be fooled into thinking that doubling their wages makes them better off if the price level has also doubled during the same time period.

Money illusion

Reacting to changes in money prices rather than relative prices. If a worker whose wages double when the price level also doubles thinks he or she is better off, that worker is suffering from money illusion.

The classical economists concluded, after taking account of the four major assumptions, that the role of government in the economy should be minimal. They assumed that pure competition prevails, all prices and wages are flexible, and people are self-interested and do not experience money illusion. If so, they argued, then any problems in the macroeconomy will be temporary. The market will correct itself.

FIGURE 11-1

Say's Law and the Circular Flow

Here we show the circular flow of income and output. The very act of supplying a certain level of goods and services necessarily equals the level of goods and services demanded, in Say's simplified world.

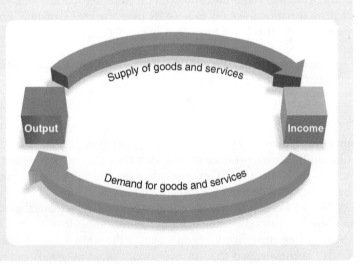

Equilibrium in the Credit Market

When income is saved, it is not reflected in product demand. It is a type of *leakage* from the circular flow of income and output because saving withdraws funds from the income stream. Therefore, total planned consumption spending *can* fall short of total current real GDP. In such a situation, it appears that supply does not necessarily create its own demand.

THE RELATIONSHIP BETWEEN SAVING AND INVESTMENT The classical economists did not believe that the complicating factor of saving in the circular flow model of income and output was a problem. They contended that each dollar saved would be invested by businesses so that the leakage of saving would be matched by the injection of business investment. *Investment* here refers only to additions to the nation's capital stock. The classical economists believed that businesses as a group would intend to invest as much as households wanted to save.

THE EQUILIBRIUM INTEREST RATE Equilibrium between the saving plans of consumers and the investment plans of businesses comes about, in the classical model, through the working of the credit market. In the credit market, the *price* of credit is the interest rate. At equilibrium, the price of credit—the interest rate—ensures that the amount of credit demanded equals the amount of credit supplied. Planned investment just equals planned saving, so there is no reason to be concerned about the leakage of saving. This fact is illustrated graphically in Figure 11-2 below.

In the figure, the vertical axis measures the rate of interest in percentage terms, and the horizontal axis measures flows of desired saving and desired investment per unit time period. The desired saving curve is really a supply curve of saving. It shows that people wish to save more at higher interest rates than at lower interest rates.

In contrast, the higher the rate of interest, the less profitable it is to invest and the lower is the level of desired investment. Thus, the desired investment curve slopes downward. In this simplified model, the equilibrium rate of interest is 5 percent, and the equilibrium quantity of saving and investment is $2 trillion per year.

FIGURE 11-2

Equating Desired Saving and Desired Investment in the Classical Model

The schedule showing planned investment is labeled "Desired investment." The desired saving curve is shown as an upward-sloping supply curve of saving. The equilibrating force here is, of course, the interest rate. At higher interest rates, people desire to save more. At higher interest rates, however, businesses wish to engage in less investment because it is less profitable to invest. In this model, at an interest rate of 5 percent, planned investment just equals planned saving, which is $2 trillion per year.

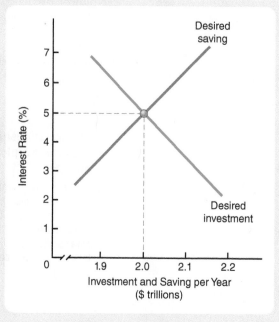

FIGURE 11-3

Equilibrium in the Labor Market

The demand for labor is downward sloping. At higher wage rates, firms will employ fewer workers. The supply of labor is upward sloping. At higher wage rates, more workers will work longer, and more people will be willing to work. The equilibrium wage rate is $22 with an equilibrium employment per year of 160 million workers.

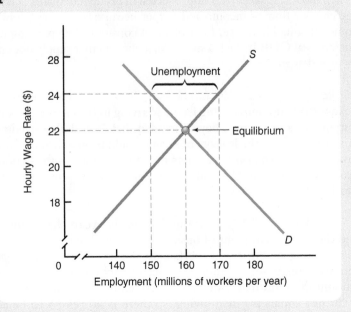

Equilibrium in the Labor Market

Now consider the labor market. If an excess quantity of labor is supplied at a particular wage level, the wage level must be above equilibrium. By accepting lower wages, unemployed workers will quickly be put back to work. We show equilibrium in the labor market in Figure 11-3 above.

Assume that equilibrium exists at $22 per hour and 160 million workers employed. If the wage rate were $24 per hour, there would be unemployment—170 million workers would want to work, but businesses would want to hire only 150 million. In the classical model, this unemployment is eliminated rather rapidly by wage rates dropping back to $22 per hour, as seen in Figure 11-3 above.

THE RELATIONSHIP BETWEEN EMPLOYMENT AND REAL GDP Employment is not to be regarded simply as some isolated figure that government statisticians estimate. Rather, the level of employment in an economy determines its real GDP (output), other things held constant. A hypothetical relationship between input (number of employees) and the value of output (real GDP per year) is shown in Table 11-1 below. The row that has

TABLE 11-1

The Relationship between Employment and Real GDP

Other things being equal, an increase in the quantity of labor input increases real GDP. In this example, if 160 million workers are employed, real GDP is $18 trillion in base-year dollars.

Labor Input per Year (millions of workers)	Real GDP per Year ($ trillions)
150	15
154	16
158	17
160	18
164	19
166	20

FIGURE 11-4

Classical Theory and Increases in Aggregate Demand

The classical theorists believed that Say's law and flexible interest rates, prices, and wages would always lead to full employment at real GDP of $18 trillion, in base-year dollars, along the vertical aggregate supply curve, *LRAS*. With aggregate demand AD_1, the price level is 110. An increase in aggregate demand shifts AD_1 to AD_2. At price level 110, the quantity of real GDP demanded per year would be $18.5 trillion at point *A* on AD_2. But $18.5 trillion in real GDP per year is greater than real GDP at full employment. Prices rise, and the economy quickly moves from E_1 to E_2, at the higher price level of 120.

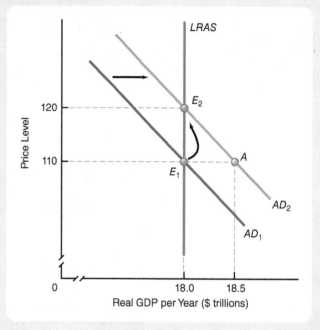

160 million workers per year as the labor input is highlighted. That might be considered a hypothetical level of full employment, and it is related to a rate of real GDP, in base-year dollars, of $18 trillion per year. MyEconLab Concept Check

Classical Theory, Vertical Aggregate Supply, and the Price Level

In the classical model, unemployment greater than the natural unemployment rate is impossible. Say's law, coupled with flexible interest rates, prices, and wages, would always tend to keep workers fully employed so that the aggregate supply curve, as shown in Figure 11-4 above, is vertical at the real GDP of $18 trillion, in base-year dollars. We have labeled the supply curve *LRAS*, which is the long-run aggregate supply curve introduced in Chapter 10. It was defined there as the real GDP that would be produced in an economy with full information and full adjustment of wages and prices year in and year out. *LRAS* therefore corresponds to the long-run rate of unemployment.

In the classical model, this happens to be the *only* aggregate supply curve. The classical economists made little distinction between the long run and the short run. Prices adjust so fast that the economy is essentially always on or quickly moving toward *LRAS*. Furthermore, because the labor market adjusts rapidly, real GDP is always at, or soon to be at, full employment. Full employment does not mean zero unemployment because there is always some frictional and structural unemployment (discussed in Chapter 7), which yields the natural rate of unemployment.

EFFECT OF AN INCREASE IN AGGREGATE DEMAND IN THE CLASSICAL MODEL In this model, any change in aggregate demand will quickly cause a change in the price level. Consider starting at E_1, at price level 110, in Figure 11-4. If aggregate demand shifts to AD_2, the economy will tend toward point *A*, but because this is beyond full-employment real GDP, prices will rise, and the economy will find itself back on the vertical *LRAS* at point E_2 at a higher price level, 120. The price level will increase as a result of the increase in *AD* because employers will end up bidding up wages for workers, as well as bidding up the prices of other inputs.

FIGURE 11-5

Effect of a Decrease in Aggregate Demand in the Classical Model

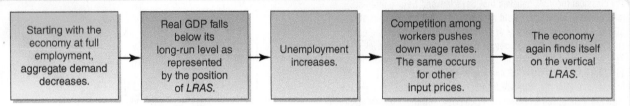

Starting with the economy at full employment, aggregate demand decreases.	Real GDP falls below its long-run level as represented by the position of *LRAS*.	Unemployment increases.	Competition among workers pushes down wage rates. The same occurs for other input prices.	The economy again finds itself on the vertical *LRAS*.

The level of real GDP per year clearly does not depend on the level of aggregate demand. Hence, we say that in the classical model, the equilibrium level of real GDP per year is completely *supply determined*. Changes in aggregate demand affect only the price level, not real GDP.

EFFECT OF A DECREASE IN AGGREGATE DEMAND IN THE CLASSICAL MODEL The effect of a decrease in aggregate demand in the classical model is the converse of the analysis just presented for an increase in aggregate demand. You can simply reverse AD_2 and AD_1 in Figure 11-4 on the previous page. To help you see how this analysis works, consider the flowchart in Figure 11-5 above.

MyEconLab Concept Check

MyEconLab Study Plan

SELF CHECK   Visit MyEconLab to practice these and other problems and to get instant feedback in your Study Plan.

Say's law states that _____ creates its own _____ and therefore *desired* expenditures will equal *actual* expenditures.

The classical model assumes that (1) _____ _____ exists, (2) _____ and _____ are completely flexible, (3) individuals are motivated by _____-_____, and (4) they cannot be fooled by _____ _____.

When saving is introduced into the model, equilibrium occurs in the credit market through changes in the

interest rate such that desired _____ equals desired _____ at the equilibrium rate of interest.

In the labor market, full employment occurs at a _____ _____ at which quantity demanded equals quantity supplied. That particular level of employment is associated with the full-employment level of real GDP per year.

In the classical model, because *LRAS* is _____, the equilibrium level of real GDP is supply determined. Any changes in aggregate demand simply change the _____ _____.

11.2 Discuss the essential features of Keynesian economics and explain the short-run aggregate supply curve

Keynesian Economics and the Keynesian Short-Run Aggregate Supply Curve

The classical economists' world was one of fully utilized resources. There would be no unused capacity and no unemployment. But then in the 1930s, Europe and the United States entered a period of economic decline that seemingly could not be explained by the classical model. John Maynard Keynes developed an explanation that has since become known as the Keynesian model.

Keynes and his followers argued that prices, especially the price of labor (wages), were inflexible downward due to the existence of unions and long-term contracts between businesses and workers. This meant that prices were "sticky." Keynes contended that in such a world, which has large amounts of excess capacity and unemployment, an increase in aggregate demand will not raise the price level, and a decrease in aggregate demand will not cause firms to lower prices.

MyEconLab Animation

FIGURE 11-6

Demand-Determined Equilibrium Real GDP at Less Than Full Employment

Keynes assumed that prices will not fall when aggregate demand falls and that there is excess capacity, so prices will not rise when aggregate demand increases. Thus, the short-run aggregate supply curve is simply a horizontal line at the given price level, 110, represented by *SRAS*. An aggregate demand shock that increases aggregate demand to AD_2 will increase the equilibrium level of real GDP per year to $18.5 trillion. An aggregate demand shock that decreases aggregate demand to AD_3 will decrease the equilibrium level of real GDP to $17.5 trillion. The equilibrium price level will not change.

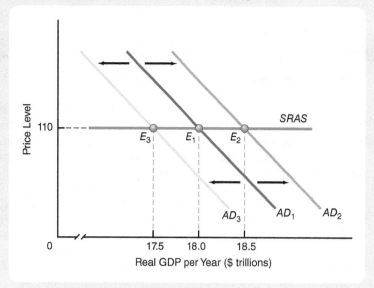

Demand-Determined Real GDP

This situation is depicted in Figure 11-6 above. For simplicity, Figure 11-6 does not show the point where the economy reaches capacity, and that is why the *short-run aggregate supply curve* (to be discussed later) never starts to slope upward and is simply the horizontal line labeled *SRAS*. Moreover, we don't show *LRAS* in Figure 11-6 either. It would be a vertical line at the level of real GDP per year that is consistent with full employment.

If we start out in equilibrium with aggregate demand at AD_1, the equilibrium level of real GDP per year, measured in base-year dollars, is $18 trillion at point E_1, and the equilibrium price level is 110. If there is a rise in aggregate demand, so that the aggregate demand curve shifts outward to the right to AD_2, the equilibrium price level at point E_2 will not change. Only the equilibrium level of real GDP per year will increase, to $18.5 trillion. Conversely, if there is a fall in aggregate demand that shifts the aggregate demand curve to AD_3, the equilibrium price level will again remain at 110 at point E_3, but the equilibrium level of real GDP per year will fall to $17.5 trillion.

Under such circumstances, the equilibrium level of real GDP per year is completely *demand determined*.

MyEconLab Concept Check

The Keynesian Short-Run Aggregate Supply Curve

The horizontal short-run aggregate supply curve represented in Figure 11-6 above is often called the **Keynesian short-run aggregate supply curve**. According to Keynes, unions and long-term contracts are real-world factors that explain the inflexibility of *nominal* wage rates. Such stickiness of wages makes *involuntary* unemployment of labor a distinct possibility, because leftward movements along the Keynesian short-run aggregate supply curve reduce real production and, hence, employment. The classical assumption of everlasting full employment no longer holds.

Data from the 1930s offer evidence of a nearly horizontal aggregate supply curve. Between 1934 and 1940, the GDP deflator stayed in a range from about 7.7 to just over 8.1, implying that the price level changed by less than 6 percent. Yet the level of real GDP measured in 2009 dollars varied between nearly $0.9 trillion and close to $1.3 trillion, or by nearly 50 percent. Thus, between 1934 and 1940, the U.S. short-run aggregate supply curve was almost flat.

Keynesian short-run aggregate supply curve
The horizontal portion of the aggregate supply curve in which there is excessive unemployment and unused capacity in the economy.

How could government requirements for firms to provide more expensive benefits to workers help to perpetuate high unemployment?

EXAMPLE

Are Higher Costs of Worker Benefits Keeping Unemployment High?

Today, the level of unemployment is about 10 million people, or almost 3 million more than at the beginning of 2008. Unemployment occurs when the quantity of labor supplied by workers at the current inflation-adjusted, or *real*, wage rate exceeds the quantity of labor demanded at that real wage rate. In other words, unemployment is a surplus in the market for labor. Reducing this labor-market surplus requires the overall inflation-adjusted real wage rate to decline toward the equilibrium real wage rate.

New government requirements for firms to provide health benefits have contributed to *higher* total real compensation (wages and benefits) to workers, however. Since 2008, increased costs to firms of benefits to workers contributed about one-fourth of a 3.3 percent rise in the federal government's inflation-adjusted index measure of total compensation paid to U.S. workers. During recent years, the rise in real benefits has

more than offset lower explicit real wage payments. Thus, instead of falling toward a level consistent with a considerable reduction in unemployment, aggregate real worker compensation—inclusive of benefits—has *increased*. This rise in overall compensation to workers arguably has contributed to the still substantial labor surplus—that is, persistently high unemployment.

FOR CRITICAL THINKING

How might a new policy of health care subsidies to low-income people contribute to unemployment by giving recipients incentives not to work and earn wage income?

Sources are listed at the end of this chapter.

MyEconLab Concept Check

Output Determination Using Aggregate Demand and Aggregate Supply

The underlying assumption of the simplified Keynesian model is that the relevant range of the short-run aggregate supply schedule (*SRAS*) is horizontal, as depicted in panel (a) of Figure 11-7 below. There you see that short-run aggregate supply is fixed at price level 110. If aggregate demand is AD_1, then the equilibrium level of real GDP, in base-year dollars, is

MyEconLab Animation

FIGURE 11-7

Real GDP Determination with Fixed versus Flexible Prices

In panel (a), the price level index is fixed at 110. An increase in aggregate demand from AD_1 to AD_2 moves the equilibrium level of real GDP from $18 trillion per year to $19 trillion per year in base-year dollars. In panel (b),

SRAS is upward sloping. The same shift in aggregate demand yields an equilibrium level of real GDP of only $18.5 trillion per year and a higher price level index at 120.

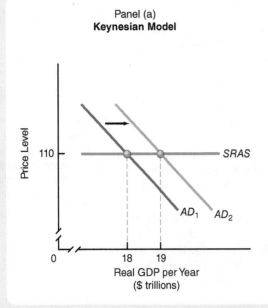

Panel (a)
Keynesian Model

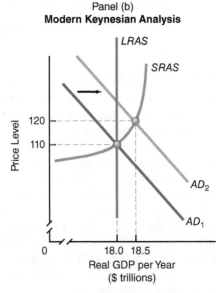

Panel (b)
Modern Keynesian Analysis

$18 trillion per year. If aggregate demand increases to AD_2, then the equilibrium level of real GDP increases to $19 trillion per year.

AN UPWARD-SLOPING SHORT-RUN AGGREGATE SUPPLY CURVE As discussed in Chapter 10, the price level has drifted upward during recent decades. Hence, prices are not totally sticky. Modern Keynesian analysis recognizes that *some*—but not complete—price adjustment takes place in the short run. Panel (b) of Figure 11-7 on the previous page displays a more general **short-run aggregate supply curve** (*SRAS*). This curve represents the relationship between the price level and real GDP with incomplete price adjustment and in the absence of complete information in the short run. Allowing for partial price adjustment implies that *SRAS* slopes upward, and its slope is steeper after it crosses long-run aggregate supply, *LRAS*. This is because higher and higher prices are required to induce firms to raise their production of goods and services to levels that temporarily exceed full-employment real GDP.

With partial price adjustment in the short run, if aggregate demand is AD_1, then the equilibrium level of real GDP in panel (b) is also $18 trillion per year, at a price level of 110, too. An increase in aggregate demand to AD_2 such as occurred in panel (a) produces a different short-run equilibrium, however. Equilibrium real GDP increases to $18.5 trillion per year, which is less than in panel (a) because an increase in the price level to 120 causes planned purchases of goods and services to decline.

Short-run aggregate supply curve
The relationship between total planned economywide production and the price level in the short run, all other things held constant. If prices adjust incompletely in the short run, the curve is positively sloped.

EXPLAINING THE SHORT-RUN AGGREGATE SUPPLY CURVE'S UPWARD SLOPE In the modern Keynesian short run, when the price level rises partially, real GDP can be expanded beyond the level consistent with its long-run growth path, discussed in Chapter 10, for a variety of reasons:

1. In the short run, most labor contracts implicitly or explicitly call for flexibility in hours of work at the given wage rate. Therefore, firms can use existing workers more intensively: They can get workers to work harder, to work more hours per day, and to work more days per week.

2. Existing capital equipment can be used more intensively. Machines can be worked more hours per day. Some can be made to operate faster. Maintenance can be delayed.

3. Finally, if wage rates are held constant, a higher price level leads to increased profits from additional production, which induces firms to hire more workers. The duration of unemployment falls, and thus the unemployment rate falls. Furthermore, people who were previously not in the labor force (homemakers and younger or older workers) can be induced to enter it.

All these adjustments cause real GDP to rise as the price level increases.

MyEconLab Concept Check
MyEconLab Study Plan

SELF CHECK Visit MyEconLab to practice these and other problems and to get instant feedback in your Study Plan.

If we assume that the economy is operating on a horizontal short-run aggregate supply curve, the equilibrium level of real GDP per year is completely _____ determined.

The horizontal short-run aggregate supply curve has been called the **Keynesian short-run aggregate supply curve** because Keynes believed that many prices, especially wages, would not be _____ even when aggregate demand decreased.

In modern Keynesian theory, the **short-run aggregate supply curve, SRAS**, shows the relationship between

the price level and real GDP without full adjustment or full information. It is upward sloping because it allows for only _____ price adjustment in the short run.

Real GDP can be expanded in the short run because firms can use existing workers and capital equipment more _____. Also, in the short run, when input prices are fixed, a higher price level means _____ profits, which induce firms to hire more workers.

11.3 Explain what factors cause shifts in the short-run and long-run aggregate supply curves

Shifts in the Aggregate Supply Curve

Just as non-price-level factors can cause a shift in the aggregate demand curve, there are non-price-level factors that can cause a shift in the aggregate supply curve. The analysis here is more complicated than the analysis for the non-price-level determinants for aggregate demand, for here we are dealing with both the short run and the long run—*SRAS* and *LRAS*. Still, anything other than the price level that affects the production of final goods and services will shift aggregate supply curves.

Shifts in Both Short- and Long-Run Aggregate Supply

There is a core class of events that cause a shift in both the short-run aggregate supply curve and the long-run aggregate supply curve. These include any change in our endowments of the factors of production. Any change in factors of production—labor, capital, or technology—that influence economic growth will shift *SRAS* and *LRAS*. Look at Figure 11-8 below. Initially, the two curves are $SRAS_1$ and $LRAS_1$. Now consider a situation in which large amounts of irreplaceable resources are lost *permanently* in a major oil spill and fire. This shifts $LRAS_1$ to $LRAS_2$ at $17.5 trillion of real GDP, measured in base-year dollars. $SRAS_1$ also shifts leftward horizontally to $SRAS_2$.

MyEconLab Concept Check

Shifts in *SRAS* Only

Some events, particularly those that are short lived, will temporarily shift *SRAS* but not *LRAS*. One of the most obvious is a change in production input prices, particularly those caused by external events that are not expected to last forever. Consider a major hurricane that temporarily shuts down a significant portion of U.S. oil production. Oil is an important input in many production activities. The resulting drop in oil production would cause at least a temporary increase in the price of this input. In this case, the long-run aggregate supply curve would remain at $LRAS_1$ in Figure 11-8.

The short-run aggregate supply curve *alone* would shift from $SRAS_1$ to $SRAS_2$, reflecting the increase in input prices—the higher price of oil. This is because the rise in

MyEconLab Animation

FIGURE 11-8

Shifts in Long-Run and Short-Run Aggregate Supply

Initially, the two aggregate supply curves are $SRAS_1$ and $LRAS_1$. An event that permanently reduces reserves of a key productive resource such as oil shifts $LRAS_1$ to $LRAS_2$ at $17.5 trillion of real GDP, in base-year dollars, and also shifts $SRAS_1$ horizontally leftward to $SRAS_2$. If, instead, a temporary increase in an input price occurred, $LRAS_1$ would remain unchanged, and only the short-run aggregate supply curve would shift, from $SRAS_1$ to $SRAS_2$.

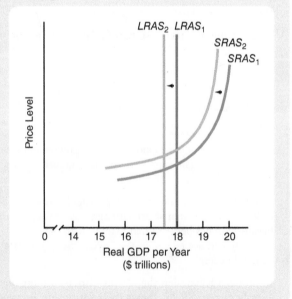

TABLE 11-2

Determinants of Aggregate Supply

The determinants listed here can affect short-run or long-run aggregate supply (or both), depending on whether they are temporary or permanent.

Changes That Cause an Increase in Aggregate Supply	Changes That Cause a Decrease in Aggregate Supply
Discoveries of new raw materials	Depletion of raw materials
Increased competition	Decreased competition
A reduction in international trade barriers	An increase in international trade barriers
Fewer regulatory impediments to business	More regulatory impediments to business
An increase in the supply of labor	A decrease in labor supplied
Increased training and education	Decreased training and education
A decrease in marginal tax rates	An increase in marginal tax rates
A reduction in input prices	An increase in input prices

the costs of production at each level of real GDP per year would require a higher price level to cover those increased costs.

We summarize the possible determinants of aggregate supply in Table 11-2 above. These determinants will cause a shift in the short-run or the long-run aggregate supply curve or both, depending on whether they are temporary or permanent.

MyEconLab Concept Check
MyEconLab Study Plan

SELF CHECK Visit MyEconLab to practice these and other problems and to get instant feedback in your Study Plan.

Any change in factors influencing _____ -run output, such as _____, capital, or _____, will shift both the *SRAS* curve and the *LRAS* curve.

A temporary change in input prices will shift only the _____ curve.

Consequences of Changes in Aggregate Demand

11.4 Evaluate the effects of aggregate demand and supply shocks on equilibrium real GDP in the short run

We now have a basic model to apply when evaluating short-run adjustments of the equilibrium price level and equilibrium real GDP when there are shocks to the economy. Whenever there is a shift in the aggregate demand or short-run aggregate supply curves, the short-run equilibrium price level or real GDP level (or both) may change. These shifts are called **aggregate demand shocks** on the demand side and **aggregate supply shocks** on the supply side.

How might uncertainty about the government's economic policies influence aggregate demand and aggregate supply shocks?

Aggregate demand shock
Any event that causes the aggregate demand curve to shift inward or outward.

Aggregate supply shock
Any event that causes the aggregate supply curve to shift inward or outward.

POLICY EXAMPLE

Economic Policy Uncertainty as a Source of Shocks

In recent years, a number of observers have argued that increases in the degree of uncertainty that people have about governmental economic policies can create aggregate demand and aggregate supply shocks. After all, households base changes in their spending decisions partly on

perceptions of the effects of altered governmental policies, and those changed expenditure choices generate shifts in the aggregate demand curve. Likewise, firms decide how much to vary their production at any given price level, taking into account anticipated changes in governmental

(continued)

policies, which determines variations in the position of the aggregate supply curve.

Figure 11-9 displays recent values of an index measure of economic policy uncertainty developed by Scott Baker and Nicholas Bloom of Stanford University and Steven Davis of the University of Chicago. These economists find evidence that increases in their measure of economic policy uncertainty are associated with reductions in real GDP. Hence, greater economic policy uncertainty appears to generate leftward shifts

in both the aggregate demand and aggregate supply curves—that is, negative aggregate demand and aggregate supply shocks.

FOR CRITICAL THINKING

Why do you suppose that uncertainty about governmental economic policy actions is more likely to discourage households from spending and business firms from producing than it is to encourage such behaviors?

Sources are listed at the end of this chapter.

FIGURE 11-9

Variations in a Measure of Economic Policy Uncertainty

This figure displays changes over time in an index measure of uncertainty about the government's economic policies. This measure indicates greatest economic policy uncertainty during the 1990–1991, 2001–2002, and 2008–2009 periods of economic downturn and during the most recent period.

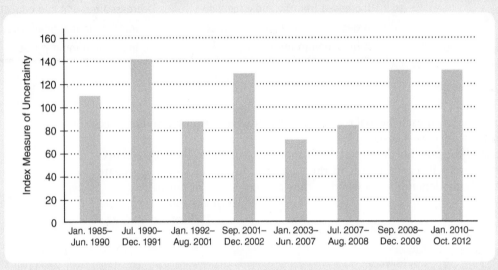

Source: Scott Baker, Nicholas Bloom, and Steven Davis, "Measuring Economic Policy Uncertainty," Stanford University and University of Chicago, May 19, 2013.

Recessionary gap

The gap that exists whenever equilibrium real GDP per year is less than full-employment real GDP as shown by the position of the long-run aggregate supply curve.

When Aggregate Demand Falls While Aggregate Supply Is Stable

Now we can show what happens in the short run when aggregate supply remains stable but aggregate demand falls. The short-run outcome will be a rise in the unemployment rate. In Figure 11-10 on the next page, you see that with AD_1, both long-run and short-run equilibrium are at $18 trillion (in base-year dollars) of real GDP per year (because $SRAS$ and $LRAS$ also intersect AD_1 at that level of real GDP). The long-run equilibrium price level is 110. A reduction in aggregate demand shifts the aggregate demand curve to AD_2. The new intersection with $SRAS$ is at $17.8 trillion per year, which is less than the long-run equilibrium level of real GDP. The difference between $18 trillion and $17.8 trillion is called a **recessionary gap**, defined as the difference between the short-run equilibrium level of real GDP and real GDP if the economy were operating at full employment on its $LRAS$.

In effect, at E_2, the economy is in short-run equilibrium at less than full employment. With too many unemployed inputs, input prices will begin to fall. Eventually, $SRAS$ will have to shift vertically downward.   MyEconLab Concept Check

Short-Run Effects When Aggregate Demand Increases

We can reverse the situation and have aggregate demand increase to AD_2, as is shown in Figure 11-11 on the next page. The initial equilibrium conditions are exactly the same as in Figure 11-10 on the next page. The move to AD_2 increases the short-run equilibrium from E_1 to E_2 such that the economy is operating at $18.2 trillion of real

FIGURE 11-10

The Short-Run Effects of Stable Aggregate Supply and a Decrease in Aggregate Demand: The Recessionary Gap

If the economy is at equilibrium at E_1, with price level 110 and real GDP per year of $18 trillion, a shift inward of the aggregate demand curve to AD_2 will lead to a new short-run equilibrium at E_2. The equilibrium price level will fall to 105, and the short-run equilibrium level of real GDP per year will fall to $17.8 trillion. There will be a recessionary gap of $200 billion.

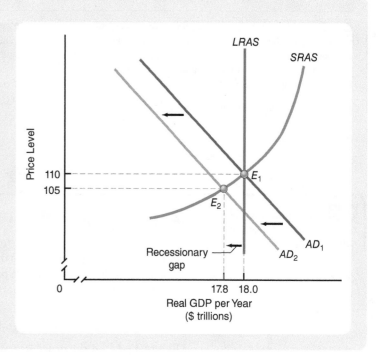

FIGURE 11-11

The Effects of Stable Aggregate Supply with an Increase in Aggregate Demand: The Inflationary Gap

The economy is at equilibrium at E_1. An increase in aggregate demand to AD_2 leads to a new short-run equilibrium at E_2, with the price level rising from 110 to 115 and equilibrium real GDP per year rising from $18 trillion to $18.2 trillion. The difference, $200 billion, is called the inflationary gap.

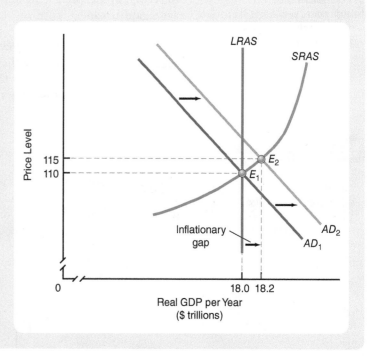

GDP per year, which exceeds *LRAS*. This is a condition of an overheated economy, typically called an **inflationary gap**.

At E_2 in Figure 11-11, the economy is at a short-run equilibrium that is beyond full employment. In the short run, more can be squeezed out of the economy than occurs in the long-run, full-information, full-adjustment situation. Firms will be operating beyond long-run capacity. Inputs will be working too hard. Input prices will begin to rise. That will eventually cause *SRAS* to shift vertically upward.   MyEconLab Concept Check
MyEconLab Study Plan

Inflationary gap
The gap that exists whenever equilibrium real GDP per year is greater than full-employment real GDP, as shown by the position of the long-run aggregate supply curve.

_____-run equilibrium occurs at the intersection of the aggregate demand curve, *AD*, and the short-run aggregate supply curve, *SRAS*. _____-run equilibrium occurs at the intersection of *AD* and the long-run aggregate supply curve, *LRAS*.

Any unanticipated shifts in aggregate demand or supply are called aggregate demand _____ or aggregate supply _____.

When aggregate demand decreases while aggregate supply is stable, a _____ gap can occur, defined as the difference between how much the economy could be producing if it were operating on its *LRAS* and the equilibrium level of real GDP. An increase in aggregate demand leads to an _____ gap.

11.5 Determine the causes of short-run variations in the inflation rate

Explaining Short-Run Variations in Inflation

In Chapter 10, we noted that in a growing economy, the explanation for persistent inflation is that aggregate demand increases over time at a faster pace than the full-employment level of real GDP. Short-run variations in inflation, however, can arise as a result of both demand *and* supply factors.

Demand-Pull versus Cost-Push Inflation

Figure 11-11 on the previous page presents a demand-side theory explaining a short-run jump in prices, sometimes called *demand-pull inflation*. Whenever the general level of prices rises in the short run because of increases in aggregate demand, we say that the economy is experiencing **demand-pull inflation**—inflation caused by increases in aggregate demand.

Demand-pull inflation

Inflation caused by increases in aggregate demand not matched by increases in aggregate supply.

An alternative explanation for increases in the price level comes from the supply side. Look at Figure 11-12 below. The initial equilibrium conditions are the same as in Figure 11-10. Now, however, there is a leftward shift in the short-run aggregate supply curve, from *SRAS*₁ to *SRAS*₂. Equilibrium shifts from *E*₁ to *E*₂. The price level increases from 110 to 115, while the equilibrium level of real GDP per year decreases

---

FIGURE 11-12

Cost-Push Inflation

If aggregate demand remains stable but *SRAS*₁ shifts to *SRAS*₂, equilibrium changes from *E*₁ to *E*₂. The price level rises from 110 to 115. If there are continual decreases in aggregate supply of this nature, the situation is called cost-push inflation.

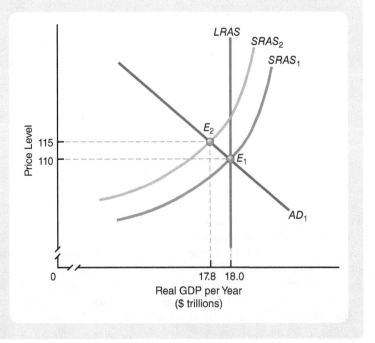

from $18 trillion to $17.8 trillion. Persistent decreases in aggregate supply causes what is called **cost-push inflation**.

As the example of cost-push inflation shows, if the economy is initially in equilibrium on its *LRAS*, a decrease in *SRAS* will lead to a rise in the price level. Thus, any abrupt change in one of the factors that determine aggregate supply will alter the equilibrium level of real GDP per year and the equilibrium price level. If the economy is for some reason operating to the left of its *LRAS*, an increase in *SRAS* will lead to a simultaneous *increase* in the equilibrium level of real GDP per year and a *decrease* in the price level. You should be able to show this in a graph similar to Figure 11-12.

MyEconLab Concept Check

Cost-push inflation
Inflation caused by decreases in short-run aggregate supply.

Aggregate Demand and Supply in an Open Economy

In many of the international examples in the early chapters of this book, we had to translate foreign currencies into dollars when the open economy was discussed. We used the exchange rate, or the dollar price of other currencies. In Chapter 10, you also learned that the open economy effect was one of the reasons why the aggregate demand curve slopes downward. When the domestic price level rises, U.S. residents want to buy cheaper-priced foreign goods. The opposite occurs when the U.S. domestic price level falls. Currently, the foreign sector of the U.S. economy constitutes more than 15 percent of all economic activities.

HOW A STRONGER DOLLAR AFFECTS AGGREGATE SUPPLY Assume that the dollar becomes stronger in international foreign exchange markets. If last year the dollar could buy 50 *rupees*, the Indian currency, but this year it buys 60 rupees, the dollar has become stronger. To the extent that U.S. companies import physical inputs and labor services from India, a stronger dollar can lead to lower input prices.

For instance, if a U.S. firm purchases 5 million rupees' worth of labor services per year from an Indian company, then before the strengthening of the dollar, that company paid $100,000 per year for those labor services. After the dollar's strengthening, however, the U.S. firm's Indian-labor-input expense drops to $83,333. This U.S. firm's cost reduction generated by the dollar's strengthening, as well as similar reductions in foreign-input expenses at other U.S. firms, will induce those firms to produce more final goods and services per year at any given price level.

Thus, a general strengthening of the dollar against the rupee and other world currencies will lead the short-run aggregate supply curve to shift outward to the right, as shown in panel (a) of Figure 11-13 on the next page. In that simplified model, equilibrium real GDP would rise, and the price level would decline. Employment would also tend to increase.

HOW A STRONGER DOLLAR AFFECTS AGGREGATE DEMAND A stronger dollar has another effect that we must consider. Foreign residents will find that U.S.-made goods are now more expensive, expressed in their own currency. Suppose that as a result of the dollar's strengthening, the dollar, which previously could buy 0.70 euro, can now buy 0.75 euro. Before the dollar strengthened, a U.S.-produced $10 downloadable music album cost a French resident 7.00 euros at the exchange rate of 0.70 euro per $1. After the dollar strengthens and the exchange rate changes to 0.75 euro per $1, that same $10 digital album will cost 7.50 euros. Conversely, U.S. residents will find that the stronger dollar makes imported goods less expensive. The result for U.S. residents is fewer exports and more imports, or lower net exports (exports minus imports). If net exports fall, employment in export industries will fall: This is represented in panel (b) of Figure 11-13 on the next page. After the dollar becomes stronger, the aggregate demand curve shifts inward from AD_1 to AD_2. The result is a tendency for equilibrium real GDP and the price level to fall and for unemployment to increase.

THE NET EFFECTS ON INFLATION AND REAL GDP We have learned, then, that a stronger dollar *simultaneously* leads to an increase in *SRAS* and a decrease in *AD*. In such situations, the equilibrium price level definitely falls. A stronger dollar contributes to deflation.

FIGURE 11-13
The Two Effects of a Stronger Dollar

When the dollar increases in value in the international currency market, there are two effects. The first is lower prices for imported inputs, causing a shift in the short-run aggregate supply schedule outward and to the right, from $SRAS_1$ to $SRAS_2$ in panel (a). Equilibrium tends to move from E_1 to E_2 at a lower price level and a higher equilibrium real GDP per year. Second, a stronger dollar can also affect the aggregate demand curve

because it will lead to lower net exports and cause AD_1 to shift inward to AD_2 in panel (b). Due to this effect, equilibrium will move from E_1 to E_2 at a lower price level and a lower equilibrium real GDP per year. On balance, the combined effects of the decrease in aggregate demand and increase in aggregate supply will be to push down the price level, but real GDP may rise or fall.

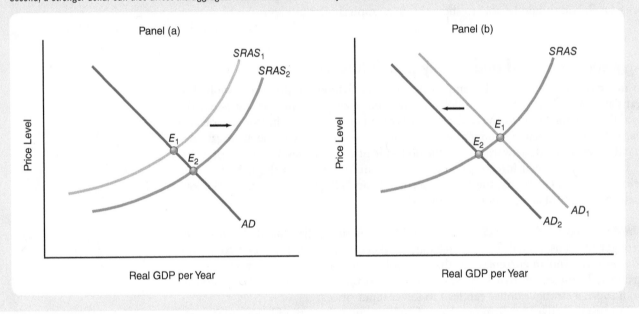

The effect of a stronger dollar on real GDP depends on which curve—*AD* or *SRAS*—shifts more. If the aggregate demand curve shifts more than the short-run aggregate supply curve, equilibrium real GDP will decline. Conversely, if the aggregate supply curve shifts more than the aggregate demand curve, equilibrium real GDP will rise. You should be able to redo this entire analysis for a weaker dollar.

WHAT IF...

a country's government tries to "cool down" real GDP growth that it views to be too rapid by pushing up the exchange value of the nation's currency?

On the one hand, increasing the exchange value of the currency would make the nation's export goods more expensive in foreign currencies, thereby generating less foreign spending on home exports and, hence, reducing domestic aggregate demand. On the other hand, the rise in the foreign value of the nation's currency would cause home-currency prices of inputs that domestic firms import from abroad to decrease. This

change would induce the country's firms to boost production of final goods and services at any given price level. As a consequence, domestic aggregate supply would increase, which would reinforce the rapid growth in real GDP already in progress. On net, therefore, pushing up the exchange value of the home currency might not necessarily help to slow real GDP growth.

MyEconLab Concept Check
MyEconLab Study Plan

SELF CHECK   Visit MyEconLab to practice these and other problems and to get instant feedback in your Study Plan.

With stable aggregate supply, an abrupt outward shift in *AD* may lead to what is called _____-_____ inflation.

With stable aggregate demand, an abrupt shift inward in *SRAS* may lead to what is called _____-_____ inflation.

A _____ dollar will reduce the cost of imported inputs, thereby causing *SRAS* to shift outward to the right. At the same time, a _____ dollar will also lead to lower net exports, causing the aggregate demand curve to shift inward. The equilibrium price level definitely falls, but the net effect on equilibrium real GDP depends on which shift is larger.

YOU ARE THERE

A Drought Suddenly Dries Up a Portion of U.S. Aggregate Supply

Water is a key resource for production of goods and services. Water in the nation's lakes and rivers provides waterways for shipping. When directed into forceful currents, water spins turbines that generate electricity. Water from rivers and streams irrigates farmland. Scenic lakefront and riverfront views also attract tourists to restaurants and hotels in many locales.

Much of the country has experienced a sharp drought. Pete Clark, co-owner of Carlos' n Charlie's, a restaurant located next to Lake Travis in Austin, Texas, has depended on water as a tourist attraction. Lake Travis is at 33 percent of its capacity, and tourists are not attracted by a mostly empty lakebed. "We hung in there for the first bad year, the second bad year, and now this third bad year," Clark says, "and we knew if we hung on for a fourth, we would create a financial hole we couldn't dig out of."

Clark's business closure is one of many nationwide related to the drought. Farms lacking water for irrigation are cutting production.

Power companies are shifting away from water to more costly sources of power for electrical turbines. For a time, shipping routes disappeared in the Great Lakes and along rivers flowing from those lakes as water levels dropped too low to support craft carrying freight. In short, the reduction in water resources available for use reduced the nation's short-run aggregate supply, thereby generating an aggregate supply shock.

CRITICAL THINKING QUESTIONS

1. How has the drought affected the position of the U.S. *SRAS* curve?

2. *Ceteris paribus*, what is the effect of the drought on the equilibrium price level?

Sources are listed at the end of this chapter.

ISSUES & APPLICATIONS

MyEconLab Video

How Do Large Firms Influence Macroeconomic Shocks?

Cliff Hide News/Alamy

CONCEPTS APPLIED

» Aggregate Demand Shock

» Aggregate Supply Shock

» Aggregate Demand and Aggregate Supply in an Open Economy

During the past four decades, the relative importance of large firms in the U.S. economy, such as Apple and General Electric, has increased. The inflation-adjusted revenues of the largest 100 companies accounted for just over 25 percent of real GDP in the 1970s, but today these firms' revenues make up more than 35 percent of real GDP.

How has the growth in large firms' percentage of total sales of final goods and services affected the transmission of aggregate demand and aggregate supply shocks? The answer is that the growing importance of large firms has had two effects. First, it has altered the ways in which aggregate demand and aggregate supply shocks occur within the economy and influence real GDP. Second, it has changed the way in which variations in the value of a nation's currency affect aggregate demand, aggregate supply, and equilibrium real GDP.

Sales of Large Firms and the Variability of Real GDP

The sales revenues of the largest U.S. companies can vary considerably during and across years. The total revenues of a typical large firm, which vary because of changes both in desired consumer expenditures and in the flow of produc-

tion that the firm itself chooses to undertake, fluctuate by an average amount of about 12 percent per year.

Of course, sales at some large U.S. firms typically are increasing at the same time that revenues at other large companies are decreasing. Nevertheless, at any given time, swings in sales of a few firms can generate significant net effects on aggregate demand and aggregate supply. As large firms' share of real GDP has risen over time, their influence on the magnitudes of these shocks has increased. Today, variations in levels of inflation-adjusted sales revenues at the largest U.S. companies account for more than 40 percent of U.S. real GDP volatility.

Large Firms, Exports, and Imports, and Real GDP Volatility

Large companies are more adept than small firms in shielding their exports and imports from effects of either a dollar strengthening or a dollar weakening. Thus, the growth in large companies' shares of exports and imports has also tended to make exports and imports—and hence aggregate demand and aggregate supply—less volatile in the face of changing currency values.

Summing up, the growing relative economic importance of large firms has two key macroeconomic effects. First, the increasing share of real GDP contributed by large companies' sales has caused swings in these firms' sales to generate greater portions of shocks to the aggregate demand and aggregate supply curves. Second, as large companies that do more to protect themselves from variations in currency values account for growing shares of exports and imports, aggregate demand and supply effects of strengthening or weakening currencies are reduced. On net, the largest firms now can have a greater influence on variations in real GDP, but their increased share of exports

and imports helps to shield real GDP from fluctuations in international currency values.

For Critical Thinking

1. Does the fact that sales at larger firms now contribute more to aggregate demand shocks or aggregate supply shocks necessarily imply that these shocks have greater magnitudes than in the past? Explain your reasoning.

2. Does the net effect of a dollar strengthening on equilibrium real GDP remain theoretically uncertain even if the effects on aggregate demand and aggregate supply are smaller? Explain.

Web Resources

1. For a ranking of the top U.S. companies according to their sales, see the Web Links in MyEconLab.

2. To see how the sales of the largest corporations match up against the real GDP levels of individual countries, see the Web Links in MyEconLab.

> ## MyEconLab
>
> For more questions on this chapter's Issues & Applications, go to MyEconLab.
>
> In the Study Plan for this chapter, select Section I: Issues and Applications.

Sources are listed at the end of this chapter.

Fundamental Points

1. In classical macroeconomic theory, the classical *LRAS* curve is vertical at the full-employment real GDP, and intersection of the *LRAS* curve with the aggregate demand curve determines the equilibrium price level.

2. In modern Keynesian theory, there is only partial price adjustment in the short run, so the short-run aggregate supply curve slopes upward.

3. A temporary event such as a temporary change in input prices causes only the short-run aggregate supply curve to shift but leaves the position of the *LRAS* curve unaffected.

4. A sudden shift in the aggregate demand curve is an aggregate demand shock that generates either a recessionary gap or an inflationary gap. A sudden shift in the short-run aggregate supply curve is an aggregate supply shock.

5. With stable aggregate supply, an abrupt outward shift in the aggregate demand curve can generate demand-side inflation. With stable aggregate demand, an abrupt shift inward in the short-run aggregate supply curve can generate supply-side inflation.

WHAT YOU SHOULD KNOW

Here is what you should know after reading this chapter. MyEconLab will help you identify what you know, and where to go when you need to practice.

LEARNING OBJECTIVES	KEY TERMS	WHERE TO GO TO PRACTICE
11.1 Describe the short-run determination of equilibrium real GDP and the price level in the classical model *The classical model assumes (1) pure competition, (2) flexible wages and prices, (3) self-interest, and (4) no money illusion. The short-run aggregate supply curve is vertical at full-employment real GDP. Variations in aggregate demand along aggregate supply generate changes in the equilibrium price level.*	Say's law, 243 money illusion, 244 **Key Figures** Figure 11-2, 245 Figure 11-3, 246 Figure 11-4, 247 Figure 11-5, 248	• MyEconLab Study Plan 11.1 • Animated Figures 11-2, 11-3, 11-4, 11-5

WHAT YOU SHOULD KNOW *continued*

LEARNING OBJECTIVES	KEY TERMS	WHERE TO GO TO PRACTICE
11.2 **Discuss the essential features of Keynesian economics and explain the short-run aggregate supply curve** *If product prices and wages and other input prices are "sticky," the short-run aggregate supply schedule can be horizontal over much of its range. This is the Keynesian short-run aggregate supply curve. More generally, however, to the extent that there is incomplete adjustment of prices in the short run, the short-run aggregate supply curve slopes upward.*	Keynesian short-run aggregate supply curve, 249 short-run aggregate supply curve, 251 **Key Figures** Figure 11-6, 249 Figure 11-7, 250	• MyEconLab Study Plan 11.2 • Animated Figures 11-6, 11-7
11.3 **Explain what factors cause shifts in the short-run and long-run aggregate supply curves** *Both the long-run aggregate supply curve and the short-run aggregate supply curve shift in response to changes in the availability of labor or capital or to changes in technology and productivity. A widespread temporary change in the prices of factors of production, however, can cause a shift in the short-run aggregate supply curve without affecting the long-run aggregate supply curve.*	**Key Figure** Figure 11-8, 252 **Key Table** Table 11-2, 253	• MyEconLab Study Plan 11.3 • Animated Figure 11-8
11.4 **Evaluate the effects of aggregate demand and supply shocks on equilibrium real GDP in the short run** *An aggregate demand shock that causes the aggregate demand curve to shift leftward pushes equilibrium real GDP below the level of full-employment real GDP in the short run, so there is a recessionary gap. An aggregate demand shock that induces a rightward shift in the aggregate demand curve results in an inflationary gap, in which short-run equilibrium real GDP exceeds full-employment real GDP.*	aggregate demand shock, 253 aggregate supply shock, 253 recessionary gap, 254 inflationary gap, 255 **Key Figures** Figure 11-9, 254 Figure 11-10, 255 Figure 11-11, 255	• MyEconLab Study Plan 11.4 • Animated Figures 11-10, 11-11
11.5 **Determine the causes of short-run variations in the inflation rate** *Demand-pull inflation occurs when the aggregate demand curve shifts rightward along an upward-sloping short-run aggregate supply curve. Cost-push inflation occurs when the short-run aggregate supply curve shifts leftward along the aggregate demand curve. A strengthening of the dollar shifts the short-run aggregate supply curve rightward and the aggregate demand curve leftward, which causes inflation but has uncertain effects on real GDP.*	demand-pull inflation, 256 cost-push inflation, 257	• MyEconLab Study Plan 11.5 • Animated Figure 11-12

Log in to MyEconLab, take a chapter test, and get a personalized Study Plan that tells you which concepts you understand and which ones you need to review. From there, MyEconLab will give you further practice, tutorials, animations, videos, and guided solutions. For more information, visit http://www.myeconlab.com

PROBLEMS

All problems are assignable in MyEconLab. Answers to odd-numbered problems appear in MyEconLab.

11-1. Consider a country whose economic structure matches the assumptions of the classical model. After reading a recent best-seller documenting a growing population of low-income elderly people who were ill prepared for retirement, most residents of this country decide to increase their saving at any given interest rate. Explain whether or how this could affect the following (see page 245):

   a. The current equilibrium interest rate

   b. Current equilibrium real GDP

   c. Current equilibrium employment

   d. Current equilibrium investment

   e. Future equilibrium real GDP (see Chapter 9)

11-2. Consider a country with an economic structure consistent with the assumptions of the classical model. Suppose that businesses in this nation suddenly anticipate higher future profitability from investments they undertake today. Explain whether or how this could affect the following (see page 245):

   a. The current equilibrium interest rate

   b. Current equilibrium real GDP

   c. Current equilibrium employment

   d. Current equilibrium saving

   e. Future equilibrium real GDP (see Chapter 9)

11-3. "There is *absolutely no distinction* between the classical model and Chapter 10's model of long-run equilibrium." Is this statement true or false? Support your answer. (See pages 243–248.)

11-4. Suppose that the Keynesian short-run aggregate supply curve is applicable for a nation's economy. Use appropriate diagrams to assist in answering the following questions (see pages 249–250):

   a. What are two events that can cause the nation's real GDP to increase in the short run?

   b. What are two events that can cause the nation's real GDP to increase in the long run?

11-5. What determines how much real GDP responds to changes in the price level along the short-run aggregate supply curve? (See page 251.)

11-6. Suppose that there is a temporary, but significant, increase in oil prices in an economy with an upward-sloping *SRAS* curve. If policymakers wish to prevent the equilibrium price level from changing in response to the oil price increase, should they increase or decrease the quantity of money in circulation? Why? (See page 256.)

11-7. As in Problem 11-6, suppose that there is a temporary, but significant, increase in oil prices in an economy with an upward-sloping *SRAS* curve. In this case, however, suppose that policymakers wish to prevent equilibrium real GDP from changing in response to the oil price increase. Should they increase or decrease the quantity of money in circulation? Why? (See page 256.)

11-8. Based on your answers to Problems 11-6 and 11-7, can policymakers stabilize *both* the price level *and* real GDP simultaneously in response to a short-lived but sudden rise in oil prices? Explain briefly. (See page 256.)

11-9. Between early 2005 and late 2007, total planned expenditures by U.S. households substantially increased in response to an increase in the quantity of money in circulation. Explain, from a short-run Keynesian perspective, the predicted effects of this event on the equilibrium U.S. price level and equilibrium U.S. real GDP. Be sure to discuss the spending gap that the Keynesian model indicates would result in the short run. (See page 255.)

11-10. Between early 2008 and the beginning of 2009, a gradual stock-market downturn and plummeting home prices generated a substantial reduction in U.S. household wealth that induced most U.S. residents to reduce their planned real spending at any given price level. Explain, from a short-run Keynesian perspective, the predicted effects of this event on the equilibrium U.S. price level and equilibrium U.S. real GDP. Be sure to discuss the spending gap that the Keynesian model indicates would result in the short run. (See page 255.)

11-11. For each question that follows, suppose that the economy *begins* at point *A*. Identify which of the

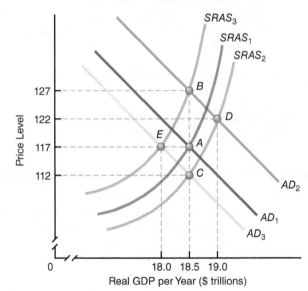

other points on the diagram—point *B*, *C*, *D*, or *E*—could represent a *new* short-run equilibrium after the described events take place and move the economy away from point *A*. Briefly explain your answers. (See pages 254–256.)

a. Most workers in this nation's economy are union members, and unions have successfully negotiated large wage boosts. At the same time, economic conditions suddenly worsen abroad, reducing real GDP and disposable income in other nations of the world.

b. A major hurricane has caused short-term halts in production at many firms and created major bottlenecks in the distribution of goods and services that had been produced prior to the storm. At the same time, the nation's central bank has significantly pushed up the rate of growth of the nation's money supply.

c. A strengthening of the value of this nation's currency in terms of other countries' currencies affects both the *SRAS* curve and the *AD* curve.

11-12. Consider an open economy in which the aggregate supply curve slopes upward in the short run. Firms in this nation do not import raw materials or any other productive inputs from abroad, but foreign residents purchase many of the nation's goods and services. What is the most likely short-run effect on this nation's economy if there is a significant downturn in economic activity in other nations around the world? (See page 255.)

REFERENCES

EXAMPLE: Are Higher Costs of Worker Benefits Keeping Unemployment High?

Bureau of Labor Statistics, "Employment Cost Index," 2014. (http://www.bls.gov/news.release/eci.toc.htm)

Federal Reserve Bank of St. Louis, FRED2, "Employment Cost Index," 2014. (http://research.stlouisfed.org/fred2/categories/4)

"Health Reform and Employment," *The Economist*, August 21, 2013.

POLICY EXAMPLE: Economic Policy Uncertainty as a Source of Shocks

Federal Reserve Bank of St. Louis, "Economic Policy Uncertainty Index for the United States," FRED2, 2014. (https://research.stlouisfed.org/fred2/series/USEPUINDXD)

William Galston, "Policy Uncertainty Paralyzes the Economy," *The Wall Street Journal*, September 24, 2013.

Ezra Klein, "Studies behind Austerity and Uncertainty," *The Washington Post*, April 30, 2013.

YOU ARE THERE: A Drought Suddenly Dries Up a Portion of U.S. Aggregate Supply

Jeff Beckham, "With Lakes Drying Up Businesses Are Parched," *The New York Times*, September 21, 2013.

Jim Carlton, "Decade of Drought Threatens West," *The Wall Street Journal*, August 16, 2013.

Adam Nagourney and Ian Lovett, "Severe Drought Has U.S. West Fearing Worst," *The New York Times*, February 1, 2014.

ISSUES & APPLICATIONS: How Do Large Firms Influence Macroeconomic Shocks?

Julian de Giovanni, Andrei Levchenko, and Isabelle Méjean, "The Role of Firms in Aggregate Fluctuations," Vox, November 16, 2013 (Summary of "Firms, Destinations, and Fluctuations," NBER Working Paper No. 20061, April 2014).

Michael Derby, "Large Firms Shield Consumers from Forex Volatility," *The Wall Street Journal*, February 11, 2013.

"The Goliaths," *The Economist*, June 22, 2013.

Pavel Losevsky/Fotolia

12 Consumption, Real GDP, and the Multiplier

LEARNING OBJECTIVES

After reading this chapter, you should be able to:

12.1 Explain the key determinants of consumption and saving in the Keynesian model

12.2 Identify the primary determinants of planned investment

12.3 Describe how equilibrium real GDP is established in the Keynesian model

12.4 Evaluate why autonomous changes in total planned expenditures have a multiplier effect on equilibrium real GDP

12.5 Understand the relationship between total planned expenditures and the aggregate demand curve

MyEconLab helps you master each objective and study more efficiently. See the end of the chapter for details.

The growth of spending on the part of U.S. households during the period of recovery following the 2007–2009 recession has been the slowest since the Great Depression of the 1930s. In particular, spending on services such as health care and insurance which typically accounts for about two-thirds of consumption expenditures, has been particularly slow to increase since the recession. By the time you have completed this chapter, you will have an understanding of the importance of household consumption spending in the traditional economic theory of the short-run determination of real GDP. In addition, you will be able to analyze the mechanism through which slowed growth of household spending on services has influenced the growth of equilibrium real GDP during the most recent economic recovery.

the share of real GDP allocated to real consumption spending by households is about 60 percent in Germany, 66 percent in the United Kingdom, and 70 percent in the United States, but less than 41 percent in China? In all of the world's nations, inflation-adjusted consumption spending on domestically produced final goods and services is a significant component of real GDP. In this chapter, you will learn how an understanding of households' real consumption spending and saving decisions can assist in evaluating fluctuations in any country's real GDP.

Determinants of Planned Consumption and Planned Saving

12.1 Explain the key determinants of consumption and saving in the Keynesian model

To contemplate the determinants of planned consumption and planned saving in the Keynesian tradition, we will assume that the short-run aggregate supply curve within the current range of real GDP is horizontal. That is, we assume that it is similar to Figure 11-6 on page 249. Thus, the equilibrium level of real GDP is demand determined. This is why Keynes wished to examine the elements of desired aggregate expenditures. Because of the Keynesian assumption of inflexible prices, inflation is not a concern in this analysis. Hence, real values are identical to nominal values.

Some Simplifying Assumptions in a Keynesian Model

To simplify the income determination model that follows, a number of assumptions are made:

1. Businesses pay no indirect taxes (for example, sales taxes).

2. Businesses distribute all of their profits to shareholders.

3. There is no depreciation (capital consumption allowance), so gross private domestic investment equals net investment.

4. The economy is closed—that is, there is no foreign trade.

Given all these simplifying assumptions, **real disposable income**, or after-tax real income, will be equal to real GDP minus net taxes—taxes paid less transfer payments received.

Real disposable income
Real GDP minus net taxes, or after-tax real income.

ANOTHER LOOK AT DEFINITIONS AND RELATIONSHIPS You can do only two things with a dollar of disposable income: Consume it or save it. If you consume it, it is gone forever. If you save the entire dollar, however, you will be able to consume it (and perhaps more if it earns interest) at some future time. That is the distinction between **consumption** and **saving**. Consumption is the act of using income for the purchase of consumption goods. **Consumption goods** are goods purchased by households for immediate satisfaction. (These also include services.) Consumption goods are such things as food and movies. By definition, whatever you do not consume you save and can consume at some time in the future.

Consumption
Spending on new goods and services to be used up out of a household's current income. Whatever is not consumed is saved. Consumption includes such things as buying food and going to a concert.

Saving
The act of not consuming all of one's current income. Whatever is not consumed out of spendable income is, by definition, saved. *Saving* is an action measured over time (a flow), whereas *savings* are a stock, an accumulation resulting from the act of saving in the past.

Stocks and Flows: The Difference between Saving and Savings It is important to distinguish between *saving* and *savings*. *Saving* is an action that occurs at a particular rate—for example, $40 per week or $2,080 per year. This rate is a flow. It is expressed per unit of time, usually a year. Implicitly, then, when we talk about saving, we talk about a *flow*, or rate, of saving. *Savings*, by contrast, are a *stock* concept, measured at a certain point or instant in time. Your current *savings* are the result of past *saving*. You may currently have *savings* of $8,000 that are the result of four years' *saving* at a rate of $2,000 per year. Consumption is also a flow concept. You consume from after-tax income at a certain rate per week, per month, or per year.

Consumption goods
Goods bought by households to use up, such as food and movies.

Relating Income to Saving and Consumption A dollar of take-home income can be allocated either to consumption or to saving. Realizing this, we can see the relationship among saving, consumption, and disposable income from the following expression:

$$\text{Consumption} + \text{saving} \equiv \text{disposable income}$$

This is called an *accounting identity*, meaning that it has to hold true at every moment in time. (To indicate that the relationship is always true, we use the $\equiv$ symbol.)

From this relationship, we can derive the following definition of saving:

$$\text{Saving} \equiv \text{disposable income} - \text{consumption}$$

Hence, saving is the amount of disposable income that is not spent to purchase consumption goods.

INVESTMENT SPENDING **Investment** is also a flow concept. As noted in Chapter 8, *investment* as used in economics differs from the common use of the term. In common speech, it is often used to describe putting funds into the stock market or real estate. In economic analysis, investment primarily is defined to include expenditures on new machines and buildings—**capital goods**—that are expected to yield a future stream of income. This is called *fixed investment*. We also include changes in business inventories in our definition. This we call *inventory investment*.

In the classical model discussed in Chapter 11 on pages 243–248, the supply of saving was determined by the rate of interest. Specifically, the higher the rate of interest, the more people wanted to save and consequently the less people wanted to consume.

In contrast, according to Keynes, the interest rate is *not* the most important determinant of an individual's real saving and consumption decisions. In his view, the flow of income, not the interest rate, is the main determinant of consumption and saving. MyEconLab Concept Check

How Income Flows Can Influence Consumption and Saving

When a person decides how much to consume and save today, Keynes reasoned, that individual must take into account both current and anticipated future incomes. After all, a higher income this year enables an individual *both* to purchase more final goods and services *and* to increase the flow of saving during the current year. Furthermore, a person's anticipation about the *future* flow of income likely influences how much of *current* income is allocated to consumption and how much to saving.

THE LIFE-CYCLE THEORY OF CONSUMPTION The most realistic and detailed theory of consumption, often called the **life-cycle theory of consumption**, considers how a person varies consumption and saving as income ebbs and flows during the course of an entire life span. This theory predicts that when an individual anticipates a higher income in the future, the individual will tend to consume more and save less in the current period than would have been the case otherwise. In contrast, when a person expects the flow of income to drop in the future, the individual responds in the present by allocating less of current income to consumption and more to saving.

THE PERMANENT INCOME HYPOTHESIS In a related theory, called the **permanent income hypothesis**, the income level that matters for a person's decision about current consumption and saving is *permanent income*, or expected average lifetime income. The permanent income hypothesis suggests that people increase their flow of consumption only if their anticipated average lifetime income rises. Thus, if a person's flow of income temporarily rises without an increase in average lifetime income, the person responds by saving the extra income and leaving consumption unchanged.

Investment
Spending on items such as machines and buildings, which can be used to produce goods and services in the future. (It also includes changes in business inventories.) The investment part of real GDP is the portion that will be used in the process of producing goods *in the future*.

Capital goods
Producer durables; nonconsumable goods that firms use to make other goods.

Life-cycle theory of consumption
A theory in which a person bases decisions about current consumption and saving on both current income and anticipated future income.

Permanent income hypothesis
A theory of consumption in which an individual determines current consumption based on anticipated average lifetime income.

THE KEYNESIAN THEORY OF CONSUMPTION AND SAVING Keynes recognized that expectations about future income could affect current consumption and saving decisions. For purposes of developing a basic theory of consumption and saving, however, Keynes focused solely on the relationship between current income and current consumption and saving. Thus:

> *Keynes argued that real consumption and saving decisions depend primarily on a household's current real disposable income.*

The relationship between planned real consumption expenditures of households and their current level of real disposable income has been called the **consumption function**. It shows how much all households plan to consume per year at each level of real disposable income per year. Columns (1) and (2) of Table 12-1 below illustrate a consumption function for a hypothetical household.

We see from Table 12-1 that as real disposable income rises, planned consumption also rises, but by a smaller amount, as Keynes suggested. Planned saving also increases with disposable income. Notice, however, that below an income of $60,000, the planned saving of this hypothetical household is actually negative. (See column 3.) The further that income drops below that level, the more the household engages in **dissaving**, either by going into debt or by using up some of its existing wealth.

GRAPHING THE NUMBERS We now graph the consumption and saving relationships presented in Table 12-1. In the upper part of Figure 12-1 on the next page, the vertical axis measures the level of planned real consumption per year, and the horizontal axis

Consumption function
The relationship between amount consumed and disposable income. A consumption function tells us how much people plan to consume at various levels of disposable income.

Dissaving
Negative saving; a situation in which spending exceeds income. Dissaving can occur when a household is able to borrow or use up existing assets.

TABLE 12-1

Real Consumption and Saving Schedules: A Hypothetical Case

Column 1 presents real disposable income from zero up to $120,000 per year. Column 2 indicates planned real consumption per year. Column 3 presents planned real saving per year. At levels of real disposable income below $60,000, planned real saving is negative. In column 4, we see the average propensity to consume, which is merely planned consumption divided by disposable income. Column 5 lists average propensity to save, which is planned saving divided by disposable income. Column 6 is the marginal propensity to consume, which shows the proportion of *additional* income that will be consumed. Finally, column 7 shows the proportion of *additional* income that will be saved, or the marginal propensity to save. (Δ represents "change in.")

Combination	(1) Real Disposable Income per Year (Y_d)	(2) Planned Real Consumption per Year (C)	(3) Planned Real Saving per Year ($S \equiv Y_d - C$) (1) − (2)	(4) Average Propensity to Consume ($APC \equiv C/Y_d$) (2) ÷ (1)	(5) Average Propensity to Save ($APS \equiv S/Y_d$) (3) ÷ (1)	(6) Marginal Propensity to Consume ($MPC \equiv \Delta C/\Delta Y_d$)	(7) Marginal Propensity to Save ($MPS \equiv \Delta S/\Delta Y_d$)
A	$ 0	$ 12,000	$−12,000	–	–	–	–
B	12,000	21,600	−9,600	1.8	−0.8	0.8	0.2
C	24,000	31,200	−7,200	1.3	−0.3	0.8	0.2
D	36,000	40,800	−4,800	1.133	−0.133	0.8	0.2
E	48,000	50,400	−2,400	1.05	−0.05	0.8	0.2
F	60,000	60,000	0	1.0	0.0	0.8	0.2
G	72,000	69,600	2,400	0.967	0.033	0.8	0.2
H	84,000	79,200	4,800	0.943	0.057	0.8	0.2
I	96,000	88,800	7,200	0.925	0.075	0.8	0.2
J	108,000	98,400	9,600	0.911	0.089	0.8	0.2
K	120,000	108,000	12,000	0.9	0.1	0.8	0.2

FIGURE 12-1

The Consumption and Saving Functions

If we plot the combinations of real disposable income and planned real consumption from columns 1 and 2 in Table 12-1 on the previous page, we get the consumption function.

At every point on the 45-degree line, a vertical line drawn to the income axis is the same distance from the origin as a horizontal line drawn to the consumption axis. Where the consumption function crosses the 45-degree line at *F*, we know that planned real consumption equals real disposable income and there is zero saving. The vertical distance between the 45-degree line and the consumption function measures the rate of real saving or dissaving at any given income level.

If we plot the relationship between column 1 (real disposable income) and column 3 (planned real saving) from Table 12-1 on the previous page, we arrive at the saving function shown in the lower part of this diagram. It is the complement of the consumption function presented above it.

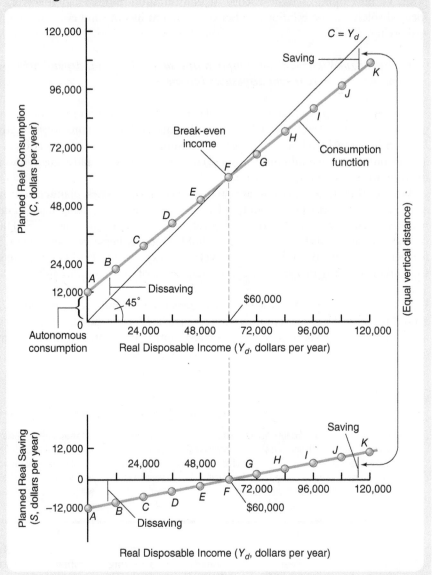

measures the level of real disposable income per year. In the lower part of the figure, the horizontal axis is again real disposable income per year, but now the vertical axis is planned real saving per year. All of these are on a dollars-per-year basis, which emphasizes the point that we are measuring flows, not stocks.

Consumption and Saving Functions As you can see, we have taken income-consumption and income-saving combinations *A* through *K* and plotted them. In the upper part of Figure 12-1 above, the result is called the *consumption function*. In the lower part, the result is called the *saving function*.

Mathematically, the saving function is the *complement* of the consumption function because consumption plus saving always equals disposable income. What is not consumed is, by definition, saved. The difference between actual disposable income and the planned rate of consumption per year *must* be the planned rate of saving per year.

The 45-Degree Reference Line How can we find the rate of saving or dissaving in the upper part of Figure 12-1? We begin by drawing a line that is equidistant from both the horizontal and the vertical axes. This line is 45 degrees from either axis and is often called the **45-degree reference line**. At every point on the 45-degree reference line, a vertical line drawn to the income axis is the same distance from the origin as a horizontal line drawn to the consumption axis. Thus, at point *F*, where the consumption function intersects the 45-degree line, real disposable income equals planned real consumption.

Point *F* is sometimes called the *break-even income point* because there is neither positive nor negative real saving. This can be seen in the lower part of Figure 12-1 as well. The planned annual rate of real saving at a real disposable income level of $60,000 is indeed zero.

DISSAVING AND AUTONOMOUS CONSUMPTION To the left of point *F* in either part of Figure 12-1, this hypothetical family engages in dissaving, either by going into debt or by consuming existing assets. The rate of real saving or dissaving in the upper part of the figure can be found by measuring the vertical distance between the 45-degree line and the consumption function. This simply tells us that if our hypothetical household sees its real disposable income fall to less than $60,000, it will not limit its consumption to this amount. It will instead go into debt or consume existing assets in some way to compensate for part of the lost income.

Autonomous Consumption Now look at the point on the diagram where real disposable income is zero but planned consumption is $12,000. This amount of real planned consumption, which does not depend at all on actual real disposable income, is called **autonomous consumption**. The autonomous consumption of $12,000 is *independent* of disposable income. That means that no matter how low the level of real income of our hypothetical household falls, the household will always attempt to consume at least $12,000 per year. (We are, of course, assuming here that the household's real disposable income does not equal zero year in and year out. There is certainly a limit to how long our hypothetical household could finance autonomous consumption without any income.)

The $12,000 of yearly consumption is determined by things other than the level of income. We don't need to specify what determines autonomous consumption. We merely state that it exists and that in our example it is $12,000 per year.

Autonomous consumption
The part of consumption that is independent of (does not depend on) the level of disposable income. Changes in autonomous consumption shift the consumption function.

The Meaning of Autonomous Spending Just remember that the word *autonomous* means "existing independently." In our model, autonomous consumption exists independently of the hypothetical household's level of real disposable income. (Later we will review some of the determinants of consumption other than real disposable income.)

There are many possible types of autonomous expenditures. Hypothetically, we can assume that investment is autonomous—independent of income. We can assume that government expenditures are autonomous. We will do just that at various times in our discussions to simplify our analysis of income determination.

AVERAGE PROPENSITY TO CONSUME AND TO SAVE Let's now go back to Table 12-1 on page 267, and this time let's look at columns 4 and 5: **average propensity to consume (APC)** and **average propensity to save (APS)**. They are defined as follows:

$$APC \equiv \frac{\text{real consumption}}{\text{real disposable income}}$$

$$APC \equiv \frac{\text{real saving}}{\text{real disposable income}}$$

Notice from column 4 in Table 12-1 that for this hypothetical household, the average propensity to consume decreases as real disposable income increases. This decrease simply means that the fraction of the household's real disposable income going to consumption falls as income rises. Column 5 shows that the average propensity to

Average propensity to consume (APC)
Real consumption divided by real disposable income. For any given level of real income, the proportion of total real disposable income that is consumed.

Average propensity to save (APS)
Real saving divided by real disposable income. For any given level of real income, the proportion of total real disposable income that is saved.

save, which at first is negative, finally hits zero at an income level of $60,000 and then becomes positive. In this example, the APS reaches a value of 0.1 at income level $120,000. This means that the household saves 10 percent of a $120,000 income.

It's quite easy for you to figure out your own average propensity to consume or to save. Just divide the value of what you consumed by your total real disposable income for the year, and the result will be your personal APC at your current level of income. Also, divide your real saving during the year by your real disposable income to calculate your own APS.

MARGINAL PROPENSITY TO CONSUME AND TO SAVE Now we go to the last two columns in Table 12-1 on page 267: **marginal propensity to consume (MPC)** and **marginal propensity to save (MPS)**. The term *marginal* refers to a small incremental or decremental change (represented by the Greek letter delta, Δ, in Table 12-1). The marginal propensity to consume, then, is defined as

$$\text{MPC} \equiv \frac{\text{change in real consumption}}{\text{change in real disposable income}}$$

The marginal propensity to save is defined similarly as

$$\text{MPS} \equiv \frac{\text{change in real saving}}{\text{change in real disposable income}}$$

Marginal propensity to consume (MPC)
The ratio of the change in consumption to the change in disposable income. A marginal propensity to consume of 0.8 tells us that an additional $100 in take-home pay will lead to an additional $80 consumed.

Marginal propensity to save (MPS)
The ratio of the change in saving to the change in disposable income. A marginal propensity to save of 0.2 indicates that out of an additional $100 in take-home pay, $20 will be saved. Whatever is not saved is consumed. The marginal propensity to save plus the marginal propensity to consume must always equal 1, by definition.

Marginal versus Average Propensities What do MPC and MPS tell you? They tell you what percentage of a given increase or decrease in real income will go toward consumption and saving, respectively. The emphasis here is on the word *change*. The marginal propensity to consume indicates how much you will change your planned real consumption if there is a change in your actual real disposable income.

If your marginal propensity to consume is 0.8, that does *not* mean that you consume 80 percent of *all* disposable income. The percentage of your total real disposable income that you consume is given by the average propensity to consume, or APC. As Table 12-1 on page 267 indicates, the APC is not equal to 0.8 anywhere in its column. Instead, an MPC of 0.8 means that you will consume 80 percent of any *increase* in your disposable income. Hence, the MPC cannot be less than zero or greater than one. It follows that households increase their planned real consumption by between 0 and 100 percent of any increase in real disposable income that they receive.

Distinguishing the MPC from the APC Consider a simple example in which we show the difference between the average propensity to consume and the marginal propensity to consume. Assume that your consumption behavior is exactly the same as our hypothetical household's behavior depicted in Table 12-1. You have an annual real disposable income of $108,000. Your planned consumption rate, then, from column 2 of Table 12-1 is $98,400. Your average propensity to consume, then, is $98,400/$108,000 = 0.911. Now suppose that at the end of the year, your boss gives you an after-tax bonus of $12,000.

What would you do with that additional $12,000 in real disposable income? According to the table, you would consume $9,600 of it and save $2,400. In that case, your *marginal* propensity to consume would be $9,600/$12,000 = 0.8 and your marginal propensity to save would be $2,400/$12,000 = 0.2. What would happen to your *average* propensity to consume? To find out, we add $9,600 to $98,400 of planned consumption, which gives us a new consumption rate of $108,000. The average propensity to consume is then $108,000 divided by the new higher salary of $120,000. Your APC drops from 0.911 to 0.9.

In contrast, your MPC remains, in our simplified example, 0.8 all the time. Look at column 6 in Table 12-1. The MPC is 0.8 at every level of income. (Therefore, the MPS is always equal to 0.2 at every level of income.) The constancy of MPC reflects the assumption that the amount you are willing to consume out of additional income will remain the same in percentage terms no matter what level of real disposable income is your starting point.

SOME RELATIONSHIPS Consumption plus saving must equal income. Both your total real disposable income and the change in total real disposable income are either consumed or saved. The sums of the proportions of either measure that are consumed and saved must equal 1, or 100 percent. This allows us to make the following statements:

$$APC + APS \equiv 1 \ (= 100 \text{ percent of total income})$$

$$MPC + MPS \equiv 1 \ (= 100 \text{ percent of the } \textit{change} \text{ income})$$

The average propensities as well as the marginal propensities to consume and save must total 1, or 100 percent. Check the two statements by adding the figures in columns 4 and 5 for each level of real disposable income in Table 12-1 on page 267. Do the same for columns 6 and 7.

How is total real consumption spending distributed across U.S. households?

EXAMPLE

The Distribution of U.S. Real Consumption Spending

Consistent with the Keynesian theory of real consumption expenditures, the average propensity to consume declines as household real disposable income rises. The average propensity to consume is lower for households receiving the highest levels of disposable income than for households with lower disposable incomes.

Nevertheless, the 20 percent of households receiving the highest real disposable incomes contribute about 38 percent of all U.S. real consumption expenditures. Recipients of the second-highest 20 percent of real disposable incomes contribute approximately 22 percent. The

60 percent of households with lower real disposable incomes account for the remaining 40 percent of real consumption spending.

FOR CRITICAL THINKING

What must be true about the average propensity to save for higher-income recipients compared with lower-income recipients? Explain briefly.

Sources are listed at the end of this chapter.

CAUSES OF SHIFTS IN THE CONSUMPTION FUNCTION A change in any other relevant economic variable besides real disposable income will cause the consumption function to shift. The number of such nonincome determinants of the position of the consumption function is almost unlimited. Real household **net wealth** is one determinant of the position of the consumption function. An increase in the real net wealth of the average household will cause the consumption function to shift upward. A decrease in real net wealth will cause it to shift downward. So far we have been talking about the consumption function of an individual or a household. Now let's move on to the national economy.

MyEconLab Concept Check
MyEconLab Study Plan

Net wealth
The stock of assets owned by a person, household, firm, or nation (net of any debts owed). For a household, net wealth can consist of a house, cars, personal belongings, stocks, bonds, bank accounts, and cash (minus any debts owed).

SELF CHECK Visit MyEconLab to practice these and other problems and to get instant feedback in your Study Plan.

_____ is a flow, something that occurs over time. It equals disposable income minus consumption. In contrast, _____ are a stock. They are the accumulation resulting from saving.

_____ is also a flow. It includes expenditures on new machines, buildings, and equipment and changes in business inventories.

The **consumption function** shows the relationship between planned rates of real consumption and real _____ _____ per year. The saving function is the complement of the consumption function because real saving plus real _____ must equal real disposable income.

The _____ propensity to consume is equal to real consumption divided by real disposable income. The

_____ propensity to save is equal to real saving divided by real disposable income.

The _____ propensity to consume is equal to the change in planned real consumption divided by the change in real disposable income. The _____ propensity to save is equal to the change in planned real saving divided by the change in real disposable income.

Any change in real disposable income will cause the planned rate of consumption to change. This is represented by a _____ _____ the consumption function. Any change in a nonincome determinant of consumption will cause a _____ _____ the consumption function.

12.2 Identify the primary determinants of planned investment

Determinants of Investment

Investment, you will remember, consists of expenditures on new buildings and equipment and changes in business inventories. Historically, real gross private domestic investment in the United States has been extremely volatile over the years, relative to real consumption. If we were to look at net private domestic investment (investment after depreciation has been deducted), we would see that in the depths of the Great Depression and at the peak of the World War II effort, the figure was negative. In other words, we were eating away at our capital stock—we weren't even maintaining it by fully replacing depreciated equipment.

If we compare real investment expenditures historically with real consumption expenditures, we find that the latter are less variable over time than the former. Why is this so? One possible reason is that the real investment decisions of businesses are based on highly variable, subjective estimates of how the economic future looks.

The Planned Investment Function

Consider that at all times, businesses perceive an array of investment opportunities. These investment opportunities have rates of return ranging from zero to very high, with the number (or dollar value) of all such projects increasing if the rate of return rises. Because a project is profitable only if its rate of return exceeds the opportunity cost of the investment—the rate of interest—it follows that as the interest rate falls, planned investment spending increases, and vice versa. Even if firms use retained earnings (internal financing) to fund an investment, the lower the market rate of interest, the smaller the *opportunity cost* of using those retained earnings.

Thus, it does not matter in our analysis whether the firm must seek financing from external sources or can obtain such financing by using retained earnings. Whatever the method of financing, as the interest rate falls, more investment opportunities will be profitable, and planned investment will be higher.

It should be no surprise, therefore, that the investment function is represented as an inverse relationship between the rate of interest and the value of planned real investment. In Figure 12-2 on the next page, a hypothetical investment schedule is given in panel (a) and plotted in panel (b). We see from this schedule that if, for example, the rate of interest is 5 percent, the dollar value of planned investment will be $2.8 trillion per year. Notice that planned investment is also given on a per-year basis, showing that it represents a flow, not a stock. (The stock counterpart of investment is the stock of capital in the economy measured in inflation-adjusted dollars at a point in time.)

U.S interest rates have been at historically low levels since 2008. What happened during a recent summer when interest rates suddenly rose slightly?

EXAMPLE

An Interest Rate Blip Flattens Spending

Following nearly five years of persistently very low interest rates, in the late spring of 2013 the general level interest rates increased by more than one-half of a percentage point. During the summer months that followed, real investment spending on construction of new structures decreased noticeably, and real investment expenditures on new equipment for plant facilities declined slightly.

When interest rates dropped back closer to prior levels later that summer, the flow of investment expenditures began to recover. By the end of the summer, the pace of investment spending had returned to its previous level.

FOR CRITICAL THINKING

Why might the desired flow of real investment expenditures be more sensitive to a one-half percentage-point increase when interest rates are in a range between 2 and 4 percent than when interest rates are in a range between 6 and 8 percent? (Hint: What proportionate change in the opportunity cost of real investment spending is a rise in the interest rate from 3 to 3.5 percent as compared with the proportionate change in the interest rate from 6 to 6.5 percent?)

Sources are listed at the end of this chapter.

FIGURE 12-2

Planned Real Investment

As shown in the hypothetical planned investment schedule in panel (a), the rate of planned real investment is inversely related to the rate of interest. If we plot the data pairs from panel (a), we obtain the investment function, *I*, in panel (b). It is negatively sloped.

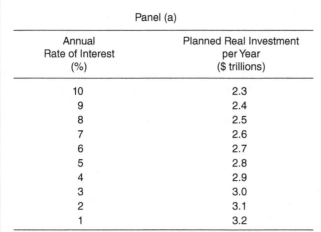

Panel (a)

Annual Rate of Interest (%)	Planned Real Investment per Year ($ trillions)
10	2.3
9	2.4
8	2.5
7	2.6
6	2.7
5	2.8
4	2.9
3	3.0
2	3.1
1	3.2

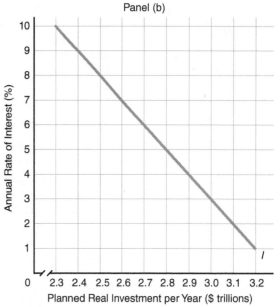

MyEconLab Concept Check

What Causes the Investment Function to Shift?

Because planned real investment is assumed to be a function of the rate of interest, any non-interest-rate variable that changes can have the potential of shifting the investment function. One of those variables is the expectations of businesses. If higher profits are expected, more machines and bigger plants will be planned for the future. More investment will be undertaken because of the expectation of higher profits. In this case, the investment function, *I*, in panel (b) of Figure 12-2, would shift outward to the right, meaning that more investment would be desired at all rates of interest.

Any change in productive technology can potentially shift the investment function. A positive change in productive technology would stimulate demand for additional capital goods and shift *I* outward to the right. Changes in business taxes can also shift the investment schedule. If they increase, we predict a leftward shift in the planned investment function because higher taxes imply a lower (after-tax) rate of return.

MyEconLab Concept Check
MyEconLab Study Plan

The planned investment schedule shows the relationship between real investment and the _____ _____; it slopes _____.

The non-interest-rate determinants of planned investment are _____, innovation and technological changes, and _____ _____.

Any change in the non-interest-rate determinants of planned investment will cause a _____ _____ the planned investment function so that at each and every rate of interest a different amount of planned investment will be made.

12.3 Describe how equilibrium real GDP is established in the Keynesian model

Determining Equilibrium Real GDP

We are interested in determining the equilibrium level of real GDP per year. When we examined the consumption function earlier in this chapter, however, it related planned real consumption expenditures to the level of real disposable income per year. We have already shown where adjustments must be made to GDP in order to get real disposable income (see Table 8-2 on page 183). Real disposable income turns out to be less than real GDP because real net taxes (real taxes minus real government transfer payments) are usually about 14 to 21 percent of GDP. A representative average is about 18 percent, so disposable income, on average, has in recent years been around 82 percent of GDP.

Consumption as a Function of Real GDP

To simplify our model, assume that real disposable income, Y_d, differs from real GDP by the same absolute amount every year. Therefore, we can relatively easily substitute real GDP for real disposable income in the consumption function.

We can now plot any consumption function on a diagram in which the horizontal axis is no longer real disposable income but rather real GDP, as in Figure 12-3 below. Notice that there is an autonomous part of real consumption that is so labeled. The difference between this graph and the graphs presented earlier in this chapter is the change in the horizontal axis from real disposable income to real GDP per year. For the rest of this chapter, assume that the MPC out of real GDP equals 0.8, so that 20 percent of changes in real disposable income is saved. Of an additional after-tax $100 earned, an additional $80 will be consumed.   MyEconLab Concept Check

The 45-Degree Reference Line

As in the earlier graphs, Figure 12-3 below shows a 45-degree reference line. The 45-degree line bisects the quadrant into two equal spaces. Thus, along the 45-degree reference line, planned real consumption expenditures, C, equal real GDP per year, Y. One can see, then, that at any point where the consumption function intersects the

---

FIGURE 12-3

Consumption as a Function of Real GDP

This consumption function shows the rate of planned expenditures for each level of real GDP per year. Autonomous consumption is $0.2 trillion. Along the 45-degree reference line, planned real consumption expenditures per year, C, are identical to real GDP per year, Y. The consumption curve intersects the 45-degree reference line at a value of $1 trillion per year in base-year dollars (the value of current GDP expressed in prices in a base year).

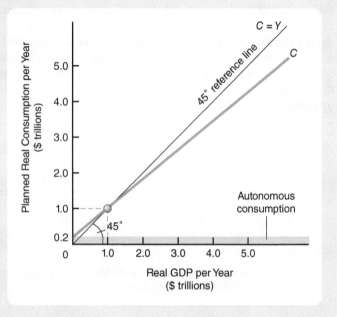

45-degree reference line, planned real consumption expenditures will be exactly equal to real GDP per year, or $C = Y$.

Note that in this graph, because we are looking only at planned real consumption on the vertical axis, the 45-degree reference line is where planned real consumption, C, is always equal to real GDP per year, Y. Later, when we add real investment, government spending, and net exports to the graph, *all* planned real expenditures will be labeled along the vertical axis. In any event, real consumption and real GDP are equal at $1 trillion per year. That is where the consumption curve, C, intersects the 45-degree reference line. At that GDP level, all real GDP is consumed.   MyEconLab Concept Check

Adding the Investment Function

Another component of private aggregate demand is, of course, real investment spending, I. We have already looked at the planned investment function, which related real investment, which includes changes in inventories of final products, to the rate of interest.

PLANNED INVESTMENT AND THE INTEREST RATE In panel (a) of Figure 12-4 below, you see that at an interest rate of 5 percent, the rate of real investment is $2.8 trillion per year. The $2.8 trillion of real investment per year is *autonomous* with respect to real GDP— that is, it is independent of real GDP.

In other words, given that we have a determinant investment level of $2.8 trillion at a 5 percent rate of interest, we can treat this level of real investment as constant, regardless of the level of GDP. This is shown in panel (b) of Figure 12-4. The vertical distance of real investment spending is $2.8 trillion. Businesses plan on investing a particular amount—$2.8 trillion per year—and will do so no matter what the level of real GDP.

COMBINING PLANNED INVESTMENT AND CONSUMPTION How do we add this amount of real investment spending to our consumption function? We simply add a line above the C line that we drew in Figure 12-3 on the previous page that is higher by the vertical

---

FIGURE 12-4

Combining Consumption and Investment

In panel (a), we show that at an interest rate of 5 percent, real investment is equal to $2.8 trillion per year. In panel (b), investment is a constant $2.8 trillion per year. When we add this amount to the consumption line, we obtain in panel (c) the $C + I$ line, which is vertically higher than the C line by exactly $2.8 trillion. Real GDP is equal to $C + I$ at $15 trillion per year where total planned real expenditures, $C + I$, are equal to actual real GDP, for this is where the $C + I$ line intersects the 45-degree reference line, on which $C + I$ is equal to Y at every point. (For simplicity, we ignore the fact that the dependence of saving on income can influence investment.)

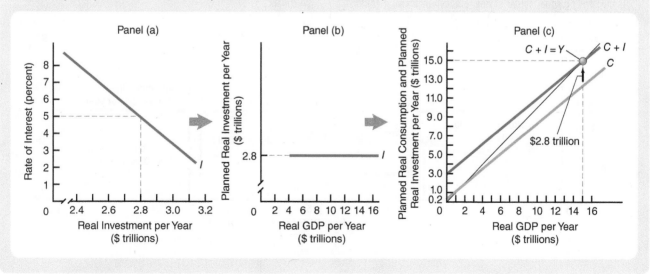

distance equal to $2.8 trillion of autonomous real investment spending. This is shown by the arrow in panel (c) of Figure 12-4 on the previous page.

Our new line, now labeled $C + I$, is called the *consumption plus investment line*. In our simple economy without real government expenditures and net exports, the $C + I$ curve represents total planned real expenditures as they relate to different levels of real GDP per year. Because the 45-degree reference line shows all the points where planned real expenditures (now $C + I$) equal real GDP, we label it $C + I = Y$. Thus, in equilibrium, the sum of consumption spending (C) and investment spending (I) equals real GDP (Y), which is $15 trillion per year. Equilibrium occurs when total planned real expenditures equal real GDP (given that any amount of production of goods and services in this model in the short run can occur without a change in the price level).   MyEconLab Concept Check

Saving and Investment: Planned versus Actual

Figure 12-5 below shows the planned investment curve as a horizontal line at $2.8 trillion per year in base-year dollars. Real investment is completely autonomous in this simplified model—it does not depend on real GDP.

The planned saving curve is represented by S. Because in our model whatever is not consumed is, by definition, saved, the planned saving schedule is the complement of the planned consumption schedule, represented by the C line in Figure 12-3 on page 274. For better exposition, we look at only a part of the saving and investment schedules—annual levels of real GDP between $13 trillion and $17 trillion.

Why does equilibrium have to occur at the intersection of the planned saving and planned investment schedules? If we are at E in Figure 12-5, planned saving equals planned investment. All anticipations are validated by reality. There is no tendency for businesses to alter the rate of production or the level of employment because they are neither increasing nor decreasing their inventories in an unplanned way.

UNPLANNED CHANGES IN BUSINESS INVENTORIES If real GDP is $17 trillion instead of $15 trillion, planned investment, as usual, is $2.8 trillion per year. It is exceeded, however, by planned saving, which is $3.2 trillion per year.

MyEconLab Animation

FIGURE 12-5

Planned and Actual Rates of Saving and Investment

Only at the equilibrium level of real GDP of $15 trillion per year will planned saving equal actual saving, planned investment equal actual investment, and hence planned saving equal planned investment.

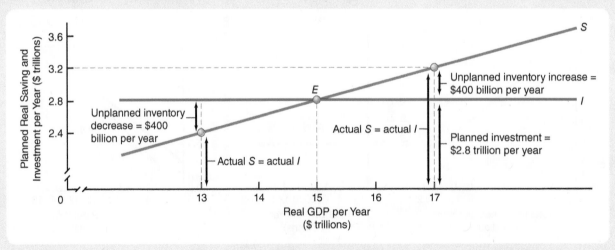

A Mismatch between Actual and Anticipated Purchases The additional $0.4 trillion ($400 billion) in saving by households over and above planned investment represents less consumption spending. The fact that consumption is lower than planned will translate into unsold goods that accumulate as unplanned business inventory investment.

Thus, consumers will *actually* purchase fewer goods and services than businesses had *planned*. This will leave firms with unsold products, and their inventories will begin to rise above the levels they had planned.

How Businesses Adjust Unplanned business inventories will now rise at the rate of $400 billion per year, or $3.2 trillion in actual investment (including inventories) minus $2.8 trillion in planned investment by firms that had not anticipated an inventory buildup. This situation, though, cannot continue for long. Businesses will respond to the unplanned increase in inventories by cutting back production of goods and services and reducing employment, and we will move toward a lower level of real GDP.

Naturally, the adjustment process works in reverse if real GDP is less than the equilibrium level. For instance, if real GDP is $13 trillion per year, an unintended inventory decrease of $0.4 trillion ultimately brings about an increase in real GDP toward the equilibrium level of $15 trillion.

Every time the saving rate planned by households differs from the investment rate planned by businesses, there will be a shrinkage or an expansion in the circular flow of income and output (introduced in Chapter 8) in the form of unplanned inventory changes. Real GDP and employment will change until unplanned inventory changes are again zero—that is, until we have attained the equilibrium level of real GDP.

MyEconLab Concept Check
MyEconLab Study Plan

SELF CHECK Visit MyEconLab to practice these and other problems and to get instant feedback in your Study Plan.

We assume that the consumption function has an _____ part that is independent of the level of real GDP per year. It is labeled "_____ consumption."

For simplicity, we assume that real investment is _____ with respect to real GDP and therefore unaffected by the level of real GDP per year.

The _____ level of real GDP can be found where planned saving equals planned investment.

Whenever planned saving exceeds planned investment, there will be unplanned inventory _____, and real GDP will fall as producers cut production of goods and services. Whenever planned saving is less than planned investment, there will be unplanned inventory _____, and real GDP will rise as producers increase production of goods and services.

Keynesian Equilibrium with Government and the Foreign Sector Added

12.4 Evaluate why autonomous changes in total planned expenditures have a multiplier effect on equilibrium real GDP

To this point, we have ignored the role of government in our model. We have also left out the foreign sector of the economy. Let's think about what happens when we also consider these as elements of the model.

Government

To add real government spending, *G*, to our macroeconomic model, we assume that the level of resource-using government purchases of goods and services (federal, state, and local), *not* including transfer payments, is determined by the political process. In other words, *G* will be considered autonomous, just like real investment (and a certain relatively small component of real consumption). In the United States, resource-using federal government expenditures account for almost 20 percent of real GDP.

The other side of the coin, of course, is that there are real taxes, which are used to pay for much of government spending. We will simplify our model greatly by assuming

TABLE 12-2

The Determination of Equilibrium Real GDP with Government and Net Exports Added

Figures are trillions of dollars.

(1) Real GDP	(2) Real Taxes	(3) Real Disposable Income	(4) Planned Real Consumption	(5) Planned Real Saving	(6) Planned Real Investment	(7) Real Government Spending	(8) Real Net Exports (exports minus imports)	(9) Total Planned Real Expenditures	(10) Unplanned Inventory Changes	(11) Direction of Change in Real GDP
12.0	3.2	8.8	7.6	1.2	2.8	3.2	−0.4	13.0	−1.2	Increase
13.0	3.2	9.8	8.4	1.4	2.8	3.2	−0.4	14.0	−1.0	Increase
14.0	3.2	10.8	9.2	1.6	2.8	3.2	−0.4	14.8	−0.8	Increase
15.0	3.2	11.8	10.0	1.8	2.8	3.2	−0.4	15.6	−0.6	Increase
16.0	3.2	12.8	10.8	2.0	2.8	3.2	−0.4	13.4	−0.4	Increase
17.0	3.2	13.8	11.6	2.2	2.8	3.2	−0.4	14.2	−0.2	Increase
18.0	3.2	14.8	12.4	2.4	2.8	3.2	−0.4	18.0	0	Neither (equilibrium)
19.0	3.2	15.8	13.2	2.6	2.8	3.2	−0.4	15.8	+0.2	Decrease
20.0	3.2	16.8	14.0	2.8	2.8	3.2	−0.4	16.6	+0.4	Decrease

Lump-sum tax

A tax that does not depend on income. An example is a $1,000 tax that every household must pay, irrespective of its economic situation.

that there is a constant **lump-sum tax** of $3.2 trillion a year to finance $3.2 trillion of government spending. This lump-sum tax will reduce disposable income by the same amount. We show this above in Table 12-2 (column 2) above, where we give the numbers for a complete model.   MyEconLab Concept Check

The Foreign Sector

For years, the media have focused attention on the nation's foreign trade deficit. We have been buying merchandise and services from foreign residents—real imports—the value of which exceeds the value of the real exports we have been selling to them. The difference between real exports and real imports is *real net exports*, which we will label X in our graphs. The level of real exports depends on international economic conditions, especially in the countries that buy our products. Real imports depend on economic conditions here at home. For simplicity, assume that real imports exceed real exports (real net exports, X, is negative) and furthermore that the level of real net exports is autonomous—independent of real national income. Assume a level of X of –$0.4 trillion per year, as shown in column 8 of Table 12-2 above.   MyEconLab Concept Check

Determining the Equilibrium Level of GDP per Year

We are now in a position to determine the equilibrium level of real GDP per year under the continuing assumptions that the price level is unchanging; that investment, government, and the foreign sector are autonomous; and that planned consumption expenditures are determined by the level of real GDP. As can be seen in Table 12-2, total planned real expenditures of $18 trillion per year equal real GDP of $18 trillion per year, and this is where we reach equilibrium.

Remember that equilibrium *always* occurs when total planned real expenditures equal real GDP. Now look at Figure 12-6 on the next page, which shows the equilibrium

FIGURE 12-6

The Equilibrium Level of Real GDP

The consumption function, with no government and thus no taxes, is shown as C. When we add autonomous investment, government spending, and net exports, we obtain $C + I + G + X$. We move from E_1 to E_2. Equilibrium real GDP is $18 trillion per year.

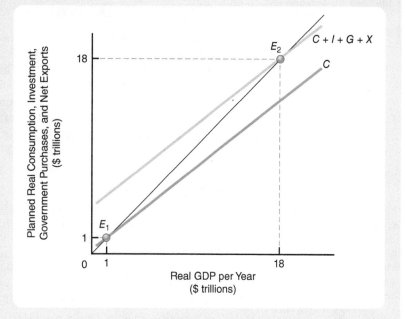

level of real GDP. There are two curves: one showing the consumption function, which is the exact duplicate of the one as it was in Figure 12-3 on page 274, before we added the government and taxes, and the other being the $C + I + G + X$ curve, which intersects the 45-degree reference line (representing equilibrium) at $18 trillion per year.

Whenever total planned real expenditures differ from real GDP, there are unplanned inventory changes. When total planned real expenditures are greater than real GDP, inventory levels drop in an unplanned manner. To get inventories back up, firms seek to expand their production of goods and services, which increases real GDP. Real GDP rises toward its equilibrium level. Whenever total planned real expenditures are less than real GDP, the opposite occurs. There are unplanned inventory increases, causing firms to cut back on their production of goods and services in an effort to push inventories back down to planned levels. The result is a drop in real GDP toward the equilibrium level.

MyEconLab Concept Check
MyEconLab Study Plan

SELF CHECK Visit MyEconLab to practice these and other problems and to get instant feedback in your Study Plan.

When we add autonomous investment, I, and autonomous government spending, G, to the consumption function, we obtain the $C + I + G$ curve, which represents total _____ _____ for a closed economy. In an open economy, we add the foreign sector, which consists of exports minus imports, or net exports, X. Total planned expenditures are thus represented by the $C + I + G + X$ curve.

Equilibrium real GDP can be found by locating the intersection of the total planned real expenditures curve with the _____-_____ reference line. At that level of

real GDP per year, planned real consumption plus planned real investment plus real government expenditures plus real net exports will equal real GDP.

Whenever total planned real expenditures exceed real GDP, there will be unplanned _____ in inventories. Production of goods and services will increase, and a higher level of equilibrium real GDP will prevail. Whenever total planned real expenditures are less than real GDP, there will be unplanned _____ in inventories. Production of goods and services will decrease, and equilibrium real GDP will decrease.

12.5 Understand the relationship between total planned expenditures and the aggregate demand curve

The Multiplier, Total Expenditures, and Aggregate Demand

Look again at panel (c) of Figure 12-4 on page 275. Assume for the moment that the only real expenditures included in real GDP are real consumption expenditures. Where would the equilibrium level of real GDP be in this case? It would be where the consumption function (C) intersects the 45-degree reference line, which is at $1 trillion per year. Now we add the autonomous amount of planned real investment, $2.8 trillion, and then determine what the new equilibrium level of real GDP will be. It turns out to be $15 trillion per year. Adding $2.8 trillion per year of investment spending increased equilibrium real GDP by *five* times that amount, or by $14 trillion per year.

The Multiplier Effect

What is operating here is the multiplier effect of changes in autonomous spending. The **multiplier** is the number by which a permanent change in autonomous real investment or autonomous real consumption is multiplied to get the change in the equilibrium level of real GDP. Any permanent increases in autonomous real investment or in any autonomous component of consumption will cause an even larger increase in real GDP. Any permanent decreases in autonomous real spending will cause even larger decreases in real GDP per year. To understand why this multiple expansion (or contraction) in equilibrium real GDP occurs, let's look at a simple numerical example.

Multiplier
The ratio of the change in the equilibrium level of real GDP to the change in autonomous real expenditures. The number by which a change in autonomous real investment or autonomous real consumption, for example, is multiplied to get the change in equilibrium real GDP.

AN EXAMPLE We'll use the same figures we used for the marginal propensity to consume and to save. MPC will equal 0.8, or $\frac{4}{5}$ and MPS will equal 0.2, or $\frac{1}{5}$ Now let's run an experiment and say that businesses decide to increase planned real investment permanently by $100 billion a year.

We see in Table 12-3 below that during what we'll call the first round in column 1, investment is increased by $100 billion. This also means an increase in real GDP of

MyEconLab Animation

TABLE 12-3

The Multiplier Process

We trace the effects of a *permanent* $100 billion increase in autonomous real investment spending on real GDP per year. If we assume a marginal propensity to consume of 0.8, such an increase will eventually elicit a $500 billion increase in equilibrium real GDP per year.

	Assumption: MPC = 0.8, or $\frac{4}{5}$		
(1) Round	(2) Annual Increase in Real GDP ($ billions)	(3) Annual Increase in Planned Real Consumption ($ billions)	(4) Annual Increase in Planned Real Saving ($ billions)
1 ($100 billion per year increase in I)	100.00 → 80.000	80.000	20.000
2	80.00 ← → 64.000	64.000	16.000
3	64.00 ← → 51.200	51.200	12.800
4	51.20 ← → 40.960	40.960	10.240
5	40.96 ← → 32.768	32.768	8.192
.	.	.	.
.	.	.	.
.	.	.	.
All later rounds	163.84	131.072	32.768
Totals	500.00	400.000	100.000

$100 billion, because the spending by one group represents income for another, shown in column 2. Column 3 gives the resultant increase in consumption by households that received this additional $100 billion in income. This rise in consumption spending is found by multiplying the MPC by the increase in real GDP. Because the MPC equals 0.8, real consumption expenditures during the first round will increase by $80 billion.

THE MULTIPLIER PROCESS That's not the end of the story, however. This additional household consumption is also spending, and it will provide $80 billion of additional income for other individuals. Thus, during the second round, we see an increase in real GDP of $80 billion. Now, out of this increased real GDP, what will be the resultant increase in consumption expenditures? It will be 0.8 times $80 billion, or $64 billion.

We continue these induced expenditure rounds and find that an initial increase in autonomous investment expenditures of $100 billion will eventually cause the equilibrium level of real GDP to increase by $500 billion. A permanent $100 billion increase in autonomous real investment spending has induced an additional $400 billion increase in real consumption spending, for a total increase in real GDP of $500 billion. In other words, equilibrium real GDP will change by an amount equal to five times the change in real investment.

WHAT IF...

> the government tried to generate a multiplier-boosted increase in the equilibrium annual level of real GDP by engaging in greater spending financed by taxing private consumption and investment?

It is possible that this government policy action might lead to a net upward shift in the C + I + G + X curve and thereby an increase in equilibrium real GDP. Nevertheless, taxing private consumption would reduce autonomous real consumption spending and shift the C + I + G + X curve in a downward direction. Taxing private real investment expenditures likewise would reduce desired investment spending and consequently would shift the C + I + G + X curve downward as well. Consequently, taxing private real consumption and investment expenditures to fund the government's increased real spending would tend to undermine the desired multiplier effect on real GDP.

MyEconLab Concept Check

The Multiplier Formula

It turns out that the autonomous spending multiplier is equal to 1 divided by the marginal propensity to save. In our example, the MPC was 0.8, or $\frac{4}{5}$. Therefore, because MPC + MPS = 1, the MPS was equal to 0.2, or $\frac{1}{5}$. When we divide 1 by $\frac{1}{5}$ we get 5. That was our multiplier. A $100 billion increase in real planned investment led to a $500 billion increase in the equilibrium level of real GDP. Our multiplier will always be the following:

$$\text{Multiplier} \equiv \frac{1}{1 - \text{MPC}} \equiv \frac{1}{\text{MPS}}$$

DETERMINING THE MULTIPLIER WITH EITHER MPC OR MPS You can always figure out the multiplier if you know either the MPC or the MPS. Let's consider an example. If MPS = 0.25, or $\frac{1}{4}$,

$$\text{Multiplier} = \frac{1}{\frac{1}{4}} = 4$$

Because MPC + MPS = 1, it follows that MPS = 1 − MPC. Hence, we can always figure out the multiplier if we are given the marginal propensity to consume. In this example, if the marginal propensity to consume is given as 0.75, or $\frac{3}{4}$

$$\text{Multiplier} = \frac{1}{1 - \frac{3}{4}} = \frac{1}{\frac{1}{4}} = 4$$

HOW THE VALUES OF MPC AND MPS AFFECT THE MULTIPLIER By taking a few numerical examples, you can demonstrate to yourself an important property of the multiplier:

The smaller the marginal propensity to save, the larger the multiplier.

Otherwise stated:

The larger the marginal propensity to consume, the larger the multiplier.

Demonstrate this to yourself by computing the multiplier when the marginal propensity to save equals $\frac{3}{4}$, $\frac{1}{2}$, and $\frac{1}{4}$. What happens to the multiplier as the MPS gets smaller?

When you have the multiplier, the following formula will then give you the change in equilibrium real GDP due to a permanent change in autonomous spending:

Change in equilibrium real GDP = multiplier × change in autonomous spending

The multiplier, as noted earlier, works for a permanent increase or a permanent decrease in autonomous spending per year. In our earlier example, if the autonomous component of real consumption had fallen permanently by $100 billion, the reduction in equilibrium real GDP would have been $500 billion per year. MyEconLab Concept Check

Significance of the Multiplier

Depending on the size of the multiplier, it is possible that a relatively small change in planned investment or in autonomous consumption can trigger a much larger change in equilibrium real GDP per year. In essence, the multiplier magnifies the fluctuations in yearly equilibrium real GDP initiated by changes in autonomous spending.

As was just noted, the larger the marginal propensity to consume, the larger the multiplier. If the marginal propensity to consume is $\frac{1}{2}$, the multiplier is 2. In that case, a $1 billion decrease in (autonomous) real investment will elicit a $2 billion decrease in equilibrium real GDP per year. Conversely, if the marginal propensity to consume is $\frac{9}{10}$, the multiplier will be 10. That same $1 billion decrease in planned real investment expenditures with a multiplier of 10 will lead to a $10 billion decrease in equilibrium real GDP per year.

Is there evidence of multiplier effects of real-world changes in autonomous spending?

POLICY EXAMPLE

Evidence of a Multiplier Effect in Federal Highway Spending

A number of economists contend that government spending on so-called infrastructure investments in roads, bridges, and other physical structures are particularly likely to exert multiplier effects. For one thing, the economists argue, these forms of spending are unlikely to replace any private real expenditures, because private firms rarely build and operate their own roads and bridges. In addition, the expenditures generate real disposable income for construction firms and their workers, whose consumption then generates real disposable income for others throughout the surrounding areas.

A study by Federal Reserve Bank of San Francisco economists Sylvain Leduc and Daniel Wilson offers evidence supporting this position. They find that each additional dollar of federal highway grants provided to state governments to spend on highway construction generates at least two dollars in overall additional spending. Thus, their analysis indicates that federal grants for highway infrastructure spending exert a multiplier effect equal to two times the initial federal expenditure.

FOR CRITICAL THINKING

Why is a federal grant to a state to build hospital facilities that private firms otherwise might have built less likely to generate any multiplier effect—and perhaps no net additional effect—on equilibrium real GDP?

Sources are listed at the end of this chapter.

FIGURE 12-7

Effect of a Rise in Autonomous Spending on Equilibrium Real GDP

A $100 billion increase in autonomous spending (investment, government, or net exports) moves AD_1 to AD_2. If the price index increases from 110 to 115, equilibrium real GDP goes up only to, say, $18.3 trillion per year instead of $18.5 trillion per year.

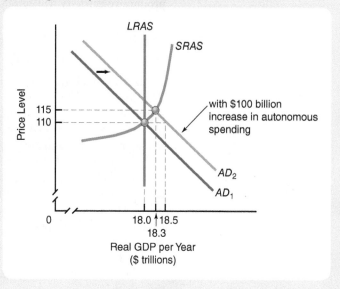

How a Change in Real Autonomous Spending Affects Real GDP When the Price Level Can Change

So far, our examination of how changes in real autonomous spending affect equilibrium real GDP has considered a situation in which the price level remains unchanged. Thus, our analysis has indicated only how much the aggregate demand curve shifts in response to a change in investment, government spending, net exports, or lump-sum taxes.

TAKING AGGREGATE SUPPLY INTO CONSIDERATION Of course, when we take into account the aggregate supply curve, we must also consider responses of the equilibrium price level to a multiplier-induced change in aggregate demand. We do so in Figure 12-7 above.

The intersection of AD_1 and $SRAS$ is at a price level of 110 with equilibrium real GDP of $18 trillion per year. An increase in autonomous spending shifts the aggregate demand curve outward to the right to AD_2. If the price level remained at 110, the short-run equilibrium level of real GDP would increase to $18.5 trillion per year because, for the $100 billion increase in autonomous spending, the multiplier would be 5, as it was in Table 12-3 on page 280.

ACCOUNTING FOR A PRICE LEVEL CHANGE The price level does not stay fixed, however, because ordinarily the $SRAS$ curve is positively sloped. In this diagram, the new short-run equilibrium level of real GDP is hypothetically $18.3 trillion. The ultimate effect on real GDP is smaller than the multiplier effect on nominal income because part of the additional income is used to pay higher prices. Not all is spent on additional goods and services, as is the case when the price level is fixed.

If the economy is at an equilibrium level of real GDP that is greater than $LRAS$, the implications for the eventual effect on real GDP are even more severe. Look again at Figure 12-7 above. The $SRAS$ curve starts to slope upward more dramatically after $18 trillion of real GDP per year. Therefore, any increase in aggregate demand will lead to a proportionally greater increase in the price level and a smaller increase in equilibrium real GDP per year. The ultimate effect on real GDP of any increase in autonomous spending will be relatively small because most of the changes will be in the price level. Moreover, any increase in the short-run equilibrium level of real GDP will tend to be temporary because the economy is temporarily above *LRAS*—the strain on its productive capacity will raise the price level.   MyEconLab Concept Check

The Relationship between Aggregate Demand and the *C + I + G + X* Curve

A relationship clearly exists between the aggregate demand curves that you studied in Chapters 10 and 11 and the *C + I + G + X* curve developed in this chapter. After all, aggregate demand consists of consumption, investment, and government purchases, plus the foreign sector of our economy. There is a major difference, however, between the aggregate demand curve, *AD*, and the *C + I + G + X* curve: The latter is drawn with the price level held constant, whereas the former is drawn, by definition, with the price level changing. To derive the aggregate demand curve from the *C + I + G + X* curve, we must now allow the price level to change. Look at the upper part of Figure 12-8 below. Here we see the *C + I + G + X* curve at a price level equal to 100, and at $18 trillion of real GDP per year, planned real expenditures exactly equal real GDP. This gives us point *A* in the lower graph, for it shows what real GDP would be at a price level of 100.

Now let's assume that in the upper graph, the price level increases to 125. What are the effects?

FIGURE 12-8

The Relationship between *AD* and the *C + I + G + X* Curve

In the upper graph, the *C + I + G + X* curve at a price level equal to 100 intersects the 45-degree reference line at E_1, or $18 trillion of real GDP per year. That gives us point *A* (price level = 100; real GDP = $18 trillion) in the lower graph. When the price level increases to 125, the *C + I + G + X* curve shifts downward, and the new level of real GDP at which planned real expenditures equal real GDP is at E_2 at $16 trillion per year. This gives us point *B* in the lower graph. Connecting points *A* and *B*, we obtain the aggregate demand curve.

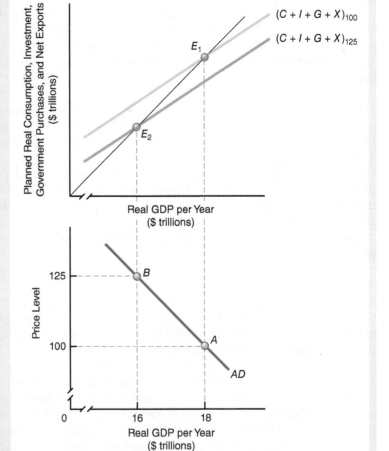

1. A higher price level can decrease the purchasing power of any cash that people hold (the real-balance effect). This is a decrease in real wealth, and it causes consumption expenditures, C, to fall, thereby putting downward pressure on the $C + I + G + X$ curve.

2. Because individuals attempt to borrow more to replenish their real cash balances, interest rates will rise, which will make it more costly for people to buy houses and cars (the interest rate effect). Higher interest rates also make it less profitable to install new equipment and to erect new buildings. Therefore, the rise in the price level indirectly causes a reduction in total planned spending on goods and services.

3. In an open economy, our higher price level causes foreign spending on our goods to fall (the open economy effect). Simultaneously, it increases our demand for others' goods. If the foreign exchange price of the dollar stays constant for a while, there will be an increase in imports and a decrease in exports, thereby reducing the size of X, again putting downward pressure on the $C + I + G + X$ curve.

The result is that a new $C + I + G + X$ curve at a price level equal to 125 generates an equilibrium at E_2 at \$16 trillion of real GDP per year. This gives us point B in the lower part of Figure 12-8 on the previous page. When we connect points A and B, we obtain the aggregate demand curve, AD.

MyEconLab Concept Check
MyEconLab Study Plan

SELF CHECK Visit MyEconLab to practice these and other problems and to get instant feedback in your Study Plan.

Any change in autonomous spending shifts the expenditure curve and causes a _____ effect on equilibrium real GDP per year.

The **multiplier** is equal to 1 divided by the _____ propensity to _____.

The smaller the marginal propensity to _____, the larger the **multiplier**. Otherwise stated, the larger the marginal propensity to _____, the larger the **multiplier**.

The $C + I + G + X$ curve is drawn with the price level held constant, whereas the AD curve allows the price level to _____. Each different price level generates a new $C + I + G + X$ curve.

YOU ARE THERE

Hukou's Depressing Effect on Autonomous Consumption in China

Wei Yinping, a 26-year-old worker at a watchband factory in the city of Shenzhen, China, saves about half of her monthly after-tax income. She saves such a large portion of her disposable income because she is one of China's 230 million residents classified by the government's *hukou* registration system as a rural dweller instead of as a resident of Shenzhen. Under the *hukou* system, which has its 4,000-year-old roots in the Xia Dynasty but was established in its current form in 1949, Yinping is officially classified as a resident of the rural area where she was born. As a consequence, even though she pays taxes like any other city resident, she is not eligible for city services, including health care services. "If I had a local *hukou* [classification]," Yinping says, "I would have many social security benefits and would not have to save so much."

Economists agree that most young and healthy city residents such as Yinping save more than is really required, on average, to cover the actual costs of services from which the *hukou* system excludes access. Thus, at every level of real disposable income, these people save more than they would in the absence of the *hukou* system, which artificially reduces the nation's annual level of autonomous consumption spending. In this way, the hukou system artificially shifts China's consumption function downward.

CRITICAL THINKING QUESTIONS

1. If the *hukou* system were ended, what would happen to China's $C + I + G + X$ curve?

2. Why do you think some economists argue that the hukou system artificially depresses China's equilibrium annual real GDP?

Sources are listed at the end of this chapter.

ISSUES & APPLICATIONS

MyEconLab Video

A Recovery Hampered by Meager Spending on Services

Pavel Losevsky/Fotolia

CONCEPTS APPLIED

➤ Consumption

➤ Consumption Goods

➤ Net Wealth

Historically, aggregate U.S. real consumption spending has recovered quickly and strongly within the months of recovery following recessions. During the recovery from the most recent recession, however, real consumption expenditures rose slowly and weakly. The main reason was that households boosted their spending on services much less than their expenditures on physical goods.

The Subdued Recovery in Household Spending on Services

Recall that consumption goods are any items—whether physical goods or services—that households purchase and then use up. Physical consumption goods include items such as clothing, shoes, and foods. Services include haircuts, services of health clubs, and services of lawn care firms.

During past recoveries of the U.S. economy from recessions, as real disposable income has risen, spending on physical goods typically has risen at a comparable or somewhat faster pace than have expenditures on services. As shown in Figure 12-9, however, during the months following the end of the 2007–2009 recession, there was a much sharper difference, compared with prior recoveries, in spending growth for physical goods versus services. The

---

Figure 12-9

Percentage Increases in Household Spending on Physical Goods and Services during the First Nine Months of Past Economic Recoveries

This figure shows that it is not unusual during economic recoveries from recessions for household spending growth on physical goods to be greater than the growth in spending on services. During the most recent recovery, however, there was a significant difference because of unusually meager growth in spending on services.

Source: Bureau of Economic Analysis.

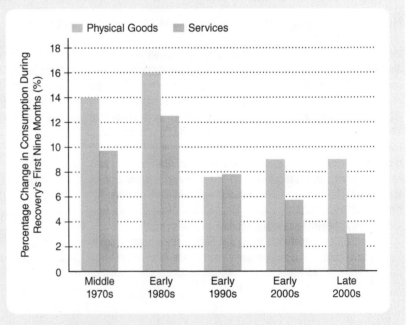

explanation for this greater difference was an unusually small increase in household spending on services as disposable income increased following the recession.

Why Expenditures on Services Grew So Slowly

Most economists agree that the fainter response of household spending on services during the most recent recovery resulted from a decline in overall household net wealth. According to this view, it is the services component of total real consumption spending that is most sensitive to changes in net wealth. When the value of household wealth is lower, people tend to wait longer between haircuts and end their health club memberships.

If this theory is correct, then the drop in net wealth reduced the amount of household spending on services at any given level of real disposable income, which shifted the consumption function downward. Then, when disposable income rose during the recovery from the recession, real spending on services began to rise but remained lower than before.

For Critical Thinking

1. Why do both movements along and any shifts in the consumption function simultaneously explain observed changes in desired aggregate consumption spending?

2. If the decline in net wealth following the financial meltdown contributed to the observed slow growth of household spending on services, did the value of the multiplier change? Explain.

Web Resources

1. To track aggregate consumption spending as a percentage of real GDP in recent years for individual nations, see the Web Links in MyEconLab.

2. For an analysis of the slow rates of increase in U.S. consumption spending following the most recent recession, see the Web Links in MyEconLab.

MyEconLab

For more questions on this chapter's Issues & Applications, go to MyEconLab.

In the Study Plan for this chapter, select Section I: Issues and Applications.

Sources are listed at the end of this chapter.

Fundamental Points

1. The consumption and saving functions show planned real consumption and saving in relation to real disposable income per year. The marginal propensities to consume and to save equal changes in real consumption and real saving divided by the change in real disposable income.

2. The downward-sloping planned investment schedule shows the inverse relationship between real investment and the interest rate. Non-interest-rate determinants of planned investment include expectations, innovation and technological changes, and business taxes.

3. The equilibrium level of real GDP, at which total planned expenditures equal real GDP, can be found where planned saving equals planned investment.

4. The intersection of the total expenditures curve, $C + I + G + X$, with the 45-degree reference line determines equilibrium real GDP. At this point, real consumption plus planned real investment plus real government expenditures plus real net exports equal real GDP.

5. Any change in autonomous spending shifts the expenditure curve and causes a multiplier effect on equilibrium real GDP per year. The multiplier is equal to 1 divided by the marginal propensity to save.

WHAT YOU SHOULD KNOW

Here is what you should know after reading this chapter. MyEconLab will help you identify what you know, and where to go when you need to practice.

LEARNING OBJECTIVES ——————— KEY TERMS ——————— WHERE TO GO TO PRACTICE—

12.1 Explain the key determinants of consumption and saving in the Keynesian model *In the Keynesian model, as real disposable income increases, so does the flow of real consumption expenditures. The portion of consumption unrelated to disposable income is autonomous consumption. The ratio of the flow of saving to disposable income is the average propensity to save (APS), and the ratio of consumption to disposable income is the average propensity to consume (APC). A change in saving divided by the corresponding change in disposable income is the marginal propensity to save (MPS), and a change in consumption divided by the corresponding change in disposable income is the marginal propensity to consume (MPC).*

real disposable income, 265
consumption, 265
saving, 265
consumption goods, 265
investment, 266
capital goods, 266
life-cycle theory of consumption, 266
permanent income hypothesis, 266
consumption function, 267
dissaving, 267
45-degree reference line, 269
autonomous consumption, 269
average propensity to consume (APC), 269
average propensity to save (APS), 269
marginal propensity to consume (MPC), 270
marginal propensity to save (MPS), 270
net wealth, 271
Key Figure
Figure 12-1, 268

- MyEconLab Study Plan 12.1
- Animated Figure 12-1

12.2 Identify the primary determinants of planned investment *Planned investment varies inversely with the interest rate, so the investment schedule slopes downward. Changes in business expectations, productive technology, or business taxes cause the investment schedule to shift.*

- MyEconLab Study Plan 12.2

12.3 Describe how equilibrium real GDP is established in the Keynesian model *In equilibrium, total planned real consumption, investment, government, and net export expenditures equal real GDP, so C + I + G + X = Y. This occurs at the point where the C + I + G + X curve crosses the 45-degree reference line. In a world without government spending and taxes, equilibrium also occurs when planned saving is equal to planned investment.*

Key Figure
Figure 12-5, 276

- MyEconLab Study Plan 12.3
- Animated Figure 12-5

12.4 Evaluate why autonomous changes in total planned expenditures have a multiplier effect on equilibrium real GDP *Any increase in autonomous expenditures causes a direct rise in real GDP. The resulting increase in disposable income in turn stimulates increased consumption by an amount equal to the marginal propensity to consume multiplied by the rise in disposable income that results. The ultimate expansion of real GDP is equal to the multiplier, 1/(1 MPC), or 1/MPS, times the increase in autonomous expenditures.*

lump-sum tax, 278
Key Figure
Figure 12-6, 279

- MyEconLab Study Plan 12.4
- Animated Figure 12-6

WHAT YOU SHOULD KNOW *continued*

LEARNING OBJECTIVES	KEY TERMS	WHERE TO GO TO PRACTICE
12.5 Understand the relationship between total planned expenditures and the aggregate demand curve *An increase in the price level induces households and businesses to cut back on spending. Thus, the C + I + G + X curve shifts downward following a rise in the price level, so that equilibrium real GDP falls. This yields the downward-sloping aggregate demand curve.*	multiplier, 280 **Key Figures** Figure 12-7, 283 Figure 12-8, 284 **Key Table** Table 12-3, 280	• MyEconLab Study Plan 12.5 • Animated Figures 12-7, 12-8 • Animated Table 12-3

Log in to MyEconLab, take a chapter test, and get a personalized Study Plan that tells you which concepts you understand and which ones you need to review. From there, MyEconLab will give you further practice, tutorials, animations, videos, and guided solutions. For more information, visit http://www.myeconlab.com

PROBLEMS

All problems are assignable in MyEconLab. Answers to odd-numbered problems appear in MyEconLab.

12-1. Classify each of the following as either a stock or a flow. (See page 265.)

   a. Myung Park earns $850 per week.

   b. Time Warner purchases $100 million in new telecommunications equipment this month.

   c. Sally Schmidt has $1,000 in a savings account at a credit union.

   d. XYZ, Inc., produces 200 units of output per week.

   e. Giorgio Giannelli owns three private jets.

   f. Apple's production declines by 750 digital devices per month.

   g. Russia owes $25 billion to the International Monetary Fund.

12-2. Consider the table below when answering the following questions. For this hypothetical economy, the marginal propensity to save is constant at all levels of real GDP, and investment spending is autonomous. There is no government. (See pages 270–276.)

Real GDP	Consumption	Saving	Investment
$ 2,000	$2,200	$_____	$400
4,000	4,000	_____	_____
6,000	_____	_____	_____
8,000	_____	_____	_____
10,000	_____	_____	_____
12,000	_____	_____	_____

   a. Complete the table. What is the marginal propensity to save? What is the marginal propensity to consume?

   b. Draw a graph of the consumption function. Then add the investment function to obtain C + I.

   c. Under the graph of C + I, draw another graph showing the saving and investment curves. Note that the C + I curve crosses the 45-degree reference line in the upper graph at the same level of real GDP where the saving and investment curves cross in the lower graph. (If not, redraw your graphs.) What is this level of real GDP?

   d. What is the numerical value of the multiplier?

   e. What is equilibrium real GDP without investment? What is the multiplier effect from the inclusion of investment?

   f. What is the average propensity to consume at equilibrium real GDP?

   g. If autonomous investment declines from $400 to $200, what happens to equilibrium real GDP?

12-3. Consider the table below when answering the following questions. For this economy, the marginal propensity to consume is constant at all levels of real GDP, and investment spending is autonomous. Equilibrium real GDP is equal to $8,000. There is no government. (See pages 270–276.)

Real GDP	Consumption	Saving	Investment
$ 2,000	$ 2,000	_____	_____
4,000	3,600	_____	_____
6,000	5,200	_____	_____
8,000	6,800	_____	_____
10,000	8,400	_____	_____
12,000	10,000	_____	_____

a. Complete the table. What is the marginal propensity to consume? What is the marginal propensity to save?

b. Draw a graph of the consumption function. Then add the investment function to obtain $C + I$.

c. Under the graph of $C + I$, draw another graph showing the saving and investment curves. Does the $C + I$ curve cross the 45-degree reference line in the upper graph at the same level of real GDP where the saving and investment curves cross in the lower graph, at the equilibrium real GDP of $8,000? (If not, redraw your graphs.)

d. What is the average propensity to save at equilibrium real GDP?

e. If autonomous consumption were to rise by $100, what would happen to equilibrium real GDP?

12-4. Calculate the multiplier for the following cases. (See page 281.)

a. MPS = 0.25

b. MPC = $\frac{5}{6}$

c. MPS = 0.125

d. MPC = $\frac{6}{7}$

12-5. Given each of the following values for the multiplier, calculate both the MPC and the MPS. (See page 281.)

a. 20

b. 10

c. 8

d. 5

12-6. The marginal propensity to consume is equal to 0.80. An increase in household wealth causes autonomous consumption to rise by $10 billion. By how much will equilibrium real GDP increase at the current price level, other things being equal? (See page 281.)

12-7. Assume that the multiplier in a country is equal to 4 and that autonomous real consumption spending is $1 trillion. If current real GDP is $18 trillion, what is the current value of real consumption spending? (See page 281.)

12-8. The multiplier in a country is equal to 5, and households pay no taxes. At the current equilibrium real GDP of $14 trillion, total real consumption spending by households is $12 trillion. What is real autonomous consumption in this country? (See page 281.)

12-9. At an initial point on the aggregate demand curve, the price level is 125, and real GDP is $18 trillion. When the price level falls to a value of 120, total autonomous expenditures increase by $250 billion. The marginal propensity to consume is 0.75. What is the level of real GDP at the new point on the aggregate demand curve? (See pages 284–285.)

12-10. At an initial point on the aggregate demand curve, the price level is 100, and real GDP is $18 trillion. After the price level rises to 110, however, there is an upward movement along the aggregate demand curve, and real GDP declines to $14 trillion. If total planned spending declined by $200 billion in response to the increase in the price level, what is the marginal propensity to consume in this economy? (See pages 284–285.)

12-11. In an economy in which the multiplier has a value of 3, the price level has decreased from 115 to 110. As a consequence, there has been a movement along the aggregate demand curve from $18 trillion in real GDP to $18.9 trillion in real GDP. (See pages 284–285.)

a. What is the marginal propensity to save?

b. What was the amount of the change in planned expenditures generated by the decline in the price level?

12-12. Consider the diagram below, which applies to a nation with no government spending, taxes, and net exports. Use the information in the diagram to answer the following questions, and explain your answers. (See pages 265–266.)

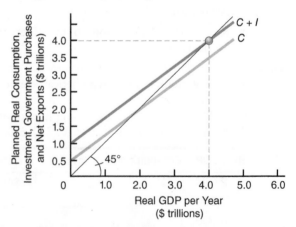

a. What is the marginal propensity to save?

b. What is the present level of planned investment spending for the present period?

c. What is the equilibrium level of real GDP for the present period?

d. What is the equilibrium level of saving for the present period?

e. If planned investment spending for the present period increases by $25 billion, what will be the resulting *change* in equilibrium real GDP? What will be the new equilibrium level of real GDP if other things, including the price level, remain unchanged?

REFERENCES

EXAMPLE: The Distribution of U.S. Real Consumption Spending

Brenda Cronin and Ben Casselman, "Wealthier Households Carry the Spending Load," *The Wall Street Journal*, March 3, 2013.

Christopher Rugaber, "Consumers in U.S. and Other Rich Countries Step up Spending," Associated Press, January 21, 2014.

Dan Weil, "Wealthy Households Keeping Consumer Sector Afloat," Moneynews, March 7, 2013.

EXAMPLE: An Interest Rate Blip Flattens Spending

Board of Governors of the Federal Reserve System, "Why Are Interest Rates Being Kept at a Low Level?" Current FAQs, 2014. (www.federalreserve.gov/faqs/money_12849.htm)

John Hilsenrath and Victoria McGrane, "Business Feels Pinch of Swift Rate Rise," *The Wall Street Journal*, June 26, 2013.

Ylan Mui, "Fed Officials Spend Week Trying to Calm Investors' Fears of Rising Interest Rates," *The Washington Post*, June 28, 2013.

POLICY EXAMPLE: Evidence of a Multiplier Effect in Federal Highway Spending

Congressional Budget Office, "The Budget and Economic Outlook: 2014 to 2024," February 4, 2014.

Sylvain Leduc and Daniel Wilson, "Are State Governments Roadblocks to Federal Stimulus? Evidence from Highway Grants in the 2009 Recovery Act," Federal Reserve Bank of San Francisco Working Paper 2013–16, July 2013.

Laura D'Andrea Tyson, "The U.S. Growth Opportunity in Infrastructure," McKinsey Insights & Publications Interview, August 2013.

YOU ARE THERE: Hukou's Depressing Effect on Autonomous Consumption in China

Harry den Hargo, "China's Hukou System: Attempts to Control Urbanization by Strictly Separating Urban and Regional," The Volume Project, April 3, 2014. (http://volumeproject.org/2014/04/chinas-hukou-system-attempts-to-control-urbanization-by-strictly-separating-urban-and-rural/)

Liyan Qi, "Is *Hukou* Reform the Key to Reviving China's Economy?" *The Wall Street Journal*, August 19, 2013.

Dexter Roberts, "China's Savers Block the Consumer Economy," *Bloomberg Businessweek*, July 21, 2013.

ISSUES & APPLICATIONS: A Recovery Hampered by Meager Spending on Services

Martin Crutsinger, "Consumer Spending Again Tepid," Associated Press, August 31, 2013.

Tami Luhby, "Health Care Spending Growth Is at a Record Low. Here's the Catch," CNN Money, April 29, 2013.

Jeanna Smialek, "Growth Freezes Up as U.S. Business Spending Slumps," Bloomberg, April 30, 2014.

The Keynesian Model and the Multiplier

We can see the multiplier effect more clearly if we look at Figure C-1 below, in which we see only a small section of the graphs that we used in Chapter 12. We start with equilibrium real GDP of $17.5 trillion per year. This equilibrium occurs with total planned real expenditures represented by $C + I + G + X$. The $C + I + G + X$ curve intersects the 45-degree reference line at $17.5 trillion per year. Now we increase real investment, I, by $100 billion. This increase in investment shifts the entire $C + I + G + X$ curve vertically to $C + I' + G + X$. The vertical shift represents that $100 billion increase in autonomous investment. With the higher level of planned expenditures per year, we are no longer in equilibrium at E. Inventories are falling. Production of goods and services will increase as firms try to replenish their inventories.

Eventually, real GDP will catch up with total planned expenditures. The new equilibrium level of real GDP is established at E' at the intersection of the new $C + I' + G + X$ curve and the 45-degree reference line, along which $C + I + G + X = Y$ (total planned expenditures equal real GDP). The new equilibrium level of real GDP is $18 trillion per year. Thus, the increase in equilibrium real GDP is equal to five times the permanent increase in planned investment spending.

FIGURE C-1

Graphing the Multiplier

We can translate Table 12-3 on page 274 into graphic form by looking at each successive round of additional spending induced by an autonomous increase in planned investment of $100 billion. The total planned expenditures curve shifts from $C + I + G + X$, with its associated equilibrium level of real GDP of $17.5 trillion, to a new curve labeled $C + I' + G + X$. The new equilibrium level of real GDP is $18 trillion. Equilibrium is again established.

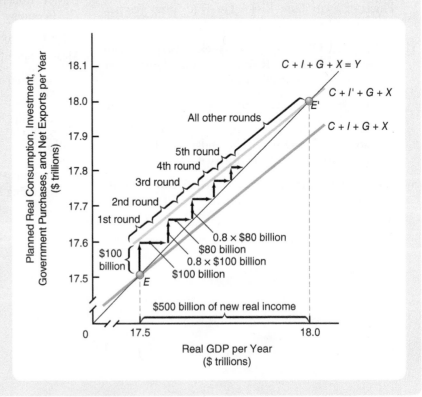

Fiscal Policy

Vince Streano/Documentary Value/Corbis

The Keynesian theory of real GDP determination indicates that changes in autonomous real expenditures—real spending unrelated to the level of real income—have a multiplier effect on the equilibrium flow of real GDP per year. In principle, this means that an increase in government spending can boost equilibrium real GDP by an amount equal to that spending increase times the multiplier. In practice, however, the observed effect of higher government expenditures on real GDP per year tends to be lower than this amount, both within a short time after the spending increase and after a longer interval has passed. To gauge the short-run effect of an increase in government spending, economists estimate an *impact fiscal multiplier*. To measure the longer-term effect, they estimate a *cumulative fiscal multiplier*. In this chapter, you will learn why both of these fiscal policy multipliers are smaller than the multiplier in the Keynesian model.

LEARNING OBJECTIVES

After reading this chapter, you should be able to:

13.1 Use traditional Keynesian analysis to evaluate the effects of discretionary fiscal policies

13.2 Discuss ways in which indirect crowding out and direct expenditure offsets can reduce the effectiveness of fiscal policy actions

13.3 List and define fiscal policy time lags and explain why they complicate efforts to engage in fiscal "fine-tuning"

13.4 Describe how certain aspects of fiscal policy function as automatic stabilizers for the economy

MyEconLab helps you master each objective and study more efficiently. See the end of the chapter for details.

the U.S. government's American Recovery and Reinvestment Act of 2009 entailed a greater overall expenditure of funds than the eight-year-long Iraqi conflict? Military and other U.S. government spending related to the war effort in Iraq totaled $709 billion, or about 4.7 percent of the value of a typical year's output of goods and services. The 2009 "Stimulus Act," which was intended to boost economic activity and reduce the unemployment rate, authorized $862 billion in spending, or about 5.7 percent of the value of annual U.S. production at that time. In this chapter, you will learn how variations in government spending and taxation affect both real GDP and the price level.

13.1 Use traditional Keynesian analysis to evaluate the effects of discretionary fiscal policies

Fiscal policy
The discretionary changing of government expenditures or taxes to achieve national economic goals, such as high employment with price stability.

Discretionary Fiscal Policy

The making of deliberate, discretionary changes in federal government expenditures or taxes (or both) to achieve certain national economic goals is the realm of **fiscal policy**. Some national goals are high employment (low unemployment), price stability, and economic growth. Fiscal policy can be thought of as a deliberate attempt to cause the economy to move to full employment and price stability more quickly than it otherwise might.

Fiscal policy has typically been associated with the economic theories of John Maynard Keynes and what is now called *traditional* Keynesian analysis. Recall from Chapter 11 that Keynes's explanation of the Great Depression was that there was insufficient aggregate demand. Because he believed that wages and prices were "sticky downward," he argued that the classical economists' picture of an economy moving automatically and quickly toward full employment was inaccurate. To Keynes and his followers, government had to step in to increase aggregate demand. Expansionary fiscal policy initiated by the federal government was the preferred way to ward off recessions and depressions.

Changes in Government Spending

In Chapter 11, we looked at the recessionary gap and the inflationary gap (see Figures 11-9 and 11-10 on page 255). The recessionary gap was defined as the amount by which the current level of real GDP falls short of the economy's *potential* production if it were operating on its *LRAS* curve. The inflationary gap was defined as the amount by which the short-run equilibrium level of real GDP exceeds the long-run equilibrium level as given by *LRAS*. Let us examine fiscal policy first in the context of a recessionary gap.

WHEN THERE IS A RECESSIONARY GAP The government, along with firms, individuals, and foreign residents, is one of the spending entities in the economy. When the government spends more, all other things held constant, the dollar value of total spending initially must rise. Look at panel (a) of Figure 13-1 on the next page. We begin by assuming that some negative shock in the near past has left the economy at point E_1, which is a short-run equilibrium in which AD_1 intersects *SRAS* at $17.5 trillion of real GDP per year. There is a recessionary gap of $500 billion of real GDP per year—the difference between *LRAS* (the economy's long-run potential) and the short-run equilibrium level of real GDP per year.

When the government decides to spend more (expansionary fiscal policy), the aggregate demand curve shifts to the right to AD_2. Here we assume that the government knows exactly how much more to spend so that AD_2 intersects *SRAS* at $18 trillion, or at *LRAS*. Because of the upward-sloping *SRAS*, the price level rises from 110 to 120 as real GDP goes to $18 trillion per year.

WHEN THERE IS AN INFLATIONARY GAP The entire process shown on the next page in panel (a) of Figure 13-1 can be reversed, as shown in panel (b). There, we assume that a recent

Expansionary and Contractionary Fiscal Policy: Changes in Government Spending

If there is a recessionary gap and short-run equilibrium is at E_1, in panel (a), fiscal policy can presumably increase aggregate demand to AD_2. The new equilibrium is at E_2 at higher real GDP per year and a higher price level. In panel (b), the economy is at short-run equilibrium at E_1, which is at a

higher real GDP than the *LRAS*. To reduce this inflationary gap, fiscal policy can be used to decrease aggregate demand from AD_1 to AD_2. Eventually, equilibrium will fall to E_2, which is on the *LRAS*.

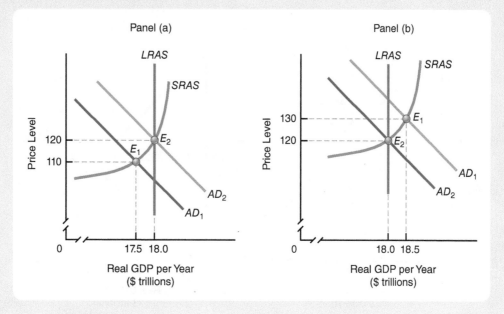

shock has left the economy at point E_1, at which an inflationary gap exists at the intersection of *SRAS* and AD_1. Real GDP cannot be sustained at $18.5 trillion indefinitely, because this exceeds long-run aggregate supply, which in real terms is $18 trillion. If the government recognizes this and reduces its spending (pursues a contractionary fiscal policy), this action reduces aggregate demand from AD_1 to AD_2. Equilibrium will fall to E_2 on the *LRAS*, where real GDP per year is $18 trillion. The price level will fall from 130 to 120.   MyEconLab Concept Check

Changes in Taxes

The spending decisions of firms, individuals, and other countries' residents depend on the taxes levied on them. Individuals in their role as consumers look to their disposable (after-tax) income when determining their desired rates of consumption. Firms look at their after-tax profits when deciding on the levels of investment per year to undertake. Foreign residents look at the tax-inclusive cost of goods when deciding whether to buy in the United States or elsewhere. Therefore, holding all other things constant, an increase in taxes causes a reduction in aggregate demand because it reduces consumption, investment, or net exports.

WHEN THE CURRENT SHORT-RUN EQUILIBRIUM IS TO THE LEFT OF *LRAS* Look at panel (a) in Figure 13-2 on the next page. The aggregate demand curve AD_1 intersects *SRAS* at E_1, with real GDP at $17.5 trillion, less than the *LRAS* of $18 trillion. In this situation, a decrease in taxes shifts the aggregate demand curve outward to the right. At AD_2, equilibrium is established at E_2, with the price level at 120 and equilibrium real GDP at $18 trillion per year.

WHEN THE CURRENT SHORT-RUN EQUILIBRIUM IS TO THE RIGHT OF *LRAS* Assume that aggregate demand is AD_1 in panel (b) of Figure 13-2 on the next page. This aggregate demand curve intersects *SRAS* at E_1, which yields real GDP greater than *LRAS*. In this

FIGURE 13-2

Expansionary and Contractionary Fiscal Policy: Changes in Taxes

In panel (a), the economy is initially at E_1, where real GDP is less than long-run equilibrium real GDP. Expansionary fiscal policy via a tax reduction can move aggregate demand to AD_2 so that the new equilibrium is at E_2 at a higher price level. Real GDP is now consistent with $LRAS$, which eliminates the recessionary gap. In panel (b), with an inflationary gap (in this case of $500 billion), taxes are increased. AD_1 moves to AD_2. The economy moves from E_1 to E_2, and real GDP is now at $18 trillion per year, the long-run equilibrium level.

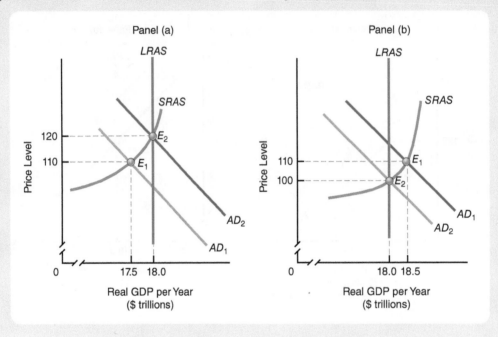

situation, an increase in taxes shifts the aggregate demand curve inward to the left. For argument's sake, assume that it intersects $SRAS$ at E_2, or exactly where $LRAS$ intersects AD_2. In this situation, the level of real GDP falls from $18.5 trillion per year to $18 trillion per year. The price level falls from 110 to 100.   MyEconLab Concept Check
MyEconLab Study Plan

Fiscal policy is defined as making discretionary changes in government _____ or _____ to achieve such national goals as high employment or reduced inflation.

To address a situation in which there is a _____ gap and the economy is operating at less than long-run aggregate supply ($LRAS$), the government can _____ its spending. This policy action shifts the aggregate demand curve to the right, causing the equilibrium level of real GDP per year to increase.

To address a situation in which there is an _____ gap, the government can _____ its spending and cause the aggregate demand curve to shift to the left, which reduces the equilibrium level of real GDP per year.

Changes in taxes can have similar effects on the equilibrium rate of real GDP and the price level. If there is an inflationary gap, an _____ in taxes can lead to a decrease in the equilibrium level of real GDP per year. In contrast, if there is a recessionary gap, a _____ in taxes can increase equilibrium real GDP per year.

13.2 Discuss ways in which indirect crowding out and direct expenditure offsets can reduce the effectiveness of fiscal policy actions

Possible Offsets to Fiscal Policy

Fiscal policy does not operate in a vacuum. Important questions must be answered: If government spending rises by, say, $300 billion, how is the spending financed, and by whom? If taxes are increased, what does the government do with the taxes? What will happen if individuals anticipate higher *future* taxes because the government is spending more today without raising current taxes? These questions involve *offsets* to the effects of current fiscal policy. We consider them in detail here.

Indirect Crowding Out

Let's take the first example of fiscal policy in this chapter—an increase in government expenditures. If government expenditures rise and taxes are held constant, something has to give. Our government does not simply take goods and services when it wants them. It has to pay for them. When it pays for them and does not simultaneously collect the same amount in taxes, it must borrow. This means that an increase in government spending without raising taxes creates additional government borrowing from the private sector (or from other countries' residents).

INDUCED INTEREST RATE CHANGES If the government attempts to borrow in excess of $500 billion more per year from the private sector, as it has since 2009, it will have to offer a higher interest rate to lure the additional funds from savers. This is the interest rate effect of expansionary fiscal policy financed by borrowing from the public. Consequently, when the federal government finances increased spending by additional borrowing, it will push interest rates up. When interest rates go up, firms' borrowing costs rise, which induces them to cut back on planned investment spending. Borrowing costs also increase for households, who reduce planned expenditures on cars and homes.

Thus, a rise in government spending, holding taxes constant (that is, deficit spending), tends to crowd out private spending, dampening the positive effect of increased government spending on aggregate demand. This is called the **crowding-out effect**. In the extreme case, the crowding out may be complete, with the increased government spending having no net effect on aggregate demand. The final result is simply more government spending and less private investment and consumption. Figure 13-3 below shows how the crowding-out effect occurs.

THE FIRM'S INVESTMENT DECISION To understand the crowding-out effect better, consider a firm that is contemplating borrowing $100,000 to expand its business. Suppose that the interest rate is 5 percent. The interest payments on the debt will be 5 percent times $100,000, or $5,000 per year ($417 per month). A rise in the interest rate to 8 percent will push the payments to 8 percent of $100,000, or $8,000 per year ($667 per month). The extra $250 per month in interest expenses will discourage some firms from making the investment. Consumers face similar decisions when they purchase houses and cars. An increase in the interest rate causes their monthly payments to go up, thereby discouraging some of them from purchasing cars and houses.

Crowding-out effect
The tendency of expansionary fiscal policy to cause a decrease in planned investment or planned consumption in the private sector. This decrease normally results from the rise in interest rates.

MyEconLab Animation

FIGURE 13-3

The Crowding-Out Effect, Step by Step

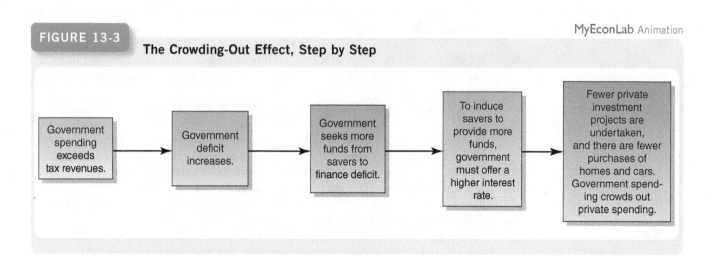

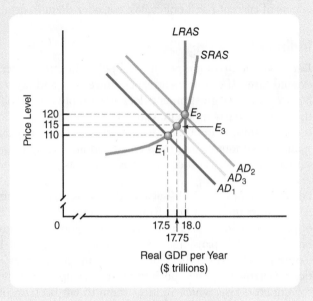

FIGURE 13-4

The Crowding-Out Effect

Expansionary fiscal policy that causes deficit financing initially shifts AD_1 to AD_2. Equilibrium initially moves toward E_2. Expansionary fiscal policy, however, pushes up interest rates, thereby reducing interest-sensitive spending. This effect causes the aggregate demand curve to shift inward to AD_3, and the new short-run equilibrium is at E_3.

GRAPHICAL ANALYSIS You see in Figure 13-4 above that the economy is in a situation in which, at point E_1, equilibrium real GDP is below the long-run level consistent with the position of the *LRAS* curve. Suppose, however, that government expansionary fiscal policy in the form of increased government spending (without increasing current taxes) attempts to shift aggregate demand from AD_1 to AD_2. In the absence of the crowding-out effect, real GDP would increase to $18 trillion per year, and the price level would rise to 120 (point E_2). With the (partial) crowding-out effect, however, as investment and consumption decline, partly offsetting the rise in government spending, the aggregate demand curve shifts inward to the left to AD_3.

The new short-run equilibrium is now at E_3, with real GDP of $17.75 trillion per year at a price level of 115. In other words, crowding out dilutes the effect of expansionary fiscal policy, and a recessionary gap remains. MyEconLab Concept Check

Planning for the Future: Ricardian Equivalence

Economists have often implicitly assumed that people look at changes in taxes or changes in government spending only in the present. What if people actually think about the size of *future* tax payments? Does this have an effect on how they react to an increase in government spending with no current tax increases? Some economists believe that the answer is yes.

CURRENT TAX CUTS AND FUTURE DEBTS What if people's horizons extend beyond this year? Don't we then have to take into account the effects of today's government policies on the future?

Consider an example. The government wants to reduce taxes by $200 billion today, as it did in 2008 and 2009 via tax "rebate" programs. Assume that government spending remains constant. Assume further that the government initially has a balanced budget. Thus, the only way for the government to pay for this $200 billion tax cut is to borrow $200 billion today. The public will owe $200 billion plus interest later. Realizing that a $200 billion tax cut today is mathematically equivalent to $200 billion plus interest later, people may wish to save the proceeds from the tax cut to meet future tax liabilities—payment of interest and repayment of debt.

Consequently, a tax cut may not affect total planned expenditures. A reduction in taxes without a reduction in government spending may therefore have no impact on aggregate demand. Similarly, an increase in taxes without an increase in government spending may not have a large (negative) impact on aggregate demand.

THE RICARDIAN EQUIVALENCE THEOREM Suppose that a decrease in taxes shifts the aggregate demand curve from AD_1 to AD_2 in Figure 13-4 on the previous page. If consumers partly compensate for a higher future tax liability by saving more, the aggregate demand curve shifts leftward, to a position such as AD_3. In the extreme case in which individuals fully take into account their increased tax liabilities, the aggregate demand curve shifts all the way back to AD_1, so that there is no effect on the economy. This is known as the **Ricardian equivalence theorem**, after the nineteenth-century economist David Ricardo, who first developed the argument publicly.

According to the Ricardian equivalence theorem, it does not matter how government expenditures are financed—by taxes or by borrowing. Is the theorem correct? Research indicates that Ricardian equivalence effects likely exist but has not provided much compelling evidence about their magnitudes. MyEconLab Concept Check

Ricardian equivalence theorem
The proposition that an increase in the government budget deficit has no effect on aggregate demand.

Restrained Consumption Effects of Temporary Tax Changes

Recall from Chapter 12 (page 266) that a person's consumption and saving decisions realistically depend on *both* current income *and* anticipated future income. On the basis of this fact, the theory of consumption known as the *permanent income hypothesis* proposes that an individual's current flow of consumption depends on the individual's permanent, or anticipated lifetime, income.

Sometimes, the government seeks to provide a short-term "stimulus" to economic activity through temporary tax cuts that last no longer than a year or two or by rebating lump-sum amounts back to taxpayers. According to the permanent income hypothesis, such short-term tax policies at best have minimal effects on total consumption spending. The reason is that *temporary* tax cuts or one-time tax rebates fail to raise the recipients' *permanent* incomes. Even after receiving such a temporary tax cut or rebate, therefore, people usually do not respond with significant changes in their consumption. Instead of spending the tax cut or rebate, they typically save most of the funds or use the funds to make payments on outstanding debts.

Thus, temporary tax cuts or rebates tend to have minimal effects on aggregate consumption, as the U.S. government has discovered when it has provided temporary tax rebates. For instance, one-time federal tax rebates totaling at least $200 billion in 2008 and again in 2009 boosted real disposable income temporarily in each year but had no perceptible effects on flows of real consumption spending.

Are European residents increasing their saving as European governments collect fewer taxes than they spend and consequently add to public debts?

INTERNATIONAL POLICY EXAMPLE

Europeans Save More as Public Spending Outstrips Taxes

Government debts build up when tax collections persistently fail to cover public spending. The logic of Ricardian equivalence indicates that the public will recognize that eventually they will have to pay the interest on these accumulated debts and will respond by boosting their private saving. As a result, there should be a positive relationship between the amounts of government indebtedness and of accumulated private savings.

Economists have found European evidence in support of this prediction. Among the nations of the European Union, those with higher levels of government indebtedness also have higher levels of private savings. That is, as government debts increase over time as a consequence of insufficient tax collections to fund greater government spending, private household savings increase as people add more to their accumulated savings each year. Consistent with the Ricardian equivalence theorem, European residents save more each year as governments borrow more funds to finance spending not fully covered by tax collections.

FOR CRITICAL THINKING

If European governments were to bring their public spending and taxation into closer balance, what does the Ricardian equivalence theorem predict would happen to the annual saving flow and, eventually, accumulated household savings?

Sources are listed at the end of this chapter.

Direct Expenditure Offsets

Government has a distinct comparative advantage over the private sector in certain activities such as diplomacy and national defense. Otherwise stated, certain resource-using activities in which the government engages do not compete with the private sector. In contrast, some of what government does, such as public education, competes directly with the private sector. When government competes with the private sector, **direct expenditure offsets** to fiscal policy may occur. For example, if the government starts providing milk at no charge to students who are already purchasing milk, there is a direct expenditure offset. Direct household spending on milk decreases, but government spending on milk increases.

Direct expenditure offsets
Actions on the part of the private sector in spending income that offset government fiscal policy actions. Any increase in government spending in an area that competes with the private sector will have some direct expenditure offset.

Normally, the impact of an increase in government spending on aggregate demand is analyzed by implicitly assuming that government spending is *not* a substitute for private spending. This is clearly the case for a cruise missile. Whenever government spending is a substitute for private spending, however, a rise in government spending causes a direct reduction in private spending to offset it.

THE EXTREME CASE In the extreme case, the direct expenditure offset is dollar for dollar, so we merely end up with a relabeling of spending from private to public. Assume that you have decided to spend $100 on groceries. Upon your arrival at the checkout counter, you find a U.S. Department of Agriculture official. She announces that she will pay for your groceries—but only the ones in the cart. Here increased government spending is $100. You leave the store in bliss. Just as you are deciding how to spend the $100, though, an Internal Revenue Service agent appears. He announces that as a result of the current budgetary crisis, your taxes are going to rise by $100. You have to pay on the spot. Increases in taxes have now been $100. We have a balanced-budget increase in government spending. In this scenario, *total* spending does not change. We simply end up with higher government spending, which directly offsets exactly an equal reduction in consumption. Aggregate demand and GDP are unchanged. Otherwise stated, if there is a full direct expenditure offset, the government spending multiplier is zero.

THE LESS EXTREME CASE Much government spending has a private-sector substitute. When government expenditures increase, private spending tends to decline somewhat (but generally not dollar for dollar), thereby mitigating the upward impact on total aggregate demand. To the extent that there are some direct expenditure offsets to expansionary fiscal policy, predicted changes in aggregate demand will be lessened. Consequently, real GDP and the price level will be less affected.

WHAT IF...

the federal government seeks to generate increases in aggregate demand and equilibrium levels of real GDP per year through public spending on all-electric and hybrid vehicles?

In recent years, the U.S. government has provided grants and other subsidies to producers of all-electric and hybrid vehicles. Government officials commonly claim that a positive by-product of these subsidy programs is that they help to boost aggregate demand. One effect of such programs is to reduce the net prices consumers have to pay for these vehicles. As a consequence of these price reductions, a number of consumers have responded by buying more all-electric and hybrid vehicles. Nevertheless, many of these consumers have substituted away from purchasing gasoline-fueled vehicles, so their spending on gasoline-powered vehicles has decreased. Thus, government-funded spending on all-electric and hybrid vehicles has been accompanied by offsetting reductions in expenditures on gasoline-powered vehicles. Consequently, the overall *net* effect of these grants and subsidies on *aggregate* desired spending, and hence aggregate demand and real GDP, has been negligible.

MyEconLab Concept Check

The Supply-Side Effects of Changes in Taxes

We have talked about changing taxes and changing government spending, the traditional tools of fiscal policy. Let's now consider the possibility of changing *marginal* tax rates.

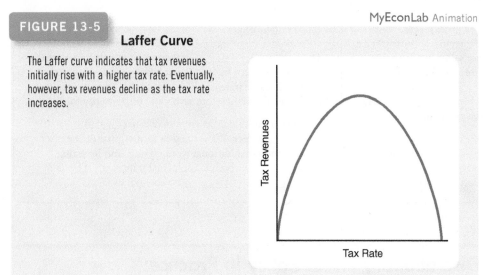

FIGURE 13-5

MyEconLab Animation

Laffer Curve

The Laffer curve indicates that tax revenues initially rise with a higher tax rate. Eventually, however, tax revenues decline as the tax rate increases.

(Vertical axis: Tax Revenues; Horizontal axis: Tax Rate)

ALTERING MARGINAL TAX RATES Recall from Chapter 6 that the marginal tax rate is the rate applied to the last, or highest, bracket of taxable income. In our federal tax system, higher marginal tax rates are applied as income rises. In that sense, the United States has a progressive federal individual income tax system. Expansionary fiscal policy could involve reducing marginal tax rates. Advocates of such changes argue that lower tax rates will lead to an increase in productivity. They contend that individuals will work harder and longer, save more, and invest more and that increased productivity will lead to more economic growth, which will lead to higher real GDP. The government, by applying lower marginal tax rates, will not necessarily lose tax revenues, for the lower marginal tax rates will be applied to a growing tax base because of economic growth—after all, tax revenues are the product of a tax rate times a tax base.

The relationship between tax rates and tax revenues, which you may recall from the discussion of sales taxes in Chapter 6, is sometimes called the *Laffer curve*, named after economist Arthur Laffer, who explained the relationship to some journalists and politicians in 1974. It is reproduced in Figure 13-5 above. On the vertical axis are tax revenues, and on the horizontal axis is the marginal tax rate. As you can see, total tax revenues initially rise but then eventually fall as the tax rate continues to increase after reaching some unspecified tax-revenue-maximizing rate at the top of the curve.

SUPPLY-SIDE ECONOMICS People who support the notion that reducing tax rates does not necessarily lead to reduced tax revenues are called supply-side economists. **Supply-side economics** involves changing the tax structure to create incentives to increase productivity. Due to a shift in the aggregate supply curve to the right, there can be greater real GDP without upward pressure on the price level.

Consider the supply-side effects of changes in marginal tax rates on labor. An increase in tax rates reduces the opportunity cost of leisure, thereby inducing individuals to reduce their work effort and to consume more leisure. An increase in tax rates, however, will also reduce spendable income, thereby shifting the demand curve for leisure inward to the left, which tends to increase work effort. The outcome of these two effects on the choice of leisure (and thus work) depends on which of them is stronger. Supply-side economists argue that the first effect often dominates: Increases in marginal tax rates cause people to work less, and decreases in marginal tax rates induce workers to work more.

MyEconLab Concept Check

MyEconLab Study Plan

Supply-side economics
The suggestion that creating incentives for individuals and firms to increase productivity will cause the aggregate supply curve to shift outward.'

Indirect crowding out occurs because of an interest rate effect in which the government's efforts to finance its deficit spending cause interest rates to _____, thereby crowding out private investment and spending, particularly on cars and houses. This is called the **crowding-out effect.**

_____ _____ _____ occur when government spending competes with the private sector and is increased. A direct crowding-out effect may occur.

The _____ _____ theorem holds that an increase in the government budget deficit has no effect on aggregate demand because individuals anticipate that their future taxes will increase and therefore save more today to pay for them.

Changes in marginal tax rates may cause _____- _____ effects if a reduction in marginal tax rates induces enough additional work, saving, and investing. Government tax receipts can actually increase. This is called _____-_____ economics.

13.3 List and define fiscal policy time lags and explain why they complicate efforts to engage in fiscal "fine-tuning"

Discretionary Fiscal Policy in Practice: Coping with Time Lags

We can discuss fiscal policy in a relatively precise way. We draw graphs with aggregate demand and supply curves to show what we are doing. We could in principle estimate the offsets that we just discussed. Even if we were able to measure all of these offsets exactly, however, would-be fiscal policymakers still face a problem: The conduct of fiscal policy involves a variety of time lags.

Policy Time Lags

Policymakers must take time lags into account. Not only is it difficult to measure economic variables, but it also takes time to collect and assimilate such data. Consequently, policymakers must contend with the **recognition time lag**, the months that may elapse before national economic problems can be identified.

After an economic problem is recognized, a solution must be formulated. Thus, there will be an **action time lag** between the recognition of a problem and the implementation of policy to solve it. For fiscal policy, the action time lag is particularly long. Such policy must be approved by Congress and is subject to political wrangling and infighting. The action time lag can easily last a year or two. Then it takes time to actually implement the policy. After Congress enacts fiscal policy legislation, it takes time to decide such matters as who gets new federal construction contracts.

Finally, there is the **effect time lag**: After fiscal policy is enacted, it takes time for the policy to affect the economy. To demonstrate the effects, economists need only shift curves on a chalkboard, a whiteboard, or a piece of paper, but in the real world, such effects take quite a while to work their way through the economy.

MyEconLab Concept Check

Recognition time lag
The time required to gather information about the current state of the economy.

Action time lag
The time between recognizing an economic problem and implementing policy to solve it. The action time lag is quite long for fiscal policy, which requires congressional approval.

Effect time lag
The time that elapses between the implementation of a policy and the results of that policy.

Problems Posed by Time Lags

Because the various fiscal policy time lags are long, a policy designed to combat a significant recession such as the recession of the late 2000s might not produce results until the economy is already out of that recession and perhaps experiencing inflation, in which case the fiscal policy action would worsen the situation. Or a fiscal policy designed to eliminate inflation might not produce effects until the economy is in a recession. In that case, too, fiscal policy would make the economic problem worse rather than better.

Furthermore, because fiscal policy time lags tend to be *variable* (each lasting anywhere from one to three years), policymakers have a difficult time fine-tuning the economy. Clearly, fiscal policy is more guesswork than science.

MyEconLab Concept Check
MyEconLab Study Plan

Time lags of various sorts reduce the effectiveness of fiscal policy. The _____ time lag is the time required to gather information about the current state of the economy.

The _____ time lag is the time between recognition of a perceived need for a policy response and implementation of that response.

The _____ time lag is the time between implementation of a policy and the policy's results.

Automatic Stabilizers

13.4 Describe how certain aspects of fiscal policy function as automatic stabilizers for the economy

Not all changes in taxes (or in tax rates) or in government spending (including government transfers) constitute discretionary fiscal policy. There are several types of automatic (or nondiscretionary) fiscal policies. Such policies do not require new legislation on the part of Congress. Specific automatic fiscal policies—called **automatic,** or **built-in, stabilizers**—include the tax system itself, unemployment compensation, and income transfer payments.

Automatic, or built-in, stabilizers
Special provisions of certain federal programs that cause changes in desired aggregate expenditures without the action of Congress and the president. Examples are the federal progressive tax system and unemployment compensation.

The Tax System as an Automatic Stabilizer

You know that if you work less, you are paid less, and therefore you pay fewer taxes. The amount of taxes that our government collects falls automatically during a recession. Basically, as observed in the U.S. economy during the severe recession of the late 2000s, incomes and profits fall when business activity slows down, and the government's tax revenues drop, too. Some economists consider this an automatic tax cut, which therefore may stimulate aggregate demand. It thereby may reduce the extent of any negative economic fluctuation.

The progressive nature of the federal personal and corporate income tax systems magnifies any automatic stabilization effect that might exist. If your hours of work are reduced because of a recession, you still pay some federal personal income taxes. But because of our progressive system, you may drop into a lower tax bracket, thereby paying a lower marginal tax rate. As a result, your disposable income falls by a smaller percentage than your before-tax income falls.   MyEconLab Concept Check

Unemployment Compensation and Income Transfer Payments

Like our tax system, unemployment compensation payments stabilize aggregate demand. Throughout the course of business fluctuations, unemployment compensation reduces *changes* in people's disposable income. When business activity drops, most laid-off workers automatically become eligible for unemployment compensation from their state governments. Their disposable income therefore remains positive, although at a lower level than when they were employed. During boom periods, there is less unemployment, and consequently fewer unemployment payments are made to the labor force. Less purchasing power is being added to the economy because fewer unemployment checks are paid out. In contrast, during recessions the opposite is true.

Income transfer payments act similarly as an automatic stabilizer. When a recession occurs, more people become eligible for income transfer payments, such as Supplemental Security Income and Temporary Assistance to Needy Families. Therefore, those people do not experience as dramatic a drop in disposable income as they otherwise would have.   MyEconLab Concept Check

Stabilizing Impact

The key stabilizing impact of our tax system, unemployment compensation, and income transfer payments is their ability to mitigate changes in disposable income, consumption, and the equilibrium level of real GDP. If disposable income is prevented

FIGURE 13-6

Automatic Stabilizers

Here we assume that as real GDP rises, tax revenues rise and government transfers fall, other things remaining constant. Thus, as the economy expands from Y_f to Y_1, a budget surplus automatically arises. As the economy contracts from Y_f to Y_2, a budget deficit automatically arises. Such automatic changes tend to reduce the magnitude of fluctuations in real GDP.

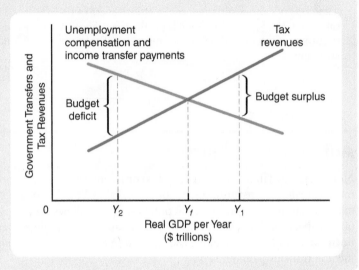

from falling as much as it otherwise would during a recession, the downturn will be moderated. In contrast, if disposable income is prevented from rising as rapidly as it otherwise would during a boom, the boom is less likely to get out of hand. The progressive income tax and unemployment compensation thus provide automatic stabilization to the economy. We present the argument graphically in Figure 13-6 above.

Why might food stamps be among the most effective automatic stabilizers?

POLICY EXAMPLE

Are Traditional Automatic Stabilizers Aimed at the Wrong People?

Traditionally, automatic fiscal stabilizers operate through systems of taxes and transfers. When real GDP decreases during downturns, tax collections decline automatically, and unemployment benefits and income transfer payments increase automatically.

Alidair McKay of Boston University and Ricardo Reis of Columbia University argue that traditional systems of taxes and transfers do little to stabilize real GDP. They contend that tax-based stabilizers assist employed people who typically do not respond by boosting their spending, while unemployment insurance and income transfer payments give the newly unemployed incentives to remain unemployed.

Automatic stabilizers that do the most to reduce real GDP variability, McKay and Reis argue, automatically transfer more resources to people who already do not have income-generating jobs. The Supplemental Nutritional Assistance (SNAP, or "food stamps") Program provides transfers to already unemployed people. McKay and Reis conclude that for this reason, SNAP is particularly effective at stabilizing desired expenditures on final goods and services.

FOR CRITICAL THINKING

McKay and Reis find evidence that individuals who are already unemployed before a downturn have higher marginal propensities to consume than other people. Why might this fact support their argument that transfers aimed at already unemployed people can do most to boost aggregate demand? (Hint: What is the relationship between the overall marginal propensity to consume and the spending multiplier?)

Sources are listed at the end of this chapter.

MyEconLab Concept Check

What Do We Really Know about Fiscal Policy?

There are two ways of looking at fiscal policy. One prevails during normal times and the other during abnormal times.

FISCAL POLICY DURING NORMAL TIME During normal times (without "excessive" unemployment, inflation, or unusual problems in the national economy), we know that due to the recognition time lag and the modest size of any fiscal policy action that Congress will actually take, discretionary fiscal policy is probably not very effective. Congress ends up doing too little too late to help in a minor recession. Moreover, fiscal policy that generates repeated tax changes (as has happened) creates uncertainty, which may do more harm than good. To the extent that fiscal policy has any effect during normal times, it probably achieves this by way of automatic stabilizers rather than by way of discretionary policy.

FISCAL POLICY DURING ABNORMAL TIMES During abnormal times, fiscal policy may be effective. Consider some classic examples: the Great Depression and war periods.

The Great Depression When there is a catastrophic drop in real GDP, as there was during the Great Depression, fiscal policy may be able to stimulate aggregate demand. Because so many people have few assets left and thus are income-constrained during such periods, government spending is a way to get income into their hands—income that they are likely to spend immediately.

Wartime Wars are in fact reserved for governments. War expenditures are not good substitutes for private expenditures—they have little or no direct expenditure offsets. Consequently, war spending as part of expansionary fiscal policy usually has noteworthy effects, such as occurred while we were waging World War II, when real GDP increased dramatically (though much of the output of new goods and services was expended for military uses).

THE "SOOTHING" EFFECT OF KEYNESIAN FISCAL POLICY One view of traditional Keynesian fiscal policy does not call for it to be used on a regular basis but nevertheless sees it as potentially useful. As you have learned in this chapter, many problems are associated with attempting to use fiscal policy. If, however, we should encounter a severe downturn, fiscal policy is available. Knowing this may reassure consumers and investors. Thus, the availability of fiscal policy may induce more buoyant and stable expectations of the future, thereby smoothing investment spending. MyEconLab Concept Check
MyEconLab Study Plan

SELF CHECK Visit MyEconLab to practice these and other problems and to get instant feedback in your Study Plan.

Two _____, or built-in, stabilizers are the progressive income tax and unemployment compensation.

Built-in stabilizers automatically tend to _____ changes in disposable income resulting from changes in overall business activity. Although discretionary fiscal policy

may not necessarily be a useful policy tool in normal times because of time lags, it may work well during _____ times, such as depressions and wartimes.

The existence of fiscal policy may have a _____ effect on consumers and investors.

YOU ARE THERE

Do Social Security Payments Boost Real GDP?

Andrew Biggs, former principal deputy commissioner of the Social Security Administration, has just read claims about the effect of Social Security payments on U.S. economic activity. The American Association of Retired Persons (AARP) has issued a number of press releases arguing that Social Security payments stimulate economic activity in various states and in the United States as a whole. The AARP argues that every dollar the federal government pays to Social Security recipients generates about two dollars of private spending. The result, the AARP contends, is that Social Security adds about $1.4 trillion to U.S. real GDP.

Biggs thinks that there are flaws in the logic laid out in the text of the AARP's press releases. First, Social Security payments to recipients are

funded from payroll taxes on workers' wages. Each dollar of payments from which recipients can spend is one less dollar of earned income from which taxed workers can spend. Biggs finds a footnote in an AARP press release acknowledging this issue: "A net analysis would subtract the economic effects of payroll taxes from those of benefit payments." Second, if recipients and workers consume the same shares of income they receive, additional spending that Social Security payments make possible for recipients will exactly equal decreased spending by taxed workers. Thus, a counterargument to the claims of the press releases is that instead of adding $1.4 trillion to real GDP, the more likely actual effect is the addition of closer to $0 to real GDP.

(continued)

1. In the short run, could Social Security add to equilibrium real GDP on net if recipients allocate a larger share of income to consumption than taxed workers?

2. If the assessment of Social Security payroll taxes on workers and payment of benefits to recipients tends to reduce the U.S. saving rate, could real GDP turn out to be lower in the long run? Explain.

Sources are listed at the end of this chapter.

ISSUES & APPLICATIONS

MyEconLab Video

Why Fiscal Policy Multipliers Typically Are Small

Vince Streano/Documentary Value/Corbis

CONCEPTS APPLIED

» Discretionary Fiscal Policy

» Crowding-Out Effect and Direct Expenditure Offsets

» Policy Time Lags

This chapter has discussed the ways in which fiscal policies potentially can influence equilibrium real GDP. To assess the effects of change in government spending on real GDP, economists often utilize *fiscal multipliers*, which are measures of how much real GDP changes in response to a given increase in government expenditures.

The Impact Fiscal Multiplier

In Chapter 12, you learned about the Keynesian spending multiplier, which has a value equal to 1 divided by the difference between 1 and the marginal propensity to consume (MPC). For instance, if the economy's MPC is equal to 0.80, then the Keynesian spending multiplier equals $1/(1 - \text{MPC}) = 1/(1 - 0.80) = 1/0.20 = 5$. This Keynesian multiplier, however, measures the *maximum feasible* effect that an increase in government spending value can exert on real GDP. The reason why is that it does not take into account direct fiscal offsets and any other short-term crowding out of private spending.

Economists who wish to gauge the actual immediate effects of discretionary fiscal policy actions on real GDP are interested in what they call the *impact fiscal multiplier*. The impact fiscal multiplier measures the direct, contemporaneous effect on equilibrium real GDP of an increase in government spending after accounting for direct fiscal offsets and any other short-term crowding out of private spending. The average value of the immediate fiscal multiplier across most studies is just below 1.0. This value implies that a $1 increase in government spending typically adds, after taking into account direct fiscal offsets and short-term crowding-out effects, slightly less than $1 to desired aggregate spending.

The Cumulative Fiscal Multiplier

The full effects of increases in government spending on real GDP do not occur immediately. For instance, when the U.S. federal government borrows more funds that it spends on final goods and services, increases in interest rates caused by its higher borrowing often take time to occur, as do the induced reductions in private spending. Hence, the fullest extent of crowding-out effects is reached after the passage of time. In addition, the existence of policy time lags—in particular, the effect time lag—implies that the adjustments of equilibrium real GDP to discretionary fiscal policy actions can be assessed only after time has passed. For instance, adjustments in the price level that tend to reduce the long-run effects of discretionary fiscal policy actions on real GDP can require a number of months. Furthermore, after some time passes following initial increases in spending, the government may decide to enact tax increases to help fund the higher spending, and such tax hikes also depress the net real GDP effects of higher government spending.

For this reason, economists also are interested in the *cumulative fiscal multiplier*, which applies to a long-run period after which all influences of discretionary fiscal policy actions on equilibrium real GDP are complete. Estimates of the cumulative fiscal multiplier indicate that its value is very small. Indeed, most estimates are very close to zero. Thus, after discretionary fiscal offsets, crowding-out effects, and long-run adjustments are taken into account, discretionary increases in government spending typically generate little net change in equilibrium real GDP per year.

For Critical Thinking

1. How could the Keynesian spending multiplier have a value of 5 while the value of the impact fiscal multiplier is only equal to 1?

2. Some economists have estimated negative values for the cumulative fiscal multiplier. How could a negative value be possible? (Hint: What would happen if there were both a 100

percent direct fiscal offset and a crowding-out effect associated with a particular increase in government spending?

Web Resources

1. To consider a discussion of estimates for the short-run fiscal multiplier, see the Web Links in MyEconLab.

2. For an explanation of why the long-run fiscal multiplier may be approximately equal to zero, see the Web Links in MyEconLab.

> ### MyEconLab
>
> For more questions on this chapter's Issues & Applications, go to MyEconLab.
>
> In the Study Plan for this chapter, select Section I: Issues and Applications.

Sources are listed at the end of this chapter.

Fundamental Points

1. Fiscal policy involves discretionary changes in government spending or taxes to achieve goals such as high employment or reduced inflation. To address a recessionary gap, the government can increase spending. To address an inflationary gap, it can reduce spending.

2. Indirect crowding out occurs when the financing of deficit spending boosts the interest rate, which in turn generates lower private investment. Direct fiscal offsets occur when higher government spending displaces private spending that otherwise would have taken place.

3. Time lags reduce fiscal policy's effectiveness. They include the recognition time lag, which is the time required to gather information; the action time lag, which is the time required for policy implementation; and the effect time lag necessary for policy to have results.

4. Automatic, or built-in, stabilizers, such as the progressive income tax system and unemployment insurance programs, automatically tend to offset changes in disposable income resulting from changes in overall business activity.

WHAT YOU SHOULD KNOW

Here is what you should know after reading this chapter. MyEconLab will help you identify what you know, and where to go when you need to practice.

LEARNING OBJECTIVES	KEY TERMS	WHERE TO GO TO PRACTICE
13.1 Use traditional Keynesian analysis to evaluate the effects of discretionary fiscal policies *In short-run Keynesian analysis, an increase in government spending or tax decrease shifts the aggregate demand curve outward and thereby closes a recessionary gap in which current real GDP is less than the long-run level of real GDP. Likewise, a reduction in government spending or a tax increase shifts the aggregate demand curve inward and closes an inflationary gap in which current real GDP exceeds the long-run level of real GDP.*	Fiscal policy, 294 **Key Figures** Figure 13-1, 295 Figure 13-2, 296	• MyEconLab Study Plan 13.1 • Animated Figures 13-1, 13-2

WHAT YOU SHOULD KNOW *continued*

LEARNING OBJECTIVES	KEY TERMS	WHERE TO GO TO PRACTICE
13.2 **Discuss ways in which indirect crowding out and direct expenditure offsets can reduce the effectiveness of fiscal policy actions** *Indirect crowding out occurs when the government must borrow from the private sector because government spending exceeds tax revenues. To obtain the necessary funds, the government must offer a higher interest rate, thereby driving up market interest rates. This reduces, or crowds out, interest-sensitive private spending. Increased government spending may also substitute directly for private expenditures and thereby offset the increase in total planned expenditures that the government had intended to bring about.*	crowding-out effect, 297 Ricardian equivalence theorem, 299 direct expenditure offsets, 300 supply-side economics, 301 **Key Figures** Figure 13-3, 297 Figure 13-4, 298 Figure 13-5, 301	• MyEconLab Study Plan 13.2 • Animated Figures 13-3, 13-4, 13-5
13.3 **List and define fiscal policy time lags and explain why they complicate efforts to engage in fiscal "fine-tuning"** *Efforts to use fiscal policy to bring about changes in aggregate demand are complicated by policy time lags. One of these is the recognition time lag, which is the time required to collect information about the economy's current situation. Another is the action time lag, the period between recognition of a problem and implementation of a policy intended to address it. Finally, there is the effect time lag, which is the interval between the implementation of a policy and its having an effect on the economy.*	Recognition time lag, 302 action time lag, 302 effect time lag, 302	• MyEconLab Study Plan 13.3
13.4 **Describe how certain aspects of fiscal policy function as automatic stabilizers for the economy** *Income taxes diminish automatically when economic activity drops, and unemployment compensation and income transfer payments increase. Thus, when there is a decline in real GDP, the automatic reduction in income tax collections and increases in unemployment compensation and income transfer payments tend to minimize the reduction in total planned expenditures that would otherwise have resulted.*	automatic, or built-in, stabilizers, 303 **Key Figure** Figure 13-6, 304	• MyEconLab Study Plan 13.4 • Animated Figure 13-6

Log in to MyEconLab, take a chapter test, and get a personalized Study Plan that tells you which concepts you understand and which ones you need to review. From there, MyEconLab will give you further practice, tutorials, animations, videos, and guided solutions. For more information, visit http://www.myeconlab.com

PROBLEMS

All problems are assignable in MyEconLab. Answers to odd-numbered problems appear in MyEconLab.

13-1. Suppose that Congress and the president decide that the nation's economic performance is weakening and that the government should "do something" about the situation. They make no tax changes but do enact new laws increasing government spending on a variety of programs. (See pages 296–300.)

    a. Prior to the congressional and presidential action, careful studies by government economists indicated that the Keynesian multiplier effect of a rise in government expenditures on equilibrium real GDP per year is equal to 3. In the 12 months since the increase in government spending, however, it has become clear that the actual ultimate effect on real GDP will be less than half of that amount. What factors might account for this?

    b. Another year and a half elapses following passage of the government spending boost. The government has undertaken no additional policy actions, nor have there been any other events of significance. Nevertheless, by the end of the second year, real GDP has returned to its original level, and the price level has increased sharply. Provide a possible explanation for this outcome.

13-2. Suppose that Congress enacts a significant tax cut with the expectation that this action will stimulate aggregate demand and push up real GDP in the short run. In fact, however, neither real GDP nor the price level changes significantly as a result of the tax cut. What might account for this outcome? (See pages 296–299.)

13-3. Explain how time lags in discretionary fiscal policymaking could thwart the efforts of Congress and the president to stabilize real GDP in the face of an economic downturn. Is it possible that these time lags could actually cause discretionary fiscal policy to *destabilize* real GDP? (See page 302.)

13-4. Determine whether each of the following is an example of a situation in which a direct expenditure offset to fiscal policy occurs. (See page 300.)

    a. In an effort to help rejuvenate the nation's railroad system, a new government agency buys unused track, locomotives, and passenger and freight cars, many of which private companies would otherwise have purchased and put into regular use.

    b. The government increases its expenditures without raising taxes. To cover the resulting budget deficit, it borrows more funds from the private sector, thereby pushing up the market interest rate and discouraging private planned investment spending.

    c. The government finances the construction of a classical music museum that otherwise would never have received private funding.

13-5. Determine whether each of the following is an example of a situation in which there is indirect crowding out resulting from an expansionary fiscal policy action. (See pages 297–298.)

    a. The government provides a subsidy to help keep an existing firm operating, even though a group of investors otherwise would have provided a cash infusion that would have kept the company in business.

    b. The government reduces its taxes without decreasing its expenditures. To cover the resulting budget deficit, it borrows more funds from the private sector, thereby pushing up the market interest rate and discouraging private planned investment spending.

    c. Government expenditures fund construction of a high-rise office building on a plot of land where a private company otherwise would have constructed an essentially identical building.

13-6. The U.S. government is in the midst of spending more than $1 billion on seven buildings containing more than 100,000 square feet of space to be used for study of infectious diseases. Prior to the government's decision to construct these buildings, a few universities had been planning to build essentially the same facilities using privately obtained funds. After construction on the government buildings began, however, the universities dropped their plans. Evaluate whether the government's $1 billion expenditure is actually likely to push U.S. real GDP above the level it would have reached in the absence of the government's construction spree. (See page 300.)

13-7. Determine whether each of the following is an example of a discretionary fiscal policy action. (See page 294.)

    a. A recession occurs, and government-funded unemployment compensation is paid to laid-off workers.

    b. Congress votes to fund a new jobs program designed to put unemployed workers to work.

c. The Federal Reserve decides to reduce the quantity of money in circulation in an effort to slow inflation.

d. Under powers authorized by an act of Congress, the president decides to authorize an emergency release of funds for spending programs intended to head off economic crises.

13-8. Determine whether each of the following is an example of an automatic fiscal stabilizer. (See pages 303–304.)

a. A federal agency must extend loans to businesses whenever an economic downturn begins.

b. As the economy heats up, the resulting increase in equilibrium real GDP per year immediately results in higher income tax payments, which dampen consumption spending somewhat.

c. As the economy starts to recover from a severe recession and more people go back to work, government-funded unemployment compensation payments begin to decline.

d. To stem an overheated economy, the president, using special powers granted by Congress, authorizes emergency impoundment of funds that Congress had previously authorized for spending on government programs.

13-9. Consider the diagram below, in which the current short-run equilibrium is at point A, and answer the questions that follow. (See pages 294–296.)

a. What type of gap exists at point A?

b. If the marginal propensity to save equals 0.20, what change in government spending financed by borrowing from the private sector could eliminate the gap identified in part (a)? Explain.

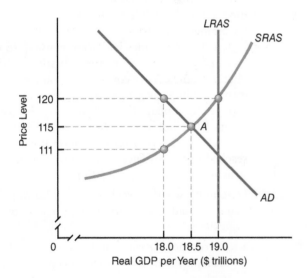

13-10. Consider the diagram in the next column, in which the current short-run equilibrium is at point A, and answer the questions that follow. (See pages 294–296.)

a. What type of gap exists at point A?

b. If the marginal propensity to consume equals 0.75, what change in government spending financed by borrowing from the private sector could eliminate the gap identified in part (a)? Explain.

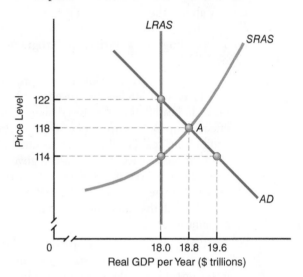

13-11. Currently, a government's budget is balanced. The marginal propensity to consume is 0.80. The government has determined that each additional $10 billion it borrows to finance a budget deficit pushes up the market interest rate by 0.1 percentage point. It has also determined that every 0.1-percentage-point change in the market interest rate generates a change in planned investment expenditures equal to $2 billion. Finally, the government knows that to close a recessionary gap and take into account the resulting change in the price level, it must generate a net rightward shift in the aggregate demand curve equal to $200 billion. Assuming that there are no direct expenditure offsets to fiscal policy, how much should the government increase its expenditures? (See pages 294–296. Hint: How much private investment spending will each $10 billion increase in government spending crowd out?)

13-12. A government is currently operating with an annual budget deficit of $40 billion. The government has determined that every $10 billion reduction in the amount it borrows each year would reduce the market interest rate by 0.1 percentage point. Furthermore, it has determined that every 0.1-percentage-point change in the market interest rate generates a change in planned investment expenditures in the opposite direction equal to $5 billion. The marginal propensity to consume is 0.75. Finally, the government knows that to eliminate an inflationary gap and take into account the resulting change in the price level, it must generate a net leftward shift in the aggregate demand curve equal to $40 billion. Assuming that there are no direct expenditure offsets to fiscal policy, how much should the government increase taxes? (See pages 294–300. Hint: How much new private investment spending is induced by each $10 billion decrease in government spending?)

13-13. Assume that the Ricardian equivalence theorem is not relevant. Explain why an income-tax-rate cut should affect short-run equilibrium real GDP. (See pages 298–299.)

13-14. Suppose that Congress enacts a lump-sum tax cut of $750 billion. The marginal propensity to consume is equal to 0.75. Assuming that Ricardian equivalence holds true, what is the effect on equilibrium real GDP? On saving? (See page 298.)

13-15. In May and June of 2008, the federal government issued one-time tax rebates—checks returning a small portion of taxes previously paid—to millions of U.S residents, and U.S. real disposable income temporarily jumped by nearly $500 billion. Household real consumption spending did not increase in response to the short-lived increase in real disposable income. Explain how the logic of the permanent income hypothesis might help to account for this apparent non-relationship between real consumption and real disposable income in the late spring of 2008. (See pages 298–299.)

13-16. It is late 2017, and the U.S. economy is showing signs of slipping into a potentially deep recession. Government policymakers are searching for income-tax-policy changes that will bring about a significant and lasting boost to real consumption spending. According to the logic of the permanent income hypothesis, should the proposed income-tax-policy changes involve tax increases or tax reductions, and should the policy changes be short-lived or long-lasting? (See pages 295–299.)

REFERENCES

INTERNATIONAL POLICY EXAMPLE: Europeans Save More as Public Spending Outstrips Taxes

Thomas Grennes and Andris Stards, "Another Look at Ricardian Equivalence: The Case of the European Union," Vox, February 28, 2013. (www.voxeu.org/article/another-look-ricardian-equivalence-case-european-union)

Christiane Nickel and Andreas Tuyka, "Fiscal Stimulus in Times of High Debt: Reconsidering Multipliers and Twin Deficits," European Central Bank Working Paper No. 1513, February 2013.

European Commission, Eurostat, "Taxation Trends in the European Union," 2014. (Published annually)

POLICY EXAMPLE: Are Traditional Automatic Stabilizers Aimed at the Wrong People?

U.S. Department of Agriculture, "Supplemental Nutrition Assistance Program (SNAP)," 2014. (www.fns .usda.gov/snap/supplemental-nutrition-assistance-program-snap)

Alisdair McKay and Ricardo Reis, "The Role of Automatic Stabilizers in the U.S. Business Cycle," Working Paper, Boston University and Columbia University, April 2013.

Evan Soltas, "Best Stimulus Package May Be Food Stamps," Bloomberg, May 6, 2013.

YOU ARE THERE: Do Social Security Payments Boost Real GDP?

American Association of Retired Persons, "Social Security Generates Nearly $1.4 Trillion in Economic Activity and Supports More Than Nine Million Jobs," AARP Press Release, October 1, 2013. (www.aarp.org/about-aarp/press-center/info-10-2013/Social-Security-Generates-Nearly-1-4-Trillion-in-Economic-Activity-Supports-More-Than-Nine-Million-Jobs.html)

Andrew Biggs, "AARP's Fuzzy Math on Social Security," *The Wall Street Journal*, October 16, 2013.

Christina Romer and David Romer, "Transfer Payments and the Macroeconomy: The Effects of Social Security Benefit Changes, 1952–1991," University of California-Berkeley, April 2014. (http://elsa.berkeley .edu/users/cromer/Romer%20and%20Romer%20NBER%20Working%20Paper.pdf)

ISSUES & APPLICATIONS: Why Fiscal Policy Multipliers Typically Are Small

Ethan Ilzetzki, Enrique Mendoza, and Carlos Végh, "How Big (Small?) Are Fiscal Multipliers?" *Journal of Monetary Economics*, 60 (2013), 239–254.

Michael Owyang, Valerie Ramey, and Sarah Zubairy, "Are Government Spending Multipliers Greater during Periods of Slack? Evidence from Twentieth-Century Historical Data," *American Economic Review Papers and Proceedings*, 103 (3, May 2013), 129–134.

Mark Thoma, "Explainer: Understanding Fiscal Multipliers," MoneyWatch, *The Wall Street Journal*, February 27, 2014.

Fiscal Policy: A Keynesian Perspective

The traditional Keynesian approach to fiscal policy differs in three ways from that presented in Chapter 13. First, it emphasizes the underpinnings of the components of aggregate demand. Second, it assumes that government expenditures are not substitutes for private expenditures and that current taxes are the only taxes taken into account by consumers and firms. Third, the traditional Keynesian approach focuses on the short run and so assumes that as a first approximation, the price level is constant.

Changes in Government Spending

Figure D-1 below measures real GDP along the horizontal axis and total planned real expenditures (aggregate demand) along the vertical axis. The components of aggregate demand are real consumption (C), investment (I), government spending (G), and net exports (X). The height of the schedule labeled $C + I + G + X$ shows total planned real expenditures (aggregate demand) as a function of real GDP. This schedule slopes upward because consumption depends positively on real GDP. Everywhere along the 45-degree reference line, planned real spending equals real GDP.

At the point Y^*, where the $C + I + G + X$ line intersects the 45-degree line, planned real spending is consistent with real GDP per year. At any income less than Y^*, spending exceeds real GDP, and so real GDP and thus real spending will tend to rise. At any level of real GDP greater than Y^*, planned spending is less than real GDP,

The Impact of Higher Government Spending on Aggregate Demand

Government spending increases, causing $C + I + G + X$ to move to $C + I + G' + X$. Equilibrium real GDP per year increases to Y^{**}.

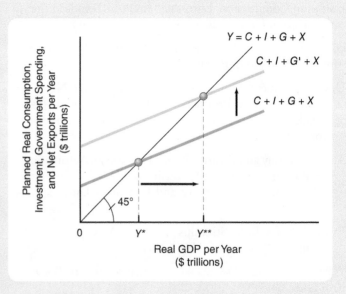

and so real GDP and thus spending will tend to decline. Given the determinants of C, I, G, and X, total real spending (aggregate demand) will be Y^*.

The Keynesian approach assumes that changes in government spending cause no direct offsets in either consumption or investment spending because G is not a substitute for C, I, or X. Hence, a rise in government spending from G to G' causes the $C + I + G + X$ line to shift upward by the full amount of the rise in government spending, yielding the line $C + I + G' + X$. The rise in real government spending causes real GDP to rise, which in turn causes consumption spending to rise, which further increases real GDP. Ultimately, aggregate demand rises to the level Y^{**}, where spending again equals real GDP. A key conclusion of the traditional Keynesian analysis is that total spending rises by *more* than the original rise in government spending because consumption spending depends positively on real GDP.   MyEconLab Concept Check

Changes in Taxes

According to the Keynesian approach, changes in current taxes affect aggregate demand by changing the amount of real disposable (after-tax) income available to consumers. A rise in taxes reduces disposable income and thus reduces real consumption; conversely, a tax cut raises disposable income and thus causes a rise in consumption spending. The effects of a tax increase are shown in Figure D-2 below. Higher taxes cause consumption spending to decline from C to C', causing total spending to shift downward to $C' + I + G + X$. In general, the decline in consumption will be less than the increase in taxes because people will also reduce their saving to help pay the higher taxes.

   MyEconLab Concept Check

The Balanced-Budget Multiplier

One interesting implication of the Keynesian approach concerns the impact of a balanced-budget change in government real spending. Suppose that the government increases spending by $1 billion and pays for it by raising current taxes by $1 billion. Such a policy is called a *balanced-budget increase in real spending*. Because the higher

---

MyEconLab Animation

FIGURE D-2

The Impact of Higher Taxes on Aggregate Demand

Higher taxes cause consumption to fall to C'. Equilibrium real GDP per year decreases to Y''.

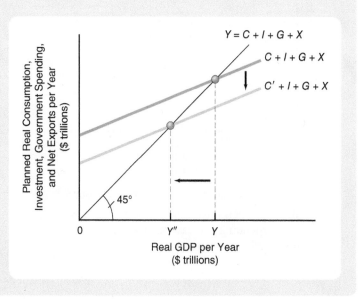

spending tends to push aggregate demand *up* by *more* than $1 billion while the higher taxes tend to push aggregate demand *down* by *less* than $1 billion, a most remarkable thing happens: A balanced-budget increase in *G* causes total spending to rise by *exactly* the amount of the rise in *G*—in this case, $1 billion. We say that the *balanced-budget multiplier* is equal to 1. Similarly, a balanced-budget reduction in government spending will cause total spending to fall by exactly the amount of the government spending cut.

MyEconLab Concept Check

The Fixed Price Level Assumption

The final key feature of the traditional Keynesian approach is that it typically assumes that as a first approximation, the price level is fixed. Recall that nominal GDP equals the price level multiplied by real GDP. If the price level is fixed, an increase in government spending that causes nominal GDP to rise will show up exclusively as a rise in *real* GDP. This will in turn be accompanied by a decline in the unemployment rate because the additional real GDP can be produced only if additional factors of production, such as labor, are utilized.

MyEconLab Concept Check
MyEconLab Study Plan

PROBLEMS

All problems are assignable in MyEconLab. *Answers to odd-numbered problems appear in* MyEconLab.

D-1. Assume that equilibrium real GDP is $18.2 trillion and full-employment equilibrium (*FE*) is $18.55 trillion. The marginal propensity to save is $\frac{1}{7}$. Answer the questions using the data in the following graph. (See pages 312–313.)

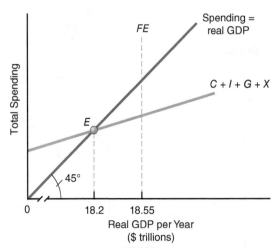

a. What is the marginal propensity to consume?

b. By how much must new investment or government spending increase to bring the economy up to full employment?

c. By how much must government cut personal taxes to stimulate the economy to the full-employment equilibrium?

D-2. Assume that MPC $= \frac{4}{5}$ when answering the following questions. (See pages 312–313.)

a. If government expenditures rise by $2 billion, by how much will the aggregate expenditure curve shift upward? By how much will equilibrium real GDP per year change?

b. If taxes increase by $2 billion, by how much will the aggregate expenditure curve shift downward? By how much will equilibrium real GDP per year change?

D-3. Assume that MPC $= \frac{4}{5}$ when answering the following questions. (See pages 312–313.)

a. If government expenditures rise by $1 billion, by how much will the aggregate expenditure curve shift upward?

b. If taxes rise by $1 billion, by how much will the aggregate expenditure curve shift downward?

c. If both taxes and government expenditures rise by $1 billion, by how much will the aggregate expenditure curve shift? What will happen to the equilibrium level of real GDP?

d. How does your response to the second question in part (c) change if MPC $= \frac{3}{4}$? If MPC $= \frac{1}{2}$?

Deficit Spending and the Public Debt

14

Tony Foggon/Alamy

Twenty years ago, the U.S. *net public debt*— the total value of outstanding government securities issued to finance the federal government's borrowing—was slightly over 50 percent of U.S. GDP. Today that percentage is closer to 90 percent. The U.S. government is not the only government that is borrowing larger amounts in relation to its nation's annual production level, however. The average ratio of the net public debts of western European governments to their nations' GDP levels has risen as well during the past two decades, from less than 50 percent to nearly 75 percent. In Japan, the net public debt as a percentage of GDP has grown from about 20 percent to more than 150 percent. What are the economic implications of increased government indebtedness relative to a country's GDP? In this chapter, you will contemplate the answer to this question.

LEARNING OBJECTIVES

After reading this chapter, you should be able to:

14.1 Explain how federal government budget deficits occur and define the public debt

14.2 Evaluate circumstances under which the public debt could be a burden to future generations

14.3 Analyze the macroeconomic effects of government budget deficits

14.4 Describe possible ways to reduce the government budget deficit

MyEconLab helps you master each objective and study more efficiently. See the end of the chapter for details.

if the net public debt rises as projected, by 2030 about 8 percent of a typical family's income will go toward paying interest on the debt? Hence, if your future family income turned out to be $100,000 per year, $8,000 of it would have to be directed to paying interest on the public debt. Projections indicate that by 2040, paying interest on the debt would require approximately $17,000 out of the same annual income, and by 2050 about $30,000 would be necessary.

Every year since 2001, the U.S. government has spent more than it collected in taxes. The government anticipates that it will continue to spend more than it receives indefinitely. Should you be worried about this? The answer, as you will see in this chapter, is both yes and no. First, let's examine what the government does when it spends more than it receives.

14.1 Explain how federal government budget deficits occur and define the public debt

Public Deficits and Debts

A **government budget deficit** exists if the government spends more than it receives in taxes during a given period of time. The government has to finance this shortfall somehow. Barring any resort to money creation (the subject matter of Chapters 15 and 16), the U.S. Treasury sells IOUs on behalf of the U.S. government, in the form of securities that are normally called bonds. In effect, the federal government asks U.S. and foreign households, businesses, and governments to lend funds to the government to cover its deficit. For example, if the federal government spends $500 billion more than it receives in revenues, the Treasury will obtain that $500 billion by selling $500 billion of new Treasury bonds. Those who buy the Treasury bonds (lend funds to the U.S. government) will receive interest payments over the life of the bond plus eventual repayment of the entire amount lent. In return, the U.S. Treasury receives immediate purchasing power. In the process, it also adds to its indebtedness to bondholders.

Government budget deficit
An excess of government spending over government revenues during a given period of time.

Distinguishing between Deficits and Debts

You have already learned about flows. GDP, for instance, is a flow because it is a dollar measure of the total amount of final goods and services produced within a given period of time, such as a year.

The federal deficit is also a flow. Suppose that the current federal deficit is $500 billion. Consequently, the federal government is currently spending at a rate of $500 billion *per year* more than it is collecting in taxes and other revenues.

Of course, governments do not always spend more each year than the revenues they receive. If a government spends an amount exactly equal to the revenues it collects during a given period, then during this interval the government operates with a **balanced budget**. If a government spends less than the revenues it receives during a given period, then during this interval it experiences a **government budget surplus**.

MyEconLab Concept Check

Balanced budget
A situation in which the government's spending is exactly equal to the total taxes and other revenues it collects during a given period of time.

Government budget surplus
An excess of government revenues over government spending during a given period of time.

The Public Debt

You have also learned about stocks, which are measured at a point in time. Stocks change between points in time as a result of flows. For instance, as you learned in Chapter 12, household savings is a stock of accumulated household wealth. Suppose that total household savings turns out to equal $75 trillion at the end of 2016 and then increases to $75.5 trillion at the end of 2017. This means that there would be a net flow of household saving equal to $0.5 trillion during 2017.

Likewise, the total accumulated **public debt** is a stock measured at a given point in time, and it changes from one time to another as a result of government budget deficits or surpluses. For instance, as of January 1, 2014, one measure of the public debt was about $12.9 trillion. During 2014, the federal government operated at a deficit of about $0.5 trillion. As a consequence, as of January 1, 2015, this measure of the public debt had increased to about $13.4 trillion.

MyEconLab Concept Check

Public debt
The total value of all outstanding federal government securities.

Government Finance: Spending More Than Tax Collections

Following four consecutive years—1998 through 2001—of official budget surpluses, the federal government began to experience budget deficits once more beginning in 2002. Since then, government spending has increased considerably, and tax revenues have failed to keep pace. Consequently, the federal government has operated with a deficit. Indeed, after 2009 the federal budget deficit widened dramatically—to inflation-adjusted levels not seen since World War II.

THE HISTORICAL RECORD OF FEDERAL BUDGET DEFICITS Figure 14-1 below charts inflation-adjusted expenditures and revenues of the federal government since 1940. The *real* annual budget deficit is the arithmetic difference between real expenditures and real revenues during years in which the government's spending has exceeded its revenues. As you can see, this nation has experienced numerous years of federal budget deficits. Indeed, the annual budget surpluses of 1998 through 2001 were somewhat out of the ordinary. The 1998 budget surplus was the first since 1968, when the government briefly operated with a surplus. Before the 1998–2001 budget surpluses, the U.S. government had not experienced back-to-back annual surpluses since the 1950s.

Indeed, since 1940 the U.S. government has operated with an annual budget surplus for a total of only 13 years. In all other years, it has collected insufficient taxes and other revenues to fund its spending. Every year this has occurred, the federal government has borrowed to finance its additional expenditures.

Even though Figure 14-1 below accounts for inflation, it does not give a clear picture of the size of the federal government's deficits or surpluses in relation to overall economic activity in the United States. Figure 14-2 on the next page provides a

MyEconLab Real-time data
MyEconLab Animation

FIGURE 14-1

Federal Budget Deficits and Surpluses since 1940

Federal budget deficits (expenditures in excess of receipts, in red) have been much more common than federal budget surpluses (receipts in excess of expenditures, in green).
Source: Office of Management and Budget.

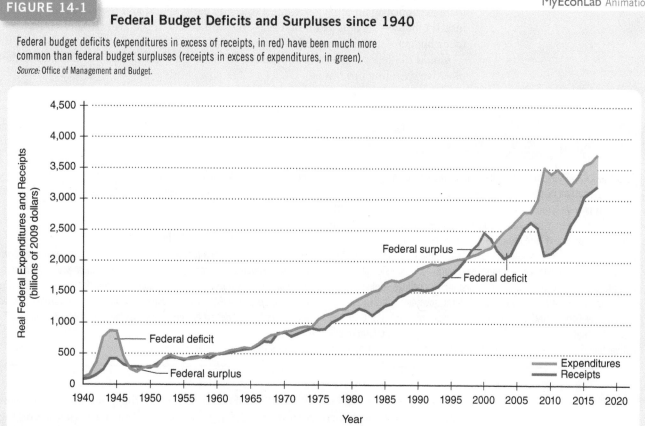

MyEconLab Real-time data
MyEconLab Animation

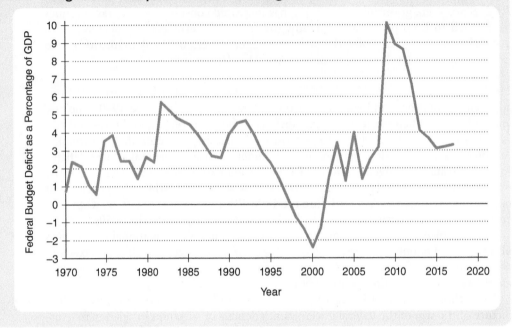

FIGURE 14-2

The Federal Budget Deficit Expressed as a Percentage of GDP

During the early 2000s, the federal budget deficit rose as a share of GDP and then declined somewhat until 2007. Then it increased dramatically until 2010. (Note that the negative values for the 1998–2001 period designate budget surpluses as a percentage of GDP during those years.)

Sources: Economic Report of the President; Economic Indicators, various issues; estimates after 2015.

clearer view of the size of government deficits or surpluses relative to the size of the U.S. economy by expressing them as percentages of GDP. As you can see, the federal budget deficit rose to nearly 6 percent of GDP in the early 1980s. It then fell back, increased once again during the late 1980s and early 1990s, and then declined steadily into the budget surplus years of 1998–2001. Since 2001, the average annual government budget deficit has exceeded 3 percent of GDP.

Could the federal government reduce its annual budget deficit by eliminating duplicative spending programs?

POLICY EXAMPLE

A Government Agency's Ideas for Reducing the Federal Deficit

Does the federal government really require three different programs for conducting catfish inspections? Are contracts with 159 different organizations that provide foreign language instructional support for the Department of Defense truly necessary? Do military veterans actually require six different employment and training programs operated by two different government agencies? Do students really "need" the support of twenty-one general federal assistance programs and eight direct subsidy programs that provide them with tax-financed assistance for college studies?

These are questions to which the federal government's General Accountability Office (GAO) has provided answers of "No." The GAO has concluded that at least 162 federal government programs perform duplicative functions. Combining such functions into individual programs,

the GAO estimates, could save tens of billions of taxpayer dollars every single year, thereby immediately reducing the annual federal budget deficit.

FOR CRITICAL THINKING

The GAO has complained that many government agencies also have overlapping accounting offices and consequently cannot provide accurate estimates of how much the agencies spend on duplicative functions. Why do you suppose the GAO has suggested that the federal government could reduce its budget deficit by combining overlapping accounting offices?

Sources are listed at the end of this chapter.

THE RESURGENCE OF FEDERAL GOVERNMENT DEFICITS Why has the government's budget slipped from a surplus equal to nearly 2.5 percent of GDP into a deficit averaging more than 3 percent of GDP? The answer is that the government has been spending more than its revenues. Spending has increased at a faster pace since the beginning of this century—particularly in light of the ongoing bailout of financial institutions and a sharp rise in discretionary fiscal expenditures—than during any other decade since World War II.

The more complex answer also considers government revenues. In 2001, Congress and the executive branch slightly reduced income tax rates, and in 2003 they also cut federal capital gains tax rates and estate tax rates. Because tax rates were reduced toward the end of a recession, when real income growth was relatively low, government tax revenues were stagnant for a time.

When economic activity began to expand into the middle of the first decade of this century, tax revenues started rising at a pace closer to the rapid rate of growth of government spending. Then, later in that decade, economic activity dropped significantly. Thus, annual tax collections declined at the same time that annual federal expenditures increased. Since 2011, tax revenues have increased but have continued to be less than government spending. As long as this situation persists, the U.S. government will operate with budget deficits such as those observed in recent years.

MyEconLab Concept Check

MyEconLab Study Plan

SELF CHECK Visit MyEconLab to practice these and other problems and to get instant feedback in your Study Plan.

Whenever the federal government spends more than it receives during a given year, it operates with a _____ _____. If federal government spending exactly equals government revenues, then the government experiences a _____ _____. If the federal government collects more revenues than it spends, then it operates with a _____ _____.

The federal budget deficit is a flow, whereas accumulated budget deficits represent a _____, called the **public debt**.

The federal budget deficit expressed as a percentage of GDP rose to around 6 percent in the early 1980s. Between 1998 and 2001, the federal government experienced a budget _____, but since then its budget has once more been in _____. Currently, the budget _____ is more than 3 percent of GDP.

Evaluating the Rising Public Debt

14.2 Evaluate circumstances under which the public debt could be a burden to future generations

All federal public debt, taken together, is called the **gross public debt**. We arrive at the **net public debt** when we subtract from the gross public debt the portion that is held by government agencies (in essence, what the federal government owes to itself). For instance, if the Social Security Administration holds U.S. Treasury bonds, the U.S. Treasury makes debt payments to another agency of the government. On net, therefore, the U.S. government owes these payments to itself.

The net public debt increases whenever the federal government experiences a budget deficit. That is, the net public debt increases when government outlays are greater than total government receipts.

Gross public debt
All federal government debt irrespective of who owns it.

Net public debt
Gross public debt minus all government interagency borrowing.

Accumulation of the Net Public Debt

Table 14-1 on the next page displays, for various years since 1940, real values, in base-year 2009 dollars, of the federal budget deficit, the total and per capita net public debt (the amount owed on the net public debt by a typical individual), and the net interest cost of the public debt in total and as a percentage of GDP. It shows that the level of the real net public debt and the real net public debt per capita grew following the early 1980s and rose again very dramatically after 2007. Thus, the real, inflation-adjusted amount that a typical individual owes to holders of the net public debt has varied considerably over time.

The net public debt levels reported in Table 14-1 do not provide a basis of comparison with the overall size of the U.S. economy. Figure 14-3 on page 321 does this

Table 14-1

The Federal Deficit, Our Public Debt, and the Interest We Pay on It

The inflation-adjusted net public debt in column 3 is defined as total federal debt *excluding* all loans between federal government agencies. Per capita net public debt shown in column 4 is obtained by dividing the net public debt by the population.

(1) Year	(2) Federal Budget Deficit (billions of 2009 dollars)	(3) Net Public Debt (billions of 2009 dollars)	(4) Per Capita Net Public Debt (2009 dollars)	(5) Net Interest Costs (billions of 2009 dollars)	(6) Net Interest as a Percentage of GDP
1940	49.0	536.6	4,061.9	11.3	0.9
1945	498.1	2,173.6	15,537.1	28.6	1.45
1950	21.3	1,506.6	9,892.6	33.0	1.68
1955	18.2	1,375.4	8,290.58	29.7	1.23
1960	1.6	1,266.9	7,011.2	36.9	1.37
1965	8.0	1,301.5	6,698.4	42.8	1.26
1970	11.6	1,181.6	5,761.0	59.7	1.47
1975	135.5	1,192.7	5,521.5	70.0	1.52
1980	155.9	1,498.4	6,634.4	110.9	1.92
1985	347.7	2,456.0	10,356.9	212.0	3.22
1990	309.8	3,373.0	13,492.1	245.7	3.23
1995	203.3	4,468.9	16,762.5	287.8	3.24
2000	−270.0*	3,894.3	13,789.9	254.7	2.34
2005	346.0	4,992.1	16,829.0	200.0	1.38
2010	1,354.9	8,910.6	32,707.6	193.8	1.35
2013	675.2	11,252.7	37,341.0	207.4	1.40
2014	617.4	11,890.9	39,373.8	206.0	1.27
2015	509.9	12,292.4	40,568.9	227.8	1.37

Sources: U.S. Department of the Treasury; Office of Management and Budget.

Note: Data for 2015 are estimates.

*A surplus

by displaying the net public debt as a percentage of GDP. We see that after World War II, this ratio fell steadily until the early 1970s (except for a small rise in the late 1950s) and then leveled off until the 1980s. After that, the ratio of the net public debt to GDP more or less continued to rise to around 50 percent of GDP, before dropping slightly in the late 1990s. The ratio has been rising once again since 2001 and has jumped dramatically since 2007.   MyEconLab Concept Check

Annual Interest Payments on the Public Debt

Columns 5 and 6 of Table 14-1 show an important consequence of the net public debt. This is the interest that the government must pay to those who hold the bonds it has issued to finance past budget deficits. Those interest payments started rising dramatically around 1975 and then declined into the middle of the first decade of this century. Deficits have recently been higher. Interest payments expressed as a percentage of GDP will rise in the years to come.

If U.S. residents were the sole owners of the government's debts, the interest payments on the net public debt would go only to U.S. residents. In this situation, we would owe the debt to ourselves, with most people being taxed so that the government could pay interest to others (or to ourselves). During the 1970s, however, the share of the net public debt owned by foreign individuals, businesses, and governments started to rise, reaching 20 percent in 1978. From there it declined until the late 1980s, when it began to rise rapidly. Today, foreign residents, businesses, and governments hold more than 50 percent of the net public debt. Thus, we do not owe the debt just to ourselves.

FIGURE 14-3

The Official Net U.S. Public Debt as a Percentage of GDP

During World War II, the net public debt grew dramatically. After the war, it fell until the 1970s, started rising in the 1980s, and then declined once more in the 1990s. Recently, it has increased significantly.

Source: U.S. Department of the Treasury.

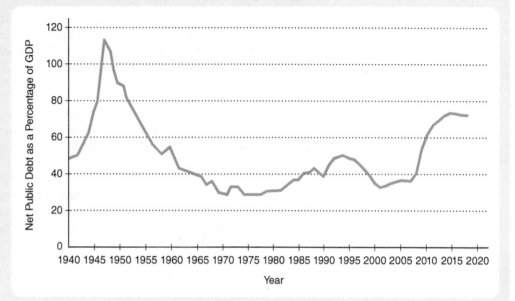

WHAT IF...

> **the federal government sought to cut the public debt by raising taxes sufficiently to cover its annual spending on goods and services?**

Eliminating government budget deficits would halt annual additions to the existing public debt (but not completely). After all, if the government succeeds only in bringing tax collections into balance with its flows of spending on goods and services, it will not have the necessary funds to cover required interest payments on the debt. Furthermore, the total debt accumulated from past deficits would remain in place. Thus, raising taxes to cover only current flows of spending on goods and services would fail to reduce the amount of outstanding debt.

MyEconLab Concept Check

Burdens of the Public Debt

Do current budget deficits and the accumulating public debt create social burdens? One perspective on this question considers possible burdens on future generations. Another focuses on transfers from U.S. residents to residents of other nations.

HOW TODAY'S BUDGET DEFICITS MIGHT BURDEN FUTURE GENERATIONS If the federal government wishes to purchase goods and services valued at $300 billion, it can finance this expenditure either by raising taxes by $300 billion or by selling $300 billion in bonds. Many economists maintain that the second option, deficit spending, would lead to a higher level of national consumption and a lower level of national saving than the first option.

The reason, say these economists, is that if people are taxed, they will have to forgo private consumption now as society substitutes government goods for private goods. If the government does not raise taxes but instead sells bonds to finance the $300 billion in expenditures, the public's disposable income remains the same. Members of the public have merely shifted their allocations of assets to include $300 billion in additional government bonds.

Two possible circumstances could cause people to treat government borrowing differently than they treat taxes. One is if people fail to realize that their liabilities (in the form of higher future taxes due to increased interest payments on the public debt) have *also* increased by $300 billion. Another is if people believe that they can consume the governmentally provided goods without forgoing any private consumption because the bill for the government goods will be paid by *future* taxpayers.

THE CROWDING-OUT EFFECT But if full employment exists, and society raises its present consumption by adding consumption of government-provided goods to the original quantity of privately provided goods, then something must be *crowded out*. In a closed economy, investment expenditures on capital goods must decline. As you learned in Chapter 13, the mechanism by which investment is crowded out is an increase in the interest rate. Deficit spending increases the total demand for credit but leaves the total supply of credit unaltered. The rise in interest rates causes a reduction in the growth of investment and capital formation, which in turn slows the growth of productivity and improvement in society's living standard.

This perspective suggests that deficit spending can impose a burden on future generations in two ways. First, unless the deficit spending is allocated to purchases that lead to long-term increases in real GDP, future generations will have to be taxed at a higher rate. That is, only by imposing higher taxes on future generations will the government be able to retire the higher public debt resulting from the present generation's consumption of governmentally provided goods. Second, the increased level of spending by the present generation crowds out investment and reduces the growth of capital goods, leaving future generations with a smaller capital stock and thereby reducing their wealth.

PAYING OFF THE PUBLIC DEBT IN THE FUTURE Suppose that after years of running substantial deficits financed by selling bonds to U.S. residents, the public debt has become so large that each adult person's implicit share of the net public debt liability is $60,000. Assume that all of the debt is owed to ourselves. Suppose further that the government chooses (or is forced) to pay off the debt at that time. Will that generation be burdened with our government's overspending?

It is true that every adult will have to come up with $60,000 in taxes to pay off the debt, but then the government will use these funds to pay off the bondholders. Sometimes the bondholders and taxpayers will be the same people. Thus, *some* people will be burdened because they owe $60,000 and own less than $60,000 in government bonds. Others, however, will receive more than $60,000 for the bonds they own. Nevertheless, as a generation within society, they could—if all government debt were issued within the nation's borders—pay and receive about the same amount of funds.

Of course, there could be a burden on some low-income adults who will find it difficult or impossible to obtain $60,000 to pay off the tax liability. Still, nothing says that taxes to pay off the debt must be assessed equally. Indeed, it seems likely that a special tax would be levied, based on the ability to pay.

OUR DEBT TO FOREIGN RESIDENTS So far we have been assuming that we owe all of the public debt to ourselves. As we saw earlier, though, that is not the case. What about the more than 50 percent owned by foreign residents?

It is true that if foreign residents buy U.S. government bonds, we do not owe that debt to ourselves. Thus, when debts held by foreign residents come due, future U.S. residents will be taxed to repay these debts plus accumulated interest. Portions of the incomes of future U.S. residents will then be transferred abroad. In this way, a potential burden on future generations may result.

Note that this transfer of income from U.S. residents to residents of other nations will not necessarily be a burden. It is important to realize that if the rate of return on projects that the government funds by operating with deficits exceeds the interest rate paid to foreign residents, both foreign residents and future U.S. residents will be better off. If funds obtained by selling bonds to foreign residents are expended on wasteful projects, however, a burden will be placed on future generations.

We can apply the same reasoning to the problem of current investment and capital creation being crowded out by current deficits. If deficits lead to slower growth rates, future generations will be poorer. If the government expenditures are really investments, and if the rate of return on such public investments exceeds the interest rate paid on the bonds, however, both present and future generations will be economically better off.

MyEconLab Concept Check
MyEconLab Study Plan

SELF CHECK Visit MyEconLab to practice these and other problems and to get instant feedback in your Study Plan.

When we subtract the funds that government agencies borrow from each other from the _____ public debt, we obtain the _____ public debt.

The public debt may impose a burden on _____ generations if they have to be taxed at higher rates to pay for the _____ generation's increased consumption of governmentally provided goods. In addition, there may be a burden if the debt leads to crowding out of current

investment, resulting in _____ capital formation and hence a _____ economic growth rate.

If foreign residents hold a significant part of our public debt, then we no longer "owe it to ourselves." If the rate of return on the borrowed funds is _____ than the interest to be paid to foreign residents, future generations can be made better off by government borrowing. Future generations will be worse off, however, if the opposite is true.

Growing U.S. Government Deficits: Implications for U.S. Economic Performance

14.3 Analyze the macroeconomic effects of government budget deficits

Many economists argue that it is no accident that foreign residents hold such a large portion of the U.S. public debt. Their reasoning suggests that a U.S. trade deficit—a situation in which the value of U.S. imports of goods and services exceeds the value of its exports—will often accompany a government budget deficit. In addition, most economists contend that government budget deficits can have significant implications, as well, for the overall economy.

Trade Deficits and Government Budget Deficits

Figure 14-4 on the next page shows U.S. trade deficits and surpluses compared with federal budget deficits and surpluses. In the mid-1970s, imports of goods and services began to consistently exceed exports of those items on an annual basis in the United States. At the same time, the federal budget deficit rose dramatically. Both deficits increased once again in the early 2000s. Then, during the economic turmoil of the late 2000s, the budget deficit exploded while the trade deficit shrank somewhat.

Overall, however, it appears that larger trade deficits tend to accompany larger government budget deficits.

DOMESTIC DEFICITS PARTLY FINANCED ABROAD Intuitively, there is a reason why we would expect federal budget deficits to be associated with trade deficits. You might call this the unpleasant arithmetic of trade and budget deficits.

Suppose that, initially, the government's budget is balanced. Government expenditures are matched by an equal amount of tax collections and other government revenues. Now assume that the federal government begins to operate with a budget deficit. It increases its spending, collects fewer taxes, or both. Assume further that domestic consumption and domestic investment do not decrease relative to GDP. Where, then, do the funds come from to finance the government's budget deficit? A portion of these funds must come from abroad. That is to say, dollar holders abroad ultimately will purchase newly created government bonds. This is the first link in the relationship between government budget deficits and trade deficits.

WHY THE TWO DEFICITS TEND TO BE RELATED The second link relating government budget deficits to trade deficits arises because foreign dollar holders will choose to hold the new U.S. government bonds only if there is an economic inducement to do so, such

MyEconLab Real-time data
MyEconLab Animation

FIGURE 14-4

The Related U.S. Deficits

The United States exported more than it imported until the mid-1970s. Then it started experiencing large trade deficits, as shown in this diagram. The federal budget has been in deficit most years since the 1960s.

The question is, has the federal budget deficit created the trade deficit?
Sources: Economic Report of the President; Economic Indicators, various issues; author's estimates.

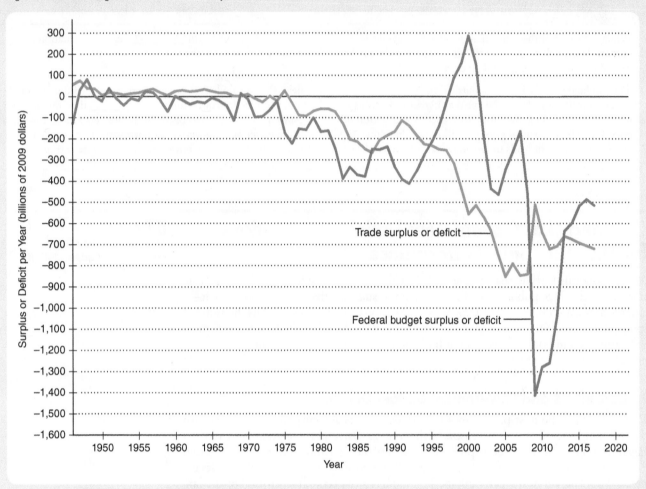

as an increase in U.S. interest rates. Given that private domestic spending and other factors are unchanged, interest rates will indeed rise whenever there is an increase in deficits financed by increased borrowing.

When foreign dollar holders purchase new U.S. government bonds, they will have fewer dollars to spend on U.S. items, including U.S. export goods. Hence, when our nation's government operates with a budget deficit, we should expect to see foreign dollar holders spending more on U.S. government bonds and less on U.S.-produced goods and services. As a consequence of the U.S. government deficit, therefore, we should generally anticipate a decline in U.S. exports relative to U.S. imports, or a higher U.S. trade deficit. MyEconLab Concept Check

The Macroeconomic Consequences of Budget Deficits

We have seen that one consequence of higher U.S. government budget deficits tends to be higher international trade deficits. Higher budget deficits, such as the much higher deficits of recent years (especially during the recession at the end of the last decade), are also likely to have broader consequences for overall economic performance.

When evaluating additional macroeconomic effects of government deficits, two important points must be kept well in mind. First, given the level of government expenditures, the main alternative to the deficit is higher taxes. Therefore, the effects of a deficit should be compared to the effects of higher taxes, not to zero. Second, it is important to distinguish between the effects of deficits when full employment exists and the effects when substantial unemployment exists.

SHORT-RUN MACROECONOMIC EFFECTS OF HIGHER BUDGET DEFICITS How do increased government budget deficits affect the economy in the short run? The answer depends on the initial state of the economy. Recall from Chapter 13 that higher government spending and lower taxes that generate budget deficits typically add to total planned expenditures, even after taking into account direct and indirect expenditure offsets. When there is a recessionary gap, the increase in aggregate demand can eliminate the recessionary gap and push the economy toward its full-employment real GDP level. In the presence of a short-run recessionary gap, therefore, government deficit spending can influence both real GDP and employment.

If the economy is at the full-employment level of real GDP, however, increased total planned expenditures and higher aggregate demand generated by a larger government budget deficit create an inflationary gap. Although greater deficit spending temporarily raises equilibrium real GDP above the full-employment level, the price level also increases.

LONG-RUN MACROECONOMIC EFFECTS OF HIGHER BUDGET DEFICITS In a long-run macroeconomic equilibrium, the economy has fully adjusted to changes in all factors. These factors include changes in government spending and taxes and, consequently, the government budget deficit. Although increasing the government budget deficit raises aggregate demand, in the long run equilibrium real GDP remains at its full-employment level. Further increases in the government deficit via higher government expenditures or tax cuts can only be inflationary. They have no effect on equilibrium real GDP, which remains at the full-employment level in the long run.

The fact that long-run equilibrium real GDP is unaffected in the face of increased government deficits has an important implication:

> *In the long run, higher government budget deficits have no effect on equilibrium real GDP per year. Ultimately, therefore, government spending in excess of government receipts simply redistributes a larger share of real GDP per year to government-provided goods and services.*

Thus, if the government operates with higher deficits over an extended period, the ultimate result is a shrinkage in the share of privately provided goods and services. By continually spending more than it collects in taxes and other revenue sources, the government takes up a larger portion of economic activity. MyEconLab Concept Check

MyEconLab Study Plan

SELF CHECK Visit MyEconLab to practice these and other problems and to get instant feedback in your Study Plan.

To obtain the dollars required to purchase newly issued U.S. government bonds, foreign residents must sell _____ goods and services in the United States than U.S. residents sell abroad. Thus, U.S. imports must _____ U.S. exports. For this reason, the federal budget deficit and the international trade _____ tend to be related.

Higher government deficits arise from increased government spending or tax cuts, which raise aggregate demand. Thus, larger government budget deficits can raise real GDP in a _____ gap situation. If the economy is

already at the full-employment level of real GDP, however, higher government deficits can only temporarily push equilibrium real GDP _____ the full-employment level.

In the long run, higher government budget deficits cause the equilibrium price level to rise but fail to raise equilibrium real GDP above the full-employment level. Thus, the long-run effect of increased government deficits is simply a redistribution of real GDP per year from _____ provided goods and services to _____ provided goods and services.

14.4 Describe possible ways to reduce the government budget deficit

How Could the Government Reduce All of Its Red Ink?

There have been many suggestions about how to reduce the government deficit. One way to reduce the deficit is to increase tax collections.

Increasing Taxes for Everyone

From an arithmetic point of view, a federal budget deficit can be wiped out by simply increasing the amount of taxes collected. Let's see what this would require. Projections for 2015 are instructive. The Office of Management and Budget estimated the 2015 federal budget deficit at about $563 billion. To have prevented this deficit from occurring by raising taxes, in 2015 the government would have had to collect nearly $4,000 in additional taxes from *every worker* in the United States. Needless to say, reality is such that we will never see annual federal budget deficits wiped out by simple tax increases.   MyEconLab Concept Check

Taxing the Rich

Some people suggest that the way to eliminate the deficit is to raise taxes on the rich. What does it mean to tax the rich more? If you talk about taxing "millionaires," you are referring to those who pay taxes on more than $1 million in income per year. There are fewer than 300,000 of them. Even if you were to double the taxes they now pay, the reduction in the deficit would be relatively trivial. Changing marginal tax rates at the upper end will produce similarly unimpressive results. The Internal Revenue Service (IRS) has determined that an increase in the top marginal tax rate from 35 percent to 45 percent would raise, at best, only about $40 billion in additional taxes. (This assumes that people do not figure out a way to avoid the higher tax rate.) Extra revenues of $40 billion per year represent only about 7 percent of the estimated 2015 federal budget deficit.

The reality is that the data do not support the notion that tax increases can completely *eliminate* deficits. Although eliminating a deficit in this way is possible arithmetically, politically just the opposite has occurred. When more tax revenues have been collected, Congress has usually responded by increasing government spending.

Why is the International Monetary Fund proposing a one-time "wealth tax"?

INTERNATIONAL POLICY EXAMPLE

Reducing Public Debts by Imposing One-Time Wealth Taxes

Residents of most U.S. states pay property taxes, which usually are assessed annually as small percentages of the assessed values of houses and surrounding properties. Residents of a few countries pay taxes on a wider array of assets. In France, for instance, anyone owning real estate, vehicles, shares of others' debts, furniture, horses, jewelry, stocks, and bonds valued at more than $1.8 million must pay an annual wealth tax. The tax is equal to at least 0.25 percent of the assessed valuation, which works out to more than $4,500 per year. People with higher levels of wealth must pay higher tax rates.

The International Monetary Fund has suggested that European governments and governments of other nations such as the United States might consider reducing their ratios of public debts to GDP to pre-2008 levels by imposing substantial, *one-time* wealth taxes. According to the IMF, European nations could achieve this objective by imposing a "tax rate of about 10

percent on households with positive net worth." Thus, instead of limiting a wealth tax to people who own relatively large amounts of assets, the IMF proposes applying it to households with any positive wealth. In addition, the IMF's proposed one-time wealth tax rate is 40 times higher than the annual wealth tax rate in France. Essentially, the IMF's proposal would entail confiscating 10 percent of the wealth of everyone who has some wealth to tax—and promising to do so only one time for the purpose of reducing the currently high public debt levels.

FOR CRITICAL THINKING

Could governments possibly devote funds raised from imposing wealth taxes to finance new spending instead of using the funds to pay off debts? Explain.

Sources are listed at the end of this chapter.

Reducing Expenditures

Reducing expenditures is another way to decrease the federal budget deficit. Figure 14-5 below shows various components of government spending as a percentage of total expenditures. There you see that military spending (national defense) as a share of total federal expenditures has risen slightly in some recent years, though it remains much lower than in most previous years.

During the period from the conclusion of World War II until 1972, military spending was the most important aspect of the federal budget. Figure 14-5 shows that it no longer is, even taking into account the war on terrorism that began in late 2001. **Entitlements**, which are legislated federal government payments that anyone who qualifies is entitled to receive, are now the most important component of the federal budget. These include payments for Social Security and other income security programs and for Medicare and other health programs such as Medicaid. Entitlements are consequently often called **noncontrollable expenditures**, or nondiscretionary expenditures unrelated to national defense that automatically change without any direct action by Congress.

Entitlements
Guaranteed benefits under a government program such as Social Security, Medicare, or Medicaid.

Noncontrollable expenditures
Government spending that changes automatically without action by Congress.

MyEconLab Animation

FIGURE 14-5

Components of Federal Expenditures as Percentages of Total Federal Spending

Although military spending as a percentage of total federal spending has risen and fallen with changing national defense concerns, national defense expenditures as a percentage of total spending have generally trended downward since the mid-1950s. Social Security and other income security programs and Medicare and other health programs now account for larger shares of total federal spending than any other programs.

Source: Office of Management and Budget.

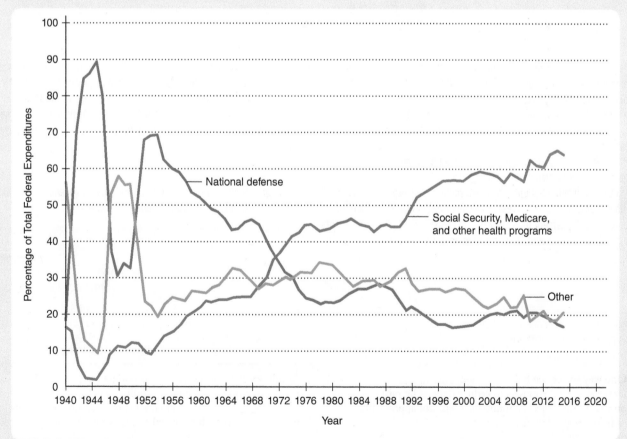

Is It Time to Begin Whittling Away at Entitlements?

In 1960, spending on entitlements represented about 20 percent of the total federal budget. Today, entitlement expenditures make up more than 60 percent of total federal spending. Consider Social Security, Medicare, and Medicaid. In constant 2009 dollars, in 2015 Social Security, Medicare, and Medicaid represented about $2.3 trillion of estimated federal expenditures. (This calculation excludes military and international payments and interest on the government debt.)

Entitlement payments for Social Security, Medicare, and Medicaid now exceed all other domestic spending. Entitlements are growing faster than any other part of the federal government budget. During the past two decades, real spending on entitlements (adjusted for inflation) grew between 7 and 8 percent per year, while the economy grew less than 3 percent per year. Social Security payments are growing in real terms at about 6 percent per year, but Medicare and Medicaid are growing at double-digit rates. The passage of Medicare prescription drug benefits in 2003 and the new federal health care legislation in 2010 simply added to the already rapid growth of these health care entitlements.

Many people believe that entitlement programs are "necessary" federal expenditures. Interest on the public debt must be paid, but Congress can change just about every other federal expenditure labeled "necessary." The federal budget deficit is not expected to drop in the near future because entitlement programs are not likely to be reduced. Governments have trouble cutting government benefit programs once they are established. One must conclude that containing federal budget deficits is likely to prove a difficult task.

Why are governments of some countries offering to let non-citizens reside within their nations' borders in exchange for "donations"?

INTERNATIONAL POLICY EXAMPLE

Help Us Fund Our Debt, and We'll Let You Reside in Our Country

As public debts continue to pile up worldwide, a growing number of governments have found a new way to raise funds to help reduce outstanding public debts. They sell residency rights. Ireland's government, for instance, will provide you with a visa giving the right to live and travel within Ireland and the rest of the European Union if you are willing to spend €500,000 (about $700,000) for it. You can obtain a "Golden Residence Permit" in Portugal if you buy at least €1 million (about $1.4 million) in Portuguese government securities during a five-year period.

Countries outside Europe also are selling residency rights. Macedonia will provide you with a residency permit for $500,000. Malta requires an $880,000 payment plus $677,000 in investments. Smaller payments are required for living and traveling in Caribbean nations such as Antigua and Barbuda, Dominica, and St. Kitts and Nevis. To obtain residency rights in Australia, you do not have to provide funds directly to the government, but you have to make investments within the nation's borders valued at more than about $850,000. The Australian government will then tax your flows of income from those investments to help pay its debts.

FOR CRITICAL THINKING

Why might people value residency permits offered by governments of some countries more highly than permits offered by others?

Sources are listed at the end of this chapter.

MyEconLab Concept Check
MyEconLab Study Plan

SELF CHECK   Visit MyEconLab to practice these and other problems and to get instant feedback in your Study Plan.

One way to reduce federal budget _____ is to increase taxes. Proposals to reduce deficits by raising taxes on the highest-income individuals will not appreciably reduce budget deficits, however.	Another way to decrease federal budget _____ is to cut back on government spending, particularly on _____, defined as benefits guaranteed under government programs such as Social Security and Medicare.

YOU ARE THERE

A Long Line of "Austerity" Budgets in Ireland

In 2006, Ireland's government operated with a slight annual budget surplus, and its net public debt was equal to just over 11 percent of the nation's gross domestic product. Today, following several straight years of substantial government deficit spending, the country's net public debt exceeds 107 percent of the nation's GDP. Michael Noonan, the finance minister for the Irish government, has been working hard to halt the rapid growth of these deficit and debt numbers. Noonan has aimed to achieve these objectives through what have come to be known as "austerity" budgets for the government. These budgets have combined government spending reductions and tax increases that have totaled nearly $38 billion, or 17 percent of the nation's GDP.

As Noonan proposes the budget for the coming year, he quotes the famous Irish poet William Butler Yeats: "Too long a sacrifice can make a stone of the heart." Noonan is convinced that the government's budget deficit is finally low enough that the net public debt as a percentage of the country's GDP is shrinking. The Irish government, Noonan has decided, is near the end of its "sacrifice." It can now maintain its current flow of annual spending, albeit at a lower level than in years past, and stick with its current flow of taxation, though at a higher level than in past years. The government, Noonan concludes, can operate with less austerity.

CRITICAL THINKING QUESTIONS

1. Why was an "austerity" budget consistent with a lower annual public deficit?

2. Why do you suppose that Ireland's government required several straight years of "austerity" budgets to reduce the nation's net public debt?

Sources are listed at the end of this chapter.

ISSUES & APPLICATIONS
MyEconLab Video

The Global Public Debt Upswing

Tony Foggon/Alamy

CONCEPTS APPLIED

» Public Debt

» Gross Public Debt

» Net Public Debt

The United States is not the only country that has experienced a significant increase in its public debt in recent years. Government indebtedness has increased considerably across the world's advanced nations.

Public Debt as a Share of Gross Domestic Product

To assess the changes in a nation's degree of public indebtedness, economists typically examine variations over time in the ratio of the nation's government's public debt to the country's level of annual economic activity, measured by GDP. Some economists consider ratios of gross public debt to GDP, but most regard ratios of net public debt to GDP as most appropriate to consider, given that the latter tracks outstanding debts held by the public in relation to economic activity. Figure 14-6 on the next page displays the latter ratios since 1991 for Japan, the United States, the euro area (the combined set of European nations that utilize the euro as their common currency), all countries with advanced economies, and all nations in the world combined.

As you can see, between the late 1990s and the early years of this century, most nations observed declines in the ratio of the net public debt to GDP. Beginning in the latter part of the past decade, however, this ratio increased worldwide. The extent of public indebtedness rose in all nations but particularly in Japan, the euro area, the United States, and, as a consequence, all advanced nations combined and the world as a whole.

FIGURE 14-6

Ratios of the Net Public Debt to Gross Domestic Product for Selected Regions

The ratio of net public debt to GDP increased noticeably after 2007 in Japan, the United States, nations that use the euro as their circulating currency, and, hence, all advanced economies and the world as a whole.

Source: Organization for Economic Cooperation and Development and the World Bank. (Post-2014 ratios are values projected by national governments.)

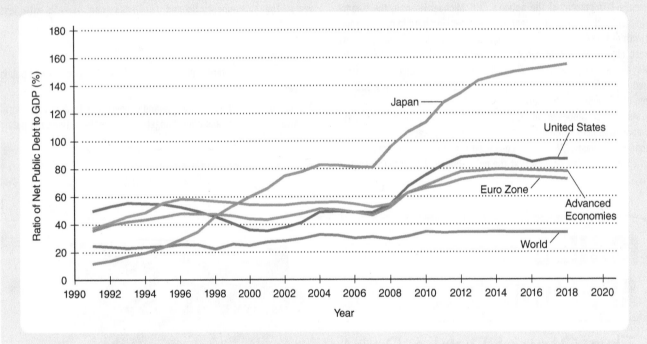

Are Projections for Future Years Too Rosy?

The post-2014 public debt–GDP ratios displayed in Figure 14-6 are estimates based on official government projections. In past years, such projections often have turned out to be overly optimistic. That is, governments commonly release predictions that magnitudes of net public debt will decrease but then end up issuing more debt than they had projected.

Thus, it remains to be seen whether the governments' predictions of gradually trailing off public debt–GDP ratios will turn out to be accurate. Even if the predictions end up being correct, the ratios of net public debt to GDP will still be very high by historical standards.

For Critical Thinking

1. Are historically high ratios of the net public debt to GDP necessarily "bad"? Explain your answer.

2. Why do you think that most economists examine ratios of the net public debt to GDP instead of ratios of the gross public debt to GDP?

Web Resources

1. To review data on net public debt as a percentage of GDP in a number of countries, see the Web Links in MyEconLab.

2. To examine information about gross public debt as a share of GDP in many nations, see the Web Links in MyEconLab.

MyEconLab

For more questions on this chapter's Issues & Applications, go to MyEconLab.

In the Study Plan for this chapter, select Section I: Issues and Applications.

Sources are listed at the end of this chapter.

Fundamental Points

1. A budget deficit occurs in any year in which the federal government operates with a flow of spending in excess of its tax collections. This deficit is added to the government's stock of outstanding debts, which is the public debt.

2. The public debt may impose a burden on future generations if they have to be taxed at higher rates to fund current government consumption, if the debt crowds out current capital investment, and if the rate of return on the borrowed funds is less than interest paid to foreign residents and governments.

3. If there is a recessionary gap, larger budget deficits generated by higher government spending or tax cuts can raise real GDP. If the economy is already at full-employment real GDP, a larger budget deficit redistributes real GDP per year from private spending to government spending.

4. Key alternatives for reducing federal budget deficits are to increase taxes or to reduce government spending, particularly in the form of expenditures on entitlement programs such as Social Security and Medicare that together account for the largest share of public spending.

WHAT YOU SHOULD KNOW

Here is what you should know after reading this chapter. MyEconLab will help you identify what you know, and where to go when you need to practice.

LEARNING OBJECTIVES	KEY TERMS	WHERE TO GO TO PRACTICE
14.1 **Explain how federal government budget deficits occur and define the public debt** *A budget deficit occurs whenever the flow of government expenditures exceeds the flow of government revenues during a period of time. Accumulated budget deficits are a stock, called the public debt. The gross public debt is the stock of total government bonds, and the net public debt is the difference between the gross public debt and the amount of government agencies' holdings of government bonds.*	government budget deficit, 316 balanced budget, 316 government budget surplus, 316 public debt, 316 **Key Figures** Figure 14-1, 317 Figure 14-2, 318	• MyEconLab Study Plan 14.1 • Animated Figures 14-1, 14-2
14.2 **Evaluate circumstances under which the public debt could be a burden to future generations** *People taxed at a higher rate must forgo private consumption as society substitutes government goods for private goods. Any current crowding out of investment as a consequence of additional debt accumulation can reduce capital formation and future economic growth. Furthermore, if capital invested by foreign residents who purchase some of the U.S. public debt has not been productively used, future generations will be worse off.*	gross public debt, 319 net public debt, 319 **Key Figure** Figure 14-3, 321	• MyEconLab Study Plan 14.2
14.3 **Analyze the macroeconomic effects of government budget deficits** *Higher government deficits contribute to a rise in total planned expenditures and aggregate demand. If there is a short-run recessionary gap, higher government deficits can thereby push equilibrium real GDP toward the full-employment level. If the economy is already at the full-employment level of real GDP, however, then a higher deficit creates a short-run inflationary gap.*	**Key Figure** Figure 14-4, 324	• MyEconLab Study Plan 14.3 • Animated Figure 14-4

WHAT YOU SHOULD KNOW *continued*

LEARNING OBJECTIVES	KEY TERMS	WHERE TO GO TO PRACTICE
14.4 Describe possible ways to reduce the government budget deficit *Suggested ways to reduce the deficit are to increase taxes, particularly on the rich, and to reduce expenditures, particularly on entitlements, defined as guaranteed benefits under government programs such as Social Security and Medicare.*	entitlements, 327 noncontrollable expenditures, 327 **Key Figure** Figure 14-5, 327	• MyEconLab Study Plan 14.4 • Animated Figure 14-5

Log in to MyEconLab, take a chapter test, and get a personalized Study Plan that tells you which concepts you understand and which ones you need to review. From there, MyEconLab will give you further practice, tutorials, animations, videos, and guided solutions. For more information, visit http://www.myeconlab.com

PROBLEMS

All problems are assignable in MyEconLab; exercises that update with real-time data are marked with 🌐. Answers to odd-numbered problems appear in MyEconLab.

14-1. In 2017, government spending is $4.3 trillion, and taxes collected are $3.9 trillion. What is the federal government deficit in that year? (See page 316.)

14-2. Suppose that the Office of Management and Budget provides the estimates of federal budget receipts, federal budget spending, and GDP at the right, all expressed in billions of dollars. Calculate the implied estimates of the federal budget deficit as a percentage of GDP for each year. (See pages 317–318.)

Year	Federal Budget Receipts	Federal Budget Spending	GDP
2017	3,829.8	4,382.6	15,573.2
2018	3,892.4	4,441.6	16,316.0
2019	3,964.2	4,529.3	16,852.1
2020	4,013.5	4,600.1	17,454.4

14-3. It may be argued that the effects of a higher public debt are the same as the effects of a higher deficit. Why? (See pages 316–318.)

14-4. What happens to the net public debt if the federal government operates next year with the following (see page 319):

a. A budget deficit?

b. A balanced budget?

c. A budget surplus?

14-5. What is the relationship between the gross public debt and the net public debt? (See page 319.)

14-6. Explain how each of the following will affect the net public debt, other things being equal. (See page 319.)

a. Previously, the government operated with a balanced budget, but recently there has been a sudden increase in federal tax collections.

b. The government had been operating with a very small annual budget deficit until three hurricanes hit the Atlantic Coast, and now government spending has risen substantially.

c. The Government National Mortgage Association, a federal government agency that purchases certain types of home mortgages, buys U.S. Treasury bonds from another government agency.

14-7. Explain in your own words why there is likely to be a relationship between federal budget deficits and U.S. international trade deficits. (See pages 323–324.)

14-8. Suppose that the share of U.S. GDP going to domestic consumption remains constant. Initially, the federal government was operating with a balanced budget, but this year it has increased its spending well above its collections of taxes and other sources of revenues. To fund its deficit spending, the government has issued bonds. So far, very few foreign residents have shown any interest in purchasing the bonds. (See page 322.)

a. What must happen to induce foreign residents to buy the bonds?

b. If foreign residents desire to purchase the bonds, what is the most important source of dollars to buy them?

14-9. Suppose that the economy is experiencing the short-run equilibrium position depicted at point *A* in the diagram below. Then the government raises its spending and thereby runs a budget deficit in an effort to boost equilibrium real GDP to its long-run equilibrium level of $18 trillion (in base-year dollars). Explain the effects of an increase in the government deficit on equilibrium real GDP and the equilibrium price level. In addition, given that many taxes and government benefits vary with real GDP, discuss what change we might expect to see in the budget deficit as a result of the effects on equilibrium real GDP. (See pages 324–325.)

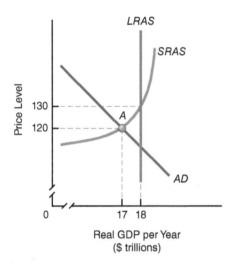

Real GDP per Year
($ trillions)

14-10. Suppose that the economy is experiencing the short-run equilibrium position depicted at point *B* in the diagram below. Explain the short-run effects of an increase in the government deficit on equilibrium real GDP and the equilibrium price level.

What will be the long-run effects? (See pages 324–325.)

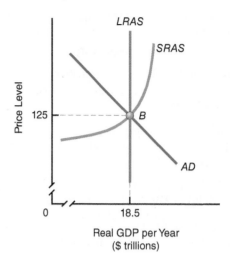

Real GDP per Year
($ trillions)

14-11. To eliminate the deficit (and halt the growth of the net public debt), a politician suggests that "we should tax the rich." The politician makes a simple arithmetic calculation in which he applies a higher tax rate to the total income reported by "the rich" in a previous year. He says that the government could thereby solve the deficit problem by taxing "the rich." What is the major fallacy in such a claim? (See page 326.)

14-12. Refer back to Problem 14-11. If the politician defines "the rich" as people with annual taxable incomes exceeding $1 million per year, what is another difficulty with the politician's reasoning, given that "the rich" rarely earn a combined taxable income exceeding $1 trillion, yet the federal deficit has regularly exceeded $1 trillion in recent years? (See page 326.)

14-13. In each of the past few years, the federal government has regularly borrowed funds to pay for at least one-third of expenditures that tax revenues were insufficient to cover. More than 60 percent of all federal expenditures now go for entitlement spending. What does this fact imply about how the government is paying for most of its discretionary expenditures? (See page 327.)

REFERENCES

POLICY EXAMPLE: A Government Agency's Ideas for Reducing the Federal Deficit

General Accounting Office, "Federal Funds Support Multiple Programs with Similar Goals," February 5, 2014.

Ben Goad, "GAO Finds Billions in Wasteful, Duplicative Federal Spending," The Hill, April 9, 2013.

Josh Hicks, "Duplicative Programs Wasting Government Funds, Report Says," *The Washington Post*, April 9, 2013.

INTERNATIONAL POLICY EXAMPLE: Reducing Public Debts by Imposing One-Time Wealth Taxes

Ambrose Evans-Pritchard, "IMF Paper Warns of 'Savings Tax' and Mass Write-Offs as West's Debt Hits 200-Year High," *The Telegraph*, January 2, 2014.

Bill Frezza, "The International Monetary Fund Lays the Groundwork for Global Wealth Confiscation," *Forbes*, October 15, 2013.

International Monetary Fund, "Taxing Times," Fiscal Monitor, World Economic and Financial Surveys, October 2013.

INTERNATIONAL POLICY EXAMPLE: Help Us Fund Our Debt, and We'll Let You Reside in Our Country

Bilefsky, Dan, "Give Malta Your Tired and Huddled, and Rich," *The New York Times*, January 31, 2014.

"Selling Citizenship: Papers, Please," *The Economist*, September 28, 2013.

"Want to Buy Citizenship? It Helps if You're One of the Super-Rich," *The Guardian*, December 10, 2013.

YOU ARE THERE: A Long Line of "Austerity" Budgets in Ireland

"Budget 2014," Article compendium, *Irish Times*, 2014.

"The Eighth Austerity Budget," *The Economist*, October 19, 2013.

Graeme Wearden, "Ireland Austerity Budget Announced as Markets Cling to Debt Ceiling Deal Hopes," *The Guardian*, October 15, 2013.

ISSUES & APPLICATIONS: The Global Public Debt Upswing

John Glover, "Global Debt Exceeds $100 Trillion as Governments Binge," Bloomberg, March 9, 2014.

"Sovereign Doubts," *The Economist*, September 28, 2013.

Sudeep Reddy, "Total World Debt Load at 313 Percent of GDP," *The Wall Street Journal*, May 11, 2013.

Money, Banking, and Central Banking

Uros Zunic/Alamy

To "mine" a digital currency called *bitcoins*—money in the form of secure computer code stored on microchips and other computing devices—some people go to considerable lengths. One individual's bitcoin-mining computer generates so much heat trying to solve the online mathematical puzzles for mining bitcoins that he keeps it next to a chimney flue in his basement. Another person's bitcoin-mining device pushed room temperatures so high in his dwelling that he purchased a second air-conditioning system. Most bitcoin "miners" report that their activities significantly raise expenditures on electricity—often by as much as 100 percent. Why do some people go to such trouble to solve mathematical problems for locating bitcoins, and why are federal and state government officials worried about the growing use of bitcoins? To understand the answers, you must learn about money and its functions, which are key topics of this chapter.

LEARNING OBJECTIVES

After reading this chapter, you should be able to:

15.1 Define the fundamental functions of money and identify key properties that any good that functions as money must possess

15.2 Explain official definitions of the quantity of money in circulation

15.3 Understand why financial intermediaries such as banks exist

15.4 Describe the basic structure and functions of the Federal Reserve System

15.5 Determine the maximum potential extent that the money supply will change following a Federal Reserve monetary policy action

15.6 Explain the essential features of federal deposit insurance

MyEconLab helps you master each objective and study more efficiently. See the end of the chapter for details.

a single loan that the Federal Reserve recently extended to a single bank in Tennessee accounted for more than 25 percent of the Federal Reserve's *total* lending to the entire U.S. banking system during a three-month interval? On the day before Thanksgiving that year, a technology breakdown halted the bank's ability to settle more than $1 billion in securities trades—the equivalent of 4 percent of the bank's total assets. The Federal Reserve granted the bank an emergency loan so that it would be able to cover its obligations to other parties. The bank then repaid to the Federal Reserve the loan, plus interest, after a technology repair was completed during the Thanksgiving holiday.

As you will learn in this chapter, making emergency loans to banks is one function of the Federal Reserve System. Nevertheless, traditionally the primary task of the Federal Reserve System has been to regulate the quantity of money in circulation in the U.S. economy—that is, to conduct *monetary policy*. Money has been important to society for thousands of years. In the fourth century B.C.E., Aristotle claimed that everything had to "be accessed in money, for this enables men always to exchange their services, and so makes society possible." Money is indeed a part of our everyday existence. Nevertheless, we have to be careful when we talk about money. Often we hear a person say, "I wish I had more money," instead of "I wish I had more wealth," thereby confusing the concepts of money and wealth. Economists use the term **money** to mean anything that people generally accept in exchange for goods and services. Table 15-1 below provides a list of some items that various civilizations have used as money. The best way to understand how these items served this purpose is to examine the functions of money.

Money
Any medium that is universally accepted in an economy both by sellers of goods and services as payment for those goods and services and by creditors as payment for debts.

15.1 Define the fundamental functions of money and identify key properties that any good that functions as money must possess

The Functions of Money

Money traditionally has four functions. The one that most people are familiar with is money's function as a *medium of exchange*. Money also serves as a *unit of accounting*, a *store of value* or *purchasing power*, and a *standard of deferred payment*. Anything that serves these four functions is money. Anything that could serve these four functions could be considered money.

Money as a Medium of Exchange

When we say that money serves as a **medium of exchange**, we mean that sellers will accept it as payment in market transactions. Without some generally accepted medium of exchange, we would have to resort to *barter*. In fact, before money was used, transactions took place by means of barter. **Barter** is simply a direct exchange of goods for goods. In a barter economy, the shoemaker who wants to obtain a dozen water glasses must seek out a glassmaker who at exactly the same time is interested in obtaining a pair of shoes. For this to occur, there has to be a high likelihood of a *double coincidence*

Medium of exchange
Any item that sellers will accept as payment.

Barter
The direct exchange of goods and services for other goods and services without the use of money.

TABLE 15-1

Examples of Money

This is a partial list of items that have been used as money. Native Americans used *wampum*, beads made from shells. Fijians used whale teeth. The early colonists in North America used tobacco. And cigarettes were used in post–World War II Germany and in Poland during the breakdown of Communist rule in the late 1980s.

Boar tusk	Goats	Rice
Boats	Gold	Round stones with centers removed
Cigarettes	Horses	Rum
Copper	Iron	Salt
Corn	Molasses	Silver
Cows	Polished beads (wampum)	Tobacco
Feathers	Pots	Tortoise shells
Glass	Red woodpecker scalps	Whale teeth

Source: Author's research.

of wants for each specific item to be exchanged. If there isn't, the shoemaker must go through several trades in order to obtain the desired dozen glasses—perhaps first trading shoes for jewelry, then jewelry for some pots and pans, and then the pots and pans for the desired glasses.

How are numerous Spanish residents coordinating barter arrangements?

INTERNATIONAL EXAMPLE

For Many Spaniards, Barter Replaces Money Exchange

More than 25 percent of the Spanish labor force has been unemployed for several years. Consequently, hundreds of thousands of unemployed people have few sources of income and have drawn down much of their wealth—and hence possess relatively few euros.

A number of Spanish residents have adjusted to life with very few available euros by establishing bartering networks. Through these networks, people who have moved back to family-held lands can, for instance, arrange exchanges of vegetables with individuals who can provide elder- or child-care services for an agreed-upon number of hours. Such barter agreements satisfy a double coincidence of wants: The vegetable gardeners can devote more time to growing vegetables to exchange for other goods and services. Individuals who provide elder- or child-care services can offer those services for food items. In addition to fresh produce and elder- and child-care

services, people barter goods such as books or furniture and services such as English lessons, appliance repairs, or rides in vehicles.

Dozens of barter networks operate in Madrid, Barcelona, and other cities. People can access most networks online to arrange barter trades, which has simplified their tasks of finding double coincidences of wants.

FOR CRITICAL THINKING

Why do you suppose a growing number of Spanish barter networks have begun utilizing informal currencies, with names such as "berries," "cougars," and "sweet potatoes" as media of exchange?

Sources are listed at the end of this chapter.

Money facilitates exchange by reducing the transaction costs associated with means-of-payment uncertainty. That is, the existence of money means that individuals no longer have to hold a diverse collection of goods as an exchange inventory. As a medium of exchange, money allows individuals to specialize in producing those goods for which they have a comparative advantage and to receive money payments for their labor. Money payments can then be exchanged for the fruits of other people's labor. The use of money as a medium of exchange permits more specialization and the inherent economic efficiencies that come with it (and hence greater economic growth).

MyEconLab Concept Check

Money as a Unit of Accounting

A **unit of accounting** is a way of placing a specific price on economic goods and services. It is the common denominator, the commonly recognized measure of value. The dollar is the unit of accounting in the United States. It is the yardstick that allows individuals easily to compare the relative value of goods and services. Accountants at the U.S. Department of Commerce use dollar prices to measure national income and domestic product. A business uses dollar prices to calculate profits and losses. A typical household budgets regularly anticipated expenses using dollar prices as its unit of accounting.

Another way of describing money as a unit of accounting is to say that it serves as a *standard of value* that allows people to compare the relative worth of various goods and services. This allows for comparison shopping, for example. MyEconLab Concept Check

Unit of accounting
A measure by which prices are expressed; the common denominator of the price system; a central property of money.

Money as a Store of Value

One of the most important functions of money is that it serves as a **store of value** or purchasing power. The money you have today can be set aside to purchase things later on. If you have $1,000 in your checking account, you can choose to spend it today on goods and services, spend it tomorrow, or spend it a month from now. In this way, money provides a way to transfer value (wealth) into the future. MyEconLab Concept Check

Store of value
The ability to hold value over time; a necessary property of money.

Money as a Standard of Deferred Payment

Standard of deferred payment
A property of an item that makes it desirable for use as a means of settling debts maturing in the future; an essential property of money.

The fourth function of the monetary unit is as a **standard of deferred payment**. This function involves the use of money both as a medium of exchange and as a unit of accounting. Debts are typically stated in terms of a unit of accounting, and they are paid with a monetary medium of exchange. That is to say, a debt is specified in a dollar amount and paid in currency (or by debit card or check). A corporate bond, for example, has a face value—the dollar value stated on it, which is to be paid upon maturity. The periodic interest payments on that corporate bond are specified and paid in dollars, and when the bond comes due (at maturity), the corporation pays the face value in dollars to the holder of the bond.　　　　MyEconLab Concept Check

Properties of Money

Money is an asset—something of value—that accounts for part of personal wealth. Wealth in the form of money can be exchanged for other assets, goods, or services. Although money is not the only form of wealth that can be exchanged for goods and services, it is the most widely and readily accepted one.

Liquidity
The degree to which an asset can be acquired or disposed of without much danger of any intervening loss in *nominal* value and with small transaction costs. Money is the most liquid asset.

MONEY—THE MOST LIQUID ASSET Money's attribute as the most readily tradable asset is called **liquidity**. We say that an asset is *liquid* when it can easily be acquired or disposed of without high transaction costs and with relative certainty as to its value. Money is by definition the most liquid asset. People can easily convert money to other asset forms. Therefore, most individuals hold at least a part of their wealth in the form of the most liquid of assets, money. You can see how assets rank in liquidity relative to one another in Figure 15-1 below.

When we hold money, however, we incur a cost for this advantage of liquidity. Because cash in your pocket and many checking or debit account balances do not earn interest, that cost is the interest yield that could have been obtained had the asset been held in another form—for example, in the form of stocks and bonds.

> *The cost of holding money (its opportunity cost) is measured by the alternative interest yield obtainable by holding some other asset.*

MONETARY STANDARDS, OR WHAT BACKS MONEY In the past, many different monetary standards have existed. For example, commodity money, which is a physical good that may be valued for other uses it provides, has been used (see Table 15-1 on page 336). The main forms of commodity money were gold and silver. Today, though, most people

MyEconLab Animation

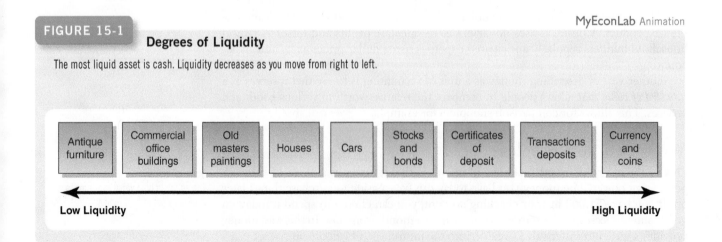

FIGURE 15-1

Degrees of Liquidity

The most liquid asset is cash. Liquidity decreases as you move from right to left.

| Antique furniture | Commercial office buildings | Old masters paintings | Houses | Cars | Stocks and bonds | Certificates of deposit | Transactions deposits | Currency and coins |

Low Liquidity ← → **High Liquidity**

throughout the world accept coins, paper currency, and balances held on deposit as **transactions deposits** (debitable and checkable accounts with banks and other financial institutions) in exchange for items sold, including labor services.

These forms of money, however, raise a question: Why are we willing to accept as payment something that has no intrinsic value? After all, you could not sell checks or debit cards to very many producers for use as a raw material in manufacturing. The reason is that payments in the modern world arise from a **fiduciary monetary system**. This concept refers to the fact that the value of the payments rests on the public's confidence that such payments can be exchanged for goods and services. *Fiduciary* comes from the Latin *fiducia*, which means "trust" or "confidence."

In our fiduciary monetary system, there is no legal requirement for money, in the form of currency or transactions deposits, to be convertible to a fixed quantity of gold, silver, or some other precious commodity. The bills are just pieces of paper. Coins have a value stamped on them that today is usually greater than the market value of the metal in them. Nevertheless, currency and transactions deposits are money because of their acceptability and predictability of value.

Acceptability Transactions deposits and currency are money because they are accepted in exchange for goods and services. They are accepted because people have confidence that these items can later be exchanged for other goods and services. This confidence is based on the knowledge that such exchanges have occurred in the past without problems.

Predictability of Value Money retains its usefulness even if its purchasing power is declining year in and year out, as during periods of inflation, if it still retains the characteristic of predictability of value. If you anticipate that the inflation rate is going to be around 3 percent during the next year, you know that any dollar you receive a year from now will have a purchasing power (see page 157) equal to 3 percent less than that same dollar today. Thus, you will not necessarily refuse to accept money in exchange simply because you know that its value will decline by the rate of inflation during the next year.

MyEconLab Concept Check
MyEconLab Study Plan

Transactions deposits
Checkable and debitable account balances in commercial banks and other types of financial institutions, such as credit unions and savings banks. Any accounts in financial institutions from which you can easily transmit debit-card and check payments without many restrictions.

Fiduciary monetary system
A system in which money is issued by the government and its value is based uniquely on the public's faith that the currency represents command over goods and services and will be accepted in payment for debts.

SELF CHECK Visit MyEconLab to practice these and other problems and to get instant feedback in your Study Plan.

Money is defined by its functions, which are as a _____ of _____, _____ of _____, _____ of _____, and _____ of _____ _____.

Money is a highly _____ asset because it can be disposed of with low transaction costs and with relative certainty as to its value.

Modern nations have _____ monetary systems—national currencies are not convertible into a fixed quantity of a commodity such as gold or silver.

Money is accepted in exchange for goods and services because people have confidence that it can later be exchanged for other goods and services. In addition, money has _____ value.

Defining Money

Money is important. Changes in the total **money supply**—the amount of money in circulation—and changes in the rate at which the money supply increases or decreases affect important economic variables, such as the rate of inflation, interest rates, and (at least in the short run) employment and the level of real GDP. Economists have struggled to reach agreement about how to define and measure money, however. There are two basic approaches: the **transactions approach**, which stresses the role of money as a medium of exchange, and the **liquidity approach**, which stresses the role of money as a temporary store of value.

15.2 Explain official definitions of the quantity of money in circulation

Money supply
The amount of money in circulation.

Transactions approach
A method of measuring the money supply by looking at money as a medium of exchange.

Liquidity approach
A method of measuring the money supply by looking at money as a temporary store of value.

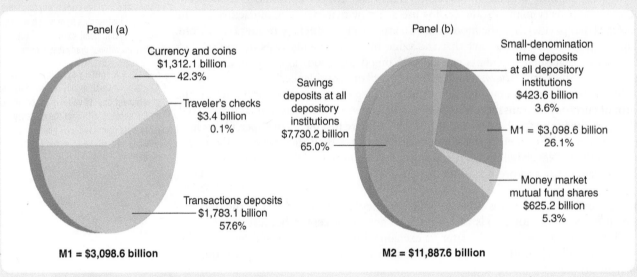

FIGURE 15-2

Composition of the U.S. M1 and M2 Money Supply, 2015

Panel (a) shows estimates of the M1 money supply, of which the largest component (over 52 percent) is transactions deposits. M2 consists of M1 plus three other components, the most important of which is savings deposits at all depository institutions.

Panel (a)

Currency and coins
$1,312.1 billion
42.3%

Traveler's checks
$3.4 billion
0.1%

Transactions deposits
$1,783.1 billion
57.6%

M1 = $3,098.6 billion

Panel (b)

Small-denomination time deposits at all depository institutions
$423.6 billion
3.6%

M1 = $3,098.6 billion
26.1%

Money market mutual fund shares
$625.2 billion
5.3%

Savings deposits at all depository institutions
$7,730.2 billion
65.0%

M2 = $11,887.6 billion

Sources: *Federal Reserve Bulletin; Economic Indicators*, various issues; author's estimates.

The Transactions Approach to Measuring Money: M1

According to the transactions approach to measuring money, the money supply consists of currency, transactions deposits, and traveler's checks not issued by banks. One key designation of the money supply, including currency, transactions deposits, and traveler's checks not issued by banks, is **M1**. The various elements of M1 for a typical year are presented in panel (a) of Figure 15-2 above.

CURRENCY The largest component of U.S. currency is paper bills called Federal Reserve notes, which are designed and printed by the U.S. Bureau of Engraving and Printing. U.S. currency also consists of coins minted by the U.S. Treasury. Federal Reserve banks (to be discussed shortly) issue paper notes and coins throughout the U.S. banking system.

TRANSACTIONS DEPOSITS Individuals transfer ownership of deposits in financial institutions by using debit cards and checks. Hence, debitable and checkable transactions deposits are normally acceptable as a medium of exchange. The **depository institutions** that offer transactions deposits are numerous and include commercial banks and almost all **thrift institutions**—savings banks, savings and loan associations (S&Ls), and credit unions.

TRAVELER'S CHECKS **Traveler's checks** are paid for by the purchaser at the time of transfer. The total quantity of traveler's checks outstanding issued by institutions other than banks is part of the M1 money supply. American Express and other institutions issue traveler's checks.

MyEconLab Concept Check

The Liquidity Approach to Measuring Money: M2

The liquidity approach to defining and measuring the U.S. money supply views money as a temporary store of value and so includes all of M1 *plus* several other highly liquid

M1
The money supply, measured as the total value of currency plus transactions deposits plus traveler's checks not issued by banks.

Depository institutions
Financial institutions that accept deposits from savers and lend funds from those deposits out at interest.

Thrift institutions
Financial institutions that receive most of their funds from the savings of the public. They include savings banks, savings and loan associations, and credit unions.

Traveler's checks
Financial instruments obtained from a bank or a nonbanking organization and signed during purchase that can be used in payment upon a second signature by the purchaser.

assets. Panel (b) of Figure 15-2 on the previous page shows the components of **M2**—money as a temporary store of value. These components include the following:

1. *Savings deposits*. Total *savings deposits*—deposits with no set maturities—are the largest component of the M2 money supply.

2. *Small-denomination time deposits*. With a *time deposit*, the funds must be left in a financial institution for a given period before they can be withdrawn without penalty. To be included in the M2 definition of the money supply, time deposits must be less than $100,000—hence, the designation *small-denomination time deposits*.

3. *Money market mutual fund balances*. Many individuals keep part of their assets in the form of shares in *money market mutual funds*—highly liquid funds that investment companies obtain from the public. All money market mutual fund balances except those held by large institutions (which typically use them more like large time deposits) are included in M2 because they are very liquid.

When all of these assets are added together, the result is M2, as shown in panel (b) of Figure 15-2.

OTHER MONEY SUPPLY DEFINITIONS Economists and other researchers have come up with additional definitions of money. Some businesspeople and policymakers prefer a monetary aggregate known as *MZM*. The MZM aggregate is the so-called money-at-zero-maturity money stock. Obtaining MZM entails adding to M1 those deposits without set maturities, such as savings deposits, that are included in M2. MZM includes *all* money market funds but excludes all deposits with fixed maturities, such as small-denomination time deposits.

MyEconLab Concept Check
MyEconLab Study Plan

> **M2**
> M1 plus (1) savings deposits at all depository institutions, (2) small-denomination time deposits, and (3) balances in retail money market mutual funds.

SELF CHECK Visit MyEconLab to practice these and other problems and to get instant feedback in your Study Plan.

The **money supply** can be defined in a variety of ways, depending on whether we use the transactions approach or the liquidity approach. According to the _____ approach, the money supply consists of currency, **transactions deposits,** and traveler's checks. This is called _____.

_____ deposits are any deposits in financial institutions from which the deposit owner can transfer funds using a debit card or checks.

When we add savings deposits, small-denomination time deposits, and retail money market mutual fund balances to _____, we obtain the measure known as _____.

Financial Intermediation and Banks

Most nations, including the United States, have a banking system that encompasses two types of institutions. One type consists of privately owned profit-seeking institutions, such as commercial banks and thrift institutions. The other type of institution is a **central bank**, which typically serves as a banker's bank and as a bank for the national treasury or finance ministry.

Direct versus Indirect Financing

When individuals choose to hold some of their savings in new bonds issued by a corporation, their purchases of the bonds are in effect direct loans to the business. This is an example of *direct finance*, in which people lend funds directly to a business. Business financing is not always direct. Individuals might choose instead to hold a time deposit at a bank. The bank may then lend to the same company. In this way, the same people can provide *indirect finance* to a business. The bank makes this possible by *intermediating* the financing of the company.

> **15.3** Understand why financial intermediaries such as banks exist

> **Central bank**
> A banker's bank, usually an official institution that also serves as a bank for a nation's government treasury. Central banks normally regulate commercial banks.

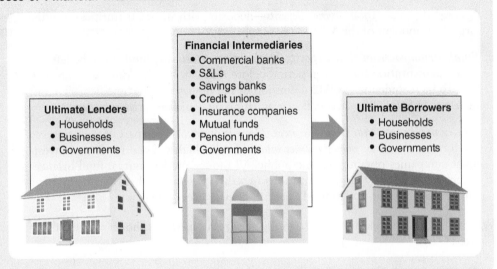

FIGURE 15-3

The Process of Financial Intermediation

The process of financial intermediation is depicted here. Note that ultimate lenders and ultimate borrowers are the same economic units—households, businesses, and governments—but not necessarily the same individuals. Whereas individual households can be net lenders or borrowers, households as an economic unit typically are net lenders. Specific businesses or governments similarly can be net lenders or borrowers. As economic units, both are net borrowers.

Ultimate Lenders
- Households
- Businesses
- Governments

Financial Intermediaries
- Commercial banks
- S&Ls
- Savings banks
- Credit unions
- Insurance companies
- Mutual funds
- Pension funds
- Governments

Ultimate Borrowers
- Households
- Businesses
- Governments

MyEconLab Concept Check

Financial Intermediation

Banks and other financial institutions are all in the same business—transferring funds from savers to investors. This process is known as **financial intermediation**, and its participants, such as banks and savings institutions, are **financial intermediaries**. The process of financial intermediation is illustrated in Figure 15-3 above.

Financial intermediation

The process by which financial institutions accept savings from businesses, households, and governments and lend the savings to other businesses, households, and governments.

Financial intermediaries

Institutions that transfer funds between ultimate lenders (savers) and ultimate borrowers.

Asymmetric information

Information possessed by one party in a financial transaction but not by the other party.

Adverse selection

The tendency for high-risk projects and clients to be overrepresented among borrowers.

Moral hazard

The possibility that a borrower might engage in riskier behavior after a loan has been obtained.

ASYMMETRIC INFORMATION, ADVERSE SELECTION, AND MORAL HAZARD Why might people wish to deposit their funds in a bank instead of lending them directly to a business? One important reason is **asymmetric information**—the fact that the business may have better knowledge of its own current and future prospects than potential lenders do. For instance, the business may know that it intends to use borrowed funds for projects with a high risk of failure that would make repaying the loan difficult.

This potential for borrowers to use the borrowed funds in high-risk projects is known as **adverse selection**. Alternatively, a business that had intended to undertake low-risk projects may change management after receiving a loan, and the new managers may use the borrowed funds in riskier ways. The possibility that a borrower might engage in behavior that increases risk after borrowing funds is called **moral hazard**.

To minimize the possibility that a business might fail to repay a loan, people thinking about lending funds directly to the business must study the business carefully before making the loan, and they must continue to monitor its performance afterward. Alternatively, they can choose to avoid the trouble by holding deposits with financial intermediaries, which then specialize in evaluating the creditworthiness of business borrowers and in keeping tabs on their progress until loans are repaid. Thus, adverse selection and moral hazard both help explain why people use financial intermediaries.

LARGER SCALE AND LOWER MANAGEMENT COSTS Another important reason that financial intermediaries exist is that they make it possible for many people to pool their funds, thereby increasing the size, or *scale*, of the total amount of savings managed by an intermediary. This centralization of management reduces costs and risks below the levels savers would incur if all were to manage their savings alone.

Pension fund companies, which are institutions that specialize in managing funds that individuals save for retirement, owe their existence largely to their abilities to provide such cost savings to individual savers. Likewise, *investment companies*, which are institutions that manage portfolios of financial instruments called mutual funds on behalf of shareholders, also exist largely because of cost savings from their greater scale of

Financial Intermediaries and Their Assets and Liabilities

Financial Intermediary	Assets	Liabilities
Commercial banks, savings and loan associations, savings banks, and credit unions	Car loans and other consumer debt, business loans, government securities, home mortgages	Transactions deposits, savings deposits, various other time deposits
Insurance companies	Mortgages, stocks, bonds, real estate	Insurance contracts, annuities, pension plans
Pension and retirement funds	Stocks, bonds, mortgages, time deposits	Pension plans
Money market mutual funds	Short-term credit instruments such as large-denomination certificates of deposit, Treasury bills, and high-grade commercial paper	Fund shares with limited checking privileges
Government-sponsored financial institutions	Home mortgages	Mortgage-backed securities issued to investors

operations. In addition, *government-sponsored financial institutions*, such as the Federal National Mortgage Association, seek to reduce overall lending costs by pooling large volumes of funds from investors in order to buy groups of mortgage loans.

FINANCIAL INSTITUTION LIABILITIES AND ASSETS Every financial intermediary has its own sources of funds, which are **liabilities** of that institution. When you place $100 in your transactions deposit at a bank, the bank creates a liability—it owes you $100—in exchange for the funds deposited. A commercial bank gets its funds from transactions and savings accounts, and an insurance company gets its funds from insurance policy premiums.

Each financial intermediary has a different primary use of its **assets**. For example, a credit union usually makes small consumer loans, whereas a savings bank makes mainly mortgage loans. Table 15-2 above lists the assets and liabilities of typical financial intermediaries. Be aware, though, that the distinctions between different types of financial institutions are becoming more and more blurred. As laws and regulations change, there will be less need to make any distinction. All may ultimately be treated simply as financial intermediaries.

Why are foreign banks accepting fewer deposits from U.S. residents?

Liabilities
Amounts owed; the legal claims against a business or household by nonowners.

Assets
Amounts owned; all items to which a business or household holds legal claim.

INTERNATIONAL POLICY EXAMPLE

Yankees, We Don't Want Your Deposits at Our Banks!

In 2010, the U.S. Congress passed the Foreign Account Tax Compliance Act (FATCA). In an effort to ensure that U.S. residents do not hide funds subject to taxation in foreign bank accounts, FATCA requires foreign banks to compile and report information about U.S. residents' deposit balances to the U.S. government. Failure to do so to the U.S. government's satisfaction can result in a 30 percent withholding of dividends, interest, or proceeds of asset sales that a foreign bank's customers receive from U.S. sources. Such penalties would include all interest and fees accruing to the foreign banks, thereby rendering accounts subject to such penalties highly unprofitable to those banks. Even compiling and reporting the information to the U.S. government's satisfaction pushes up foreign banks' costs, which can significantly reduce the profitability of U.S. depositors' accounts.

A growing number of foreign banks have responded to U.S. enforcement of FATCA by refusing to allow U.S. residents to open new deposit accounts. Indeed, many foreign banks have even been closing U.S. depositors' existing accounts and returning the depositors' funds rather than incurring the costs of complying with FATCA.

FOR CRITICAL THINKING

How have foreign banks' decisions to accept fewer deposits from U.S. residents affected their total liabilities, other things being unchanged?

Sources are listed at the end of this chapter.

FIGURE 15-4

How a Debit-Card Transaction Clears

A college student named Jill Jones uses a debit card issued by Bank of America to purchase clothing valued at $200 from Macy's, which has an account with Citibank. The debit-card transaction creates an electronic record that is transmitted to Citibank. The debit-card system forwards this record to Bank of America, which deducts $200 from Jill Jones's transactions deposit account. Then the debit-card system transmits the $200 payment to Citibank, which credits the $200 to Macy's account.

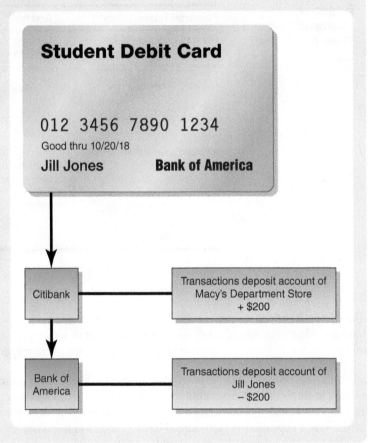

Transmitting Payments via Debit-Card Transactions

Since 2006, the dollar volume of payments transmitted using debit cards has exceeded the value of checking transactions. To see how a debit-card transaction clears, take a look at Figure 15-4 above. Suppose that Bank of America has provided a debit card to a college student named Jill Jones, who in turn uses the card to purchase $200 worth of clothing from Macy's, which has an account at Citibank. The debit-card transaction generates an electronic record, which the debit-card system transmits to Citibank.

The debit-card system also automatically uses the electronic record to determine the bank that issued the debit card used to purchase the clothing. It transmits this information to Bank of America. Then Bank of America verifies that Jill Jones is an account holder, deducts $200 from her transactions deposit account, and transmits these funds electronically, via the debit-card system, to Citibank. Finally, Citibank credits $200 to Macy's transactions deposit account, and payment for the clothing purchase is complete.

MyEconLab Concept Check
MyEconLab Study Plan

SELF CHECK Visit MyEconLab to practice these and other problems and to get instant feedback in your Study Plan.

_____ intermediaries, including depository institutions such as commercial banks and savings institutions, insurance companies, mutual funds, and pension funds, transfer funds from ultimate lenders (savers) to ultimate borrowers.

Financial intermediaries specialize in tackling problems of _____ information. They address the _____

_____ problem by carefully reviewing the creditworthiness of loan applicants, and they deal with the _____ _____ problem by monitoring borrowers after they receive loans. Many financial intermediaries also take advantage of cost reductions arising from the centralized management of funds pooled from the savings of many individuals.

The Federal Reserve System: The U.S. Central Bank

The Federal Reserve System, which serves as the nation's central bank, is one of the key banking institutions in the United States. It is partly a creature of government and partly privately owned.

The Federal Reserve System

The Federal Reserve System, also known simply as **the Fed**, is the most important regulatory agency in the U.S. monetary system and is usually considered the monetary authority. The Fed was established by the Federal Reserve Act, signed on December 13, 1913, by President Woodrow Wilson.

The Fed
The Federal Reserve System; the central bank of the United States.

ORGANIZATION OF THE FEDERAL RESERVE SYSTEM Figure 15-5 below shows how the Federal Reserve System is organized. It is managed by the Board of Governors, composed of seven full-time members appointed by the U.S. president with the approval of the Senate. The chair of the Board of Governors is the leading official of the Board of Governors and of the Federal Reserve System. Since 2013, Janet Yellen has held this position.

The 12 Federal Reserve district banks have a total of 25 branches. The boundaries of the 12 Federal Reserve districts and the cities in which Federal Reserve banks are located are shown in Figure 15-6 on the next page. The Federal Open Market

MyEconLab Animation

FIGURE 15-5

Organization of the Federal Reserve System

The 12 Federal Reserve district banks are headed by 12 separate presidents. The main authority of the Fed resides with the Board of Governors of the Federal Reserve System, whose seven members are appointed for 14-year terms by the president of the United States and confirmed by the Senate. Open market operations are carried out through the Federal Open

Market Committee (FOMC), consisting of the seven members of the Board of Governors plus five presidents of the district banks (always including the president of the New York bank, with the others rotating).

Source: Board of Governors of the Federal Reserve System, *The Federal Reserve System: Purposes and Functions*, 7th ed. (Washington, D.C., 1984), p. 5.

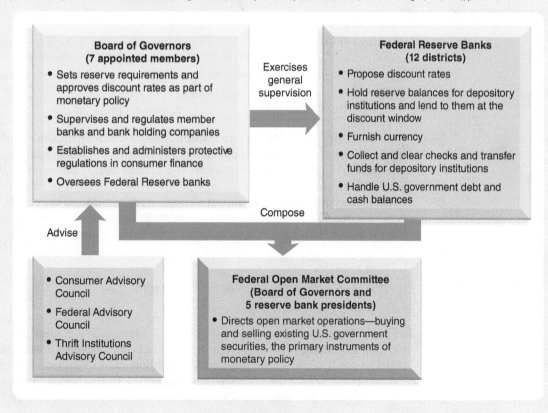

FIGURE 15-6

The Federal Reserve System

The Federal Reserve System is divided into 12 districts, each served by one of the Federal Reserve district banks, located in the cities indicated. The Board of Governors meets in Washington, D.C.

Source: Board of Governors of the Federal Reserve System.

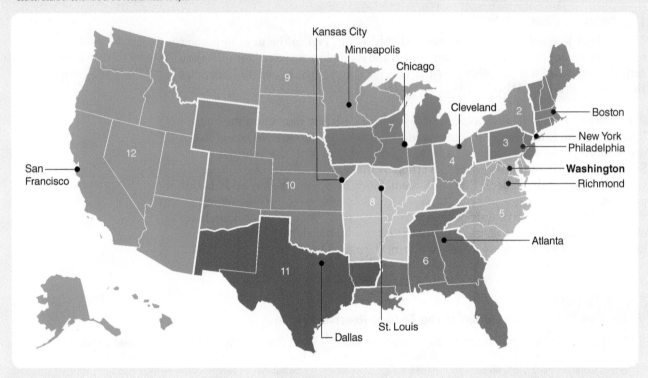

Committee (FOMC) determines the future growth of the money supply and other important variables. This committee is composed of the members of the Board of Governors, the president of the New York Federal Reserve Bank, and presidents of four other Federal Reserve banks, rotated periodically. The chair of the Board of Governors also chairs the FOMC.

DEPOSITORY INSTITUTIONS Depository institutions—all financial institutions that accept deposits—comprise our monetary system, consisting of about 5,800 commercial banks, 900 savings and loan associations and savings banks, and nearly 7,000 credit unions. All depository institutions may purchase services from the Federal Reserve System on an equal basis. Also, almost all depository institutions are required to keep a certain percentage of their deposits in reserve at the Federal Reserve district banks or as vault cash. This percentage depends on the bank's volume of business.

MyEconLab Concept Check

Functions of the Federal Reserve System

The Federal Reserve performs several functions:

1. *The Fed supplies the economy with fiduciary currency.* The Federal Reserve banks supply the economy with paper currency called Federal Reserve notes. Even though all Federal Reserve notes are printed at the Bureau of Engraving and Printing in Washington, D.C., each note is assigned a code indicating which of the 12 Federal Reserve banks first introduced the note into circulation. Moreover, each of these

notes is an obligation (liability) of the Federal Reserve System, *not* the U.S. Treasury.

2. *The Fed holds depository institutions' reserves and provides payment-clearing systems.* The 12 Federal Reserve district banks hold the reserves (other than vault cash) of depository institutions. Depository institutions are required by law to keep a certain percentage of their transactions deposits as reserves. Even if they weren't required to do so by law, they would still wish to keep some reserves on which they can draw funds as needed for expected and unexpected transactions. The Federal Reserve System also operates systems for transmitting and clearing payments among depository institutions' reserve accounts. Federal Reserve banks all offer check-clearing services and electronic payments transfer services to commercial banks, savings institutions, and credit unions.

3. *The Fed acts as the government's fiscal agent.* The Federal Reserve is the primary banker and fiscal agent for the federal government. Consequently, the U.S. Treasury has a transactions account with the Federal Reserve, which helps the government collect certain tax revenues and aids in the purchase and sale of government securities.

4. *The Fed supervises depository institutions.* The Fed (along with the Comptroller of the Currency, the Federal Deposit Insurance Corporation, the Office of Thrift Supervision in the Treasury Department, and the National Credit Union Administration) is a supervisor and regulator of depository institutions.

5. *The Fed conducts monetary policy.* Perhaps the Fed's most important task is to regulate the nation's money supply. To understand how the Fed manages the money supply, we must examine more closely its reserve-holding function and the way in which depository institutions aid in expansion and contraction of the money supply. We will do this later in this chapter.

6. *The Fed intervenes in foreign currency markets.* Sometimes the Fed attempts to keep the value of the dollar from changing. It does this by buying and selling U.S. dollars in foreign exchange markets.

7. *The Fed acts as the "lender of last resort."* From time to time, an individual bank that is otherwise in good financial condition may be temporarily low on cash and other liquid assets. Such an institution is said to be illiquid. A key justification for the formation of the Federal Reserve System was that the Fed would stand ready to prevent temporarily illiquid banks from failing by serving as the financial system's **lender of last resort**. In this capacity, the Fed stands ready to lend to any temporarily illiquid but otherwise financially healthy banking institution. In this way, the Fed seeks to prevent illiquidity at a few banks from leading to a general loss of depositors' confidence in the overall soundness of the banking system.

Lender of last resort
The Federal Reserve's role as an institution that is willing and able to lend to a temporarily illiquid bank that is otherwise in good financial condition to prevent the bank's illiquid position from leading to a general loss of confidence in that bank or in others.

WHAT IF...

the Fed were to act as lender of *first* resort?

If the Fed were the first-resort lender for private banks, any time a bank desired to obtain funds, it could borrow the desired amount of funds from the Fed and make additional loans to customers or buy more securities. By making such loans directly to a bank, the Fed would create new reserves and hence expand the amount of total reserves in the banking system. In effect, by acting as lender of first resort, the Fed would enable the banking system to determine the aggregate amount of reserves. In contrast, by acting as lender of *last* resort, the Fed maintains final authority over the creation of new reserves. The Fed consequently preserves control over the total quantity of reserves in the banking system.

MyEconLab Concept Check
MyEconLab Study Plan

The central bank in the United States is the _____ _____ _____, which was established on December 13, 1913.

There are 12 Federal Reserve district banks, with 25 branches. The Federal Reserve System is managed by the _____ of _____ in Washington, D.C. The Fed interacts with almost all depository institutions in the United States, most of which must keep a certain percentage of their transactions deposits on reserve with the Fed. The Fed serves as the chief regulatory agency for all

depository institutions that have Federal Reserve System membership.

The functions of the Federal Reserve System are to supply fiduciary _____, provide payment-clearing services, hold depository institution _____, act as the government's fiscal agent, supervise depository institutions, regulate the supply of money, intervene in foreign currency markets, and act as the _____ of _____ _____.

15.5 Determine the maximum potential extent that the money supply will change following a Federal Reserve monetary policy action

Fractional Reserve Banking, the Federal Reserve, and the Money Supply

As early as 1000 B.C.E., uncoined gold and silver were being used as money in Mesopotamia. Goldsmiths weighed and assessed the purity of those metals. Later they started issuing paper notes indicating that the bearers held gold or silver of given weights and purity on deposit with the goldsmith. These notes could be transferred in exchange for goods and became the first paper currency. The gold and silver on deposit with the goldsmiths were the first bank deposits. Eventually, goldsmiths realized that inflows of gold and silver for deposit always exceeded the average amount of gold and silver withdrawn at any given time—often by a predictable ratio.

These goldsmiths started making loans by issuing to borrowers paper notes that exceeded in value the amount of gold and silver the goldsmiths actually kept on hand. They charged interest on these loans. This constituted the earliest form of what is now called **fractional reserve banking**. We know that goldsmiths operated this way in Delphi, Didyma, and Olympia in Greece as early as the seventh century B.C.E. In Athens, fractional reserve banking was well developed by the sixth century B.C.E.

Depository Institution Reserves

In a fractional reserve banking system, banks do not keep sufficient funds on hand to cover 100 percent of their depositors' accounts. Also, the funds held by depository institutions in the United States are not kept in gold and silver, as they were with the early goldsmiths. Instead, the funds are held as **reserves** in the form of cash in banks' vaults and deposits that banks hold on deposit with Federal Reserve district banks.

The fraction of deposits that banks hold as reserves is called the **reserve ratio**. There are two determinants of the size of this ratio. One is the quantity of reserves that the Federal Reserve requires banks to hold, which are called *required reserves*. The other determinant of the reserve ratio is whatever additional amount of reserves that banks voluntarily hold, known as *excess reserves*.

To show the relationship between reserves and deposits at an individual bank, let's examine the **balance sheet**, or statement of assets owned and liabilities (amounts owed to others), for a particular depository institution. Balance Sheet 15-1 on the next page displays a balance sheet for a depository institution called Typical Bank. Liabilities for this institution consist solely of $1 million in transactions deposits. Assets consist of $100,000 in reserves and $900,000 in loans to customers. Total assets of $1 million equal total liabilities of $1 million. Because Typical Bank has $100,000 of reserves and $1 million of transactions deposits, its reserve ratio is 10 percent. Thus, Typical Bank is part of a system of fractional reserve banking, in which it holds only 10 percent of its deposits as reserves.

Fractional reserve banking
A system in which depository institutions hold reserves that are less than the amount of total deposits.

Reserves
In the U.S. Federal Reserve System, deposits held by Federal Reserve district banks for depository institutions, plus depository institutions' vault cash.

Reserve ratio
The fraction of transactions deposits that banks hold as reserves.

Balance sheet
A statement of the assets and liabilities of any business entity, including financial institutions and the Federal Reserve System. Assets are what is owned; liabilities are what is owed.

Typical Bank

Assets		Liabilities	
Reserves	$100,000	Transactions deposits	$1,000,000
Loans	$900,000		
Total	$1,000,000	Total	$1,000,000

MyEconLab Concept Check

Fractional Reserve Banking and Money Expansion

Under fractional reserve banking, the Federal Reserve can add to the quantity of money in circulation by bringing about an expansion of deposits within the banking system. To understand how the Fed can create money within the banking system, we must look at how depository institutions respond to Fed actions that increase reserves in the entire system.

Let's consider the effect of a Fed **open market operation**, which is a Fed purchase or sale of existing U.S. government securities in the open market—the private secondary market in which people exchange securities that have not yet matured. Assume that the Fed engaged in an *open market purchase* by buying a $100,000 U.S. government security from a bond dealer. The Fed does this by electronically transferring $100,000 to the bond dealer's transactions deposit account at Bank 1. Thus, as shown in Balance Sheet 15-2 below, Bank 1's transactions deposit liabilities increase by $100,000.

Let's suppose that the reserve ratio for Bank 1 and all other depository institutions is 10 percent. As shown in Balance Sheet 15-2, therefore, Bank 1 responds to this $100,000 increase in transactions deposits by adding 10 percent of this amount, or $10,000, to its reserves. The bank allocates the remaining $90,000 of additional deposits to new loans, so its loans increase by $90,000.

Open market operations
The purchase and sale of existing U.S. government securities (such as bonds) in the open private market by the Federal Reserve System.

Bank 1

Assets		Liabilities	
Reserves	+$10,000	Transactions deposits	+$100,000
Loans	+$90,000		
Total	+$100,000	Total	+$100,000

EFFECT ON THE MONEY SUPPLY At this point, the Fed's purchase of a $100,000 U.S. government security from a bond dealer has increased the money supply immediately by $100,000. This occurs because transactions deposits held by the public—bond dealers are part of the public—are part of the money supply. Hence, the addition of $100,000 to deposits with Bank 1, with no corresponding deposit reduction elsewhere in the banking system, raises the money supply by $100,000. (If another member of the public, instead of the Fed, had purchased the bond, that person's transactions deposit would have been reduced by $100,000, so there would have been no change in the money supply.)

The process of money creation does not stop here. The borrower who receives the $90,000 loan from Bank 1 will spend these funds, which will then be deposited in other banks. In this instance, suppose that the $90,000 spent by Bank 1's borrower is deposited in a transactions deposit account at Bank 2. At this bank, as shown in Balance

Sheet 15-3 below, transactions deposits and hence the money supply increase by $90,000. Bank 2 adds 10 percent of these deposits, or $9,000, to its reserves. It uses the remaining $81,000 of new deposits to add $81,000 to its loans.

BALANCE SHEET 15-3

Bank 2

Assets		Liabilities	
Reserves	+$9,000	Transactions deposits	+$90,000
Loans	+$81,000		
Total	+$90,000	Total	+$90,000

CONTINUATION OF THE DEPOSIT CREATION PROCESS Look at Bank 3's account in Balance Sheet 15-4 below. Assume that the borrower receiving the $81,000 loan from Bank 2 spends these funds, which then are deposited in an account at Bank 3. Transactions deposits and the money supply increase by $81,000. Reserves of Bank 3 rise by 10 percent of this amount, or $8,100. Bank 3 uses the rest of the newly deposited funds, or $72,900, to increase its loans.

BALANCE SHEET 15-4

Bank 3

Assets		Liabilities	
Reserves	+$8,100	Transactions deposits	+$81,000
Loans	+$72,900		
Total	+$81,000	Total	+$81,000

This process continues to Banks 4, 5, 6, and so forth. Each bank obtains smaller and smaller increases in deposits because banks hold 10 percent of new deposits as reserves. Thus, each succeeding depository institution makes correspondingly smaller loans. Table 15-3 below shows new deposits, reserves, and loans for the remaining depository institutions.

TABLE 15-3

Maximum Money Creation with 10 Percent Reserve Ratio

This table shows the maximum new loans that banks can make, given the Fed's electronic transfer of $100,000 to a transactions deposit account at Bank 1. The reserve ratio is 10 percent.

Bank	New Deposits	New Reserves	Maximum New Loans
1	$100,000 (from Fed)	$10,000	$90,000
2	90,000	9,000	81,000
3	81,000	8,100	72,900
4	72,900	7,290	65,610
.	.	.	.
.	.	.	.
.	.	.	.
All other banks	656,100	65,610	590,490
Totals	$1,000,000	$100,000	$900,000

FIGURE 15-7

The Multiple Expansion in the Money Supply Due to $100,000 in New Reserves

When the Reserve Ratio Is 10 Percent

The banks are all aligned in decreasing order of new deposits created. Bank 1 receives the $100,000 in new reserves and lends out $90,000. Bank 2 receives the $90,000 and lends out $81,000. The process continues through Banks 3 to 19 and then the rest of the banking system. Ultimately, assuming no leakages into currency, the $100,000 of new reserves results in an increase in the money supply of $1 million, or 10 times the new reserves, because the reserve ratio is 10 percent.

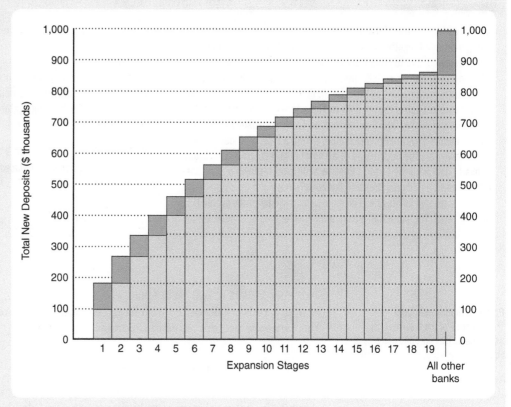

EFFECT ON TOTAL DEPOSITS AND THE MONEY SUPPLY In this example, deposits and the money supply increased initially by the $100,000 that the Fed paid the bond dealer in exchange for a U.S. government security. Deposits and the money supply were further increased by a $90,000 deposit in Bank 2, and they were again increased by an $81,000 deposit in Bank 3. Eventually, total deposits and the money supply increase by $1 million, as shown in Table 15-3. This $1 million expansion of deposits and the money supply consists of the original $100,000 created by the Fed, plus an extra $900,000 generated by deposit-creating bank loans. The deposit creation process is portrayed graphically in Figure 15-7 above.

You should be able to work through the foregoing example to show the reverse process when there is a *decrease* in reserves because the Fed engages in an *open market sale* by selling a $100,000 U.S. government security. The result is a multiple contraction of deposits and, therefore, of the total money supply in circulation. MyEconLab Concept Check

The Money Multiplier

In the example just given, a $100,000 increase in reserves generated by the Fed's purchase of a security yielded a $1 million increase in transactions deposits and, hence, the money supply. Thus, deposits and the money supply increased by a multiple of 10 times the initial $100,000 increase in overall reserves. Conversely, a $100,000 decrease in reserves generated by a Fed sale of a security will yield a decrease in total deposits of $1 million—that is, a multiple of 10 times the initial $100,000 decrease in overall reserves.

We can now make a generalization about the extent to which the total money supply will change when the banking system's reserves are increased or decreased. The **money multiplier** gives the change in the money supply due to a change in reserves. In our example, the value of the money multiplier is 10.

How will a new bank regulatory policy affect the money multiplier?

Money multiplier

A number that, when multiplied by a change in reserves in the banking system, yields the resulting change in the money supply.

POLICY EXAMPLE

New Bank Liquidity Requirements and the Money Multiplier

At various times during 2008 and 2009, some of the largest U.S. banks struggled to pull together sufficient funds to transmit payments due to their customers and to other banks. In an attempt to ensure that such a situation does not recur, U.S. bank regulators soon will be imposing a new liquidity requirement on thirty banks that have more than $50 billion in total assets. Each of these banks will have to keep on hand at all times an amount of highly liquid assets judged to be sufficient to cover the bank's volume of payments transmitted during a typical 30-day period.

Reserves are the most liquid of all assets, so regulators will require banks to hold with the Federal Reserve additional reserves to help satisfy the new liquidity requirement. For any given level of deposits, therefore, bank reserve holdings will increase, which will boost the overall U.S. reserve ratio. The potential money multiplier equals 1 divided by the reserve ratio, so the increase in the reserve ratio generated by the liquidity requirement will reduce the potential money multiplier. Thus, once the new liquidity requirement goes into effect, the value of the potential money multiplier will drop. Other things being equal, the actual money multiplier likely will decrease as well, meaning that a given change in total reserves in the banking system then will bring about a smaller change in the money supply.

FOR CRITICAL THINKING

Will the money multiplier be reduced as much if bank regulators allow banks to hold government securities in place of reserves in meeting their liquidity requirements?

Sources are listed at the end of this chapter.

Potential money multiplier
The reciprocal of the reserve ratio, assuming no leakages into currency. It is equal to 1 divided by the reserve ratio.

POTENTIAL VERSUS ACTUAL MONEY MULTIPLIERS If we assume, as in our example, that all loan proceeds are deposited with banks, we obtain the **potential money multiplier**— the *maximum* possible value of the money multiplier:

$$\text{Potential money multiplier} = \frac{1}{\text{reserve ratio}}$$

That is, the potential money multiplier is equal to 1 divided by the fraction of transactions deposits that banks hold as reserves. In our example, the reserve ratio was 10 percent, or 0.10 expressed as a decimal fraction. Thus, in the example the value of the potential money multiplier was equal to 1 divided by 0.10, which equals 10.

What happens if the entire amount of a loan from a depository institution is not redeposited? When borrowers want to hold a portion of their loans as currency outside the banking system, these funds cannot be held by banks as reserves from which to make loans. The greater the amount of cash leakage, the smaller the *actual* money multiplier. Typically, borrowers do hold a portion of loan proceeds as currency, so the actual money multiplier usually is smaller than the potential money multiplier.

REAL-WORLD MONEY MULTIPLIERS The potential money multiplier is rarely attained for the banking system as a whole. Furthermore, each definition of the money supply, M1 or M2, will yield a different actual money multiplier.

In most years, the actual M1 multiplier has been in a range between 1 and 3. The actual M2 multiplier showed an upward trend until recently, rising from 6.5 in the 1960s to over 12 in the mid-2000s. Since then, however, it has dropped to about 4.

MyEconLab Concept Check
MyEconLab Study Plan

SELF CHECK Visit MyEconLab to practice these and other problems and to get instant feedback in your Study Plan.

_____ of depository institutions consist of their vault cash and deposits that they hold with _____ _____ district banks.

The fraction of transactions deposit liabilities that depository institutions hold as reserves is the _____ _____.

The _____ _____ _____ is equal to 1 divided by the reserve ratio.

Federal Deposit Insurance

As you have seen, fractional reserve banking enables the Federal Reserve to use an open market purchase (or sale) of U.S. government bonds to generate an expansion (or contraction) of deposits. The change in the money supply is a multiple of the open market purchase (or sale). Another effect of fractional reserve banking is to make depository institutions somewhat fragile. After all, the institutions have only a fraction of reserves on hand to honor their depositors' requests for withdrawals.

If many depositors simultaneously rush to their bank to withdraw all of their transactions and time deposits—a phenomenon called a **bank run**—the bank would be unable to satisfy their requests. The result would be the failure of that depository institution. Widespread bank runs could lead to the failure of many institutions.

Seeking to Limit Bank Failures with Deposit Insurance

When businesses fail, they create hardships for creditors, owners, and customers. When a depository institution fails, however, an even greater hardship results, because many individuals and businesses depend on the safety and security of banks. As Figure 15-8 below shows, during the 1920s an average of about 600 banks failed each year. In the early 1930s, during the Great Depression, that average soared to nearly 3,000 failures each year.

In 1933, at the height of these bank failures, the **Federal Deposit Insurance Corporation (FDIC)** was founded to insure the funds of depositors and remove the reason for ruinous runs on banks. In 1934, federal deposit insurance was extended to deposits in savings and loan associations and mutual savings banks, and in 1971 it was offered for deposits in credit unions.

> **15.6** Explain the essential features of federal deposit insurance

Bank run
Attempt by many of a bank's depositors to convert transactions and time deposits into currency out of fear that the bank's liabilities may exceed its assets.

Federal Deposit Insurance Corporation (FDIC)
A government agency that insures the deposits held in banks and most other depository institutions. All U.S. banks are insured this way.

FIGURE 15-8   Bank Failures

A tremendous number of banks failed prior to the creation of federal deposit insurance in 1933. Thereafter, bank failures were few until the mid-1980s. Annual failure rates jumped again in the early and late 2000s.
Source: Federal Deposit Insurance Corporation.

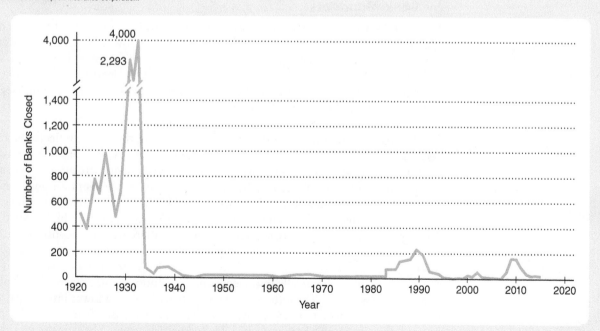

As can be seen in Figure 15-8 on the previous page, bank failure rates dropped dramatically after passage of the early federal legislation. The long period from 1935 until the 1980s was relatively quiet. From World War II to 1984, fewer than nine banks failed per year. From 1995 until 2008, failures again averaged about nine per year. Since 2009, however, more than 400 banks have failed, and many more are still in danger of failing. We will examine the reasons for this shortly. First, though, we need to understand how deposit insurance works.   MyEconLab Concept Check

The Rationale for Deposit Insurance

Consider the following scenario. A bank begins to look shaky. Its assets do not seem sufficient to cover its liabilities. If the bank has no deposit insurance, depositors in this bank (and any banks associated with it) will all want to withdraw their funds from the bank at the same time. Their concern is that this shaky bank is insolvent and will not have enough assets to return their deposits to them in the form of currency.

Indeed, this is what happens in a bank failure when insurance doesn't exist. Just as when a regular business fails, the creditors of the bank may not all get paid, or if they do, they will get paid less than 100 percent of what they are owed. Depositors are creditors of a bank because their funds are "on loan" to the bank. As explained earlier, however, banks do not hold 100 percent of their depositors' funds as cash. Instead, banks lend out most of their deposit funds to borrowers. Consequently, all depositors cannot withdraw all their funds simultaneously. Hence, the intent of the legislation enacted in the 1930s was to assure depositors that they could have their deposits converted into cash when they wished, no matter how serious the financial situation of the bank.

Federal deposit insurance provided this assurance. The FDIC charged depository institutions premiums based on their total deposits, and these premiums went into funds that would reimburse depositors in the event of bank failures. By insuring deposits, the FDIC bolstered depositors' trust in the banking system and provided depositors with the incentive to leave their deposits with the bank, even in the face of widespread talk of bank failures. In 1933, it was sufficient for the FDIC to cover each account up to $2,500. The current maximum is $250,000 per depositor per institution.   MyEconLab Concept Check

How Deposit Insurance Causes Increased Risk Taking by Bank Managers

Until the 1990s, all insured depository institutions paid the same small fee for coverage. The fee that they paid was completely unrelated to how risky their assets were. A depository institution that made loans to companies such as Apple, Inc., and Google, Inc., paid the same deposit insurance premium as another depository institution that made loans (at higher interest rates) to the governments of developing countries that were teetering on the brink of financial collapse.

Although deposit insurance premiums for a while were adjusted somewhat in response to the riskiness of a depository institution's assets, they never reflected all of the relative risk. Indeed, between the late 1990s and the late 2000s, very few depository institutions paid *any* deposit insurance premiums. This lack of correlation between risk and premiums can be considered a fundamental flaw in the deposit insurance scheme. Because bank managers do not have to pay higher insurance premiums when they make riskier loans, they have an incentive to invest in more assets of higher yield, and therefore necessarily higher risk, than they would if there were no deposit insurance.

ARTIFICIALLY LOW INSURANCE PREMIUMS The problem with the insurance scheme is that the premium rate is artificially low. Depository institution managers are able to obtain deposits at less than full cost (because depositors will accept a lower interest payment on insured deposits). Consequently, managers can increase their profits by using insured deposits to purchase higher-yield, higher-risk assets. The gains to risk taking accrue to the managers and stockholders of the depository institutions. The losses go to the deposit insurer (and, as we will see, ultimately to taxpayers).

A REGULATORY SOLUTION To combat these flaws in the financial industry and in the deposit insurance system, a vast regulatory apparatus oversees depository institutions. The FDIC and other federal deposit insurance agencies possess regulatory powers to offset the risk-taking temptations to depository institution managers.

These regulatory powers include the ability to require higher capital investment; to regulate, examine, and supervise bank affairs; and to enforce regulatory decisions. Higher capital requirements were imposed in the early 1990s and then adjusted some- what shortly after the turn of the century, but the recent jump in bank failures reveals that basic flaws remain.   MyEconLab Concept Check

Deposit Insurance, Adverse Selection, and Moral Hazard

As a deposit insurer, the FDIC effectively acts as a government-run insurance com- pany. This means that the FDIC's operations expose the federal government to the same kinds of asymmetric information problems that other financial intermediaries face.

ADVERSE SELECTION IN DEPOSIT INSURANCE One of these problems is *adverse selection*, which is often a problem when insurance is involved because people or firms that are relatively poor risks are sometimes able to disguise that fact from insurers. It is instructive to examine the way this works with the deposit insurance provided by the FDIC. Deposit insurance shields depositors from the potential adverse effects of risky decisions and so makes depositors willing to accept riskier investment strategies by their banks. Clearly, protection of depositors from risks encourages more high-flying, risk-loving entrepreneurs to become managers of banks.

Moreover, because depositors have so little incentive to monitor the activities of insured banks, it is also likely that the insurance actually encourages outright crooks— embezzlers and con artists—to enter the industry. The consequences for the FDIC— and for taxpayers—are larger losses.

MORAL HAZARD IN DEPOSIT INSURANCE Moral hazard is also an important phenomenon in the presence of insurance contracts, such as the deposit insurance provided by the FDIC. Insured depositors know that they will not suffer losses if their bank fails. Hence, they have little incentive to monitor their bank's investment activities or to punish their bank by withdrawing their funds if the bank assumes too much risk. This means that insured banks have incentives to take on more risks than they otherwise would.   MyEconLab Concept Check

Can Deposit Insurance Be Reformed?

Since 2005, Congress has sought to reform federal deposit insurance. These efforts are still under way.

A REFORM EFFORT THAT CAME TOO LATE The Federal Deposit Insurance Reform Act of 2005 aimed to reform federal deposit insurance. On the one hand, this legislation expanded deposit insurance coverage and potentially added to the system's moral hazard problems. It increased deposit insurance coverage for Individual Retirement Accounts (IRAs) offered by depository institutions from $100,000 to $250,000 and authorized the FDIC to periodically adjust the insurance limit on all deposits to reflect inflation.

On the other hand, the act provided the FDIC with improved tools for addressing moral hazard risks. The law changed a rule that had prevented the FDIC from charg- ing deposit insurance premiums if total insurance funds exceeded 1.25 percent of all insured deposits. This limit had enabled practically all U.S. depository institutions to avoid paying deposit insurance premiums for about a decade. Now the FDIC can adjust deposit insurance premiums at any time.

A NEW STRUCTURAL REFORM During the banking troubles of the late 2000s, Congress sought to increase the public's confidence in depository institutions by extending coverage to virtually all liabilities in the banking system. Although this move succeeded in boosting trust in banks, it also expanded the scope of deposit insurance. To reflect this fact, in late 2010 the FDIC altered the structure for deposit insurance premiums. The FDIC now assesses premium rates on banks' total liabilities—that is, the banks' deposits plus their borrowings from other sources.

The FDIC also raised its premium rates. Because the base for assessing premiums and the premium rates are both higher, the FDIC is now collecting premiums and adding to its reserve fund at a faster pace. Nevertheless, most economists agree that, on net, the FDIC's exposure to moral hazard risks has increased considerably in recent years.

Does the U.S. government guarantee the FDIC insurance system?

POLICY EXAMPLE

Does the Government Provide Taxpayer Guarantees to the FDIC?

According to the Federal Deposit Insurance Corporation, each dollar of insured deposits held by each individual at any given bank is "backed by the full faith and credit of the United States government." The upper limit on this government "backing" is $250,000 for each person's deposit account at that bank.

In fact, however, the 1933 law that created the FDIC specified only that reserves accumulated by charging premiums to banks would back deposits. The law said nothing about government backing. Not until the 1980s, when Congress passed nonbinding resolutions—votes that did not constitute a legal commitment—did Congress mention government backing. In 1989, Congress also instructed a special insurance agency for savings banks and savings and loan associations to require those institutions to display signs indicating that the government backed customer's deposits. Nevertheless, Congress later eliminated that agency.

Thus, in spite of the FDIC's claim of full government support, Congress has never formally committed taxpayer dollars for the purpose of backing deposits. Indeed, when the FDIC's reserve fund ran out of cash as a result of bank failures between 2008 and 2010, the U.S. Treasury provided a *loan* to enable the FDIC to make refunds to failed banks' insured depositors. The FDIC had to repay the loan, plus interest, from funds collected by imposing higher premiums on insured banks.

FOR CRITICAL THINKING

From an economic standpoint, why might a taxpayer loan to the FDIC be equivalent to "backing" insured deposits with the "full faith and credit" of the government?

Sources are listed at the end of this chapter.

MyEconLab Concept Check
MyEconLab Study Plan

SELF CHECK Visit MyEconLab to practice these and other problems and to get instant feedback in your Study Plan.

To limit the fallout from systemwide failures and bank runs, Congress created the _____ _____ _____ _____ in 1933. Since the advent of federal deposit insurance, there have been no true bank runs at federally insured banks.

Federal insurance of bank deposits insulates depositors from risks, so depositors are _____ concerned about riskier investment strategies by depository institutions. Thus, bank managers have an incentive to invest in _____ assets to make _____ rates of return.

On the one hand, the Federal Deposit Insurance Reform Act of 2005 expanded the _____ hazard risks associated with deposit insurance by increasing limits for insured retirement deposits and indexing limits for other deposits to inflation. On the other hand, the law granted the FDIC greater discretion to assess risk-based deposit insurance _____ intended to restrain _____ hazard risks.

YOU ARE THERE

In Kenya, Mobile-Phone Airtime Is Money

Bob Collymore is the chief executive officer of a company called Safaricom, the top provider of mobile-phone services in the African nation of Kenya. Safaricom also operates a mobile-phone payments system called M-Pesa, which customers can use to make payments denominated in the national currency, the *shilling*. Alternatively, customers can employ a different means of payment: prepaid mobile-phone usage minutes called "airtime." If a customer has unused minutes of airtime that she prefers to exchange for an item sold online, she can arrange a purchase of that item at a price expressed in terms of airtime minutes.

Because so many consumers now use both forms of payment when shopping online with their mobile phones, sellers usually display prices both in units of shilling and in minutes of airtime. Thus, the M-Pesa system offers Kenyan mobile-phone users the ability to use two different means of payment: shillings or airtime.

Collymore has a problem. The M-Pesa system has become so popular that expanded usage of Safaricom's mobile-phone network has strained its capability of handling the increased flows of transactions. The network occasionally has become overloaded, and Safaricom's employees have experienced difficulties in rerouting transmissions to prevent breakdowns. The company is already in the process of upgrading its network capacity, but Collymore has decided to conduct routine upgrades thereafter to help the firm keep up with growing M-Pesa usage.

CRITICAL THINKING QUESTIONS

1. What is one key function of money performed by airtime minutes? Explain.

2. What other key function of money do airtime minutes exhibit? Explain.

Sources are listed at the end of this chapter.

ISSUES & APPLICATIONS

MyEconLab Video

A Virtual Currency's Private Wins and Public Losses

Uros Zunic/Alamy

CONCEPTS APPLIED

» Medium of Exchange

» Unit of Accounting

» Store of Value

One of the world's newest currencies is available only online and in a digital form. It is called the bitcoin, and it is neither issued nor backed by a government. The digital currency was developed in 2009 by an individual or group going by the name "Satoshi Nakamoto." To obtain bitcoins, people must utilize computer programs that "mine" the currency by solving ever-more-complex mathematical puzzles that enable the entire bitcoin network to keep track of transactions using the currency. About 21 million bitcoins can feasibly be obtained via computer mining, and the roughly 12 million bitcoins that have been mined so far circulate as a currency alongside the world's other currencies.

Private Motives for Exchanging and Holding Bitcoins

Originally, people could mine bitcoins using basic home desktop and laptop devices. Now, some hardware companies sell specialized bitcoin "mining rigs" that are equipped with computer graphics cards designed solely to find bitcoins.

Why do people go to so much trouble to locate bitcoins? The answer is that the digital currency functions as a form of money. Many individuals utilize bitcoins as a medium of exchange, and a growing number of businesses accept bitcoins in payment for goods and services. Some sellers even quote online bitcoin prices and thereby use the currency as a unit of accounting. The fact that the number of bitcoins has an upper limit tends to place a lower bound on the bitcoin's value in terms of dollars or other traditional currencies, so the digital currency also has served as a store of value. Indeed, in recent years, the dollar value of a bitcoin has risen from just over $10 per digital coin to about $100 per coin.

Public Battles over Bitcoins

Federal and state government officials are less enthused about bitcoins. Some people who exchange the currency and hold stockpiles of it do so because online transactions involving the currency are difficult for governments to track. Individuals have been known to use the currency to hide payments of incomes and thereby avoid paying income taxes. Other people have engaged in underground bitcoin trades involving illegal gambling and illicit drugs. Furthermore, recently hackers successfully broke into bitcoin clearinghouses and impeded the flows of bitcoin transactions. In one case, hackers stole hundreds of millions of dollars' worth of the digital currency (much of which later was recovered).

To combat such activities, federal and state governments are contemplating requiring companies that coordinate bitcoin trading to obtain funds-transferral licenses and to submit themselves to regular supervisory audits. In effect, governments are considering treating bitcoin holdings as akin to deposits and the coordination of bitcoin transmissions as analogous to bank processing of debit and check transactions. If governments pursue this avenue, firms that specialize in holding and trading bitcoins would be licensed and regulated much like banks. From the perspective of bitcoin enthusiasts, such requirements would undermine a fundamental advantage of using bitcoins—namely, that people can trade and hold bitcoins outside the banking system.

For Critical Thinking

1. In principle, which functions of money can digital currencies such as bitcoins perform? Explain.

2. What do you suppose is the main economic interest of federal and state governments in the fact that people are trading and holding bitcoins? (Hint: Think IRS.)

Web Resources

1. To learn more about the mechanics of the Bitcoin Network, see the Web Links in MyEconLab.

2. For a discussion of various issues associated with bitcoins, see the Web Links in MyEconLab.

> ### MyEconLab
>
> For more questions on this chapter's Issues & Applications, go to MyEconLab.
>
> In the Study Plan for this chapter, select Section I: Issues and Applications.

Sources are listed at the end of this chapter.

Fundamental Points

1. Money is defined by its functions, which are as a medium of exchange, unit of accounting, store of value, and standard of deferred payment.

2. The transactions approach to defining money yields M1, or the sum of currency, transactions deposits, and traveler's checks. The liquidity approach yields M2, which adds to M1 savings deposits, small-denomination time deposits, and retail money market mutual fund balances.

3. Financial intermediaries such as depository institutions specialize in addressing asymmetric information problems such as adverse selection and moral hazard. They take advantage of cost reductions from pooling the savings of many individuals under centralized management.

4. The Federal Reserve supplies fiduciary currency, clears payments, holds depository institution reserves, acts as the government's fiscal agent, supervises depository institutions, regulates the money supply, intervenes in foreign currency markets, and acts as lender of last resort.

5. Depository institutions hold as reserves their vault cash and deposits that they have with the Federal Reserve banks, and the reserve ratio is the fraction they maintain as reserves. The potential money multiplier is equal to 1 divided by the reserve ratio.

6. The objective of the Federal Deposit Insurance Corporation is to provide federal deposit insurance coverage to depository institutions with an intent to limit the negative consequences from systemwide depository institution failures and bank runs.

WHAT YOU SHOULD KNOW

Here is what you should know after reading this chapter. MyEconLab will help you identify what you know, and where to go when you need to practice.

LEARNING OBJECTIVES	KEY TERMS	WHERE TO GO TO PRACTICE
15.1 Define the fundamental functions of money and identify key properties that any good that functions as money must possess *Money is a medium of exchange that people use to make payments for goods, services, and financial assets. It is also a unit of accounting for quoting prices in terms of money values. In addition, money is a store of value, so people can hold money for future use in exchange. Finally, money is a standard of deferred payment, enabling lenders to make loans and buyers to repay those loans with money. A good will function as money only if people are widely willing to accept the good in exchange for other goods and services. People will use money only if its value is relatively predictable.*	money, 336 medium of exchange, 336 barter, 336 unit of accounting, 337 store of value, 337 standard of deferred payment, 338 liquidity, 338 transactions deposits, 339 fiduciary monetary system, 339 **Key Figure** **Figure 15-1**, 338	• MyEconLab Study Plan 15.1 • Animated Figure 15-1
15.2 Explain official definitions of the quantity of money in circulation *The narrow definition of the quantity of money in circulation, called M1, includes only currency, transactions deposits, and traveler's checks. A broader definition, called M2, is equal to M1 plus savings deposits, small-denomination time deposits, and noninstitutional holdings of money market mutual fund balances.*	money supply, 339 transactions approach, 339 liquidity approach, 339 M1, 340 depository institutions, 340 thrift institutions, 340 traveler's checks, 340 M2, 341	• MyEconLab Study Plan 15.2
15.3 Understand why financial intermediaries such as banks exist *Financial intermediaries help reduce problems stemming from the existence of asymmetric information. Adverse selection arises when uncreditworthy individuals and firms seek loans, Moral hazard problems exist when an individual or business that has been granted credit begins to engage in riskier practices. Financial intermediaries may also permit savers to benefit from economies of scale, which is the ability to reduce the costs and risks of managing funds by pooling funds and spreading costs and risks across many savers.*	central bank, 341 financial intermediation, 342 financial intermediaries, 342 asymmetric information, 342 adverse selection, 342 moral hazard, 342 liabilities, 343 assets, 343 **Key Figures** Figure 15-3, 342 Figure 15-4, 344	• MyEconLab Study Plan 15.3 • Animated Figures 15-3, 15-4
15.4 Describe the basic structure and functions of the federal reserve system *The Federal Reserve System consists of 12 district banks overseen by the Board of Governors. The Fed's main functions are supplying fiduciary currency, holding banks' reserves and clearing payments, acting as the government's fiscal agent, supervising banks, regulating the money supply, intervening in foreign exchange markets, and acting as a lender of last resort.*	The Fed, 345 lender of last resort, 347 **Key Figure** Figure 15-6, 346	• MyEconLab Study Plan 15.4 • Animated Figures 15-5, 15-6

WHAT YOU SHOULD KNOW *continued*

LEARNING OBJECTIVES	KEY TERMS	WHERE TO GO TO PRACTICE
15.5 Determine the maximum potential extent that the money supply will change following a Federal Reserve monetary policy action *When a bond dealer deposits funds received from the Fed in payment for a security following a Fed open market purchase, there is an increase in the total deposits in the banking system. The money supply increases by the amount of the initial deposit. The bank receiving this deposit can lend out funds in excess of those it holds as reserves, which will generate a rise in deposits at another bank. The maximum potential change in deposits throughout the banking system equals the amount of reserves injected (or withdrawn) by the Fed times the potential money multiplier, which is 1 divided by the reserve ratio.*	fractional reserve banking, 348 reserves, 348 reserve ratio, 348 balance sheet, 348 open market operations, 349 money multiplier, 351 potential money multiplier, 352 **Key Table** Table 15-3, 350 **Key Figure** Figure 15-7, 351	• MyEconLab Study Plan 15.5 • Animated Figure 15-7
15.6 Explain the essential features of federal deposit insurance *The Federal Deposit Insurance Corporation (FDIC) charges some depository institutions premiums and places these funds in accounts for use in reimbursing failed banks' depositors.*	bank run, 353 Federal Deposit Insurance Corporation (FDIC, 353	• MyEconLab Study Plan 15.6

Log in to MyEconLab, take a chapter test, and get a personalized Study Plan that tells you which concepts you understand and which ones you need to review. From there, MyEconLab will give you further practice, tutorials, animations, videos, and guided solutions. For more information, visit http://www.myeconlab.com

PROBLEMS

All problems are assignable in MyEconLab; exercises that update with real-time data are marked with ⊕ . Answers to odd-numbered problems appear in MyEconLab.

15-1. Until 1946, residents of the island of Yap used large doughnut-shaped stones as financial assets. Although prices of goods and services were not quoted in terms of the stones, the stones were often used in exchange for particularly large purchases, such as livestock. To make the transaction, several individuals would insert a large stick through a stone's center and carry it to its new owner. A stone was difficult for any one person to steal, so an owner typically would lean it against the side of his or her home as a sign to others of accumulated purchasing power that would hold value for later use in exchange. Loans would often be repaid using the stones. In what ways did these stones function as money? (See pages 336–338.)

15-2. During the late 1970s, prices quoted in terms of the Israeli currency, the shekel, rose so fast that grocery stores listed their prices in terms of the U.S. dollar and provided customers with dollar-shekel conversion tables that they updated daily. Although people continued to buy goods and services and make loans using shekels, many Israeli citizens converted shekels to dollars to avoid a reduction in their wealth due to inflation. In what way did the U.S. dollar function as money in Israel during this period? (See pages 336–338.)

15-3. During the 1945–1946 Hungarian hyperinflation, when the rate of inflation reached 41.9 *quadrillion* percent per month, the Hungarian government discovered that the real value of its tax receipts was falling dramatically. To keep real tax revenues more stable, it created a good called a "tax pengö," in which all bank deposits were denominated for purposes of taxation. Nevertheless, payments for goods and services were made only in terms of the regular Hungarian currency, whose value tended to fall rapidly even though the value of a tax pengö remained stable. Prices were also quoted only in terms of the regular currency. Lenders, however, began denominating loan payments in terms of tax pengös. In what ways did the tax pengö function as money in Hungary in 1945 and 1946? (See pages 336–338.)

15-4. Considering the following data (expressed in billions of U.S. dollars), calculate M1 and M2. (See pages 340–341.)

Currency	1,050
Savings deposits	5,500
Small-denomination time deposits	1,000
Traveler's checks outside banks and thrifts	10
Total money market mutual funds	800
Institution-only money market mutual funds	1,800
Transactions deposits	1,140

15-5. Considering the following data (expressed in billions of U.S. dollars), calculate M1 and M2. (See pages 340–341.)

Transactions deposits	1,025
Savings deposits	3,300
Small-denomination time deposits	1,450
Money market deposit accounts	1,950
Noninstitution money market mutual funds	1,900
Traveler's checks outside banks and thrifts	25
Currency	1,050
Institution-only money market mutual funds	1,250

15-6. Identify whether each of the following amounts is counted in M1 only, M2 only, both M1 and M2, or neither. (See pages 340–341.)

a. $50 billion in U.S. Treasury bills

b. $15 billion in small-denomination time deposits

c. $5 billion in traveler's checks not issued by a bank

d. $20 billion in money market deposit accounts

15-7. Identify whether each of the following items is counted in M1 only, M2 only, both M1 and M2, or neither. (See pages 340–341.)

a. A $1,000 balance in a transactions deposit at a mutual savings bank

b. A $100,000 time deposit in a New York bank

c. A $10,000 time deposit an elderly widow holds at her credit union

d. A $50 traveler's check not issued by a bank

e. A $50,000 savings deposit

15-8. Match each of the rationales for financial intermediation listed below with at least one of the following financial intermediaries: insurance company, pension fund, savings bank. Explain your choices. (See pages 342–343.)

a. Adverse selection

b. Moral hazard

c. Lower management costs generated by larger scale

15-9. Identify whether each of the following events poses an adverse selection problem or a moral hazard problem in financial markets. (See page 342.)

a. A manager of a savings and loan association responds to reports of a likely increase in federal deposit insurance coverage. She directs loan officers to extend mortgage loans to less creditworthy borrowers.

b. A loan applicant does not mention that a legal judgment in his divorce case will require him to make alimony payments to his ex-wife.

c. An individual who was recently approved for a loan to start a new business decides to use some of the funds to take a Hawaiian vacation.

15-10. In what sense is currency a liability of the Federal Reserve System? (See pages 346–347.)

15-11. In what respects is the Fed like a private banking institution? In what respects is it more like a government agency? (See pages 346–347.)

15-12. Take a look at the map of the locations of the Federal Reserve districts and their headquarters in Figure 15-6 on page 346. Today, the U.S. population is centered just west of the Mississippi River—that is, about half of the population is either to the west or the east of a line running roughly just west of this river. Can you reconcile the current locations of Fed districts and banks with this fact? Why do you suppose the Fed has its current geographic structure? (See page 346.)

15-13. Draw an empty bank balance sheet, with the heading "Assets" on the left and the heading "Liabilities" on the right. Then place the following items on the proper side of the balance sheet (see pages 348–349):

a. Loans to a private company

b. Borrowings from a Federal Reserve district bank

c. Deposits with a Federal Reserve district bank

d. U.S. Treasury bills

e. Vault cash

f. Transactions deposits

15-14. Draw an empty bank balance sheet, with the heading "Assets" on the left and the heading "Liabilities" on the right. Then place the following items on the proper side of the balance sheet. (See pages 348–349.)

    a. Borrowings from another bank in the interbank loans market

    b. Deposits this bank holds in an account with another private bank

    c. U.S. Treasury bonds

    d. Small-denomination time deposits

    e. Mortgage loans to household customers

    f. Money market deposit accounts

15-15. The reserve ratio is 11 percent. What is the value of the potential money multiplier? (See page 352.)

15-16. The Federal Reserve purchases $1 million in U.S. Treasury bonds from a bond dealer, and the dealer's bank credits the dealer's account. The reserve ratio is 15 percent. Assuming that no currency leakage occurs, how much will the bank lend to its customers following the Fed's purchase? (See pages 349–350.)

15-17. Suppose that the value of the potential money multiplier is equal to 4. What is the reserve ratio? (See page 352.)

15-18. Consider a world in which there is no currency and depository institutions issue only transactions deposits. The reserve ratio is 20 percent. The central bank sells $1 billion in government securities. What ultimately happens to the money supply? (See page 352.)

15-19. Assume a 1 percent reserve ratio and no currency leakages. What is the potential money multiplier? How will total deposits in the banking system ultimately change if the Federal Reserve purchases $5 million in U.S. government securities? (See page 352.)

REFERENCES

INTERNATIONAL EXAMPLE: For Many Spaniards, Barter Replaces Money Exchange

Meritxell Mir, "In Hard-Hit Spain, Bartering Becomes a Means of Getting By," *USA Today*, February 20, 2013.

Sinikka Tarvainen, "Everything's Almost Free in Spain's Parallel Barter Economy," Europe Online Magazine, September 3, 2013.

"Spain's Unemployment Rate Inches Up, Checking Talk of Recovery," Reuters, January 23, 2014.

INTERNATIONAL POLICY EXAMPLE: Yankees, We Don't Want Your Deposits at Our Banks!

Lynnley Browning, "Complying with U.S. Tax Evasion Law Is Vexing Foreign Banks," *The New York Times*, September 16, 2013.

Patrick Temple-West, "Foreigners' Accounts in U.S. Banks Eyed in Tax Crackdown," Reuters, February 4, 2013.

Robert Wood, "Even U.S. Banks Must Aid IRS Hunt for Offshore Accounts," *Forbes*, January 16, 2014.

POLICY EXAMPLE: New Bank Liquidity Requirements and the Money Multiplier

Jesse Hamilton, "Fed Liquidity Proposal Seen Trading Safety for Costlier Credit," *Bloomberg Businessweek*, October 25, 2013.

Ronald Orol, "Fed Approves Tough Bank Liquidity Rule," The Street, February 19, 2014.

Ryan Tracy and Michael Crittenden, "Fed Proposes Stricter Liquidity Rules for Largest U.S. Banks," *The Wall Street Journal*, October 24, 2013.

POLICY EXAMPLE: Does the Government Provide Taxpayer Guarantees to the FDIC?

Federal Deposit Insurance Corporation, "Deposit Insurance Summary," www.fdic.gov/deposit/deposits/dis/, 2014.

Marcie Geffner, "FDIC Insures Bank Deposits to $250,000," Bankrate, September 2013.

Alex Pollock, "Deposits Guaranteed Up to $250,000—Maybe," *The Wall Street Journal*, May 28, 2013.

YOU ARE THERE: In Kenya, Mobile-Phone Airtime Is Money

"Airtime Is Money," *The Economist*, January 19, 2013.

Rachel Botsman, "Mobile Money: The African Lesson We Can Learn," Financial Review, February 14, 2014.

"Why Does Kenya Lead the World in Mobile Money?" *The Economist*, May 27, 2013.

ISSUES & APPLICATIONS: A Virtual Currency's Private Wins and Public Losses

Joe Light, "For Virtual Prospectors, Life in the Bitcoin Mines Gets Real," *The Wall Street Journal*, September 18, 2013.

Robin Sidel and Andrew Johnson, "States Put Heat on Bitcoin," *The Wall Street Journal*, June 25, 2013.

Craig Timberg, "Mt. Gox Collapse Spurs Calls to Regulate Bitcoin," *The Washington Post*, February 28, 2014.

Domestic and International Dimensions of Monetary Policy

16

Federal Reserve/Alamy

A few years ago, the Federal Reserve began a policy of purchasing $85 billion in securities each month—a policy program that was the third in a series of sustained securities purchases it had first initiated late in 2008. The Fed continued with these regular monthly purchases for well over a year. Many of the securities purchased by the Fed were U.S. Treasury bills, notes, and bonds. As a consequence, the Fed gradually began to accumulate a growing share of ownership of the federal government's debts. Why did the Fed engage in a series of sustained purchases of securities? What implications did the Fed's actions have for the market clearing interest rate that the Treasury had to pay on its securities? When you have finished this chapter, you will know the answers to these questions.

LEARNING OBJECTIVES

After reading this chapter, you should be able to:

16.1 Identify the key factors that influence the quantity of money that people desire to hold

16.2 Describe how Federal Reserve monetary policy actions influence market interest rates

16.3 Evaluate how expansionary and contractionary monetary policy actions affect equilibrium real GDP and the price level in the short run

16.4 Understand the equation of exchange and its importance in the quantity theory of money and prices

16.5 Explain how the Federal Reserve has implemented credit policy since 2008

MyEconLab helps you master each objective and study more efficiently. See the end of the chapter for details.

> **DID YOU KNOW THAT...**
>
> banks now hold about $3 trillion of excess reserves on deposit with Federal Reserve banks, or more than *1,000 times more* excess reserves than they typically held prior to 2008? Since late 2008, the Fed has paid banks an annual interest rate of 0.25 percent on their excess reserve holdings. Consequently, banks receive from the Fed more than $6 billion in interest per year to keep idle reserves with Federal Reserve banks instead of lending those reserves to households and businesses.
>
> Later in this chapter, you will learn about the Fed's rationale for paying banks to hold such massive volumes of excess reserves. First, though, you must find out how interest rates influence how much money private individuals and firms desire to hold—that is, about their *demand for money*.

16.1 Identify the key factors that influence the quantity of money that people desire to hold

The Demand for Money

In the previous chapter, we saw how the Federal Reserve's open market operations can increase or decrease the money supply. Our focus was on the effects of the Fed's actions on the banking system. In this chapter, we widen our discussion to see how Fed monetary policy actions have an impact on the broader economy by influencing market interest rates. First, though, you must understand the factors that determine how much money people desire to hold—in other words, you must understand the demand for money.

All of us engage in a flow of transactions. We buy and sell things all of our lives. Because we use money—dollars—as our medium of exchange, however, all *flows* of nonbarter transactions involve a *stock* of money. We can restate this as follows:

To use money, one must hold money.

Given that everybody must hold money, we can now talk about the *demand* to hold it. People do not demand to hold money just to look at pictures of past leaders. They hold it to be able to use it to buy goods and services.

The Demand for Money: What People Wish to Hold

Money balances
Synonymous with money, money stock, money holdings.

People have certain motivations that cause them to want to hold **money balances**. Individuals and firms could try to do without non-interest-bearing money balances. Life, though, is inconvenient without a ready supply of money balances. Thus, the public has a demand for money, motivated by several factors.

THE TRANSACTIONS DEMAND The main reason people hold money is that money can be used to purchase goods and services. People are paid at specific intervals (once a week, once a month, and the like), but they wish to make purchases more or less continuously. To free themselves from having to buy goods and services only on payday, people find it beneficial to hold money. The benefit they receive is convenience: They willingly forgo interest earnings in order to avoid the inconvenience of cashing in nonmoney assets such as bonds every time they wish to make a purchase. Thus, people hold money to make regular, *expected* expenditures under the **transactions demand**. As nominal GDP (see page 175 in Chapter 8) rises, people will want to hold more money because they will be making more transactions.

Transactions demand
Holding money as a medium of exchange to make payments. The level varies directly with nominal GDP.

THE PRECAUTIONARY DEMAND The transactions demand involves money held to make *expected* expenditures. People also hold money for the **precautionary demand** to make *unexpected* purchases or to meet emergencies. When people hold money for the precautionary demand, they incur a cost in forgone interest earnings that they balance against the benefit of having cash on hand. The higher the rate of interest, the lower the precautionary money balances people wish to hold.

Precautionary demand
Holding money to meet unplanned expenditures and emergencies.

THE ASSET DEMAND Remember that one of the functions of money is to serve as a store of value. People can hold money balances as a store of value, or they can hold bonds or stocks or other interest-earning assets. The desire to hold money as a store of value leads to the **asset demand** for money. People choose to hold money rather than other assets for two reasons: its liquidity and the lack of risk.

Asset demand

Holding money as a store of value instead of other assets such as corporate bonds and stocks.

The disadvantage of holding money balances as an asset, of course, is the interest earnings forgone. Each individual or business decides how much money to hold as an asset by looking at the opportunity cost of holding money. The higher the interest rate—which is the opportunity cost of holding money—the lower the money balances people will want to hold as assets. Conversely, the lower the interest rate offered on alternative assets, the higher the money balances people will want to hold as assets.

MyEconLab Concept Check

The Demand for Money Curve

Assume for simplicity's sake that the amount of money demanded for transactions purposes is proportionate to income. That leaves the precautionary and asset demands for money, both determined by the opportunity cost of holding money. If we assume that the interest rate represents the cost of holding money balances, we can graph the relationship between the interest rate and the quantity of money demanded.

In Figure 16-1 below, the demand for money curve shows a familiar downward slope. The horizontal axis measures the quantity of money demanded, and the vertical axis is the interest rate. The rate of interest is the cost of holding money. At a higher interest rate, a lower quantity of money is demanded, and vice versa.

To see this, imagine two scenarios. In the first one, you can earn 20 percent a year if you put your funds into purchases of U.S. government securities. In the other scenario, you can earn 1 percent if you put your funds into purchases of U.S. government securities. If you have $1,000 average cash balances in a non-interest-bearing checking account, in the first scenario over a one-year period, your opportunity cost would be 20 percent of $1,000, or $200. In the second scenario, the opportunity cost that you would incur would be 1 percent of $1,000, or $10. Under which scenario would you hold more funds in your checking account instead of securities?

MyEconLab Concept Check
MyEconLab Study Plan

SELF CHECK Visit MyEconLab to practice these and other problems and to get instant feedback in your Study Plan.

To use money, people must hold money. Therefore, they have a _____ for money balances.

The determinants of the demand for money balances are the _____ demand, the _____ demand, and the _____ demand.

Holding money carries an _____ cost—the interest income forgone. Hence, the demand for money curve showing the relationship between the quantity of money balances demanded and the interest rate slopes _____.

FIGURE 16-1

The Demand for Money Curve

If we use the interest rate as a proxy for the opportunity cost of holding money balances, the demand for money curve, M_d, is downward sloping, similar to other demand curves

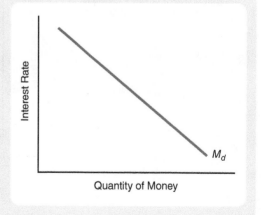

16.2 Describe how Federal Reserve monetary policy actions influence market interest rates

How the Fed Influences Interest Rates

When the Fed takes actions that alter the rate of growth of the money supply, it is seeking to influence investment, consumption, and total aggregate expenditures. In taking these monetary policy actions, the Fed in principle has four tools at its disposal: open market operations, changes in the reserve ratio, changes in the interest rates paid on reserves, and discount rate changes. The first two tools were introduced in Chapter 15. The discount rate and interest rates paid on reserves will be discussed later in this chapter. Let's consider the effects of open market operations, the tool that the Fed regularly employs on a day-to-day basis.

Open Market Operations

As we saw in the previous chapter, the Fed changes the amount of reserves in the banking system by its purchases and sales of government bonds issued by the U.S. Treasury. To understand how these actions by the Fed influence the market interest rate, we start out in an equilibrium in which all individuals, including the holders of bonds, are satisfied with the current situation. There is some equilibrium level of interest rate (and bond prices).

Now, if the Fed wants to conduct open market operations, it must somehow induce individuals, businesses, and foreign residents to hold more or fewer U.S. Treasury bonds. The inducement must take the form of making people better off. So, if the Fed wants to buy bonds, it will have to offer to buy them at a higher price than exists in the marketplace. If the Fed wants to sell bonds, it will have to offer them at a lower price than exists in the marketplace. Thus, an open market operation must cause a change in the price of bonds.

GRAPHING THE SALE OF BONDS The Fed sells some of the bonds it has on hand. This is shown in panel (a) of Figure 16-2 below. Notice that the supply of bonds in the private market is shown here as a vertical line with respect to price. The demand for bonds is downward sloping. If the Fed offers more bonds it owns for sale, the supply curve shifts from S_1 to S_2. People will not be willing to buy the extra bonds at the initial equilibrium bond price, P_1. They will be satisfied holding the additional bonds at the new equilibrium price, P_2.

MyEconLab Animation

FIGURE 16-2

Determining the Price of Bonds

In panel (a), the Fed offers more bonds for sale. The price drops from P_1 to P_2. In panel (b), the Fed purchases bonds. This is the equivalent of a reduction in the supply of bonds available for private investors to hold. The price of bonds must rise from P_1 to P_3 to clear the market.

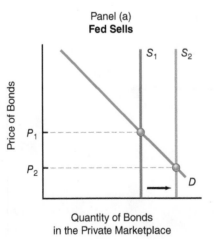

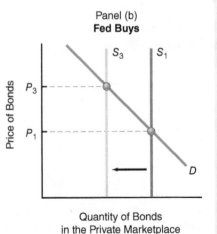

THE FED'S PURCHASE OF BONDS The opposite occurs when the Fed purchases bonds. You can view this purchase of bonds as a reduction in the stock of bonds available for private investors to hold. In panel (b) of Figure 16-2, the original supply curve is S_1. The new supply curve of outstanding bonds will end up being S_3 because of the Fed's purchases of bonds. To get people to give up these bonds, the Fed must offer them a more attractive price. The price will rise from to P_1 to P_3.   MyEconLab Concept Check

Relationship between the Price of Existing Bonds and the Rate of Interest

The price of existing bonds and the rate of interest are inversely related. Assume that the average yield on bonds is 5 percent. You decide to purchase a bond. A local corporation agrees to sell you a bond that will pay you $50 a year forever. What is the price you are willing to pay for the bond? It is $1,000. Why? Because $50 divided by $1,000 equals 5 percent, which is as good as the best return you can earn elsewhere. You purchase the bond. The next year something happens in the economy, and you can now obtain bonds that have effective yields of 10 percent. (In other words, the prevailing interest rate in the economy is now 10 percent.) What will happen to the market price of the existing bond that you own, the one you purchased the year before? It will fall.

If you try to sell the bond for $1,000, you will discover that no investors will buy it from you. Why should they when they can obtain the same $50-a-year yield from someone else by paying only $500? Indeed, unless you offer your bond for sale at a price that is no higher than $500, no buyers will be forthcoming. Hence, an increase in the prevailing interest rate in the economy has caused the market value of your existing bond to fall.

The important point to be understood is this:

> *The market price of **existing** bonds (and all fixed-income assets) is inversely related to the rate of interest prevailing in the economy.*

As a consequence of the inverse relationship between the price of existing bonds and the interest rate, the Fed is able to influence the interest rate by engaging in open market operations. A Fed open market sale that reduces the equilibrium price of bonds brings about an increase in the interest rate. A Fed open market purchase that boosts the equilibrium price of bonds generates a decrease in the interest rate.   MyEconLab Concept Check
MyEconLab Study Plan

SELF CHECK   Visit MyEconLab to practice these and other problems and to get instant feedback in your Study Plan.

When the Fed sells bonds, it must offer them at a _____ price. When the Fed buys bonds, it must pay a _____ price.

There is an _____ relationship between the prevailing rate of interest in the economy and the market price of *existing* bonds (and all fixed-income assets).

A Federal Reserve open market sale generates a _____ in the price of *existing* bonds and an _____ in the market interest rate. An open market purchase brings about an _____ in the price of *existing* bonds and a _____ in the market rate of interest.

Effects of an Increase in the Money Supply

16.3 Evaluate how expansionary and contractionary monetary policy actions affect equilibrium real GDP and the price level in the short run

Now that we've seen how the Fed's monetary policy actions influence the market interest rate, we can ask a broader question: How does monetary policy influence real GDP and the price level? To understand how monetary policy works in its simplest form, we are going to run an experiment in which you increase the money supply in a very direct way. Assume that the government has given you hundreds of millions of dollars in just-printed bills. You then fly around the country in a helicopter, dropping the money out of the window. People pick it up and put it in their pockets. Some deposit the money in their transactions deposit accounts. As a result, they now have too much money—not in the sense that they want to throw it away but rather in relation to other assets that they own. There are a variety of ways to dispose of this "new" money.

Direct Effect of an Increase in the Money Supply

The simplest thing that people can do when they have excess money balances is to go out and spend them on goods and services. Here they have a direct impact on aggregate demand. Aggregate demand rises because with an increase in the money supply, at any given price level people now want to purchase more output of real goods and services.   MyEconLab Concept Check

Indirect Effect of an Increase in the Money Supply

Not everybody will necessarily spend the newfound money on goods and services. Some people may wish to deposit a portion or all of those excess money balances in banks.

BANKS' LENDING RESPONSES AND AGGREGATE DEMAND The recipient banks now discover that they have higher reserves than they wish to hold. As you learned in Chapter 15, one thing that banks can do to get higher-interest-earning assets is to lend out the excess reserves.

Banks, however, cannot induce people to borrow more funds than they were borrowing before unless the banks lower the interest rate that they charge on loans. This lower interest rate encourages people to take out those loans. Businesses will therefore engage in new investment with the funds loaned. Individuals will engage in more consumption of durable goods such as housing, autos, and home entertainment centers. In both ways, the increased loans generate a rise in aggregate demand. More people will be involved in more spending—even those who did not pick up any of the money that was originally dropped out of your helicopter.

LOW INTEREST RATES AND QUANTITATIVE EASING What happens if the market interest rate on bonds falls close to zero, as has occurred in recent years? In that case, monetary policy traditionally must rely on the direct effect of a change in bank reserves and, through the money multiplier effect, the quantity of money in circulation. Monetary policy cannot depend on the indirect effect of an interest rate that is already at zero. A policy action in which the Federal Reserve conducts open market purchases to increase bank reserves without seeking to alter the interest rate, which is already zero, is called **quantitative easing**.   MyEconLab Concept Check

Quantitative easing
Federal Reserve open market purchases intended to generate an increase in bank reserves at a nearly zero interest rate.

Graphing the Effects of an Expansionary Monetary Policy

To consider the effects of an expansionary monetary policy on real GDP and the price level, look at Figure 16-3 on the next page. We start out in a situation in which the economy is operating at less than full employment. You see a recessionary gap in the figure, which is measured as the horizontal difference between the long-run aggregate supply curve, *LRAS*, and the current equilibrium. Short-run equilibrium is at E_1, with a price level of 120 and real GDP of $17.5 trillion. The *LRAS* curve is at $18 trillion. Assume now that the Fed increases the money supply. Because of the direct and indirect effects of this increase in the money supply, aggregate demand shifts outward to the right to AD_2. The new equilibrium is at an output rate of $18 trillion of real GDP per year and a price level of 125. Here expansionary monetary policy can move the economy toward its *LRAS* curve sooner than otherwise.

FIGURE 16-3

Expansionary Monetary Policy with Underutilized Resources

If we start out with equilibrium at E_1, expansionary monetary policy will shift AD_1 to AD_2. The new equilibrium will be at E_2.

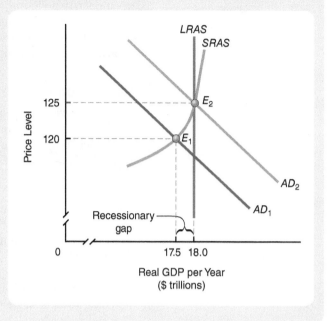

Graphing the Effects of Contractionary Monetary Policy

Assume that there is an inflationary gap as shown in Figure 16-4 below. There you see that the short-run aggregate supply curve, $SRAS$, intersects aggregate demand, AD_1, at E_1. This is to the right of the $LRAS$ of real GDP per year of $18 trillion. Contractionary monetary policy can eliminate this inflationary gap. Because of both the direct and indirect effects of monetary policy, the aggregate demand curve shifts inward from AD_1 to AD_2. Equilibrium is now at E_2, which is at a lower price level, 120. Equilibrium real GDP has now fallen from $18.5 trillion to $18 trillion.

FIGURE 16-4

Contractionary Monetary Policy with Overutilized Resources

If we begin at short-run equilibrium at point E_1, contractionary monetary policy will shift the aggregate demand curve from AD_1 to AD_2. The new equilibrium will be at point E_2.

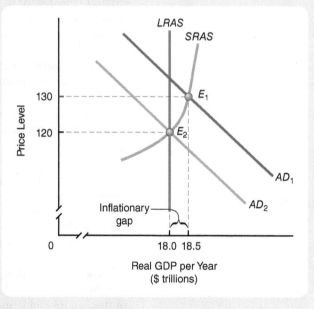

Note that contractionary monetary policy involves a reduction in the money supply, with a consequent decline in the price level (deflation). In the real world, contractionary monetary policy more commonly involves reducing the *rate of growth* of the money supply, thereby reducing the rate of increase in the price level (inflation). Similarly, real-world expansionary monetary policy typically involves increasing the rate of growth of the money supply.　　　　　　　　　　　　　　　　MyEconLab Concept Check

Open Economy Transmission of Monetary Policy

So far we have discussed monetary policy in a closed economy. When we move to an open economy, with international trade and the international purchases and sales of all assets including dollars and other currencies, monetary policy becomes more complex. Consider first the effect of monetary policy on exports.

THE NET EXPORT EFFECT OF EXPANSIONARY MONETARY POLICY To see how a change in monetary policy can affect net exports, suppose that the Federal Reserve implements an expansionary policy that reduces the market interest rate. The lower U.S. interest rate, in turn, tends to discourage foreign investment in U.S. financial assets, such as U.S. government securities.

A Dollar Depreciation If residents of foreign countries decide that they want to purchase fewer U.S. government securities or other U.S. assets, they will require fewer U.S. dollars with which to purchase these U.S. assets. As a consequence, the demand for dollars decreases in foreign exchange markets. The international price of the dollar therefore falls. This is called a *depreciation* of the dollar.

A dollar depreciation tends to boost net exports because it makes our exports cheaper in terms of foreign currency and imports more expensive in terms of dollars. Foreign residents demand more of our goods and services, and we demand fewer of theirs.

A Positive Net Export Effect The preceding reasoning implies that when expansionary monetary policy reduces the U.S. interest rate at the current price level, there will be a positive net export effect because foreign residents will want fewer U.S. financial instruments. Hence, they will demand fewer dollars, thereby causing the international price of the dollar to decline.

This fall in the dollar's international value makes our exports less expensive for the rest of the world. Consequently, foreign residents demand a larger quantity of our exports. The decline in the dollar's value also means that foreign goods and services are more expensive in the United States, so we therefore demand fewer imports. We come up with this conclusion:

> *Expansionary monetary policy causes interest rates to fall. Such a decrease will induce international outflows of funds, thereby reducing the international value of the dollar and making U.S. goods more attractive abroad. The net export effect of expansionary monetary policy will be in the same direction as the monetary policy effect, thereby amplifying the effect of such policy.*

THE NET EXPORT EFFECT OF CONTRACTIONARY MONETARY POLICY Now assume that the Federal Reserve wants to pursue a contractionary monetary policy. In so doing, it will cause interest rates to increase in the short run, as discussed earlier. Rising interest rates will cause funds to flow into the United States. The demand for dollars will increase, and the international price of the dollar will rise. Foreign goods will now look less expensive to U.S. residents, and imports will rise. Foreign residents will desire fewer of our exports, and exports will fall. The result will be a decrease in net exports. Again, the international consequences reinforce the domestic consequences of monetary policy, in this case by inducing a reduction in aggregate demand.

On a broader level, the Fed's ability to control the rate of growth of the money supply may be hampered as U.S. money markets become less isolated. With the push of a computer button, billions of dollars can change hands halfway around the world. If the Fed reduces the growth of the money supply, individuals and firms in the United States can obtain dollars from other sources. People in the United States who want more liquidity can obtain their dollars from foreign residents. Indeed, as world markets become increasingly integrated, U.S. residents, who can already hold U.S. bank accounts denominated in foreign currencies, more regularly conduct transactions using other nations' currencies.

MyEconLab Concept Check
MyEconLab Study Plan

SELF CHECK Visit MyEconLab to practice these and other problems and to get instant feedback in your Study Plan.

The _____ effect of an increase in the money supply arises because people desire to spend more on real goods and services when they have excess money balances.

The _____ effect of an increase in the money supply works through a _____ in the interest rate, which encourages businesses to make new investments with the funds loaned to them. Individuals will also engage in more consumption (on consumer durables) because of _____ interest rates.

If contractionary monetary policy raises U.S. interest rates, there is a _____ net export effect because

foreign residents will demand _____ U.S. financial instruments, thereby demanding _____ dollars and hence causing the international price of the dollar to rise. This makes our exports more expensive for the rest of the world.

When expansionary monetary policy causes interest rates to fall, foreign residents will want _____ U.S. financial instruments. The resulting _____ in the demand for dollars will reduce the dollar's value in foreign exchange markets, leading to an _____ in net exports.

Monetary Policy and Inflation

16.4 Understand the equation of exchange and its importance in the quantity theory of money and prices

Most media discussions of inflation focus on the short run. The price index can fluctuate in the short run because of events such as oil price shocks, labor union strikes, or discoveries of large amounts of new natural resources. In the long run, however, empirical studies show that excessive growth in the money supply results in inflation.

If the supply of money rises relative to the demand for money, people have more money balances than desired. They adjust their mix of assets to reduce money balances in favor of other items. This ultimately causes their spending on goods and services to increase. The result is a rise in the price level, or inflation.

The Equation of Exchange and the Quantity Theory

A simple way to show the relationship between changes in the quantity of money in circulation and the price level is through the **equation of exchange**, developed by Irving Fisher (note that $\equiv$ refers to an identity or truism):

$$M_sV \equiv PY$$

where M_s = actual money balances held by the nonbanking public
V = **income velocity of money**, which is the number of times, on average per year, each monetary unit is spent on final goods and services
P = price level or price index
Y = real GDP per year

Equation of exchange
The formula indicating that the number of monetary units (M_s) times the number of times each unit is spent on final goods and services (V) is identical to the price level (P) times real GDP (Y).

Income velocity of money (V)
The number of times per year a dollar is spent on final goods and services; identically equal to nominal GDP divided by the money supply.

Consider a numerical example involving the entire economy. Assume that in this economy, the total money supply, Ms, is $15 trillion; real GDP, Y, is $20 trillion (in base-year dollars); and the price level, P, is 1.5 (150 in index number terms). Using the equation of exchange,

$$M_sV \equiv PY$$

$$\$15 \text{ trillion} \times V \equiv 1.5 \times \$20 \text{ trillion}$$

$$\$15 \text{ trillion} \times V \equiv \$30 \text{ trillion}$$

$$V \equiv 2.0$$

Thus, each dollar is spent an average of 2 times per year.

THE EQUATION OF EXCHANGE AS AN IDENTITY The equation of exchange must always be true—it is an *accounting identity*. The equation of exchange states that the total amount of funds spent on final output, M_sV, is equal to the total amount of funds *received* for final output, PY. Thus, a given flow of funds can be viewed from either the buyers' side or the producers' side. The value of goods purchased is equal to the value of goods sold.

If Y represents real GDP and P is the price level, PY equals the dollar value of national output of goods and services or *nominal* GDP. Thus,

$$M_sV \equiv PY \equiv \text{nominal GDP}$$

THE QUANTITY THEORY OF MONEY AND PRICES If we now make some assumptions about different variables in the equation of exchange, we come up with the simplified theory of why the price level changes, called the **quantity theory of money and prices**. If we assume that the velocity of money, V, is constant and that real GDP, Y, is also constant, the simple equation of exchange tells us that a change in the money supply can lead only to an equiproportional change in the price level. Continue with our numerical example. Y is \$20 trillion. V equals 2.0. If the money supply increases by 20 percent, to \$18 trillion, the only thing that can happen is that the price level, P, has to go up from 1.5 to 1.8. In other words, the price level must also increase by 20 percent. Otherwise the equation is no longer in balance. An increase in the money supply of 20 percent results in a rise in the price level (inflation) of 20 percent.

Quantity theory of money and prices
The hypothesis that changes in the money supply lead to equiproportional changes in the price level.

EMPIRICAL VERIFICATION There is considerable evidence of the empirical validity of the relationship between monetary growth and high rates of inflation. Figure 16-5 below tracks the correspondence between money supply growth and the rates of inflation in various countries around the world.

FIGURE 16-5

The Relationship between Money Supply Growth Rates and Rates of Inflation

If we plot rates of inflation and rates of monetary growth for different countries, we come up with a scatter diagram that reveals an obvious direct relationship. If you were to draw a line through the "average" of the points in this figure, it would be upward sloping, showing that an increase in the rate of growth of the money supply leads to an increase in the rate of inflation.

Sources: International Monetary Fund and national central banks. Data are for latest available periods.

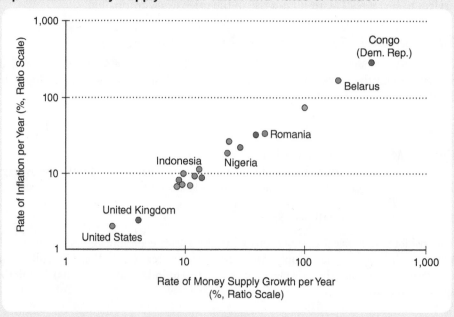

How does the quantity equation help in understanding the effect of recent policies of the Bank of Japan?

Japan Rediscovers Inflation via the Quantity Equation

Between 1999 and 2012, even though the Bank of Japan increased the nation's money supply at an average annual pace just below 2 percent, the income velocity of money *fell* at an annual rate equal to about –2 percent. On net, therefore, the quantity $M \times V$ on the left-hand side of the quantity equation, $M \times V = P \times Y$, tended to decrease slightly from year to year even as real GDP, or Y in the right-hand side of the equation, increased in most years. As a consequence, the price level, P, *decreased* in most years. The average annual rate of change in Japan's price index during the 1999–2012 interval was equal to approximately –0.3 percent, so that Japan experienced deflation in a typical year during this period.

Beginning in early 2013, however, Japan's government induced the Bank of Japan to raise the pace of the nation's money supply growth to an annualized rate exceeding 4 percent. Thus, even though Japan's income velocity of money continued to decrease at a rate close to –2 percent, the overall value of the left-hand side of the quantity equation, $M \times V$, began to grow once more. Within a few months, the annualized rate of growth of the Japanese price level exceeded 1 percent. By 2015, the nation's inflation rate averaged about 2 percent. Thus, Japan now experiences persistently positive, rather than negative, annual inflation rates.

FOR CRITICAL THINKING

If Japan's income velocity of money and real GDP had remained unchanged from 2013 onward and the money growth rate had remained at 4 percent per year, what would have been the nation's rate of inflation per year?

Sources are listed at the end of this chapter.

SELF CHECK   Visit MyEconLab to practice these and other problems and to get instant feedback in your Study Plan.

The _____ of _____ states that the expenditures by some people will equal income receipts by others, or $M_s V \equiv PY$ (money supply times velocity equals nominal GDP).

Viewed as an accounting identity, the equation of exchange is always _____, because the amount of

funds _____ on final output of goods and services must equal the total amount of funds _____ for final output.

The quantity theory of money and prices states that a change in the _____ _____ will bring about a proportional change in the _____ _____ .

Monetary Policy Transmission and Credit Policy at Today's Fed

> **16.5** Explain how the Federal Reserve has implemented credit policy since 2008

Earlier in this chapter, we talked about the direct and indirect effects of monetary policy. The direct effect is simply that an increase in the money supply causes people to have excess money balances. To get rid of these excess money balances, people increase their expenditures. The indirect effect, depicted in Figure 16-6 below, as the interest-rate-based money transmission mechanism, occurs because some people have decided to purchase interest-bearing assets with their excess money balances. This

FIGURE 16-6

The Interest-Rate-Based Money Transmission Mechanism

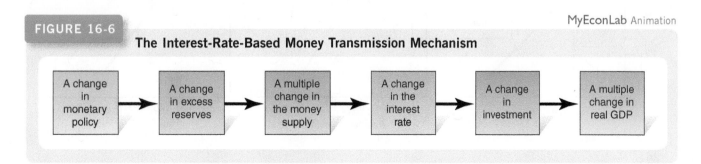

A change in monetary policy → A change in excess reserves → A multiple change in the money supply → A change in the interest rate → A change in investment → A multiple change in real GDP

causes the price of such assets—bonds—to go up. Because of the inverse relationship between the price of existing bonds and the interest rate, the interest rate in the economy falls. This lower interest rate induces people and businesses to spend more than they otherwise would have spent.

An Interest-Rate-Based Transmission Mechanism

The indirect, interest-rate-based transmission mechanism can be seen explicitly in Figure 16-7 below. In panel (a), you see that an increase in the money supply reduces the interest rate. The economywide demand curve for money is labeled M_d in panel (a). At first, the money supply is at M_s, a vertical line determined by the Federal Reserve. The equilibrium interest rate is r_1. This occurs where the money supply curve intersects the money demand curve.

Now assume that the Fed increases the money supply, say, via open market operations. This will shift the money supply curve outward to the right to M'_s. People find themselves with too much cash (liquidity). They buy bonds. When they buy bonds, they bid up the prices of bonds, thereby lowering the interest rate. The interest rate falls to r_2, where the new money supply curve M'_s intersects the money demand curve M_d. This reduction in the interest rate from r_1 to r_2 has an effect on planned investment, as can be seen in panel (b). Planned investment per year increases from I_1 to I_2. An increase in investment will increase aggregate demand, as shown in panel (c). Aggregate demand increases from AD_1 to AD_2. Equilibrium in the economy increases from real GDP per year of $17.5 trillion, which is not on the $LRAS$, to equilibrium real GDP per year of $18 trillion, which is on the $LRAS$.

TARGETING THE FEDERAL FUNDS RATE As we have seen, the Fed can influence interest rates only by actively entering the market for federal government securities (usually Treasury

FIGURE 16-7

Adding Monetary Policy to the Aggregate Demand–Aggregate Supply Model

In panel (a), we show a demand for money function, M_d. It slopes downward to show that at lower rates of interest, a larger quantity of money will be demanded. The money supply is given initially as M_s, so the equilibrium rate of interest will be r_1. At this rate of interest, we see from the planned investment schedule given in panel (b) that the quantity of

planned investment demanded per year will be I_1. After the shift in the money supply to M'_s, the resulting increase in tment from I_1 to I_2 shifts the aggregate demand curve in panel (c) outward from AD_1 to AD_2. Equilibrium moves from E_1 to E_2, at real GDP of $18 trillion per year.

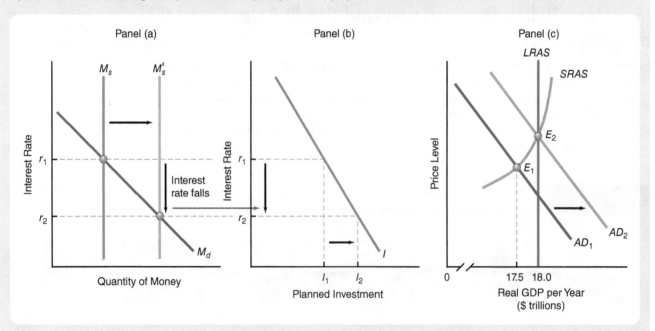

bills). So, if the Fed wants to raise "the" interest rate, it essentially must engage in contractionary open market operations. That is to say, it must sell more Treasury securities than it buys, thereby reducing total reserves in the banking system and, hence, the money supply. This tends to boost the rate of interest. Conversely, when the Fed wants to decrease "the" rate of interest, it engages in expansionary open market operations, thereby increasing reserves and the money supply. But what interest rate is the Fed attempting to change?

In reality, more than one interest rate matters for Fed policymaking. Three interest rates are particularly relevant.

1. **The Federal Funds Rate.** In normal times, depository institutions wishing to borrow funds rarely seek to borrow directly from the Fed. In years past, this was because the Fed would not lend them all they wanted to borrow. Instead, the Fed encouraged banks to obtain funds in the **federal funds market** when they wanted to expand their reserves. The federal funds market is an interbank market in reserves where one bank borrows the excess reserves—resources held voluntarily over and above required reserves—of another. The generic term *federal funds* refers to the borrowing or lending of reserve funds that are usually repaid within the same 24-hour period.

   Depository institutions that borrow in the federal funds market pay an interest rate called the **federal funds rate**. Because the federal funds rate is a ready measure of the cost that banks must incur to raise funds, the Federal Reserve often uses it as a yardstick by which to measure the effects of its policies. Consequently, the federal funds rate is closely watched as an indicator of the Fed's intentions.

2. **The Discount Rate.** When the Fed does lend reserves directly to depository institutions, the rate of interest that it charges is called the **discount rate**. When depository institutions borrow reserves from the Fed at this rate, they are said to be borrowing through the Fed's "discount window." Borrowing from the Fed increases reserves and thereby expands the money supply, other things being equal.

   Since 2003, the Fed has set the discount rate above the federal funds rate. The differential has ranged from 0.25 percentage point to 1.0 percentage point. An increase in this differential reduces depository institutions' incentive to borrow from the Fed and thereby generates a reduction in discount window borrowings.

3. **The Interest Rate on Reserves.** In October 2008, Congress granted the Fed authority to pay interest on both required reserves and excess reserves of depository institutions. Initially, the Fed paid different rates of interest on required and excess reserves, but since late 2008 the Fed has paid the same interest rate on both categories of reserves.

Why have European central banks considered proposals for a *negative* interest rate on excess reserves—that is, an interest *charge* on private banks' excess reserves held with those central banks?

Federal funds market
A private market (made up mostly of banks) in which banks can borrow reserves from other banks that want to lend them. Federal funds are usually lent for overnight use.

Federal funds rate
The interest rate that depository institutions pay to borrow reserves in the interbank federal funds market.

Discount rate
The interest rate that the Federal Reserve charges for reserves that it lends to depository institutions. It is sometimes referred to as the *rediscount rate* or, in Canada and England, as the *bank rate*.

POLICY EXAMPLE

European Central Banks Contemplate Negative Interest Rates

Even as the Fed continued to pay U.S. banks and U.S. branches of foreign banks interest on the excess reserves held at Federal Reserve banks, European central banks were considering a radically different plan. The key element of this plan was to charge banks for holding excess reserves at European central banks. In effect, this plan called for a negative interest rate on European excess reserves.

The basic idea behind this plan was to give European banks a greater incentive to lend their excess reserves to households and firms instead of allowing the funds to sit "unused' in deposits with central banks. According to proponents of the plan, an upsurge in bank lending generated by the threat of a central bank interest charge on idle excess reserves would help to stimulate household consumption spending and business fixed investment.

So far, this idea of charging interest on excess reserves has not been adopted by European central banks. Nevertheless, the European Central Bank has indicated that eventually it might consider a negative interest rate on the excess reserve deposits of European banks.

FOR CRITICAL THINKING

If European central banks were to charge interest on excess reserves held in Europe while the Fed continued to pay interest on excess reserves held in the United States, why might we expect an increased flow of funds from banks in Europe to their U.S. branches?

Sources are listed at the end of this chapter.

Varying the interest rate on reserves alters the incentives that banks face when deciding whether to hold any additional reserves they obtain as excess reserves or to lend those reserves out to other banks in the federal funds market. If the Fed raises the interest rate it pays on reserves and thereby reduces the differential between the federal funds rate and the interest rate on reserves, banks have less incentive to lend reserves in the federal funds market. Thus because the interest rate on reserves is now positive rather than zero, it is not surprising that excess reserves in the U.S. banking system now amount to about $3 trillion, as discussed in more detail later in this chapter.

Establishing the Fed Policy Strategy The policy decisions that determine open market operations by which the Fed pursues its announced objective for the federal funds rate are made by the Federal Open Market Committee (FOMC). Every six to eight weeks, the voting members of the FOMC—the seven Fed board governors and five regional bank presidents—determine the Fed's general strategy of open market operations.

The FOMC outlines its strategy in a document called the **FOMC Directive**. This document lays out the FOMC's general economic objectives, establishes short-term federal funds rate objectives, and specifies target ranges for money supply growth. After each meeting, the FOMC issues a brief statement to the media, which then publish stories about the Fed's action or inaction and what it is likely to mean for the economy. Typically, these stories have headlines such as "Fed Cuts Key Interest Rate," "Fed Acts to Push Up Interest Rates," or "Fed Decides to Leave Interest Rates Alone."

The Trading Desk The FOMC leaves the task of implementing the Directive to officials who manage an office at the Federal Reserve Bank of New York known as the **Trading Desk**. The media spend little time considering how the Fed's Trading Desk conducts its activities, taking for granted that the Fed can implement the policy action that it has announced to the public. The Trading Desk's open market operations typically are confined within a one-hour interval each weekday morning.

THE TAYLOR RULE In 1990, John Taylor of Stanford University suggested a relatively simple equation that the Fed might use for the purpose of selecting a federal funds rate target. This equation would direct the Fed to set the federal funds rate target based on an estimated long-run real interest rate (see page 161 in Chapter 7), the current deviation of the actual inflation rate from the Fed's inflation objective, and the proportionate gap between actual real GDP per year and a measure of potential real GDP per year. Taylor and other economists have applied his equation, which has become known as the **Taylor rule**, to actual Fed policy choices. They have concluded that the Taylor rule's recommendations for federal funds rate target values come close to the actual targets the Fed has selected over time.

Plotting the Taylor Rule on a Graph The Federal Reserve Bank of St. Louis now regularly tracks target levels for the federal funds rate predicted by a basic Taylor-rule equation. Figure 16-8 on the next page displays paths of both the actual federal funds rate (the orange line) and the Taylor-rule recommendation if the Fed's inflation objective (the green line) is 0 percent inflation.

Assessing the Stance of Fed Policy with the Taylor Rule Suppose that the actual federal funds rate is *below* the rate implied by a 0 percent inflation goal. In this situation, the Taylor rule implies that the Fed's policymaking is expansionary. As a consequence, the actual inflation rate will rise above 0 percent. Thus, during the 2004–2005 interval, the actual federal funds rate was well below the level consistent with a 0 percent inflation rate. This implies that Fed policymaking was very expansionary during this period, sufficiently so as to be expected to yield a long-run inflation rate substantially in excess of 0 percent per year. The Taylor-rule graph implies that in 2006, the Fed's policy stance became more contractionary, with the actual federal funds rate above the

---

FOMC Directive
A document that summarizes the Federal Open Market Committee's general policy strategy, establishes near-term objectives for the federal funds rate, and specifies target ranges for money supply growth.

Trading Desk
An office at the Federal Reserve Bank of New York charged with implementing monetary policy strategies developed by the Federal Open Market Committee.

Taylor rule
An equation that specifies a federal funds rate target based on an estimated long-run real interest rate, the current deviation of the actual inflation rate from the Federal Reserve's inflation objective, and the gap between actual real GDP per year and a measure of potential real GDP per year.

FIGURE 16-8

Actual Federal Funds Rates and Values Predicted by a Taylor Rule

This figure displays both the actual path of the federal funds rate since 2004 and the target paths specified by a Taylor-rule equation for a Federal Reserve annual inflation objective of 0 percent.

Source: Federal Reserve Bank of St. Louis; *Monetary Trends,* various issues.

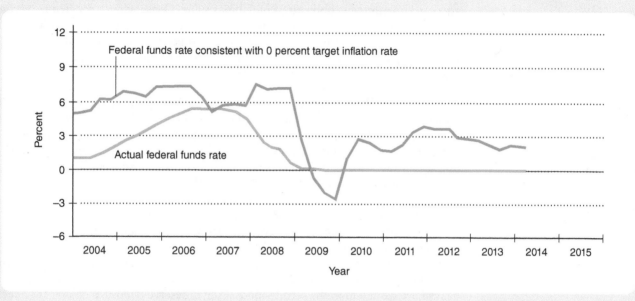

level consistent with 0 percent inflation. Then, the graph suggests, Fed policymaking became expansionary once more beginning in late 2007.

Until just after beginning of this century, the actual federal funds rate remained close to the Taylor-rule predictions over time. In recent years, however, the Fed has failed to set its federal funds rate target in a manner consistent with the Taylor rule.

Credit Policy at Today's Fed

Federal Reserve policymakers continue to announce and to try to achieve a target value for the federal funds rate. Since the financial meltdown of the last decade, however, the Fed has pursued a new approach to policymaking, called **credit policy**, under which it directly extends credit to specific banks, other financial intermediaries, and even nonfinancial companies. When Fed officials initiated this new policy approach in 2008, they indicated their intention to make it a temporary undertaking. In reality, the Fed continues to use credit policy alongside traditional monetary policy and appears unlikely to end its direct extensions of credit in the near future.

Credit policy
Federal Reserve policymaking involving direct lending to financial and nonfinancial firms.

THE CREDIT POLICY APPROACH IN PRACTICE When hundreds of banking institutions found themselves struggling to avoid severe illiquidity and bankruptcy in 2008, the Fed introduced a number of programs through which it provided credit directly to these institutions. The Fed auctioned funds to banking institutions and also bought many debt securities held by a number of these institutions.

In addition, the Fed purchased some of the debts of auto finance companies and then later allowed the companies to obtain bank charters so that they could receive direct loans from the Fed's discount window. The Fed also provided short-term emergency financing arrangements for nonfinancial firms, such as Caterpillar, Inc. and Toyota. Even though the Fed had engaged in none of these varied forms of credit policy activities prior to 2008, *as of 2015, more than $2.5 trillion, or 40 percent, of the Fed's asset holdings, relate to its conduct of credit policy.*

In recent years, the Fed has slowed its extension of credit to institutions and firms. Nevertheless, many of the debts that it purchased from banks and other firms have long *maturities*—periods of time before full repayments are due. This situation is quite different from the situation prior to 2008, when only a small portion of the Fed's assets had lengthy maturities.

Furthermore, a number of the debts the Fed has purchased from private institutions are based on mortgage obligations of dubious value. Consequently, the Fed faces considerable risk that at least some of the debts will never be fully repaid. This state of affairs is also quite different from the situation in preceding years, when the bulk of the Fed's assets, about 80 percent of which were U.S. government securities, offered very low risks of loss.

HOW THE FED FINANCES THE CREDIT IT EXTENDS In an important sense, the Fed's credit policy results in its activities more closely resembling those of a private bank than a central bank. Like a private banking institution, the Fed extends credit by lending out funds that it obtains from depositors. Unlike private banks, however, the Fed holds deposits of banking institutions instead of deposits of households and firms. These deposits consist of the reserve deposits that banks hold with Federal Reserve banks.

To engage in its active and substantial credit policy, the Fed must induce private banks to maintain substantial reserve deposits with the Federal Reserve banks. A key inducement is the interest rate the Fed pays on reserves. Even though the Fed has paid a very low interest rate of about 0.25 percent on reserve deposits since 2008, throughout most this period, the market clearing federal funds rate has been even lower. Thus, banks have earned more by setting funds aside in reserve deposit accounts at Federal Reserve banks than by lending to other banks in the federal funds market. This means that the Fed essentially has paid banks a per-unit *subsidy* to keep hundreds of billions of dollars on deposit with the Fed.

All such funds held at Federal Reserve banks do not remain idle, though. Just as private banks can use the deposits of households and firms to fund loans and purchases of securities, the Fed can use the reserve deposits of private banks to fund its own lending and securities-buying activities. Since 2008, total reserve deposits at Federal Reserve banks have risen from less than $50 billion to more than *$2.5 trillion* in 2015. A large portion of these funds have financed the Fed's credit policy—lending to domestic and foreign banks, nonfinancial companies, and central banks and buying risky, longer-term mortgage obligations.

ARGUMENTS IN FAVOR OF THE FED'S CREDIT POLICY Three arguments support the Federal Reserve's credit policy:

1. *Giving Banks Time to Recover from the Financial Meltdown.* The original rationale for initiating the credit policy was to address the deteriorating condition of the U.S. banking industry that began in 2007. As more and more banks weakened during 2008 and 2009, the Fed created an array of lending programs aimed at countering the fact that institutions were less willing to lend to one another in private markets. These new Fed lending programs made banks much more liquid than they would have been otherwise, which ensured their ability to withstand bank runs. The Fed's lending programs also succeeded in keeping many otherwise insolvent banks—those for which the value of assets dropped below the value of liabilities—afloat until they could become more economically viable. A few large institutions ultimately could not continue as stand-alone banks, and hundreds of smaller community banks failed. Nevertheless, the programs provided "breathing space" until other financial institutions could acquire those banks and their lower-valued assets.

2. *Making Financial Markets and Institutions More Liquid and Solvent.* The Fed's purchases of debt securities also helped make financial markets and institutions more liquid and solvent. At the height of the financial crisis, the Fed's purchases of

debt securities from companies such as Ford Motor Company and Harley-Davidson, Inc. ensured that these otherwise profitable and solvent firms remained liquid. The Fed's later purchases of mortgage-obligation debt securities removed many high-risk assets from banks' balance sheets and thereby improved the banks' longer-term solvency prospects.

3. **Contributing to International Financial Liquidity.** Finally, the credit extended by the Fed to foreign private banks and central banks enabled these institutions to maintain holdings of U.S. dollars. This credit policy action helped ensure liquidity in international financial markets.

Thus, the Fed's credit policy activities did much to help prevent banks, firms, and financial markets from becoming illiquid, which undoubtedly forestalled possible bank runs in 2008 and 2009. Its credit policy actions also prevented a number of bank failures.

ARGUMENTS AGAINST THE FED'S CREDIT POLICY Critics of the Fed's credit policy have offered three arguments against it.

1. **Providing an Incentive for Institutions to Operate Less Efficiently.** Critics point out that the Fed is capable of creating as much liquidity as desired via open market purchases. These critics worry that the Fed encourages institutions to which it directs credit to operate with less attention to minimizing operating costs than they would otherwise.

2. **Reducing Incentives to Screen and Monitor in Order to Limit Asymmetric Information Problems.** Critics of the Fed argue that preventing insolvencies via this credit policy interferes with the functions of private institutions and markets in identifying and addressing asymmetric information problems (see Chapter 15). If banks know the Fed will bail them out, critics suggest, banks will do poorer jobs of screening and monitoring borrowers. Hence, in the longer term, the Fed's credit policy could broaden the scope of asymmetric information problems.

3. **Making Monetary Policy Less Effective.** Critics suggest that the Fed has pursued its credit policy so vigorously that its performance in the realm of monetary policy has worsened. They point out that while the Fed was providing credit to many individual institutions and firms, difficulties in predicting how these actions would affect the money supply contributed to substantial swings in monetary aggregates. In fact, although quantitative easing policies when the interest rate was near zero raised bank reserves by more than $3 trillion, the Fed's payment of interest on reserves induced banks to hold those reserves idle at Federal Reserve banks. Thus, the reserve ratio increased, and the money multiplier fell. On net, therefore, the money supply failed to grow very much in response to the Fed's quantitative easing. Indeed, over some intervals the money supply even declined.

WHAT IF...

the Federal Reserve chooses to pay interest on reserves at the same time that the federal government seeks to induce banks to extend more credit to companies?

Payment of interest on reserves by the Fed increases the incentive for banks to hold excess reserves on deposit with the Fed instead of lending those funds to households and firms. This policy provides the Fed with funds to engage in its own credit policies but conflicts with any federal government policy intended to induce banks to lend to private firms. Indeed, such a policy conflict actually has occurred in recent years. Even as the Fed began paying banks interest on excess reserves, the government sought to induce banks to direct taxpayer-provided funds to small business loans. Thus, while the federal government was pursuing a policy aimed at boosting bank business lending, the Fed was implementing a policy that reduced the incentive for banks to lend to firms.

SELF CHECK Visit MyEconLab to practice these and other problems and to get instant feedback in your Study Plan.

At present, the policy strategy of the Federal Open Market Committee (FOMC) focuses on aiming for a target value of the _____ _____ rate, which the FOMC seeks to achieve via _____ _____ _____ that alter the supply of reserves to the banking system.

The FOMC outlines the Fed's general monetary policy strategy in the FOMC _____, which it transmits to the Trading Desk of the Federal Reserve Bank of _____ _____ for implementation.

Since 2008, the Fed has implemented _____ policy, under which it has extended _____ directly to selected financial institutions and has purchased debt securities that have lost much of their market value.

Advantages of the Fed's _____ policy are that it has provided institutions with more liquidity, has helped to limit the number of bank _____, and has provided more dollars for use in international markets. Disadvantages include reduced incentives for banks to minimize operating costs and to screen and to _____ borrowers and potential conflicts of _____ policy with the Fed's monetary policy responsibilities.

YOU ARE THERE

The Fed Struggles to Communicate Its Policies

Securities traders know that open market purchases associated with Fed quantitative easing tend to push up bond prices and tend to push down interest rates. Traders also know that open market sales will tend to reduce bond prices and lead to higher interest rates. Thus, these traders pay close attention to signals of future Fed policies imbedded in Fed officials' pronouncements. Nevertheless, after months of Fed statements that traders thought signaled an end to quantitative easing, the Fed unexpectedly continued the quantitative easing policy. A headline summed up the reaction: "In Bid for Clarity, Fed Delivers Opacity."

In an effort to improve Fed policy communications, the Fed chair resorted to using metaphors—figures of speech meant to suggest similarities. In this respect, he sought to follow the example of previous Fed chairs, such as William Martin, who in 1955 said that the Fed's duty was to "take away the punch bowl just as the party gets going." Unfortunately for the chair of the Fed, his metaphors failed to communicate Fed policy intentions very clearly. Traders were not quite sure what he meant, for instance, when he said, "We're going to be shifting the mix of our tools as we try to land the ship in a smooth way onto the aircraft carrier." Then he said that the Fed's quantitative easing effort was "akin to letting up a bit on the gas pedal as the car picks up speed" but the interest rate effect would be like "beginning to apply the brakes." Afterward, many traders indicated that they remained deeply confused about the Fed's plans.

CRITICAL THINKING QUESTIONS

1. Why are *future* Fed policy intentions, such as those communicated by today's Fed chair, Janet Yellen, of particular interest to securities traders?

2. Why do you think traders regard Martin's metaphor as clearer than the recent Fed chair's?

Sources are listed at the end of this chapter.

ISSUES & APPLICATIONS

MyEconLab Video

Federal Reserve/Alamy

How Fed Policies Have Helped to Fund Federal Deficits

CONCEPTS APPLIED

» Quantitative Easing

» Credit Policy

» Money Balances

At various times over the past several years, the Federal Reserve has engaged in quantitative easing by purchasing securities. These purchases increase the quantity of bank reserves, which provides the Fed with funds to engage in credit policy. Because the purchases often involve U.S. Treasury securities, the Fed's quantitative easing programs also have boosted its share of ownership of the public debt discussed in Chapter 14.

The Fed's Acquisition of Treasury Debts: QE1, QE2, and QE3

Since 2008, the Fed has conducted three quantitative easing policy programs: QE1—$1.6 trillion, November 2008–March 2009; QE2—$600 billion, November 2010–June 2011; and QE3—$1.6 trillion, September 2012–October 2014. During QE1, many of the securities that the Fed

bought were short-term, 3-to-6-month-maturity securities that the U.S. Treasury since has paid off. QE2 and QE3, however, involved more purchases of longer-term Treasury debts that have not been paid off. Consequently, as shown in Figure 16-9, the Fed's share of the net public debt outstanding has grown considerably, to more than 18 percent.

MyEconLab Real-time data

FIGURE 16-9

Share of the Net Public Debt Held by the Federal Reserve System

As the Federal Reserve has implemented quantitative easing programs since 2008, the percentage of the net public debt that the Fed holds has more than doubled.

Source: Federal Reserve Bank of St. Louis; author's estimates.

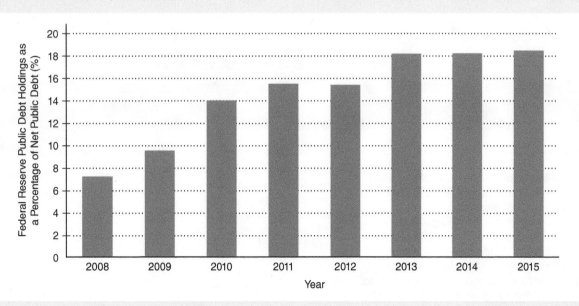

Benefits for the U.S. Treasury, but Monetary Concerns

The Fed's credit policies have sought to stabilize the banking system, but the combination of its credit and monetary policies has also been a boon to the U.S. Treasury. The Fed does not purchase newly issued securities directly from the U.S. Treasury, but the Fed's policies have held down market interest rates and hence the U.S. Treasury's costs of borrowing.

The Fed has paid interest to banks to induce them to hold reserves with the Fed, which the Fed in turn has used to fund its QE and credit-policy programs. Hence, the Fed's substantial expansion of reserves has not generated a significant increase in the money supply. As a result, even though the Fed's current share of ownership of the net public debt is at its highest since the 1970s, the rate of money growth has remained lower than it was in that earlier decade.

For Critical Thinking

1. If the public's desired money balances were to increase and the Fed were to allow the quantity of money in circulation to rise, how would such a Fed policy response influence the short-run equilibrium price level and level of real GDP per year?

2. According to the quantity equation, if the U.S. money growth rate were to double as a consequence of the Fed's quantitative easing policies, what would be the effect on the inflation rate, other things being equal?

Web Resources

1. Read an article describing the use of quantitative easing programs at the Federal Reserve and three other central banks in the Web Links in MyEconLab.

2. Track the dollar amount of Treasury debt held by the Federal Reserve in the Web Links in MyEconLab.

> ### MyEconLab
>
> For more questions on this chapter's Issues & Applications, go to MyEconLab.
>
> In the Study Plan for this chapter, select Section I: Issues and Applications.

Sources are listed at the end of this chapter.

Fundamental Points

1. The determinants of the demand for money balances are the transactions demand, the precautionary demand, and the asset demand.

2. An inverse relationship exists between the prevailing rate of interest and the market price of *existing* bonds (and all fixed-income assets). A Fed open market purchase generates an increase in the price of *existing* bonds and a decrease in the market interest rate.

3. The direct effect of a money supply increase occurs because people wish to spend more when they have excess money balances, and the indirect effect arises from a decrease in the interest rate, which encourages firms to make new investments with borrowed funds.

4. The equation of exchange states that $M_sV \equiv PY$ (money supply times velocity equals nominal GDP). The quantity theory of money and prices states that a change in the money supply will generate a proportional change in the price level.

5. The policy strategy of the Federal Open Market Committee (FOMC) involves maintaining a target for the federal funds rate. Since 2008, the Fed has implemented credit policy by extending loans directly to banks and by purchasing debt securities.

WHAT YOU SHOULD KNOW

Here is what you should know after reading this chapter. MyEconLab will help you identify what you know, and where to go when you need to practice.

LEARNING OBJECTIVES	KEY TERMS	WHERE TO GO TO PRACTICE
16.1 Identify the key factors that influence the quantity of money that people desire to hold *People desire to hold more money to make transactions when nominal GDP increases. In addition, money is a store of value that people may hold alongside bonds, stocks, and other interest-earning assets. The opportunity cost of holding money as an asset is the interest rate, so the quantity of money demanded declines as the market interest rate increases.*	money balances, 364 transactions demand, 364 precautionary demand, 364 asset demand, 365 **Key Figure** Figure 16-1, 365	• MyEconLab Study Plan 16.1

WHAT YOU SHOULD KNOW *continued*

LEARNING OBJECTIVES	KEY TERMS	WHERE TO GO TO PRACTICE
16.2 Describe how federal reserve monetary policy actions influence market interest rates *When the Fed sells U.S. government bonds, it must offer them for sale at a lower price to induce buyers to purchase the bonds. The market price of existing bonds and the prevailing interest rate in the economy are inversely related, so the market interest rate rises when the Fed sells bonds.*	**Key Figure** Figure 16-2, 366	• MyEconLab Study Plan 16.2 • Animated Figure 16-2
16.3 Evaluate how expansionary and contractionary monetary policy actions affect equilibrium real GDP and the price level in the short run *An expansionary monetary policy action increases the money supply and causes a decrease in market interest rates. The aggregate demand curve shifts rightward, which can eliminate a short-run recessionary gap in real GDP. In contrast, a contractionary monetary policy action reduces the money supply and causes an increase in market interest rates. This results in a leftward shift in the aggregate demand curve, which can eliminate a short-run inflationary gap.*	quantitative easing, 368 **Key Figures** Figure 16-3, 369 Figure 16-4, 369	• MyEconLab Study Plan 16.3 • Animated Figures 16-3, 16-4
16.4 Understand the equation of exchange and its importance in the quantity theory of money and prices *The equation of exchange states that the quantity of money times the average number of times a unit of money is used in exchange—the income velocity of money—must equal the price level times real GDP. The quantity theory of money and prices assumes that the income velocity of money is constant and real GDP is relatively stable. Thus, a rise in the quantity of money leads to an equiproportional increase in the price level.*	equation of exchange, 371 income velocity of money (V), 371 quantity theory of money and prices, 372	• MyEconLab Study Plan 16.4
16.5 Explain how the Federal Reserve has implemented credit policy since 2008 *The interest-rate-based approach to the monetary policy transmission mechanism operates through effects of monetary policy actions on market interest rates, which bring about changes in desired investment and thereby affect equilibrium real GDP via the multiplier effect. At present, the Fed uses an interest rate target, which is the federal funds rate. Since the late 2000s, the Federal Reserve has used credit policy, which involves direct lending to financial and nonfinancial firms.*	federal funds market, 375 federal funds rate, 375 discount rate, 375 FOMC Directive, 376 Trading Desk, 376 Taylor rule, 376 credit policy, 377 **Key Figures** Figure 16-6, 373 Figure 16-7, 374 Figure 16-8, 377	• MyEconLab Study Plan 16.5 • Animated Figures 16-6, 16-7

Log in to MyEconLab, take a chapter test, and get a personalized Study Plan that tells you which concepts you understand and which ones you need to review. From there, MyEconLab will give you further practice, tutorials, animations, videos, and guided solutions. For more information, visit http://www.myeconlab.com

PROBLEMS

All problems are assignable in MyEconLab; exercises that update with real-time data are marked with 🌐 . *Answers to odd-numbered problems appear in MyEconLab.*

16-1. Let's denote the price of a nonmaturing bond (called a *consol*) as P_b. The equation that indicates this price is $P_b = I/r$, where I is the annual net income the bond generates and r is the nominal market interest rate. (See pages 364–367.)

   a. Suppose that a bond promises the holder $500 per year forever. If the nominal market interest rate is 5 percent, what is the bond's current price?

   b. What happens to the bond's price if the market interest rate rises to 10 percent?

16-2. On the basis of Problem 16-1, imagine that initially the market interest rate is 5 percent and at this interest rate you have decided to hold half of your financial wealth as bonds and half as holdings of non-interest-bearing money. You notice that the market interest rate is starting to rise, however, and you become convinced that it will ultimately rise to 10 percent. (See pages 365–367.)

   a. In what direction do you expect the value of your bond holdings to go when the interest rate rises?

   b. If you wish to prevent the value of your financial wealth from declining in the future, how should you adjust the way you split your wealth between bonds and money? What does this imply about the demand for money?

16-3. You learned in Chapter 11 that if there is an inflationary gap in the short run, then in the long run a new equilibrium arises when input prices and expectations adjust upward, causing the short-run aggregate supply curve to shift upward and to the left and pushing equilibrium real GDP per year back to its long-run value. In this chapter, however, you learned that the Federal Reserve can eliminate an inflationary gap in the short run by undertaking a policy action that reduces aggregate demand. (See page 369.)

   a. Propose one monetary policy action that could eliminate an inflationary gap in the short run.

   b. In what way might society gain if the Fed implements the policy you have proposed instead of simply permitting long-run adjustments to take place?

16-4. You learned in Chapter 11 that if a recessionary gap occurs in the short run, then in the long run a new equilibrium arises when input prices and expectations adjust downward, causing the short-run aggregate supply curve to shift downward and to the right and pushing equilibrium real GDP per year back to its long-run value. In this chapter, you learned that the Federal Reserve can eliminate a recessionary gap in the short run by undertaking a policy action that increases aggregate demand. (See page 369.)

   a. Propose one monetary policy action that could eliminate the recessionary gap in the short run.

   b. In what way might society gain if the Fed implements the policy you have proposed instead of simply permitting long-run adjustments to take place?

16-5. Suppose that the economy currently is in long-run equilibrium. Explain the short- and long-run adjustments that will take place in an aggregate demand–aggregate supply diagram if the Fed expands the quantity of money in circulation. (See page 369.)

16-6. Explain why the net export effect of a contractionary monetary policy reinforces the usual impact that monetary policy has on equilibrium real GDP per year in the short run. (See page 370.)

16-7. Suppose that, initially, the U.S. economy was in an aggregate demand–aggregate supply equilibrium at point A along the aggregate demand curve AD in the diagram below. Now, however, the value of the U.S. dollar suddenly appreciates relative to foreign currencies. This appreciation happens to have no measurable effects on either the short-run or the long-run aggregate supply curve in the United States. It does, however, influence U.S. aggregate demand. (See pages 369–370.)

    a. Explain in your own words how the dollar appreciation will affect net export expenditures in the United States.

    b. Of the alternative aggregate demand curves depicted in the figure—AD_1 versus AD_2—which could represent the aggregate demand effect of the U.S. dollar's appreciation? What effects does the appreciation have on real GDP and the price level?

    c. What policy action might the Federal Reserve take to prevent the dollar's appreciation from affecting equilibrium real GDP in the short run?

16-8. Suppose that the quantity of money in circulation is fixed but the income velocity of money doubles. If real GDP remains at its long-run potential level, what happens to the equilibrium price level? (See pages 371–372.)

16-9. Suppose that following adjustment to the events in Problem 16-8, the Fed cuts the money supply in half. How does the price level now compare with its value before the income velocity and the money supply changed? (See pages 371–372.)

16-10. Consider the following data: The money supply is $1 trillion, the price level equals 2, and real GDP is $5 trillion in base-year dollars. What is the income velocity of money? (See page 372.)

16-11. Consider the data in Problem 16-10. Suppose that the money supply increases by $100 billion and real GDP and the income velocity remain unchanged. (See pages 371–372.)

    a. According to the quantity theory of money and prices, what is the new equilibrium price level after full adjustment to the increase in the money supply?

    b. What is the percentage increase in the money supply?

    c. What is the percentage change in the price level?

    d. How do the percentage changes in the money supply and price level compare?

16-12. Assuming that the Fed judges inflation to be the most significant problem in the economy and that it wishes to employ all of its policy instruments except interest on reserves, what should the Fed do with its three policy tools? (See pages 373–375.)

16-13. Suppose that the Fed implements each of the policy changes you discussed in Problem 16-12.

Now explain how the net export effect resulting from these monetary policy actions will reinforce their effects that operate through interest rate changes. (See page 370.)

16-14. Imagine working at the Trading Desk at the New York Fed. Explain whether you would conduct open market purchases or sales in response to each of the following events. Justify your recommendation. (See page 375.)

    a. The latest FOMC Directive calls for an increase in the target value of the federal funds rate.

    b. For a reason unrelated to monetary policy, the Fed's Board of Governors has decided to raise the differential between the discount rate and the federal funds rate. Nevertheless, the FOMC Directive calls for maintaining the present federal funds rate target.

16-15. To implement a credit policy intended to expand liquidity of the banking system, the Fed desires to increase its assets by lending to a substantial number of banks. How might the Fed adjust the interest rate that it pays banks on reserves in order to induce them to hold the reserves required for funding this credit policy action? What will happen to the Fed's liabilities if it implements this policy action? (See pages 377–378.)

16-16. Suppose that to finance its credit policy, the Fed pays an annual interest rate of 0.25 percent on bank reserves. During the course of the current year, banks hold $1 trillion in reserves. What is the total amount of interest the Fed pays banks during the year? (See pages 377–378.)

16-17. During an interval between mid-2010 and early 2011, the Federal Reserve embarked on a policy it termed "quantitative easing." Total reserves in the banking system increased. Hence, the Federal Reserve's liabilities to banks increased, and at the same time its assets rose as it purchased more assets—many of which were securities with private market values that had dropped considerably. The money multiplier declined, so the net increase in the money supply was negligible. Indeed, during a portion of the period, the money supply actually declined before rising near its previous value. Evaluate whether the Fed's "quantitative easing" was a monetary policy or credit policy action. (See pages 368 and 374–379.)

REFERENCES

INTERNATIONAL POLICY EXAMPLE: Japan Rediscovers Inflation via the Quantity Equation

Phred Dvorak and Eleanor Warnock, "Stagnant Japan Rolls Dice on New Era of Easy Money," *The Wall Street Journal*, March 20, 2013.

Toru Fujioka and Andy Sharp, "Bank of Japan Sticks to Record Easing as Inflation Picks Up," Bloomberg, January 22, 2014.

"Monetary Policy in Japan: Opening the Floodgates," *The Economist*, April 13, 2013.

POLICY EXAMPLE: European Central Banks Contemplate Negative Interest Rates

Brian Blackstone, "ECB: Negative Deposit Rate, Asset Purchases Are Options," *The Wall Street Journal*, November 13, 2013.

"European Monetary Policy: The Negative Option," *The Economist*, June 1, 2013.

Christopher Lawton, "ECB Considers Negative Deposit Rate," *The Wall Street Journal*, February 12, 2014.

YOU ARE THERE: The Fed Struggles to Communicate Its Policies

Binyamin Appelbaum, "Yellen Sets a Familiar Direction for the Fed," *The New York Times*, February 11, 2014.

Victoria McGrane, "Fedspeak: Complex Monetary Policy Spawns Flights of Metaphors," *The Wall Street Journal*, July 4, 2013.

Pedro Niccolaci, "Ground Control, We Have a Fed Communications Problem," *Reuters*, September 19, 2013.

ISSUES & APPLICATIONS: How Fed Policies Have Helped to Fund Federal Deficits

Enrique Castro-Mendivil, "Federal Reserve Owns More than $2 Trillion in U.S. Debt," *Reuters*, August 20, 2013.

Terence Jeffrey, "Fed's Holdings of U.S. Government Debt Hit Record," *CBS News*, January 24, 2013.

Floyd Norris, "No Surprise, Fed Was Biggest Buyer of Treasuries in 2013," *The New York Times*, February 21, 2014.

Monetary Policy: A Keynesian Perspective

According to the traditional Keynesian approach to monetary policy, changes in the money supply can affect the level of aggregate demand only through their effect on interest rates. Moreover, interest rate changes act on aggregate demand solely by changing the level of real planned investment spending. Finally, the traditional Keynesian approach argues that there are plausible circumstances under which monetary policy may have little or no effect on interest rates and thus on aggregate demand.

Figure E-1 below measures real GDP per year along the horizontal axis and total planned expenditures (aggregate demand) along the vertical axis. The components of aggregate demand are real consumption (C), investment (I), government spending (G), and net exports (X). The height of the schedule labeled $C + I + G + X$ shows total real planned expenditures (aggregate demand) as a function of real GDP per year. This schedule slopes upward because consumption depends positively on real GDP. All along the line labeled $Y = C + I + G + X$, real planned spending equals real GDP per year. At point Y^*, where the $C + I + G + X$ line intersects this 45-degree reference line, real planned spending is consistent with real GDP.

At any real GDP level less than Y^*, spending exceeds real GDP, so real GDP and thus spending will tend to rise. At any level of real GDP greater than Y^*, real planned spending is less than real GDP, so real GDP and thus spending will tend to decline. Given the determinants of C, I, G, and X, total spending (aggregate demand) will be Y^*.

FIGURE E-1

An Increase in the Money Supply

An increase in the money supply increases real GDP by lowering interest rates and thus increasing investment from I to I'.

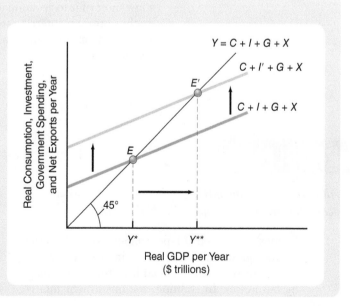

Increasing the Money Supply

According to the Keynesian approach, an increase in the money supply pushes interest rates down. This induces firms to increase the level of investment spending from I to I'. As a result, the $C + I + G + X$ line shifts upward in Figure E-1 on the previous page by the full amount of the rise in investment spending, thus yielding the line $C + I' + G + X$. The rise in investment spending causes real GDP to rise, which in turn causes real consumption spending to rise, further increasing real GDP. Ultimately, aggregate demand rises to Y^{**}, where spending again equals real GDP. A key conclusion of the Keynesian analysis is that total spending rises by *more* than the original rise in investment spending because consumption spending depends positively on real GDP.

MyEconLab Concept Check

Decreasing the Money Supply

Not surprisingly, contractionary monetary policy works in exactly the reverse manner. A reduction in the money supply pushes interest rates up. Firms respond by reducing their investment spending, and this pushes real GDP downward. Consumers react to the lower real GDP by scaling back on their real consumption spending, which further depresses real GDP. Thus, the ultimate decline in real GDP is larger than the initial drop in investment spending. Indeed, because the change in real GDP is a multiple of the change in investment, Keynesians note that changes in investment spending (similar to changes in government spending) have a *multiplier* effect on the economy.

MyEconLab Concept Check

Arguments against Monetary Policy

It might be thought that this multiplier effect would make monetary policy a potent tool in the Keynesian arsenal, particularly when it comes to getting the economy out of a recession. In fact, however, many traditional Keynesians argue that monetary policy is likely to be relatively ineffective as a recession fighter.

According to their line of reasoning, although monetary policy has the potential to reduce interest rates, changes in the money supply have little *actual* impact on interest rates. Instead, during recessions, people try to build up as much as they can in liquid assets to protect themselves from risks of unemployment and other losses of income. When the monetary authorities increase the money supply, individuals are willing to allow most of it to accumulate in their bank accounts. This desire for increased liquidity thus prevents interest rates from falling very much, which in turn means that there will be almost no change in investment spending and thus little change in aggregate demand.

MyEconLab Concept Check
MyEconLab Study Plan

PROBLEMS

All problems are assignable in MyEconLab. *Answers to odd-numbered problems appear in* MyEconLab.

E-1. Suppose that each 0.1-percentage-point decrease in the equilibrium interest rate induces a $10 billion increase in real planned investment spending by businesses. In addition, the investment multi-plier is equal to 5, and the money multiplier is equal to 4. Furthermore, every $20 billion increase in the money supply brings about a 0.1-percentage-point reduction in the equilibrium interest rate. Use this information to answer the following questions under the assumption that all other things are equal. (See pages 387–388.)

a. How much must real planned investment increase if the Federal Reserve desires to bring about a $100 billion increase in equilibrium real GDP?

b. How much must the money supply change for the Fed to induce the change in real planned investment calculated in part (a)?

c. What dollar amount of open market operations must the Fed undertake to bring about the money supply change calculated in part (b)?

E-2. Suppose that each 0.1-percentage-point increase in the equilibrium interest rate induces a $5 billion decrease in real planned investment spending by businesses. In addition, the investment multiplier is equal to 4, and the money multiplier is equal to 3. Furthermore, every $9 billion decrease in the money supply brings about a 0.1-percentage-point increase in the equilibrium interest rate. Use this information to answer the following questions under the assumption that all other things are equal. (See pages 387–388.)

a. How much must real planned investment decrease if the Federal Reserve desires to bring about an $80 billion decrease in equilibrium real GDP?

b. How much must the money supply change for the Fed to induce the change in real planned investment calculated in part (a)?

c. What dollar amount of open market operations must the Fed undertake to bring about the money supply change calculated in part (b)?

E-3. Assume that the following conditions exist (see pages 387–388):

a. All banks are fully loaned up—there are no excess reserves, and desired excess reserves are always zero.

b. The money multiplier is 3.

c. The planned investment schedule is such that at a 6 percent rate of interest, investment is $1,200

billion; at 5 percent, investment is $1,225 billion.

d. The investment multiplier is 3.

e. The initial equilibrium level of real GDP is $18 trillion.

f. The equilibrium rate of interest is 6 percent.

Now the Fed engages in expansionary monetary policy. It buys $1 billion worth of bonds, which increases the money supply, which in turn lowers the market rate of interest by 1 percentage point. Determine how much the money supply must have increased, and then trace out the numerical consequences of the associated reduction in interest rates on all the other variables mentioned.

E-4. Assume that the following conditions exist (see pages 387–388):

a. All banks are fully loaned up—there are no excess reserves, and desired excess reserves are always zero.

b. The money multiplier is 4.

c. The planned investment schedule is such that at a 4 percent rate of interest, investment is $1,400 billion. At 5 percent, investment is $1,380 billion.

d. The investment multiplier is 5.

e. The initial equilibrium level of real GDP is $19 trillion.

f. The equilibrium rate of interest is 4 percent.

Now the Fed engages in contractionary monetary policy. It sells $2 billion worth of bonds, which reduces the money supply, which in turn raises the market rate of interest by 1 percentage point. Determine how much the money supply must have decreased, and then trace out the numerical consequences of the associated increase in interest rates on all the other variables mentioned.

17

Stabilization in an Integrated World Economy

Jim Weber/The Commercial Appeal/Zumapress/Newscom

LEARNING OBJECTIVES

After reading this chapter, you should be able to:

17.1 Explain why the actual unemployment rate might depart from the natural rate of unemployment

17.2 Describe why there may be an inverse relationship between the inflation rate and the unemployment rate and evaluate how expectations affect this relationship

17.3 Understand the rational expectations hypothesis and its implications for economic policymaking

17.4 Distinguish among alternative modern approaches to strengthening the case for active policymaking

MyEconLab helps you master each objective and study more efficiently. See the end of the chapter for details.

In November 2010, in excess of 14 million people were unemployed, and the unemployment rate was above 9 percent. The Fed chair at that time promised that the Fed's policies would foster economic conditions that would rapidly bring down unemployment. Just over two years later, nearly 13 million people remained unemployed, and the unemployment rate remained above 8 percent. In 2012, the Fed promised not to allow market interest rates to rise again until the unemployment rate declined below a target level. In 2014 however, the Fed announced an end to this commitment by 2015, whether or not the unemployment target had been reached. In this chapter, you will learn why the Fed theorized that this monetary policy strategy might help to bring down unemployment. You will also learn why the Fed abandoned its promise.

analysis of prices posted on Internet Web sites and processed by automatic scanners in brick-and-mortar stores verifies that by far the most common ending number in a price for an item priced as high as $11 is "9"? In addition, prices ending in the number "9" change less often than prices ending in other numbers. When prices ending in the number "9" *do* change, though, the price changes typically are larger than those from prices ending in numbers other than "9." Some economists who study these and other data relating to how firms price their goods and services suggest that these facts contribute to "price stickiness"—that is, a generalized tendency for prices to adjust sluggishly over time.

In this chapter, you will learn about possible consequences of widespread price stickiness. Among these is that sticky prices may help to make macroeconomic policies aimed at stabilizing the economy more potent.

Active versus Passive Policymaking and the Natural Rate of Unemployment

17.1 Explain why the actual unemployment rate might depart from the natural rate of unemployment

If it is true that monetary and fiscal policy actions aimed at exerting significant stabilizing effects on overall economic activity are likely to succeed, then this would be a strong argument for **active (discretionary) policymaking**. This is the term for actions that monetary and fiscal policymakers undertake in reaction to or in anticipation of a change in economic performance. On the other side of the debate is the view that the best way to achieve economic stability is through **passive (nondiscretionary) policymaking**, in which there is no deliberate stabilization policy at all. Policymakers follow a rule and do not attempt to respond in a discretionary manner to actual or potential changes in economic activity.

Recall from Chapter 13 that there are lags between the time when the national economy enters a recession or a boom and the time when that fact becomes known and acted on by policymakers. Proponents of passive policy argue that such time lags often render short-term stabilization policy ineffective or, worse, procyclical.

To take a stand on this debate concerning active versus passive policymaking, you first need to know the potential trade-offs that policymakers believe they face. Then you need to see what the data actually show. One possible policy trade-off may be between price stability and unemployment. Before exploring that, however, we need to look at the economy's natural, or long-run, rate of unemployment.

Active (discretionary) policymaking
All actions on the part of monetary and fiscal policymakers that are undertaken in response to or in anticipation of some change in the overall economy.

Passive (nondiscretionary) policymaking
Policymaking that is carried out in response to a rule. It is therefore not in response to an actual or potential change in overall economic activity.

The Natural Rate of Unemployment

Recall from Chapter 7 that there are different types of unemployment: frictional, cyclical, structural, and seasonal. *Frictional unemployment* arises because individuals take the time to search for the best job opportunities. Much unemployment is of this type, except when the economy is in a recession or a depression, when cyclical unemployment rises.

THE ROLE OF STRUCTURAL UNEMPLOYMENT Note that we did not say that frictional unemployment was the *sole* form of unemployment during normal times. *Structural unemployment* is caused by a variety of "rigidities" throughout the economy. Structural unemployment results from factors such as these:

1. Government-imposed minimum wage laws, laws restricting entry into occupations, and welfare and unemployment insurance benefits that reduce incentives to work

2. Union activity that sets wages above the equilibrium level and also restricts the mobility of labor

All of these factors reduce individuals' abilities or incentives to choose employment rather than unemployment.

Consider the effect of unemployment insurance benefits on the probability of an unemployed person's finding a job. When unemployment benefits run out, according to economists Lawrence Katz and Bruce Meyer, the probability of an unemployed person's finding a job doubles. The conclusion is that unemployed workers are more serious about finding a job when they are no longer receiving such benefits.

THE NATURAL UNEMPLOYMENT RATE Frictional unemployment and structural unemployment both exist even when the economy is in long-run equilibrium—they are a natural consequence of costly information (the need to conduct a job search) and the existence of rigidities such as those noted above. Because these two types of unemployment are a natural consequence of imperfect and costly information and rigidities, they are components of what economists call the **natural rate of unemployment**. As we discussed in Chapter 7, this is defined as the rate of unemployment that would exist in the long run after everyone in the economy fully adjusted to any changes that have occurred.

Recall that real GDP per year tends to return to the level implied by the long-run aggregate supply curve (*LRAS*). Thus, whatever rate of unemployment the economy tends to return to in long-run equilibrium can be called the natural rate of unemployment.

According to the U.S. government, what is the natural unemployment rate?

Natural rate of unemployment

The rate of unemployment that is estimated to prevail in long-run macroeconomic equilibrium, when all workers and employers have fully adjusted to any changes in the economy.

POLICY EXAMPLE

The U.S. Government's Estimate of the Natural Rate of Unemployment

The Congressional Budget Office (CBO), an agency that tracks economic data for the U.S. Congress, estimates the natural rate of unemployment each year. The CBO forms these estimates based on its projections of "potential real GDP," or the level of real GDP per year that CBO determines that the economy is capable of producing given available national resources.

Figure 17-1 on the next page displays both the actual unemployment rate and the CBO's estimates of the natural unemployment rate since 1966. As you can see, according to the CBO, the natural rate of unemploy-

ment steadily increased from just over 5.7 percent in 1966 to nearly 6.3 percent in the late 1970s before dropping to 5 percent at the beginning of this century. The CBO estimates that the natural unemployment rate has risen to 5.5 percent in 2015.

FOR CRITICAL THINKING

Why does the natural rate of unemployment differ from the actual rate of unemployment?

Sources are listed at the end of this chapter.

MyEconLab Concept Check

Departures from the Natural Rate of Unemployment

The unemployment rate has a strong tendency to stay at and return to the natural rate. It is possible for other factors, such as changes in private spending or fiscal and monetary policy actions, however, to move the actual unemployment rate away from the natural rate, at least in the short run. Deviations of the actual unemployment rate from the natural rate are called *cyclical unemployment* because they are observed over the course of nationwide business fluctuations. During recessions, the overall unemployment rate exceeds the natural rate, so cyclical unemployment is positive. During periods of economic booms, the overall unemployment rate can go below the natural rate. At such times, cyclical unemployment is negative.

To see how departures from the natural rate of unemployment can occur, let's consider two examples. In Figure 17-2 on the next page, we begin in equilibrium at point E_1 with the associated price level 117 and real GDP per year of $18 trillion.

THE IMPACT OF EXPANSIONARY POLICY Now imagine that the government decides to use fiscal or monetary policy to stimulate the economy. Further suppose, for reasons that will soon become clear, that this policy surprises decision makers throughout the economy in the sense that they did not anticipate that the policy would occur.

MyEconLab Real-time data
MyEconLab Animation

FIGURE 17-1

The Actual U.S. Unemployment Rate and Congressional Budget Office Estimates of the Natural Rate of Unemployment

As you can see, the actual U.S. rate of unemployment has exhibited considerable variability in recent decades. Congressional Budget Office esti- mates of the natural unemployment rate have exhibited considerably less short-term variation but instead have changed more gradually over time.

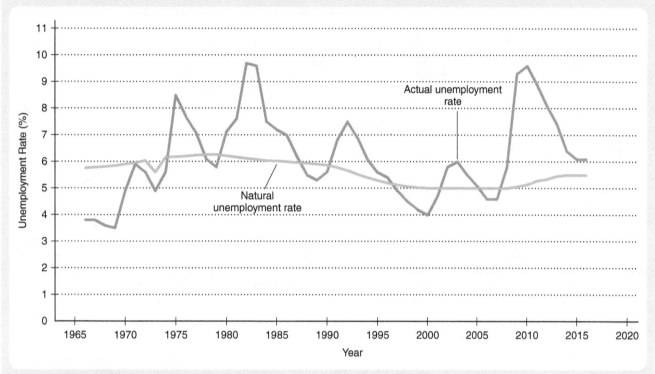

Sources: Economic Report of the President; Economic Indicators, various issues; author's estimates; Congressional Budget Office

MyEconLab Animation

FIGURE 17-2

Impact of an Increase in Aggregate Demand on Real GDP and Unemployment

Point E_1 is an initial short-run and long-run equilibrium. An expansionary monetary or fiscal policy shifts the aggregate demand curve outward to AD_2. The price level rises from 117 to 120 at point E_2, and real GDP per year increases to $18.4 trillion in base-year dollars. The unemployment rate is now below its natural rate at the short-run equilibrium point E_2. As expectations of input owners are revised, the short-run aggregate supply curve shifts from $SRAS_1$ to $SRAS_2$ because of higher prices and higher resource costs. Real GDP returns to the $LRAS$ level of $18 trillion per year, at point E_3. The price level increases to 122. The unemployment rate returns to the natural rate.

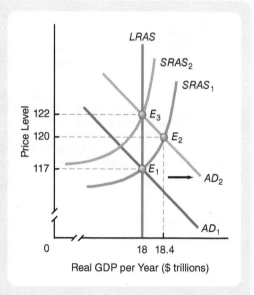

As shown in Figure 17-2, the expansionary policy action causes the aggregate demand curve to shift from AD_1 to AD_2. The price level rises from 117 to 120. Real GDP, measured in base-year dollars, increases from $18 trillion to $18.4 trillion.

In the labor market, individuals find that conditions have improved markedly relative to what they expected. Firms seeking to expand output want to hire more workers. To accomplish this, they recruit more actively and possibly ask workers to work overtime, so individuals in the labor market find more job openings and more possible hours they can work. Consequently, as you learned in Chapter 7, the average duration of unemployment falls, and so does the unemployment rate.

The *SRAS* curve does not stay at $SRAS_1$ indefinitely, however. Input owners, such as workers and owners of capital and raw materials, revise their expectations. The short-run aggregate supply curve shifts to $SRAS_2$ as input prices rise. We find ourselves at a new equilibrium at E_3, which is on the *LRAS*. Long-run real GDP per year is $18 trillion again, but at a higher price level, 122. The unemployment rate returns to its original, natural level.

WHAT IF...

> the government attempted to generate a long-term economic expansion by providing people with tax "rebates," or returns of portions of taxes they had paid during the year?

In fact, the U.S. government provided temporary tax rebates three times in the past decade. In each case, the fact that the rebates were fully anticipated and temporary resulted in the tax policy actions having no measurable long-term effects on equilibrium real GDP. Thus, the economy adjusted to the same long-run levels of real GDP that it would have reached in the absence of the policy actions. The fully anticipated, temporary tax rebates did not bring about long-term economic expansions. Indeed, estimates by a number of economists have indicated that in every instance, the tax rebates generated very small *short-term* real GDP effects.

THE CONSEQUENCES OF CONTRACTIONARY POLICY Instead of expansionary policy, the government could have decided to engage in contractionary (or deflationary) policy. As shown in Figure 17-3 below, the sequence of events would have been in the opposite direction of those in Figure 17-2 on the previous page.

Beginning from an initial equilibrium E_1, an unanticipated reduction in aggregate demand puts downward pressure on both prices and real GDP. The price level falls from 120 to 118, and real GDP declines from $18 trillion to $17.7 trillion. Fewer firms are hiring, and those that are hiring offer fewer overtime possibilities. Individuals

MyEconLab Animation

FIGURE 17-3

Impact of a Decline in Aggregate Demand on Real GDP and Unemployment

Starting from equilibrium at E_1, a decline in aggregate demand to AD_2 leads to a lower price level, 118, and real GDP declines to $17.7 trillion. The unemployment rate will rise above the natural rate of unemployment. Equilibrium at E_2 is temporary, however. At the lower price level, the expectations of input owners are revised. $SRAS_1$ shifts to $SRAS_2$. The new long-run equilibrium is at E_3, with real GDP equal to $18 trillion and a price level of 116. The actual unemployment rate is once again equal to the natural rate of unemployment.

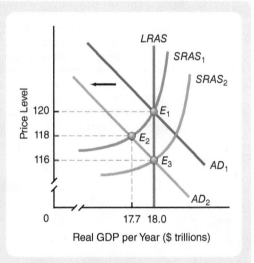

looking for jobs find that it takes longer than predicted. As a result, unemployed individuals remain unemployed longer. The average duration of unemployment rises, and so does the rate of unemployment.

The equilibrium at E_2 is only a short-run situation, however. As input owners change their expectations about future prices, $SRAS_1$ shifts to $SRAS_2$, and input prices fall. The new long-run equilibrium is at E_3, which is on the long-run aggregate supply curve, *LRAS*. In the long run, the price level declines further, to 116, as real GDP returns to \$18 trillion. Thus, in the long run the unemployment rate returns to its natural level.

MyEconLab Concept Check
MyEconLab Study Plan

The **natural rate of unemployment** is the rate that exists in _____-run equilibrium, when workers' _____ are consistent with actual conditions.

Departures from the natural rate of unemployment can occur when individuals encounter unanticipated changes in fiscal or monetary policy. An unexpected _____ in aggregate demand will reduce unemployment below the natural rate, whereas an unanticipated _____ in aggregate demand will push unemployment above the natural rate.

The Phillips Curve: A Rationale for Active Policymaking?

17.2 Describe why there may be an inverse relationship between the inflation rate and the unemployment rate and evaluate how expectations affect this relationship

Let's recap what we have just observed. In the short run, an *unexpected increase* in aggregate demand causes the price level to rise and the unemployment rate to fall. Conversely, in the short run, an *unexpected decrease* in aggregate demand causes the price level to fall and the unemployment rate to rise. Moreover, although not shown explicitly in either diagram, two additional points are true:

1. The greater the unexpected increase in aggregate demand, the greater the amount of inflation that results in the short run, and the lower the unemployment rate.

2. The greater the unexpected decrease in aggregate demand, the greater the deflation that results in the short run, and the higher the unemployment rate.

The Negative Short-Run Relationship between Inflation and Unemployment

Figure 17-4 on the next page summarizes these findings. The inflation rate (*not* the price level) is measured along the vertical axis, and the unemployment rate is measured along the horizontal axis. Panel (a) shows the unemployment rate at a natural rate denoted U^* that is assumed to be 6 percent at point A. At this point, the actual inflation rate and anticipated inflation rate are both equal to 0 percent. Panel (b) of Figure 17-4 depicts the effects of unanticipated changes in aggregate demand. In panel (b), an unexpected increase in aggregate demand causes the price level to rise—the inflation rate rises to 3 percent—and causes the unemployment rate to fall to 5 percent. Thus, the economy moves upward to the left from A to B.

Conversely, in the short run, unexpected decreases in aggregate demand cause the price level to fall and the unemployment rate to rise above the natural rate. In panel (b), the price level declines—the *deflation* rate is −1 percent—and the unemployment rate rises to 8 percent. The economy moves from point A to point C. If we look at both increases and decreases in aggregate demand, we see that high inflation rates tend to be associated with low unemployment rates (as at B) and that low (or negative) inflation rates tend to be accompanied by high unemployment rates (as at C).

FIGURE 17-4

The Phillips Curve

Unanticipated changes in aggregate demand produce a negative relationship between the inflation rate and unemployment. In panel (a), U^* is the natural rate of unemployment, and the rate of inflation is zero at this unemployment rate at point A. Panel (b) indicates that a higher inflation rate at point B is associated with a lower unemployment rate. Deflation at point C is associated with a higher unemployment rate.

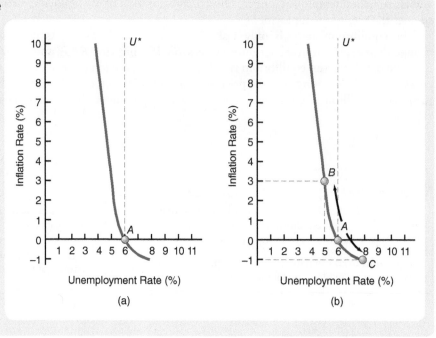

(a)

(b)

Is There a Trade-Off?

The apparent negative relationship between the inflation rate and the unemployment rate shown in panels (a) and (b) of Figure 17-4 has come to be called the **Phillips curve**, after A. W. Phillips, who discovered that a similar relationship existed historically in Great Britain. Although Phillips presented his findings only as an empirical regularity, economists quickly came to view the relationship as representing a *trade-off* between inflation and unemployment.

In particular, policymakers who favored active policymaking believed that they could *choose* alternative combinations of unemployment and inflation. Thus, it seemed that a government that disliked unemployment could select a point like B in panel (b) of Figure 17-4 above, with a positive inflation rate but a relatively low unemployment rate. Conversely, a government that feared inflation could choose a stable price level at A, but only at the expense of a higher associated unemployment rate. Indeed, the Phillips curve seemed to suggest that it was possible for discretionary policymakers to fine-tune the economy by selecting the policies that would produce the exact mix of unemployment and inflation that suited current government objectives. As it turned out, matters are not so simple.

The Importance of Expectations

The reduction in unemployment that takes place as the economy moves from A to B in Figure 17-4 occurs because the wage offers encountered by unemployed workers are unexpectedly high. As far as the workers are concerned, these higher *nominal* wages appear, at least initially, to be increases in *real* wages. It is this perception that induces them to reduce the duration of their job search. This is a sensible way for the workers to view the world if aggregate demand fluctuates up and down at random, with no systematic or predictable variation one way or another. If activist policymakers attempt to exploit the apparent trade-off in the Phillips curve, however, according to economists who support passive policymaking, aggregate demand will no longer move up and down in an *unpredictable* way.

Phillips curve

A curve showing the relationship between unemployment and changes in wages or prices. It was long thought to reflect a trade-off between unemployment and inflation.

FIGURE 17-5

A Shift in the Phillips Curve

When there is a change in the expected inflation rate, the Phillips curve (*PC*) shifts to incorporate the new expectations. PC_0 shows expectations of zero inflation. PC_3 reflects a higher expected inflation rate, such as 3 percent.

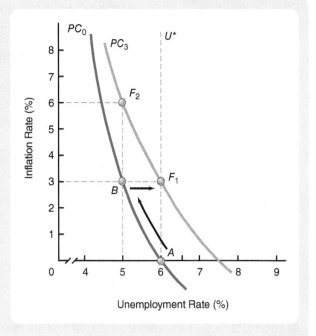

THE EFFECTS OF AN UNANTICIPATED POLICY Consider, for example, Figure 17-5 above. If the Federal Reserve attempts to reduce the unemployment rate to 5 percent, it must increase the rate of growth of the money supply enough to produce an inflation rate of 3 percent. If this is an unexpected one-shot action in which the rate of growth of the money supply is first increased and then returned to its previous level, the inflation rate will temporarily rise to 3 percent, and the unemployment rate will temporarily fall to 5 percent. Proponents of passive policymaking contend that past experience with active policies indicates that after the money supply stops growing, the inflation rate will soon return to zero and unemployment will return to 6 percent, its natural rate. Thus, an unexpected temporary increase in money supply growth will cause a movement from point *A* to point *B*, and the economy will move on its own back to *A*.

ADJUSTING EXPECTATIONS AND A SHIFTING PHILLIPS CURVE Why do those advocating passive policymaking argue that variations in the unemployment rate from its natural rate typically are temporary? If, for instance, activist Federal Reserve policymakers wish to prevent the unemployment rate from returning to $U^* = 6$ percent in Figure 17-5 above, they will conclude that the money supply must grow fast enough to keep the inflation rate up at 3 percent. But if the Fed does this, argue those who favor passive policymaking, all of the economic participants in the economy—workers and job seekers included—will come to *expect* that inflation rate to continue. This, in turn, will change their expectations about wages.

AN EXAMPLE Consider again an example in which the expected inflation rate is zero. In this situation, a 3 percent rise in nominal wages meant a 3 percent expected rise in real wages, and this was sufficient to induce some individuals to take jobs rather than remain unemployed. It was this expectation of a rise in real wages that reduced search duration and caused the unemployment rate to drop from $U^* = 6$ percent to 5 percent.

If the expected inflation rate becomes 3 percent, though, a 3 percent rise in nominal wages means *no* rise in *real* wages. Once workers come to expect the higher inflation rate, rising nominal wages will no longer be sufficient to entice them out of unemployment. As a result, as the *expected* inflation rate moves up from 0 percent to 3 percent, the unemployment rate will move up also.

IMPLICATIONS FOR THE PHILLIPS CURVE In terms of Figure 17-5, as authorities initially increase aggregate demand, the economy moves from point A to point B. If the authorities continue the stimulus in an effort to keep the unemployment rate down, workers' expectations will adjust, causing the unemployment rate to rise. In this second stage, the economy moves from B to point F_1. The unemployment rate returns to the natural rate, $U^* = 6$ percent, but the inflation rate is now 3 percent instead of zero.

Once the adjustment of expectations has taken place, any further short-run adjustments to future unanticipated policy actions will take place along a curve such as PC_3, say, a movement from F_1 to F_2. This new schedule is also a Phillips curve, differing from the first, PC_0, in that the actual inflation rate consistent with a 3 percent unemployment rate is higher, at 6 percent, because the expected inflation rate is higher. Of course, if future changes in policies generating a rise in the inflation rate from 3 percent to 6 percent are fully anticipated, instead of a movement from F_1 to F_2, yet another outward shift in the Phillips curve would take place.

Why did an effort by the Bank of England to influence expectations fail to work out as planned?

INTERNATIONAL POLICY EXAMPLE

The Bank of England's Bad Timing for "Forward Guidance"

In August 2013, the Bank of England announced that it did not intend to allow market interest rates to increase until at least the summer of 2016. That 2016 date was the earliest, the Bank of England determined, that the British economy's unemployment and inflation rates would reach desired levels.

The objective of the Bank of England's announcement, which it called "forward guidance," was to convince British households and businesses that they should *not* anticipate any monetary policy changes for the three years to come. In this way, the Bank of England hoped that people's expectations of inflation would swing to a level consistent with its objectives for inflation, unemployment, and the level of economic activity.

In fact, however, the United Kingdom's economic activity had sharply improved only three *months* after the Bank of England's statement that policy would not change for three *years*. Households and firms anticipated that continuation of the central bank's low-interest-rate policy would lead to higher inflation. Consequently, inflation expectations began to rise above the Bank of England's inflation objective.

FOR CRITICAL THINKING
What do you think happened to the short-run Phillips curve when British households and firms began to anticipate higher inflation?

Sources are listed at the end of this chapter.

MyEconLab Concept Check
MyEconLab Study Plan

SELF CHECK Visit MyEconLab to practice these and other problems and to get instant feedback in your Study Plan.

The _____ curve exhibits a negative short-run relationship between the inflation rate and the unemployment rate that can be observed when there are *unanticipated* changes in aggregate _____.

A movement along the Phillips curve occurs when actual inflation changes with _____ expectations

unchanged. If expected _____ changes, there is a shift in the position of the Phillips curve.

_____ policymakers seek to take advantage of a proposed Phillips curve trade-off between inflation and unemployment.

17.3 Understand the rational expectations hypothesis and its implications for economic policymaking

Rational Expectations, the Policy Irrelevance Proposition, and Real Business Cycles

You already know that economists assume that economic participants act *as though* they were rational and calculating. We assume that firms rationally maximize profits when they choose today's rate of output and that consumers rationally maximize satisfaction when they choose how much of what goods to consume today. One of the pivotal features of current macro policy research is the assumption that economic participants think rationally about the future as well as the present. This relationship was developed by Robert Lucas, who won the Nobel Prize in 1995 for his work. In particular, there is widespread agreement among many macroeconomics researchers that the **rational expectations hypothesis** extends our understanding of the behavior of the macroeconomy. This hypothesis has two key elements:

1. Individuals base their forecasts (expectations) about the future values of economic variables on all readily available past and current information.

2. These expectations incorporate individuals' understanding about how the economy operates, including the operation of monetary and fiscal policy.

In essence, the rational expectations hypothesis holds that Abraham Lincoln was correct when he said, "You can fool all the people some of the time. You can even fool some of the people all of the time. But you can't fool *all* of the people *all* the time."

If we further assume that there is pure competition in all markets and that all prices and wages are flexible, we obtain what many call the *new classical* approach to evaluating the effects of macroeconomic policies. To see how rational expectations operate in the new classical perspective, let's take a simple example of the economy's response to a change in monetary policy. MyEconLab Concept Check

Flexible Wages and Prices, Rational Expectations, and Policy Irrelevance

Consider Figure 17-6 below, which shows the long-run aggregate supply curve (*LRAS*) for the economy, as well as the initial aggregate demand curve (*AD*$_1$) and the short-run aggregate supply curve (*SRAS*$_1$). The money supply is initially given by $M_1 = \$12$ trillion, and the price level and real GDP are equal to 110 and $18 trillion, respectively. Consequently, point *A* represents the initial long-run equilibrium.

Suppose now that the money supply is unexpectedly increased to $M_2 = \$13$ trillion, thereby causing the aggregate demand curve to shift outward to *AD*$_2$. Given the location of the short-run aggregate supply curve, this increase in aggregate demand will cause the price level and real GDP to rise to 120 and $18.3 trillion, respectively. The new short-run equilibrium is at *B*. Because real GDP is *above* the long-run equilibrium

Rational expectations hypothesis
A theory stating that people combine the effects of past policy changes on important economic variables with their own judgment about the future effects of current and future policy changes.

MyEconLab Animation

FIGURE 17-6

Responses to Anticipated and Unanticipated Increases in Aggregate Demand

A $1 trillion increase in the money supply causes the aggregate demand curve to shift rightward. If people *anticipate* the increase in the money supply and insist on higher nominal wages, the short-run aggregate supply curve shifts leftward immediately, from *SRAS*$_1$ to *SRAS*$_2$. There is a direct movement, indicated by the green arrow, from point *A* to point *C*. In contrast, an *unanticipated* increase in the money supply causes an initial upward movement along *SRAS*$_1$ from point *A* to point *B*, indicated by the upward-sloping black arrow. In the long run, workers recognize that the price level has increased and demand higher wages, causing the *SRAS* curve to shift leftward, resulting in a movement from point *B* to point *C*.

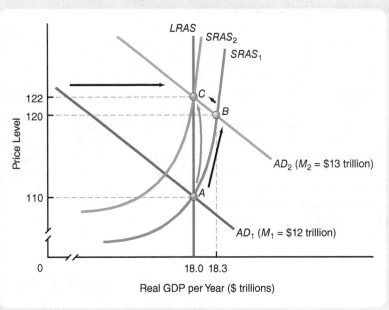

level of $18 trillion, unemployment must be below long-run levels (the natural rate), and so workers will soon respond to the higher price level by insisting on higher nominal wages. The resulting increase in firms' labor expenses will cause the short-run aggregate supply curve to shift upward vertically. As indicated by the upward-sloping black arrow, the economy moves from point *B* to a new long-run equilibrium at *C*.

The price level thus continues its rise to 122, even as real GDP declines back down to $18 trillion (and unemployment returns to the natural rate). So, as we have seen before, even though an increase in the money supply can raise real GDP and lower unemployment in the short run, it has no effect on either variable in the long run.

ANTICIPATED POLICY AND THE POLICY IRRELEVANCE PROPOSITION What if people *anticipate* the policy action discussed above? Let's look again at Figure 17-6 on the previous page to consider the answer to this question. In the initial equilibrium at point *A* of the figure, the short-run aggregate supply curve *SRAS*$_1$ corresponds to a situation in which the expected money supply and the actual money supply are equal. When the money supply changes in a way that is anticipated by economic participants, the aggregate supply curve will shift to reflect this expected change in the money supply. The new short-run aggregate supply curve *SRAS*$_2$ results. According to the rational expectations hypothesis, the short-run aggregate supply curve will shift upward *simultaneously* with the rise in aggregate demand. As a result, the economy will move directly from point *A* to point *C*, without passing through *B*, as depicted by the green arrow in Figure 17-6.

The *only* response to the rise in the money supply is a rise in the price level from 110 to 122. Neither output nor unemployment changes at all. This conclusion—that fully anticipated monetary policy is irrelevant in determining the levels of real variables—is called the **policy irrelevance proposition**:

Policy irrelevance proposition
The conclusion that policy actions have no real effects in the short run if the policy actions are anticipated and none in the long run even if the policy actions are unanticipated.

> *Under the assumption of rational expectations on the part of decision makers in the economy,* anticipated *monetary policy cannot alter either the rate of unemployment or the level of real GDP. Regardless of the nature of the anticipated policy, the unemployment rate will equal the natural rate, and real GDP will be determined solely by the economy's long-run aggregate supply curve.*

Can the rest of us benefit from the Fed's forecasts?

POLICY EXAMPLE

Are the Fed's Expectations Useful in Forming Our Expectations?

To forecast inflation correctly, one essentially must also accurately forecast other measures of economic activity, such as real GDP growth and the unemployment rate. The Federal Reserve employs hundreds of statisticians and economists to collect data and use the data in forecasting. These individuals at the Fed compile economic predictions that we might anticipate would help us in forming our own expectations.

In recent years, however, the Fed's economic forecasts have been far off the mark. In 2013, the Fed predicted that the rate of real GDP growth in 2015 would be above 3.5 percent. In 2014, the Fed reduced its forecast for 2013 real GDP growth to about 3 percent. By 2015, its forecast for real GDP growth in that year was just above 2.5 percent, which was close to the actual pace of growth. The Fed likewise adjusted its 2015 unemployment rate forecasts as the actual unemployment rate gradually declined.

A consequence of the Fed's inaccurate predictions for economic growth and unemployment was that the Fed persistently *overestimated* the 2015 inflation rate. The Fed's initial forecast exceeded 2 percent, but the actual 2015 inflation rate was about 1.8 percent. Basing our own 2015 inflation expectations on Fed predictions would have been a certain way to overestimate the year's inflation rate.

FOR CRITICAL THINKING
How might political factors influence Fed economic forecasts? (Hint: Recall that the Fed's legal structure and powers are determined by Congress, and its top officials are presidential appointees.)

Sources are listed at the end of this chapter.

MyEconLab Concept Check

Another Challenge to Policy Activism: Real Business Cycles

When confronted with the policy irrelevance proposition, many economists began to reexamine the first principles of macroeconomics with fully flexible wages and prices.

THE DISTINCTION BETWEEN REAL AND MONETARY SHOCKS Some economists argue that real, as opposed to purely monetary, forces might help explain aggregate economic fluctuations. These shocks may take various forms, such as technological advances that improve productivity, changes in the composition of the labor force, or changes in availability of a key resource. Consider Figure 17-7 below, which illustrates the concept of *real business cycles*. We begin at point E_1 with the economy in both short- and long-run equilibrium, with the associated supply curves, $SRAS_1$ and $LRAS_1$. Initially, the level of real GDP is $18 trillion, and the price level is 118. Because the economy is in long-run equilibrium, the unemployment rate must be at the natural rate.

A permanent reduction in the supply of a key productive resource, such as oil, causes both the $SRAS$ and $LRAS$ curves to shift to the left, to $SRAS_2$ and $LRAS_2$, because fewer goods will be available for sale due to the reduced supplies. In the short run, two adjustments begin to occur simultaneously. First, the prices of oil and petroleum-based products begin to rise, so the overall price level rises to 121. Second, the higher costs of production occasioned by the rise in oil prices induce firms to cut back production, so real GDP falls to $17.7 trillion in the short run. The new temporary short-run equilibrium occurs at E_2, with a higher price level (121) and a lower level of real GDP ($17.7 trillion).

This is not the full story, however. Owners of nonoil inputs, such as labor, are also affected by the reduction in oil supplies. For instance, as the real wage falls as a result of the higher price level, some workers who were willing to continue on the job at lower real wages in the short run will eventually decide to switch from full-time to part-time employment or to drop out of the labor force altogether. Thus, there will be a fall in the supply of nonoil inputs, reflected in an upward shift in the $SRAS$ curve from $SRAS_2$ to $SRAS_3$. This puts additional upward pressure on the price level and exerts a downward force on real GDP. Thus, the final long-run equilibrium occurs at point E_3, with the price level at 123 and real GDP at $17.5 trillion.

MyEconLab Animation

FIGURE 17-7

Effects of a Reduction in the Supply of Resources

The position of the *LRAS* depends on our endowments of all types of resources. Hence, a permanent reduction in the supply of one of those resources, such as oil, causes a reduction—an inward shift—in the aggregate supply curve from $LRAS_1$ to $LRAS_2$. In addition, there is a rise in the equilibrium price level and a fall in the equilibrium rate of real GDP per year to 123 and $17.7 trillion, respectively.

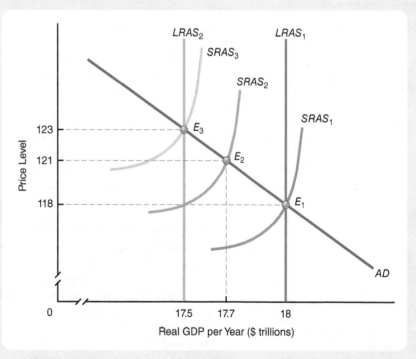

STAGFLATION Notice that in the example depicted in Figure 17-7 on the previous page, real GDP declines over the same interval that the price level increases. If these effects persist over additional periods, then the decline in real GDP will be associated with lower employment and a higher unemployment rate. Inflation also will result. Such a situation involving lower real GDP and increased inflation is called **stagflation**.

The most recent prolonged periods of stagflation in the United States occurred during the 1970s and early 1980s. One factor contributing to stagflation episodes during those years was sharp reductions in the supply of oil, as in the example illustrated in Figure 17-7 on the previous page. In addition, Congress enacted steep increases in marginal tax rates and implemented a host of new federal regulations on firms in the early 1970s. All these factors together acted to reduce long-run aggregate supply and hence contributed to stagflation. Increases in oil supplies, cuts in marginal tax rates, and deregulation during the 1980s and 1990s helped to prevent stagflation episodes from occurring after the early 1980s.

MyEconLab Concept Check
MyEconLab Study Plan

Stagflation
A situation characterized by lower real GDP, lower employment, and a higher unemployment rate during the same period that the rate of inflation increases.

SELF CHECK Visit MyEconLab to practice these and other problems and to get instant feedback in your Study Plan.

The _____ _____ hypothesis assumes that individuals' forecasts incorporate all readily available information, including an understanding of government policy and its effects on the economy.

If the **rational expectations hypothesis** is valid, there is pure competition, and all prices and wages are flexible, then the _____ _____ proposition follows: Fully anticipated monetary policy actions cannot alter either the rate of unemployment or the level of real GDP.

Even if all prices and wages are perfectly flexible, aggregate _____ shocks such as sudden changes in technology or in the supplies of factors of production can cause national economic fluctuations. To the extent that these _____ _____ cycles predominate as sources of economic fluctuations, the case for active policymaking is weakened.

17.4 Distinguish among alternative modern approaches to strengthening the case for active policymaking

Modern Approaches to Justifying Active Policymaking

The policy irrelevance proposition and the idea that real shocks are important causes of business fluctuations undermine the desirability of trying to stabilize economic activity with activist policies that exert effects on aggregate demand. Both criticisms of activist policies arise from combining the rational expectations hypothesis with the assumptions of pure competition and flexible wages and prices. It should not be surprising, therefore, to learn that economists who see a role for activist policymaking do not believe that market clearing models of the economy can explain business cycles. They contend that the "sticky" wages and prices assumed by Keynes in his major work (see Chapter 11) remain important in today's economy. To explain how aggregate demand shocks and policies can influence a nation's real GDP and unemployment rate, these economists, who are sometimes called *new Keynesians*, have tried to refine the theory of aggregate supply.

Small Menu Costs and Sticky Prices

One approach to explaining why many prices might be sticky in the short run supposes that much of the economy is characterized by imperfect competition and that it is costly for firms to change their prices in response to changes in demand. The costs associated with changing prices are called *menu costs*. These include the costs of renegotiating contracts, printing price lists (such as menus), and informing customers of price changes.

Many such costs may not be very large, so economists call them **small menu costs**. Some of the costs of changing prices, however, such as those incurred in bringing

Small menu costs
Costs that deter firms from changing prices in response to demand changes—for example, the costs of renegotiating contracts or printing new price lists.

together business managers from points around the nation or the world for meetings on price changes or renegotiating deals with customers, may be significant.

MyEconLab Concept Check

Real GDP and the Price Level in a Sticky-Price Economy

According to the new Keynesians, sticky prices strengthen the argument favoring active policymaking as a means of preventing substantial short-run swings in real GDP and, as a consequence, employment.

NEW KEYNESIAN INFLATION DYNAMICS To see why the idea of price stickiness strengthens the case for active policymaking, consider panel (a) of Figure 17-8 below. If a significant portion of all prices do not adjust rapidly, then in the short run the aggregate supply curve effectively is horizontal, as assumed in the traditional Keynesian theory discussed in Chapter 11. This means that a decline in aggregate demand, such as the shift from AD_1 to AD_2 shown in panel (a), will induce the largest possible decline in equilibrium real GDP, from $18 trillion to $17.7 trillion at E_2. When prices are sticky, economic contractions induced by aggregate demand shocks are as severe as they can be.

As panel (a) shows, in contrast to the traditional Keynesian theory, the new Keynesian sticky-price theory indicates that the economy will find its own way back to a long-run equilibrium. The theory presumes that small menu costs induce many firms not to change their prices in the short run, because the menu costs exceed the small profit gains that the firms would experience from raising their prices. Nevertheless, the profit gains that firms reap over additional periods accumulate, which ultimately gives them incentives to reduce their prices in the long run. Thus, in a long-run equilibrium the price level declines in response to the decrease in aggregate demand. As firms

FIGURE 17-8

Short- and Long-Run Adjustments in the New Keynesian Sticky-Price Theory

In panel (a), when prices are sticky, the short-run aggregate supply curve is horizontal at a price level of 118. Hence, the short-run effect of a fall in aggregate demand from AD_1 to AD_2 generates the largest possible decline in real GDP, from $18 trillion at point E_1 to $17.7 trillion at point E_2. In the long run, producers incur menu costs of reducing prices to boost their profits, which shifts the *SRAS* curve downward. The price level falls to 116 and real GDP returns to $18 trillion at point E_3. In panel (b), instead of waiting for long-run adjustments to occur, policymakers engage in expansionary policies that shift the aggregate demand curve back to its original position, thereby shortening or even eliminating a recession.

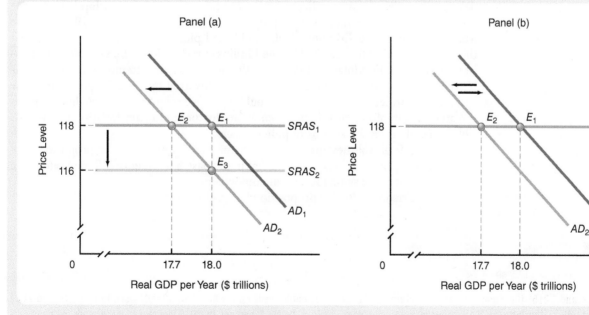

reduce their prices, the horizontal aggregate supply curve shifts downward, from $SRAS_1$ to $SRAS_2$, and equilibrium real GDP returns to its former level at E_3, other things being equal.

Of course, an increase in aggregate demand would have effects opposite to those depicted in panel (a) of Figure 17-8. A rise in aggregate demand would cause real GDP to rise in the short run. In the long run, firms would gain sufficient profits from raising their prices to compensate for incurring menu costs, and the short-run aggregate supply curve would shift upward. Consequently, an economy with growing aggregate demand should exhibit so-called **new Keynesian inflation dynamics**: initial sluggish adjustment of the price level in response to aggregate demand increases followed by higher inflation later on.

New Keynesian inflation dynamics
In new Keynesian theory, the pattern of inflation exhibited by an economy with growing aggregate demand—initial sluggish adjustment of the price level in response to increased aggregate demand followed by higher inflation later.

WHY ACTIVE POLICYMAKING CAN PAY OFF WHEN PRICES ARE STICKY To think about why the new Keynesian sticky-price theory supports the argument for active policymaking, let's return to the case of a decline in aggregate demand illustrated in panel (a) of Figure 17-8 on the previous page. Panel (b) shows the same decline in aggregate demand as in panel (a) and the resulting maximum contractionary effect on real GDP.

Monetary and fiscal policy actions that influence aggregate demand are as potent as possible when prices are sticky and short-run aggregate supply is horizontal. In principle, therefore, all that a policymaker confronted by the leftward shift in aggregate demand depicted in panel (b) must do is to conduct the appropriate policy to induce a rightward shift in the *AD* curve back to its previous position. Indeed, if the policymaker acts rapidly enough, the period of contraction experienced by the economy may be very brief. Active policymaking can thereby moderate or even eliminate recessions.

MyEconLab Concept Check

Is There a New Keynesian Phillips Curve?

A fundamental thrust of the new Keynesian theory is that activist policymaking can promote economic stability. Assessing this implication requires evaluating whether policymakers face an *exploitable* relationship between the inflation rate and the unemployment rate and between inflation and real GDP. By "exploitable," economists mean a relationship that is sufficiently predictable (for policymakers only) and long-lived to allow enough time for policymakers to reduce unemployment or to push up real GDP when economic activity falls below its long-run level.

THE U.S. EXPERIENCE WITH THE PHILLIPS CURVE For more than fifty years, economists have debated the existence of a policy-exploitable Phillips curve relationship between the inflation rate and the rate of unemployment. In separate articles in 1968, the late Milton Friedman and Edmond Phelps published pioneering studies suggesting that the apparent trade-off suggested by the Phillips curve could *not* be exploited by activist policymakers. Friedman and Phelps both argued that any attempt to reduce unemployment by boosting inflation would soon be thwarted by the incorporation of the new higher inflation rate into the public's expectations. The Friedman-Phelps research thus implies that for any given unemployment rate, *any* inflation rate is possible, depending on the actions of policymakers.

Figure 17-9 on the next page appears to provide support for the propositions of Friedman and Phelps. It clearly shows that in the past, a number of inflation rates have proved feasible at the same rates of unemployment.

Can the Friedman-Phelps proposition be applied to other nations?

INTERNATIONAL EXAMPLE

Has European Inflation Been "Too Low"?

Between 2012 and 2015, the European region containing the 18 countries that utilize the euro as their common currency—commonly called the "euro zone"—fell into a recession. The region's unemployment rate, which had already risen to 10 percent in 2012 from below 8 percent in 2010, increased once more, to nearly 12 percent.

FIGURE 17-9

The Phillips Curve: Theory versus Data

If we plot points representing the rate of inflation and the rate of unemployment for the United States from 1953 to the present, there does not appear to be any trade-off between the two variables.

Sources: Economic Report of the President; Economic Indicators, various issues.

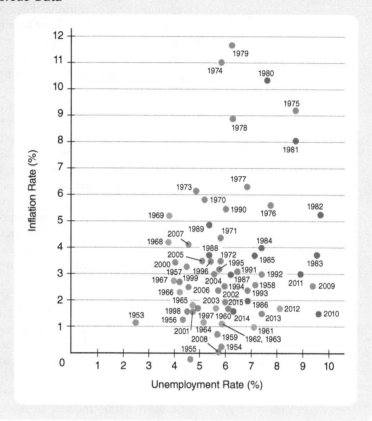

As the euro zone's unemployment rate rose between 2012 and 2015, inflation declined, from nearly 3 percent to about 1 percent. Based on the logic of the short-run Phillips curve trade-off, many observers argued that the region's inflation rate was "too low." If the European Central Bank (ECB) would simply push up money growth and thereby boost the inflation rate, they argued, the unemployment rate would begin to decline.

Other economists countered that observation of an increase in the actual inflation rate would push up euro-zone inflation expectations. The likely long-run consequence of higher inflation, these economists contended, would be little change in the region's unemployment rate.

FOR CRITICAL THINKING

Why do you suppose that European nations have observed over the past two decades that the rate of unemployment generally has not been closely related to variations in the inflation rate?

Sources are listed at the end of this chapter.

THE NEW KEYNESIAN PHILLIPS CURVE Today's new Keynesian theorists are not concerned about the lack of an apparent long-lived relationship between inflation and unemployment revealed by Figure 17-9. From their point of view, the issue is not whether a relationship between inflation and unemployment or between inflation and real GDP breaks down over a period of years. All that matters for policymakers, the new Keynesians suggest, is whether such a relationship is exploitable in the near term. If so, policymakers can intervene in the economy as soon as actual unemployment and real GDP vary from their long-run levels. Appropriate activist policies, new Keynesians conclude, can dampen cyclical fluctuations and make them shorter-lived.

Evaluating New Keynesian Inflation Dynamics To assess the predictions of new Keynesian inflation dynamics, economists seek to evaluate whether inflation is closely related to two key factors that theory indicates should determine the inflation rate. The first of these factors is anticipated future inflation. The new Keynesian theory implies that menu costs reduce firms' incentive to adjust their prices. When some firms *do* adjust their prices, however, they will seek to set prices at levels based on expected future positions of demand curves for their products. The expected future inflation rate signals to firms how much equilibrium prices are likely to increase during future months, so firms will take into account the expected future inflation rate when setting prices at the present time.

The second key factor that new Keynesian theory indicates should affect current inflation is the average inflation-adjusted (real) per-unit costs that firms incur in producing goods and services. Thus, new Keynesians propose a positive relationship between inflation and an aggregate measure of real per-unit costs faced by firms throughout the economy. If firms' average inflation-adjusted per-unit costs increase, the prediction is that there will be higher prices charged by that portion of firms that do adjust their prices in the current period and, hence, greater current inflation.

Empirical evidence does indicate that increases in expected future inflation and greater real per-unit production costs are indeed associated with higher observed rates of inflation. In light of this support for these key predictions of the new Keynesian theory, the theory is exerting increasing influence on U.S. policymakers. For instance, media reports commonly refer to Fed officials' careful attention to changes in inflation expectations and firms' production costs that they interpret as signals of altered inflationary pressures.

Just How Exploitable Is the New Keynesian Phillips Curve? Not all economists are persuaded that the new Keynesian theory is correct. They point out that new classical theory already indicates that when prices are *flexible*, higher inflation expectations should reduce short-run aggregate supply. Such a decline in aggregate supply should, in turn, contribute to increased inflation.

Even if one were convinced that new Keynesian theory is correct, a fundamental issue is whether the new Keynesian theory has truly identified *exploitable* relationships. At the heart of this issue is just how often firms adjust their prices.

MyEconLab Concept Check

Summing Up: Economic Factors Favoring Active versus Passive Policymaking

To many people who have never taken a principles of economics course, it seems apparent that the world's governments should engage in active policymaking aimed at achieving high and stable real GDP growth and a low and stable unemployment rate. As you have learned in this chapter, the advisability of policy activism is not so obvious.

Several factors are involved in assessing whether policy activism is really preferable to passive policymaking. Table 17-1 on the next page summarizes the issues involved in evaluating the case for active policymaking versus the case for passive policymaking.

The current state of thinking on the relative desirability of active or passive policymaking may leave you somewhat frustrated. On the one hand, most economists agree that active policymaking is unlikely to exert sizable long-run effects on any nation's economy. Most also agree that aggregate supply shocks contribute to business cycles. Consequently, it is generally agreed that there are limits on the effectiveness of monetary and fiscal policies. On the other hand, a number of economists continue to argue that there is evidence indicating stickiness of prices and wages. They argue, therefore, that monetary and fiscal policy actions can offset, at least in the short run and perhaps even in the long run, the effects that aggregate demand shocks would otherwise have on real GDP and unemployment.

These diverging perspectives help explain why economists reach differing conclusions about the advisability of pursuing active or passive approaches to macroeconomic policymaking. Different interpretations of evidence on the issues summarized in Table 17-1 on the next page will likely continue to divide economists for years to come.

TABLE 17-1

Issues That Must Be Assessed in Determining the Desirability of Active versus Passive Policymaking

Economists who contend that active policymaking is justified argue that for each issue listed in the first column, there is evidence supporting the conclusions listed in the second column. In contrast, economists who suggest that passive policymaking is appropriate argue that for each issue in the first column, there is evidence leading to the conclusions in the third column.

Issue	Support for Active Policymaking	Support for Passive Policymaking
Phillips curve inflation–unemployment trade-off	Stable in the short run; perhaps predictable in the long run	Varies with inflation expectations; at best fleeting in the short run and nonexistent in the long run
Aggregate demand shocks	Induce short-run and perhaps long-run effects on real GDP and unemployment	Have little or no short-run effects and certainly no long-run effects on real GDP and unemployment
Aggregate supply shocks	Can, along with aggregate demand shocks, influence real GDP and unemployment	Cause movements in real GDP and unemployment and hence explain most business cycles
Pure competition	Is not typical in most markets, where imperfect competition predominates	Is widespread in markets throughout the economy
Price flexibility	Is uncommon because factors such as small menu costs induce firms to change prices infrequently	Is common because firms adjust prices immediately when demand changes
Wage flexibility	Is uncommon because labor market adjustments occur relatively slowly	Is common because nominal wages adjust speedily to price changes, making real wages flexible

MyEconLab Concept Check
MyEconLab Study Plan

SELF CHECK   Visit MyEconLab to practice these and other problems and to get instant feedback in your Study Plan.

Some new Keynesian economists suggest that _____ _____ costs inhibit many firms from making speedy changes in their prices and that this price stickiness can make the short-run aggregate supply curve _____. Variations in aggregate demand have the largest possible effects on real GDP in the short run, so policies that influence aggregate demand also have the greatest capability to stabilize real GDP in the face of aggregate demand shocks.

Even though there is little evidence supporting a long-run trade-off between inflation and unemployment, new Keynesian theory suggests that activist policymaking may be able to stabilize real GDP and employment in the _____ run. This is possible, according to the theory, if stickiness of _____ adjustment is sufficiently great that policymakers can exploit a _____-run trade-off between inflation and real GDP.

YOU ARE THERE

A New Fed Chair Confronts the Fed's Low-Interest-Rate Promise

Fed chair Janet Yellen was a prior member of the Board of Governors and an architect of the Fed's policy to hold interest rates low as long as the unemployment rate remains above 6.5 percent. Just before Yellen agreed to take over as the chair, groups of Fed staff economists independently had conducted studies of the effects of the Fed's unemployment-rate-based monetary policy. One of these studies argued that the Fed should consider allowing the annual inflation rate to rise above the Fed's currently targeted level of 2 percent. Higher inflation, the study concluded, would be required to generate a measurable drop in the unemployment rate. The other study contended that, if anything, the Fed's 6.5 percent threshold for the unemployment rate was too high. A more appropriate unemployment-rate threshold for the Fed's low-interest-rate promise, the study concluded, was 5.5 percent.

(continued)

Now that Yellen has assumed the role of Fed chair, she is considering the contention by Fed critics that the low-interest-rate promise eventually could give Fed policymaking a bias toward higher inflation. These critics worry that the natural unemployment rate has drifted higher, so that trying to push down the unemployment rate could push up inflation. After reading the studies, Yellen decides effectively to side with the critics. Her first major official act as Fed chair is to end the Fed's explicit link between interest rates and the unemployment rate.

CRITICAL THINKING QUESTIONS

1. Did Fed critics perceive the position of the long-run Phillips curve as being to the right or left of an unemployment rate of 6.5 percent? Explain.

2. Which of the Fed studies emphasizes the short-run Phillips curve? Which focuses more on the long-run Phillips curve? Explain.

Sources are listed at the end of this chapter.

ISSUES & APPLICATIONS

MyEconLab Video

The Fed's Complicated Effort to Balance Active and Passive Policymaking

Jim Weber/The Commercial Appeal/
Zumapress/Newscom

CONCEPTS APPLIED

» Active (Discretionary) Policymaking

» Passive (Nondiscretionary) Policymaking

» Phillips Curve

Prior to 2012, the Federal Reserve had never before linked its interest rate policy settings directly to any single specific macroeconomic objectives. Between 2012 and 2014, however, the Fed experimented with using the unemployment rate as a key benchmark for its interest-rate-targeting policy.

Striving for a Combination of Active and Passive Policymaking

One attractive feature of an unemployment-based objective for Fed policymakers was that it offered a way to blend active and passive policymaking. Critics of active monetary policymaking have long argued that a monetary policy rule would be preferable to making a series of discretionary policy changes. Discretionary actions, the critics argue, are as likely to add to economic instability as reduce it. Proponents of active monetary policymaking, in contrast, have contended that the problem with passive policymaking is that an unvarying strategy lacks flexibility to adjust to changing economic conditions.

By tying its interest rate target to the unemployment rate in 2012, the Fed sought to find a middle path between the two extremes. On the one hand, an unemployment-conditioned monetary policy is passive in the sense that the Fed stays with its interest rate target as long as the unemployment rate remains elevated. On the other hand, the policy is active in the sense that the level of the interest rate

target hinges on the unemployment rate and is adjusted by the Fed whenever the unemployment rate falls to a level viewed as sufficiently low.

Balancing Inflation and Unemployment Objectives

The Fed also viewed its unemployment-rate-based monetary policy strategy as consistent with containing inflation even as it sought to generate a lower unemployment rate. Keeping the money supply growing sufficiently fast to maintain very low market interest rates, the Fed reasoned, provided a persistent aggregate demand stimulus. The Fed's plan was to cut back on its stimulus as the unemployment rate declined toward the natural unemployment rate. At this point, the Fed automatically would begin to allow market interest rates to rise, which would slow the growth of aggregate demand and prevent a jump in inflation.

The problem for Fed policymakers turned out to be deciding whether they actually would follow through by allowing interest rates to increase. Ultimately, in 2014

Fed officials dodged having to face this decision. They opted out of maintaining a link between interest rates and the unemployment rate. By the beginning of 2015, the Fed had returned to a largely active approach in which officials relied on discretion instead of any semblance of a rule.

For Critical Thinking

1. Why would the Fed likely have faced difficulties in its effort to combine activist and passive policymaking if the inflation rate had increased substantially while the unemployment rate remained above the Fed's threshold unemployment rate?

2. In the long run, are either active or passive Fed policies likely to influence the unemployment rate? Explain briefly.

Web Resources

1. Learn more about the Fed's unemployment-based monetary policy strategy in the Web Links in MyEconLab.

2. Read about the Fed's "dual mandate" to balance inflation and employment/unemployment objectives in the Web Links in MyEconLab.

> ### MyEconLab
>
> For more questions on this chapter's Issues & Applications, go to MyEconLab.
>
> In the Study Plan for this chapter, select Section I: Issues and Applications.

Sources are listed at the end of this chapter.

Fundamental Points

1. Active policies may be able to cause the actual unemployment rate to deviate in the short run from the natural unemployment rate.

2. *Unanticipated* changes in aggregate demand can cause movements along the Phillips curve.

3. According to the policy irrelevance proposition, if people's expectations are rational, pure competition prevails, and prices and wages are flexible, fully anticipated monetary policies cannot affect real GDP or unemployment.

4. New Keynesian theory indicates that small menu costs can generate stickiness that makes the short-run aggregate supply curve horizontal for periods of time. If so, activist policymaking may be able to stabilize real GDP and employment in the short run.

What You Should Know

Here is what you should know after reading this chapter. MyEconLab will help you identify what you know, and where to go when you need to practice.

LEARNING OBJECTIVES	KEY TERMS	WHERE TO GO TO PRACTICE
17.1 Explain why the actual unemployment rate might depart from the natural rate of unemployment *An unexpected increase in aggregate demand can cause real GDP to rise in the short run, which results in a reduction in the unemployment rate below the natural rate of unemployment. Likewise, an unanticipated reduction in aggregate demand can push down real GDP in the short run, thereby causing the actual unemployment rate to rise above the natural unemployment rate.*	active (discretionary) policymaking, 391 passive (nondiscretionary) policymaking, 391 natural rate of unemployment, 392 **Key Figures** Figure 17-1, 393 Figure 17-2, 393 Figure 17-3, 394	• MyEconLab Study Plan 17.1 • Animated Figures 17-1, 17-2, 17-3
17.2 Describe why there may be an inverse relationship between the inflation rate and the unemployment rate and evaluate how expectations affect this relationship *An unexpected increase in aggregate demand that causes a drop in the unemployment rate also induces inflation. Thus, there should be an inverse relationship between the inflation rate and the unemployment rate. If people anticipate that efforts to exploit this Phillips curve trade-off will boost inflation, the Phillips curve will shift outward.*	Phillips curve, 396 **Key Figures** Figure 17-4, 396 Figure 17-5, 397	• MyEconLab Study Plan 17.2 • Animated Figures 17-4, 17-5

WHAT YOU SHOULD KNOW *continued*

LEARNING OBJECTIVES	KEY TERMS	WHERE TO GO TO PRACTICE

17.3 **Understand the rational expectations hypothesis and its implications for economic policymaking** *The rational expectations hypothesis suggests that people form expectations of inflation using all available past and current information and an understanding of how the economy functions. If pure competition prevails, wages and prices are flexible, and people completely anticipate the actions of policymakers, so real GDP remains unaffected by anticipated policy actions. Technological changes and labor market shocks such as variations in the composition of the labor force can induce business fluctuations, called real business cycles, which weaken the case for active policymaking.*

rational expectations hypothesis, 399
policy irrelevance proposition, 400
stagflation, 402
Key Figures
Figure 17-6, 399
Figure 17-7, 401

- MyEconLab Study Plan 17.3
- Animated Figures 17-6, 17-7

17.4 **Distinguish among alternative modern approaches to strengthening the case for active policymaking** *New Keynesian approaches suggest that firms may be slow to change prices in the face of variations in demand. Thus, the short-run aggregate supply curve is horizontal, and changes in aggregate demand have the largest possible effects on real GDP in the short run. If prices and wages are sufficiently inflexible in the short run that there is an exploitable trade-off between inflation and real GDP, discretionary policy actions can stabilize real GDP.*

small menu costs, 402
new Keynesian inflation dynamics, 404

- MyEconLab Study Plan 17.4

Log in to MyEconLab, take a chapter test, and get a personalized Study Plan that tells you which concepts you understand and which ones you need to review. From there, MyEconLab will give you further practice, tutorials, animations, videos, and guided solutions. For more information, visit http://www.myeconlab.com

PROBLEMS

All problems are assignable in MyEconLab. Answers to odd-numbered problems appear in MyEconLab.

17-1. Suppose that the government altered the computation of the unemployment rate by including people in the military as part of the labor force. (See pages 391–392 and 395–396.)

   a. How would this affect the actual unemployment rate?

   b. How would such a change affect estimates of the natural rate of unemployment?

   c. If this computational change were made, would it in any way affect the logic of the short-run and long-run Phillips curve analysis and its implications for policymaking? Why might the government wish to make such a change?

17-2. The natural rate of unemployment depends on factors that affect the behavior of both workers

and firms. Make lists of possible factors affecting workers and firms that you believe are likely to influence the natural rate of unemployment. (See pages 391–392.)

17-3. Suppose that more unemployed people who are classified as part of frictional unemployment decide to stop looking for work and start their own businesses instead. What is likely to happen to each of the following, other things being equal? (See pages 391–392 and 395–396.)

   a. The natural unemployment rate

   b. The economy's Phillips curve

17-4. Suppose that people who previously had held jobs become cyclically unemployed at the same time the inflation rate declines. Would the result be a movement along or a shift of the short-run Phillips curve? Explain your reasoning. (See pages 395–398.)

17-5. Suppose that people who previously had held jobs become structurally unemployed due to establishment of new government regulations during a period in which the inflation rate remains unchanged. Would the result be a movement along or a shift of the short-run Phillips curve? Explain your reasoning. (See pages 395–398.)

17-6. Suppose that the greater availability of online job placement services generates a reduction in frictional unemployment during an interval in which the inflation rate remains unchanged. Would the result be a movement along or a shift of the short-run Phillips curve? Explain your reasoning. (See pages 395–398.)

17-7. Consider a situation in which a future president has appointed Federal Reserve leaders who conduct monetary policy much more erratically than in past years. The consequence is that the quantity of money in circulation varies in a much more unsystematic and, hence, hard-to-predict manner. According to the policy irrelevance proposition, is it more or less likely that the Fed's policy actions will cause real GDP to change in the short run? Explain. (See pages 398–400.)

17-8. People called "Fed watchers" earn their living by trying to forecast what policies the Federal Reserve will implement within the next few weeks and months. Suppose that Fed watchers discover that the current group of Fed officials is following very systematic and predictable policies intended to reduce the unemployment rate. The Fed watchers then sell this information to firms, unions, and others in the private sector. If pure competition prevails, prices and wages are flexible, and people form rational expectations, are the Fed's policies enacted after the information sale likely to have their intended effects on the unemployment rate? (See pages 398–400.)

17-9. Suppose that economists were able to use U.S. economic data to demonstrate that the rational expectations hypothesis is true. Would this be sufficient to demonstrate the validity of the policy irrelevance proposition? (See pages 398–400.)

17-10. Evaluate the following statement: "In an important sense, the term *policy irrelevance proposition* is misleading because even if the rational expectations hypothesis is valid, economic policy actions can have significant effects on real GDP and the unemployment rate." (See pages 398–400.)

17-11. Consider the diagram below, which is drawn under the assumption that the new Keynesian sticky-price theory of aggregate supply applies. Assume that at present, the economy is in long-run equilibrium at point *A*. Answer the following questions. (See page 403.)

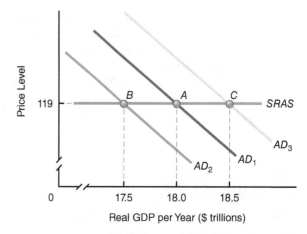

a. Suppose that there is a sudden increase in desired investment expenditures. Which of the alternative aggregate demand curves—AD_2 or AD_3—will apply after this event occurs? Other things being equal, what will happen to the equilibrium price level and to equilibrium real GDP in the *short run*? Explain.

b. Other things being equal, after the event and adjustments discussed in part (a) have taken place, what will happen to the equilibrium price level and to equilibrium real GDP in the *long run*? Explain.

17-12. Both the traditional Keynesian theory discussed in Chapter 11 and the new Keynesian theory considered in this chapter indicate that the short-run aggregate supply curve is horizontal. (See page 403.)

a. In terms of their *short-run* implications for the price level and real GDP, is there any difference between the two approaches?

b. In terms of their *long-run* implications for the price level and real GDP, is there any difference between the two approaches?

17-13. The real-business-cycle approach attributes even short-run increases in real GDP largely to aggregate supply shocks. Rightward shifts in aggregate supply tend to push down the equilibrium price level. How could the real-business-cycle perspective explain the low but persistent inflation that the United States experienced until 2007? (See pages 401–402.)

17-14. Normally, when aggregate demand increases, firms find it more profitable to raise prices than to leave prices unchanged. The idea behind the small-menu-cost explanation for price stickiness is that firms will leave their prices unchanged if their profit gain from adjusting prices is less than the menu costs they would incur if they change prices. If firms anticipate that a rise in demand is likely to last for a long time, does this make them more or less likely to adjust their prices when they face small menu costs? (See pages 402–403. Hint: Profits are a flow that firms earn from week to week and month to month, but small menu costs are a one-time expense.)

17-15. The policy relevance of new Keynesian inflation dynamics based on the theory of small menu costs and sticky prices depends on the exploitability of

the implied relationship between inflation and real GDP. Explain in your own words why the average time between price adjustments by firms is a crucial determinant of whether policymakers can actively exploit this relationship to try to stabilize real GDP. (See pages 404–406.)

REFERENCES

POLICY EXAMPLE: The U.S. Government's Estimate of the Natural Rate of Unemployment

Congressional Budget Office, "Key Assumptions in Projecting Potential GDP," February 5, 2013.

Federal Reserve Economic Data, Federal Reserve Bank of St. Louis, 2014.

Terence Jeffrey, "Full Employment? Actual versus Natural Unemployment Rates, CBS News, March 26, 2013.

INTERNATIONAL POLICY EXAMPLE: The Bank of England's Bad Timing for "Forward Guidance"

David Cottle, "When Reality Gets in the Way of Forward Guidance," The Wall Street Journal, November 13, 2013.

David Milliken and Ana Nicolaci Da Costa, "Bank of England Points to 2015 Rate Rise, Blurs Guidance," Reuters, February 12, 2014.

Paul Waldie, "Carney Defends His Forward Guidance Policy," The Globe and Mail, November 13, 2013.

POLICY EXAMPLE: Are the Fed's Expectations Useful in Forming Our Expectations?

Michael Derby, "Fed Dilemma: Forecasting Inflation Is Hard," The Wall Street Journal, September 17, 2013.

"Fed Lowers U.S. Growth Projections for 2014, 2015," RTE News, March 19, 2014.

Dylan Matthews, "How Bad the Fed Is at Predicting the Future," Washington Post, June 19, 2013.

INTERNATIONAL EXAMPLE: Has European Inflation Been "Too Low"?

Brian Blackstone, "Euro Zone Faces Threat of Too Little Inflation," The Wall Street Journal, October 31, 2013.

"In the Danger Zone: The Euro Area Is Getting Perilously Close to Deflation," The Economist, January 11, 2014.

"The Price Is a Blight: The Rich World, and Especially the Euro Zone, Risks Harmfully Low Inflation," The Economist, November 9, 2013.

YOU ARE THERE: A New Fed Chair Confronts the Fed's Low-Interest-Rate Promise

Peter Coy, "Two Papers That Could Persuade the Fed to Prolong Stimulus," Bloomberg Businessweek, November 5, 2013.

"Janet Yellen: Clarity Gap," The Economist, March 23, 2014.

Joshua Zumbrun and Craig Torres, "Yellen Seeking New Low-Rate Guidance Can Use Forecasts," Bloomberg, February 24, 2014.

ISSUES & APPLICATIONS: The Fed's Complicated Effort to Balance Active and Passive Policymaking

Michael Derby, "Fed Forward Guidance Proves Effective, New York Fed Research Says," The Wall Street Journal, November 5, 2013.

Victoria McGrane and Jon Hilsenrath, "Fed Tweaks Rate Guidance, Lessening Weight on Unemployment Rate," The Wall Street Journal, March 19, 2014.

Joshua Zumbrun and Craig Torres, "Fed to Change Rate Guidance as Unemployment Falls, Minutes Show," Bloomberg, February 19, 2014.

Policies and Prospects for Global Economic Growth

RunPhoto/Digital Vision/Getty Images

If a nation's real GDP per year is unchanged, its level of per capita real GDP shrinks when the country's population increases. Likewise, if a nation's rate of annual real GDP growth is constant, its rate of growth of per capita real GDP decreases when the country's population growth rate rises. This fact helps to explain why many media observers and policymakers express the view that worldwide population growth ultimately must reduce the global economic growth rate. Most economists agree that this view is not necessarily correct, however. By the time you have finished reading this chapter, you will understand why economists tend to have a less negative view about the economic-growth implications of world population growth.

LEARNING OBJECTIVES

After reading this chapter, you should be able to:

18.1 Explain why population growth can have uncertain effects on economic growth

18.2 Understand why the existence of dead capital retards investment and economic growth in much of the developing world

18.3 Discuss the sources of international investment funds for developing nations and identify obstacles to international investment in these nations

18.4 Identify the key functions of the World Bank and the International Monetary Fund

MyEconLab helps you master each objective and study more efficiently. See the end of the chapter for details.

> **DID YOU KNOW THAT...**
>
> even though people in India own a total of 280 million cows, the average rate of return from owning a cow in India, once the cost of food—about $160 per year—and a person's labor is taken into account, is negative? Some economists have argued that so many people in rural India own cows in spite of this negative return because there are so few nearby bank branches at which they otherwise can save extra cash. The economists contend that because these people do not have access to financial institutions offering deposits, they purchase cows as repositories of value that allow them to retain at least a fraction of unspent income—savings—over long periods. Poor accessibility to banks and negative returns on cow owner-ship, these economists conclude, help to explain why the saving rate in rural India is very low.
>
> Economists have long recognized that people save more when they are able to earn higher returns on their saving. Increased saving, in turn, can be used to finance larger volumes of capital investment, which gener-ates higher rates of economic growth. This logic suggests that improved accessibility of Indian residents to alternative savings instruments that offer *positive* returns likely would help to boost India's overall economic growth rate. After reading this chapter, you will be equipped to undertake your own evaluation of the prospects for global economic growth.

18.1 Explain why population growth can have uncertain effects on economic growth

Labor Resources and Economic Growth

You learned in Chapter 9 that the main determinants of economic growth are the growth of labor and capital resources and the rates of growth of labor and capital pro-ductivity. Human resources are abundant around the globe. Currently, the world's population increases by more than 70 million people each year. This population growth is not spread evenly over the earth's surface. Among the relatively wealthy na-tions of Europe, women bear an average of just over one child during their lifetimes. In the United States, a typical woman bears about 1.5 children. In the generally poor-er nations of Africa, however, women bear an average of six children.

Population growth does not necessarily translate into an increase in labor resources in the poorest regions of the world. Many people in poor nations do not join the labor force. Many who do so have trouble obtaining employment.

A common assumption is that high population growth in a less developed nation hinders the growth of its per capita GDP. Certainly, this is the presumption in China, where the government has imposed an absolute limit of one child per female resident. In fact, however, the relationship between population growth and economic growth is not really so clear-cut.

Basic Arithmetic of Population Growth and Economic Growth

Does a larger population raise or lower per capita real GDP? If a country has fixed borders and an unchanged level of aggregate real GDP, a higher population directly reduces per capita real GDP. After all, if there are more people, then dividing a con-stant amount of real GDP by a larger number of people reduces real GDP per capita.

This basic arithmetic works for growth rates too. We can express the growth rate of per capita real GDP in a nation as

$$\text{Rate of growth of per capita real GDP} = \text{rate of growth in real GDP} - \text{rate of growth of population}$$

Hence, if real GDP grows at a constant rate of 4 percent per year and the annual rate of population growth increases from 2 percent to 3 percent, the annual rate of growth of per capita real GDP will decline, from 2 percent to 1 percent.

HOW POPULATION GROWTH CAN CONTRIBUTE TO ECONOMIC GROWTH The arithmetic of the relationship between economic growth and population growth can be misleading. Certainly, it is a mathematical fact that the rate of growth of per capita real GDP

TABLE 18-1

Population Growth and Growth in Per Capita Real GDP in Selected Nations since 1970		
Country	**Average Annual Population Growth Rate (%)**	**Average Annual Rate of Growth of Per Capita Real GDP (%)**
Central African Republic	2.5	−1.1
Chile	1.5	2.8
China	1.1	7.2
Congo Democratic Republic	3.1	−3.4
Egypt	2.2	3.2
Haiti	1.8	0.1
Indonesia	1.8	4.0
Liberia	2.4	−1.3
Madagascar	2.9	−0.6
Malaysia	2.3	4.6
Togo	3.0	−0.9
United States	1.0	1.7

Source: Penn World Tables, International Monetary Fund.

equals the difference between the rate of growth in real GDP and the rate of growth of the population. Economic analysis, however, indicates that population growth can affect the rate of growth of real GDP. Thus, these two growth rates generally are not independent.

Recall from Chapter 9 that a higher rate of labor force participation by a nation's population contributes to increased growth of real GDP. If population growth is also accompanied by growth in the rate of labor force participation, then population growth can positively contribute to *per capita* real GDP growth. Even though population growth by itself tends to reduce the growth of per capita real GDP, greater labor force participation by an expanded population can boost real GDP growth sufficiently to more than compensate for the increase in population. On balance, the rate of growth of per capita real GDP can thereby increase.

WHETHER POPULATION GROWTH HINDERS OR CONTRIBUTES TO ECONOMIC GROWTH DEPENDS ON WHERE YOU LIVE On net, does an increased rate of population growth detract from or add to the rate of economic growth? Table 18-1 above indicates that the answer depends on which nation one considers. In some nations that have experienced relatively high rates of population growth, such as Egypt, Indonesia, and Malaysia, and, to a lesser extent, Chile and China, economic growth has accompanied population growth. In contrast, in nations such as the Congo Democratic Republic, Liberia, and Togo, there has been a negative relationship between population growth and per capita real GDP growth. Other factors apparently must affect how population growth and economic growth ultimately interrelate. MyEconLab Concept Check

The Role of Economic Freedom

A crucial factor influencing economic growth is the relative freedom of a nation's residents. Particularly important is the degree of **economic freedom**—the rights to own private property and to exchange goods, services, and financial assets with minimal government interference—available to the residents of a nation.

Approximately two-thirds of the world's people reside in about three dozen nations with governments unwilling to grant residents significant economic freedom. The

Economic freedom
The rights to own private property and to exchange goods, services, and financial assets with minimal government interference.

economies of these nations, even though they have the majority of the world's population, produce less than 10 percent of the world's total output. Some of these countries have experienced rates of economic growth at or above the 1.2 percent annual average for the world's nations during the past 30 years, but many are growing much more slowly. More than 30 of these countries have experienced negative rates of per capita income growth.

Only 17 nations, with 17 percent of the world's people, grant their residents high degrees of economic freedom. These nations together account for 81 percent of total world output. All of the countries that grant considerable economic freedom have experienced positive rates of economic growth, and most are close to or above the world's average rate of economic growth.

What has motivated many Hungarians to move to Britain?

INTERNATIONAL EXAMPLE

Hungarian Entrepreneurs Choose London over Budapest

In 2004, when Britain was home to only about 5,000 people of Hungarian descent, Hungary joined the European Union (EU). This action enabled Hungarian citizens to move anywhere within the EU to work. Since then, nearly 50,000 people have migrated from Hungary to Britain, which soon is likely to become the top EU destination for Hungarian immigrants.

Why are so many Hungarians moving to Britain? The answer has two parts. The first is that Hungary is not among the world's easiest nations in which entrepreneurs can start new businesses. Opening a firm in Hungary requires about three months and payment of at least $1,000 of fees to attorneys, architects, and the government. The second part of the answer is that Britain is one of the easiest countries in which to open

a firm. An entrepreneur must wait no more than two days for government approval, and a new company can be registered online for fees that total less than $25. In short, setting up a new business in Hungary is much more time-consuming and expensive than doing so in Britain. As a consequence, the steady of flow of entrepreneurs from Hungary to Britain continues.

FOR CRITICAL THINKING
Why do you suppose that the Hungarian government is contemplating trimming some of the required steps and fees for starting a new firm within that country?

Sources are listed at the end of this chapter.

MyEconLab Concept Check

The Role of Political Freedom

Interestingly, *political freedom*—the right to openly support and democratically select national leaders—appears to be less important than economic freedom in determining economic growth. Some countries that grant considerable economic freedom to their citizens have relatively strong restrictions on their residents' freedoms of speech and the press.

When nondemocratic countries have achieved high standards of living through consistent economic growth, they tend to become more democratic over time. This suggests that economic freedom tends to stimulate economic growth, which then leads to more political freedom.

MyEconLab Concept Check
MyEconLab Study Plan

SELF CHECK   Visit MyEconLab to practice these and other problems and to get instant feedback in your Study Plan.

For a given rate of growth of aggregate real GDP, higher population growth tends to _____ the growth of per capita real GDP.

To the extent that increased population growth also leads to greater _____ _____ participation that raises the growth of total real GDP, a higher population growth

rate can potentially _____ the rate of growth in per capita real GDP.

In general, the extent of _____ freedom does not necessarily increase the rate of economic growth. A greater degree of _____ freedom, however, does have a positive effect on a nation's growth prospects.

Capital Goods and Economic Growth

A fundamental problem developing countries face is that a significant portion of their capital goods and land that may be used to produce other items in the future, is what economists call **dead capital**, a term coined by economist Hernando de Soto. This term describes a capital resource lacking clear title of ownership. Dead capital may actually be put to some productive purpose, but individuals and firms face difficulties in exchanging, insuring, and legally protecting their rights to this resource. Thus, dead capital is a resource that people cannot readily allocate to its *most efficient* use. As economists have dug deeper into the difficulties confronting residents of the world's poorest nations, they have found that dead capital is among the most significant impediments to growth of per capita incomes in these countries.

Dead Capital and Inefficient Production

Physical structures used to house both business operations and labor resources are forms of capital goods. Current estimates indicate that unofficial, nontransferable physical structures valued at more than $10 trillion are found in developing nations around the world. Because people in developing countries do not officially own this huge volume of capital goods, they cannot easily trade these resources. Thus, it is hard for many of the world's people to use capital goods in ways that will yield the largest feasible output of goods and services.

AN EXAMPLE Consider, for instance, a hypothetical situation faced by an individual in Cairo, Egypt, a city in which an estimated 95 percent of all physical structures are unofficially owned. Suppose this person unofficially owns a run-down apartment building but has no official title of ownership for this structure. Also suppose that the building is better suited for use as a distribution center for a new import-export firm.

Now consider a situation in which the individual would like to sell or lease the structure to the new firm. Because this individual does not formally own the building, however, he or she is unable to do so.

THE PROBLEM OF NO FORMAL TITLE OF OWNERSHIP The difficulty that the person in the above example confronts is faced by millions of other people in Egypt. If the costs of obtaining formal title to the property are sufficiently high relative to the potential benefit—as they apparently are at present for more than 9 of every 10 Cairo businesses and households—this individual's capital resource will likely not be allocated to its highest-valued use.

This example illustrates a basic problem of dead capital. People who unofficially own capital goods are commonly constrained in their ability to employ them in their most productive uses. As a result, large quantities of capital goods throughout the developing world are inefficiently employed. MyEconLab Concept Check

Dead Capital and Economic Growth

Recall from Chapter 2 that when we take into account production choices over time, any society faces a trade-off between consumption goods and capital goods. Whenever we make a choice to produce more consumption goods today, we incur an opportunity cost of fewer goods in the future. Hence, when we make a choice to aim for more future economic growth to permit consumption of more goods in the future, we must allocate more resources to producing capital goods today. Making this choice entails incurring an opportunity cost today because society must allocate fewer resources to the current production of consumption goods.

This growth trade-off applies to any society, whether in a highly industrialized nation or a developing country. In a developing country, however, the inefficiencies of dead capital greatly reduce the rate of return on investment by individuals and firms.

18.2 Understand why the existence of dead capital retards investment and economic growth in much of the developing world

Dead capital
Any capital resource that lacks clear title of ownership.

The resulting disincentives to invest in new capital goods can greatly hinder economic growth.

GOVERNMENT INEFFICIENCIES, INVESTMENT, AND GROWTH A major factor contributing to the problem of dead capital in many developing nations is significant and often highly inefficient government regulation. Governments in many of the world's poorest nations place tremendous obstacles in the way of entrepreneurs interested in owning capital goods and directing them to profitable opportunities.

In addition to creating dead capital, overzealously administered government regulations that impede private resource allocation tend to reduce investment in new capital goods. If newly produced capital goods cannot be easily devoted to their most efficient uses, there is less incentive to invest. In a nation with a stifling government bureaucracy regulating the uses of capital goods, newly created capital will all too likely become dead capital.

Thus, government inefficiency can be a major barrier to economic growth. Figure 18-1 below depicts the relationship between average growth of per capita incomes and index measures of governmental inefficiency for various nations. As you can see, the economies of countries with less efficient governments tend to grow at relatively slower rates. The reason is that bureaucratic inefficiencies complicate private individuals' efforts to direct capital goods to their most efficient uses.

ACCESS TO CREDIT MATTERS The 2006 Nobel Peace Prize went to Muhammad Yunus of Bangladesh. Yunus contends that access to private credit is vital for promoting economic growth in poverty-stricken countries, where, in his view, present credit arrangements are inadequate. Yunus received the Nobel Peace Prize for his efforts to operate a *microlender*—a banking institution that specializes in making very small loans to entrepreneurs seeking to lift themselves up from the lowest rungs of poverty.

MyEconLab Animation

FIGURE 18-1

Bureaucratic Inefficiency and Economic Growth

Inefficiencies in government bureaucracies reduce the incentive to invest and thereby detract from economic growth.

Sources: International Monetary Fund; World Bank.

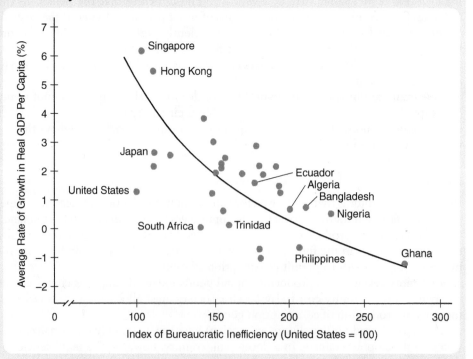

FIGURE 18-2

The Ratio of Private Credit to GDP in Selected Nations

This figure displays the top five and bottom five nations of the world ranked according to ratios of private credit to GDP.

Source: Federal Reserve Bank of St. Louis.

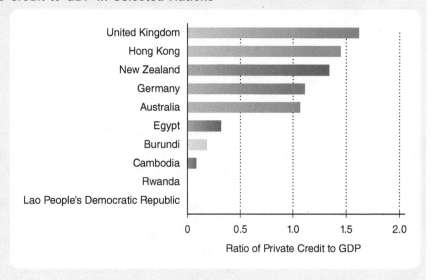

Private lenders such as microlenders, Yunus suggests, are more likely to grant loans if borrowers can provide marketable collateral in the form of capital assets that lenders can obtain if a borrower defaults. Loan applicants cannot offer as collateral capital assets that they do not officially own, however. Even if an applicant has legal title to capital assets, a lender is unlikely to accept them as collateral if government rules and inefficiencies inhibit the marketability of those assets in the event that the borrower defaults.

Figure 18-2 above displays both the top five and the bottom five nations of the world ranked by their ratios of private credit to GDP. Common features of the bottom five nations are significant stocks of informally used but officially unowned capital goods and very inefficient government bureaucracies. Access to credit in these nations is very limited, so ratios of private credit to GDP are low.

In some of the poorest nations in which microlending activities are beginning to flourish, tens of millions of people are obtaining access to credit for the first time in their lives. As a consequence, ratios of private credit to GDP are climbing.

Why is microlending expanding beyond developing nations?

EXAMPLE

Microloans Catch On in Advanced Nations, Too

Even as the U.S. economy has experienced its most sluggish recovery from a recession since World War II, the economy of the European Union has not yet fully recovered. In the aftermath of the 2007–2009 economic and financial meltdown, U.S. and European banks have toughened the criteria under which they will grant loans to individuals or small businesses. Even small loans can be difficult to obtain for households with families who are struggling to get by between jobs or for firms that desire to make capital investments intended to generate longer-term cost savings.

In both Europe and the United States, a growing number of individuals and businesses are turning to microloans. In Europe, microlenders have advanced more than 250,000 new microloans since 2008, which, when measured in dollars, now total nearly $2 billion in credit extended. About 400 U.S. microlenders have advanced almost $200 million in loans. Microlending has grown rapidly even in high-tech Silicon Valley, where an increasing number of entrepreneurs have experienced drops in annual incomes but confront very high costs of living. Hundreds of entrepreneurs in Silicon Valley have received loans of $15,000 or less. These microloans permit the entrepreneurs to subsist on small incomes until they are able to build up business operations that can generate larger incomes.

FOR CRITICAL THINKING

How do you suppose the recent U.S. and European recessions affected the demand for microloans? Explain.

Sources are listed at the end of this chapter.

SELF CHECK Visit MyEconLab to practice these and other problems and to get instant feedback in your Study Plan.

Dead capital is a capital resource without clear title of _____. It is difficult for a buyer to trade, insure, or maintain a right to use dead capital.

The inability to put dead capital to its most efficient use contributes to _____ economic growth, particularly

in _____ nations, where dead capital can be a relatively large portion of total capital goods.

Inefficient government _____ contribute to the dead capital problem, which reduces the incentive to invest in additional capital goods.

18.3 Discuss the sources of international investment funds for developing nations and identify obstacles to international investment in these nations

Private International Financial Flows as a Source of Global Growth

Given the large volume of inefficiently employed capital goods in developing nations, what can be done to promote greater global growth? One approach is to rely on private markets to find ways to direct capital goods toward their best uses in most nations. Another is to entrust the world's governments with the task of developing and implementing policies that enhance economic growth in developing nations. Let's begin by considering the market-based approach to promoting global growth.

Private Investment in Developing Nations

Between 1995 and 2007, at least $150 billion per year in private funds flowed to developing nations in the form of loans or purchases of bonds or stock. Of course, in some years, international investors stop lending to developing countries or sell off government-issued bonds and private-company stocks of those countries. When these international outflows of funds are taken into account, the *net* flows of funds to developing countries have averaged just over $80 billion per year since 1995. This is nearly 5 percent of the annual net investment within the United States.

Nearly all the funds that flow into developing countries do so to finance investment projects in those nations. Economists group these international flows of investment funds into three categories. One is loans from banks and other sources. The second is **portfolio investment**, or purchases of less than 10 percent of the shares of ownership in a company. The third is **foreign direct investment**, or the acquisition of stocks to obtain more than a 10 percent share of a firm's ownership.

Portfolio investment
The purchase of less than 10 percent of the shares of ownership in a company in another nation.

Foreign direct investment
The acquisition of more than 10 percent of the shares of ownership in a company in another nation.

Figure 18-3 on the next page displays percentages of each type of international investment financing provided to developing nations since 1981. As you can see, three decades ago, bank loans accounted for the bulk of international funding of investment in the world's less developed nations. Today, direct ownership shares in the form of portfolio investment and foreign direct investment together account for most international investment financing.　　　　　　　　　　　　　　　MyEconLab Concept Check

Obstacles to International Investment

There is an important difficulty with depending on international flows of funds to finance capital investment in developing nations. The markets for loans, bonds, and stocks in developing countries are particularly susceptible to problems relating to *asymmetric information* (see Chapter 15). International investors are well aware of the informational problems to which they are exposed in developing nations, so many stand ready to withdraw their financial support at a moment's notice.

ASYMMETRIC INFORMATION AS A BARRIER TO FINANCING GLOBAL GROWTH Recall from Chapter 15 that asymmetric information in financial markets exists when institutions that make loans or investors who hold bonds or stocks have less information than those who seek to use the funds. *Adverse selection* problems arise when those who wish to obtain funds for the least worthy projects are among those who attempt to borrow or issue bonds or stocks. If banks and investors have trouble identifying these higher-risk individuals

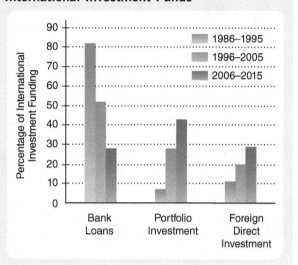

MyEconLab Animation

FIGURE 18-3

Sources of International Investment Funds

Since 1981, international funding of capital investment in developing nations has shifted from lending by banks to ownership shares via portfolio investment and foreign direct investment.

Source: International Monetary Fund (including estimates).

and firms, they may be less willing to channel funds to even creditworthy borrowers. Another asymmetric information problem is *moral hazard*. This is the potential for recipients of funds to engage in riskier behavior after receiving financing.

In light of the adverse selection problem, anyone thinking about funding a business endeavor in any locale must study the firm carefully before extending financial support. The potential for moral hazard requires a lender to a firm or someone who has purchased the firm's bonds or stock to continue to monitor the company's performance after providing financial support.

By definition, financial intermediation is still relatively undeveloped in less advanced regions of the world. Consequently, individuals interested in financing potentially profitable investments in developing nations typically cannot rely on financial intermediaries based in these countries. Asymmetric information problems may be so great in some developing nations that very few private lenders or investors will wish to direct their funds to capital investment projects. In some countries, therefore, concerns about adverse selection and moral hazard can be a significant obstacle to economic growth.

Why is Rwanda suddenly attracting more private foreign investment funds?

INTERNATIONAL EXAMPLE

Rwanda Attracts Foreign Investment through Transparency

A generation ago, many governmental activities within the East African nation of Rwanda were highly obscure to outsiders. Today, global investment firms that specialize in rating governments' levels of transparency—that is, openness about the making of and enforcement of government rules—rank Rwanda above nations such as Poland and Hungary. This now-higher level of transparency, Rwanda's government has discovered, generates greater inflows of foreign investors.

Rwanda's experience is consistent with conclusions reached by numerous economic studies over the years. Foreign investors quickly lose confidence that they will receive high returns on their investments in countries with governments that enact rules in secret and impose regulations unexpectedly. Within weeks, or sometimes even more quickly, flows of funds to nontransparent countries halt, and convincing foreign investors to renew such flows can require costly efforts and lengthy

waits. In contrast, countries with governments that have in place open mechanisms for establishing and enforcing their laws tend to attract steady flows of investment funds from abroad. Rwanda's switch from opaque governmental activities to more nearly transparent dealings has induced foreign investors to provide stable flows of funds to finance growth-generating capital investment.

FOR CRITICAL THINKING

Why do you suppose that private companies sometimes object when required to open their records of interactions with national governments to greater public scrutiny? (Hint: Why might firms make secret payments to government officials?)

Sources are listed at the end of this chapter.

INCOMPLETE INFORMATION AND INTERNATIONAL FINANCIAL CRISES Those who are willing to contemplate making loans or buying bonds or stocks issued in developing nations must either do their own careful homework or follow the example of other lenders or investors whom they regard as better informed. Many relatively unsophisticated lenders and investors, such as relatively small banks and individual savers, rely on larger lenders and investors to evaluate risks in developing nations.

International financial crisis
The rapid withdrawal of foreign investments and loans from a nation.

This state of affairs has led some economists to suggest that a herding mentality can influence international flows of funds. In extreme cases, they contend, the result can be an **international financial crisis**. This is a situation in which lenders rapidly withdraw loans made to residents of developing nations and investors sell off bonds and stocks issued by firms and governments in those countries.

An international financial crisis began in 2008. Unlike the crisis that started in 1997 and radiated outward from Southeast Asia, Central Asia, and Latin America, the more recent crisis began in the United States. It then spread to Europe before adversely affecting most developing nations. Although economies of several Asian nations have weathered the crisis relatively well so far, the world economy shrank for the first time in decades. Undoubtedly, this has contributed to a decline in flows of private funds to developing nations.

MyEconLab Concept Check
MyEconLab Study Plan

SELF CHECK Visit MyEconLab to practice these and other problems and to get instant feedback in your Study Plan.

The three main categories of international flows of investment funds are loans by _____, _____ investment that involves purchasing less than 10 percent of the shares of ownership in a company, and _____ _____ investment that involves purchasing more than 10 percent of a company's ownership shares.

On net, an average of about $ _____ billion in international investment funds flows to developing nations each year. In years past, bank loans were the source of most foreign funding of investment in developing countries, but recently _____ investment and _____ _____ investment have increased.

Obstacles to private financing of capital accumulation and growth in developing nations include _____ _____ and _____ _____ problems caused by asymmetric information, which can restrain and sometimes destabilize private flows of funds.

18.4 Identify the key functions of the World Bank and the International Monetary Fund

International Institutions and Policies for Global Growth

There has long been a recognition that adverse selection and moral hazard problems can both reduce international flows of private funds to developing nations and make these flows relatively variable. Since 1945, the world's governments have taken an active role in supplementing private markets. Two international institutions, the World Bank and the International Monetary Fund, have been at the center of government-directed efforts to attain higher rates of global economic growth.

The World Bank

World Bank
A multinational agency that specializes in making loans to about 100 developing nations in an effort to promote their long-term development and growth.

The **World Bank** specializes in extending relatively long-term loans for capital investment projects that otherwise might not receive private financial support. When the World Bank was first formed in 1945, it provided assistance in the post–World War II rebuilding period. In the 1960s, the World Bank broadened its mission by widening its scope to encompass global antipoverty efforts.

Today, the World Bank makes loans to about 100 developing nations containing roughly half the world's population. Governments and firms in these countries typically seek loans from the World Bank to finance specific projects, such as better irrigation systems, road improvements, and better hospitals.

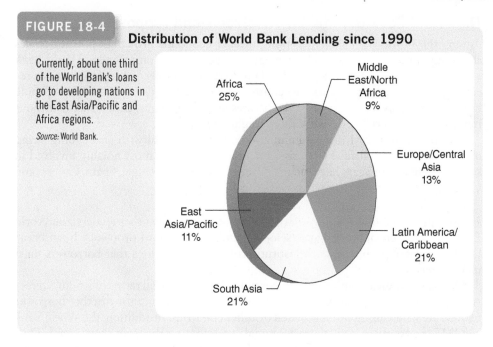

FIGURE 18-4

Distribution of World Bank Lending since 1990

Currently, about one third of the World Bank's loans go to developing nations in the East Asia/Pacific and Africa regions.

Source: World Bank.

Africa 25%

Middle East/North Africa 9%

Europe/Central Asia 13%

Latin America/ Caribbean 21%

East Asia/Pacific 11%

South Asia 21%

The World Bank is actually composed of five separate institutions: the International Development Association, the International Bank for Reconstruction and Development, the International Finance Corporation, the Multinational Investment Guarantee Agency, and the International Center for Settlement of Investment Disputes. These World Bank organizations each have between 150 and 188 member nations, and on their behalf, the approximately 10,000 people employed by World Bank institutions coordinate the funding of investment activities undertaken by various governments and private firms in developing nations. Figure 18-4 above displays the current regional distribution of about $50 billion yearly in World Bank lending. Governments of the world's wealthiest countries provide most of the funds that the World Bank lends each year, although the World Bank also raises some of its funds in private financial markets.   MyEconLab Concept Check

The International Monetary Fund

The **International Monetary Fund (IMF)** is an international organization that aims to promote global economic growth by fostering financial stability. Currently, the IMF has more than 180 member nations.

When a country joins the IMF, it deposits funds to an account called its **quota subscription**. These funds are measured in terms of an international unit of accounting called *special drawing rights* (*SDRs*), which have a value based on a weighted average of a basket of four key currencies: the euro, the pound sterling, the yen, and the dollar. At present, one SDR is equivalent to about $1.50.

The IMF assists developing nations primarily by making loans to their governments. Originally, the IMF's primary function was to provide short-term loans, and it continues to offer these forms of assistance.

After the 1970s, however, nations' demands for short-term credit declined, and the IMF adapted by expanding its other lending programs. It now provides certain types of credit directly to poor and heavily indebted countries, either as long-term loans intended to support growth-promoting projects or as short- or long-term assistance aimed at helping countries experiencing problems in repaying existing debts. Under these funding programs, the IMF seeks to assist any qualifying member experiencing an unusual fluctuation in exports or imports, a loss of confidence in its own financial system, or spillover effects from financial problems originating elsewhere.

MyEconLab Concept Check

International Monetary Fund (IMF)
A multinational organization that aims to promote world economic growth through more financial stability.

Quota subscription
A nation's account with the International Monetary Fund, denominated in special drawing rights.

The World Bank and the IMF: Problems and Proposals

Among the World Bank's client nations, meager economic growth in recent decades shows up in numerous ways. The average resident in a nation receiving World Bank assistance lives on less than $2 per day. Hundreds of millions of people in nations receiving its financial support will never attend school, and tens of thousands of people in these countries die of preventable diseases every day. Thus, there is an enormous range of areas where World Bank funds might be put to use.

The International Monetary Fund also continues to deal with an ongoing string of major international financial crisis situations. Countries most notably involved in such crises in recent years have included Ireland, Iceland, Portugal, Spain, Greece, and Cyprus.

ASYMMETRIC INFORMATION AND THE WORLD BANK AND IMF Like any other lenders, the World Bank and IMF encounter adverse selection and moral hazard problems. In an effort to address these problems, both institutions impose conditions that borrowers must meet to receive funds.

Officials of these organizations do not publicly announce all terms of lending agreements, however, so it is largely up to the organizations to monitor whether borrower nations are wisely using funds donated by other countries. In addition, the World Bank and IMF tend to place very imprecise initial conditions on the loans they extend. They typically toughen conditions only after a borrowing nation has violated the original arrangement. By giving nations that are most likely to try to take advantage of vague conditions a greater incentive to seek funding, this policy worsens the adverse selection problem the World Bank and IMF face.

RETHINKING LONG-TERM DEVELOPMENT LENDING Since the early 1990s, one of the main themes of development economics has been the reform of market processes in developing nations. Markets work better at promoting growth when a developing nation has more effective institutions, such as basic property rights, well-run legal systems, and uncorrupt government agencies.

Hence, there is considerable agreement that a top priority of the World Bank and the IMF should be to identify ways to put basic market foundations into place by guaranteeing property and contract rights. Doing so would require constructing legal systems that can credibly enforce laws protecting these rights. Another key requirement is simplifying the processes for putting capital goods to work most efficiently in developing countries.

ALTERNATIVE INSTITUTIONAL STRUCTURES FOR LIMITING FINANCIAL CRISES In recent years, economists have advanced a wide variety of proposals on the appropriate role for the International Monetary Fund in anticipating and reacting to international financial crises. Many of these proposals share common features, such as more frequent and in-depth releases of information both by the IMF and by countries that borrow from this institution. Nearly all economists also recommend improved financial and accounting standards for those receiving funds from the World Bank and the IMF, as well as other changes that might help reduce moral hazard problems in such lending.

Nevertheless, proposals for change diverge sharply. The IMF and its supporters have suggested maintaining its current structure but working harder to develop so-called early warning systems of financial crises so that aid can be provided to head off crises before they develop. Some economists have proposed establishing an international system of rules restricting capital outflows that might threaten international financial stability.

Other economists call for more dramatic changes. For instance, one proposal suggests creating a board composed of finance ministers of member nations to be directly in charge of day-to-day management of the IMF. Another recommends providing government incentives, in the form of tax breaks and subsidies, for increased private-sector lending that would supplement or even replace loans now made by the IMF.

WHAT IF...

the International Monetary Fund keeps secret some of the conditions of its loans to nations' governments?

If the IMF were to fail to make public all of the conditions that it places on loans to countries' governments, then private foreign investors could be exposed to negative spillover effects resulting from problems that those governments experience in repaying IMF loans. In fact, on the basis of transparency, or openness to public scrutiny of its lending activities, the IMF rated only twenty-eighth in a recent ranking of 67 international funding organizations. Thus, the IMF does keep some of its lending conditions secret, which exposes foreign investors to potential negative outcomes. For instance, secret arrangements between the IMF and countries' governments might lead to sudden government policy changes that would reduce the values of companies' investments in those nations. Foreign investors know this, and they respond by reducing their investment in countries that borrow from the IMF.

MyEconLab Concept Check
MyEconLab Study Plan

SELF CHECK   Visit MyEconLab to practice these and other problems and to get instant feedback in your Study Plan.

The **World Bank** is an umbrella institution for _____ international organizations, each of which has at least 150 member nations, which coordinate _____-term loans to governments and private firms in developing nations.

The **International Monetary Fund** is an organization with more than 180 member nations. It coordinates mainly _____-term and some longer-term financial assistance to developing nations in an effort to _____ international flows of funds.

Like other lenders, the World Bank and the IMF confront _____ _____ and _____ _____ problems. Recently, there have been suggestions for restructuring the operations of both institutions, but so far there is little agreement about how to do so.

YOU ARE THERE

Seeking to Unlock Kenya's Growth Potential via Ownership Rights

In recent years, foreign investment has increased considerably in the nations of Sub-Saharan Africa. One country among these is Kenya, in which most cities contain sprawling shantytowns populated with residences and thousands of tiny businesses. Also commonplace, particularly in shantytowns, are unsightly piles of rubble strewn along unpaved, rutted paths and criminals who lie in wait to prey on residents. Nevertheless, many homes and firms situated within the borders of these shantytowns have significant value to their residents. The values of these structures undoubtedly would increase as investment funds flow into Kenya—if only private ownership rights to shantytown structures existed.

Evans Omondi Jack, a 60-year-old Nairobi man who over the years has been forcibly evicted four times from the shantytown in which he was born, has launched a court case to establish who has titles of ownership in shantytowns. Omondi's attorneys argue that under Kenyan law, most parcels of shantytown lands, which largely are government-owned, should have been sold at public auction years ago. They are hopeful that Omondi and the other two-thirds of Kenyan citizens who reside within the 2 percent of Kenyan lands containing the shantytowns will be granted or offered a chance to buy formal titles of ownership to existing buildings. If so, the structures may be transformed from dead capital to tradable capital goods that people can further develop as foreign investment in Kenya increases.

CRITICAL THINKING QUESTIONS

1. Why do residents of the shantytowns have little incentive to remove rubble?

2. How might granting titles of ownership lead to improved shantytown conditions?

Sources are listed at the end of this chapter.

ISSUES & APPLICATIONS

MyEconLab Video

Will Population Growth End Economic Growth— or Fuel It?

RunPhoto/Digital Vision/Getty Images

CONCEPTS APPLIED

» Population Growth

» Global Economic Growth

» Economic Development

Today, more than 7.2 billion people inhabit planet Earth, and current population forecasts indicate that by 2050 nearly 9.6 billion will do so. If this forecast turns out to be accurate, will the increase in the world's population doom economic growth prospects? Or will a one-third expansion of human resources provide a net contribution to global economic growth and development? You have learned that whether the answers to these opposing questions will turn out to be "yes and no" or "no and yes" depends on choices that people make. To think about why, let's compare and contrast the experiences of two countries: Russia and South Korea.

Growth Arithmetic and Russia

Recall that the basic arithmetic of economic growth indicates that a nation's economic growth rate is equal to the rate of growth of its overall real GDP minus its rate of population growth. People without training in economics who look at this relationship often jump to the conclusion that this relationship implies that a positive rate of population growth necessarily reduces economic growth. By implication, humanity would be economically better off with a shrinking population.

Russia's experience is instructive in evaluating this logic. Russia's birthrate has declined steadily over the past two decades. Hence, as of 2015 there are almost 24 million Russian residents who are in their twenties, but in another decade there will be only 14 million. By the logic of population-growth critics, Russia's rate of economic growth should be higher than it once was. In fact, Russia's annual rate of economic growth has steadily decreased and has averaged only 0.5 percent over the past 20 years. Current projections indicate that the nation's long-term economic growth rate likely will be at or even less than zero within a decade from now, largely because a growing percentage of Russia's shrinking population is poorly educated.

Lessons from the Experience of South Korea

Unlike Russia's rate of population growth, that of South Korea has remained positive, and its population of young

people in their twenties has increased slightly over time. Yet South Korea's average annual rate of economic growth over the past twenty years has exceeded 4 percent—more than eight times Russia's. As South Korea has added new young people to its population, its residents have spent in excess of 3 percent of their total incomes on education, the highest percentage of all of the world's advanced nations. Higher labor productivity has allowed South Korea to maintain a sufficiently high rate of real GDP growth to more than compensate for population growth's negative effect on economic growth.

The contrasting experiences of Russia and South Korea sum up what economic reasoning adds to the basic arithmetic of economic growth. On the one hand, a growing world population will maintain or boost positive economic growth if the young people who replace their elders are highly productive and economically free human resources. If so, real GDP growth can rise at a faster pace than the population. On the other hand, a shrinking world population yields lower economic growth and development if new generations are poorly trained and have fewer economic freedoms.

For Critical Thinking

1. Why might Russia's long-run economic growth rate increase if it allows increased immigration from China and other nations?

2. How could South Korea's long-run rate of growth of real GDP per capita shrink to or below zero if its long-term rate

of total real GDP growth were to drop to nearly zero? (Hint: What is the difference between the rate of economic growth and the rate of growth of real GDP?)

Web Resources

1. Take a look at the population projections of the United Nations in the Web Links in MyEconLab.
2. View data on sources of economic growth for various nations in the Web Links in MyEconLab.

MyEconLab

For more questions on this chapter's Issues & Applications, go to MyEconLab.

In the Study Plan for this chapter, select Section I: Issues and Applications.

Sources are listed at the end of this chapter.

Fundamental Points

1. With real GDP unchanged, higher population growth tends to reduce the growth of per capita real GDP, but if increased population growth raises the growth of total real GDP, a higher population growth rate can potentially increase the rate of growth in per capita real GDP.
2. The inability to put dead capital, a capital resource without clear ownership title, to its most efficient use contributes to lower economic growth.

3. The three types of international flows of investment funds are bank loans, portfolio investment, and foreign direct investment.
4. The World Bank organizes long-term loans to governments and private firms in developing nations. The International Monetary Fund coordinates primarily short-term and some longer-term financial assistance to developing countries to stabilize international flows of funds.

WHAT YOU SHOULD KNOW

Here is what you should know after reading this chapter. MyEconLab will help you identify what you know, and where to go when you need to practice.

LEARNING OBJECTIVES	KEY TERMS	WHERE TO GO TO PRACTICE
18.1 Explain why population growth can have uncertain effects on economic growth *Increased population growth has contradictory effects on economic growth. On the one hand, for a given growth rate of real GDP, increased population growth tends to reduce growth of per capita real GDP. On the other hand, if increased population growth is accompanied by higher labor productivity and participation, the growth rate of real GDP can increase.*	economic freedom, 415	• MyEconLab Study Plan 18.1
18.2 Understand why the existence of dead capital retards investment and economic growth in much of the developing world *Relatively few people in less developed countries establish legal ownership of capital goods. Unofficially owned resources are known as dead capital. Inability to trade, insure, and enforce rights to dead capital makes it difficult to employ these resources most efficiently, and this tends to limit economic growth.*	dead capital, 417 **Key Figure** Figure 18-1, 418	• MyEconLab Study Plan 18.2 • Animated Figure 18-1

WHAT YOU SHOULD KNOW *continued*

LEARNING OBJECTIVES ───	KEY TERMS ───	WHERE TO GO TO PRACTICE ───
18.3 **Discuss the sources of international investment funds for developing nations and identify obstacles to international investment in these nations** *International flows of funds to developing nations promote global economic growth. Asymmetric information problems, such as adverse selection and moral hazard problems, hinder international flows of funds and thereby slow economic growth in developing nations.*	portfolio investment, 420 foreign direct investment, 420 international financial crisis, 422 **Key Figure** Figure 18-3, 421	• MyEconLab Study Plan 18.3 • Animated Figure 18-3
18.4 **Identify the key functions of the World bank and the International Monetary Fund** *Adverse selection and moral hazard problems faced by private investors can both limit and destabilize international flows of funds to developing countries. The World Bank finances capital investment in countries that have trouble attracting funds from private sources. The International Monetary Fund attempts to stabilize international financial flows by extending loans to countries caught up in international financial crises.*	World Bank, 422 International Monetary Fund (IMF), 423 quota subscription, 423	• MyEconLab Study Plan 18.4

Log in to MyEconLab, take a chapter test, and get a personalized Study Plan that tells you which concepts you understand and which ones you need to review. From there, MyEconLab will give you further practice, tutorials, animations, videos, and guided solutions. For more information, visit http://www.myeconlab.com

PROBLEMS

All problems are assignable in MyEconLab; exercises that update with real-time data are marked with 🌐. Answers to odd-numbered problems appear in MyEconLab.

18-1. A country's real GDP is growing at an annual rate of 3.1 percent, and the current rate of growth of per capita real GDP is 0.3 percent per year. What is the population growth rate in this nation? (See page 414.)

18-2. The annual rate of growth of real GDP in a developing nation is 0.3 percent. Initially, the country's population was stable from year to year. Recently, however, a significant increase in the nation's birthrate has raised the annual rate of population growth to 0.5 percent. (See page 414.)

    a. What was the rate of growth of per capita real GDP before the increase in population growth?

    b. If the rate of growth of real GDP remains unchanged, what is the new rate of growth of per capita real GDP following the increase in the birthrate?

18-3. A developing country has determined that each additional $1 billion of net investment in capital goods adds 0.01 percentage point to its long-run average annual rate of growth of per capita real GDP. (See pages 417–418.)

    a. Domestic entrepreneurs recently began to seek official approval to open a range of businesses employing capital resources valued at $20 billion. If the entrepreneurs undertake these investments, by what fraction of a percentage point will the nation's long-run average annual rate of growth of per capita real GDP increase, other things being equal?

b. After weeks of effort trying to complete the first of 15 stages of bureaucratic red tape necessary to obtain authorization to start their businesses, a number of entrepreneurs decide to drop their investment plans completely, and the amount of official investment that actually takes place turns out to be $10 billion. Other things being equal, by what fraction of a percentage point will this decision reduce the nation's long-run average annual rate of growth of per capita real GDP from what it would have been if investment had been $20 billion?

18-4. Consider the estimates that the World Bank has assembled for the following nations:

Country	Legal Steps Required to Start a Business	Days Required to Start a Business	Cost of Starting a Business as a Percentage of Per Capita GDP
Angola	14	146	838%
Bosnia-Herzegovina	12	59	52%
Morocco	11	36	19%
Togo	14	63	281%
Uruguay	10	27	47%

Rank the nations in order, starting with the one you would expect to have the highest rate of economic growth, other things being equal. Explain your reasoning. (See pages 417–419.)

18-5. Suppose that every $500 billion of dead capital reduces the average rate of growth in worldwide per capita real GDP by 0.1 percentage point. If there is $10 trillion in dead capital in the world, by how many percentage points does the existence of dead capital reduce average worldwide growth of per capita real GDP? (See pages 417–419.)

18-6. Assume that each $1 billion in net capital investment generates 0.3 percentage point of the average percentage rate of growth of per capita real GDP, given the nation's labor resources. Firms have been investing exactly $6 billion in capital goods each year, so the annual average rate of growth of per capita real GDP has been 1.8 percent. Now a government that fails to consistently adhere to the rule of law has come to power, and firms must pay $100 million in bribes to gain official approval for every $1 billion in investment in capital goods. In response, companies cut back their total investment spending to $4 billion per year. If other things are equal and companies maintain this rate of investment, what will be the

nation's new average annual rate of growth of per capita real GDP? (See pages 420–421.)

18-7. During the past year, several large banks extended $200 million in loans to the government and several firms in a developing nation. International investors also purchased $150 million in bonds and $350 million in stocks issued by domestic firms. Of the stocks that foreign investors purchased, $100 million were shares that amounted to less than a 10 percent interest in domestic firms. This was the first year this nation had ever permitted inflows of funds from abroad. (See page 420.)

a. Based on the investment category definitions discussed in this chapter, what was the amount of portfolio investment in this nation during the past year?

b. What was the amount of foreign direct investment in this nation during the past year?

18-8. Last year, $100 million in outstanding bank loans to a developing nation's government were not renewed, and the developing nation's government paid off $50 million in maturing government bonds that had been held by foreign residents. During that year, however, a new group of banks participated in a $125 million loan to help finance a major government construction project in the capital city. Domestic firms also issued $50 million in bonds and $75 million in stocks to foreign investors. All of the stocks issued gave the foreign investors more than 10 percent shares of the domestic firms. (See page 420.)

a. What was gross foreign investment in this nation last year?

b. What was net foreign investment in this nation last year?

18-9. Identify which of the following situations currently faced by international investors are examples of adverse selection and which are examples of moral hazard. (See pages 420–421.)

a. Among the governments of several developing countries that are attempting to issue new bonds this year, it is certain that a few will fail to collect taxes to repay the bonds when they mature. It is difficult, however, for investors considering buying government bonds to predict which governments will experience this problem.

b. Foreign investors are contemplating purchasing stock in a company that, unknown to them, may have failed to properly establish legal ownership over a crucial capital resource.

c. Companies in a less developed nation have already issued bonds to finance the purchase of new capital goods. After receiving the funds from the bond issue, however, the company's managers pay themselves large bonuses instead.

d. When the government of a developing nation received a bank loan three years ago, it ultimately repaid the loan but had to reschedule its payments after officials misused the funds for unworthy projects. Now the government, which still has many of the same officials, is trying to raise funds by issuing bonds to foreign investors, who must decide whether or not to purchase them.

18-10. Identify which of the following situations currently faced by the World Bank or the International Monetary Fund are examples of adverse selection and which are examples of moral hazard. (See pages 420–424.)

a. The World Bank has extended loans to the government of a developing country to finance construction of a canal with a certain future flow of earnings. Now, however, the government has decided to redirect those funds to build a casino that may or may not generate sufficient profits to allow the government to repay the loan.

b. The IMF is considering extending loans to several nations that failed to fully repay loans they received from the IMF during the past decade but now claim to be better credit risks. Now the IMF is not sure in advance which of these nations are unlikely to fully repay new loans.

c. The IMF recently extended a loan to a government directed by democratically elected officials that would permit the nation to adjust to an abrupt reduction in private flows of funds from abroad. A coup has just occurred, however, in response to newly discovered corruption within the government's elected leadership. The new military dictator has announced tentative plans to disburse some of the funds in equal shares to all citizens.

18-11. For each of the following situations, explain which of the policy issues discussed in this chapter relates to the stance the institution has taken. (See pages 420–424.)

a. The World Bank offers to make a loan to a company in an impoverished nation at a lower interest rate than the company had been about to agree to pay to borrow the same amount from a group of private banks.

b. The World Bank makes a loan to a company in a developing nation that has not yet received

formal approval to operate there, even though the government approval process typically takes 15 months.

c. The IMF extends a loan to a developing nation's government, with no preconditions, to enable the government to make already overdue payments on a loan it had previously received from the World Bank.

18-12. For each of the following situations, explain which of the policy issues discussed in this chapter relates to the stance the institution has taken. (See pages 420–424.)

a. The IMF extends a long-term loan to a nation's government to help it maintain publicly supported production of goods and services that the government otherwise would have turned over to private companies.

b. The World Bank makes a loan to companies in an impoverished nation in which government officials typically demand bribes equal to 50 percent of companies' profits before allowing them to engage in any new investment projects.

c. The IMF offers to make a loan to banks in a country in which the government's rulers commonly require banks to extend credit to finance high-risk investment projects headed by the rulers' friends and relatives.

18-13. Answer the following questions concerning proposals to reform long-term development lending programs currently offered by the IMF and World Bank. (See pages 424–425.)

a. Why might the World Bank face moral hazard problems if it were to offer to provide funds to governments that promise to allocate the funds to major institutional reforms aimed at enhancing economic growth?

b. How does the IMF face an adverse selection problem if it is considering making loans to governments in which the ruling parties have already shown predispositions to try to "buy" votes by creating expensive public programs in advance of elections? How might following an announced rule in which the IMF cuts off future loans to governments that engage in such activities reduce this problem and promote increased economic growth in nations that do receive IMF loans?

REFERENCES

INTERNATIONAL EXAMPLE: Hungarian Entrepreneurs Choose London over Budapest

Asa Bennett, "Migrant Entrepreneurs' 'Breathtaking Contribution' to UK Economy," Huffington Post UK, March 4, 2014.

Agnes Lovasz and Edith Balazs, "Hungary's Entrepreneurs Flock to London," *Bloomberg Businessweek*, July 25, 2013.

Jennifer Walker, "New British Business Center to Boost Hungary Ties," *The Budapest Times*, November 8, 2013.

EXAMPLE: Microloans Catch On in Advanced Nations, Too

Ilan Brat and Giavanni Legorano, "Microloans Catch on in Europe, Too," *The Wall Street Journal*, November 4, 2013.

Ina Paiva Cordle, "OUR Microlending Receives $600,000 Grant to Offer Microloans in South Florida," *Miami Herald*, February 3, 2014.

Martha Mendoza, "Microloans Surging in Silicon Valley," *Bloomberg Businessweek*, September 21, 2013.

INTERNATIONAL EXAMPLE: Rwanda Attracts Foreign Investment through Transparency

Carol Matlack, "Investors Like What They See in Rwanda," *Bloomberg Businessweek*, April 25, 2013.

Doy Santos, "What the Philippines Can Learn from Rwanda," Propinoy Project, January 14, 2014.

"Transparent Money: Clarity about Public Spending Can Make Poor Countries Richer," *The Economist*, November 2, 2013.

YOU ARE THERE: Seeking to Unlock Kenya's Growth Potential via Ownership Rights

Mark Anderson, "Kenyan Women Sue for Ownership of Nairobi Slum," *The Guardian*, October 2, 2013.

Christine Lagarde, "Kenya at the Economic Frontier: Challenges and Opportunities," International Monetary Fund, January 6, 2014.

"Tangles over Tenure: Deciding Who Owns Shantytowns Would Help Their Residents," *The Economist*, September 22, 2013.

ISSUES & APPLICATIONS: Will Population Growth End Economic Growth—or Fuel It?

Mark Adomanis, "Russia Just Recorded Its First Natural Population Growth since the Collapse of the Soviet Union," *Forbes*, February 7, 2014.

Oliver Bullough, "The Russians Are Shrinking!" *The Wall Street Journal*, May 3, 2013.

Andrew MacAskill, "Korea Tries to Curb Its High Achievers," *Bloomberg Businessweek*, June 14, 2013.

19

Comparative Advantage and the Open Economy

Fernando Vergara / AP/Corbis

LEARNING OBJECTIVES

After reading this chapter, you should be able to:

19.1 Explain why nations can gain from specializing in production and engaging in international trade

19.2 Understand common arguments against free trade

19.3 Describe ways that nations restrict foreign trade

19.4 Identify key international agreements and organizations that adjudicate trade disputes among nations

MyEconLab helps you master each objective and study more efficiently. See the end of the chapter for details.

Two decades ago, there were fewer than 40 actively functioning *regional trade blocs*—groups of countries that grant members special privileges regarding international trade of goods and services. Today, the number of functioning regional trade blocs is more than nine times larger. As a consequence, the average country is now a member of two regional trade blocs. What do nations gain from participating in regional trade blocs? What might they stand to lose? To be able to answer questions such as these, you must first learn about the economic gains that residents of countries can obtain by engaging in trade across national borders, which is a central subject of this chapter.

the United States is a net exporter of robotic toilets? These toilets utilize motion-detector and remote-control technologies to open and close their seats automatically. Some models also feature leg-warming porcelain, built-in stereo systems, and bidet settings. Although U.S. firms export robotic toilets for purchase by residents of a number of different nations, the primary net importers of these robotic toilets are residents of China. In this chapter, you will learn about the fundamental economic determinants of whether a nation's residents become net exporters or importers of particular goods and services.

Why We Trade: Comparative Advantage and Mutual Gains from Exchange

19.1 Explain why nations can gain from specializing in production and engaging in international trade

You have already been introduced to the concept of specialization and mutual gains from trade in Chapter 2. These concepts are worth repeating because they are essential to understanding why the world is better off on net because of more international trade. First, however, let's take a look at the growing volumes of international trade undertaken by the world's peoples in recent years.

The Worldwide Importance of International Trade

Look at panel (a) of Figure 19-1 on the next page. Since the end of World War II, world output of goods and services (world real gross domestic product, or world real GDP) has increased almost every year. It is now about 11 times what it was then. Look at the top line in panel (a) of Figure 19-1. Even taking into account its recent dip, world trade has increased to about 31 times its level in 1950.

The United States has figured prominently in this expansion of world trade. In panel (b) of Figure 19-1 on the next page, you see imports and exports expressed as a percentage of total annual yearly income (GDP). Whereas imports amounted to barely 4 percent of annual U.S. GDP in 1950, today they account for more than 17 percent. International trade has become more important to the U.S. economy, and it may become even more so as other countries loosen their trade restrictions.

MyEconLab Concept Check

The Output Gains from Specialization

The best way to understand the gains from trade among nations is first to understand the output gains from specialization between individuals. Suppose that a creative advertising specialist can come up with two pages of ad copy (written words) an hour or generate one computerized art rendering per hour. At the same time, a computer art specialist can write one page of ad copy per hour or complete one computerized art rendering per hour. Here the ad specialist can come up with more pages of ad copy per hour than the computer specialist and seemingly is just as good as the computer specialist at doing computerized art renderings. Is there any reason for the ad specialist and the computer specialist to "trade"? The answer is yes because such trading will lead to higher output.

THE SITUATION WITH NO TRADE Consider the scenario of no trading. Assume that during each eight-hour day, the ad specialist and the computer whiz devote half of their day to writing ad copy and half to computerized art rendering. The ad specialist would create eight pages of ad copy (4 hours × 2) and four computerized art renderings (4 × 1).

During that same period, the computer specialist would create four pages of ad copy (4 hours × 1) and four computerized art renderings (4 × 1). Each day, the combined output for the ad specialist and the computer specialist would be 12 pages of ad copy and eight computerized art renderings.

FIGURE 19-1

The Growth of World Trade

In panel (a), you can see the growth in world trade in relative terms because we use an index of 100 to represent real world trade in 1950. By the early 2010s, that index had exceeded 3,100. At the same time, the index of world real GDP (annual world real income) had gone up to only about 1,100. Thus, generally world trade has been on the rise. In the United States, both imports and exports, expressed as a percentage of annual national income (GDP) in panel (b), generally rose after 1950 and recovered following the 2008–2009 recession.

Sources: Steven Husted and Michael Melvin, *International Economics*, 3rd ed. (New York: HarperCollins, 1995), p. 11, used with permission; World Trade Organization; Federal Reserve System; U.S. Department of Commerce.

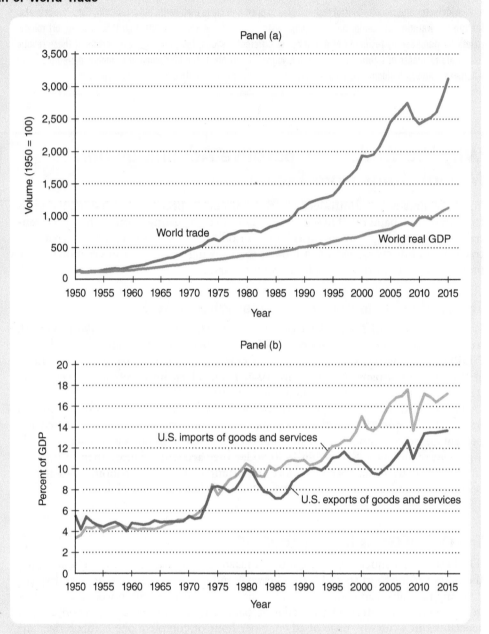

SPECIALIZATION AND TRADE If the ad specialist specialized only in writing ad copy and the computer whiz specialized only in creating computerized art renderings, their combined output would rise to 16 pages of ad copy (8 × 2) and eight computerized art renderings (8 × 1). Overall, production would increase by four pages of ad copy per day with no decline in art renderings.

Note that this example implies that to create one additional computerized art rendering during a day, the ad specialist has to sacrifice the creation of two pages of ad copy. The computer specialist, in contrast, has to give up the creation of only one page of ad copy to generate one more computerized art rendering. Thus, the ad specialist has a comparative advantage in writing ad copy, and the computer specialist has a comparative advantage in doing computerized art renderings. **Comparative advantage** is simply the ability to produce something at a lower *opportunity cost* than other producers, as we pointed out in Chapter 2.

Comparative advantage
The ability to produce a good or service at a lower opportunity cost than other producers.

TABLE 19-1

Maximum Feasible Hourly Production Rates of Either Digital Apps or Tablet Devices Using All Available Resources

This table indicates maximum feasible rates of production of digital apps and tablet devices if all available resources are allocated to producing either one item or the other. If U.S. residents allocate all resources to producing a single good, they can produce either 90 digital apps per hour or 225 tablets per hour. If residents of India allocate all resources to manufacturing one good, they can produce either 100 apps per hour or 50 tablets per hour.

Product	United States	India
Digital apps	90	100
Tablet devices	225	50

Specialization among Nations

To demonstrate the concept of comparative advantage for nations, let's consider a simple two-country, two-good world. As a hypothetical example, let's suppose that the nations in this world are India and the United States.

PRODUCTION AND CONSUMPTION CAPABILITIES IN A TWO-COUNTRY, TWO-GOOD WORLD In Table 19-1 above, we show maximum feasible quantities of high-performance commercial digital apps (apps) and tablet devices (tablets) that can be produced during an hour using all resources—labor, capital, land, and entrepreneurship—available in the United States and in India. As you can see from the table, U.S. residents can utilize all their resources to produce either 90 apps per hour or 225 tablets per hour. If residents of India utilize all their resources, they can produce either 100 apps per hour or 50 tablets per hour.

COMPARATIVE ADVANTAGE Suppose that in each country, there are constant opportunity costs of producing apps and tablets. Table 19-1 above implies that to allocate all available resources to production of 50 tablets, residents of India would have to sacrifice the production of 100 apps. Thus, the opportunity cost in India of producing 1 tablet is equal to 2 apps. At the same time, the opportunity cost of producing 1 app in India is 0.5 tablet.

In the United States, to allocate all available resources to production of 225 tablets, U.S. residents would have to give up producing 90 apps. This means that the opportunity cost in the United States of producing 1 tablet is equal to 0.4 app. Alternatively, we can say that the opportunity cost to U.S. residents of producing 1 app is 2.5 tablets ($225 \div 90 = 2.5$).

The opportunity cost of producing a tablet is lower in the United States than in India. At the same time, the opportunity cost of producing apps is lower in India than in the United States. Consequently, the United States has a comparative advantage in manufacturing tablets, and India has a comparative advantage in producing apps.

PRODUCTION WITHOUT TRADE Table 19-2 on the next page tabulates two possible production choices in a situation in which U.S. and Indian residents choose not to engage in international trade. Let's suppose that in the United States, residents choose to produce and consume 30 digital apps. To produce this number of apps requires that 75 fewer tablets (30 apps times 2.5 tablets per app) be produced than the maximum feasible tablet production of 225 tablets, or 150 tablets. Thus, in the absence of trade, 30 apps and 150 tablets are produced and consumed in the United States.

TABLE 19-2

U.S. and Indian Production and Consumption without Trade

This table indicates two possible hourly combinations of production and consumption of digital apps and tablet devices in the absence of trade in a "world" encompassing the United States and India. U.S. residents produce 30 apps, and residents of India produce 25 apps, so the total apps that can be consumed worldwide is 55. In addition, U.S. residents produce 150 tablets, and Indian residents produce 37.5 tablets, so worldwide production and consumption of tablets amount to 187.5 tablets per hour.

Product	United States	India	Actual World Output
Digital apps (per hour)	30	25	55
Tablet devices (per hour)	150	37.5	187.5

Table 19-2 indicates that during an hour's time in India, residents choose to produce and consume 37.5 tablets. Obtaining this number of tablets entails the production of 75 fewer apps (37.5 tablets times 2 apps per tablet) than the maximum of 100 apps, or 25 apps. Hence, in the absence of trade, 37.5 tablets and 25 apps are produced and consumed in India.

Finally, Table 19-2 displays production of apps and tablets for this two-country world, given the nations' production (and, implicitly, consumption) choices in the absence of trade. In an hour's time, U.S. app production is 30 units, and Indian app production is 25 units, so the total apps produced and available for consumption worldwide is 55. Hourly U.S. tablet production is 150 tablets, and Indian tablet production is 37.5 tablets, so a total of 187.5 tablets per hour is produced and available for consumption in this two-country world.

SPECIALIZATION IN PRODUCTION More realistically, residents of the United States will choose to specialize in the activity for which they experience a lower opportunity cost. In other words, U.S. residents will specialize in the activity in which they have a comparative advantage—the production of tablet devices, which they can offer in trade to residents of India. Likewise, Indian residents will specialize in the manufacturing industry in which they have a comparative advantage—the production of digital apps, which they can offer in trade to U.S. residents.

By specializing, the two countries can gain from engaging in international trade. To see why, suppose that U.S. residents allocate all available resources to producing 225 tablets, the good in which they have a comparative advantage. In addition, residents of India utilize all resources they have on hand to produce 100 apps, the good in which they have a comparative advantage.

CONSUMPTION WITH SPECIALIZATION AND TRADE U.S. residents will be willing to buy an Indian digital app as long as they must provide in exchange no more than 2.5 tablet devices, which is the opportunity cost of producing 1 app at home. At the same time, residents of India will be willing to buy a U.S. tablet as long as they must provide in exchange no more than 2 apps, which is their opportunity cost of producing a tablet.

Suppose that residents of both countries agree to trade at a rate of exchange of 1 tablet for 1 app and that they agree to trade 75 U.S. tablets for 75 Indian apps. Table 19-3 on the next page displays the outcomes that result in both countries. By specializing in tablet production and engaging in trade, U.S. residents can continue to consume 150 tablets. In addition, U.S. residents are also able to import and consume 75 apps produced in India. At the same time, specialization and exchange allow residents of India to continue to consume 25 apps. Producing 75 more apps for export to the United States allows India to import 75 tablets.

TABLE 19-3

U.S. and Indian Production and Consumption with Specialization and Trade

According to this table, U.S. residents produce 225 tablet devices and no digital apps, and Indian residents produce 100 digital apps and no tablets. Residents of the two nations then agree to a rate of exchange of 1 tablet for 1 app and proceed to trade 75 U.S. tablets for 75 Indian apps.

Specialization and trade allow U.S. residents to consume 75 apps imported from India and to consume 150 tablets produced at home. By specializing and engaging in trade, Indian residents consume 25 apps produced at home and import 75 tablets from the United States.

Product	U.S. Production and Consumption with Trade		Indian Production and Consumption with Trade	
Digital apps (per hour)	U.S. production	0	Indian production	100
	+Imports from India	75	−Exports to U.S.	75
	Total U.S. consumption	75	Total Indian consumption	25
Tablet devices (per hour)	U.S. production	225	Indian production	0
	−Exports to India	75	+Imports from U.S.	75
	Total U.S. consumption	150	Total Indian consumption	75

GAINS FROM TRADE Table 19-4 below summarizes the rates of consumption of U.S. and Indian residents with and without trade. Column 1 displays U.S. and Indian app and tablet consumption rates with specialization and trade from Table 19-3, and it sums these to determine total consumption rates in this two-country world. Column 2 shows U.S., Indian, and worldwide consumption rates without international trade from Table 19-2 on the previous page. Column 3 gives the differences between the two columns.

Table 19-4 below indicates that by producing 75 additional tablets for export to India in exchange for 75 apps, U.S. residents are able to expand their app consumption from 30 to 75. Thus, the U.S. gain from specialization and trade is 45 apps. This is a net gain in app consumption for the two-country world as a whole, because neither country had to give up consuming any tablets for U.S. residents to realize this gain from trade.

TABLE 19-4

National and Worldwide Gains from Specialization and Trade

This table summarizes the consumption gains experienced by the United States, India, and the two-country world. U.S. and Indian app and tablet consumption rates with specialization and trade from Table 19-3 above are listed in column 1, which sums the national consumption rates to determine total worldwide consumption with

trade. Column 2 shows U.S., Indian, and worldwide consumption rates without international trade, as reported in Table 19-2 on the previous page. Column 3 gives the differences between the two columns, which are the resulting national and worldwide gains from international trade.

Product	(1) National and World Consumption with Trade		(2) National and World Consumption without Trade		(3) Worldwide Consumption Gains from Trade	
Digital apps (per hour)	U.S. consumption	75	U.S. consumption	30	Change in U.S. consumption	+45
	+Indian consumption	25	+Indian consumption	25	Change in Indian consumption	+0
	World consumption	100	World consumption	55	**Change in world consumption**	**+45**
Tablet devices (per hour)	U.S. consumption	150	U.S. consumption	150	Change in U.S. consumption	+0
	+Indian consumption	75	+Indian consumption	37.5	Change in Indian consumption	+37.5
	World consumption	225	World consumption	187.5	**Change in world consumption**	**+37.5**

In addition, without trade, residents of India could have used all resources to produce and consume only 37.5 tablets and 25 apps. By using all resources to specialize in producing 100 apps and engaging in trade, residents of India can consume 37.5 *more* tablets than they could have produced and consumed alone without reducing their app consumption. Thus, the Indian gain from trade is 37.5 tablets. This represents a world-wide gain in tablet consumption, because neither country had to give up consuming any tablets for Indian residents to realize this gain from trade.

SPECIALIZATION IS THE KEY This example shows that when nations specialize in producing goods for which they have a comparative advantage and engage in international trade, considerable consumption gains are possible for those nations and hence for the world. Why is this so?

Why Specialization Yields Gains from Trade The answer is that specialization and trade enable Indian residents to obtain each tablet device at an opportunity cost of 1 digital app instead of 2 apps and permit U.S. residents to obtain each app at an opportunity cost of 1 tablet instead of 2.5 tablets.

Indian residents effectively experience a gain from trade of 1 app for each tablet purchased from the United States, and U.S. residents experience a gain from trade of 1.5 tablets for each app purchased from India. Thus, specializing in producing goods for which the two nations have a comparative advantage allows both nations to produce more efficiently. As a consequence, worldwide production capabilities increase. This makes greater worldwide consumption possible through international trade.

The Losers from Trade Of course, not everybody in our example is better off when free trade occurs. In our example, the U.S. app industry and Indian tablet industry have disappeared. Thus, U.S. app makers and Indian tablet manufacturers are worse off.

Some people worry that the United States (or any country, for that matter) might someday "run out of exports" because of overaggressive foreign competition. The analysis of comparative advantage tells us the contrary. No matter how much other countries compete for our business, the United States (or any other country) will always have a comparative advantage in something that it can export. In 10 or 20 years, that something may not be what we export today, but it will be exportable nonetheless because we will have a comparative advantage in producing it. Thus, the significant flows of world trade of exports and imports of both goods and services shown in Figure 19-2 on the next page will continue because the United States and other nations will retain comparative advantages in producing various goods and services.

Why are there significant export flows of U.S. trash to China every year?

EXAMPLE

A U.S. Comparative Advantage in Trash

In the United States, where people have been producing many paper- and metal-based products for decades, recyclable trash abounds. Each year, U.S. consumers and firms throw out millions of tons of unwanted trash, including paper, plastics, and scrap metal. As a consequence, the opportunity cost of obtaining reusable paper, plastics, and metal is much lower in the United States than in most other nations. In contrast, China has been producing products containing these materials for a considerably shorter time. Much smaller amounts of recyclable paper, plastics, and metals have made their way to trash dumpsters and landfills, so the opportunity cost of obtaining these materials is significantly higher in China.

The consequence is that at least 15 million tons of recyclable trash makes its way each year from the United States to China. Indeed, trash has been one of the top U.S. exports to China for more than a decade, with the export flow of recyclable materials typically valued at more than $10 billion per year.

FOR CRITICAL THINKING

Why do you suppose that a recently imposed Chinese regulation requiring U.S. trash to be washed prior to export has increased the Chinese opportunity cost of obtaining recyclable trash?

Sources are listed at the end of this chapter.

FIGURE 19-2

World Trade Flows

International trade in goods and services amounts to nearly $44 trillion worldwide. The percentage figures show the proportion of trade flowing in the various directions among the nations that engage in the most trade.

Sources: International Monetary Fund and author's estimates (data are for 2015).

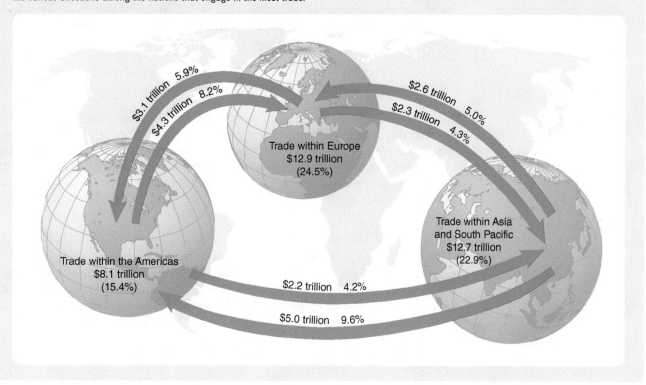

$3.1 trillion 5.9%
$4.3 trillion 8.2%
$2.6 trillion 5.0%
$2.3 trillion 4.3%

Trade within Europe
$12.9 trillion
(24.5%)

Trade within Asia
and South Pacific
$12.7 trillion
(22.9%)

Trade within the Americas
$8.1 trillion
(15.4%)

$2.2 trillion 4.2%

$5.0 trillion 9.6%

MyEconLab Concept Check

Other Benefits from International Trade: The Transmission of Ideas

Beyond the fact that comparative advantage results in an overall increase in the output of goods produced and consumed, there is another benefit to international trade. International trade also aids in the transmission of ideas. According to economic historians, international trade has been the principal means by which new goods, services, and processes have spread around the world. For example, coffee was initially grown in Arabia near the Red Sea. Around 675 A.D., it began to be roasted and consumed as a beverage. Eventually, it was exported to other parts of the world, and the Dutch started cultivating it in their colonies during the seventeenth century and the French in the eighteenth century. The lowly potato is native to the Peruvian Andes. In the sixteenth century, it was brought to Europe by Spanish explorers. Thereafter, its cultivation and consumption spread rapidly. Finally, it became part of the North American agricultural scene in the early eighteenth century.

New processes have also been transmitted through international trade. An example is the Japanese manufacturing innovation that emphasized redesigning the system rather than running the existing system in the best possible way. Inventories were reduced to just-in-time levels by reengineering machine setup methods.

In addition, international trade has enabled *intellectual property* to spread throughout the world. New music, such as rock and roll in the 1950s and 1960s and hip-hop in the 1990s and 2000s, has been transmitted in this way, as have the digital devices applications and application tools that are common for online and wireless users everywhere.

MyEconLab Concept Check

The Relationship between Imports and Exports

The basic proposition in understanding all of international trade is this:

> *In the long run, imports are paid for by exports.*

The reason that imports are ultimately paid for by exports is that foreign residents want something in exchange for the goods that are shipped to the United States. For the most part, they want U.S.-made goods and services. From this truism comes a remarkable corollary:

> *Any restriction of imports ultimately reduces exports.*

This is a shocking revelation to many people who want to restrict foreign competition to protect domestic jobs. Although it is possible to "protect" certain U.S. jobs by restricting foreign competition, it is impossible to make *everyone* better off by imposing import restrictions. Why? The reason is that ultimately such restrictions lead to a reduction in employment and output—and hence incomes—in the export industries of the nation.   MyEconLab Concept Check

International Competitiveness

"The United States is falling behind." "We need to stay competitive internationally." Statements such as these are often heard when the subject of international trade comes up. There are two problems with such talk. The first has to do with a simple definition. What does "global competitiveness" really mean? When one company competes against another, it is in competition. Is the United States like one big corporation, in competition with other countries? Certainly not. The standard of living in each country is almost solely a function of how well the economy functions *within that country*, not relative to other countries.

Another point relates to real-world observations. According to the Institute for Management Development in Lausanne, Switzerland, the United States is among the top ten nations in overall productive efficiency. According to the report, the relatively high ranking of the United States over the years has been due to widespread entrepreneurship, economic restructuring, and information-technology investments. Other factors include the open U.S. financial system and large investments in scientific research.   MyEconLab Concept Check
   MyEconLab Study Plan

SELF CHECK   Visit MyEconLab to practice these and other problems and to get instant feedback in your Study Plan.

A nation has a **comparative advantage** when its residents are able to produce a good or service at a _____ opportunity cost than residents of another nation.

Specializing in production of goods and services for which residents of a nation have a _____ _____ allows the nation's residents to _____ more of all goods and services.

_____ from trade arise for all nations in the world that engage in international trade because specialization and trade allow countries' residents to _____ more goods and services without necessarily giving up consumption of other goods and services.

19.2 Understand common arguments against free trade

Arguments Against Free Trade

Numerous arguments are raised against free trade. These arguments focus mainly on the costs of trade. They do not consider the benefits or the possible alternatives for reducing the costs of free trade while still reaping benefits.

The Infant Industry Argument

A nation may feel that if a particular industry is allowed to develop domestically, it will eventually become efficient enough to compete effectively in the world market. Therefore, the nation may impose some restrictions on imports to give domestic producers time to reach the point at which they can compete in the domestic market without any restrictions on imports.

THE BASIS OF THE ARGUMENT In graphic terminology, we would expect that if the protected industry truly does experience improvements in production techniques or technological breakthroughs toward greater efficiency in the future, the supply curve will shift outward to the right so that the domestic industry can produce larger quantities at each and every price.

National policymakers often assert that this **infant industry argument** has some merit in the short run. They have used it to protect a number of industries in their infancy around the world.

PROBLEMS WITH INFANT INDUSTRY PROTECTION Such a policy can be abused, however. Often the protective import-restricting arrangements remain even after the infant has matured. If other countries can still produce more cheaply, the people who benefit from this type of situation are obviously the stockholders (and specialized factors of production that will earn higher-than-normal rates of return in the industry that is still being protected from world competition.

The people who lose out are the consumers, who must pay a price higher than the world price for the product in question. In any event, because it is very difficult to know beforehand which industries will eventually survive, it is possible, perhaps even likely, that policymakers will choose to protect industries that have no reasonable chance of competing on their own in world markets. Note that when we speculate about which industries "should" be protected, we are in the realm of *normative economics*. We are making a value judgment, a subjective statement of what *ought to be*.

MyEconLab Concept Check

Infant industry argument
The contention that tariffs should be imposed to protect from import competition an industry that is trying to get started. Presumably, after the industry becomes technologically efficient, the tariff can be lifted.

Countering Foreign Subsidies and Dumping

Another common argument against unrestricted foreign trade is that a nation might wish to counter other nations' subsidies to their own producers. When a foreign government subsidizes its producers, our producers claim that they cannot compete fairly with these subsidized foreign producers. To the extent that such subsidies fluctuate, it can be argued that unrestricted free trade will seriously disrupt domestic producers. They will not know when foreign governments are going to subsidize their producers and when they are not. Our competing industries will be expanding and contracting too frequently.

At the same time, however, per-unit subsidies provided by foreign governments to foreign firms raise total domestic market supply, which depresses the domestic price of the subsidized foreign product. In this sense, foreign subsidies effectively are gifts to domestic consumers on the part of foreign taxpayers.

What U.S. agency specializes in responding to subsidies to foreign sellers by offering subsidized credit to foreign buyers of U.S.-made goods?

POLICY EXAMPLE

The U.S. Export-Import Bank Fights Subsidies with Subsidies

Each year, a U.S. government agency called the Export-Import (Ex-Im) Bank specializes in granting loans to *foreign* buyers. The Ex-Im Bank's loan terms are generous, because U.S. taxpayers subsidize the loans.

The rationale for the Ex-Im Bank's activities is based on the observation that many U.S. firms face competition from foreign companies that receive subsidies from their home governments. The Ex-Im Bank's task is to fight the effects of these foreign-government subsidies with countering U.S. government subsidies. It seeks to help U.S. firms competing against foreign-subsidized foreign firms by providing subsidized loans to foreign consumers that purchase U.S. goods.

Recent examples of loans extended by the Ex-Im Bank include the following:

- $1.1 billion to an Indonesian airline to buy a fleet of U.S.-produced jets
- $694 million to an Australian mining firm planning to buy U.S.-manufactured construction equipment
- $187 million to an Irish aircraft firm to buy a fleet of U.S.-made helicopters

- $183 million to a Hong Kong aerospace firm to buy U.S.-produced satellites

Each year, the Ex-Im Bank grants more than $100 billion in loans to foreign buyers.

FOR CRITICAL THINKING

Why do you suppose that U.S. airline firms, which compete against Indonesian and other foreign airlines that receive subsidized loans, are unhappy about the Ex-Im Bank's activities?

Sources are listed at the end of this chapter.

Dumping

Selling a good or a service abroad below the price charged in the home market or at a price below its cost of production.

The phenomenon called *dumping* is also used as an argument against unrestricted trade. **Dumping** is said to occur when a producer sells its products abroad below the price that is charged in the home market or at a price below its cost of production. Often, when a foreign producer is accused of dumping, further investigation reveals that the foreign nation is in the throes of a recession. The foreign producer does not want to slow down its production at home. Because it anticipates an end to the recession and doesn't want to hold large inventories, it dumps its products abroad at prices below home prices. U.S. competitors may also allege that the foreign producer sells its output at prices below its full costs to be assured of covering variable costs of production.   MyEconLab Concept Check

Protecting Domestic Jobs

Perhaps the argument used most often against free trade is that unrestrained competition from other countries will eliminate jobs in the United States because other countries have lower-cost labor than we do. Less restrictive environmental standards in other countries might also lower their private costs relative to ours.

PROPOSED BENEFITS OF DOMESTIC JOBS PROTECTION For many people, and particularly for politicians from areas that might be threatened by foreign competition, the jobs-protection argument is compelling. For example, a representative from an area with shoe factories would certainly be upset about the possibility of lower employment of their U.S. constituents because of competition from lower-priced shoe manufacturers in Brazil and Italy. Of course, this argument against free trade is equally applicable to trade between the states within the United States.

Economists David Gould, G. L. Woodbridge, and Roy Ruffin examined the data on the relationship between increases in imports and the unemployment rate. They concluded that there is no causal link between the two. Indeed, in half the cases they studied, when imports increased, the unemployment rate fell.

COSTS OF PROTECTING DOMESTIC JOBS Another issue involves the cost of protecting U.S. jobs by restricting international trade. The Institute for International Economics examined the restrictions on foreign textiles and apparel goods. The study found that U.S. consumers pay $9 billion a year more than they would otherwise pay for those goods to protect jobs in those industries. That comes out to $50,000 *a year* for each job saved in an industry in which the average job pays only $20,000 a year.

Similar studies have yielded similar results: Restrictions on imports of Japanese cars have cost $160,000 *per year* for every job saved in the auto industry. Every job preserved in the glass industry has cost $200,000 each and every year. Every job preserved in the U.S. steel industry has cost an astounding $750,000 per year.   MyEconLab Concept Check

Emerging Arguments against Free Trade

In recent years, two new antitrade arguments have been advanced. One of these focuses on environmental and safety concerns. For instance, many critics of free trade have suggested that genetic engineering of plants and animals could lead to accidental production of new diseases and that people, livestock, and pets could be harmed by tainted foods imported for human and animal consumption. These worries have induced the European Union to restrain trade in such products.

Another argument against free trade arises from national defense concerns. Major espionage successes by China in the late 1990s and 2000s led some U.S. strategic experts to propose sweeping restrictions on exports of new technology.

Free trade proponents counter that at best these are arguments for the judicious regulation of trade. They continue to argue that, by and large, broad trade restrictions mainly harm the interests of the nations that impose them.

MyEconLab Concept Check
MyEconLab Study Plan

Ways to Restrict Foreign Trade

19.3 Describe ways that nations restrict foreign trade

International trade can be stopped or at least stifled in many ways. These include quotas and taxes (the latter are usually called *tariffs* when applied to internationally traded items). Let's talk first about quotas.

Quotas

Under a **quota system**, individual countries or groups of foreign producers are restricted to a certain amount of trade. An import quota specifies the maximum amount of a commodity that may be imported during a specified period of time. For example, the government might allow no more than 200 million barrels of foreign crude oil to enter the United States in a particular month.

Consider the example of quotas on textiles. Figure 19-3 on the next page presents the demand and supply curves for imported textiles. In an unrestricted import market, the equilibrium quantity imported is 900 million yards at a price of $1 per yard (expressed in constant-quality units). When an import quota is imposed, the supply curve is no longer S. Instead, the supply curve becomes vertical at some amount less than the equilibrium quantity—here, 800 million yards per year. The price to the U.S. consumer increases from $1.00 to $1.50.

Clearly, the output restriction generated by a quota on foreign imports of a particular item has the effect of raising the domestic price of the imported item. Two groups benefit. One group is importers that are able to obtain the rights to sell imported items domestically at the higher price, which raises their revenues and boosts their profits. The other group is domestic producers. Naturally, a rise in the price of an imported item induces an increase in the demand for domestic substitutes. Thus, the domestic prices of close substitutes for the item subject to the

Quota system
A government-imposed restriction on the quantity of a specific good that another country is allowed to sell in the United States. In other words, quotas are restrictions on imports. These restrictions are usually applied to one or several specific countries.

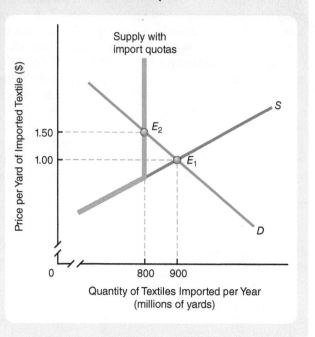

FIGURE 19-3

The Effect of Quotas on Textile Imports

Without restrictions, at point E_1, 900 million yards of textiles would be imported each year into the United States at the world price of $1.00 per yard. If the federal government imposes a quota of only 800 million yards, the effective supply curve becomes vertical at that quantity. It intersects the demand curve at point E_2, so the new equilibrium price is $1.50 per yard.

import restriction also increase, which generates higher revenues and profits for domestic producers.

WHAT IF...

> the government were to "protect American jobs" by placing quotas on imports of all goods and services from abroad?

Imposing quotas on all imported items would constrain quantities supplied in all affected markets for imported goods and services, which would push up the prices of these items. As a consequence, the demands for close domestic substitutes would increase, and prices of the substitute domestic goods and services would rise, which would boost revenues and profits of domestic firms. The domestic firms' demand for home labor also would increase, so more home workers would be employed. Domestic consumers, however, would pay the higher prices for imported goods and for domestic substitute items, and their higher expenditures would fund the increases in domestic firms' revenues and profits—as well as the new jobs.

Voluntary restraint agreement (VRA)
An official agreement with another country that "voluntarily" restricts the quantity of its exports to the United States.

Voluntary import expansion (VIE)
An official agreement with another country in which it agrees to import more from the United States.

VOLUNTARY QUOTAS Quotas do not have to be explicit and defined by law. They can be "voluntary." Such a quota is called a **voluntary restraint agreement (VRA)**. In the early 1980s, Japanese automakers voluntarily restrained exports to the United States. These restraints stayed in place into the 1990s. Today, there are VRAs on machine tools and textiles.

The opposite of a VRA is a **voluntary import expansion (VIE)**. Under a VIE, a foreign government agrees to have its companies import more foreign goods from another country. The United States almost started a major international trade war with Japan in 1995 over just such an issue. The U.S. government wanted Japanese automobile manufacturers to voluntarily increase their imports of U.S.-made automobile parts. Ultimately, Japanese companies did make a token increase in their imports of U.S. auto parts.

Tariffs

We can analyze tariffs by using standard supply and demand diagrams. Let's use as our commodity smartphones, some of which are made in China and some of which are

FIGURE 19-4

The Effect of a Tariff on Chinese-Made Smartphones

Without a tariff, the United States buys 10 million smartphones per year imported from China at an average price of $200, at point E_1 in panel (a). U.S. producers sell 5 million domestically made smartphones, also at $200 each, at point E_1 in panel (b). A $50 tariff per smartphone will shift the Chinese import supply curve to S_2 in panel (a), so that the new

equilibrium is at E_2 with price increased to $225 and quantity sold reduced to 8 million per year. The demand curve for U.S.-made smartphones (for which there is no tariff) shifts to D_2, in panel (b). Domestic sales increase to 6.5 million per year, at point E_2.

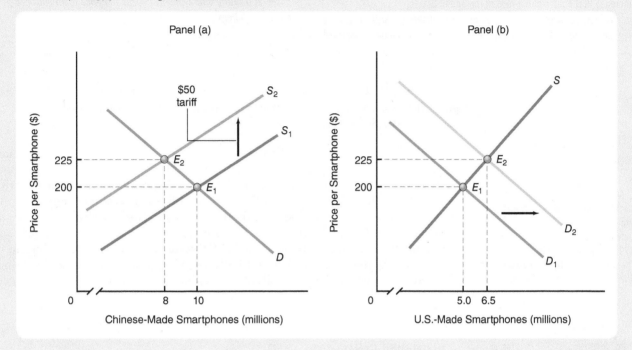

made domestically. In panel (a) of Figure 19-4 above, you see the demand for and supply of Chinese smartphones. The equilibrium price is $200 per constant-quality unit, and the equilibrium quantity is 10 million per year. In panel (b), you see the same equilibrium price of $200, and the *domestic* equilibrium quantity is 5 million units per year.

Now a tariff of $50 is imposed on all smartphones imported from China. The supply curve shifts upward by $50 to S_2. For purchasers of Chinese smartphones, the price increases to $225. The quantity demanded falls to 8 million per year. In panel (b), you see that at the higher price of smartphones imported from China, the demand curve for U.S.-made smartphones shifts outward to the right to D_2. The equilibrium price increases to $225, and the equilibrium quantity increases to 6.5 million units per year. The tariff benefits domestic smartphone producers, then, because it increases the demand for their products due to the higher price of a close substitute, Chinese smartphones. This causes a redistribution of income from Chinese producers and U.S. consumers of smartphones to U.S. producers of smartphones.

Why did U.S. plywood prices rise when the U.S. government announced a tariff on Chinese imports, even though the government later canceled the tariff?

POLICY EXAMPLE

How a Never-Implemented Tariff Plan Still Managed to Boost U.S. Plywood Prices

Recently, the U.S. government tentatively decided that U.S. plywood firms had been harmed by subsidies that China's government provides to that nation's plywood producers and by alleged dumping on the part of Chinese firms. When the government announced this judgment, it also announced an intention to impose a special 45 percent tariff on most plywood imports from China.

During the weeks following this announcement, U.S. consumers and producers of lumber both anticipated that this tariff would raise the demand for U.S.-produced plywood and reduce the supply of Chinese-produced plywood. Thus, they expected that the price of plywood would rise in the *future*. U.S. plywood consumers reacted by increasing their current demand for plywood. U.S. and Chinese firms decreased their current supplies of plywood. The result was an immediate, nearly 10 percent increase in the price of plywood in the United States.

In fact, however, the U.S. government reversed its tariff decision a few months later. When U.S. plywood consumers and producers learned that no tariff would be imposed after all, their expectations of future plywood prices decreased. Market demand and supply curves returned to their previous positions, and the equilibrium price of plywood dropped back near its previous level.

FOR CRITICAL THINKING

Why do you suppose that the announcement of an import quota to be imposed at a future date typically causes the price of an imported good to rise immediately?

Sources are listed at the end of this chapter.

TARIFFS IN THE UNITED STATES In Figure 19-5 below, we see that tariffs on all imported goods have varied widely. The highest rates in the twentieth century occurred with the passage of the Smoot-Hawley Tariff in 1930.

CURRENT TARIFF LAWS The Trade Expansion Act of 1962 gave the president the authority to reduce tariffs by up to 50 percent. Subsequently, tariffs were reduced by about 35 percent. In 1974, the Trade Reform Act allowed the president to reduce tariffs further. In 1984, the Trade and Tariff Act resulted in the lowest tariff rates ever. All such trade agreement obligations of the United States were carried out under the auspices of the **General Agreement on Tariffs and Trade (GATT),** which was signed in 1947. Member nations of the GATT account for more than 85 percent of world trade. As you can see in Figure 19-5 below, U.S. tariff rates have declined since the early 1960s, when several rounds of negotiations under the GATT were initiated.

General Agreement on Tariffs and Trade (GATT)

An international agreement established in 1947 to further world trade by reducing barriers and tariffs. The GATT was replaced by the World Trade Organization in 1995.

MyEconLab Animation

FIGURE 19-5

Tariff Rates in the United States since 1820

Tariff rates in the United States have bounced around like a football. Indeed, in Congress, tariffs are a political football. Import-competing industries prefer high tariffs. In the twentieth century, the highest tariff was the Smoot-Hawley Tariff of 1930, which was about as high as the "tariff of abominations" in 1828.
Source: U.S. Department of Commerce.

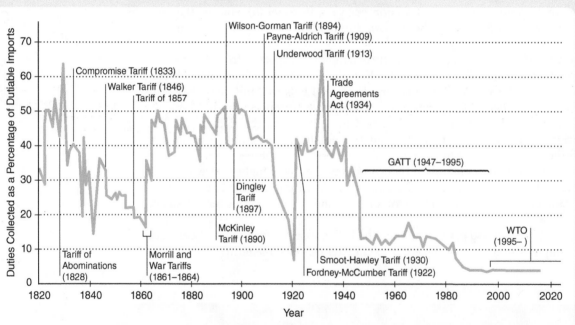

MyEconLab Concept Check
MyEconLab Study Plan

One means of restricting foreign trade is an import quota, which specifies a _____ amount of a good that may be imported during a certain period. The resulting increase in import prices benefits domestic _____ that receive higher prices resulting from substitution to domestic goods.

Another means of restricting imports is a **tariff**, which is a _____ on imports only. An import tariff _____ import-competing industries and harms consumers by raising prices.

International Trade Organizations

19.4 Identify key international agreements and organizations that adjudicate trade disputes among nations

The widespread effort to reduce tariffs around the world has generated interest among nations in joining various international trade organizations. These organizations promote trade by granting preferences in the form of reduced or eliminated tariffs, duties, or quotas.

The World Trade Organization (WTO)

The most important international trade organization with the largest membership is the **World Trade Organization (WTO)**, which was ratified by the final round of negotiations of the General Agreement on Tariffs and Trade at the end of 1993. The WTO, which as of 2015 had 159 member nations and included 30 observer governments, began operations on January 1, 1995. The WTO has fostered important and far-reaching global trade agreements. There is considerable evidence that since the WTO was formed, many of its member nations have adopted policies promoting international trade. The WTO also adjudicates trade disputes between nations in an effort to reduce the scope of protectionism around the globe.

World Trade Organization (WTO)
The successor organization to the GATT that handles trade disputes among its member nations.

What recent trade policy breakthrough occurred under multilateral trade negotiations sponsored by the WTO?

INTERNATIONAL POLICY EXAMPLE

After a Two-Decade Wait, the WTO Makes Some Progress Again

Following considerable progress in the 1990s, the World Trade Organization experienced nearly a decade of failure to advance significant actions to increase global trade. Recently, however, the 159 nations participating in a round of trade talks first initiated in Doha, Qatar—and hence known as the "Doha Round"—agreed on a new set of multilateral efforts to bring about substantial reductions in international trade costs.

In Bali, Indonesia, delegates to WTO negotiations over global rules governing trade agreed to various measures—reduced tariffs, subsidies, and quotas—aimed at cutting average costs of shipping goods by as much as 10 percent. Some estimates indicate that if these measures are implemented,

trade may be sufficiently stimulated to generate a global gain in trade equivalent to as much as $400 billion in real GDP *per year*—or about 7 percent of world real GDP. WTO officials are hoping that the Bali agreement will mark only the first step toward enacting additional reductions in costs of conducting international trade.

FOR CRITICAL THINKING
Why can once-and-for-all reductions in tariffs, subsidies, and quotas generate gains from trade throughout the years that follow?

Sources are listed at the end of this chapter.

MyEconLab Concept Check

Regional Trade Agreements

Numerous other international trade organizations exist alongside the WTO. Sometimes known as **regional trade blocs**, these organizations are created by special deals among groups of countries that grant trade preferences only to countries within their groups. Currently, more than 475 bilateral or regional trade agreements are in effect

Regional trade bloc
A group of nations that grants members special trade privileges.

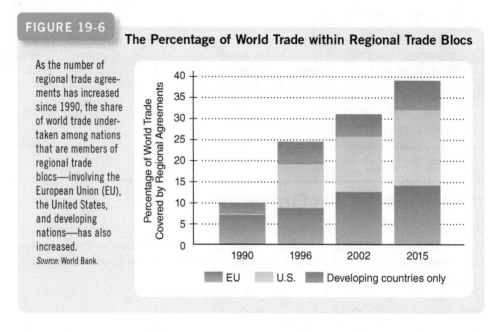

FIGURE 19-6

The Percentage of World Trade within Regional Trade Blocs

As the number of regional trade agreements has increased since 1990, the share of world trade undertaken among nations that are members of regional trade blocs—involving the European Union (EU), the United States, and developing nations—has also increased.

Source: World Bank.

around the globe. Examples include groups of industrial powerhouses, such as the European Union, the North American Free Trade Agreement, and the Association of Southeast Asian Nations. Nations in South America with per capita real GDP nearer the world average have also formed regional trade blocs called Mercosur and the Andean Community. In addition, less developed nations have formed regional trade blocs, such as the Economic Community of West African States and the Community of East and Southern Africa.

DO REGIONAL TRADE BLOCS SIMPLY DIVERT TRADE? Figure 19-6 above shows that the formation of regional trade blocs, in which the European Union and the United States are often key participants, is on an upswing. An average African nation participates in four separate regional trading agreements. A typical Latin American country belongs to eight different regional trade blocs.

In the past, economists worried that the formation of regional trade blocs could mainly result in **trade diversion**, or the shifting of trade from countries outside a regional trade bloc to nations within a bloc. Indeed, a study by Jeffrey Frankel of Harvard University found evidence that some trade diversion does take place. Nevertheless, Frankel and other economists have concluded that the net effect of regional trade agreements has been to boost overall international trade, in some cases considerably.

THE TRADE DEFLECTION ISSUE Today, the primary issue associated with regional trade blocs is **trade deflection**. This occurs when a company located in a nation outside a regional trade bloc moves goods that are not quite fully assembled into a member country, completes assembly of the goods there, and then exports them to other nations in the bloc. To try to reduce incentives for trade deflection, regional trade agreements often include **rules of origin**, which are regulations carefully defining categories of products that are eligible for trading preferences under the agreements. Some rules of origin, for instance, require any products trading freely among members of a bloc to be composed mainly of materials produced within a member nation.

Proponents of free trade worry, however, about the potential for parties to regional trade agreements to use rules of origin to create barriers to trade. Sufficiently complex rules of origin, they suggest, can provide disincentives for countries to utilize the trade-promoting preferences that regional trade agreements ought to provide. Indeed, some free trade proponents applaud successful trade deflection. They contend that it helps to circumvent trade restrictions and thus allows nations within regional trade blocs to experience additional gains from trade.

MyEconLab Concept Check
MyEconLab Study Plan

Trade diversion
Shifting existing international trade from countries outside a regional trade bloc to nations within the bloc.

Trade deflection
Moving partially assembled products into a member nation of a regional trade bloc, completing assembly, and then exporting them to other nations within the bloc, so as to benefit from preferences granted by the trade bloc.

Rules of origin
Regulations that nations in regional trade blocs establish to delineate product categories eligible for trading preferences.

The main international institution created to improve trade among nations was the General Agreement on Tariffs and Trade (GATT). The last round of trade talks under the GATT led to the creation of the _____ _____ _____.

_____ _____ agreements among numerous nations of the world have established more than 475 bilateral and _____ _____ blocs, which grant special trade privileges such as reduced tariff barriers and quota exemptions to member nations.

YOU ARE THERE

On Valentine's Day, Most Fresh Flowers Are Foreign

Carol Medeiros, global associate produce buyer for Whole Foods Market, Inc., increasingly is relying on imported flowers, which, she says, "help keep a lot of favorites in our mix" of available bouquets for holidays such as Valentine's Day. Currently, more than 95 percent of U.S. imported flowers arrive by plane. Nevertheless, "something we are hearing more and more about," she says, is shipment of flowers from South America via ocean freighters. To cut down on the flowers' air respiration rate so that they remain fresh during a two-week ocean trek, the blooms are chilled to nearly freezing temperatures following harvest. The flowers are then placed in refrigerated shipping containers, which are moved by trucks to ports. Ships carry the flowers to U.S. ports, from which they are distributed to retailers such as Whole Foods.

Since 1990, the imported share of sales of U.S. fresh flowers—mainly from South America, but increasingly from Africa as well—has risen from just over 40 percent to nearly 65 percent. Thus, international trade now accounts for nearly two of every three flowers sold by Whole Foods and other U.S. retailers.

CRITICAL THINKING QUESTIONS

1. Why might South American and African growers confront a lower opportunity cost than U.S. growers in producing fresh flowers during early February each year before the U.S. Valentine's Day?

2. Why do you suppose that non-U.S. flower growers might have a comparative advantage over U.S. growers in producing fresh flowers throughout each year?

Sources are listed at the end of this chapter.

ISSUES & APPLICATIONS

MyEconLab Video

Regional Trade Blocs Are the New Trade Bandwagon

Fernando Vergara / AP/Corbis

CONCEPTS APPLIED

» Regional Trade Bloc

» Trade Diversion

» Trade Deflection

Before 1990, there were only a few actively functioning regional trade blocs. In the 1970s and 1980s, just a few select country groups granted member nations special trade privileges. During the 1990s, the number of regional trade blocs began to grow at a much faster pace. As a consequence, a substantial number of these trade blocs are in existence today.

Nearly Everyone Seems to Want to Join Regional Trade Blocs

Figure 19-7 shows how the number of regional trade blocs has evolved since 1948. Shown in blue is the total number of regional trade blocs to which the world's nations have been members. Today, there are approximately 575 of these blocs on record.

Nearly every year, some countries stop abiding by regional trade agreements, even though technically they

FIGURE 19-7

Evolution of Regional Trade Agreements since 1948

Shown in blue are the total regional trade agreements to which the world's nations have claimed to be committed. Shown in red are actively functioning regional trade blocs, after subtracting out "paper" agreements to which countries no longer abide.

Source: World Trade Organization.

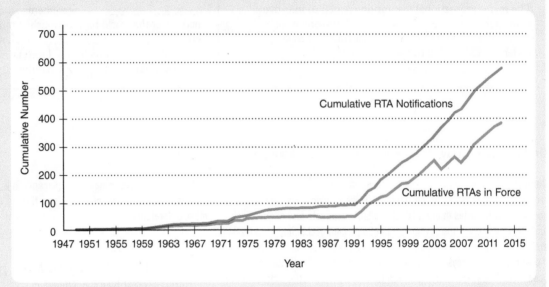

remain in force. Today, about 200 of these agreements are known as "paper" agreements that the member nations no longer honor and that thereby serve no actual economic purpose. Shown in red in the figure is the number of actively functioning regional trade blocs after such "paper" agreements have been subtracted out, which currently totals about 375. There are 192 nations in the world, so an average nation is a member of about 2 active regional trade blocs.

Could Regional Trade Blocs Displace the World Trade Organization?

As regional trade blocs have proliferated, some observers have questioned whether the future of formal global trade arrangements lies with these blocs instead of the World Trade Organization. After all, they note, regional tie-ups involving advanced nations, such as the proposed Trans-Atlantic Trade and Investment Partnership involving the United States and the European Union, involve large percentages of global trade. What is the point, these observers question, of having a multinational trade organization such as the WTO?

Many policymakers and economists contend that a role remains for the WTO to oversee international trading arrangements. The WTO, they argue, can ensure that members of regional blocs do not begin to engage in trade diversion, by shifting trade toward bloc members, or in trade deflection, by using regional systems to benefit artificially from bloc preferences. According to this view, WTO oversight can help to contain trade diversion and trade

deflection effects of regional trade agreements. Thus, the continued proliferation of regional trade blocs may continue to promote overall global trade growth.

For Critical Thinking

1. If trade diversion were the main consequence of the formation of regional trade blocs, would such arrangements contribute to the growth of global trade? Explain your reasoning.

2. Why do "paper agreements" do little to generate increased international trade?

Web Resources

1. Find out more about regional trade agreements in the Web Links in MyEconLab.

2. Learn about pros and cons of the formation of regional trade blocs in the Web Links in MyEconLab.

MyEconLab

For more questions on this chapter's Issues & Applications, go to MyEconLab.

In the Study Plan for this chapter, select Section I: Issues and Applications.

Sources are listed at the end of this chapter.

Fundamental Points

1. A nation possesses a comparative advantage if it is able to produce a good or service at a lower opportunity cost than the item can be produced in other countries.

2. Key arguments against free trade include the idea that new ("infant") industries cannot thrive without protection, that foreign subsidies and dumping should be countered, and that domestic jobs should be protected.

3. The primary policy tools for restricting international trade are quotas and tariffs.

4. The two fundamental types of international trade organizations are the World Trade Organization and a large set of regional trade blocs.

WHAT YOU SHOULD KNOW

Here is what you should know after reading this chapter. MyEconLab will help you identify what you know, and where to go when you need to practice.

LEARNING OBJECTIVES

19.1 **Explain why nations can gain from specializing in production and engaging in international trade** *A country has a comparative advantage in producing a good if it can produce that good at a lower opportunity cost, in terms of forgone production of a second good, than another nation. Both nations can gain by specializing in producing the goods in which they have a comparative advantage and engaging in trade. Together, they can consume more than they would have in the absence of specialization and trade.*

19.2 **Understand common arguments against free trade** *One argument against free trade is that temporary import restrictions might permit an "infant industry" to develop. Another argument concerns dumping, in which foreign firms allegedly sell some of their output in domestic markets at prices below the prices in their home markets or even below their costs of production. In addition, some environmentalists support restrictions on foreign trade to protect their nations from exposure to environmental hazards. Finally, some contend that countries should limit exports of technologies that could pose a threat to their national defense.*

19.3 **Describe ways that nations restrict foreign trade** *One way to restrain trade is to impose a quota, or a limit on imports of a good. This action restricts the supply of the good in the domestic market, thereby pushing up the equilibrium price of the good. Another way to reduce trade is to place a tariff on imported goods. This reduces the supply of foreign-made goods and increases the demand for domestically produced goods, thereby bringing about a rise in the price of the good.*

KEY TERMS

comparative advantage, 434
Key Figure
Figure 19-1, 434
Figure 19-2, 439

infant industry argument, 441
dumping, 442

quota system, 443
voluntary restraint agreement (VRA), 444
voluntary import expansion (VIE), 444
General Agreement on Tariffs and Trade (GATT), 446
Key Figures
Figure 19-3, 444
Figure 19-4, 445
Figure 19-5, 446

WHERE TO GO TO PRACTICE

- MyEconLab Study Plan 19.1
- Animated Figures 19-1, 19-2

- MyEconLab Study Plan 19.2

- MyEconLab Study Plan 19.3
- Animated Figures 19-3, 19-4, 19-5

WHAT YOU SHOULD KNOW *continued*

LEARNING OBJECTIVES ———————— KEY TERMS ———————— WHERE TO GO TO PRACTICE ——

19.4 Identify key international agreements and organizations that adjudicate trade disputes among nations *From 1947 to 1995, nations agreed to abide by the General Agreement on Tariffs and Trade (GATT), which laid an international legal foundation for relaxing quotas and reducing tariffs. Since 1995, the World Trade Organization (WTO) has adjudicated trade disputes that arise between or among nations. Now there are also more than 475 bilateral and regional trade blocs, including the North American Free Trade Agreement and the European Union, that provide special trade preferences to member nations.*

World Trade Organization, 447
regional trade bloc, 447
trade diversion, 448
trade deflection, 448
rules of origin, 448

• MyEconLab Study Plan 19.4

Log in to MyEconLab, take a chapter test, and get a personalized Study Plan that tells you which concepts you understand and which ones you need to review. From there, MyEconLab will give you further practice, tutorials, animations, videos, and guided solutions. For more information, visit http://www.myeconlab.com

PROBLEMS

All problems are assignable in MyEconLab. *Answers to the odd-numbered problems appear in* MyEconLab.

19-1. To answer the questions below, consider the following table for the neighboring nations of Northland and West Coast. The table lists maximum feasible hourly rates of production of pastries if no sandwiches are produced and maximum feasible hourly rates of production of sandwiches if no pastries are produced. Assume that the opportunity costs of producing these goods are constant in both nations. (See page 435.)

Product	Northland	West Coast
Pastries (per hour)	50,000	100,000
Sandwiches (per hour)	25,000	200,000

a. What is the opportunity cost of producing pastries in Northland? Of producing sandwiches in Northland?

b. What is the opportunity cost of producing pastries in West Coast? Of producing sandwiches in West Coast?

19-2. Based on your answers to Problem 19-1, which nation has a comparative advantage in producing pastries? Which nation has a comparative advantage in producing sandwiches? (See page 435.)

19-3. Suppose that the two nations in Problems 19-1 and 19-2 choose to specialize in producing the goods for which they have a comparative advantage. They agree to trade at a rate of exchange of 1 pastry for 1 sandwich. At this rate of exchange, what are the maximum possible numbers of pastries and sandwiches that they could agree to trade? (See page 436.)

19-4. Residents of the nation of Border Kingdom can forgo production of digital televisions and utilize all available resources to produce 300 bottles of high-quality wine per hour. Alternatively, they can forgo producing wine and instead produce 60 digital TVs per hour. In the neighboring country of Coastal Realm, residents can forgo production of digital TVs and use all resources to produce 150 bottles of high-quality wine per hour, or they can forgo wine production and produce 50 digital TVs per hour. In both nations, the opportunity costs of producing the two goods are constant. (See pages 435–436.)

a. What is the opportunity cost of producing digital TVs in Border Kingdom? Of producing bottles of wine in Border Kingdom?

b. What is the opportunity cost of producing digital TVs in Coastal Realm? Of producing bottles of wine in Coastal Realm?

19-5. Based on your answers to Problem 19-4, which nation has a comparative advantage in producing digital TVs? Which nation has a comparative advantage in producing bottles of wine? (See page 436.)

19-6. Suppose that the two nations in Problem 19-4 decide to specialize in producing the good for which they have a comparative advantage and to engage in trade. Would residents of both nations find a rate of exchange of 4 bottles of wine for 1 digital TV potentially agreeable? Why or why not? (See pages 436–437.)

To answer Problems 19-7 and 19-8, refer to the following table, which shows possible combinations of hourly outputs of modems and flash memory drives in South Shore and neighboring East Isle, in which opportunity costs of producing both products are constant.

South Shore		East Isle	
Modems	Flash Drives	Modems	Flash Drives
75	0	100	0
60	30	80	10
45	60	60	20
30	90	40	30
15	120	20	40
0	150	0	50

19-7. Consider the above table and answer the questions that follow. (See pages 435–437.)

a. What is the opportunity cost of producing modems in South Shore? Of producing flash memory drives in South Shore?

b. What is the opportunity cost of producing modems in East Isle? Of producing flash memory drives in East Isle?

c. Which nation has a comparative advantage in producing modems? Which nation has a comparative advantage in producing flash memory drives?

19-8. Refer to your answers to Problem 19-7 when answering the following questions. (See page 437.)

a. Which *one* of the following rates of exchange of modems for flash memory drives will be acceptable to *both* nations: (i) 3 modems for 1 flash drive; (ii) 1 modem for 1 flash drive; or (iii) 1 flash drive for 2.5 modems? Explain.

b. Suppose that each nation decides to use all available resources to produce only the good for which it has a comparative advantage and to engage in trade at the single feasible rate of exchange you identified in part (a). Prior to specialization and trade, residents of South Shore chose to produce and consume 30 modems per hour and 90 flash drives per hour, and residents of East Isle chose to produce and consume 40 modems per hour and 30 flash drives per hour. Now, residents of South Shore agree to export to East Isle the same quantity of South Shore's specialty good that East Isle residents were consuming prior to engaging in international trade. How many units of East Isle's specialty good does South Shore import from East Isle?

c. What is South Shore's hourly consumption of modems and flash drives after the nation specializes and trades with East Isle? What is East Isle's hourly consumption of modems and flash drives after the nation specializes and trades with South Shore?

d. What consumption gains from trade are experienced by South Shore and East Isle?

19-9. Critics of the North American Free Trade Agreement (NAFTA) suggest that much of the increase in exports from Mexico to the United States now involves goods that Mexico otherwise would have exported to other nations. Mexican firms choose to export the goods to the United States, the critics argue, solely because the items receive preferential treatment under NAFTA tariff rules. What term describes what these critics are claiming is occurring with regard to U.S.-Mexican trade as a result of NAFTA? Explain your reasoning. (See pages 447–448.)

19-10. Some critics of the North American Free Trade Agreement (NAFTA) suggest that firms outside NAFTA nations sometimes shift unassembled inputs to Mexico, assemble the inputs into final goods there, and then export the final product to the United States in order to take advantage of Mexican trade preferences. What term describes what these critics are claiming is occurring with regard to U.S.-Mexican trade as a result of NAFTA? Explain your reasoning. (See page 448.)

19-11. How could multilateral trade agreements established for all nations through the World Trade Organization help to prevent both trade diversion and trade deflection that can occur under regional trade agreements, thereby promoting more overall international trade? (See page 448.)

REFERENCES

EXAMPLE: A U.S. Comparative Advantage in Trash

Peter Ford, "China Puts Up a Green Wall to U.S. Trash," *Christian Science Monitor*, June 19, 2013.

Jason Margolis, "China's 'Green Fence' Is Cleaning Up America's Dirty Recycling," PII's World, February 18, 2014. (http://www.pri.org/stories/2014-02-18/chinas-green-fence-cleaning-americas-dirty-recycling)

Adam Minter, "To a Chinese Scrap-Metal Hunter, America's Trash Is Treasure," *Bloomberg Businessweek*, August 29, 2013.

POLICY EXAMPLE: The U.S. Export-Import Bank Fights Subsidies with Subsidies

Doug Cameron, "Boeing Cites Jitters over Airplane Financing from Ex-Im Bank," *The Wall Street Journal*, August 7, 2013.

Ted Reed, "Delta, Leader of the U.S. Airline Industry, Challenges Boeing and Export-Import Bank," *Forbes*, April 13, 2014.

Angelo Young, "Why U.S. Export-Import Bank Backs Australian Billionaire Heiress Gina Rinehart," International Business Times, December 20, 2013.

POLICY EXAMPLE: How a Never-Implemented Tariff Plan Still Managed to Boost U.S. Plywood Prices

Dan D'Ambrosio, "U.S. Plywood Industry's Plea for Help Rejected," *USA Today*, January 2, 2014.

Thomas Russell, "ITC Vote Eliminates U.S. Duties on Chinese Plywood," Furniture Today, November 7, 2013.

Greg Simon and C. Richard Titus, "Protectionists Pick Your Pocket Again," *The Wall Street Journal*, September 15, 2013.

INTERNATIONAL POLICY EXAMPLE: After a Two-Decade Wait, the WTO Makes Some Progress Again

Larry Elliot, "Bali Summit Invigorated World Trade Organization," *The Guardian*, December 18, 2013.

Pankaj Ghemawat and Steven Altman, "WTO's Baby Steps at Bali a Big Deal," CNN, January 9, 2014.

"Unaccustomed Victory: Global Trade Talks Yield a Deal for the First Time in Almost 20 Years," *The Economist*, December 14, 2013.

YOU ARE THERE: On Valentine's Day, Most Fresh Flowers Are Foreign

ABC/Univision, "What It Takes to Import Flowers for Valentine's Day," Huffington Post, February 14, 2013.

Laura Securon Palet, "Where Are Those Valentine's Day Flowers From, Anyway?" *USA Today*, February 14, 2014.

Bob Sechler, "Fresh-Cut Flowers, Shipped by Sea?" *The Wall Street Journal*, May 11, 2013.

ISSUES & APPLICATIONS: Regional Trade Blocs Are the New Trade Bandwagon

"In My Backyard: Multilateral Trade Pacts Are Increasingly Giving Way to Regional Ones," *The Economist*, October 12, 2013.

David Luhnow, "The Two Latin Americas: A Continental Divide between One Bloc That Favors State Controls and Another That Embraces Free Markets," *The Wall Street Journal*, January 3, 2014.

Evan Soltas, "Are Free-Trade Agreements Actually Protectionist?" Bloomberg, June 17, 2013.

GLOSSARY

A

Absolute advantage The ability to produce more units of a good or service using a given quantity of labor or resource inputs. Equivalently, the ability to produce the same quantity of a good or service using fewer units of labor or resource inputs.

Accounting identities Values that are equivalent by definition.

Accounting profit Total revenues minus total explicit costs.

Action time lag The time between recognizing an economic problem and implementing policy to solve it. The action time lag is quite long for fiscal policy, which requires congressional approval.

Active (discretionary) policymaking All actions on the part of monetary and fiscal policymakers that are undertaken in response to or in anticipation of some change in the overall economy.

Ad valorem **taxation** Assessing taxes by charging a tax rate equal to a fraction of the market price of each unit purchased.

Adverse selection The tendency for high-risk projects and clients to be over-represented among borrowers.

Age-earnings cycle The regular earnings profile of an individual throughout his or her lifetime. The age-earnings cycle usually starts with a low income, builds gradually to a peak at around age 50, and then gradually curves down until it approaches zero at retirement.

Aggregate demand The total of all planned expenditures in the entire economy.

Aggregate demand curve A curve showing planned purchase rates for all final goods and services in the economy at various price levels, all other things held constant.

Aggregate demand shock Any event that causes the aggregate demand curve to shift inward or outward.

Aggregate supply The total of all planned production for the economy.

Aggregate supply shock Any event that causes the aggregate supply curve to shift inward or outward.

Aggregates Total amounts or quantities. Aggregate demand, for example, is total planned expenditures throughout a nation.

Anticipated inflation The inflation rate that we believe will occur. When it

does occur, we are in a situation of fully anticipated inflation.

Antitrust legislation Laws that restrict the formation of monopolies and regulate certain anticompetitive business practices.

Appreciation An increase in the exchange value of one nation's currency in terms of the currency of another nation.

Asset demand Holding money as a store of value instead of other assets such as corporate bonds and stocks.

Assets Amounts owned; all items to which a business or household holds legal claim.

Asymmetric information Information possessed by one party in a financial transaction but not by the other party.

Automatic, or built-in, stabilizers Special provisions of certain federal programs that cause changes in desired aggregate expenditures without the action of Congress and the president. Examples are the federal progressive tax system and unemployment compensation.

Autonomous consumption The part of consumption that is independent of (does not depend on) the level of disposable income. Changes in autonomous consumption shift the consumption function.

Average fixed costs Total fixed costs divided by the number of units produced.

Average physical product Total product divided by the variable input.

Average propensity to consume (APC) Real consumption divided by real disposable income. For any given level of real income, the proportion of total real disposable income that is consumed.

Average propensity to save (APS) Real saving divided by real disposable income. For any given level of real income, the proportion of total real disposable income that is saved.

Average tax rate The total tax payment divided by total income. It is the proportion of total income paid in taxes.

Average total costs Total costs divided by the number of units produced; sometimes called *average per-unit total costs*.

Average variable costs Total variable costs divided by the number of units produced.

B

Balance of payments A system of accounts that measures transactions of goods, services, income, and financial assets between domestic households, businesses, and governments and residents of the rest of the world during a specific time period.

Balance of trade The difference between exports and imports of physical goods.

Balance sheet A statement of the assets and liabilities of any business entity, including financial institutions and the Federal Reserve System. Assets are what is owned; liabilities are what is owed.

Balanced budget A situation in which the government's spending is exactly equal to the total taxes and other revenues it collects during a given period of time.

Bank run Attempt by many of a bank's depositors to convert transactions and time deposits into currency out of fear that the bank's liabilities may exceed its assets.

Barter The direct exchange of goods and services for other goods and services without the use of money.

Base year The year that is chosen as the point of reference for comparison of prices in other years.

Base-year dollars The value of a current sum expressed in terms of prices in a base year.

Behavioral economics An approach to the study of consumer behavior that emphasizes psychological limitations and complications that potentially interfere with rational decision making.

Bilateral monopoly A market structure consisting of a monopolist and a monopsonist.

Black market A market in which goods are traded at prices above their legal maximum prices or in which illegal goods are sold.

Bond A legal claim against a firm, usually entitling the owner of the bond to receive a fixed annual coupon payment, plus a lump-sum payment at the bond's maturity date. Bonds are issued in return for funds lent to the firm.

Bounded rationality The hypothesis that people are *nearly*, but not fully, rational, so that they cannot examine every possible choice available to them but instead use simple rules of thumb to sort among the alternatives that happen to occur to them.

Budget constraint All of the possible combinations of goods that can be purchased (at fixed prices) with a specific budget.

Bundling Offering two or more products for sale as a set.

Business fluctuations The ups and downs in business activity throughout the economy.

C

Capital account A category of balance of payments transactions that measures flows of financial assets.

Capital consumption allowance Another name for depreciation, the amount that businesses would have to put aside in order to take care of deteriorating machines and other equipment.

Capital gain A positive difference between the purchase price and the sale price of an asset. If a share of stock is bought for $5 and then sold for $15, the capital gain is $10.

Capital goods Producer durables; nonconsumable goods that firms use to make other goods.

Capital loss A negative difference between the purchase price and the sale price of an asset.

Capture hypothesis A theory of regulatory behavior that predicts that regulators will eventually be captured by special interests of the industry being regulated.

Cartel An association of producers in an industry that agree to set common prices and output quotas to prevent competition.

Central bank A banker's bank, usually an official institution that also serves as a bank for a nation's government treasury. Central banks normally regulate commercial banks.

Ceteris paribus **[KAY-ter-us PEAR-uh-bus] assumption** The assumption that nothing changes except the factor or factors being studied.

Ceteris paribus **conditions** Determinants of the relationship between price and quantity that are unchanged along a curve. Changes in these factors cause the curve to shift.

Closed shop A business enterprise in which employees must belong to the union before they can be hired and must remain in the union after they are hired.

Collective bargaining Negotiation between the management of a company and the management of a union for the purpose of reaching a mutually agreeable contract that sets wages, fringe benefits, and working conditions for all employees in all the unions involved.

Collective decision making How voters, politicians, and other interested parties act and how these actions influence nonmarket decisions.

Common property Property that is owned by everyone and therefore by no one. Air and water are examples of common property resources.

Comparative advantage The ability to produce a good or service at a lower opportunity cost than other producers.

Complements Two goods are complements when a change in the price of one causes an opposite shift in the demand for the other.

Concentration ratio The percentage of all sales contributed by the leading four or leading eight firms in an industry; sometimes called the *industry concentration ratio.*

Constant dollars Dollars expressed in terms of real purchasing power, using a particular year as the base or standard of comparison, in contrast to current dollars.

Constant returns to scale No change in long-run average costs when output increases.

Constant-cost industry An industry whose total output can be increased without an increase in long-run per-unit costs. Its long-run supply curve is horizontal.

Consumer optimum A choice of a set of goods and services that maximizes the level of satisfaction for each consumer, subject to limited income.

Consumer Price Index (CPI) A statistical measure of a weighted average of prices of a specified set of goods and services purchased by typical consumers in urban areas.

Consumer surplus The difference between the total amount that consumers would have been willing to pay for an item and the total amount that they actually pay.

Consumption Spending on new goods and services to be used up out of a household's current income. Whatever is not consumed is saved. Consumption includes such things as buying food and going to a concert.

Consumption function The relationship between amount consumed and disposable income. A consumption function tells us how much people plan to consume at various levels of disposable income.

Consumption goods Goods bought by households to use up, such as food and movies.

Contraction A business fluctuation during which the pace of national economic activity is slowing down.

Cooperative game A game in which the players explicitly cooperate to make themselves jointly better off. As applied to firms, it involves companies colluding in order to make higher than perfectly competitive rates of return.

Corporation A legal entity that may conduct business in its own name just as an individual does. The owners of a corporation, called shareholders, own shares of the firm's profits and have the protection of limited liability.

Cost-of-living adjustments (COLAs) Clauses in contracts that allow for increases in specified nominal values to take account of changes in the cost of living.

Cost-of-service regulation Regulation that allows prices to reflect only the actual average cost of production and no monopoly profits.

Cost-push inflation Inflation caused by decreases in short-run aggregate supply.

Craft unions Labor unions composed of workers who engage in a particular trade or skill, such as baking, carpentry, or plumbing.

Creative response Behavior on the part of a firm that allows it to comply with the letter of the law but violate the spirit, significantly lessening the law's effects.

Credence good A product with qualities that consumers lack the expertise to assess without assistance.

Credit policy Federal Reserve policy-making involving direct lending to financial and nonfinancial firms.

Cross price elasticity of demand (E_{xy}) The percentage change in the amount of an item demanded (holding its price constant) divided by the percentage change in the price of a related good.

Crowding-out effect The tendency of expansionary fiscal policy to cause a decrease in planned investment or planned consumption in the private sector. This decrease normally results from the rise in interest rates.

Current account A category of balance of payments transactions that measures the exchange of merchandise, the exchange of services, and unilateral transfers.

Cyclical unemployment Unemployment resulting from business recessions that occur when aggregate (total) demand is insufficient to create full employment.

D

Dead capital Any capital resource that lacks clear title of ownership.

Deadweight loss The portion of consumer surplus that no one in society is able to obtain in a situation of monopoly.

Decreasing-cost industry An industry in which an increase in output leads to a reduction in long-run per-unit costs, such that the long-run industry supply curve slopes downward.

Deflation A sustained decrease in the average of all prices of goods and services in an economy.

Demand A schedule showing how much of a good or service people will purchase at any price during a specified time period, other things being constant.

Demand curve A graphical representation of the demand schedule. It is a negatively sloped line showing the inverse relationship between the price and the quantity demanded (other things being equal).

Demand-pull inflation Inflation caused by increases in aggregate demand not matched by increases in aggregate supply.

Dependent variable A variable whose value changes according to changes in the value of one or more independent variables.

Depository institutions Financial institutions that accept deposits from savers and lend funds from those deposits out at interest.

Depreciation A decrease in the exchange value of one nation's currency in terms of the currency of another nation.

Depression An extremely severe recession.

Derived demand Input factor demand derived from demand for the final product being produced.

Development economics The study of factors that contribute to the economic growth of a country.

Diminishing marginal utility The principle that as more of any good or service is consumed, its *extra* benefit declines. Otherwise stated, increases in total utility from the consumption of a good or service become smaller and smaller as more is consumed during a given time period.

Direct expenditure offsets Actions on the part of the private sector in spending income that offset government fiscal policy actions. Any increase in government spending in an area that competes with the private sector will have some direct expenditure offset.

Direct marketing Advertising targeted at specific consumers, typically in the form of postal mailings, telephone calls, or e-mail messages.

Direct relationship A relationship between two variables that is positive, meaning that an increase in one variable is associated with an increase in the other and a decrease in one variable is associated with a decrease in the other.

Discount rate The interest rate that the Federal Reserve charges for reserves that it lends to depository institutions.

It is sometimes referred to as the *rediscount rate* or, in Canada and England, as the *bank rate*.

Discounting The method by which the present value of a future sum or a future stream of sums is obtained.

Discouraged workers Individuals who have stopped looking for a job because they are convinced that they will not find a suitable one.

Diseconomies of scale Increases in long-run average costs that occur as output increases.

Disposable personal income (DPI) Personal income after personal income taxes have been paid.

Dissaving Negative saving; a situation in which spending exceeds income. Dissaving can occur when a household is able to borrow or use up existing assets.

Distribution of income The way income is allocated among the population based on groupings of residents.

Dividends Portion of a corporation's profits paid to its owners (shareholders).

Division of labor The segregation of resources into different specific tasks. For instance, one automobile worker puts on bumpers, another doors, and so on.

Dominant strategies Strategies that always yield the highest benefit. Regardless of what other players do, a dominant strategy will yield the most benefit for the player using it.

Dumping Selling a good or a service abroad below the price charged in the home market or at a price below its cost of production.

Durable consumer goods Consumer goods that have a life span of more than three years.

Dynamic tax analysis Economic evaluation of tax rate changes that recognizes that the tax base eventually declines with ever-higher tax rates, so that tax revenues may eventually decline if the tax rate is raised sufficiently.

E

Economic freedom The rights to own private property and to exchange goods, services, and financial assets with minimal government interference.

Economic goods Goods that are scarce, for which the quantity demanded exceeds the quantity supplied at a zero price.

Economic growth Increases in per capita real GDP measured by its rate of change per year.

Economic profits Total revenues minus total opportunity costs of all inputs used, or the total of all implicit and explicit costs.

Economic rent A payment for the use of any resource over and above its opportunity cost.

Economic system A society's institutional mechanism for determining the way in which scarce resources are used to satisfy human desires.

Economics The study of how people allocate their limited resources to satisfy their unlimited wants.

Economies of scale Decreases in long-run average costs resulting from increases in output.

Effect time lag The time that elapses between the implementation of a policy and the results of that policy.

Efficiency The case in which a given level of inputs is used to produce the maximum output possible. Alternatively, the situation in which a given output is produced at minimum cost.

Effluent fee A charge to a polluter that gives the right to discharge into the air or water a certain amount of pollution; also called a *pollution tax*.

Elastic demand A demand relationship in which a given percentage change in price will result in a larger percentage change in quantity demanded.

Empirical Relying on real-world data in evaluating the usefulness of a model.

Endowments The various resources in an economy, including both physical resources and such human resources as ingenuity and management skills.

Entitlements Guaranteed benefits under a government program such as Social Security, Medicare, or Medicaid.

Entrepreneurship The component of human resources that performs the functions of raising capital; organizing, managing, and assembling other factors of production; making basic business policy decisions; and taking risks.

Equation of exchange The formula indicating that the number of monetary units (M_s) times the number of times each unit is spent on final goods and services (V) is identical to the price level (P) times real GDP (Y).

Equilibrium The situation when quantity supplied equals quantity demanded at a particular price.

Exchange rate The price of one nation's currency in terms of the currency of another country.

Excise tax A tax levied on purchases of a particular good or service.

Expansion A business fluctuation in which the pace of national economic activity is speeding up.

Expenditure approach Computing GDP by adding up the dollar value at current market prices of all final goods and services.

Experience good A product that an individual must consume before the product's quality can be established.

Explicit costs Costs that business managers must take account of because they must be paid. Examples are wages, taxes, and rent.

Externality A consequence of a diversion of a private cost (or benefit) from a social cost (or benefit). A situation in which the costs (or benefits) of an action are not fully borne (or gained) by the decision makers engaged in an activity that uses scarce resources.

F

Featherbedding Any practice that forces employers to use more labor than they would otherwise or to use existing labor in an inefficient manner.

Federal Deposit Insurance Corporation (FDIC) A government agency that insures the deposits held in banks and most other depository institutions. All U.S. banks are insured this way.

Federal funds market A private market (made up mostly of banks) in which banks can borrow reserves from other banks that want to lend them. Federal funds are usually lent for overnight use.

Federal funds rate The interest rate that depository institutions pay to borrow reserves in the interbank federal funds market.

Fiduciary monetary system A system in which money is issued by the government and its value is based uniquely on the public's faith that the currency represents command over goods and services and will be accepted in payment for debts.

Final goods and services Goods and services that are at their final stage of production and will not be transformed into yet other goods or services. For example, wheat ordinarily is not considered a final good because it is usually used to make a final good, bread.

Financial capital Funds used to purchase physical capital goods, such as buildings and equipment, and patents and trademarks.

Financial intermediaries Institutions that transfer funds between ultimate lenders (savers) and ultimate borrowers.

Financial intermediation The process by which financial institutions accept savings from businesses, households, and governments and lend the savings to other businesses, households, and governments.

Firm A business organization that employs resources to produce goods or services for profit. A firm normally owns and operates at least one "plant" or facility in order to produce.

Fiscal policy The discretionary changing of government expenditures or taxes to achieve national economic goals, such as high employment with price stability.

Fixed costs Costs that do not vary with output. Fixed costs typically include such expenses as rent on a building. These costs are fixed for a certain period of time (in the long run, though, they are variable).

Fixed investment Purchases by businesses of newly produced producer durables, or capital goods, such as production machinery and office equipment.

Flexible exchange rates Exchange rates that are allowed to fluctuate in the open market in response to changes in supply and demand. Sometimes called *floating exchange rates*.

Flow A quantity measured per unit of time; something that occurs over time, such as the income you make per week or per year or the number of individuals who are fired every month.

FOMC Directive A document that summarizes the Federal Open Market Committee's general policy strategy, establishes near-term objectives for the federal funds rate, and specifies target ranges for money supply growth.

Foreign direct investment The acquisition of more than 10 percent of the shares of ownership in a company in another nation.

Foreign exchange market A market in which households, firms, and governments buy and sell national currencies.

Foreign exchange rate The price of one currency in terms of another.

Foreign exchange risk The possibility that changes in the value of a nation's currency will result in variations in the market value of assets.

45-degree reference line The line along which planned real expenditures equal real GDP per year.

Fractional reserve banking A system in which depository institutions hold reserves that are less than the amount of total deposits.

Free-rider problem A problem that arises when individuals presume that others will pay for public goods so that, individually, they can escape paying for their portion without causing a reduction in production.

Frictional unemployment Unemployment due to the fact that workers must search for appropriate job offers. This activity takes time, and so they remain temporarily unemployed.

Full employment An arbitrary level of unemployment that corresponds to "normal" friction in the labor market. In 1986, a 6.5 percent rate of unemployment was considered full employment. Today it is somewhat higher.

G

Gains from trade The sum of consumer surplus and producer surplus.

Game theory A way of describing the various possible outcomes in any situation involving two or more interacting individuals when those individuals are aware of the interactive nature of their situation and plan accordingly. The plans made by these individuals are known as *game strategies*.

GDP deflator A price index measuring the changes in prices of all new goods and services produced in the economy.

General Agreement on Tariffs and Trade (GATT) An international agreement established in 1947 to further world trade by reducing barriers and tariffs. The GATT was replaced by the World Trade Organization in 1995.

Gini coefficient On a graph with the cumulative percentage of money income measured along the vertical axis and the cumulative percentage of households measured along the horizontal axis, if A is the area between the line of perfect income equality and the Lorenz curve and B is the total area beneath the line of perfect income equality, the Gini coefficient equals $A/(A+B)$.

Goods All things from which individuals derive satisfaction or happiness.

Government budget constraint The limit on government spending and transfers imposed by the fact that every dollar the government spends, transfers, or uses to repay borrowed funds must ultimately be provided by the user charges and taxes it collects.

Government budget deficit An excess of government spending over government revenues during a given period of time.

Government budget surplus An excess of government revenues over government spending during a given period of time.

Government, or political, goods Goods (and services) provided by the public sector; they can be either private or public goods.

Government-inhibited good A good that has been deemed socially undesirable through the political process. Heroin is an example.

Government-sponsored good A good that has been deemed socially desirable through the political process. Museums are an example.

Gross domestic income (GDI) The sum of all income—wages, interest, rent, and profits—paid to the four factors of production.

Gross domestic product (GDP) The total market value of all final goods and services produced during a year by factors of production located within a nation's borders.

Gross private domestic investment The creation of capital goods, such as factories and machines, that can yield production and hence consumption in the future. Also included in this definition are changes in business inventories and repairs made to machines or buildings.

Gross public debt All federal government debt irrespective of who owns it.

H

Health insurance exchanges Government agencies to which the national health care program assigns the task of assisting individuals, families, and small businesses in identifying health insurance policies to purchase.

Hedge A financial strategy that reduces the chance of suffering losses arising from foreign exchange risk.

Herfindahl-Hirschman Index (HHI) The sum of the squared percentage sales shares of all firms in an industry.

Horizontal merger The joining of firms that are producing or selling a similar product.

Human capital The accumulated training and education of workers.

I

Implicit costs Expenses that managers do not have to pay out of pocket and hence normally do not explicitly calculate, such as the opportunity cost of factors of production that are owned. Examples are owner-provided capital and owner-provided labor.

Import quota A physical supply restriction on imports of a particular good, such as sugar. Foreign exporters are unable to sell in the United States more than the quantity specified in the import quota.

Incentive structure The system of rewards and punishments individuals face with respect to their own actions.

Incentives Rewards or penalties for engaging in a particular activity.

Income approach Measuring GDP by adding up all components of national income, including wages, interest, rent, and profits.

Income elasticity of demand (E_i) The percentage change in the amount of a good demanded, holding its price constant, divided by the percentage change in income. The responsiveness of the amount of a good demanded to a change in income, holding the good's relative price constant.

Income in kind Income received in the form of goods and services, such as housing or medical care. Income in kind differs from money income, which is simply income in dollars, or general

purchasing power, that can be used to buy *any* goods and services.

Income velocity of money (V) The number of times per year a dollar is spent on final goods and services; identically equal to nominal GDP divided by the money supply.

Increasing-cost industry An industry in which an increase in industry output is accompanied by an increase in long-run per-unit costs, such that the long-run industry supply curve slopes upward.

Independent variable A variable whose value is determined independently of, or outside, the equation under study.

Indifference curve A curve composed of a set of consumption alternatives, each of which yields the same total amount of satisfaction.

Indirect business taxes All business taxes except the tax on corporate profits. Indirect business taxes include sales and business property taxes.

Industrial unions Labor unions that consist of workers from a particular industry, such as automobile manufacturing or steel manufacturing.

Industry supply curve The locus of points showing the minimum prices at which given quantities will be forthcoming; also called the *market supply curve.*

Inefficient point Any point below the production possibilities curve, at which the use of resources is not generating the maximum possible output.

Inelastic demand A demand relationship in which a given percentage change in price will result in a less-than-proportionate percentage change in the quantity demanded.

Infant industry argument The contention that tariffs should be imposed to protect from import competition an industry that is trying to get started. Presumably, after the industry becomes technologically efficient, the tariff can be lifted.

Inferior goods Goods for which demand falls as income rises.

Inflation A sustained increase in the average of all prices of goods and services in an economy.

Inflationary gap The gap that exists whenever equilibrium real GDP per year is greater than full-employment real GDP as shown by the position of the long-run aggregate supply curve.

Information product An item that is produced using information-intensive inputs at a relatively high fixed cost but distributed for sale at a relatively low marginal cost.

Informational advertising Advertising that emphasizes transmitting knowledge about the features of a product.

Innovation Transforming an invention into something that is useful to humans.

Inside information Information that is not available to the general public about what is happening in a corporation.

Interactive marketing Advertising that permits a consumer to follow up directly by searching for more information and placing direct product orders.

Interest The payment for current rather than future command over resources; the cost of obtaining credit.

Interest rate effect One of the reasons that the aggregate demand curve slopes downward: Higher price levels increase the interest rate, which in turn causes businesses and consumers to reduce desired spending due to the higher cost of borrowing.

Intermediate goods Goods used up entirely in the production of final goods.

International financial crisis The rapid withdrawal of foreign investments and loans from a nation.

International Monetary Fund An agency founded to administer an international foreign exchange system and to lend to member countries that had balance of payments problems. The IMF now functions as a lender of last resort for national governments.

Inventory investment Changes in the stocks of finished goods and goods in process, as well as changes in the raw materials that businesses keep on hand. Whenever inventories are decreasing, inventory investment is negative. Whenever they are increasing, inventory investment is positive.

Inverse relationship A relationship between two variables that is negative, meaning that an increase in one variable is associated with a decrease in the other and a decrease in one variable is associated with an increase in the other.

Investment Spending on items such as machines and buildings, which can be used to produce goods and services in the future. (It also includes changes in business inventories.) The investment part of real GDP is the portion that will be used in the process of producing goods *in the future.*

J

Job leaver An individual in the labor force who quits voluntarily.

Job loser An individual in the labor force whose employment was involuntarily terminated.

Jurisdictional dispute A disagreement involving two or more unions over which should have control of a particular jurisdiction, such as a particular craft or skill or a particular firm or industry.

K

Keynesian short-run aggregate supply curve The horizontal portion of the aggregate supply curve in which there is excessive unemployment and unused capacity in the economy.

L

Labor Productive contributions of humans who work.

Labor force Individuals aged 16 years or older who either have jobs or who are looking and available for jobs; the number of employed plus the number of unemployed.

Labor force participation rate The percentage of noninstitutionalized working-age individuals who are employed or seeking employment.

Labor productivity Total real domestic output (real GDP) divided by the number of workers (output per worker).

Labor unions Worker organizations that seek to secure economic improvements for their members. They also seek to improve the safety, health, and other benefits (such as job security) of their members.

Land The natural resources that are available from nature. Land as a resource includes location, original fertility and mineral deposits, topography, climate, water, and vegetation.

Law of demand The observation that there is a negative, or inverse, relationship between the price of any good or service and the quantity demanded, holding other factors constant.

Law of diminishing marginal product The observation that after some point, successive equal-sized increases in a variable factor of production, such as labor, added to fixed factors of production will result in smaller increases in output.

Law of increasing additional cost The fact that the opportunity cost of additional units of a good generally increases as people attempt to produce more of that good. This accounts for the bowed-out shape of the production possibilities curve.

Law of supply The observation that the higher the price of a good, the more of that good sellers will make available over a specified time period, other things being equal.

Leading indicators Events that have been found to occur before changes in business activity.

Lemons problem The potential for asymmetric information to bring about a general decline in product quality in an industry.

Lender of last resort The Federal Reserve's role as an institution that is willing and able to lend to a temporarily illiquid bank that is otherwise in good financial condition to prevent the bank's illiquid position from leading to a general loss of confidence in that bank or in others.

Liabilities Amounts owed; the legal claims against a business or household by nonowners.

Life-cycle theory of consumption A theory in which a person bases decisions about current consumption and saving on both current income and anticipated future income.

Limited liability A legal concept in which the responsibility, or liability, of the owners of a corporation is limited to the value of the shares in the firm that they own.

Liquidity The degree to which an asset can be acquired or disposed of without much danger of any intervening loss in *nominal* value and with small transaction costs. Money is the most liquid asset.

Liquidity approach A method of measuring the money supply by looking at money as a temporary store of value.

Long run The time period during which all factors of production can be varied.

Long-run aggregate supply curve A vertical line representing the real output of goods and services after full adjustment has occurred. It can also be viewed as representing the real GDP of the economy under conditions of full employment—the full-employment level of real GDP.

Long-run average cost curve The locus of points representing the minimum unit cost of producing any given rate of output, given current technology and resource prices.

Long-run industry supply curve A market supply curve showing the relationship between prices and quantities after firms have been allowed the time to enter into or exit from an industry, depending on whether there have been positive or negative economic profits.

Lorenz curve A geometric representation of the distribution of income. A Lorenz curve that is perfectly straight represents complete income equality. The more bowed a Lorenz curve, the more unequally income is distributed.

Lump-sum tax A tax that does not depend on income. An example is a $1,000 tax that every household must pay, irrespective of its economic situation.

M

M1 The money supply, measured as the total value of currency plus transactions deposits plus traveler's checks not issued by banks.

M2 M1 plus (1) savings deposits at all depository institutions, (2) small-denomination time deposits, and (3) balances in retail money market mutual funds.

Macroeconomics The study of the behavior of the economy as a whole, including such economywide phenomena as changes in unemployment, the general price level, and national income.

Majority rule A collective decision-making system in which group decisions are made on the basis of more than 50 percent of the vote. In other words, whatever more than half of the electorate votes for, the entire electorate has to accept.

Marginal cost pricing A system of pricing in which the price charged is equal to the opportunity cost to society of producing one more unit of the good or service in question. The opportunity cost is the marginal cost to society.

Marginal costs The change in total costs due to a one-unit change in production rate.

Marginal factor cost (MFC) The cost of using an additional unit of an input. For example, if a firm can hire all the workers it wants at the going wage rate, the marginal factor cost of labor is that wage rate.

Marginal physical product The physical output that is due to the addition of one more unit of a variable factor of production. The change in total product occurring when a variable input is increased and all other inputs are held constant. It is also called *marginal product*.

Marginal physical product (MPP) of labor The change in output resulting from the addition of one more worker. The MPP of the worker equals the change in total output accounted for by hiring the worker, holding all other factors of production constant.

Marginal propensity to consume (MPC) The ratio of the change in consumption to the change in disposable income. A marginal propensity to consume of 0.8 tells us that an additional $100 in take-home pay will lead to an additional $80 consumed.

Marginal propensity to save (MPS) The ratio of the change in saving to the change in disposable income. A marginal propensity to save of 0.2 indicates that out of an additional $100 in take-home pay, $20 will be saved. Whatever is not saved is consumed. The marginal propensity to save plus the marginal propensity to consume must always equal 1, by definition.

Marginal revenue The change in total revenues resulting from a one-unit change in output (and sale) of the product in question.

Marginal revenue product (MRP) The marginal physical product (MPP) times marginal revenue (MR). The MRP gives the additional revenue obtained from a one-unit change in labor input.

Marginal tax rate The change in the tax payment divided by the change in income, or the percentage of *additional* dollars that must be paid in taxes. The marginal tax rate is applied to the highest tax bracket of taxable income reached.

Marginal utility The change in total utility due to a one-unit change in the quantity of a good or service consumed.

Market All of the arrangements that individuals have for exchanging with one another. Thus, for example, we can speak of the labor market, the automobile market, and the credit market.

Market clearing, or equilibrium, price The price that clears the market, at which quantity demanded equals quantity supplied; the price where the demand curve intersects the supply curve.

Market demand The demand of all consumers in the marketplace for a particular good or service. The summation at each price of the quantity demanded by each individual.

Market failure A situation in which an unrestrained market operation leads to either too few or too many resources going to a specific economic activity.

Mass marketing Advertising intended to reach as many consumers as possible, typically through television, newspaper, radio, or magazine ads.

Medium of exchange Any item that sellers will accept as payment.

Microeconomics The study of decision making undertaken by individuals (or households) and by firms.

Minimum efficient scale (MES) The lowest rate of output per unit time at which long-run average costs for a particular firm are at a minimum.

Minimum wage A wage floor, legislated by government, setting the lowest hourly rate that firms may legally pay workers.

Models, or theories Simplified representations of the real world used as the basis for predictions or explanations.

Money Any medium that is universally accepted in an economy both by sellers of goods and services as payment for those goods and services and by creditors as payment for debts.

Money balances Synonymous with money, money stock, money holdings.

Money illusion Reacting to changes in money prices rather than relative prices. If a worker whose wages double when the price level also doubles thinks he or she is better off, that worker is suffering from money illusion.

Money multiplier A number that, when multiplied by a change in reserves in the banking system, yields the resulting change in the money supply.

Money price The price expressed in today's dollars; also called the *absolute* or *nominal price.*

Money supply The amount of money in circulation.

Monopolist The single supplier of a good or service for which there is no close substitute. The monopolist therefore constitutes its entire industry.

Monopolistic competition A market situation in which a large number of firms produce similar but not identical products. Entry into the industry is relatively easy.

Monopolization The possession of monopoly power in the relevant market and the willful acquisition or maintenance of that power, as distinguished from growth or development as a consequence of a superior product, business acumen, or historical accident.

Monopoly A firm that can determine the market price of a good. In the extreme case, a monopoly is the only seller of a good or service.

Monopsonist The only buyer in a market.

Monopsonistic exploitation Paying a price for the variable input that is less than its marginal revenue product; the difference between marginal revenue product and the wage rate.

Moral hazard The possibility that a borrower might engage in riskier behavior after a loan has been obtained.

Multiplier The ratio of the change in the equilibrium level of real GDP to the change in autonomous real expenditures. The number by which a change in autonomous real investment or autonomous real consumption, for example, is multiplied to get the change in equilibrium real GDP.

N

National income (NI) The total of all factor payments to resource owners. It can be obtained from net domestic product (NDP) by subtracting indirect business taxes and transfers and adding net U.S. income earned abroad and other business income adjustments.

National income accounting A measurement system used to estimate national income and its components. One approach to measuring an economy's aggregate performance.

Natural monopoly A monopoly that arises from the peculiar production characteristics in an industry. It usually arises when there are large economies of scale relative to the industry's demand such that one firm can produce at a lower average cost than can be achieved by multiple firms.

Natural rate of unemployment The rate of unemployment that is estimated to prevail in long-run macroeconomic equilibrium, when all workers and employers have fully adjusted to any changes in the economy.

Negative market feedback A tendency for a good or service to fall out of favor with more consumers because other consumers have stopped purchasing the item.

Negative-sum game A game in which players as a group lose during the process of the game.

Net domestic product (NDP) GDP minus depreciation.

Net investment Gross private domestic investment minus an estimate of the wear and tear on the existing capital stock. Net investment therefore measures the change in the capital stock over a one-year period.

Net public debt Gross public debt minus all government interagency borrowing.

Net wealth The stock of assets owned by a person, household, firm, or nation (net of any debts owed). For a household, net wealth can consist of a house, cars, personal belongings, stocks, bonds, bank accounts, and cash (minus any debts owed).

Network effect A situation in which a consumer's willingness to purchase a good or service is influenced by how many others also buy or have bought the item.

New entrant An individual who has never held a full-time job lasting two weeks or longer but is now seeking employment.

New growth theory A theory of economic growth that examines the factors that determine why technology, research, innovation, and the like are undertaken and how they interact.

New Keynesian inflation dynamics In new Keynesian theory, the pattern of inflation exhibited by an economy with growing aggregate demand—initial sluggish adjustment of the price level in response to increased aggregate demand followed by higher inflation later.

Nominal rate of interest The market rate of interest observed in contracts expressed in today's dollars.

Nominal values The values of variables such as GDP and investment expressed in current dollars, also called *money values;* measurement in terms of the actual market prices at which goods and services are sold.

Noncontrollable expenditures Government spending that changes automatically without action by Congress.

Noncooperative game A game in which the players neither negotiate nor cooperate in any way. As applied to firms in an industry, this is the common situation in which there are relatively few firms and each has some ability to change price.

Nondurable consumer goods Consumer goods that are used up within three years.

Nonincome expense items The total of indirect business taxes and depreciation.

Nonprice rationing devices All methods used to ration scarce goods that are price-controlled. Whenever the price system is not allowed to work, nonprice rationing devices will evolve to ration the affected goods and services.

Normal goods Goods for which demand rises as income rises. Most goods are normal goods.

Normal rate of return The amount that must be paid to an investor to induce investment in a business. Also known as the *opportunity cost of capital*.

Normative economics Analysis involving value judgments about economic policies; relates to whether outcomes are good or bad. A statement of *what ought to be*.

Number line A line that can be divided into segments of equal length, each associated with a number.

O

Oligopoly A market structure in which there are very few sellers. Each seller knows that the other sellers will react to its changes in prices, quantities, and qualities.

Open economy effect One of the reasons that the aggregate demand curve slopes downward: Higher price levels result in foreign residents desiring to buy fewer U.S.-made goods, while U.S. residents now desire more foreign-made goods, thereby reducing net exports. This is equivalent to a reduction in the amount of real goods and services purchased in the United States.

Open market operations The purchase and sale of existing U.S. government securities (such as bonds) in the open private market by the Federal Reserve System.

Opportunistic behavior Actions that focus solely on short-run gains because long-run benefits of cooperation are perceived to be smaller.

Opportunity cost The highest-valued, next-best alternative that must be sacrificed to obtain something or to satisfy a want.

Opportunity cost of capital The normal rate of return, or the available return on the next-best alternative investment. Economists consider this a

cost of production, and it is included in our cost examples.

Optimal quantity of pollution The level of pollution for which the marginal benefit of one additional unit of pollution abatement just equals the marginal cost of that additional unit of pollution abatement.

Origin The intersection of the *y* axis and the *x* axis in a graph.

Outsourcing A firm's employment of labor outside the country in which the firm is located.

P

Par value The officially determined value of a currency.

Partnership A business owned by two or more joint owners, or partners, who share the responsibilities and the profits of the firm and are individually liable for all the debts of the partnership.

Passive (nondiscretionary) policy-making Policymaking that is carried out in response to a rule. It is therefore not in response to an actual or potential change in overall economic activity.

Patent A government protection that gives an inventor the exclusive right to make, use, or sell an invention for a limited period of time (currently, 20 years).

Payoff matrix A matrix of outcomes, or consequences, of the strategies available to the players in a game.

Perfect competition A market structure in which the decisions of *individual* buyers and sellers have no effect on market price.

Perfectly competitive firm A firm that is such a small part of the total *industry* that it cannot affect the price of the product it sells.

Perfectly elastic demand A demand that has the characteristic that even the slightest increase in price will lead to zero quantity demanded.

Perfectly elastic supply A supply characterized by a reduction in quantity supplied to zero when there is the slightest decrease in price.

Perfectly inelastic demand A demand that exhibits zero responsiveness to price changes. No matter what the price is, the quantity demanded remains the same.

Perfectly inelastic supply A supply for which quantity supplied remains constant, no matter what happens to price.

Permanent income hypothesis A theory of consumption in which an individual determines current consumption based on anticipated average lifetime income.

Personal Consumption Expenditure (PCE) Index A statistical measure of average prices that uses annually

updated weights based on surveys of consumer spending.

Personal income (PI) The amount of income that households actually receive before they pay personal income taxes.

Persuasive advertising Advertising that is intended to induce a consumer to purchase a particular product and discover a previously unknown taste for the item.

Phillips curve A curve showing the relationship between unemployment and changes in wages or prices. It was long thought to reflect a trade-off between unemployment and inflation.

Physical capital All manufactured resources, including buildings, equipment, machines, and improvements to land that are used for production.

Planning curve The long-run average cost curve.

Planning horizon The long run, during which all inputs are variable.

Plant size The physical size of the factories that a firm owns and operates to produce its output. Plant size can be defined by square footage, maximum physical capacity, and other physical measures.

Policy irrelevance proposition The conclusion that policy actions have no real effects in the short run if the policy actions are anticipated and none in the long run even if the policy actions are unanticipated.

Portfolio investment The purchase of less than 10 percent of the shares of ownership in a company in another nation.

Positive economics Analysis that is *strictly* limited to making either purely descriptive statements or scientific predictions; for example, "If A, then B." A statement of *what is*.

Positive market feedback A tendency for a good or service to come into favor with additional consumers because other consumers have chosen to buy the item.

Positive-sum game A game in which players as a group are better off at the end of the game.

Potential money multiplier The reciprocal of the reserve ratio, assuming no leakages into currency. It is equal to 1 divided by the reserve ratio.

Precautionary demand Holding money to meet unplanned expenditures and emergencies.

Present value The value of a future amount expressed in today's dollars; the most that someone would pay today to receive a certain sum at some point in the future.

Price ceiling A legal maximum price that may be charged for a particular good or service.

Price controls Government-mandated minimum or maximum prices that may be charged for goods and services.

Price differentiation Establishing different prices for similar products to reflect differences in marginal cost in providing those commodities to different groups of buyers.

Price discrimination Selling a given product at more than one price, with the price difference being unrelated to differences in marginal cost.

Price elasticity of demand (E_p) The responsiveness of the quantity demanded of a commodity to changes in its price; defined as the percentage change in quantity demanded divided by the percentage change in price.

Price elasticity of supply (E_s) The responsiveness of the quantity supplied of a commodity to a change in its price—the percentage change in quantity supplied divided by the percentage change in price.

Price floor A legal minimum price below which a good or service may not be sold. Legal minimum wages are an example.

Price index The cost of today's market basket of goods expressed as a percentage of the cost of the same market basket during a base year.

Price searcher A firm that must determine the price-output combination that maximizes profit because it faces a downward-sloping demand curve.

Price system An economic system in which relative prices are constantly changing to reflect changes in supply and demand for different commodities. The prices of those commodities are signals to everyone within the system as to what is relatively scarce and what is relatively abundant.

Price taker A perfectly competitive firm that must take the price of its product as given because the firm cannot influence its price.

Principle of rival consumption The recognition that individuals are rivals in consuming private goods because one person's consumption reduces the amount available for others to consume.

Principle of substitution The principle that consumers shift away from goods and services that become priced relatively higher in favor of goods and services that are now priced relatively lower.

Prisoners' dilemma A famous strategic game in which two prisoners have a choice between confessing and not confessing to a crime. If neither confesses, they serve a minimum sentence. If both confess, they serve a longer sentence. If one confesses and the other doesn't, the one who confesses goes free. The dominant strategy is always to confess.

Private costs Costs borne solely by the individuals who incur them. Also called *internal costs*.

Private goods Goods that can be consumed by only one individual at a time. Private goods are subject to the principle of rival consumption.

Private property rights Exclusive rights of ownership that allow the use, transfer, and exchange of property.

Producer durables, or capital goods Durable goods having an expected service life of more than three years that are used by businesses to produce other goods and services.

Producer Price Index (PPI) A statistical measure of a weighted average of prices of goods and services that firms produce and sell.

Producer surplus The difference between the total amount that producers actually receive for an item and the total amount that they would have been willing to accept for supplying that item.

Product differentiation The distinguishing of products by brand name, color, and other minor attributes. Product differentiation occurs in other than perfectly competitive markets in which products are, in theory, homogeneous, such as wheat or corn.

Production Any activity that results in the conversion of resources into products that can be used in consumption.

Production function The relationship between inputs and maximum physical output. A production function is a technological, not an economic, relationship.

Production possibilities curve (PPC) A curve representing all possible combinations of maximum outputs that could be produced, assuming a fixed amount of productive resources of a given quality.

Profit-maximizing rate of production The rate of production that maximizes total profits, or the difference between total revenues and total costs. Also, it is the rate of production at which marginal revenue equals marginal cost.

Progressive taxation A tax system in which, as income increases, a higher percentage of the additional income is paid as taxes. The marginal tax rate exceeds the average tax rate as income rises.

Property rights The rights of an owner to use and to exchange property.

Proportional rule A decision-making system in which actions are based on the proportion of the "votes" cast and are in proportion to them. In a market system, if 10 percent of the "dollar votes" are cast for blue cars, 10 percent of automobile output will be blue cars.

Proportional taxation A tax system in which, regardless of an individual's income, the tax bill comprises exactly the same proportion.

Proprietorship A business owned by one individual who makes the business decisions, receives all the profits, and is legally responsible for the debts of the firm.

Public debt The total value of all outstanding federal government securities.

Public goods Goods for which the principle of rival consumption does not apply and for which exclusion of nonpaying consumers is too costly to be feasible. They can be jointly consumed by many individuals simultaneously at no additional cost and with no reduction in quality or quantity. Furthermore, no one who fails to help pay for the good can be denied the benefit of the good.

Purchasing power The value of money for buying goods and services. If your money income stays the same but the price of one good that you are buying goes up, your effective purchasing power falls.

Purchasing power parity Adjustment in exchange rate conversions that takes into account differences in the true cost of living across countries.

Q

Quantitative easing Federal Reserve open market purchases intended to generate an increase in bank reserves at a nearly zero interest rate.

Quantity theory of money and prices The hypothesis that changes in the money supply lead to equiproportional changes in the price level.

Quota subscription A nation's account with the International Monetary Fund, denominated in special drawing rights.

Quota system A government-imposed restriction on the quantity of a specific good that another country is allowed to sell in the United States. In other words, quotas are restrictions on imports. These restrictions are usually applied to one or several specific countries.

R

Random walk theory The theory that there are no predictable trends in securities prices that can be used to "get rich quick."

Rate of discount The rate of interest used to discount future sums back to present value.

Rate-of-return regulation Regulation that seeks to keep the rate of return in an industry at a competitive level by not allowing prices that would produce economic profits.

Rational expectations hypothesis A theory stating that people combine the effects of past policy changes on important economic variables with their own judgment about the future effects of current and future policy changes.

Rationality assumption The assumption that people do not intentionally make decisions that would leave them worse off.

Reaction function The manner in which one oligopolist reacts to a change in price, output, or quality made by another oligopolist in the industry.

Real disposable income Real GDP minus net taxes, or after-tax real income.

Real rate of interest The nominal rate of interest minus the anticipated rate of inflation.

Real values Measurement of economic values after adjustments have been made for changes in the average of prices between years.

Real-balance effect The change in expenditures resulting from a change in the real value of money balances when the price level changes, all other things held constant; also called the *wealth effect*.

Real-income effect The change in people's purchasing power that occurs when, other things being constant, the price of one good that they purchase changes. When that price goes up, real income, or purchasing power, falls, and when that price goes down, real income increases.

Recession A period of time during which the rate of growth of business activity is consistently less than its long-term trend or is negative.

Recessionary gap The gap that exists whenever equilibrium real GDP per year is less than full-employment real GDP as shown by the position of the long-run aggregate supply curve.

Recognition time lag The time required to gather information about the current state of the economy.

Reentrant An individual who used to work full-time but left the labor force and has now reentered it looking for a job.

Regional trade bloc A group of nations that grants members special trade privileges.

Regressive taxation A tax system in which as more dollars are earned, the percentage of tax paid on them falls. The marginal tax rate is less than the average tax rate as income rises.

Reinvestment Profits (or depreciation reserves) used to purchase new capital equipment.

Relative price The money price of one commodity divided by the money price of another commodity; the number of units of one commodity that must be sacrificed to purchase one unit of another commodity.

Relevant market A group of firms' products that are closely substitutable and available to consumers within a geographic area.

Rent control Price ceilings on rents.

Repricing, or menu, cost of inflation The cost associated with recalculating prices and printing new price lists when there is inflation.

Reserve ratio The fraction of transactions deposits that banks hold as reserves.

Reserves In the U.S. Federal Reserve System, deposits held by Federal Reserve district banks for depository institutions, plus depository institutions' vault cash.

Resources Things used to produce goods and services to satisfy people's wants.

Retained earnings Earnings that a corporation saves, or retains, for investment in other productive activities; earnings that are not distributed to stockholders.

Ricardian equivalence theorem The proposition that an increase in the government budget deficit has no effect on aggregate demand.

Right-to-work laws Laws that make it illegal to require union membership as a condition of continuing employment in a particular firm.

Rule of 70 A rule stating that the approximate number of years required for per capita real GDP to double is equal to 70 divided by the average rate of economic growth.

Rules of origin Regulations that nations in regional trade blocs establish to delineate product categories eligible for trading preferences.

S

Sales taxes Taxes assessed on the prices paid on most goods and services.

Saving The act of not consuming all of one's current income. Whatever is not consumed out of spendable income is, by definition, saved. *Saving* is an action measured over time (a flow), whereas *savings* are a stock, an accumulation resulting from the act of saving in the past.

Say's law A dictum of economist J. B. Say that supply creates its own demand. Producing goods and services generates the means and the willingness to purchase other goods and services.

Scarcity A situation in which the ingredients for producing the things that people desire are insufficient to satisfy all wants at a zero price.

Search good A product with characteristics that enable an individual to evaluate the product's quality in advance of a purchase.

Seasonal unemployment Unemployment resulting from the seasonal pattern of work in specific industries. It is usually

due to seasonal fluctuations in demand or to changing weather conditions that render work difficult, if not impossible, as in the agriculture, construction, and tourist industries.

Secondary boycott A refusal to deal with companies or purchase products sold by companies that are dealing with a company being struck.

Secular deflation A persistent decline in prices resulting from economic growth in the presence of stable aggregate demand.

Securities Stocks and bonds.

Services Mental or physical labor or assistance purchased by consumers. Examples are the assistance of physicians, lawyers, dentists, repair personnel, housecleaners, educators, retailers, and wholesalers; items purchased or used by consumers that do not have physical characteristics.

Share of stock A legal claim to a share of a corporation's future profits. If it is *common stock*, it incorporates certain voting rights regarding major policy decisions of the corporation. If it is *preferred stock*, its owners are accorded preferential treatment in the payment of dividends but do not have any voting rights.

Share-the-gains, share-the-pains theory A theory of regulatory behavior that holds that regulators must take account of the demands of three groups: legislators, who established and oversee the regulatory agency; firms in the regulated industry; and consumers of the regulated industry's products.

Short run The time period during which at least one input, such as plant size, cannot be changed.

Shortage A situation in which quantity demanded is greater than quantity supplied at a price below the market clearing price.

Short-run aggregate supply curve The relationship between total planned economywide production and the price level in the short run, all other things held constant. If prices adjust incompletely in the short run, the curve is positively sloped.

Short-run break-even price The price at which a firm's total revenues equal its total costs. At the break-even price, the firm is just making a normal rate of return on its capital investment. (It is covering its explicit and implicit costs.)

Short-run economies of operation A distinguishing characteristic of an information product arising from declining short-run average total cost as more units of the product are sold.

Short-run shutdown price The price that covers average variable costs. It occurs just below the intersection of the marginal cost curve and the average variable cost curve.

Signals Compact ways of conveying to economic decision makers information needed to make decisions. An effective signal not only conveys information but also provides the incentive to react appropriately. Economic profits and economic losses are such signals.

Slope The change in the y value divided by the corresponding change in the x value of a curve; the "incline" of the curve.

Small menu costs Costs that deter firms from changing prices in response to demand changes–for example, the costs of renegotiating contracts or printing new price lists.

Social costs The full costs borne by society whenever a resource use occurs. Social costs can be measured by adding external costs to private, or internal, costs.

Special drawing rights (SDRs) Reserve assets created by the International Monetary Fund for countries to use in settling international payment obligations.

Specialization The organization of economic activity so that what each person (or region) consumes is not identical to what that person (or region) produces. An individual may specialize, for example, in law or medicine. A nation may specialize in the production of coffee, e-book readers, or digital cameras.

Stagflation A situation characterized by lower real GDP, lower employment, and a higher unemployment rate during the same period that the rate of inflation increases.

Standard of deferred payment A property of an item that makes it desirable for use as a means of settling debts maturing in the future; an essential property of money.

Static tax analysis Economic evaluation of the effects of tax rate changes under the assumption that there is no effect on the tax base, meaning that there is an unambiguous positive relationship between tax rates and tax revenues.

Stock The quantity of something, measured at a given point in time—for example, an inventory of goods or a bank account. Stocks are defined independently of time, although they are assessed at a point in time.

Store of value The ability to hold value over time; a necessary property of money.

Strategic dependence A situation in which one firm's actions with respect to price, quality, advertising, and related changes may be strategically countered by the reactions of one or more other firms in the industry. Such dependence can exist only when there are a limited number of major firms in an industry.

Strategy Any rule that is used to make a choice, such as "Always pick heads."

Strikebreakers Temporary or permanent workers hired by a company to replace union members who are striking.

Structural unemployment Unemployment of workers over lengthy intervals resulting from skill mismatches with position requirements of employers and from fewer jobs being offered by employers constrained by governmental business regulations and labor market policies.

Subsidy A negative tax; a payment to a producer from the government, usually in the form of a cash grant per unit.

Substitutes Two goods are substitutes when a change in the price of one causes a shift in demand for the other in the same direction as the price change.

Substitution effect The tendency of people to substitute cheaper commodities for more expensive commodities.

Supply A schedule showing the relationship between price and quantity supplied for a specified period of time, other things being equal.

Supply curve The graphical representation of the supply schedule; a line (curve) showing the supply schedule, which generally slopes upward (has a positive slope), other things being equal.

Supply-side economics The suggestion that creating incentives for individuals and firms to increase productivity will cause the aggregate supply curve to shift outward.

Surplus A situation in which quantity supplied is greater than quantity demanded at a price above the market clearing price.

Sympathy strike A work stoppage by a union in sympathy with another union's strike or cause.

T

Tariffs Taxes on imported goods.

Tax base The value of goods, services, wealth, or incomes subject to taxation.

Tax bracket A specified interval of income to which a specific and unique marginal tax rate is applied.

Tax incidence The distribution of tax burdens among various groups in society.

Tax rate The proportion of a tax base that must be paid to a government as taxes.

Taylor rule An equation that specifies a federal funds rate target based on an estimated long-run real interest rate, the current deviation of the actual inflation rate from the Federal Reserve's inflation objective, and the gap between actual real GDP per year and a measure of potential real GDP per year.

Technology The total pool of applied knowledge concerning how goods and services can be produced.

The Fed The Federal Reserve System; the central bank of the United States.

Theory of public choice The study of collective decision making.

Third parties Parties who are not directly involved in a given activity or transaction. For example, in the relationship between caregivers and patients, fees may be paid by third parties (insurance companies, government).

Thrift institutions Financial institutions that receive most of their funds from the savings of the public. They include savings banks, savings and loan associations, and credit unions.

Tie-in sales Purchases of one product that are permitted by the seller only if the consumer buys another good or service from the same firm.

Tit-for-tat strategic behavior In game theory, cooperation that continues as long as the other players continue to cooperate.

Total costs The sum of total fixed costs and total variable costs.

Total income The yearly amount earned by the nation's resources (factors of production). Total income therefore includes wages, rent, interest payments, and profits that are received by workers, landowners, capital owners, and entrepreneurs, respectively.

Total revenues The price per unit times the total quantity sold.

Trade deflection Moving partially assembled products into a member nation of a regional trade bloc, completing assembly, and then exporting them to other nations within the bloc, so as to benefit from preferences granted by the trade bloc.

Trade diversion Shifting existing international trade from countries outside a regional trade bloc to nations within the bloc.

Trading Desk An office at the Federal Reserve Bank of New York charged with implementing monetary policy strategies developed by the Federal Open Market Committee.

Transaction costs All of the costs associated with exchange, including the informational costs of finding out the price and quality, service record, and durability of a product, plus the cost of contracting and enforcing that contract.

Transactions approach A method of measuring the money supply by looking at money as a medium of exchange.

Transactions demand Holding money as a medium of exchange to make payments. The level varies directly with nominal GDP.

Transactions deposits Checkable and debitable account balances in commercial banks and other types of financial institutions, such as credit unions and savings banks. Any accounts in financial institutions from which you can easily transmit debit-card and check payments without many restrictions.

Transfer payments Money payments made by governments to individuals for which no services or goods are rendered in return. Examples are Social Security old-age and disability benefits and unemployment insurance benefits.

Transfers in kind Payments that are in the form of actual goods and services, such as food stamps, subsidized public housing, and medical care, and for which no goods or services are rendered in return.

Traveler's checks Financial instruments obtained from a bank or a nonbanking organization and signed during purchase that can be used in payment upon a second signature by the purchaser.

Two-sided market A market in which an intermediary firm provides services that link groups of producers and consumers.

U

Unanticipated inflation Inflation at a rate that comes as a surprise, either higher or lower than the rate anticipated.

Unemployment The total number of adults (aged 16 years or older) who are willing and able to work and who are actively looking for work but have not found a job.

Union shop A business enterprise that may hire nonunion members, conditional on their joining the union by some specified date after employment begins.

Unit elasticity of demand A demand relationship in which the quantity demanded changes exactly in proportion to the change in price.

Unit of accounting A measure by which prices are expressed; the common denominator of the price system; a central property of money.

Unit tax A constant tax assessed on each unit of a good that consumers purchase.

Unlimited liability A legal concept whereby the personal assets of the owner of a firm can be seized to pay off the firm's debts.

Util A representative unit by which utility is measured.

Utility The want-satisfying power of a good or service.

Utility analysis The analysis of consumer decision making based on utility maximization.

V

Value added The dollar value of an industry's sales minus the value of intermediate goods (for example, raw materials and parts) used in production.

Variable costs Costs that vary with the rate of production. They include wages paid to workers and purchases of materials.

Versioning Selling a product in slightly altered forms to different groups of consumers.

Vertical merger The joining of a firm with another to which it sells an output or from which it buys an input.

Voluntary exchange An act of trading, done on an elective basis, in which both parties to the trade expect to be better off after the exchange.

Voluntary import expansion (VIE) An official agreement with another country in which it agrees to import more from the United States.

Voluntary restraint agreement (VRA) An official agreement with another country that "voluntarily" restricts the quantity of its exports to the United States.

W

Wants What people would buy if their incomes were unlimited.

World Bank A multinational agency that specializes in making loans to about 100 developing nations in an effort to promote their long-term development and growth.

World Trade Organization (WTO) The successor organization to the GATT that handles trade disputes among its member nations.

X

x axis The horizontal axis in a graph.

Y

y axis The vertical axis in a graph.

Z

Zero-sum game A game in which any gains within the group are exactly offset by equal losses by the end of the game.

INDEX